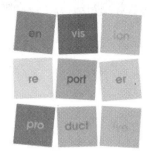

WordBu

D1235773

A Better Way To Teach Vocabulary™
Based on Frequently Used Latin and Greek Roots.

ELEMENTS LEVEL 2

word = prefix + root + suffix

Dynamic®
Literacy
Educational Publishers
Changing lives with words.™

WordBuild®

was developed by

Thomas H. Estes, Ph.D.
Professor Emeritus of Reading
University of Virginia

Rollin David Larrick, Ph.D.
Teacher of Latin, Greek, and English

Gerald V. Bailey
Managing Editor
Systems Architect

Table of Contents

Why WordBuild is *A Better Way To Teach Vocabulary*™

- Instead of relying on rote memorization of words, students learn the meanings of the key elements of words — the roots, prefixes, and suffixes. Rather than forgetting words, students remember them because they know and understand the core parts or *morphemes* of the words.

- With explicit instruction for the most frequently used Latin and Greek roots, prefixes, and suffixes, students acquire the skills to unlock meaning from more than 16,000 words.

- Best of all, WordBuild is easy to teach and takes only 15 minutes each day.

- Teachers say the biggest bonus to using WordBuild is that students like it. Not only are they actively engaged in building large vocabularies but they enjoy the word games that are the foundation of all the exercises.

WordBuild's unique organization enables you to build vocabulary and reading comprehension with many different groups of students at affordable prices:

- Regular Classroom
- Remedial
- ELL
- Intervention/RTI
- Summer School
- After School

WordBuild gets results quickly!

In a 12-week study conducted in a large urban district in the spring of 2008, students of all ability levels in both middle and high school showed significant growth in word comprehension. Struggling students improved at an even faster rate and closed the gap with higher performing students.

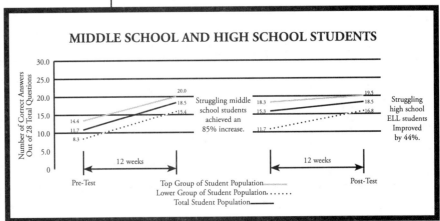

MIDDLE SCHOOL AND HIGH SCHOOL STUDENTS

Struggling middle school students achieved an 85% increase.

Struggling high school ELL students Improved by 44%.

Number of Correct Answers Out of 28 Total Questions

Pre-Test — Post-Test — 12 weeks

Top Group of Student Population
Lower Group of Student Population
Total Student Population

WordBuild successfully builds vocabulary and comprehension in just 15 minutes a day!

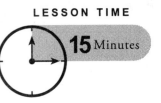

LESSON TIME

15 Minutes

Program Components

Foundations

Students learn the meanings of the most important prefixes and suffixes in the English language. Words studied are those taken directly from content area textbooks so students gain the foundation they need to build a strong academic vocabulary, and they gain the ability to understand words they have never seen before.

Foundations 1 and 2 Components

- Student Activity Books: weekly units contain a year's worth of engaging activities focusing on prefixes and suffixes.

- Teacher Editions: ready-to-go lesson plans include teaching tips, assessments, answer keys, and more.

- Web site provides access to bonus content and activities

Elements

Students build and sustain academic vocabulary as they learn the 93 most commonly used roots of our language. All of these come from Latin or Greek. As students learn these roots and combine them with prefixes and suffixes they can unlock the meaning of thousands of words.

Elements 1, 2, and 3 Components

- Student Activity Books: weekly units contain a year's worth of engaging activities focusing on the most frequently used roots of our language.

- Teacher Editions: ready-to-go lesson plans include teaching tips, assessments, comprehension boosters, answer keys, and more.

- Software: A CD based game that students love plus on-line software that provides unlimited exercises

- Optional on-line activities help teachers differentiate instruction

Grade Level Recommendation Chart						
	Regular Classroom	Remedial	ELL	Intervention RTI	Summer School	After School
	Recommended Grades	Recommended Grades	Recommended Grades	Recommended Grades	Recommended Grades	Recommended Grades
Foundations	3-5	5-9	5-9	7-12	5-9	5-9
Elements	5-10	7-12	7-12	9-12	7-12	7-12

WordBuild,
A Better Way to Teach Vocabulary™

3 Reasons why you should put WordBuild in your classrooms

1. WordBuild can dramatically improve the vocabulary and reading comprehension of your students and help them make significant gains in all content areas.

2. WordBuild can help increase your students' scores on standardized tests.

3. WordBuild can make a big difference in the lives of all the students who use it.

Why WordBuild Works

Students learn the core building blocks of academic vocabulary—the 93 most frequently used roots of the English language and the prefixes and suffixes that go with them so they develop the ability to unlock over 16,000 words without rote memorization!

Motivating puzzles and games make learning vocabulary interesting and fun. Differentiated Instruction allows students of many different reading levels to work on the same roots at the same time.

WordBuild aligns to state and national language arts standards.

Students say it best:

- This is so cool because now I know how all words work!

- I'm not afraid of big words anymore!

WordBuild Is the Result of More Than Thirty Years of Research and Practice

Dr. Thomas H. Estes has spent his career studying and teaching how children acquire reading skills. He served as professor of Reading Education in the Curry School of Education, University of Virginia for more than thirty years and was a Reading Specialist in both elementary and high schools in the early days of his career.

An award-winning teacher and author, Dr. Estes focuses on the teaching of reading at all age and grade levels, particularly the processes of comprehension and vocabulary acquisition.

Dr. Rollin David Larrick has spent his career studying and teaching about language. His specialties include the history of English, the evolution of Romance languages from Latin, and the linguistics of Germanic and classical languages.

An award-winning teacher, Dr. Larrick has taught English, Latin, and Greek for more than 35 years at both the high school and college levels.

Together, Dr. Estes and Dr. Larrick have developed a program that brings together the best research on the evolution of language and best practice in teaching vocabulary in a systematic and fun way that excites both students and teachers.

Using WordBuild,
A Better Way to Teach Vocabulary

We know that we have definitely learned something when we can take what we know and apply it successfully to new situations. For example, we can subtract 703 from 1743 even though we have never seen that exact problem before.

WordBuild works like that. It does not require students to memorize lists of new words and their definitions. Instead, the system first directs students' attention to words they already know, words they themselves bring up in a lesson. Then they analyze their words, not letter-by-letter or syllable-by syllable, but by the pieces of meaning that lie embedded in all words. These pieces of meaning are called morphemes, and by becoming aware of a few hundred morphemes, students have the tools to unlock the meanings of thousands and thousands of new words which they will encounter in their pursuit of academic and professional excellence.

Goals of WordBuild

- Teach students to discover how words work, how they are made up

- Encourage students to become independent and successful life-long learners

Basic Principles for Teachers

- Let the students propose, make observations, and question the words

- Explore words along with your students; find out answers together

- Keep the lesson moving at an enjoyable pace, no more than 15 minutes

prefix + root + suffix = WORD

Where should you start?
The overview for students on pages I-8 and I-9 is worth copying and handing out. Have students take it home and show it to their parents. Everyone will learn something!

Great Teacher Edition Features
you won't want to miss

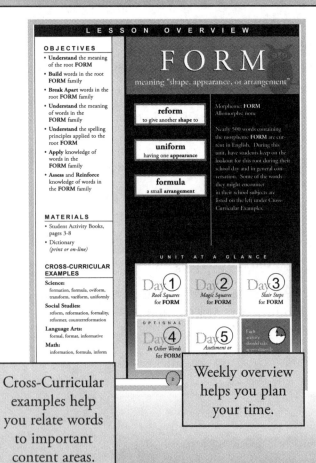

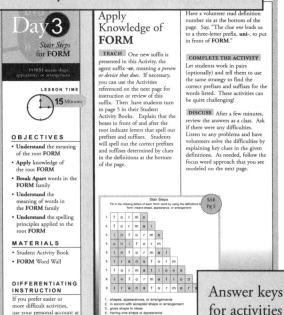

Cross-Curricular examples help you relate words to important content areas.

Weekly overview helps you plan your time.

Lessons follow the **TEACH COMPLETE DISCUSS** method (I do, you do, we do) which enables you to actively involve the whole class

Answer keys for activities in the student activity book.

Weekly, semester, and year end tests give you all you need for assessing your students

Lively information relating to words in each root family helps you become a word expert without taking an extra course!

Student Activity Book – A roadmap for a typical weekly unit

Day 1

The Root Squares activity, done on day 1 of each unit, is the keystone to the WordBuild System. This activity starts the process of observing how familiar words are constructed. Students put word pieces together to make familiar words that help them understand what each word piece means.

Root Squares
How many words can you make?

Start in any square. Your goal is to combine two or more word parts to make as many words in the 'form' family as you can. Write each word and a definition you can think of for it in the space provided at the bottom of the page. Use the back of the page if you need to.

uni	ed	al
ing	form	trans
in	at	ion

_____
_____
_____
_____
_____
_____
_____
_____
_____

Day 2

The Magic Squares activity, done on day 2, offers students a chance to see how a definition fits a word according to the pieces that make up that word. An entertaining mathematical twist provides a multi-layered enjoyment to analyzing words.

Magic Squares

Select the best answer for each of the words in the 'form' family from the numbered definitions. Put the number in the proper space in the Magic Square box. If the total of the numbers is the same both across and down, you have found the magic number!

'form' means shape, appearance, or arrangement

WORDS
A. transforming
B. informational
C. uniformity
D. uniformed
E. informative
F. transformation
G. formations
H. formalizes
I. formless

DEFINITIONS
1. to become similar in shape to something else; to comply
2. condition of having one shape or appearance
3. puts into accepted arrangement or shape
4. attired in apparel on one shape or appearance
5. shapes, appearances, or arrangements
6. act of moving across to another shape
7. relating to providing shape to shape
8. serving to provide shape to data
9. moving across to another shape or appearance
10. having no shape

Magic Square Box

A.	B.	C.
D.	E.	F.
G.	H.	I.

Magic Number _____

Day 3

The Stair Steps activity, on day 3, gives students a chance to review affixes and observe how word definitions reflect the meanings of the pieces that make up the word.

Stair Steps

Fill in the missing letters of each 'form' word by using the definitions below.
'form' means shape, appearance, or arrangement

1. f o r m
2. f o r m
3. f o r m
4. f o r m
5. f o r m
6. f o r m
7. f o r m
8. f o r m
9. f o r m

1. shapes, appearances, or arrangements
2. in accord with accepted shape or arrangement
3. gives shape to ideas
4. having one shape or appearance
5. without shape or arrangement; relaxed
6. to move across to another shape or appearance
7. shapes, appearances, or arrangements
8. knowledge arranged or shaped to be understood
9. devices that move across to another shape

Day 4

The In Other Words Activities are challenging and entertaining. The activity consists of a story written using etymological defintions of 8-10 words in the root family being studied. Students are then asked to answer a series of questions about the story by selecting from words in a word bank that reflect those etymological meanings. This activity fosters a deep understanding of both units of meaning and parts of speech.

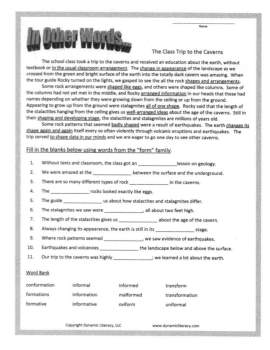

In Other Words...

Name _____

The Class Trip to the Caverns

The school class took a trip to the caverns and received an education about the earth, without textbook or <u>in the usual classroom arrangement</u>. The <u>change in appearance</u> of the landscape as we crossed from the green and bright surface of the earth into the totally dark cavern was amazing. When the tour guide Rocky turned on the lights, we gasped to see all the rock <u>shapes and arrangements</u>.

Some rock arrangements were <u>shaped like eggs</u>, and others were shaped like columns. Some of the columns had not yet met in the middle, and Rocky <u>arranged information</u> in our heads that these had names depending on whether they were growing down from the ceiling or up from the ground. Appearing to grow up from the ground were stalagmites <u>all of one shape</u>. Rocky said that the length of the stalactites hanging from the ceiling gives us <u>well-arranged ideas</u> about the age of the caverns. Still in their <u>shaping and developing stage</u>, the stalactites and stalagmites are millions of years old.

Some rock patterns that seemed <u>badly shaped</u> were a result of earthquakes. The earth <u>changes its shape again and again</u> itself every so often violently through volcanic eruptions and earthquakes. The trip served <u>to shape data in our minds</u> and we are eager to go one day to see other caverns.

<u>Fill in the blanks below using words from the "form" family.</u>

1. Without texts and classroom, the class got an _____ lesson on geology.
2. We were amazed at the _____ between the surface and the underground.
3. There are so many different types of rock _____ in the caverns.
4. The _____ rocks looked exactly like eggs.
5. The guide _____ us about how stalactites and stalagmites differ.
6. The stalagmites we saw were _____, all about two feet high.
7. The length of the stalactites gives us _____ about the age of the cavern.
8. Always changing its appearance, the earth is still in its _____ stage.
9. Where rock patterns seemed _____, we saw evidence of earthquakes.
10. Earthquakes and volcanoes _____ the landscape below and above the surface.
11. Our trip to the caverns was highly _____; we learned a lot about the earth.

Word Bank

conformation	informal	informed	transform
formations	information	malformed	transformation
formative	informative	oviform	uniformal

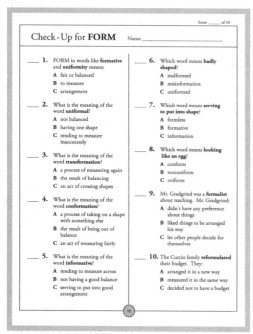

Check-Up for FORM   Name _____   Score: ____ of 10

____ 1. FORM in words like **formative** and **uniformity** means:
A fair or balanced
B to measure
C arrangement

____ 2. What is the meaning of the word **uniformal**?
A not balanced
B having one shape
C tending to measure inaccurately

____ 3. What is the meaning of the word **transformation**?
A a process of measuring again
B the result of balancing
C an act of crossing shapes

____ 4. What is the meaning of the word **conformation**?
A a process of taking on a shape with something else
B the result of being out of balance
C an act of measuring fairly

____ 5. What is the meaning of the word **informative**?
A tending to measure across
B not having a good balance
C serving to put into good arrangement

____ 6. Which word means **badly shaped**?
A malformed
B misinformation
C uniformed

____ 7. Which word means **serving to put into shape**?
A formless
B formative
C information

____ 8. Which word means **looking like an egg**?
A conform
B nonuniform
C oviform

____ 9. Mr. Gradgrind was a **formalist** about teaching. Mr. Gradgrind:
A didn't have any preference about things
B liked things to be arranged his way
C let other people decide for themselves

____ 10. The Curcio family **reformulated** their budget. They:
A arranged it in a new way
B measured it in the same way
C decided not to have a budget

Day 5

Day 5 features a standard assessment, a brief and easy-to-use check-up on each root, that measures not only knowledge of the root but of words in the root family EXPLICITLY NOT STUDIED.

The WORD WALL is a place for students to build their own dictionary by root.

BONUS ACTIVITY Morpheme Mania is a game students can play on their own or in class.

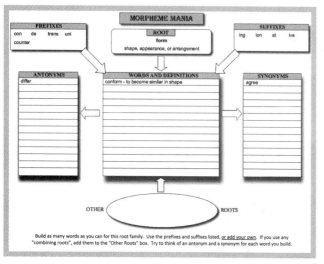

MORPHEME MANIA

PREFIXES				ROOT	SUFFIXES			
con	de	trans	uni	form	ing	ion	at	ive
counter				shape, appearance, or arrangement				

ANTONYMS	WORDS AND DEFINITIONS	SYNONYMS
differ	conform - to become similar in shape	agree

OTHER ROOTS

Build as many words as you can for this root family. Use the prefixes and suffixes listed, <u>or add your own</u>. If you use any "combining roots", add them to the "Other Roots" box. Try to think of an antonym and a synonym for each word you build.

My Word Wall   Name _____

Root: *form*

Word	Synonym / Antonym	Word	Synonym / Antonym

Morphemes for this meaning family

Prefixes	Roots	Suffixes

Our Language - An Overview for Students

You hear English spoken all day and see it in print everywhere, so you probably take it for granted. It just IS, like air and water, ever present and never changing.

But have you noticed that almost everything changes? Sometimes, change seems to be the only constant! Clothing and hair styles, music, cars, computer technology—always changing. The same goes for the language you speak. Over time, words come and go as they are needed, pronunciations change, definitions change, spellings change. Think about how many words you use that you never hear your parents use. Some of those words will be in future dictionaries, so you are yourself responsible for some of the changes we are referring to.

Lots of forces cause all these changes, but there was one big force that once changed the English language in a massive and magnificent way. It was an invasion a long time ago by an army that conquered the English people and changed the way they lived and spoke.

Let's go back in time almost a thousand years, to the early part of 1066, in England. If you heard someone speaking English then, you would hardly believe it was English. Here's an example of what you might have heard in a church:

Þu ure fæder, þe eart on heofonum: Sy þin nama gehalgod. Cume ðin riċe. Sy ðin wylla on eorðan swaswa on heofonum. Syle us to dæg urne daghwamlican hlaf, ond forgyf us ure gyltas swaswa we forgyfað ðam þe wið us agyltað. Ond ne læd þu na us on costnunge, ac alys us fram yfele. Sy hit swa.

You can recognize a few words here and there, but on the whole, it's more like a foreign language than English, isn't it?

Then came the most significant event in the history of our language. In October of the year 1066, an army from across the channel that divides England from France stormed in and took control of the country. This army spoke a Latin-based language with a bit of Norse mixed in, a language called Norman French, and the new leaders demanded that from that time on, all business, all education, all worship, all writing be in their language, and the local native language was forbidden in public affairs.

Imagine being forced to learn a foreign language in order to carry on your life in your own homeland!

Thanks to the Battle of Hastings, the words of the winning Normans make up nearly 70% of the words found in our written texts

The English people, especially the younger ones, did indeed learn the Norman French language, but they didn't forget their old mother tongue. Privately, at home, they continued to speak their English, but in public, they obeyed the rules and spoke the victorious language. Over the years, what do you think happened? The people began to mix both languages together, using their native words in certain situations, and their new language in other situations, so much so that the mixture became one new language. Today that is English. This new English still has a double personality, with some words, the original English, being used in everyday speech, and the Latin-based version of those same words being used in writing and formal speech. That is why we have in English today two ways to express nearly everything: beside the word 'teacher', for example, we have "educator". With "motherly" we have "maternal"; with "car" we have automobile", and so on in thousands of examples. It is no exaggeration to say that modern English is a bilingual language.

Harold, King of England, was killed by the invading Normans at the Battle of Hastings.

As it turns out, the words of the winning Normans still make up nearly 70% of the words found in written texts, in law, in medicine, in government— in all academic and formal English like that you see in your school textbooks. And so, just as the English speakers nearly a thousand years ago had to learn the "winning" words in order to succeed, so do we even today. The good news is that learning these winning words is not so hard—and is even fun—once you see how they work, how they are made up of pieces of meaning, called morphemes, used over and over in different combinations that build new words.

This vocabulary program is called WORDBUILD because it focuses on how words are built. The building blocks of words are actually pieces of meaning. The goal of the program is that you will never see a new word again without asking yourself what you already know about it.

Here is a formula to keep in mind:

W O R D = (prefix) + root + (suffix)

The parentheses are to show that those parts don't have to be used. All every word really needs is a root. The root is the core meaning of a word.

Figuring out the meanings of words is like solving a problem. In solving this problem, first find the root of the word. Sometimes the root is a word by itself, but most roots must have a prefix or suffix added to them to make words. Either way, the root of a word will be its core meaning. Prefixes and suffixes also have meaning. To figure out what a word means, look for any part whose meaning is familiar. When the meanings of these parts are added together, the underlying meaning of the word will begin to appear.

The Bayeux Tapestry is the most important relic to survive from the 11th century. Who do you think commissioned this stitched chronicle of the Battle of Hastings

BEFORE YOU BEGIN...

Make your WordBuild experience even better by using the additional activities and information available on-line.

Differentiated Instruction

The exercises in the Elements Level 2 Student Activity book that are directly referenced in this manual are considered mainstream, or *Mastery* level. Two additional tracks of activities are available on-line to facilitate varying student ability levels. The *Novice* track consists of Root Squares, Magic Squares, and Stair Steps activities for all 36 Elements Level 2 roots. These exercises use some simpler affixes and words and have some overlap with the mastery level exercises. This allows you to differentiate instruction within your classroom while having the whole class study the same root.

Likewise, the *Expert* level exercises are more challenging than the mastery level exercises. Detailed suggestions for a variety of ways to use differentiated instruction can be found on the Dynamic Literacy website on the Resources page.

To find these activities, log in at www. dynamicliteracy.com using your personal teacher account. Select a root in level 2 and you will be presented with all three types of exercises.

Bonus Activities

Check the website from time to time to see what's new. You will find interesting and fun activities and information on numbers, colors, body parts, and who knows what else!

The best advice we can give you:

KEEP IT FUN!

PLEASE NOTE

The first 2 roots, FORM and PON, are repeated from Elements Level 1, but the exercises are a little more difficult. This is done to introduce new students to the WordBuild system and to re-engage students who used Elements 1 last year.

OBJECTIVES

- **Understand** the meaning of the root **FORM**

- **Build** words in the root **FORM** family

- **Break Apart** words in the root **FORM** family

- **Understand** the meaning of words in the **FORM** family

- **Understand** the spelling principles applied to the root **FORM**

- **Apply** knowledge of words in the **FORM** family

- **Assess** and **Reinforce** knowledge of words in the **FORM** family

MATERIALS

- Student Activity Books, pages 3-8

- Dictionary *(print or on-line)*

CROSS-CURRICULAR EXAMPLES

Science:
    formation, formula, oviform, transform, variform, uniformly

Social Studies:
    reform, reformation, formality, reformer, counterreformation

Language Arts:
    formal, format, informative

Math:
    information, formula, inform

FORM

meaning "shape, appearance, or arrangement"

reform
to give another **shape** to

uniform
having one **appearance**

formula
a small **arrangement**

Morpheme: **FORM**
Allomorphs: none

Nearly 500 words containing the morpheme **FORM** are current in English. During this unit, have students keep on the lookout for this root during their school day and in general conversation. Some of the words they might encounter in their school subjects are listed on the left under Cross-Curricular Examples.

UNIT AT A GLANCE

Day ① *Root Squares* for **FORM**

Day ② *Magic Squares* for **FORM**

Day ③ *Stair Steps* for **FORM**

OPTIONAL
Day ④ *In Other Words* for **FORM**

Day ⑤ *Assessment or Morpheme Mania* for **FORM**

Each activity should take approximately **15 minutes.**

The root **FORM** is the Latin version of the Greek root **morph**. Both roots mean "shape, appearance, or arrangement," but Latin reversed the first and last consonant sounds of the Greek. (Such a switch is an occasional language phenomenon called **metathesis**.) Students may know of Mighty Morphin Power Rangers, Animorphs, or the X-Men character Morph, and they will know that these can be changed into various shapes and appearances.

Shapes or letter clusters that have meaning within words are called **morphemes**. Mastery of a few hundred of these pieces opens the door to understanding thousands of words, even if they have never been seen before.

A morpheme like **FORM**, which can also stand alone as a word, is called a "free" or "unbound" morpheme.

The word **formula** is a Latin word used in English, having two suffixes, **-ul** and **-a**, a Latin noun-marker. The word means "a little shape or arrangement." We discover the same two suffixes together, **-ula**, in the name of a scary character whose name means "little Dragon." Can your students figure out who that is? *(Dracula)*.

W O R D   W A L L

Every day, provide time for students to write words that they have built or found using the current root, or morpheme, in their personal Word Wall, found in the Student Activity Book with each new root. Encourage students to add words to their personal Word Walls throughout the year. Some teachers also keep versions of the Word Walls hanging in the classroom, depending on space and décor, and invite students continually to add pertinent words as they are found.

Word Alert! There are a few words that have the letters F-O-R-M in them and that seem to be in this root family, but they derive from other roots.

Words	Where they come from
former, formerly	from an Old English root family related to *fore* and *front*
formic, formaldehyde	from a Latin word meaning *ant*
Formica *(trade name)*	from *formerly* + a Latin word meaning *grainy rock (mica)*
formidable	from a Latin word meaning *fearsome* (causing something to become stiff or *firm* with fright)
perform	from a Germanic root meaning to *carry out* or to *furnish*

There are two separate and unrelated words **former**, one meaning *something that gives shape*, and the other meaning *happening earlier*. Sometimes morphemes with quite different meanings have the same spelling. The obvious difference in meanings between familiar words such as these two words **former** will be a clue to a difference in original morpheme. However, in case of uncertainty, consult a reliable dictionary.

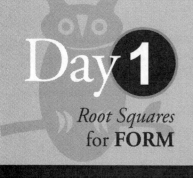

Day 1

Root Squares
for FORM

FORM means shape,
appearance, or arrangement

LESSON TIME

15 Minutes

OBJECTIVES

- **Understand** the meaning of the root **FORM**

- **Build** words in the **FORM** family

- **Understand** the meaning of words in the **FORM** family

- **Understand** the spelling principles applied to the root **FORM**

MATERIALS

- Student Activity Book

- **FORM** Word Wall

- Dictionary
  (print or on-line)

DIFFERENTIATING INSTRUCTION

If you prefer easier or more difficult activities, use your personal account at www.dynamicliteracy.com to access novice or expert versions, along with ideas on using them.

Root Squares for FORM

TEACH Have students turn to the Root Squares on page 3 in their Activity Books. Write **FORM** on the board and explain that it is a root, or morpheme, but can also stand alone as a word. Lead students to a definition *shape, appearance, or arrangement* as a noun ("We fill out *forms* for a job") or a verb ("Ice *forms* on the lake"). Do a quick spot-check review on the meanings of the affixes surrounding the center box, and explain that the affixes can attach before or after **FORM** to build other words. Then have students attach **-at** on the end of **FORM** to make *format*. Students can write *format* in a space at the bottom of the page and write a simple definition such as *to put into a certain arrangement*.

COMPLETE THE ACTIVITY Have students add other morphemes to **FORM**, list their words, and write simple definitions. If students have difficulty building words, show them how by modeling a matrix approach found on the next page, taking one affix at a time and seeing if it will connect with the root.

DISCUSS After five minutes, have volunteers write up some of their words. Remind students about doubling **t** if they add **-ed** or **-ing** to **format**. Discuss the meanings of the words, using the meanings of **FORM** and of the affixes as a guide. Emphasize that the meaning of **FORM** in each word is still *shape, appearance, or arrangement*, even with prefixes and suffixes added. If desired, use the focus word approach that you see modeled on the next page.

SAB
Pg 3

Root Squares

How many words can you make?

Start in any square. Your goal is to combine two or more word parts to make as many words in the 'form' family as you can. Write each word and a definition you can think of for it in the space provided at the bottom of the page. Use the back of the page if you need to.

uni	ed	al
ing	form	trans
in	at	ion

_____

_____

_____

_____

_____

_____

_____

www.dynamicliteracy.com

4

NEED REVIEW?	All prefixes and suffixes used with this activity were featured in earlier levels of *WordBuild* Teacher Editions. You can access information about, activities for, or Mini-Lessons for these other affixes by using your personal account number to log onto the Dynamic Literacy website. Instructions for obtaining your free account are found on the inside front cover of this book.

Focus Word: **INFORM** ⟶ Write this word on the board.

TEACH

Sample leading question:	"Let's take a minute to consider the word **inform**. What do we do when we **inform** somebody of something?"
Target response:	We tell them. We give them some **information**."
Teacher continuation:	"Right, and where is that **information** going?"
Target response:	"It's going *in* the other person's head. That's why the prefix is **in**-!"
Continuation:	"Great. And what's going *in* the other person's head?"
Response:	"Formation?" "Stuff." "Data." "Gossip."
Continuation:	What does the word say about the stuff, data, or gossip going *in* the head?"
Response:	"It makes sense - it has **form**, that is, a certain *shape or arrangement!*"

Encourage students to define **inform** using the meanings of the two pieces that make up the word: *to put into shape.*

DISCUSS Say, "The things we read and the people we listen to and respect **inform** our characters, or make us who we are." Let students provide examples of things they've read or people they've known who have **informed** them.

DEMONSTRATE Ask students to group into threes or fours and **inform** each other with **information** about the date of their birthdays.

Root Squares Matrix

You can refer to this matrix to guide students in this activity. Students could build at least these 24 words. *It really doesn't matter how many they build* – the point is that they understand the consistent meanings of the root **form** and of its prefixes and suffixes.

	no prefix	in-	trans-	uni-
no suffix	form	inform	transform	uniform
-al	formal	informal		uniformal
-at	format			
-ed	formed	informed	transformed	uniformed
-ing	forming	informing	transforming	uniforming
-at + -ion	formation	information	transformation	
-at + -ing	formatting			
-at + -ed	formatted			
-at + -ion + -al	formational	informational	transformational	

Words that students coin for empty slots are legitimate learning tools: have students who coin such words give appropriate definitions for them.

Day 2

Magic Squares for FORM

FORM means shape, appearance, or arrangement

LESSON TIME

15 Minutes

OBJECTIVES

- **Understand** the meaning of the root **FORM**
- **Break Apart** words in the **FORM** family
- **Understand** the meanings of words in the **FORM** family

MATERIALS

- Student Activity Book
- **FORM** Word Wall
- Dictionary *(print or on-line)*

DIFFERENTIATING INSTRUCTION

If you prefer easier or more difficult activities, use your personal account at www.dynamicliteracy.com to access novice or expert versions, along with ideas on using them.

Break Apart Words with FORM

TEACH A Mini-Lesson for the suffix **-ity** appears on the next page. If your students need instruction or review on any of the other affixes used with this Activity, information, activities or Mini-Lessons for them can be accessed by logging onto the Dynamic Literacy website.

Have students turn to the Magic Squares on page 4 in their Student Activity Books. Explain that 9 words from the root **FORM** family are listed in lettered order on the left. Some are words that they built using the Root Squares, and others use different affixes. To the right are 10 numbered definitions (one definition will not be used). Students are to match definitions to the lettered words by placing the number of the definition into the correct lettered box.

Model for the students: "For Word I, *formless*, I know that **FORM** means *shape or appearance* and that **-less** means *without or not having*. Looking through the definitions, I see that definition 10 reads *having no shape*, so I will write the number 10 in box I."

COMPLETE THE ACTIVITY

Let students use a similar strategy to find correct definitions for the other words and to write the number of the definition in the box that matches the letter. Tell students that if all their answers are correct, each row and each column will add up to the Magic Number.

DISCUSS After 5 minutes, go over some of the words and ask students to describe their strategies for discovering the correct answer. Add new words to the classroom **FORM** Word Wall and remind students to add these words to the Word Wall on page 8 in their Activity Books. As needed, follow the focus word approach that you see modeled on the next page.

SAB Pg 4

Magic Squares

Select the best answer for each of the words in the 'form' family from the numbered defin[itions]. Put the number in the proper space in the Magic Square box. If the total of the numbers is the same both across and down, you have found the magic number!

'form' means shape, appearance, or arrangement

WORDS	DEFINITIONS
A. transforming	1. to become similar in shape to something else; to comply
B. informational	2. condition of having one shape or appearance
C. uniformity	3. puts into accepted arrangement or shape
D. uniformed	4. attired in apparel on one shape or appearance
E. informative	5. shapes, appearances, or arrangements
F. transformation	6. act of moving across to another shape
G. formations	7. relating to providing shape to data
H. formalizes	8. serving to provide shape to data
I. formless	9. moving across to another shape or appearance
	10. having no shape

Magic Square Box

A. 9	B. 7	C. 2
D. 4	E. 8	F. 6
G. 5	H. 3	I. 10

Magic Number _18_

*** ANSWER KEY ***

6

Day ② Extend the Learning

MINI-LESSON: the Suffix *-ity*

The suffix *-ity* is one of the most common noun-forming morphemes in the English language. Attached primarily to adjective roots, *-ity* makes abstract nouns that mean the *quality or state* of whatever adjective it is suffixed onto. Write up some of these words for your students:

peculiar	elastic	equal	solid	odd	formal	human
familiar	vital	complex	real	similar	inferior	national

Have students select words they know, define them, and then add the suffix *-ity*. Have the class discuss what change in meaning or usage occurs with the added suffix. (The descriptive word becomes a noun meaning *the quality or state of having that description*).

Focus Word: **FORMALIZE** ⟶ Write this word on the board.

TEACH

Sample leading question	"Who can tell us what it means to *formalize* plans?"
Student response:	"To make them official or known."
Teacher continuation:	"And how are they made official or known?"
Target response:	"They're talked over and settled on by everybody involved."
Teacher:	"Let the word tell us about itself."
Target responses:	"I know—the plans are put into a clear shape or arrangement!" "They're made *formal*."
Teacher continuation:	"What part of the word tells you they're made *formal*?"
Response:	(consulting notes or back of Activity Book) "The suffix *-ize* means *to make or cause to be like*."

Encourage students to define *formalize* using the pieces that make up the word: *to cause to have or be like a shape or appearance.*

DISCUSS Discuss the difference between *formalized* and *unformalized*. Are there any situations when being *unformalized* might be better than *formalized*?

DEMONSTRATE Let students write a random bunch of words on the board for a minute. Then have a volunteer guide the class into *formalizing* the words into any organized pattern that might be suggested.

Tech Connect

Looking up a word in a dictionary today is as easy as clicking with a mouse on a computer. One of the best web sites is called www.dictionary.com.

Type a word you want to know more about in the search box and an array of dictionaries and word resources will appear. For the word **form**, Dictionary.com has 44 entries and a list of synonyms and antonyms.

This site, made up of many different word resources, provides access to thousands of words like **form**. Students will want to bookmark this site, and you may find yourself revisiting often. Who would have thought a dictionary could be such fun!

7

LESSON TIME

15 Minutes

OBJECTIVES

- **Understand** the meaning of the root **FORM**

- **Apply** knowledge of the root **FORM**

- **Break Apart** words in the **FORM** family

- **Understand** the meaning of words in the **FORM** family

- **Understand** the spelling principles applied to the root **FORM**

MATERIALS

- Student Activity Book
- **FORM** Word Wall

DIFFERENTIATING INSTRUCTION

If you prefer easier or more difficult activities, use your personal account at www.dynamicliteracy.com to access novice or expert versions, along with ideas on using them.

Apply Knowledge of FORM

TEACH One new suffix is presented in this Activity, the agent suffix **-er**, meaning *a person or device that does*. If necessary, you can use the Activities referenced on the next page for instruction or review of this suffix. Then have students turn to page 5 in their Student Activity Books. Explain that the boxes in front of and after the root indicate letters that spell out prefixes and suffixes. Students will spell out the correct prefixes and suffixes determined by clues in the definitions at the bottom of the page.

Have a volunteer read definition number four at the bottom of the page. Say, "The clue *one* leads us to a three-letter prefix, **uni-**, to put in front of **FORM**."

COMPLETE THE ACTIVITY

Let students work in pairs (optionally) and tell them to use the same strategy to find the correct prefixes and suffixes for the words listed. These activities can be quite challenging!

DISCUSS After a few minutes, review the answers as a class. Ask if there were any difficulties. Listen to any problems and have volunteers solve the difficulties by explaining key clues in the given definitions. As needed, follow the focus word approach that you see modeled on the next page.

Stair Steps

Fill in the missing letters of each 'form' word by using the definitions b
'form' means shape, appearance, or arrangement

SAB
Pg 5

1.	f	o	r	m	s				
2.	f	o	r	m	a	l			
3.	i	n	f	o	r	m	s		
4.	u	n	i	f	o	r	m		
5.	i	n	f	o	r	m	a	l	
6.	t	r	a	n	s	f	o	r	m
7.	f	o	r	m	a	t	i	o	n	s
8.	i	n	f	o	r	m	a	t	i	o	n
9.	t	r	a	n	s	f	o	r	m	e	r	s

1. shapes, appearances, or arrangements
2. in accord with accepted shape or arrangement
3. gives shape to ideas
4. having one shape or appearance
5. without shape or arrangement; relaxed
6. to move across to another shape or appearance
7. shapes, appearances, or arrangements
8. knowledge arranged or shaped to be understood
9. devices that move across to another shape

Day ③ Extend the Learning

Activities for teaching or reviewing the suffix **-er**, meaning *a person or device that does*, can be accessed using your personal account number to log onto the Dynamic Literacy website.

Focus Word: **TRANSFORM** ⟶ Write this word on the board.

TEACH

Sample leading question:	"I saw a great old movie recently. This nice friendly scientist would *transform* every night into a mean, nasty villain. What does it mean to *transform*?"
Target response:	"To change, to be different."
Teacher continuation:	"In what way is the person changed or different?"
Responses:	"They act different. They behave in a new way." "No—they look different, too. That's it—they have a new appearance!"

Encourage students to define *transform* using the pieces that make up the word: *to move across from one shape or appearance to another.*

DISCUSS Sample focused discussion: What does it mean if a caterpillar *transforms* into a butterfly?

DEMONSTRATE Put up the fraction 3/8 and ask if any student can *transform* that fraction into a decimal number. (The student should divide eight into three and the decimal number .375 will emerge.)

Word Play

Explore with students the difference between the words *reform* and *re-form*. *Reform* means 'to change,' usually for the better. *Re-form* means 'to put back into the same shape as before.'

transformation!

Day 4

In Other Words for FORM

FORM means shape, appearance, or arrangement

LESSON TIME

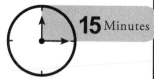

15 Minutes

OBJECTIVES

- **Understand** the meaning of the root **FORM**
- **Reinforce** knowledge of the root **FORM**
- **Understand** the meaning of words in the **FORM** family
- **Apply** knowledge of words in the **FORM** family

MATERIALS

- Student Activity Book
- **FORM** Word Wall
- Dictionary *(print or on-line)*

In Other Words for **FORM**

TEACH A new Combining Form (a root that joins with another root to build words) appears in this Activity. A Mini-Lesson for **ov** can be found on page 12, along with references to teaching or review activities for the prefixes **con-** and **mal-**, as needed.

Have students turn to page 6 of their Student Activity Books. Explain that they are going to read a little story that uses some surprising and sometimes odd phrasing. The underlined words or phrases in the story are actually definitions or synonyms for words in the **FORM** family. Then they will see sentences about the story, each containing a blank. Using context clues in the sentences, they will find a **FORM** family word in the Word Bank at the bottom to fit in each blank. Have a student read aloud the opening sentence or sentences of the story that contain the first underlined phrase. Then say, "Let's look at the first numbered sentence that contains a blank to be filled in. Clues in the sentence tell us that we want a descriptive word for **lesson**, and that there are no texts or classroom; the clue from the story says that it's *not the usual arrangement*. I see the word **informal** and it fits all the clues. Let's write **informal** in the blank for the first sentence."

COMPLETE THE ACTIVITY

This can be quite challenging, so allow students to work on this activity in small groups. Not every word in the Word Bank will be used.

DISCUSS

After about 10 minutes, ask if there were any difficulties. Have volunteers explain strategies they used that led to correct answers.

In Other Words...

SAB Pg 6

The Class Trip to the Caverns

The school class took a trip to the caverns and received an education about the earth, without textbook or <u>in the usual classroom arrangement</u>. The <u>change in appearance</u> of the landscape as we crossed from the green and bright surface of the earth into the totally dark cavern was amazing. When the tour guide Rocky turned on the lights, we gasped to see the all the rock <u>shapes and arrangements</u>.

Some rock arrangements were <u>shaped like eggs</u>, and others were shaped like columns. Some of the columns had not yet met in the middle, and Rocky <u>arranged information</u> in our heads that these had names depending on whether they were growing down from the ceiling or up from the ground. Appearing to grow up from the ground were stalagmites <u>all of one shape</u>. Rocky said that the length of the stalactites hanging from the ceiling gives us <u>well-arranged ideas</u> about the age of the caverns. Still in their <u>shaping and developing stage</u>, the stalactites and stalagmites are millions of years old.

Some rock patterns that seemed <u>badly shaped</u> were a result of earthquakes. The earth <u>changes its shape again and again</u> itself every so often violently through volcanic eruptions and earthquakes. The trip served <u>to shape data in our minds</u> and we are eager to go one day to see other caverns.

<u>Fill in the blanks below using words from the "form" family.</u>

1. Without texts and classroom, the class got an <u>informal</u> lesson on geology.

2. We were amazed at the <u>transformation</u> between the surface and the underground.

3. There are so many different types of rock <u>formations</u> in the caverns.

4. The <u>oviform</u> rocks looked exactly like eggs.

5. The guide <u>informed</u> us about how stalactites and stalagmites differ.

6. The stalagmites we saw were <u>uniformal</u>, all about two feet high.

7. The length of the stalactites gives us <u>information</u> about the age of the cavern.

8. Always changing its appearance, the earth is still in its <u>formative</u> stage.

9. Where rock patterns seemed <u>malformed</u>, we saw evidence of earthquakes.

10. Earthquakes and volcanoes <u>transform</u> the landscape below and above the surface.

11. Our trip to the caverns was highly <u>informative</u>; we learned a lot about the earth.

<u>Not Used:</u> conformation

OPTIONAL

Day 5

Morpheme Mania
for **FORM**

FORM means shape,
appearance, or arrangement

LESSON TIME

15 Minutes

OBJECTIVES

• **Build** words in the
  FORM family

• **Apply** knowledge of
  synonyms and antonyms
  to **FORM** words

Optional Morpheme Mania for **FORM**

On page 7 of their Activity Books, students will see an optional vocabulary enrichment activity that they can work on in groups, time permitting. This activity makes a great review for the formal assessment that you will find on the next page.

All the affixes presented in the week's activities are provided at the top of the page on either side of the root of the week. Students can write in up to 13 of the words they built during the week, possibly discovering additional ones.

Then students can brainstorm with each other to come up with antonyms and synonyms they may know. Starter examples are given with every Morpheme Mania in the Activity Book. Because antonyms and synonyms may require knowledge of roots which students have not yet studied, completion of this activity is not crucial. Simply remind students that they can at any time during the course of the year revisit any of their Morpheme Mania pages and add words, antonyms, and synonyms as their vocabulary grows.

Day 5 *Assessment*

Make and hand out copies.
The answer key is on page A-3.
The instructions are on page A-2.

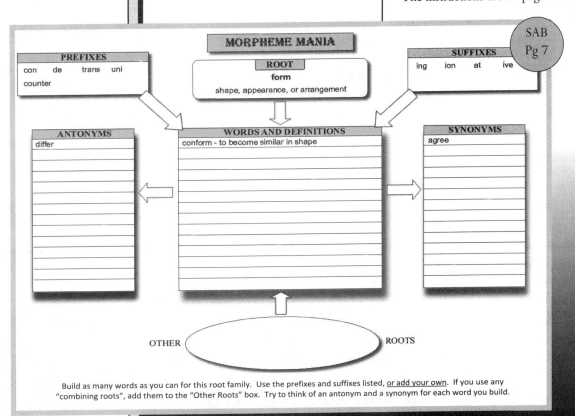

MORPHEME MANIA

SAB
Pg 7

PREFIXES
con   de   trans   uni
counter

ROOT
form
shape, appearance, or arrangement

SUFFIXES
ing   ion   at   ive

ANTONYMS
differ

WORDS AND DEFINITIONS
conform - to become similar in shape

SYNONYMS
agree

OTHER   ROOTS

Build as many words as you can for this root family. Use the prefixes and suffixes listed, <u>or add your own</u>. If you use any
"combining roots", add them to the "Other Roots" box. Try to think of an antonym and a synonym for each word you build.

conform to become similar in shape to something else; to comply

conformed became similar in shape to something else; complied

conformer a person wanting to share appearances with others; a person who complies

conformers people wanting to share appearances with others; people who comply

conforming becoming similar in shape to something else; complying

conformist a person who easily adapts to a shape or arrangement; a person who prefers to comply

conformists people who easily adapt to a shape or arrangement; people who prefer to comply

conformities similarities or agreements in shape or arrangement; qualities of complying

conformity similarity or agreement in shape or arrangement; quality of complying

conforms becomes similar in shape to something else; complies

deform to take away the nature or shape of; to ruin or contort

deformation act of taking away the nature or shape of; state of being ruined or contorted

deformations acts of taking away the nature or shape of; states of being ruined or contorted

deformed took away the nature or shape of; ruined or contorted

deformedly so as to take away the nature or shape of; in a ruined or contorted manner

deforming taking away the nature or shape of; ruining or contorting

deformities qualities of being away from an expected shape; qualities of being ruined or contorted

deformity quality of being away from an expected shape; quality of being ruined or contorted

deforms takes away the nature or shape of; ruins or contorts

form shape, appearance, or arrangement

formal in accord with accepted shape or arrangement

formality behavior for the sake of accepted arrangements

formalize to put into accepted arrangement or shape

formalized put into accepted arrangement or shape

formalizes puts into accepted arrangement or shape

formalizing putting into accepted arrangement or shape

formally so as to accord with accepted arrangement

format shape, appearance, or arrangement; a reusable pattern or structure

formation shape, appearance, arrangement

formational pertaining to shape, appearance, arrangement

formationally so as to pertain to shape, appearance, arrangement

formations shapes, appearances, or arrangements

formative related to shaping or developing

formats shapes or arranges; reusable patterns or structures

formatted shaped or arranged; put into a reusable pattern or structure

formatting shaping or arranging; putting into a reusable pattern or structure

formed shaped, arranged

former anything that gives shape or arrangement to

formers things that give shape or arrangement to

forming shaping, arranging

formless having no shape

forms shapes, appearances, or arrangements

formula a little shape or arrangement; logical arrangement of steps in a process

formulaic like a little shape or arrangement; of a logical arrangement of steps in a process

formulas little shapes or arrangements; logical arrangements of steps in processes

formulate to reduce to a small arrangement of steps or parts

formulated reduced to a small arrangement of steps or parts

formulates reduces to a small arrangement of steps or parts

formulating reducing to a small arrangement of steps or parts

formulation reduction to a small arrangement of steps or parts

formulations reductions to small arrangements of steps or parts

inform to give shape to ideas; to tell or notify

informal without shape or arrangement; relaxed

informalities qualities of not having accepted arrangement

informality quality of not having accepted arrangement

informally so as not to accord with accepted arrangement

information knowledge arranged or shaped to be understood

informational relating to providing shape to data

informative serving to provide shape to data

informatively in a manner serving to provide shape to data

informed gave shape to ideas; told or notified

informer a person who secretly provides shape to data

informers people who secretly provide shape to data

informing giving shape to ideas; telling or notifying

informingly in a manner giving shape to ideas

informs gives shape to ideas; tells or notifies

malform to shape badly

malformation bad shape or structure

malformations bad shapes or structures

malformed badly shaped

malforming causing to be shaped badly

malforms shapes badly

oviform shaped like an egg

reform to give another shape or appearance to; arrange again; to make over or improve

reformation act of shaping again

reformed changed the shape of again; made over or improved

reformer a person giving shape or arrangement to again

reformers people giving shape or arrangement to again

reforming changing the shape of again; making over or improving

reforms changes the shape of again; makes over or improves

transform to move across to another shape or appearance

transformation act of moving across to another shape

transformations acts of moving across to other shapes

transformed moved across to another shape or appearance

transformer a device that moves across to another shape

transformers devices that move across to another shape

transforming moving across to another shape or appearance

transforms moves across to another shape or appearance

uniform having one shape or appearance

uniformal pertaining to having one shape or appearance

uniformed attired in apparel of one shape or appearance

uniformities conditions of having one shape or appearance

uniformity condition of having one shape or appearance

uniformly in a manner having one shape or appearance

uniforms outfits having one shape or appearance

MINI-LESSON: the Combining Form **ov**

The Combining Form *ov* is from the Latin word for *egg*. The most familiar word using this root is the word **oval**, *egg-like in shape*.

Oviparous animals give birth through the use of eggs. Many other biological words are made with this combining form, including **ovipositor**, **oviduct**, **ovarian**, **ovocyte**, **ovoplasm**, and **oviform** as the most common ones. You may have students research and report on these and other biological terms as you think appropriate.

Review material for the prefixes **con-** and **mal-** can be accessed on the Dynamic Literacy website, as needed.

Check-Up for **FORM**   Name _____

____ **1.** FORM in words like **formative** and **uniformity** means:

A fair or balanced

B to measure

C arrangement

____ **2.** What is the meaning of the word **uniformal**?

A not balanced

B having one shape

C tending to measure inaccurately

____ **3.** What is the meaning of the word **transformation**?

A a process of measuring again

B the result of balancing

C an act of crossing shapes

____ **4.** What is the meaning of the word **conformation**?

A a process of taking on a shape with something else

B the result of being out of balance

C an act of measuring fairly

____ **5.** What is the meaning of the word **informative**?

A tending to measure across

B not having a good balance

C serving to put into good arrangement

____ **6.** Which word means **badly shaped**?

A malformed

B misinformation

C uniformed

____ **7.** Which word means **serving to put into shape**?

A formless

B formative

C information

____ **8.** Which word means **looking like an egg**?

A conform

B nonuniform

C oviform

____ **9.** Mr. Gradgrind was a **formalist** about teaching. Mr. Gradgrind:

A didn't have any preference about things

B liked things to be arranged his way

C let other people decide for themselves

____ **10.** The Curcio family **reformulated** their budget. They:

A arranged it in a new way

B measured it in the same way

C decided not to have a budget

OBJECTIVES

- **Understand** the meaning of the root **PON**
- **Build** words in the root **PON** family
- **Break Apart** words in the root **PON** family
- **Understand** the meaning of words in the **PON** family
- **Understand** the spelling principles applied to the root **PON**
- **Apply** knowledge of words in the **PON** family
- **Assess** and **Reinforce** knowledge of words in the **PON** family

MATERIALS

- Student Activity Books, pages 9-14
- Dictionary *(print or on-line)*
- Some toy blocks *(optional)*

CROSS-CURRICULAR EXAMPLES

Science:

component, compost, composite, decompose, deposit, dispose, oviposit

Social Studies:

counterpose, depose, impose, opponent, proponent

Language Arts:

apposition, composition, composer, opposite, preposition, proposal

Math:

posit, exponent, transpose

PON

meaning "to place or put"

position

to **place** (verb) or a specific **place** (noun)

compose

to **put** together

Morpheme: **PON**
Allomorphs: **PONE, POS, POSE, POST**

Over 700 words current in English use the root **PON** or one of its allomorphs. During this unit, tell students to be alert for this root in their school texts, general reading, and oral language they hear.

Some of the words they might encounter in their school subjects are listed on the left under Cross-Curricular Examples

UNIT AT A GLANCE

Day **1**
Root Squares for **PON**

Day **2**
Magic Squares for **PON**

Day **3**
Stair Steps for **PON**

OPTIONAL
Day **4**
In Other Words for **PON**

Day **5**
Assessment or Morpheme Mania for **PON**

Each activity should take approximately **15 minutes.**

Word Fun Facts

The root **PON** has other forms (allomorphs) **POS** and **POST** because of the past tense forms of the original Latin verb (similar to the differences between English **are** and **were**). Most words from this root family use the **POS** form, but we will refer to the root in its "default" form, **PON**.

If the root occurs at the end of a word (or with a final suffix **-s**), the allomorphs used are **PONE** (*postpone, postpones*) or **POSE** (*compose, composes*).

Etymologically, there are two separate words **POSE**. When you *pose* a question, you **put** it out there for someone to answer. Such a usage belongs to this root family. However, when you *pose* for a picture, you stop, or **pause**, and such a usage does not technically belong to this root family.

Similarly, when you *compose* a song, you **put** it together (from this root family), but when you *compose* yourself, you thoroughly **pause** and calm down (not from this root family). The two usages are so close in meaning, though, that any distinction in origin is now immaterial.

Word Tip

A valuable process to share with students helps to show whether a word has a specific root in it or not. It can be called the "proof" method, whereby the target root is isolated and the remaining parts of the word are analyzed. For example, if we divide the word *exponents*, we will find that every element in the word fits into a proper, meaningful category:

ex	pon	ent	s
prefix	root	suffix	suffix

This word *does* belong to the **PON** family.

However, if we divide a word like *responded* we are left with pieces that do not have meaning.

re	s	pon	d	ed
prefix	?	root	?	suffix

This word *cannot* belong to the **PON** family.
(It belongs with a root **SPOND**)

Word Alert!

There are many words that have the letters **P-O-N** or **P-O-S** in them, but they derive from other roots.

Words	Where they come from
poncho, pone, possum	American Indian words
possible, possess	Latin, *to be able*
ponder	Latin, *weight*
posy	Greek, *make*
sponge	Greek, *fungus*
respond, response	Latin, *promise*

Words	Where they come from
pontiff, pontoon	Latin, *bridge*
pond	Old English, *enclosure*
pony	Latin, *young animal*
coupon	French, *to cut*
post	Latin, *after*
typos	short for *typographical errors*

Day 1

Root Squares for PON

PON means
to place or put

LESSON TIME

15 Minutes

OBJECTIVES

- **Understand** the meaning of the root **PON**
- **Build** words in the **PON** family
- **Understand** the meaning of words in the **PON** family
- **Understand** the spelling principles applied to the root **PON**

MATERIALS

- Student Activity Book
- **PON** Word Wall
- Dictionary *(print or on-line)*

DIFFERENTIATING INSTRUCTION

If you prefer easier or more difficult activities, use your personal account at www.dynamicliteracy.com to access novice or expert versions, along with ideas on using them.

Root Squares for PON

TEACH Have students turn to page 9 in their Activity Books. Call attention to the center box. Unlike the root **FORM**, the root **PON** occurs in several different spellings, called *allomorphs*. Ask students to decide if any of those forms in the middle box can be a word. Students may see that *pose* is a word, and you can use that word to guide them to a meaning *to place or put* (we **put** ourselves into a certain shape when we *pose*). Students may also suggest that *pone* is a word, but tell them that *pone* is an American Indian word meaning *corn*. Tell students to start their list with *pose*. Say, "Notice that one of the affixes surrounding the middle box looks just like one of the allomorphs of today's root. That's just a coincidence that happens every now and then with words.

Let's talk a bit about the prefix **post-**." Use the Mini-Lesson for **post-** on the next page.

COMPLETE THE ACTIVITY

Have students add other affixes to **PON** or one of its allomorphs, list their words, and attempt simple definitions. Remind students to look in the inside covers of their Activity Books if they have questions about an affix. If students have difficulty building words with the Root Squares, show them how by modeling the matrix approach found on the next page, taking one affix at a time and seeing if it will connect with the root.

DISCUSS After five minutes, have volunteers write some of their words on the board. Focus with the class on the words they have written up and let them discuss how the meaning of the root is still *to place or put*, even when prefixes and suffixes are added. Watch for a target word that easily demonstrates the meaning to place or put. If the word *impose* is not present, ask the class, "Can anyone try to use the prefix **im-**?" and then use the target word discussion on the next page.

Root Squares

How many words can you make?

Start in any square. Your goal is to combine two or more word parts to make as many words in the 'pon, pone, pos, pose, post' family as you can. Write each word and a definition you can think of for it in the space provided at the bottom of the page. Use the back of the page if you need to.

com	er	de
ent	pon, pone, pos, pose, post	ite
post	ion	im

SAB Pg 9

MINI-LESSON: the Prefix *post-*

The prefix **post-** comes from the Latin preposition that means *after or later than* whatever it is attached to. Write up these words for your students, and let them discuss what adding the prefix **post-** does to each:

adolescent   **concert**   **convention**   **game**   **war**

Focus Word: **IMPOSE** ⟶ Write this word on the board.

TEACH

Sample leading question:	"Did you ever have a friend *impose* upon you?"
Student response:	"Would that mean they accused you of doing something they did, they put it on you?"
Teacher continuation:	"Not exactly, though that's a good suggestion."
Target response:	"Would it mean they had you carry something for them?"
Teacher:	"Maybe, but it's more than that. Let's try to figure it out from the word itself. What does the prefix **im-** mean?"
Student:	"It could mean *not*, couldn't it?" "It could mean *in* or *on*. How do we know?"
Teacher:	"We don't know until we've learned the word, but we've heard it in context already, so let's see if we can figure it out."
Student:	"I know! I've heard the expression *"to be put upon,"* meaning *to be bothered*—that's exactly what *impose* means!"
Continuation:	"Good—it's to **put** a burden on or trouble somebody."
Response:	"Then I have definitely had friends **impose** on me!"

Encourage students to define *impose* not simply as *to bother* but, using the meanings of the two pieces that make up the word, *to put upon*.

DISCUSS Sample focused discussion: What things might be an *imposition* for others, and why?

DEMONSTRATE Set a single block out on a table. Have a student take another block and *impose* it upon the other. *Impose* as many times as possible before the structure falls.

Root Squares Matrix

You can refer to this matrix to guide students in this activity. Students could build at least these 29 words. **It really doesn't matter how many they build** – the point is that they understand the consistent meanings of the root **pon** and of its prefixes and suffixes.

	no prefix	com-	de-	post-	im-
no suffix	post	compost		postpone	impost
	pose	compose	depose	postpose	impose
			depone		impone
-ent		component	deponent		imponent
-er	poser	composer	deposer	postponer	imposter
			deponer		imponer
-it(e)	posit	composite	deposit		
-it(e) + -ion	position	composition	deposition	postposition	imposition

Day 2

Magic Squares for PON

PON means
to place or put

LESSON TIME

15 Minutes

OBJECTIVES

- **Understand** the meaning of the root **PON**

- **Break Apart** words in the **PON** family

- **Understand** the meanings of words in the **PON** family

MATERIALS

- Student Activity Book

- **PON** Word Wall

- Dictionary *(print or on-line)*

DIFFERENTIATING INSTRUCTION

If you prefer easier or more difficult activities, use your personal account at www.dynamicliteracy.com to access novice or expert versions, along with ideas on using them.

Break Apart Words with PON

TEACH One variation of a familiar prefix appears in this activity. Use the Mini-Lesson for **sup-** found on the next page. Then have students turn to the Magic Squares on page 10 in their Student Activity Books. Model a Think-Aloud strategy for students: "I know that **PON** or **POS** means *to place or put.* I can use this knowledge to find the definition of a word with **PON** or **POS** as its root." Direct students to word G, *imposition.* Say, "I know that the prefix **im-** means *in or on* and that the suffix **-ion** makes a noun *like an act.* Definition 10 says *the act of putting oneself in the way,* and that seems right. The follow-up definition, *an addition of a tax or task,* makes me sure that I can write the number 10 in box G.

COMPLETE THE ACTIVITY

Ask students to use the same strategy to find the correct definitions for the other words. Tell them to write the number of the definition in the box that matches the letter for the word. Remind them that if all their answers are correct, each row and each column will add up to the same Magic number.

DISCUSS After five minutes, ask if there are any difficulties about matching the words and definitions. If there are, ask volunteers to explain clues in the definitions that will lead to the correct choice of word.

Add any new words to the classroom **PON** Word Wall and remind students to add these words to the **PON** Word Wall in their Activity Books. As needed, follow the focus word approach that you see modeled on the next page.

SAB
Pg 10

Magic Squares

Select the best answer for each of the words in the 'pon, pone, pos, pose, post' family from the numbered definitions. Put the number in the proper space in the Magic Square box. If the total of the numbers is the same both across and down, you have found the magic number!

'pon, pone, pos, pose, post' means to place or put

WORDS	DEFINITIONS
A. opposition	1. act of being put out; act of being publicly shown
B. suppose	2. placement in conflict against
C. positive	3. items put together; units that make a whole
D. postponement	4. something put outside; a math symbol denoting the 'power' of a numerical amount
E. exponent	
F. disposers	5. people who put down; people who put money into a bank for safekeeping
G. imposition	6. the act of putting off until afterwards
H. depositors	7. certain of what is said or put forth; confident and sure of what is proposed
I. components	
	8. people who put away; people who throw things away after use
	9. to put up; to offer up as a suggestion or argument
	10. the act of putting oneself in the way; the addition of a tax or task

Magic Square Box

A. 2	B. 9	C. 7
D. 6	E. 4	F. 8
G. 10	H. 5	I. 3

Magic Number __18__

*** ANSWER KEY ***

Day ② Extend the Learning

MINI-LESSON: the Prefix *sup-*

The prefix **sup-** is an assimilated form of the prefix **sub-**, meaning *below, up from below, or not enough*.

Write up these words spelled with the prefix **sub-** and have students pronounce them. They will then understand why the letter **b** becomes the letter **p**.

subport   **subpose**   **subpress**

Draw on the board a roof being ***supported*** by columns and let students discuss and visualize the morphological definition: *to carry from below*.

Lead students to visualize how the prefix **sup-** works in phrases such as ***suppressing*** a riot (*pushing it under, crushing it*) and ***supposing*** a situation (*bringing it up*).

The other prefixes and suffixes used with this activity were featured in earlier levels of ***WordBuild*** Teacher Editions. You can access information about, Activities for, or Mini-Lessons for these other affixes by using your personal account number to log onto the Dynamic Literacy website.

Focus Word: **SUPPOSE** ⟶ Write this word on the board.

TEACH

Sample leading question	"Did you ever think what it means when you **suppose** something?"
Student response:	"You think it's true." "We're **supposed** to—whoops—I just used that word! Now I'm really confused."
Teacher continuation:	"Let's solve this morphological puzzle together, step-by-step. We see the root there, right?
Target response:	"Yes, *to put or place*."
Teacher:	"And the prefix?"
Target responses:	"That's the new variation of **sub-**, *under or up from below*." "Hmm, *to put up from below*. Let me see. "I get it—you suggest something, you bring it up and put it out for others to think about."
More Response:	"But wait a minute. What about when you're ***supposed*** to do something, meaning you are required or expected to do it? How does that work?
Teacher continuation:	"Let's think it through."
Response:	"How about that it was just someone's suggestion they *put up* that it was a requirement?"
Teacher:	"That's great. Sometimes it seems like a stretch, but if we think hard, we can usually see the connection between a word's morphemes and its usage. Nicely done."

DISCUSS A ***supposition*** is something *brought up* to consider. Tell students that the exact Greek translation of ***supposition*** is *hypothesis*. See if students can detect any difference in usage or application. (A ***supposition*** is more general and less scientific or logical).

DEMONSTRATE Put up the idea that it will snow tonight. What ***suppositions*** can students make about tomorrow?

19

Day 3

Stair Steps for PON

PON means to place or put

LESSON TIME

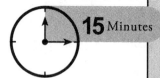

15 Minutes

OBJECTIVES

- **Understand** the meaning of the root **PON**
- **Apply** knowledge of the root **PON**
- **Break Apart** words in the **PON** family
- **Understand** the meaning of words in the **PON** family
- **Understand** the spelling principles applied to the root **PON**

MATERIALS

- Student Activity Book
- **PON** Word Wall

DIFFERENTIATING INSTRUCTION

If you prefer easier or more difficult activities, use your personal account at www.dynamicliteracy.com to access novice or expert versions, along with ideas on using them.

Apply Knowledge of PON

TEACH Have students turn to the Stair Steps activity in their Student Activity Books, page 11. Ask a volunteer to read definition number 5 at the bottom of the page. Say, "So we're looking for a clue in the definition to a four-letter prefix to put in front of and a two-letter suffix to put after **PON**." If no one offers, say, "Is there a prefix that means *afterwards*?" If still no one answers, remind students of the prefix **post**-. If no one suggests what suffix is needed, ask students to give you the past tense of the English word *put* (it is *put* as well). Since *put* can be past tense, the past tense suffix -**ed** will work.

COMPLETE THE ACTIVITY

Let students work in pairs (optionally) and tell them to use the same strategy to find the correct prefixes and suffixes for the words listed.

DISCUSS After a few minutes, review the answers as a class. Ask if there were any difficulties. Listen to any problems and have groups or individuals solve the difficulties by explaining key clues in the given definitions. As needed, follow the focus word approach that you see modeled on the next page.

Stair Steps

Fill in the missing letters of each 'pon' word by using the definitions be[low]
'pon' means to place or put

SAB Pg 11

1.	p	o	s	e	d					
2.	i	m	p	o	s	e				
3.	d	e	p	o	s	i	t			
4.	c	o	m	p	o	s	e	r		
5.	p	o	s	t	p	o	n	e	d	
6.	c	o	m	p	o	n	e	n	t	s
7.	p	r	e	p	o	s	i	t	i	o	n
8.	s	u	p	e	r	i	m	p	o	s	e	s
9.	d	e	c	o	m	p	o	s	i	t	i	o	n

1. put on a deliberate manner or look; intentionally displayed a look or stance
2. to put in the way; to add on a tax or task
3. to put down; to put money into a bank for safekeeping
4. a person who puts together; a creator, especially of music
5. put off until afterwards
6. items put together; units that make a whole
7. quality of being placed in front; a part of speech placed in front of its object
8. puts down on top of something
9. act or process of leaving off from being put together; disintegration

Prefixes used with this activity were featured in earlier levels of **WordBuild** Teacher Editions. You can access information about, Activities for, or Mini-Lessons for these prefixes by using your personal account number to log onto the Dynamic Literacy website.

Focus Word: **POSTPONE** ⟶ Write this word on the board.

TEACH

Sample leading question:	"If a game is ***postponed***, what happens to it?"
Student:	"It gets cancelled, maybe because of rain."
Teacher:	"Is it cancelled?"
Student:	"No, it's just put off until later."
Teacher:	"Is there anything in the word ***postpone*** itself that tells us this?"
Student:	"Yes! Its pieces mean exactly that—*put off until later!*"
Response:	"Great—you see, words tell us things about themselves we might never have imagined."

DISCUSS Let students give examples of events that were ***postponed***. They can talk about why the ***postponement*** occurred and when the event finally took place again.

DEMONSTRATE Say, "I was going to have you write a paper for me today, but I think I'll ***postpone*** it. For what later date shall I put that assignment?"

Day 4

In Other Words for **PON**

PON means to place or put

LESSON TIME

15 Minutes

OBJECTIVES

- **Understand** the meaning of the root **PON**
- **Reinforce** knowledge of the root **PON**
- **Understand** the meaning of words in the **PON** family
- **Apply** knowledge of words in the **PON** family

MATERIALS

- Student Activity Book
- **PON** Word Wall
- Dictionary *(print or on-line)*

In Other Words for **PON**

TEACH Have students turn to page 12 in their Student Activity Books. Explain that they are going to read a little story that uses some surprising and sometimes odd phrasing. The underlined words or phrases in the story are actually definitions or synonyms for words in the **PON** family. Then they will see sentences about the story, each containing a blank. Using context clues in the sentences, they will find a **PON** family word in the Word Bank at the bottom to fit in each blank. Have a student read aloud the opening sentence or sentences of the story that contain the first underlined phrase. Then say, "Let's look at the first numbered sentence that contains a blank to be filled in. Clues in the sentence tell us that we want a *verb* to go with the subject *announcement*. The first underlined clue back in the story itself says that the word we want means *was put out*. I see the word **exposed** in the Word Bank, and it fits all the clues. Let's write **exposed** in the blank for the first sentence."

COMPLETE THE ACTIVITY

This can be quite challenging, so allow students to work on this activity in small groups. Every word in the Word Bank will be used, so a process of elimination can help.

DISCUSS After about 10 minutes, ask if there were any difficulties. Have volunteers explain strategies they used that led to correct answers. Do not worry if the whole activity is not completed, but let students make the correlation between as many of the phrases in the story with the words in the individual sentences as time allows.

SAB Pg 12

LOCAL LONER DISCOVERED TO BE MULTI-MILLIONAIRE

It was <u>put out</u> today that a local woman who died last week had been <u>putting herself forth</u> as a poor person but had <u>put down</u> millions every week over the years into the bank's place <u>for holding back accounts</u>. She left a will <u>to put away</u> all her wealth to her twenty first cousins. Penny N. Digent, who kept to herself, had held various <u>jobs</u> over the years and her neighbors had <u>put as a suggestion</u> that she had no relatives. The bank has <u>put forward an idea</u> that those who can prove their relationship with Ms. Digent should <u>put together</u> a family chart, with all the properly documented pieces put together, and bring it to the bank. People who <u>put themselves in a false light</u> will be arrested for fraud. The bank has <u>put off until later</u> setting a deadline for the charts.

<u>Fill in the blanks below using words from the "pon, pone, pos, pose, post" family.</u>

1. The bank's announcement <u>exposed</u> that the late Ms. Digent was a multi-millionaire.
2. Although very wealthy, she had been <u>posturing</u> as a poor person.
3. Every week she had <u>deposited</u> her money into the bank.
4. The bank had a special <u>repository</u> for accounts like this one.
5. The bank wishes to <u>dispose</u> of this wealth as Ms. Digent wished.
6. Ms. Digent worked in several <u>positions</u> over many years.
7. She never spoke of her relatives; <u>supposedly</u> she had no family.
8. Official at the bank have <u>proposed</u> that qualifying relatives come forth.
9. Those qualified need to <u>compose</u> a family tree.
10. This family tree must have all the legal <u>components</u> to document the relationship.
11. This way, the bank will be able to prevent <u>imposters</u> from getting the money.
12. A decision to set the deadline for the charts has been <u>postponed</u>.

Day 5

Morpheme Mania for **PON**

PON means
to place or put

LESSON TIME

15 Minutes

OBJECTIVES

• **Build** words in the **PON** family

• **Apply** knowledge of synonyms and antonyms to **PON** words

Optional Morpheme Mania for **PON**

On page 13 of their Activity Books, students will see an optional vocabulary enrichment activity that they can work on in groups, time permitting. This activity makes a great review for the formal assessment on the next page.

All the affixes presented in the week's activities are provided at the top of the page on either side of the root of the week. Students can write in up to 13 of the words they built during the week, possibly discovering additional ones.

Then students can brainstorm with each other to come up with antonyms and synonyms they may know. Starter examples are given with every Morpheme Mania in the Activity Book. Because antonyms and synonyms may require knowledge of roots which students have not yet studied, completion of this activity is not crucial. Simply remind students that they can at any time during the course of the year revisit any of their Morpheme Mania pages and add words, antonyms, and synonyms as their vocabulary grows.

Day 5 *Assessment*

Make and hand out copies.
The answer key is on page A-3.
The instructions are on page A-2.

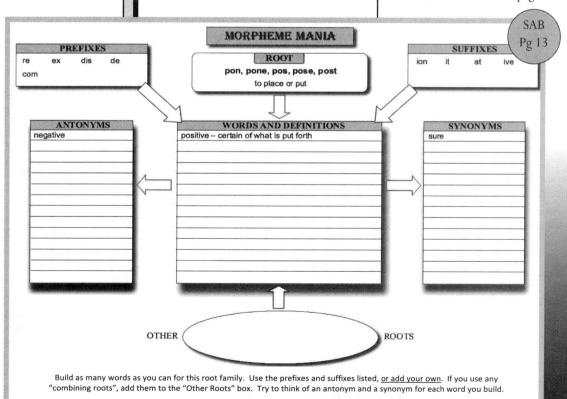

SAB
Pg 13

MORPHEME MANIA

PREFIXES			
re	ex	dis	de
com			

ROOT
pon, pone, pos, pose, post
to place or put

SUFFIXES			
ion	it	at	ive

ANTONYMS
negative

WORDS AND DEFINITIONS
positive – certain of what is put forth

SYNONYMS
sure

OTHER ROOTS

Build as many words as you can for this root family. Use the prefixes and suffixes listed, or add your own. If you use any "combining roots", add them to the "Other Roots" box. Try to think of an antonym and a synonym for each word you build.

apposition placement of two nouns near one another to explain

appositive related to being placed near to explain

component an item put together; one of the units making up a whole

components items put together; units that make a whole

compose to put together; to create or build

composed put together; created or built

composer a person who puts together; a creator, especially of music or poetry

composers people who put together; creators, especially of music or poetry

composes puts together; creates, especially music or poetry

composing putting together; creating, especially music or poetry

composite something put together from different parts

composites things put together from different parts

composition something put together; a musical or literary creation

compositional related to anything put together

compositions things put together; musical or literary creations

compost something put together; a mixture of decaying organic material

composts things put together; types of mixtures of decaying organic material

composure state of being in place with oneself; calmness or self-control

decompose to come apart after being put together; to disintegrate

decomposed came apart after being put together; disintegrated

decomposes comes apart after being put together; disintegrates

decomposing coming apart after being put together; disintegrating

decomposition act or process of coming apart after being put together; disintegration

depose to put down; to remove from power

deposed put down; removed from power

deposes puts down; removes from power

deposing putting down; removing from power

deposit to put down; to put money into a bank for safekeeping

deposited put down; put money into a bank for safekeeping

depositing putting down; putting money into a bank for safekeeping

deposition a formal statement put down

depositions formal statements put down

depositor a person who puts down; a person who puts money into a bank for safekeeping

depositors people who put down; people who put money into a bank for safekeeping

depository a place for putting down; storage unit

deposits puts down; puts money into a bank for safekeeping

disposability capability of being put away; ability to be thrown away after use

disposable capable of being put away; able to be thrown away after use

disposables things that can be put away; things that can be thrown away after use

disposal act or process of putting away; the right to throw away or use

dispose to put away; to throw away after use

disposed put away; threw away after use

disposer a person who puts away; a person who throws something away after use

disposers people who put away; people who throw things away after use

disposes puts away; throws away after use

disposing putting away; throwing away after use

disposition act or process of putting away; act of throwing away after use

dispositions acts or processes of putting away; acts of throwing away after use

exponent something put outside; a math symbol denoting numerical power

exponential related to being placed outside; pertaining to numerical power

exponentially in a manner related to being placed outside; so as to relate to numerical power

exponents things put outside; numerical powers

expose to put out; to show publicly

exposed put out; showed publicly

exposes puts out; shows publicly

exposing putting out; showing publicly

exposition a putting out; a public showing

expositions acts of putting out; public showings

exposure act of being put out; act of being publicly shown

exposures things put out; things publicly shown

impose to put upon; to add on a tax or task

imposed put upon; added on a tax or task

imposes puts upon; adds on a tax or task

imposing putting upon; adding on a tax or task

imposition the act of putting oneself in the way; the addition of a tax or task

impositions acts of putting oneself in the way; additions of taxes or tasks

indispose to put in incorrect or uncomfortable state; to make unfit

indisposed put in incorrect or uncomfortable state; made unfit

indisposes puts in incorrect or uncomfortable state; makes unfit

indisposing putting in incorrect or uncomfortable state; making unfit

indisposition act of being put into an uncomfortable state; act of making unfit

indispositions acts of being put into uncomfortable states; acts of making unfit

opponent a person who is placed against; a rival, as in a game

opponents people who are placed against; rivals, as in games

oppose to put up against; to act against or be in conflict with

opposed put up against; acted against or was in conflict with

opposer a person who puts himself or herself up against; a person who acts against or in conflict with

opposers people who put themselves up against; people who act against or in conflict with something

opposes puts up against; acts against or is in conflict with

opposing putting up against; acting against or being in conflict with

opposite a thing different from or put up against; a thing exactly contrary to

oppositely so as to be put up against; so as to be contradicting to

opposites things different from or put up against; things exactly contrary to

opposition placement in conflict against

pose to put; to ask; to put on a deliberate manner or look

posed put; asked; put on a deliberate manner or look

poser a person who puts a question; a person who seems superficial

posers people who put questions; people who seem superficial

poses puts; asks; puts on a deliberate manner or look

posing putting; asking; putting on a deliberate manner or look

position place where something is put; job

positioned put in a specific place

positions places where things are put; jobs

positive put forth with certainty; confident and sure

positively in a manner put forth with certainty; confidently and surely

post place of duty where someone is put

postage stamp allowing mail to be put out

postal related to stations that put out mail

posted put into a place of duty

posting putting into a place of duty

postpone to put off until afterwards

postponed put off until afterwards

postponement the act of putting off until afterwards

postponements acts of putting off until afterwards

postpones puts off until afterwards

postponing putting off until afterwards

posts places of duty where people are put

posture the way a person places himself or herself; a person's stance

postured placed oneself; stood or modeled one's body in a way for effect

postures places oneself; stands or models one's body in a way for effect

posturing putting one's body in a stance for effect

predispose to put aside beforehand; to show a tendency

predisposed put aside beforehand; showed a tendency

predisposes puts aside beforehand; shows a tendency

predisposing putting aside beforehand; showing a tendency

predisposition act of being put aside beforehand; a tendency

predispositions acts of being put aside beforehand; tendencies

preposition quality of being placed in front; a part of speech placed in front of its object

prepositional related to being placed in front; pertaining to being put before an object

prepositions things placed in front; words put before their objects

proposal something put forth; a suggestion offered

proposals things put forth; suggestions offered

propose to put forth; to suggest or offer an idea

proposed put forth; suggested or offered an idea

proposer a person who puts forth; a person who suggests or offers an idea

proposers people who put forth; people who suggest or offer ideas

proposes puts forth; suggests or offers an idea

proposing putting forth; suggesting or offering an idea

proposition something put forth; a suggestion or idea offered

purpose that which is put forth; a reason given

purposeful characteristic of things put forth; having many reasons

purposefully in a manner characteristic of things put forth; in a manner having many reasons

purposely in a manner put forth; for a specific reason

purposes things put forth; reasons given

repose to place oneself back; to rest

reposed placed oneself back; rested

reposes places oneself back; rests

reposing placing oneself back; resting

repository place where things are put back

superimpose to put down on top of something

superimposed put down on top of something

superimposes puts down on top of something

superimposing putting down on top of something

suppose to put up; to offer up as a suggestion or argument

supposed put up; offered up as a suggestion or argument

supposedly in a manner put up; so as to be offered up as a suggestion or argument

supposes puts up; offers up as a suggestion or argument

supposing putting up; offering up as a suggestion or argument

supposition something put up; a suggestion or argument

suppositional relating to something put up; relating to a suggestion or argument

Check-Up for **PON**

Name _____

____ **1.** **PON** or **POS** in words like **component** and **position** means:

    A to place or put

    B to save or protect

    C to seek

____ **2.** What is the meaning of the word **compose**?

    A to protect completely

    B to put together

    C to seek along with

____ **3.** What is the meaning of the word **depose**?

    A to move away from

    B to seek information from

    C to put down

____ **4.** What is the meaning of the word **proposed**?

    A put forth

    B protected

    C sat in front of

____ **5.** What is the meaning of the word **imposition**?

    A quality of not being able to sit

    B a result of seeking to protect

    C an act of putting a burden on someone

____ **6.** Which word means **a place to store things**?

    A imposter

    B repository

    C imponent

____ **7.** Which word means **the process of placing up against**?

    A opposition

    B exponent

    C depone

____ **8.** Which word means **an act of putting off until later**?

    A superimpose

    B preposition

    C postponement

____ **9.** The generous millionaire made good **disposition** of his money. He:

    A kept his money hidden from everyone

    B put his money in many different places

    C sought to double his money

____ **10.** Dickie always **transposed** the vowels in the word *their*. Dickie:

    A was careful to write the letters clearly

    B switched the letters

    C left out the letters

OBJECTIVES

- **Understand** the meaning of the root **QUEST**

- **Build** words in the root **QUEST** family

- **Break Apart** words in the root **QUEST** family

- **Understand** the meaning of words in the **QUEST** family

- **Understand** the spelling principles applied to the root **QUEST**

- **Apply** knowledge of words in the **QUEST** family

- **Assess** and **Reinforce** knowledge of words in the **QUEST** family

MATERIALS

- Student Activity Books, pages 15-20

- Dictionary *(print or on-line)*

CROSS-CURRICULAR EXAMPLES

Science:
inquiry, questionable, requirement

Social Studies:
quest, inquisition, acquisition, conquest, conquistador

Language Arts:
inquisitive, exquisite, question, unconquerable

Math:
query, inquiry, requirement, prerequisite

QUEST

meaning "to ask, seek, gain"

question
to **ask** or the act of **asking**

quest
an act of **seeking**

conquest
something **gained** completely

Morpheme: **QUEST**
Allomorphs: **QUIS, QUIR, QUIRE, QUER**

Over 300 words containing the morpheme QUEST or one of its allomorphs are current in English. During this unit, tell students to be alert for this root in their school texts, general reading, and oral language they hear. Some of the words they might encounter in their school subjects are listed on the left under Cross-Curricular Examples.

UNIT AT A GLANCE

Day ① *Root Squares* for **QUEST**

Day ② *Magic Squares* for **QUEST**

Day ③ *Stair Steps* for **QUEST**

OPTIONAL
Day ④ *In Other Words* for **QUEST**

Day ⑤ *Assessment or Morpheme Mania* for **QUEST**

Each activity should take approximately **15 minutes**.

Sometimes a root morpheme exists as a word in and of itself. That's true with the morpheme **FORM** (*a shape*), and it's true with the morpheme **QUEST** (*a search*).

Original definitions and applications of words can, over time, become broader or more generalized. An example of broadening application is with the word *exquisite*. The maker of something described as *exquisite* sought out every detail and carefully paid attention to seeking flawlessness and perfection. The word has generalized to be a synonym for *beautiful or fine*.

A *perquisite*, *thoroughly sought*, is anything that a person gains above and beyond basic expectations, such as a parking privilege or a tip. You'll most often hear and see this word shortened to *perk*, as in, "There are some great *perks* with this job."

The prefix **ad-**, when assimilated with the root **QUEST**, becomes **ac-**. Assimilation is a phonetic process. Since the letter **q** is pronounced as a **kw** sound, the **d** of the prefix **ad-** takes on a "hard" **c** sound, like a **k**, to match, or become similar to, the hard **c** sound that the letter **q** makes.

The *conquistadors* of early American history carry this root in their name. They were Spaniards seeking power and gold in South America and southern North America.

Word Alert! The French spelling of a document seeking to learn a body of information is *questionnaire*. Following the pattern of *millionaire* or *doctrinaire*, however, the word could reasonably be spelled *questionaire*.

One family of words with the letters **q-u-e-s-t** should not be confused with the morpheme that means *ask, seek, or gain*. That family of words has to do with horses, as in the word *equestrian*. Another such unrelated family has to do with *separating*, as in *sequester*.

The royal title *marquis* is not related to this root, nor are words such as *squirm* or *squish*.

The word *squirrel* derives from two Greek morphemes meaning *shadow* and *tail*.

Proof Method: *squish* and *squirm*

The correct way to split words into morphemes should be illustrated often.

Wrong: S—QUIS—H   S—QUIR—M

Since an initial letter **s** and final letters **h** or **m** do not contain meaning, the morpheme **quis** or **quir** must not be present in these words. The words *squish* and *squirm* cannot be split into more than one morpheme.

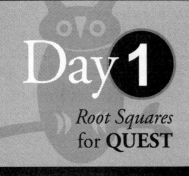

Day 1

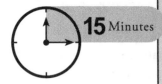

Root Squares
for **QUEST**

QUEST means
to seek, ask, gain

LESSON TIME

15 Minutes

OBJECTIVES

- **Understand** the meaning of the root **QUEST**
- **Build** words in the **QUEST** family
- **Understand** the meaning of words in the **QUEST** family
- **Understand** the spelling principles applied to the root **QUEST**

MATERIALS

- Student Activity Book
- **QUEST** Word Wall
- Dictionary *(print or on-line)*

DIFFERENTIATING INSTRUCTION

If you prefer easier or more difficult activities, use your personal account at www.dynamicliteracy.com to access novice or expert versions, along with ideas on using them.

Root Squares for QUEST

TEACH Have students turn to page 15 in their Activity Books. Say, "All of the prefixes and suffixes in the squares surrounding the shaded center are probably familiar, but if you have questions about any of the meanings, simply ask or look it up in the list inside the front and back cover of the activity book." Remember, you can access information about or Mini-Lessons for the affixes used with this and upcoming Activities for the root **QUEST** on the Dynamic Literacy website.

Call attention to the center box. Point out that the root **QUEST** has several different spellings, called *allomorphs*. Ask students to decide if any of the forms they see in the middle square can stand alone as a word. They may see that *quest* is a word, and you can use that word to guide them to the meaning *to ask, seek, or gain*. When we *seek* something, we are on a *quest*. Suggest that students start their list with *quest* and then add the suffix **-ion** to build a second word, *question*.

COMPLETE THE ACTIVITY If students have difficulty building words with the Root Squares, show them how by modeling the matrix approach found on the next page, taking one affix at a time and seeing if it will connect with any one of the allomorphs of the root.

DISCUSS After five minutes, have volunteers write some of their words on the board. Focus with the class on the words they have built and guide them in a discussion of how the meaning of the root is still *to ask, seek, or gain*, even when prefixes and suffixes are added. The sample focus word dialogue on the next page will give you some ideas about demonstrating the meanings of *to ask, seek, or gain*.

Root Squares

How many words can you make?

Start in any square. Your goal is to combine two or more word parts to make as many words in the 'quest, quis, quir, quire, quer' family as you can. Write each word and a definition you can think of for it in the space provided at the bottom of the page. Use the back of the page if you need to.

ac	ion	in
it	quest, quis, quir, quire, quer	con
ment	ive	re

SAB
Pg 15

Focus Word: **QUESTION** ⟶ Write these words on the board.

TEACH

Sample leading question:	"Here are the words *quest* and *question*. Let's take a look at all the ways the two words are alike or different."
Student: Student: Student:	"Their first five letters are the same." "They can both be nouns." "You can go on a *quest*, but you can't go on a *question*."
Student:	"*Question* can be a verb, so you can *question* somebody, but you can't *quest* somebody."
Student:	Yes, it *can* be a verb, too—dogs *quest* things like birds."
Teacher:	"These are all great observations. How are they alike in meaning?"
Student:	"I get it—the root means *seek*, and with both words, you're *seeking* something!"
Student:	"Yes—you're after something, either information or prey!"
Student:	"A *quest* seems like a big deal but a *question* can be about any little thing."
Teacher:	"Yes, word usages differ, but we see that the core meaning remains the same no matter what words are made from the root."

DISCUSS Sample focused discussion: Let groups of students brainstorm for a few minutes on words in English that ask *questions* in and of themselves (words like *who, what, when, where, how,* and *why*).

Another discussion could center on games or stories that deal with a *quest*.

DEMONSTRATE Have students tell what specific information is being *sought* with each of those *question* words (called *interrogatives*).

Root Squares Matrix

You can refer to this matrix to guide students in this activity. Students could build at least these 22 words. *It really doesn't matter how many they build* – the point is that they understand the consistent meanings of the root **QUEST** and of its prefixes and suffixes.

	no prefix	ac-	con-	in-	re-
no suffix	quest		conquest	inquest	request
			conquer		
		acquire		inquire	require
-ion	question				
-ite		acquisite			requesite
-ment		acquirement			requirement
-it + -ive		acquisitive		inquisitive	
-it + -ion		acquisition		inquisition	requisition
re- + suffixes	requestion	reaquire	reconquer	reinquire	

Words that students coin for empty slots are legitimate learning tools: have students who coin such words give appropriate definitions for them.

Day 2

Magic Squares
for **QUEST**

QUEST means
to seek, ask, gain

LESSON TIME

15 Minutes

OBJECTIVES

- **Understand** the meaning of the root **QUEST**
- **Break Apart** words in the **QUEST** family
- **Understand** the meanings of words in the **QUEST** family

MATERIALS

- Student Activity Book
- **QUEST** Word Wall
- Dictionary
  (print or on-line)

DIFFERENTIATING INSTRUCTION

If you prefer easier or more difficult activities, use your personal account at www.dynamicliteracy.com to access novice or expert versions, along with ideas on using them.

Break Apart Words with QUEST

TEACH Have students turn to the Magic Squares on page 16 in their Student Activity Books. Model a Think-Aloud strategy for students: "I know that **QUEST**, with the various spellings of this root, means *to ask, seek, or gain*. I can use this knowledge to find the definition of a word with this as its root." Direct students to word I, *exquisite*. Say, "I know that the prefix **ex-** means *out* and that the suffix **-ite** means *of, related to, suited for*. Definition #3 is the only one with the idea of *out* in its definition: *highly desirable to be sought out; superb*. Since *desirable* and *suited for* are practically the same thing, I think we'll write the number 3 in square I."

SAB Pg 16

COMPLETE THE ACTIVITY

Ask students to use the same strategy to find the correct definitions for the other words. Tell them to write the number of the definition in the box that matches the letter for the word. Remind them that if all their answers are correct, each row and each column will add up to the same Magic number.

DISCUSS After five minutes, ask if there are any difficulties about matching the words and definitions. If there are, ask volunteers to explain clues in the definitions that will lead to the correct choice of word. As needed, follow the focus word approach for *requirement* that you see modeled on the next page.

Add any new words to the classroom **QUEST** Word Wall and remind students to add these words to the **QUEST** Word Wall in their Activity Books.

Magic Squares

Select the best answer for each of the words in the 'quest, quis, quir, quire, quer' family from the numbered definitions. Put the number in the proper space in the Magic Square box. If the total of the numbers is the same both across and down, you have found the magic number!

'quest, quis, quir, quire, quer' means to ask, seek, gain

WORDS	DEFINITIONS
A. acquires	1. seeking into; searching for information
B. requisitioner	2. a person who formally seeks back; a person who demands as necessary
C. questionable	3. highly desirable to be sought out; superb
D. conquerable	4. able to be gained completely; able to be defeated
E. unquestionable	5. sought into; searched for information
F. requirement	6. not subject to being asked about; definite or secure
G. inquired	7. in a manner subject to be asked about; uncertainly
H. inquisitively	8. something that must be sought back; something demanded as necessary
I. exquisite	9. brings gain to; seeks and gains
	10. in a manner tending to seek into or ask; in a manner tending to question

Magic Square Box

A. 9	B. 2	C. 7
D. 4	E. 6	F. 8
G. 5	H. 10	I. 3

Magic Number __18__

*** ANSWER KEY ***

Focus Word: **REQUIREMENT** ➝ Write this word on the board.

TEACH

Sample leading question:	"Just what exactly is a ***requirement***?"
Student:	"It's something you must have."
Teacher:	"Name some things that are ***requirements***."
Students:	"Air, food, water." "Sun, rain." "Cell phones!"
Teacher:	"All right, good. Now let's look deeply into the word to see what is going on. Tell me about the pieces of meaning in the word."
Student:	"Well, it's definitely a thing, a noun, because **-ment** on a word makes a noun. All the things we named are nouns."
Student:	"And there's that root we're working on. A ***requirement*** is something we *seek or ask for*."
Student:	"What about the prefix **re-**? Doesn't that mean *again*? How does that work?"
Student:	"I see—a ***requirement*** is something you have to have over and over, not just once, but *again and again*."
Teacher:	"Good—now think about a driver's license as a ***requirement***."
Student:	"Sure—you need it to drive today and you'll need it again when you drive the next time!"

DISCUSS Let small groups think up a situation, like a trip to the beach or an electrical outage, and list ***requirements*** they can think of for the situation.

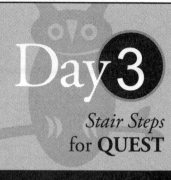

Day 3

Stair Steps
for QUEST

QUEST means
to seek, ask, gain

LESSON TIME

15 Minutes

OBJECTIVES

- **Understand** the meaning of the root **QUEST**

- **Apply** knowledge of the root **QUEST**

- **Break Apart** words in the **QUEST** family

- **Understand** the meaning of words in the **QUEST** family

- **Understand** the spelling principles applied to the root **QUEST**

MATERIALS

- Student Activity Book
- **QUEST** Word Wall

DIFFERENTIATING INSTRUCTION

If you prefer easier or more difficult activities, use your personal account at www.dynamicliteracy.com to access novice or expert versions, along with ideas on using them.

Apply Knowledge of QUEST

TEACH Have students turn to page 17 in their Student Activity Books. Explain that the boxes in front of and after the root indicate letters that spell out prefixes and suffixes. Students will spell out the correct prefixes and suffixes determined by clues in the definitions at the bottom of the page.

Have a volunteer read definition number five at the bottom of the page. Say, "The suffix **-ing** on the words *asking* and *calling* leads us to use those letters to fill in the three blanks at the end. The clue *back* leads us to a two-letter prefix, **re**-, to put in front of **QUESTING**."

COMPLETE THE ACTIVITY Let students work in pairs (optionally) and tell them to use the same strategy to find the correct prefixes and suffixes for the words listed. These activities can be quite challenging!

DISCUSS After a few minutes, review the answers as a class. Ask if there were any difficulties. Listen to any problems and have volunteers solve the difficulties by explaining key clues in the given definitions. As needed, follow the focus word approach that you see modeled on the next page.

SAB
Pg 17

Stair Steps

Fill in the missing letters of each 'quest, quis, quir, quire, quer' word by us[...]
definitions below. 'quest, quis, quir, quire, quer' means to place or pu[...]

1.	q	u	e	s	t	s				
2.	r	e	q	u	e	s	t			
3.	a	c	q	u	i	r	e	d		
4.	c	o	n	q	u	e	r	e	r	
5.	r	e	q	u	e	s	t	i	n	g
6.	i	n	q	u	i	s	i	t	i	v	e
7.	r	e	q	u	i	r	e	m	e	n	t	s
8.	u	n	c	o	n	q	u	e	r	a	b	l	e

1. acts of seeking; missions or searches
2. to ask back; to call for or ask as a favor
3. brought gain to; sought and gained
4. a person who gains completely; a person who forcefully obtains power and control over
5. asking back; calling for or asking as a favor
6. tending to seek into or ask; tending to question
7. things that must be sought back; things demanded as necessary
8. not able to be gained completely; not able to be defeated

Focus Word: **CONQUERER** ⟶ Write this word on the board.

TEACH

Sample leading question:	"Can you tell us what a ***conquerer*** is?"
Student:	"A warrior." "A winner."
Teacher:	"Why are ***conquerers*** warriors or winners?"
Student:	"They are trying to get something and they succeed."
Student:	"Right—they are *seeking* to gain something."
Student:	"I see all that, but what's the prefix **con-** doing there? Doesn't that mean *with or together*?"
Student:	"Sure—***conquerers*** don't work alone."
Student:	"Yes they do—whoever climbs Mt. Everest *conquers* Mt. Everest. The one who discovers a cure for cancer will *conquer* cancer."
Student:	"I don't think those people work alone either—they're seeking the same thing along with lots of people."
Teacher::	"Right, and does anyone remember what a prefix like **con-** can mean in addition to *with or together*?"
Student:	"I remember: *completely*! A ***conquerer*** completely gets what he or she is *seeking*!"

DISCUSS Let groups determine if they know of anyone in history actually given the name ***Conquerer***.

DEMONSTRATE Here is a good opportunity to remind the class of ***William the Conquerer***, what he was *seeking*, and his role in morphemes and the English language.

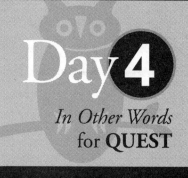

Day 4

In Other Words
for **QUEST**

QUEST means
to seek, ask, gain

LESSON TIME

15 Minutes

OBJECTIVES

- **Understand** the meaning of the root **QUEST**

- **Reinforce** knowledge of the root **QUEST**

- **Understand** the meaning of words in the **QUEST** family

- **Apply** knowledge of words in the **QUEST** family

MATERIALS

- Student Activity Book

- **QUEST** Word Wall

- Dictionary
  (print or on-line)

In Other Words for **QUEST**

TEACH Have students turn to page 18 in their Student Activity Books. Explain to students that they are going to read a little story that uses some surprising and sometimes odd phrasing. The underlined words or phrases in the story are actually definitions or synonyms for other words that use the root **QUEST**. Then they will see sentences about the story, each containing a blank.

Using context clues in the sentences, they will find a **QUEST** family word in the Word Bank at the bottom to fit in each blank. Read aloud or have a student read the first sentence. Then say, "Let's look at the first sentence. Clues in the sentence tell us that we want

a naming word, a noun that is a synonym for a *search*, and that this search for exciting things is in stories and movies. I see the word ***quest*** at the bottom of the page and that word fits all the clues. Let's write ***quest*** in the blank for the first sentence."

COMPLETE THE ACTIVITY

This can be quite challenging, so allow students to work on this activity in small groups. Not every word in the Word Bank will be used.

DISCUSS

After about 10 minutes, ask if there were any difficulties. Have volunteers explain strategies they used that led to correct answers.

LOOK IT UP

SAB
Pg 18

Even if you don't have a suit of armor or a battle-steed, you can still go on a <u>search</u> for the Holy Grail, hidden gold mines, or even Faberge eggs. All you need to <u>seek and gain</u> the riches of the universe or to <u>obtain power and control over</u> uncharted lands or dragons is a thirst to <u>seek into things</u> and the special, <u>needed</u> ticket: your library card. Armed with burning <u>uncertainties</u> and a couple hours of free time, you could be with the climbers at their <u>complete gain</u> of Mt. Everest, or you could look over the shoulders of the commission during their <u>acts of seeking into</u> the assassination of an American president.

The next time your kid brother approaches you with a look <u>that tends to seek</u> in his eyes, amaze him with your understanding of water biomes or space explorers. Explore the universe with some good books!

<u>Fill in the blanks below using words from the "quest, quis, quir, quire, quer" family.</u>

1. Stories and movies about a <u>quest</u> for rare items and adventure are exciting.

2. Through books you can <u>acquire</u> the riches of the universe.

3. In your reading you can <u>conquer</u> dragons.

4. A thirst to <u>inquire</u> into all kinds of subjects helps our minds grow.

5. A library card is a <u>requisite</u> ticket to access thousands of books.

6. It is good to ask yourself <u>questions</u> and be curious.

7. Edmund Hillary made his <u>conquest</u> of Mt. Everest in 1953.

8. The Warren Commission made several <u>inquiries</u> into the death of President Kennedy.

9. Little children and animals sometimes have an <u>inquisitive</u> look in their eyes.

<u>Not Used:</u>   requirements   questionable   unconquered

OPTIONAL

Day 5

Morpheme Mania
for **QUEST**

QUEST means
to seek, ask, gain

LESSON TIME

15 Minutes

OBJECTIVES

- **Build** words in the **QUEST** family

- **Apply** knowledge of synonyms and antonyms to **QUEST** words

Optional Morpheme Mania for **QUEST**

On page 19 of their Activity Books, students will see a vocabulary enrichment activity that they can work on in groups as a culminating activity for this week instead of, or, time permitting, in addition to, the more formal assessment.

All the affixes presented in the week's activities are provided at the top of the page on either side of the root of the week in all its forms. Students can write in up to 13 of the words they built during the week, possibly discovering additional ones.

Then students can brainstorm with each other to come up with antonyms and synonyms they may know. Starter examples are given with every Morpheme Mania in the Activity Book. Because antonyms and synonyms may require knowledge of roots which students have not yet studied, completion of this activity is not crucial. Simply remind students that they can at any time during the course of the year revisit any of their Morpheme Mania pages and add words, antonyms, and synonyms as their vocabulary grows

Day 5 *Assessment*

Make and hand out copies.
The answer key is on page A-3.
The instructions are on page A-2.

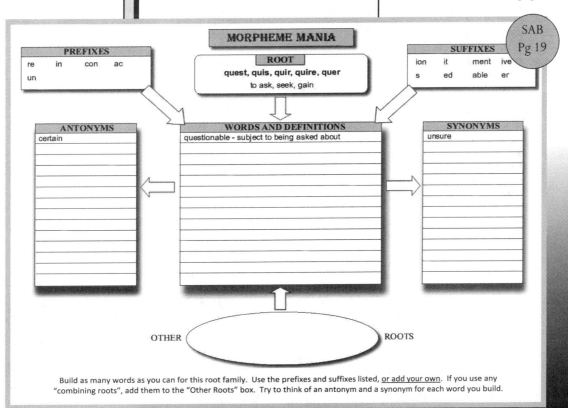

MORPHEME MANIA

PREFIXES
re   in   con   ac
un

ROOT
quest, quis, quir, quire, quer
to ask, seek, gain

SUFFIXES
ion   it   ment   ive
s   ed   able   er

SAB Pg 19

ANTONYMS
certain

WORDS AND DEFINITIONS
questionable - subject to being asked about

SYNONYMS
unsure

OTHER   ROOTS

Build as many words as you can for this root family. Use the prefixes and suffixes listed, <u>or add your own</u>. If you use any "combining roots", add them to the "Other Roots" box. Try to think of an antonym and a synonym for each word you build.

quest, quis, quir, quire, quer *to ask, seek, gain*

acquire to bring gain to; to seek and gain

acquired brought gain to; sought and gained

acquires brings gain to; seeks and gains

acquiring bringing gain to; seeking and gaining

acquisition a gain brought to; something sought and gained

acquisitions gains brought to; things sought and gained

conquer to gain completely; forcefully to obtain power and control over

conquerable able to be gained completely; able to be defeated

conquered gained completely; forcefully obtained power and control over

conquering gaining completely; forcefully obtaining power and control over

conqueringly in a manner gaining completely; in a manner forcefully obtaining power and control over

conqueror a person who gains completely; a person who forcefully obtains power and control over

conquerors people who gain completely; people who forcefully obtain power and control over

conquers gains completely; forcefully obtains control over

conquest something gained completely; something obtained by force

conquests things gained completely; things obtained by force

enquire to seek into

enquired sought into

enquirer a person who seeks into

enquirers people who seek into

enquires seeks into

enquiries acts of seeking into

enquiring seeking into

enquiry an act of seeking into

exquisite highly desirable to be sought out; superb

inquire to seek into

inquired sought into

inquirer a person who seeks into

inquirers people who seek into

inquires seeks into

inquiries acts of seeking into

inquiring seeking into

inquiringly in a manner seeking into

inquiry an act of seeking into; an act of searching for information

inquisition a formal seeking into

inquisitions groups seeking into formally

inquisitive tending to seek into or ask

inquisitively in a manner tending to seek into or ask

quest an act of seeking; a mission or search

question to ask or a thing asked; uncertainty

questionable subject to being asked about; uncertain

questionably in a manner subject to be asked about; uncertainly

questioned asked something; was uncertain

questioning asking something; being uncertain

questions asks or thinks asked; doubts; uncertainties

quests acts of seeking; missions or searches

request to ask back; to call for or ask as a favor

requested asked back; called for or asked as a favor

requesting asking back; calling for or asking as a favor

requests asks back; calls for or asks as a favor

require to seek back; to demand as necessary

required sought back; demanded as necessary

requirement something that must be sought back; something demanded as necessary

requirements things that must be sought back; things demanded as necessary

requires asks back; demands as necessary

requiring asking back; demanding as necessary

requisite sought back; needed, necessary

requisition a formal seeking back; something demanded as necessary

requisitioned formally sought back; demanded as necessary

requisitioner a person who formally seeks back; a person who demands as necessary

requisitioners people who formally seek back; people who demand as necessary

requisitioning seeking back; demanding as necessary

requisitions things sought back; things demanding as necessary

unconquerable not able to be gained completely; not able to be defeated

unconquerably in a manner not able to be gained completely; in a manner not able to be defeated

unconquered not gained completely; not forcefully taken control and power over

unquestionable not subject to being asked about; definite or sure

unquestionably in a manner not subject to being asked about; definitely or surely

Check-Up for **QUEST**   Name _____

____ **1.** **QUEST, QUIS, QUIR,** or **QUER** in words like **conquest, inquisitive, require,** and **conquer** means:

    A to seek

    B strong

    C family or birth

____ **2.** What is the meaning of the word **inquest**?

    A existing at birth

    B a search into

    C a lack of strength

____ **3.** What is the meaning of the word **acquisitive**?

    A given at birth

    B not having power to do more

    C tending to look for and gain for oneself

____ **4.** What is the meaning of the word **requisite**?

    A having the same qualities as others

    B to regain strength

    C needing to be sought after and gotten

____ **5.** What is the meaning of the word **inquisitive**?

    A tending to look into matters a lot

    B without strength

    C causing harm

____ **6.** Which word means **to gain completely**?

    A questionable

    B conquer

    C requisition

____ **7.** Which word means **to seek again and get**?

    A reacquire

    B requisitioner

    C requirements

____ **8.** Which word means **people who seek back**?

    A requisitioners

    B inquiries

    C exquisite

____ **9.** Arithmetic is a **prerequisite** for algebra. Arithmetic is:

    A not in the same family or group as algebra

    B needed before you can study algebra

    C a much harder subject than algebra

____ **10.** Albie **queried** his friends. Albie:

    A was just like family to his friends

    B was stronger than his friends

    C asked for information from his friends

OBJECTIVES

- **Understand** the meaning of the root **VAL**
- **Build** words in the root **VAL** family
- **Break Apart** words in the root **VAL** family
- **Understand** the meaning of words in the **VAL** family
- **Understand** the spelling principles applied to the root **VAL**
- **Apply** knowledge of words in the **VAL** family
- **Assess** and **Reinforce** knowledge of words in the **VAL** family

MATERIALS

- Student Activity Books, pages 21-26
- Dictionary *(print or on-line)*

CROSS-CURRICULAR EXAMPLES

Science:
valence, equivalence, evaluate

Social Studies:
availability, devaluate, prevailing

Language Arts:
valuable, ambivalence, valediction

Math:
valid, invalid, equivalent

VAL

meaning "strength, worth, health"

valor
strength and **worth**

value
worth

invalid
someone without **health**

Morpheme: **VAL**
Allomorphs: **VALI, VALE, VAIL VALU, VALUE**

Over 500 words containing the morpheme **VAL** or one of its allomorphs are current in English. During this unit, tell students to be alert for this root in their school texts, general reading, and oral language they hear. Some of the words they might encounter in their school subjects are listed on the left under Cross-Curricular Examples.

UNIT AT A GLANCE

Day 1 *Root Squares* for **VAL**

Day 2 *Magic Squares* for **VAL**

Day 3 *Stair Steps* for **VAL**

OPTIONAL **Day 4** *In Other Words* for **VAL**

Day 5 *Assessment or Morpheme Mania* for **VAL**

Each activity should take approximately **15 minutes**.

One variation of this morpheme, called an allomorph, is **value**, which can stand alone as a word. Such morphemes that can also be words are called *free* or *unbound* morphemes. As a word, **value** can be a noun (the **value** of something) or a verb (we **value** something we like).

Like many morphemes, this one has several spellings due, in part, to different vowels that serve to connect one morpheme to another to make words. Another reason is that words of French borrowing later than 1066 are spelled with the diphthong **ai** instead of **a**. Knowing which spellings go with which affixes is a matter of experimentation and experience. Pronunciation can also help: note the words **prevail** and **prevalent**, reflecting their respective pronunciations.

A **valedictory** speech is one that wishes for the *health* and success of a departing group. Note what we are really saying when we say, "Fare well" ("continue on in a *healthy* manner"). A **valediction** has come to mean *an act or declaration of saying good-bye.*

Valetudinarians, on the other hand, are people so concerned about being well that they actually feel weak and sickly (**invalid**) most of the time.

Word Alert! Many words ending with the suffix –al attached to root stems ending in the letter **v** will not belong to this root family. For example, **naval**, *pertaining to a ship*, **oval**, *shaped like an egg*, and **rival**, *sharing the same river*.

The word **avalanche**, a powerful collapse of snow, is of unknown origin, probably not even from the Indo-European family of languages, but from original inhabitants of Europe.

You might think **chivalry** had something to do with valor. In fact, **chivalry**, like **chevalier** and **cavalier**, comes from a word, **caballus**, which the Romans used for a type of horse.

Another word that looks and means like it might be related to this root is **medieval**. The root morpheme in **medieval** comes from the word **aevum**, meaning age or time of life.

The words **valley** and **valve** are from a root meaning *to roll*. This root is presented in a later section of WordBuild Elements II. The word **vale**, as *a rolling tract of land*, belongs to that root as well.

Morphemic Splitting

The word **naval** provides a good lesson on where to split a word into meaningful pieces. The word **naval** breaks into the root **nav** (*ship*, as in **navigate** or **navy**) and the suffix -al, *like or characterized by*). It does not break into a supposed prefix **na-**, which does not exist, and the root **val**.

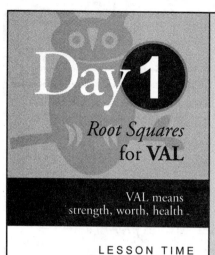

Day 1

Root Squares
for **VAL**

VAL means
strength, worth, health

LESSON TIME

15 Minutes

OBJECTIVES

- **Understand** the meaning of the root **VAL**
- **Build** words in the **VAL** family
- **Understand** the meaning of words in the **VAL** family
- **Understand** the spelling principles applied to the root **VAL**

MATERIALS

- Student Activity Book
- **VAL** Word Wall
- Dictionary *(print or on-line)*

DIFFERENTIATING INSTRUCTION

If you prefer easier or more difficult activities, use your personal account at www.dynamicliteracy.com to access novice or expert versions, along with ideas on using them.

Root Squares for VAL

TEACH Have students turn to page 21 in their Activity Books. Say, "Two new affixes appear here, so let's focus first on the suffix -**id** and the Combining Form **equi**." Refer to the Mini-Lessons on the next page as needed.

Call attention to the center box. Point out that the root **VAL** has several different spellings, called *allomorphs*. Ask students to decide if any of the forms they see in the middle square can stand alone as a word. They may see that *value* is a word, and you can use that word to guide them to the meaning *strength, worth, or health*. When we estimate the *worth* of something, we put a *value* on it. Students can start their word list with the word *value*. Then suggest

that students continue with **val** and then add -**id**, meaning *resembling or having the quality of*, onto the end to build *valid*.

COMPLETE THE ACTIVITY

Have students follow the directions to build words. If they have difficulty building words with the Root Squares, show them how by modeling the matrix approach found on the next page, taking one affix at a time and seeing if it will connect with any one of the allomorphs of the root.

DISCUSS After five minutes, have volunteers write some of their words on the board. Focus with the class on the words they have built and guide them in a discussion of how the meaning of the root is still *strength, worth, or health*, even when prefixes and suffixes are added. Watch for target words that most easily demonstrate the meanings of *strength, worth, or health*. If the word *devalue* is not present, ask the class, "Can anyone try to use the prefix **de-**?" and then continue on to the target word discussion on the next page.

Root Squares

How many words can you make?

Start in any square. Your goal is to combine two or more word parts to make as many words in the 'val, vali, vale, vail, valu, value' family as you can. Write each word and a definition you can think of for it in the space provided at the bottom of the page. Use the back of the page if you need to.

de	ent	e
ate	val, vali, vale, vail, valu, value	id
in	ion	equi

SAB
Pg 21

Focus Word: **DEVALUE** ➔ Write this word on the board.

TEACH

Sample leading question:	"Sometimes I hear that they are going to **devalue** money. What does that mean?"
Student: Student: Student:	"Does it mean make it so that it's not worth anything?" "No, I think it's reducing the worth." "How can that happen?"
Student:	"The value of a dollar is the same as how much you can buy with it. If the price of anything goes up, the value of the dollar goes down—so it's devalued. **De-** means down."
Student:	"If the price of an object goes down, then the worth of the object goes down—it gets **devalued**."
Teacher:	"Can anything besides money be **devalued**?"
Student:	"I guess if you stop liking something you liked before, you could say you have **devalued** it—you've moved its worth down."

DISCUSS Let groups talk about items that they have seen **devalued** in their lifetime.

DEMONSTRATE Put a pencil or pen out on a table and say it costs one dollar. Now add another pencil or pen and say the two now cost a dollar. What has happened to the worth of the pencils or pens? (It has been **devalued** by half).

MINI-LESSON: The suffix **-id** is from a Latin morpheme that made adjectives out of verb stems. It means *like or resembling* something that does whatever verb root it is attached to. About 35 common English adjectives still have this morpheme, all of them with a Latin bound morpheme base. Removing the suffix **-id** will not result in a free-standing English word. You can demonstrate the effect of the suffix with any of these words:

morbid	**lucid**	**rancid**	**frigid**	**rigid**	**solid**	**humid**
timid	**rapid**	**stupid**	**horrid**	**splendid**	**candid**	**vivid**

MINI-LESSON: The Combining Form **equi**, meaning *balanced or the same*, will be presented as a root morpheme later in this manual, but it is used with the root **val** as a prefix. Give students the word **equal** (or **equality**) as a good guide word for mastering this morpheme. Ask if anyone knows when the two **equinoxes** occur during the year (in March and September, when the nights and days are of the *same* length).

Root Squares Matrix

You can refer to this matrix to guide students in this activity. Students could build at least these 17 words. *It really doesn't matter how many they build* – the point is that they understand the consistent meanings of the root **VAL** and of its prefixes and suffixes.

	no prefix	de-	e-	equi-	in-
no suffix	value	devalue			
	vail				
-ate	valuate	devaluate	evaluate		
-ent	valent			equivalent	
-id	valid				invalid
-id + ate	validate				invalidate
-ion					
-at(e) + -ion	valuation	devaluation	evaluation		
-id + -at(e) + -ion	validation				invalidation

Day 2

Magic Squares for VAL

VAL means strength, worth, health

LESSON TIME

15 Minutes

OBJECTIVES

- **Understand** the meaning of the root **VAL**

- **Break Apart** words in the **VAL** family

- **Understand** the meanings of words in the **VAL** family

MATERIALS

- Student Activity Book

- **VAL** Word Wall

- Dictionary *(print or on-line)*

DIFFERENTIATING INSTRUCTION

If you prefer easier or more difficult activities, use your personal account at www.dynamicliteracy.com to access novice or expert versions, along with ideas on using them.

Break Apart Words with **VAL**

TEACH Have students turn to the Magic Squares on page 22 in their Student Activity Books. Model a Think-Aloud strategy for students: "I know that **VAL** and the various spellings of this root mean *strength, worth, health*. I can use this knowledge to find the definition of a word with this as its root." Direct students to word G, *valueless*. Say, "I know that the suffix -**less** means *without, not having*. Definition #10 is the only one with the idea of *without* in its definition: *without worth*. Since *worth* is one of the meanings of the root **VAL**, we'll write the number 10 in square G.

COMPLETE THE ACTIVITY

Ask students to use the same strategy to find the correct definitions for the other words. Tell them to write the number of the definition in the box that matches the letter for the word. Remind them that if all their answers are correct, each row and each column will add up to the same Magic number.

DISCUSS After five minutes, ask if there are any difficulties about matching the words and definitions. If there are, ask volunteers to explain clues in the definitions that will lead to the correct choice of word. As needed, follow the focus word approach for *ambivalent* that you see modeled on the next page.

Add any new words to the classroom **VAL** Word Wall and remind students to add these words to the **VAL** Word Wall in their Activity Books

---

SAB Pg 22

Magic Squares

Select the best answer for each of the words in the 'val, vali, vale, vail, valu, value' family from numbered definitions. Put the number in the proper space in the Magic Square box. If the total of the numbers is the same both across and down, you have found the magic number!

'val, vali, vale, vail, valu, value' means strength, worth, health

WORDS	DEFINITIONS
A. equivalent	1. quality of being thoroughly strongest; quality of dominance
B. evaluating	2. having the same worth or strength
C. validated	3. lack of readiness to be of use or worth to
D. devalued	4. in a manner not having worth or strength
E. invalidly	5. strong or worthy for both; having opposite feelings or attitudes
F. valiant	6. took worth away from
G. valueless	7. declared that something has worth
H. ambivalent	8. possessing strength; brave and bold
I. unavailability	9. assessing the worth of; giving a grade to
	10. without worth

Magic Square Box

A. 2	B. 9	C. 7
D. 6	E. 4	F. 8
G. 10	H. 5	I. 3

Magic Number **18**

*** ANSWER KEY ***

MINI-LESSON: the Prefix **ambi-**

The prefix **ambi-** is from a Latin morpheme that means *all around* or *on both sides* of something. It came to mean *both*, and students may know the word **ambidextrous** as a description of someone who can use *both* hands with equal ease.

Ambiguity may be another word some students may know. Lead them to discover that when something is **ambiguous**, it has *two or more meanings*. For example, the sentence, "I like flying airplanes," can mean either "I like to fly airplanes," or it can mean "I like airplanes when they are flying."

The **ambience** of a restaurant is *the mood, feeling, and décor all around*.

Focus Word: **AMBIVALENT** ⟶ Write this word on the board.

TEACH

Sample leading question:	"Has anyone ever been **ambivalent** about something?"
Student:	"Yes—it means you can't make up your mind."
Teacher:	"Why can't you make up your mind?"
Student:	"It's hard to make a choice."
Student:	"I know—look at the word. You can't make up your mind because your choices all have *worth*."
Student:	"I see it—**valent** must mean *having worth*, and **ambivalent** tells what kind of worth"
Student:	"I guess it's always a matter of a choice between two things, since **ambi-** means *both*."
Teacher:	"I guess you're right, but, remember, the basic meanings of roots and affixes can expand over time. Let's take a look in a dictionary."

Language usage changes according to the way words are spoken, written, and understood in various times and places. Check with a reliable up-do-date dictionary to see whether the force of **ambi-** in the word **ambivalent** is *two*, as originally true, or more than two.

DISCUSS Let groups think of situations they have encountered in which both of two required choices seemed good.

DEMONSTRATE Take an example or two from the groups and encourage students to see that the word **ambivalence** means, at its core, *double worth or strength*.

Day 3

Stair Steps
for VAL

**VAL means
strength, worth, health**

LESSON TIME

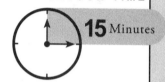

15 Minutes

OBJECTIVES

- **Understand** the meaning of the root **VAL**

- **Apply** knowledge of the root **VAL**

- **Break Apart** words in the **VAL** family

- **Understand** the meaning of words in the **VAL** family

- **Understand** the spelling principles applied to the root **VAL**

MATERIALS

- Student Activity Book

- **VAL** Word Wall

DIFFERENTIATING INSTRUCTION

If you prefer easier or more difficult activities, use your personal account at www.dynamicliteracy.com to access novice or expert versions, along with ideas on using them.

Apply Knowledge of VAL

TEACH Have students turn to page 23 in their Student Activity Books. Explain that the boxes in front of and after the root indicate letters that spell out prefixes and suffixes. Students will spell out the correct prefixes and suffixes determined by clues in the definitions at the bottom of the page.

Have a volunteer read definition number three at the bottom of the page. Say, "The idea of *manner* and *way* would suggest the suffix **-ly** to create an adverb. The idea of *having and being* lead to the suffix **-id** following

the root, so that we build the word **VALIDLY** on stair step number three."

COMPLETE THE ACTIVITY

Let students work in pairs (optionally) and tell them to use the same strategy to find the correct prefixes and suffixes for the words listed. These activities can be quite challenging!

DISCUSS After a few minutes, review the answers as a class. Ask if there were any difficulties. Listen to any problems and have volunteers solve the difficulties by explaining key clues in the given definitions. As needed, follow the focus word approach that you see modeled on the next page.

**SAB
Pg 23**

Stair Steps

Fill in the missing letters of each 'val, vali, vale, vail, valu, value' word by us[ing] definitions below. 'val, vali, vale, vail, valu, value' means to place or p[ut]

1.	v	a	l	i	d						
2.	v	a	l	u	e	s					
3.	v	a	l	i	d	l	y				
4.	i	n	v	a	l	i	d	s			
5.	d	e	v	a	l	u	i	n	g		
6.	v	a	l	i	d	a	t	i	n	g	
7.	e	v	a	l	u	a	t	i	o	n	s
8.	e	q	u	i	v	a	l	e	n	t	l	y

1. strong and worthy; legitimate and creditable
2. worthwhile things; ethics, morals, or beliefs of emotional investments
3. in a manner having worth; in a way being legitimate
4. people lacking strength; people weak as a result of illness or injury
5. taking worth away from
6. declaring that something has worth
7. assessments of worth; acts of giving grades to
8. in a manner having the same worth or strength

Focus Word: **VALIDATING** ⟶ Write this word on the board.

TEACH

Sample leading question:	"Let's talk about this word a while. Who can tell me about that suffix **-ing**?"
Student:	"That's easy—it means *happening right now, going on*."
Teacher:	"Let's hear you use it in a sentence."
Student:	"Sure. ***Validating*** your parking sticker is a way to save money."
Teacher:	"That's a great sentence. What does ***validating*** mean in that sentence?"
Student:	"Making the sticker have worth right now."
Student B:	"Yes, but as a noun, not a verb—your sentence makes ***validating*** an act or process, a noun."
Student C:	"I have a sentence. Matt's award was a ***validating*** experience for him."
Teacher:	"Explain to us what that means."
Student C:	"It means he felt a sense of *worth and strength*."
Student B:	"And you've used the word as an adjective!"
Teacher:	"Do you mean that the suffix **-ing** can make a verb, a noun, or an adjective?"
Students:	"Yes—that's right. We remember that now."

Studying morphemes can lead to strong, sound knowledge in grammar. On occasion, lead discussions like this one just for a review of the grammatical nature of suffixes.

MINI-LESSON: The Suffix *-or*

The suffix **-or** has been presented before as an *agent*, naming *a person or device that performs an act*. However, the suffix was also simply a way that the Latin language made nouns out of certain roots. Many of these nouns still survive in modern English. Show any of these words to your students and explain that they are unchanged ancient Latin nouns:

color	**labor**	**horror**	**arbor**	**odor**	**splendor**
rigor	**vigor**	**valor**	**dolor**	**armor**	**tremor**
rumor	**tumor**	**honor**	**vapor**	**furor**	**error**

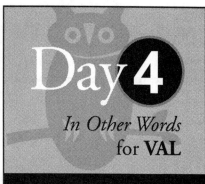

Day 4

In Other Words for **VAL**

VAL means strength, worth, health

LESSON TIME

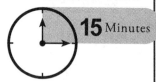

15 Minutes

OBJECTIVES

- **Understand** the meaning of the root **VAL**

- **Reinforce** knowledge of the root **VAL**

- **Understand** the meaning of words in the **VAL** family

- **Apply** knowledge of words in the **VAL** family

MATERIALS

- Student Activity Book

- **VAL** Word Wall

- Dictionary *(print or on-line)*

In Other Words for **VAL**

TEACH Have students turn to page 24 in their Student Activity Books. Explain that they are going to read a little story that uses some surprising and sometimes odd phrasing. The underlined words or phrases in the story are actually definitions or synonyms for words in the **VAL** family. Then they will see sentences about the story, each containing a blank. Using context clues in the sentences, they will find a **VAL** family word in the Word Bank at the bottom to fit in each blank. Have a student read aloud the opening sentence or sentences of the story that contain the first underlined phrase. Then say, "Let's look at the first numbered sentence that contains a blank to be filled in. Clues in the sentence tell us that we want an action word, a verb that means *check out the worth of*, and that this activity is happening in regard to a new restaurant. I see the word *evaluating* at the bottom of the page and that word fits all the clues. Let's write *evaluating* in the blank for the first sentence."

COMPLETE THE ACTIVITY

This can be quite challenging, so allow students to work on this activity in small groups. Not every word in the Word Bank will be used.

DISCUSS

After about 10 minutes, ask if there were any difficulties. Have volunteers explain strategies they used that led to correct answers.

SAB Pg 24

A Bad Start but a Good Finish

Gore Mandizer, the famous food editor, wanted to <u>check out the worth</u> of the new restaurant in town. Because the restaurant advertised that a second dinner <u>of the same worth</u> as the first would be half price, Gore took along his friend Eppie Curean.

The restaurant's host and owner didn't recognize the critic and said there were no tables <u>ready to be of use or worth</u> to them, but Gore hinted strongly that if the owner <u>considered</u> his business <u>worthy</u>, he should find them a place to sit.

The owner got the hint and led Gore and Eppie to a table and gave them menus that were stained with food. Gore and Eppie, <u>thinking that both to leave and to stay were strong choices</u>, decided to give it a try.

The rest of the experience was so good that Gore <u>in a strong manner</u> tried not to let them know who he was. The good food and service <u>took away the worth</u> of the original unpleasantry and they both though it a <u>worthwhile</u> experience. Gore and Eppie then had their parking permit <u>made worthy</u> and left.

<u>Fill in the blanks below</u> using words from the "val, vali, vale, vail, valu, value" family.

1. Gore and Eppie were <u>evaluating</u> the new restaurant.

2. The prices of the two dinners were exactly <u>equivalent</u>.

3. Fortunately a table became <u>available</u> for Gore and Eppie.

4. The owner <u>valued</u> his business and his customers.

5. The customers were <u>ambivalent</u> about whether to stay or leave.

6. The food critic <u>valiantly</u> kept his identity hidden.

7. The quality of the rest of the evening <u>invalidated</u> the original bad impressions.

8. Overall, the restaurant visit was a <u>valuable</u> experience.

9. The parking permit was <u>validated</u> for customers.

<u>Not Used:</u>   prevailed   valor   invalidity

46

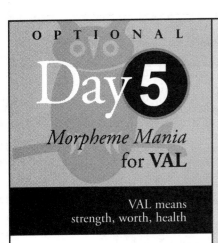

O P T I O N A L

Day 5

Morpheme Mania
for **VAL**

VAL means
strength, worth, health

LESSON TIME

15 Minutes

OBJECTIVES

- **Build** words in the **VAL** family

- **Apply** knowledge of synonyms and antonyms to **VAL** words

Optional Morpheme Mania for **VAL**

On page 25 of their Activity Books, students will see an optional vocabulary enrichment activity that they can work on in groups, time permitting. This activity makes a great review for the formal assessment on the next page.

All the affixes presented in the week's activities are provided at the top of the page on either side of the root of the week in all its forms. Students can write in up to 13 of the words they built during the week, possibly discovering additional ones.

Then students can brainstorm with each other to come up with antonyms and synonyms they may know. Starter examples are given with every Morpheme Mania in the Activity Book. Because antonyms and synonyms may require knowledge of roots which students have not yet studied, completion of this activity is not crucial. Simply remind students that they can at any time during the course of the year revisit any of their Morpheme Mania pages and add words, antonyms, and synonyms as their vocabulary grows.

Day 5 *Assessment*

Make and hand out copies.
The answer key is on page A-3.
The instructions are on page A-2.

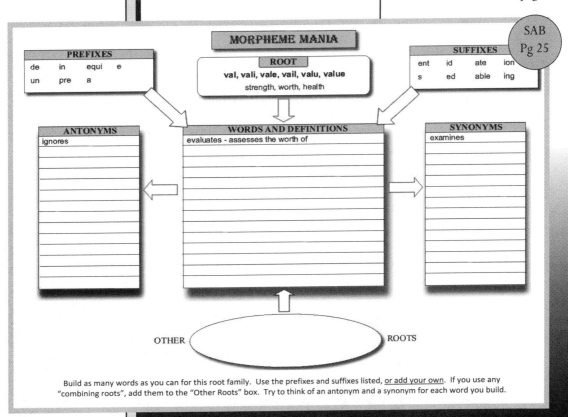

SAB Pg 25

MORPHEME MANIA

PREFIXES

de	in	equi	e
un	pre	a	

ROOT
val, vali, vale, vail, valu, value
strength, worth, health

SUFFIXES

ent	id	ate	ion
s	ed	able	ing

ANTONYMS
ignores

WORDS AND DEFINITIONS
evaluates - assesses the worth of

SYNONYMS
examines

OTHER ⬭ ROOTS

Build as many words as you can for this root family. Use the prefixes and suffixes listed, <u>or add your own</u>. If you use any "combining roots", add them to the "Other Roots" box. Try to think of an antonym and a synonym for each word you build.

ambivalence strength or worth for both; state of having opposing feelings or attitudes

ambivalences strengths or worths for both; states of having opposing feelings or attitudes

ambivalencies strengths or worths for both; states of having opposing feelings or attitudes

ambivalency strength or worth for both; state of having opposing feelings or attitudes

ambivalent strong or worthy for both; having opposing feelings or attitudes

avail to be of worth or advantage to

availability readiness to be of use and worth to

available present and ready to be of use and worth to

availed was of worth or advantage to

avails is of worth or advantage to

devaluation an act or result of taking away worth from

devalue to take worth away from

devalued took worth away from

devalues takes worth away from

devaluing taking worth away from

equivalence quality of having the same worth or strength

equivalences qualities of having the same worth or strength

equivalencies qualities of having the same worth or strength

equivalency quality of having the same worth or strength

equivalent having the same worth or strength

equivalently in a manner having the same worth or strength

equivalents things having the same worth or strength

evaluate to decide the worth of; to give a grade to

evaluated decided the worth of; gave a grade to

evaluates decides the worth of; gives a grade to

evaluating deciding the worth of; giving a grade to

evaluation decision about the worth of; act of giving a grade to

evaluations decisions about the worth of; acts of giving grades to

evaluative serving to decide the worth of; serving to give a grade to

evaluator a person who decides the worth of; a person who gives a grade to

evaluators people who decide the worth of; people who give grades

invalid not having worth or strength

invalidated made not worth anything; nullified

invalidly in a manner not having worth or strength

invalids people lacking strength; people weak as a result of illness or injury

invaluable impossible to establish the worth of; priceless

invaluably in a manner impossible to establish the worth of; pricelessly

prevail to be thoroughly stronger than another; to dominate another

prevailed was thoroughly stronger than another; dominated another

prevailing being thoroughly stronger than another; dominating another

prevailingly in a manner being thoroughly stronger than another; in a manner dominating another

prevails is thoroughly stronger than another; dominates another

prevalence quality of being thoroughly strongest; quality of dominance

prevalency quality of being thoroughly strongest; quality of dominance

prevalent thoroughly strongest; dominant

unavailability lack of readiness to be of use or worth to

unavailable not present and ready to be of use and worth to

valiant possessing strength; brave and bold

valiantly in a manner possessing strength; bravely and boldly

valid strong and worthy; legitimate and creditable

validate to declare that something has worth

validated declared that something has worth

validates declares that something has worth

validating declaring that something has worth

validities qualities of having worth; qualities of being legitimate

validity quality of having worth; quality of being legitimate

validly in a manner having worth; so as to be legitimate

valor strength and worth; bravery

valorous full of strength and worth; brave

valors acts of strength and worth; acts of bravery

valuable able to be given worth

valuably in a manner able to be given worth

valuation the estimated worth of

valuations estimations of the worth of

value worth

valued considered as worthy

valueless without worth

values worthwhile things; ethics, morals, or beliefs of emotional investments

valuing giving worth

Check-Up for **VAL**

Name _____

____ **1.** **VAL** or **VAIL** in words like **valor** and **prevail** means:

    A road or trip

    B strength or worth

    C roll or turn

____ **2.** What is the meaning of the word **devaluate**?

    A to trip while making a turn

    B to make a turn on a road

    C to take worth away from

____ **3.** What is the meaning of the word **equivalent**?

    A having balanced strength

    B rolling in an even way

    C with the same distance between two places

____ **4.** What is the meaning of the word **ambivalent**?

    A feeling that two differing things both have worth

    B taking a trip toward a specific place

    C turning around a central point

____ **5.** What is the meaning of the word **invalidly**?

    A in a manner that rolls inward

    B so as not to have any worth

    C serving to travel in comfort

____ **6.** Which word means **made to have worth**?

    A evaluation

    B validated

    C prevail

____ **7.** Which word means **thoroughly strong**?

    A prevalent

    B invaluably

    C equivalency

____ **8.** Which word means **strength and bravery**?

    A valid

    B available

    C valor

____ **9.** The star player was **devalorized** for what he did. The star player:

    A was praised by everyone

    B was forgiven because he was so good

    C lost worth in people's eyes

____ **10.** Randy needed time to **convalesce**. Randy needed time to:

    A study for exams

    B gather strength together

    C take a vacation

OBJECTIVES

- **Understand** the meaning of the root **PORT**
- **Build** words in the root **PORT** family
- **Break Apart** words in the root **PORT** family
- **Understand** the meaning of words in the **PORT** family
- **Understand** the spelling principles applied to the root **PORT**
- **Apply** knowledge of words in the **PORT** family
- **Assess** and **Reinforce** knowledge of words in the **PORT** family

MATERIALS

- Student Activity Books, pages 27-32
- Dictionary *(print or on-line)*
- pencils, paper clips *(optional)*

CROSS-CURRICULAR EXAMPLES

Science:
  insupportable, portal

Social Studies:
  imports, exports, deportation, portage

Language Arts:
  importance, disport, reportedly

Math:
  supportability, purport

PORT

meaning "to carry, bring"

porters
people who **carry** luggage

import
to **bring** into the country for sale

Morpheme: **PORT**
Allomorphs: none

About 400 words containing the morpheme **PORT** are current in English. During this unit, tell students to be alert for this root in their school texts, general reading, and oral language they hear. Some of the words they might encounter in their school subjects are listed on the left under Cross-Curricular Examples.

UNIT AT A GLANCE

Day 1
Root Squares for **PORT**

Day 2
Magic Squares for **PORT**

Day 3
Stair Steps for **PORT**

OPTIONAL
Day 4
In Other Words for **PORT**

Day 5
Assessment or Morpheme Mania for **PORT**

Each activity should take approximately **15 minutes.**

Word Fun Facts

The French word **portmanteau**, meaning *carrying case*, is used in English to name a word coined by blending two other words. For example, **smoke** and **fog** are blended to become **smog**. **Breakfast** and **lunch** are blended to become **brunch**. See if your students know any other **portmanteau** words, and explain how *carrying case* is a good image for this type of words.

To **disport** is to *carry on in different directions*, playing now here, now there. The prefix was shortened to make the word **sport**!

A **portfolio** is a folder containing examples of a person's work that he or she can *carry* around to show prospective employers or clients.

Port is an out-of-style word for *a manner of carrying oneself*, as in posture, stance, or behavior. **Comportment**, behavior, was once an entry on old school report cards. A **portly** person's carriage is obvious, leading to two threads of meaning: *stately or dignified*, and *large or stout*.

Porters, people whose job it is to *carry* packages and other burdens for others, once had a reputation for being burly and stout. A type of beer known for its stoutness and strength seemed to be a favorite of riverside and seaside **porters**, and that beer came to be called **porter**. Places that served **porter** (presumably mostly to **porters**) were called **porterhouses**, and from that we have the word **porterhouse** steak, a thick cut of beef.

A doorway carries a person from one area to another. One subgroup of words in English belongs to this family by way of the Latin word for *door*, **porta**. For example, **portico**, **portal**, and **porch** relate to doorways or passageways that *carry* people to different areas.

Another subgroup of words belonging to this root family has to do with carrying goods or property to a certain place for safe-keeping. These words all relate to **port**, as a **seaport**, **carport**, or **airport**. When ships would dock, they regularly did so with the left side of the boat facing the port. That left side came to be known as **portside**. Many place-names contain the word **port**, among which is **Oporto**, Portugal, the harbor from which a Portuguese wine, simply called **port**, was exported.

While the origins of the sofa called **davenport** and the mushroom called **portobello** remain obscure, it is likely that both terms stem ultimately from place-names that include the word **port**, meaning a harbor.

Word Alert! Words relating to **portray** and **portrait** do not belong to the root family meaning *carry*. Instead, they are come from the root **tract**, meaning *to draw or drag*.

Words relating to **portion** are not of this family, but rather from the root **part**, meaning *a section or piece*.

Day 1

Root Squares for PORT

PORT means to carry, bring

LESSON TIME

15 Minutes

OBJECTIVES

- **Understand** the meaning of the root **PORT**
- **Build** words in the **PORT** family
- **Understand** the meaning of words in the **PORT** family
- **Understand** the spelling principles applied to the root **PORT**

MATERIALS

- Student Activity Book
- **PORT** Word Wall
- Dictionary *(print or on-line)*
- pencils, paper clips *(optional)*

DIFFERENTIATING INSTRUCTION

If you prefer easier or more difficult activities, use your personal account at www.dynamicliteracy.com to access novice or expert versions, along with ideas on using them.

Root Squares for PORT

TEACH Have students turn to page 27 in their Activity Books. Say, "All of the prefixes and suffixes in the squares surrounding the shaded center are probably familiar, but if you have questions about any of the meanings, simply ask or look it up the front or back cover of the activity book."

Call attention to the center box. Point out that the root **PORT** has only one spelling. Ask students to decide if what they see in the middle square can stand alone as a word. They may recognize *port* is a word, and you can use that word to guide them to the meaning *to carry or bring*. When we *carry* something, we *port* it, though this root almost always requires a prefix or suffix to add to that meaning. With no prefix or suffix, the word most often refers to a place where ships are loaded or unloaded with the things that they *carry*. Suggest that students start their list with *port* and then add **trans-** to build a second word, *transport*. The prefix **trans-** indicates that the porting is done *across* an area.

COMPLETE THE ACTIVITY

Have students follow the directions to build words. If students have difficulty building words with the Root Squares, show them how by modeling the matrix approach found on the next page, taking one affix at a time and seeing if it will connect with any one of the allomorphs of the root.

DISCUSS After 5 minutes, have volunteers write some of their words on the board. Focus with the class on the words they have built and guide them in a discussion of how the meaning of the root is still *to carry or bring*, even when prefixes and suffixes are added. Watch for target words that best demonstrate the meanings of to *carry or bring*. If the word *export* is not present, ask the class, "Can anyone try to use the prefix **ex-**?" and then continue on to the target word discussion on the next page.

Root Squares
How many words can you make?

Start in any square. Your goal is to combine two or more word parts to make as many words in the 'port' family as you can. Write each word and a definition you can think of for it in the space provided at the bottom of the page. Use the back of the page if you need to.

er	trans	im
ed	port	re
sup	ing	ex

SAB Pg 27

Focus Word: **EXPORT** → Write this word on the board.

TEACH

Sample leading question:	"What's an *export*?"
Student:	"A product like a car or something that we sell to other countries."
Teacher:	"Does everyone agree?"
Student:	"I get it already. It's something carried out of the country, just like an *import* is something brought in from someplace else."
Student:	"But they are things to sell and buy, not just things like souvenirs or luggage."
Teacher:	"Good. You probably learned these words in other classes, and now you understand them based on their root and prefix."

DISCUSS Let students discuss what kinds of products are *exported*, and how they are *exported*. Technologically savvy students can explain the meaning of *export* (and *import*) in computer language.

DEMONSTRATE Divide the class into halves. Have someone from group A take some pencils to group B, and have someone from group B take some paper clips to group A. Have the class discuss who is *exporting* and who is *importing* each time.

Root Squares Matrix

You can refer to this matrix to guide students in this activity. Students could build at least these 29 words. *It really doesn't matter how many they build* – the point is that they understand the consistent meanings of the root **PORT** and of its prefixes and suffixes.

	no prefix	ex-	im-	re-	sup-	trans-
no suffix	port	export	import	report	support	transport
-ed	ported	exported	imported	reported	supported	transported
-er	porter	exporter	importer	reporter	supporter	transporter
-ing	porting	exporting	importing	reporting	supporting	transporting
-er + -ing	portering					
(re-)		reexport	reimport		resupport	retransport

Day 2

Magic Squares for PORT

PORT means to carry, bring

LESSON TIME

15 Minutes

OBJECTIVES

- **Understand** the meaning of the root **PORT**
- **Break Apart** words in the **PORT** family
- **Understand** the meanings of words in the **PORT** family

MATERIALS

- Student Activity Book
- **PORT** Word Wall
- Dictionary *(print or on-line)*

DIFFERENTIATING INSTRUCTION

If you prefer easier or more difficult activities, use your personal account at www.dynamicliteracy.com to access novice or expert versions, along with ideas on using them.

Break Apart Words with **PORT**

TEACH Have students turn to the Magic Squares on page 28 in their Student Activity Books. Model a Think-Aloud strategy for students: "I know that **PORT** means *to carry, bring*. I can use this knowledge to find the definition of a word with this as its root."

Direct students to word A, ***supportable***. Say, "I know that the prefix **sup-** is actually an assimilated form of the prefix **sub-**, meaning *less than normal, under, up from below* and the suffix **-able** means *having the power*. Definition 9 is the only one with the ideas of *capable* and *beneath* in its definition: *capable of being carried from beneath*. Since that definition accounts for all the parts of the word, including the

meaning of **PORT**, we'll write the number 9 in square A.

COMPLETE THE ACTIVITY

Ask students to use the same strategy to find the correct definitions for the other words. Tell them to write the number of the definition in the box that matches the letter for the word. Remind them that if all their answers are correct, each row and each column will add up to the same Magic number.

DISCUSS After five minutes, ask if there are any difficulties about matching the words and definitions. If there are, ask volunteers to explain clues in the definitions that will lead to the correct choice of word. As needed, follow the focus word approach for ***importable*** that you see modeled on the next page.

Add any new words to the classroom **PORT** Word Wall and remind students to add these words to the **PORT** Word Wall in their Activity Books.

SAB Pg 28

Magic Squares

Select the best answer for each of the words in the 'port' family from the numbered definitions. Put the number in the proper space in the Magic Square box. If the total of the numbers is the same both across and down, you have found the magic number!

'port' means to carry, bring

WORDS	DEFINITIONS
A. supportable	1. carried away from; expelled from a country
B. unsupported	2. people who bring back; people who give information about
C. reporters	3. in a manner carrying form beneath; in a manner that upholds or keeps from falling
D. transporters	4. people or vehicles that carry across
E. reporting	5. able to be brought in; able to be brought into the country to sell
F. exporters	6. people who carry out; people who send goods out of the country to sell
G. importable	7. not carried from beneath; not upheld or kept from falling
H. supportingly	8. bringing back; giving information about
I. transported	9. capable of being carried from beneath; able to be upheld or kept from falling
	10. carried across; brought from one placed to another

Magic Square Box

A. 9	B. 7	C. 2
D. 4	E. 8	F. 6
G. 5	H. 3	I. 10

Magic Number __18__

*** ANSWER KEY ***

Focus Word: **IMPORTABLE** ⟶ Write this word on the board.

TEACH

Sample leading question:	"Let's take a look at the word *importable*. How many pieces of meaning do we see?"
Student:	"Three. There's the main root **port**, and a prefix **im-** and a suffix **-able**."
Teacher:	"So adding the meanings of the three pieces together, what do we get?"
Student:	"*Able to be brought in, able to be carried in.* I don't get it."
Student:	"I know. On our vacation we were told that certain things could not be brought back in the country, like live plants or animals. So those things would not be *importable*."
Student:	"Couldn't the prefix mean *not*, so that the word means *not able to be carried*, like too heavy?"
Teacher:	"Let's check it out. (Consulting a dictionary) Yes! There are two different words *importable*, meaning exactly what everyone has said: *able to be brought in*, and *not able to be carried*. The one meaning *not able to be carried* is considered out of date."
Student:	"Then why should we know it?"
Teacher:	"Knowing how words come and go allows writers from the past to communicate with us."

DISCUSS Why would certain things be *importable* and others not? (size or safety, for example, for either meaning).

DEMONSTRATE Have the class imagine a huge elephant outside the window or door. Ask if that elephant is *importable*. (No, it can't be brought in, and yes, it can't be carried!)

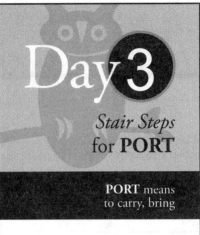

Day 3

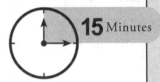

PORT means
to carry, bring

LESSON TIME

15 Minutes

OBJECTIVES

- **Understand** the meaning of the root **PORT**

- **Apply** knowledge of the root **PORT**

- **Break Apart** words in the **PORT** family

- **Understand** the meaning of words in the **PORT** family

- **Understand** the spelling principles applied to the root **PORT**

MATERIALS

- Student Activity Book
- **PORT** Word Wall

DIFFERENTIATING INSTRUCTION

If you prefer easier or more difficult activities, use your personal account at www.dynamicliteracy.com to access novice or expert versions, along with ideas on using them.

Apply Knowledge of PORT

TEACH Have students turn to page 29 in their Student Activity Books. Explain that the boxes in front of and after the root indicate letters that spell out prefixes and suffixes. Students will spell out the correct prefixes and suffixes determined by clues in the definitions at the bottom of the page.

Have a volunteer read definition number one at the bottom of the page. Say, "The ideas of *carry out* and *send goods out* suggest the prefix **ex-** to add the meaning *out of*, or *from* to the root **PORT**. If we put that prefix in the blank spaces on step two, we will have **EXPORT**, which fits the definition."

COMPLETE THE ACTIVITY

Let students work in pairs (optionally) and tell them to use the same strategy to find the correct prefixes and suffixes for the words listed. These activities can be quite challenging!

DISCUSS After a few minutes, review the answers as a class. Ask if there were any difficulties. Listen to any problems and have volunteers solve the difficulties by explaining key clues in the given definitions. As needed, follow the focus word approach that you see modeled on the next page.

Stair Steps

Fill in the missing letters of each 'port' word by using the definitions bel[ow]
'port' means to place or put

SAB Pg 29

1.	e	x	p	o	r	t				
2.	p	o	r	t	e	r	s			
3.	r	e	p	o	r	t	e	r		
4.	e	x	p	o	r	t	i	n	g	
5.	r	e	p	o	r	t	e	d	l	y
6.	i	m	p	o	r	t	a	n	t	l	y
7.	t	r	a	n	s	p	o	r	t	e	r	s
8.	u	n	s	u	p	p	o	r	t	a	b	l	e
9.	t	r	a	n	s	p	o	r	t	a	t	i	o	n

1. to carry out; to send goods out of the country to sell
2. people who carry
3. a person who brings back; a person who gives information about
4. carrying out; sending goods out of the country to sell
5. in a manner brought back; in a manner giving information about
6. in a manner worth being brought in; in a significant or relevant manner
7. people or vehicles that carry across
8. not capable of being carried from beneath; not able to be upheld or kept from falling
9. act or process of carrying across; a means of conveyance

Focus Word: **REPORTER** ⟶ Write this word on the board.

TEACH

Sample leading question:	"What does a ***reporter*** do?"
Student:	"That's somebody who writes or announces news stories."
Student:	"It's somebody who goes out to crime scenes and stuff to get the facts."
Teacher:	"You're right, but, as usual, let's see what the word itself has to tell us."
Teacher:	"Hmm. A person who *carries back*, *brings again*? Not sure."
Student:	"I know! It's a person who gets the facts and then *brings them back* to tell others. I get it."
Student:	"So, to give a ***report*** makes sense. You *bring back* what you have found out. Neat."

DISCUSS Let the class think of other usages of the word ***report*** and how *bring back* works in each situation. For example, a ***report*** can be a *rumor*. It can mean *to show up* (***report*** for work). It can be *a loud noise* (the ***report*** of a gun). It can be *a record of progress* (a ***report*** card).

DEMONSTRATE Project on a screen the nearly eight-inch-long fine-print entry for the word ***report*** in a comprehensive dictionary, such as Webster's Third New International Unabridged, just to show in how many ways a simple morphemic definition like ***carry back*** can be applied.

PORT means
to carry, bring

LESSON TIME

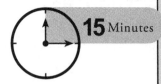

15 Minutes

OBJECTIVES

- **Understand** the meaning of the root **PORT**

- **Reinforce** knowledge of the root **PORT**

- **Understand** the meaning of words in the **PORT** family

- **Apply** knowledge of words in the **PORT** family

MATERIALS

- Student Activity Book

- **PORT** Word Wall

- Dictionary
  (print or on-line)

In Other Words for **PORT**

TEACH Have students turn to page 30 in their Student Activity Books. Explain that they are going to read a little story that uses some surprising and sometimes odd phrasing. The underlined words or phrases in the story are actually definitions or synonyms for words in the **PORT** family. Then they will see sentences about the story, each containing a blank. Using context clues in the sentences, they will find a **PORT** family word in the Word Bank at the bottom to fit in each blank. Have a student read aloud the opening sentence or sentences of the story that contain the first underlined phrase. Then say, "Let's look at the first numbered sentence that contains a blank to be filled in. Clues in the sentence tell us that we want an action word, a verb that means *carrying across*, and that this activity is happening via a limo ride between home and the airport. I see the word *transporting* at the bottom of the page and that word fits all the clues. The **trans-** part means *across* and the *porting* part means *carrying*. Let's write *transporting* in the blank for the first sentence."

COMPLETE THE ACTIVITY

This can be quite challenging, so allow students to work on this activity in small groups. Not every word in the Word Bank will be used.

DISCUSS

After about 10 minutes, ask if there were any difficulties. Have volunteers explain strategies they used that led to correct answers.

Off they Go!

SAB
Pg 30

Taiwo, Julian, and Irtefa were about to take their first airplane ride together. They were so excited. They especially liked the fact that a limousine would be <u>carrying them across</u> from their homes to the air terminal.

When they arrived at the terminal, they asked a <u>person who carries</u> to help them carry their luggage into the terminal. While they waited at the terminal, they watched trucks picking up the <u>goods sent in</u> from all over the world. They also saw cargo planes that were taking <u>goods to be sent out</u> to other places all over the world.

When they got onto the plane, Julian used his carry-on bag as a <u>carry under</u> for his feet, and Taiwo and Irtefa got out their <u>able to be carried</u> headrests and settled into their seats. The attendant <u>brought back</u> information that they would depart in ten minutes but that it was very <u>relevant</u> that they buckle up in their seatbelts now. Soon, the feel of the plane rushing into the sky felt great to the three friends and off they went.

<u>Fill in the blanks below using words from the "port" family.</u>

1. The friends were excited that a limousine would be <u>transporting</u> them to the airport.

2. The airline <u>porter</u> helped them carry all their luggage.

3. Trucks were picking up the <u>imports</u> being delivered from other countries.

4. Cargo planes were taking <u>exports</u> out to go to other countries.

5. Julian used a carry-on bag to <u>support</u> his feet.

6. The girls brought along convenient, <u>portable</u> headrests for the long trip.

7. The flight attendant <u>reported</u> that the plane would be leaving on time.

8. The friends were reminded that it is extremely <u>important</u> to buckle seatbelts.

<u>Not Used:</u>   deportment   deported   supportingly   exportable

Day 5

Morpheme Mania
for **PORT**

PORT means
to carry, bring

LESSON TIME

15 Minutes

OBJECTIVES

- **Build** words in the **PORT** family

- **Apply** knowledge of synonyms and antonyms to **PORT** words

Optional Morpheme Mania for **PORT**

On page 31 of their Activity Books, students will see an optional vocabulary enrichment activity that they can work on in groups, time permitting. This activity makes a great review for the formal assessment on the next page.

All the affixes presented in the week's activities are provided at the top of the page on either side of the root of the week in all its forms. Students can write in up to 13 of the words they built during the week, possibly discovering additional ones.

Then students can brainstorm with each other to come up with antonyms and synonyms they may know. Starter examples are given with every Morpheme Mania in the Activity Book. Because antonyms and synonyms may require knowledge of roots which students have not yet studied, completion of this activity is not crucial. Simply remind students that they can at any time during the course of the year revisit any of their Morpheme Mania pages and add words, antonyms, and synonyms as their vocabulary grows.

Day 5 *Assessment*

Make and hand out copies.
The answer key is on page A-3.
The instructions are on page A-2.

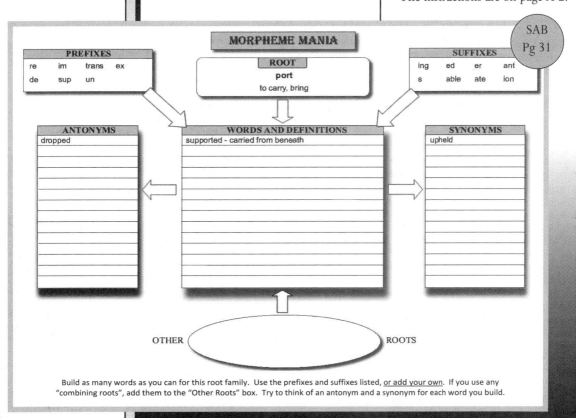

MORPHEME MANIA

PREFIXES			
re	im	trans	ex
de	sup	un	

ROOT
port
to carry, bring

SUFFIXES			
ing	ed	er	ant
s	able	ate	ion

SAB
Pg 31

ANTONYMS
dropped

WORDS AND DEFINITIONS
supported - carried from beneath

SYNONYMS
upheld

OTHER ROOTS

Build as many words as you can for this root family. Use the prefixes and suffixes listed, or add your own. If you use any "combining roots", add them to the "Other Roots" box. Try to think of an antonym and a synonym for each word you build.

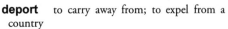
deport to carry away from; to expel from a country

deported carried away from; expelled from a country

deporting carrying away from; expelling from a country

deportment act or process of carrying away from; an act of expulsion from a country

deportments acts or processes of carrying away from; acts of expulsion from a country

deports carries away from; transfers out or expels from a country

export to carry out; to send goods out of the country to sell

exportable able to be carried out; able to be sent out of the country to sell

exported carried out; sent goods out of the country to sell

exporter a person who carries out; a person who sends goods out of the country to sell

exporters people who carry out; people who send goods out of the country to sell

exporting carrying out; sending goods out of the country to sell

exports carries out; sends good out of the country to sell

import to bring in; to bring goods into the country to sell

importable able to be brought in; able to be brought into the country to sell

importance the degree of worth for being brought in; quality or condition of being significant or relevant

important worth being brought in; significant or relevant

importantly in a manner worth being brought in; in a significant or relevant manner

importantness quality of being worth bringing in; significance or relevance

importation act or process of bringing in; an act of bringing goods into the country to sell

importations acts or processes of bringing in; acts of bringing goods into the country to sell

imported brought in; brought goods into the country to sell

importer a person who brings in; a person who brings goods into the country to sell

importers people who bring in; people who bring goods into the country to sell

importing bringing in; bringing goods into the country to sell

imports brings in; brings goods into the country to sell

port carriage or manner in which something is carried

portability ability to be carried

portable able to be carried

portal serving to carry

portals devices that carry to other places

porter a person who carries

porters people who carry

portly having carriage; large or overweight

ports carriages or manners in which things are carried

report to bring back; to give information about

reported brought back; gave information about

reportedly in a manner brought back; in a manner giving information about

reporter a person who brings back; a person who gives information about

reporters people who bring back; people who give information about

reporting bringing back; giving information about

reports brings back; gives information about

support to carry from beneath; to uphold or keep from falling

supportable capable of being carried from beneath; able to be upheld or kept from falling

supported carried from beneath; upheld or kept from falling

supporter a person who carries from beneath; a person who upholds or keeps from falling

supporters people who carry from beneath; people who uphold or keep from falling

supporting bearing or carrying from beneath; upholding or keeping from falling

supportingly in a manner carrying from beneath; so as to uphold or keep from falling

supports carries from beneath; upholds or keeps from falling

transport to carry across; to bring from one place to another

transportable able to be carried across; able to be brought from one place to another

transportation act or process of carrying across; a means of conveyance

transportations acts or processes of carrying across; various means of conveyance

transported carried across; brought from one place to another

transporter a person or vehicle that carries across

transporters people or vehicles that carry across

transporting carrying across

transports carries across; brings from one place to another

unimportant not worth being brought in; not significant or relevant

unimportantly in a manner not worth being brought in; in an insignificant or irrelevant manner

unsupportable not capable of being carried from beneath; not able to be upheld or kept from falling

unsupported not carried from beneath; not upheld or kept from falling

Check-Up for **PORT**

Name _____

____ **1.** **PORT** in words like **exports** and **transportation** means:

    A to carry

    B to save or protect

    C wealth

____ **2.** What is the meaning of the word **imported**?

    A not protected

    B brought in

    C increased wealth

____ **3.** What is the meaning of the word **portable**?

    A likely to increase wealth

    B tending to save or protect

    C able to be carried

____ **4.** What is the meaning of the word **report**?

    A to bring back

    B to protect again

    C to give money

____ **5.** What is the meaning of the word **supportingly**?

    A not being in favor of

    B so as to carry or hold up

    C to overload

____ **6.** Which word means **someone who carries things**?

    A deportation

    B important

    C porter

____ **7.** Which word means **to bring across again**?

    A importantly

    B retransport

    C unsupportable

____ **8.** Which word means **the process of sending out**?

    A exportation

    B deporting

    C reimportation

____ **9.** We liked watching the otters **disporting** in the water. The otters were:

    A having lunch

    B floating quietly

    C letting themselves be carried with fun in all directions

____ **10.** Grandmother's school record has a grade for **comportment**, or:

    A how likely people were to have success in life

    B how many times students were helpful to the teacher

    C how people carried themselves and behaved

OBJECTIVES

- **Understand** the meaning of the root **JECT**
- **Build** words in the root **JECT** family
- **Break Apart** words in the root **JECT** family
- **Understand** the meaning of words in the **JECT** family
- **Understand** the spelling principles applied to the root **JECT**
- **Apply** knowledge of words in the **JECT** family
- **Assess** and **Reinforce** knowledge of words in the **JECT** family

MATERIALS

- Student Activity Books, pages 33-38
- Dictionary *(print or on-line)*
- pencils *(optional)*

CROSS-CURRICULAR EXAMPLES

Science:
conjecture, ejector, injection

Social Studies:
objectives, subjectivist

Language Arts:
adjectival, interjection, subject

Math:
projectile, trajectory

JECT
meaning "to throw"

eject
to **throw** out

Morpheme: **JECT**
Allomorphs: none

Over 200 words containing the morpheme **JECT** are current in English. During this unit, tell students to be alert for this root in their school texts, general reading, and oral language they hear. Some of the words they might encounter in their school subjects are listed on the left under Cross-Curricular Examples.

UNIT AT A GLANCE

Day 1
Root Squares for **JECT**

Day 2
Magic Squares for **JECT**

Day 3
Stair Steps for **JECT**

OPTIONAL
Day 4
In Other Words for **JECT**

Day 5
Assessment or Morpheme Mania for **JECT**

Each activity should take approximately **15 minutes**.

One common feature of English words borrowed from French is the omission of central or other internal consonants. The original Latin verb root **ject** became the French verb **jeter**, *to throw*, (note that the internal **c** has been dropped), and from there came the English word **jet**, *a forceful rush through a narrow opening*, and, of course, the name of the plane that propels itself with such a forceful rush. The verb to **jettison**, meaning *to throw off*, comes from this source, as does a **jetty**, a pier that is *thrown* out into the space of the water.

Two of the names of parts of speech contain this morpheme: **adjective** (a word *thrown toward another* so as to describe it) and **interjection** (a word *thrown into the midst of others* for an emotional effect. In addition, the word for a major component of every sentence, the **subject**, contains this morpheme.

A **súbject**, on the one hand, is a person "thrown under" the control of someone else, as the *Queen's subjects*. On the other hand, the word means the topic which underlies (has been "thrown under") the very essence of a statement. From this usage of **subject** comes the word **gist**, the main point.

To **subjéct** someone to anything unpleasant is to throw that person underneath the unpleasantry, as in "Rudy was **subjected** to three hours of listening to an out-of-tune piano."

To **conjecture** is to throw ideas together and see what comes up.

Word Alert!
There are *no alerts*. Every English word containing the letter combination **j-e-c-t** can be traced to this root family!

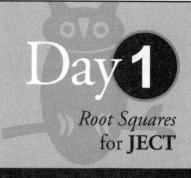

Day 1

Root Squares
for **JECT**

JECT means
to throw

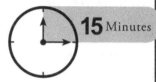
OBJECTIVES

- **Understand** the meaning of the root **JECT**

- **Build** words in the **JECT** family

- **Understand** the meaning of words in the **JECT** family

- **Understand** the spelling principles applied to the root **JECT**

MATERIALS

- Student Activity Book
- **JECT** Word Wall
- Dictionary *(print or on-line)*
- pencils *(optional)*

DIFFERENTIATING INSTRUCTION

If you prefer easier or more difficult activities, use your personal account at www.dynamicliteracy.com to access novice or expert versions, along with ideas on using them.

Root Squares for JECT

TEACH Have students turn to page 33 in their Activity Books. Say, "All of the prefixes and suffixes in the squares surrounding the shaded center are probably familiar, but if you have questions about any of them, look them up in the list inside the front and back cover of the activity book." Call attention to the center box. Point out that the root **JECT** has only one spelling. Ask students to decide if what they see in the middle square can stand alone as a word. Since it is not an independent word, it must have a prefix or a suffix to play a part in making a word. Ask students to put one of the word parts they see in the surrounding squares onto the root **JECT**. If they need help, ask them to add the prefix **re-** to build **reject**, a word they may recognize as a common word, and you can use that word to guide them to the meaning *to throw*. Since the prefix **re-** means *back*, when we **reject** something, we *throw it back*. Suggest that students start their list by adding the suffix **-ion** to **reject** to build a second word, **rejection**.

COMPLETE THE ACTIVITY
Have students follow the directions to build words. If students have difficulty building words with the Root Squares, show them how by modeling the matrix approach found on the next page, taking one affix at a time and seeing if it will connect with any one of the allomorphs of the root.

DISCUSS After 5 minutes, have volunteers write some of their words on the board. Focus with the class on the words they have built and guide them in a discussion of how the meaning of the root is still *to throw*, even when prefixes and suffixes are added. Watch for target words that demonstrate the meanings of throw. If the word **project** is not present, ask the class, "Can anyone try to use the prefix **pro-** ?" and then continue on to the target word discussion on the next page.

SAB
Pg 33

Root Squares

How many words can you make?

Start in any square. Your goal is to combine two or more word parts to make as many words in the 'ject' family as you can. Write each word and a definition you can think of for it in the space provided at the bottom of the page. Use the back of the page if you need to.

re	ion	ile
ory	ject	inter
sub	ure	pro

Focus Word: **PROJECT** ⟶ Write this word on the board.

TEACH

Lead with this:	"There are two ways to pronounce this word. Get with your 'smart buddy' and figure out the two ways."
Student:	"The accent on the word can be at the beginning or at the end."
Teacher:	"And what difference will that change in accent make?"
Student:	"A *próject*, with the accent on the first syllable, is a thing, a noun."
Student:	"And to *projéct*, with the accent on the last syllable, is an action, a verb."
Teacher:	"Good. Now let's see what the word, with either pronunciation, tells us about itself. Let's look at the pieces of meaning in the word."
Student:	"There is a prefix **pro**, meaning *forward*, and the root **ject**, meaning *to throw*. I don't see what a *project*, like a science *project*, has to do with *throw forward*."
Student:	"But I get it with the verb, to *project*. To *project* your voice is to *throw it forward* so people can hear."
Student:	"And to *project* an image on a screen is to *throw it forth*."
Student:	"Maybe *throw* is too strong a word for every meaning. If we think of it as just *putting*, rather than *throwing*, I can see how a *project* is something you *put forth*."
Teacher:	"That sounds good. An original meaning, like *throw*, can certainly go through some changes over time."

DISCUSS What are differences between the words *propose* (literally, *to put forward*) and *project* (*to throw forward*)? A way to discuss this is to list things that are *proposed* (marriage, ideas, plans) and things that are *projected* (voice, images, voting results). Such lists are called *linguistic collocations*, and they help determine variations in the meanings of morphemes.

DEMONSTRATE Hold up several pencils of uneven length, with the eraser ends all on the same level, and lead the class to see that the longest pencil *projects* or "sticks forth" out from the others.

Root Squares Matrix

You can refer to this matrix to guide students in this activity. Students could build at least these 15 words. *It really doesn't matter how many they build* – the point is that they understand the consistent meanings of the root **JECT** and of its prefixes and suffixes.

	inter-	pro-	re-	sub-
no suffix	interject	project	reject	subject
-ile		projectile		
-ion	interjection	projection	rejection	subjection
-ory	interjectory	projectory		
-ure		projecture		
re-	reinterject	reproject		resubject

Day 2

Magic Squares
for **JECT**

JECT means
to throw

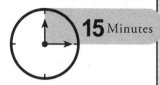

LESSON TIME

15 Minutes

OBJECTIVES

- **Understand** the meaning of the root **JECT**

- **Break Apart** words in the **JECT** family

- **Understand** the meanings of words in the **JECT** family

MATERIALS

- Student Activity Book
- **JECT** Word Wall
- Dictionary *(print or on-line)*

DIFFERENTIATING INSTRUCTION

If you prefer easier or more difficult activities, use your personal account at www.dynamicliteracy.com to access novice or expert versions, along with ideas on using them.

Break Apart Words with **JECT**

TEACH Have students turn to the Magic Squares on page 34 in their Student Activity Books. Model a Think-Aloud strategy for students: "I know that **JECT** means *to throw*. I can use this knowledge to find the definition of a word with this as its root." Direct students to word D, ***dejected***.

Say, "I know that the prefix **de-** means *down* and the suffix **-ed** makes the word *past* or *having been* or *made to become*. Definition 4 is the one with the idea of *down: thrown down*. Since that definition accounts for all the parts of the word, including the meaning of **JECT**, we'll write the number 4 in square D.

COMPLETE THE ACTIVITY
Ask students to use the same strategy to find the correct definitions for the other words. Tell them to write the number of the definition in the box that matches the letter for the word. Remind them that if all their answers are correct, each row and each column will add up to the same Magic number

DISCUSS After five minutes, ask if there are any difficulties about matching the words and definitions. If there are, ask volunteers to explain clues in the definitions that will lead to the correct choice of word. As needed, follow the focus word approach for **reject** that you see modeled on the next page.

Add any new words to the classroom **JECT** Word Wall and remind students to add these words to the **JECT** Word Wall in their Activity Books.

SAB
Pg 34

Magic Squares

Select the best answer for each of the words in the 'ject' family from the numbered definitions. Put the number in the proper space in the Magic Square box. If the total of the numbers is the same both across and down, you have found the magic number!

'ject' means to throw

WORDS	DEFINITIONS
A. adjective	1. something thrown in between; act of inserting or breaking into with a comment
B. reject	2. throwing out; driving out or expelling
C. projectile	3. throwing onto; a word that describes a noun
D. dejected	4. thrown down; disheartened or depressed
E. ejecting	5. something thrown forward; something shot forward
F. injections	6. related to throwing together; based on guesswork
G. objectionable	7. to throw back; to refuse or toss away
H. conjectural	8. able to be thrown up against; likely to be protested
I. interjection	9. acts of throwing into; acts of forcing or driving something in

Magic Square Box

A. 3	B. 7	C. 5
D. 4	E. 2	F. 9
G. 8	H. 6	I. 1

Magic Number **15**

*** ANSWER KEY ***

Focus Word: **REJECT** ⟶ Write this word on the board.

TEACH

Sample leading question:	"What does it mean to **reject** an idea?"
Student:	"You don't like it. You think it's bad."
Teacher:	"And what are you doing to the idea if you **reject** it?"
Student:	"I see it! You *throw it back*, like a fish you don't want after you've caught it!"
Student:	"Doesn't that word have two different pronunciations, just like **próject** and **projéct**?"
Student:	"Yes! There's the verb, to **rejéct**, and there's the noun, a **réject**."
Teacher:	"Good, and what is a **reject**?"
Student:	"It's something *not liked or accepted*. It's *thrown back* as not wanted."

DISCUSS Discuss *collocations* or applications of the word **reject**. For example, what does a **reject** button on a phone do? What does it mean if the body **rejects** a kidney transplant? What is happening if you are **rejected** from a team? Are the words **project** and **reject** opposites?

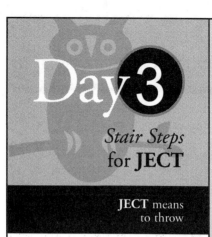
LESSON TIME

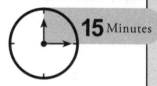

15 Minutes

OBJECTIVES

- **Understand** the meaning of the root **JECT**

- **Apply** knowledge of the root **JECT**

- **Break Apart** words in the **JECT** family

- **Understand** the meaning of words in the **JECT** family

- **Understand** the spelling principles applied to the root **JECT**

MATERIALS

- Student Activity Book
- **JECT** Word Wall

DIFFERENTIATING INSTRUCTION

If you prefer easier or more difficult activities, use your personal account at www.dynamicliteracy.com to access novice or expert versions, along with ideas on using them.

Apply Knowledge of JECT

TEACH Have students turn to page 35 in their Student Activity Books. Explain that the boxes in front of and after the root indicate letters that spell out prefixes and suffixes. Students will spell out the correct prefixes and suffixes determined by clues in the definitions at the bottom of the page.

Have a volunteer read definition number two at the bottom of the page. Say, "The suffix **-s** on the word *throws* tells me we want that suffix in the final blank. The words *into* and *in* in the definition lead me to a prefix with that meaning: **in-**

would work, and with that we get **INJECTS**. That would fit the definition very well."

COMPLETE THE ACTIVITY
Let students work in pairs (optionally) and tell them to use the same strategy to find the correct prefixes and suffixes for the words listed. These activities can be quite challenging!

DISCUSS After a few minutes, review the answers as a class. Ask if there were any difficulties. Listen to any problems and have volunteers solve the difficulties by explaining key clues in the given definitions. As needed, follow the focus word approach that you see modeled on the next page.

Stair Steps

Fill in the missing letters of each 'ject' word by using the definitions bel
'ject' means to place or put

SAB
Pg 35

1.	r	e	j	e	c	t				
2.	i	n	j	e	c	t	s			
3.	e	j	e	c	t	i	o	n		
4.	a	d	j	e	c	t	i	v	e	
5.	p	r	o	j	e	c	t	i	l	e
6.	c	o	n	j	e	c	t	u	r	a	l
7.	i	n	t	e	r	j	e	c	t	i	n	g
8.	o	b	j	e	c	t	i	o	n	a	b	l	e

1. to throw back; to refuse or toss away
2. throws into; forces or drives something in
3. act of throwing out; an act of driving out or expelling
4. throwing onto; a word that describes a noun
5. something thrown forward; something shot back
6. related to throwing together; based on guesswork
7. throwing between; inserting or breaking into with a comment
8. able to be thrown up against; likely to be protested

Focus Word: **INTERJECTING** ⟶ Write this word on the board.

TEACH

Sample leading question:	"Let's take a look at this word. We know that the suffix **-ing** does what to it?"
Student:	"Makes it mean *happening now*."
Teacher:	"So, leaving just *interject*, what pieces of meaning do we have?"
Student:	"We have the root *ject*, *throw*, and we have a prefix, *inter*."
Student:	"We had a Mini-Lesson on *inter*. That means *between or among*."
Teacher:	"Good, so adding all the meanings together, what do we get for *interjecting*?"
Student:	"*Throwing between now*. When is that ever used?"
Student:	"Somebody can be *interjecting* an opinion."
Student:	"Or *interjecting* comments."
Teacher:	"And what is somebody who is *interjecting* opinions or comments literally doing?"
Student:	"They are *throwing* opinions or comments *in among* the conversation."

DISCUSS There is a type of communication using words that are just *thrown into* a conversation to express emotion. These words are called *interjections*. Let students *interject* their sentences with such words as ouch!, whew!, or goodness!

DEMONSTRATE Write this sentence on the board: I had a banana split, and ___ was it good! Ask for appropriate *interjecting* words that would fit in the blank.

Day 4

In Other Words
for **JECT**

JECT means
to throw

LESSON TIME

15 Minutes

OBJECTIVES

- **Understand** the meaning of the root **JECT**

- **Reinforce** knowledge of the root **JECT**

- **Understand** the meaning of words in the **JECT** family

- **Apply** knowledge of words in the **JECT** family

MATERIALS

- Student Activity Book

- **JECT** Word Wall

- Dictionary
(print or on-line)

In Other Words for **JECT**

TEACH You will find a mini-lesson for **tra-** on page 72 if you need it. Have students turn to page 36 in their Student Activity Books. Explain that they are going to read a little story that uses some surprising and sometimes odd phrasing. The underlined words or phrases in the story are actually definitions or synonyms for words in the **JECT** family. Then they will see sentences about the story, each containing a blank. Using context clues in the sentences, they will find a **JECT** family word in the Word Bank at the bottom to fit in each blank. Have a student read aloud the opening sentence or sentences of the story that contain the first underlined phrase. Then

say, "Let's look at the first numbered sentence that contains a blank to be filled in. Clues in the sentence tell us that we want a descriptive word, an adjective that means *thrown down*, in the sense of a way someone might feel. I see the word **dejected** at the bottom of the page and that word fits all the clues. One of the meanings for the **de-** part is *down* and the **jected** part means *thrown*. Notice that is not the past tense of *throw* but rather the *adjectival* sense. Let's write **dejected** in the blank for the first sentence."

COMPLETE THE ACTIVITY

This can be quite challenging, so allow students to work on this activity in small groups. Not every word in the Word Bank will be used.

DISCUSS After about 10 minutes, ask if there were any difficulties. Have volunteers explain strategies they used that led to correct answers.

In Other Words...

SAB
Pg 36

Edward Jenner Takes a Bold Risk

Edward Jenner wanted to find a way to stop the disease cowpox. He had done lots of research but had found nothing. Feeling <u>thrown down</u>, he almost gave up. One day as he was tossing <u>things thrown across</u> the room at the wall, he had an idea. "Aha!" he said as he practically <u>threw</u> himself <u>out</u> of his seat. Jenner <u>threw together</u> ideas, thinking that <u>thrusting</u> a bit of the disease <u>into</u> someone could give immunity against that disease. His fellow townspeople were <u>throwing up obstacles in the way</u> against Jenner's idea and were <u>throwing</u> him <u>up</u> to harsh questions. "Excuse me," one of the locals <u>threw in between</u> the arguments, "This is just too stupid and dangerous. "

But Jenner said he would <u>throw back</u> their fear and ridicule and would one day try out his theory. He did, successfully, and that is how vaccinations came to be.

<u>Fill in the blanks below using words from the "ject" family.</u>

1. Because he felt <u>dejected</u>, Jenner almost gave up.

2. Jenner was one day wrapped in thought while hurling <u>trajectories</u> across the room.

3. He was so excited that he <u>ejected</u> himself out of his chair.

4. He <u>conjectured</u> in his thoughts that a bit of the disease could give immunity.

5. He would <u>inject</u> a small amount of cowpox into a healthy person.

6. The local citizens <u>objected</u> to this plan.

7. They <u>subjected</u> him to harsh questioning.

8. One citizen even <u>interjected</u> ridicule into the discussion.

9. Jenner <u>rejects</u> the critics and successfully stops the disease.

<u>Not Used:</u> adjective objectionable subjective

O P T I O N A L

Day 5

Morpheme Mania
for **JECT**

JECT means
to throw

LESSON TIME

15 Minutes

OBJECTIVES

- **Build** words in the **JECT** family
- **Apply** knowledge of synonyms and antonyms to **JECT** words

Optional Morpheme Mania for **JECT**

On page 37 of their Activity Books, students will see an optional vocabulary enrichment activity that they can work on in groups, time permitting. This activity makes a great review for the formal assessment on the next page.

All the affixes presented in the week's activities are provided at the top of the page on either side of the root of the week in all its forms. Students can write in up to 13 of the words they built during the week, possibly discovering additional ones.

Then students can brainstorm with each other to come up with antonyms and synonyms they may know. Starter examples are given with every Morpheme Mania in the Activity Book. Because antonyms and synonyms may require knowledge of roots which students have not yet studied, completion of this activity is not crucial. Simply remind students that they can at any time during the course of the year revisit any of their Morpheme Mania pages and add words, antonyms, and synonyms as their vocabulary grows.

Day 5 *Assessment*

Make and hand out copies.
The answer key is on page A-3.
The instructions are on page A-2.

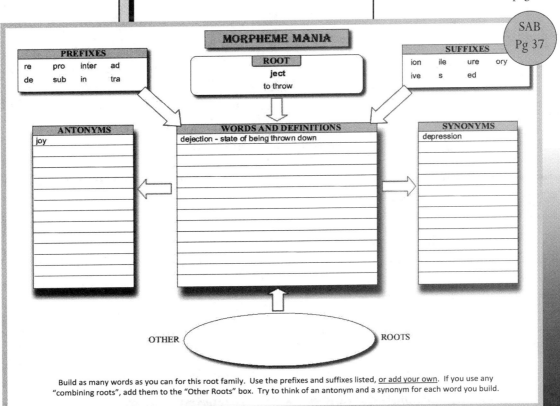

SAB
Pg 37

MORPHEME MANIA

PREFIXES			
re	pro	inter	ad
de	sub	in	tra

ROOT
ject
to throw

SUFFIXES			
ion	ile	ure	ory
ive	s	ed	

ANTONYMS
joy

WORDS AND DEFINITIONS
dejection – state of being thrown down

SYNONYMS
depression

OTHER ROOTS

Build as many words as you can for this root family. Use the prefixes and suffixes listed, or add your own. If you use any "combining roots", add them to the "Other Roots" box. Try to think of an antonym and a synonym for each word you build.

71

adjective throwing onto; a word or phrase describing a noun

adjectives things that throw onto; words or phrases describing nouns

conjectural related to throwing together; based on guesswork

conjecture an act of throwing together; a guess or a suspicion

conjectured threw together; guessed or suspected

conjectures throws together; guesses or suspects

conjecturing throwing together; guessing or suspecting

deject to throw down; to dishearten or depress

dejected thrown down; disheartened or depressed

dejectedly in a manner thrown; in a disheartened or depressed manner

dejecting throwing down; disheartening or depressing

dejection state of being thrown down; depression or state of being disheartened

dejections states of being thrown down; depressions or states of being disheartened

dejects throws down; disheartens or depresses

eject to throw out; to drive out or expel

ejected threw out; drove out or expelled

ejecting throwing out; driving out or expelling

ejection act of throwing out; an act of driving out or expelling

ejections acts of throwing out; acts of driving out or expelling

inject throw into; to force or plunge something in

injected threw into; forced or plunged something in

injecting throwing into; forcing or plunging something in

injection an act of throwing into; a thing forced or plunged in

injections acts of throwing into; things forced or plunged in

injects throws into; forces or plunges something in

interject to throw between; to insert or break in with a comment

interjected threw between; inserted or broke in with a comment

interjecting throwing between; inserting or breaking into with a comment

interjection something thrown in between; act of inserting or breaking in with a comment

interjections things thrown in between; acts of inserting or breaking in with comments

interjects throws in between; inserts or breaks in with a comment

object to throw up against; to protest

objected threw up against; protested

objecting throwing up against; protesting

objection something thrown up against; an act of protest

objectionable able to be thrown up against; likely to be protested

objections things thrown up against; acts of protest

objective anything thrown up against; a goal or a reality

objectively so as to thrown up against; in a manner fitting a goal or reality

objectives things thrown up against; goals or realities

objectivity quality of things thrown up against; quality of a goal or of reality

objects throws up against; protests

project to throw forward; to cast an image onto a surface

projected threw forward; cast an image onto a surface

projectile something thrown forward; something shot forward

projectiles things thrown forward; things shot forward

projecting throwing forward; casting an image onto a surface

projection act or process of throwing forward; anything that sticks out from a surface

projections acts or processes of throwing forward; things that stick out from a surface

projector device for throwing forward; device for casting images onto a screen

projectors devices for throwing forward; devices for casting images onto a screen

projects throws forward; casts an image onto a surface

reject to throw back; to refuse or toss away

rejected threw back; refused or tossed away

rejecting throwing back; refusing or tossing away

rejection act of throwing back; act or refusing or tossing away

rejections acts of throwing back; acts or refusing or tossing away

rejects throws back; refuses or tosses away

subject to throw under; to put under the influence of another's power

subjected threw under; put under the influence of another's power

subjects throws under; puts under the influence of another's power

trajectories things thrown across; paths across which things are thrown

trajectory something thrown across; a path across which something is thrown

---

MINI-LESSON: the prefix **tra-**

The prefix **tra-** is a simplification, a type of *assimilation*, of the prefix **trans-**, meaning *across*. The letters **ns** of **trans-** will drop in a few words, particularly before the letters **d**, **j**, and **v** (though both *transverse* and *traverse* are current). Sometimes, only consulting a current dictionary will settle whether assimilations or simplifications are taking place in English words.

You can have students try to pronounce these words with the full prefix **trans-** so that they can hear why the shortening occurs:

transduce — traduce	transjectory — trajectory
transdition — tradition	transvesty — travesty

Check-Up for **JECT**

Name _____

____ **1.** **JECT** in words like **ejected** and **projection** means:

    A to run

    B to finish

    C to throw

____ **2.** What is the meaning of the word **reject**?

    A to throw back

    B to finish again

    C to run across

____ **3.** What is the meaning of the word **projector**?

    A a person who completes work

    B a device to throw light forward

    C a measurement for a running course

____ **4.** What is the meaning of the word **interjection**?

    A something thrown in between

    B the third completion of a task

    C the process of running through

____ **5.** What is the meaning of the word **objected**?

    A stated something clearly

    B quit before finishing

    C threw up a barrier

____ **6.** Which word means **something thrown across**?

    A trajectory

    B injection

    C conjectural

____ **7.** Which word means **thrown down**?

    A ejected

    B dejected

    C reinterjected

____ **8.** Which word means **an act of throwing things together**?

    A rejection

    B conjecture

    C objection

____ **9.** The team was feeling **abject** after the game. The team felt:

    A like running a victory lap

    B neither good nor bad

    C as if thrown off a bus

____ **10.** Andy tried to arrange the **disjected** papers he had dropped. The papers had been:

    A made dirty by a mud puddle

    B thrown all over the place

    C finished the day before

OBJECTIVES

- **Understand** the meaning of the root **SIGN**

- **Build** words in the root **SIGN** family

- **Break Apart** words in the root **SIGN** family

- **Understand** the meaning of words in the **SIGN** family

- **Understand** the spelling principles applied to the root **SIGN**

- **Apply** knowledge of words in the **SIGN** family

- **Assess** and **Reinforce** knowledge of words in the **SIGN** family

MATERIALS

- Student Activity Books, pages 39-44

- Dictionary *(print or on-line)*

- Adhesive stickers or posting notes (optional)

CROSS-CURRICULAR EXAMPLES

Science:
insignificance, signify

Social Studies:
signals, signatory, reassign

Language Arts:
presignify, signature, assignment

Math:
significant, assign

SIGN

meaning "mark, meaning, indication"

sign
a **mark** with meaning

signify
to cause to have a **meaning**

signal
an **indication**

Morpheme: **SIGN**
Allomorph: **SIGNI**

Over 200 words containing the morpheme **SIGN** or its allomorph are current in English. During this unit, tell students to be alert for this root in their school texts, general reading, and oral language they hear. Some of the words they might encounter in their school subjects are listed on the left under Cross-Curricular Examples.

UNIT AT A GLANCE

Day **1**
Root Squares
for **SIGN**

Day **2**
Magic Squares
for **SIGN**

Day **3**
Stair Steps
for **SIGN**

OPTIONAL
Day **4**
In Other Words
for **SIGN**

Day **5**
Assessment or Morpheme Mania
for **SIGN**

Each activity should take approximately **15 minutes**.

This root is related to the root **sequ**, meaning *to follow*. A **sign** was originally an image or standard (such as a flag), which a person would follow. Thus, a **sign**, as in an omen, is something to pay heed to (*follow the signs*). A stop **sign** gives instructions that are best obeyed (or followed).

In place of an actual hand-written **signature** to mark ownership or authorship, a person might once have used a **signet**, a ring or seal that could be stamped into wax to leave an identifying mark.

Insignia are *marks of distinction* put onto a person, such as badges or ribbons.

An **ensign** is a *mark of identification*, often a flag, used by organizations for advertisement or alert. That same word, **ensign**, was once used to name the person who would carry the flag or identifying mark. **Ensign** then became a military title, and remains so in the navy. From its naval connections, the word **ensign** can also mean *a deep, dark blue*.

To **sign** a document is to *put your identifying mark on it*. If you do that again, you **re-sign** it. But what about the verb **resign** (notice that the **s** has become a **z** sound)? Here, the prefix **re-** takes on a meaning *back*, as in **reverse** or **refund**, similar to **un-**, so that the verb **resign** means something close to *not obeying or being a part of anymore*, or *not adding your signature to anymore*.

Who *designed* that fabulous dress?

Word Alert!

A familiar French title of respect originally given to an elder (a senior) is **monsieur**, *my sire*. The Italian form of this title is **monsignor**, and the general titles meaning *mister* and *mistress*, **signor** and **signora**, are not from the root **sign**. Words such as **signory** and **signorial**, *belonging to a master* (an elder), are also outside this root family. Otherwise, all English words containing the letter sequence **s-i-g-n** do belong to this root family.

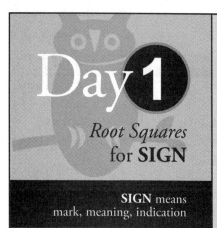

Day 1

Root Squares
for **SIGN**

SIGN means
mark, meaning, indication

LESSON TIME

15 Minutes

OBJECTIVES

- **Understand** the meaning of the root **SIGN**

- **Build** words in the **SIGN** family

- **Understand** the meaning of words in the **SIGN** family

- **Understand** the spelling principles applied to the root **SIGN**

MATERIALS

- Student Activity Book
- **SIGN** Word Wall
- Dictionary *(print or on-line)*

DIFFERENTIATING INSTRUCTION

If you prefer easier or more difficult activities, use your personal account at www.dynamicliteracy.com to access novice or expert versions, along with ideas on using them.

Root Squares for SIGN

TEACH Have students turn to page 39 in their Activity Books. Say, "All of the prefixes and suffixes in the squares surrounding the center are probably familiar, but if you aren't sure of any of the meanings, ask or look them up in the front or back of the activity book." There is one Combining Form, **fic**, and a related Mini-Lesson is available on the next page.

Point out that the root **SIGN** has two different spellings, called *allomorphs*. Ask students to decide if one of the forms they see in the middle square can stand alone as a word. They will see **sign**, and you can use that word to guide them to the meaning *mark* or *seal, meaning* or *indication*. When we **sign** something, we *make our mark on it*. Our **signature** is our *mark*. Suggest

that students start their list with **sign** and then add **de-**, meaning *down*, to build a second word, **design**. This word means *to mark down, to sketch out a plan*.

COMPLETE THE ACTIVITY

Have students follow the directions to build words. If students have difficulty building words with the Root Squares, show them how by modeling the matrix approach found on the next page, taking one affix at a time and seeing if it will connect with any one of the allomorphs of the root.

DISCUSS After five minutes, have volunteers write some of their words on the board. Focus on the words they have built and guide them in a discussion of how the meaning of the root is still *mark* or *seal, meaning* or *indication*, even when prefixes and suffixes are added. Watch for target words that most easily demonstrate the meanings of

mark or *seal, meaning* or *indication*. If the word **signer** is not present, ask the class, "Can anyone try to use the suffix **-er**?" and then continue on to the target word discussion on the next page.

Root Squares

How many words can you make?

Start in any square. Your goal is to combine two or more word parts to make as many words in the 'sign, signi' family as you can. Write each word and a definition you can think of for it in the space provided at the bottom of the page. Use the back of the page if you need to.

fic	ment	de
ant	sign, signi	er
ate	as	al

SAB
Pg 39

Focus Word: SIGNER → Write this word on the board.

TEACH

Question:	"John Hancock is one of the most famous **signers** of the Declaration of Independence. Does anybody know why?"
Student:	"I've heard people say, 'Put your John Hancock here,' when they want you to write your name."
Student:	"I know—that's the great big name on the Declaration of Independence."
Teacher:	"Do you know why he wrote his name so big? He really wanted to get his message across and he wanted to leave his **mark**."
Student:	"I get it–he left his name as a **sign**!"
Teacher:	"That's right, and let's go back and look at the word **signer** again. What does the -**er** on the end mean?"
Student:	"Somebody who *does or makes something*."
Student:	"So a **signer** is somebody who *makes his mark*."
Student:	"But **signer** can also mean somebody who uses **sign** language, can't it?"
Student:	"Hey, that's right! My cousin is a **signer** for her church group, because there are people who need sign language there."
Teacher:	"Good—so we see two great uses of the word **signer**, and in both uses, somebody is *getting meaning across with written or finger symbols*."

DISCUSS What are some symbols that can be used by **signers** to get meaning across? How is a **signer** like or different from a **signaler**?

DEMONSTRATE If someone knows any of the hand symbols used in some of the sign languages for people who cannot hear, let that person demonstrate and teach a few. Return to the concept that the person making these marks of meaning is a **signer**.

MINI-LESSON: the Combining Form *fic*

This prevalent Combining Form is a variation of the root **fac**, which was featured in the Elements Level 1 program. It comes from the Latin verb that means *to make or do*, and it is used in about 900 English words. It appears as a suffix in some familiar English words with Latin base roots. You can illustrate the effect of the suffix with these examples:

honorific: *making or causing to be an honor*
scientific: *making or causing to be known as a fact of science*
horrific: *making or causing to be a horror*
pacific: *making or causing to be peaceful*

More often the Combining Form **fic** occurs with other suffixes, as the following familiar examples will show:

artificial   **notification**   **magnificent**   **beneficial**   **identification**   **efficient**   **official**   **qualification**

Root Squares Matrix

You can refer to this matrix to guide students in this activity. Students could build at least these 14 words. *It really doesn't matter how many they build* – the point is that they understand the consistent meanings of the root **SIGN** and of its prefixes and suffixes.

	no prefix	as-	de-
no suffix	sign	assign	design
-al	signal		
-ate	signate		designate
-er	signer	assigner	designer
-fic	signific		
-fic + -ant	significant		
-fic + -ate	significate		
-ment		assignment	
-al + -ment	signalment		

Day 2

Magic Squares
for **SIGN**

SIGN means
mark, meaning, indication

LESSON TIME

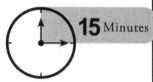

15 Minutes

OBJECTIVES

- **Understand** the meaning of the root **SIGN**

- **Break Apart** words in the **SIGN** family

- **Understand** the meanings of words in the **SIGN** family

MATERIALS

- Student Activity Book

- **SIGN** Word Wall

- Dictionary
  (print or on-line)

DIFFERENTIATING INSTRUCTION

If you prefer easier or more difficult activities, use your personal account at www.dynamicliteracy.com to access novice or expert versions, along with ideas on using them.

Break Apart Words with SIGN

TEACH   Have students turn to the Magic Squares on page 40 in their Student Activity Books. Model a Think-Aloud strategy for students: "I know that **SIGN**, with the two different spellings of this root, means *mark, seal, meaning, indication*. I can use this knowledge to find the definition of a word with this as its root." Direct students to word I, **reassign**. Say, "I know that the prefix **re-** means *again* and the prefix **as-** is an assimilation of **ad-**, meaning *toward or to*. Looking for those words in a definition, I see definition #10 is the one with those meanings in its definition: *to give a mark to again*. Since that definition accounts for all the parts of the word, including one meaning of **SIGN**, the meaning *mark*, we'll write the number 10 in square I.

COMPLETE THE ACTIVITY

Ask students to use the same strategy to find the correct definitions for the other words. Tell them to write the number of the definition in the box that matches the letter for the word. Remind them that if all their answers are correct, each row and each column will add up to the same Magic number.

DISCUSS   After five minutes, ask if there are any difficulties about matching the words and definitions.   If there are, ask volunteers to explain clues in the definitions that will lead to the correct choice of word.   As needed, follow the focus word approach for **assigning** that you see modeled on the next page.

Add any new words to the classroom **SIGN** Word Wall and remind students to add these words to the **SIGN** Word Wall in their Activity Books.

Magic Squares

SAB
Pg 40

Select the best answer for each of the words in the 'sign, signi' family from the numbered definitions. Put the number in the proper space in the Magic Square box. If the total of the numbers is the same both across and down, you have found the magic number!

'sign, signi' means mark, seal, meaning, or indication

WORDS	DEFINITIONS
A. assigning	1. to indicate completely; to hand over or deliver
B. designated	2. in a manner of no marked importance of things done; irrelevantly
C. insignificantly	3. marks of things done; importances
D. resignations	4. indications back; notifications of giving up a job or office
E. redesigning	5. a person's mark indicating who he or she is; a person's name as written by himself or herself
F. reassigned	6. gave a mark to again; gave a task again
G. signature	7. indicated; named or appointed
H. significances	8. marking down again; sketching out a new or different plan
I. reassign	9. giving a mark to; giving a task
	10. to give a mark to again; to give a task again

Magic Square Box

A. 9	B. 7	C. 2
D. 4	E. 8	F. 6
G. 5	H. 3	I. 10

Magic Number 18

*** ANSWER KEY ***

Focus Word: ASSIGNING → Write this word on the board.

TEACH

Sample leading question:	"Let's take a close look at the word *assigning*. How many morphemes do you think are in that word?"
Student:	"Three! There is a prefix, a root, and a suffix."
Student:	"I see the root **sign** and the suffix **-ing**, *going on now*, but I'm not sure what the prefix is."
Teacher:	"Let's try to figure it out."
Student:	"Oh, yes, that's the prefix **ad-** changed to **as-**."
Teacher:	"Why does it change, and how could you tell?"
Student:	"The double letter **s** after the first **a** is a clue that **ad-** is there, but changed to **as-** because of the next **s**."
Teacher:	"Does anyone remember what that change is called?"
Student:	"Assimilation!"
Student:	"Hey—the word **assimilation** has *assimilation* in it with **ad-**!"
Teacher:	"Now let's dig for the deep meaning of that well-known word."

DISCUSS Note that this discussion focused on the structure of the word **assigning**. Reviews of patterns is always valuable, and then you can proceed to an analysis of the deep-structure meaning of the word. Encourage students to experiment with the various meanings of the morphemes **ad-** and **sign** to arrive at a meaning such as *giving a mark or indication to*, and explaining how that makes sense with what they know about the word.

DEMONSTRATE Say, "I am **assigning** all of you a task. I'm **assigning** all of you to stand up. Now I'm **assigning** the guys (or the juniors or the first row, etc.) to sit back down." Then say, "Notice how I indicated the group and the task, giving the task to the group. So what other words in English mean about the same thing as **assigning**?" Lead the class to words such as **ordering**, **allotting**, **drilling**, or even **tasking**.

A feeble attempt to explain
a missing *assignment!*

LESSON TIME

15 Minutes

OBJECTIVES

- **Understand** the meaning of the root **SIGN**

- **Apply** knowledge of the root **SIGN**

- **Break Apart** words in the **SIGN** family

- **Understand** the meaning of words in the **SIGN** family

- **Understand** the spelling principles applied to the root **SIGN**

MATERIALS

- Student Activity Book

- **SIGN** Word Wall

- Stickers (Optional)

DIFFERENTIATING INSTRUCTION

If you prefer easier or more difficult activities, use your personal account at www.dynamicliteracy.com to access novice or expert versions, along with ideas on using them.

Apply Knowledge of **SIGN**

TEACH Have students turn to page 41 in their Student Activity Books. Explain that the boxes in front of and after the root indicate letters that spell out prefixes and suffixes. Students will spell out the correct prefixes and suffixes determined by clues in the definitions at the bottom of the page.

Have a volunteer read definition number two at the bottom of the page. Say, "As we have seen before, the suffix -s we see on the word **gives** tells us we want that suffix in the final blank. The little word **to** suggests the prefix **ad-**, though the word **adsign** doesn't seem right, does

it? Remember the various spellings of that prefix? The letter **d** must *assimilate* to **s** to make the prefixed word easier to pronounce. With that assimilation, we get **ASSIGN**, the word with the meaning that goes with the definition we see for step two."

COMPLETE THE ACTIVITY

Let students work in pairs (optionally) and tell them to use the same strategy to find the correct prefixes and suffixes for the words listed. These activities can be quite challenging!

DISCUSS After a few minutes, review the answers as a class. Ask if there were any difficulties. Listen to any problems and have volunteers solve the difficulties by explaining key clues in the given definitions. As needed, follow the focus word approach that you see modeled on the next page.

SAB Pg 41

Stair Steps

Fill in the missing letters of each 'sign'signi' word by using the definitions b
'sign, signi' means mark, seal; meaning; indication

1.	s	i	g	n	e	r				
2.	a	s	s	i	g	n	s			
3.	d	e	s	i	g	n	e	r		
4.	s	i	g	n	a	l	e	r	s	
5.	s	i	g	n	a	t	u	r	e	s
6.	a	s	s	i	g	n	m	e	n	t	s
7.	d	e	s	i	g	n	a	t	i	o	n	s
8.	r	e	a	s	s	i	g	n	m	e	n	t	s
9.	i	n	s	i	g	n	i	f	i	c	a	n	c	e

1. a person who indicates; a person communicating by sign language
2. gives a mark to; gives a task
3. a person who marks down; a person who sketches out a plan
4. people who indicate; people who give non-verbal massages
5. people's marks indicating who they are; people's names as written by themselves
6. acts or processes of giving a mark to; tasks
7. acts or processes of indicating; names or appointments
8. acts or processes of giving a mark to again; tasks given again
9. quality of making no marked importance; irrelevance

Focus Word: **REASSIGNMENTS** ⟶ Write this word on the board.

TEACH

Sample leading question:	"Let's take a look at this word. How many morphemes do we have?"
Student:	"Four."
Student:	"I say five."
Teacher:	Let's sort them out and count them."
Student:	"There are two prefixes and two suffixes, plus the root."
Teacher:	"Does everyone see that?"
Student:	"Oh, right. Prefixes **re-** and **ad-**, suffixes -**ment** and -**s**, root **sign**."
Teacher:	"Great, and now let's add up the meanings to see how the word **reassignments** works."
Student:	"Hey—it's just like 'translating' a word."
Student:	"Yes, I've always liked the puzzle idea of reading the pieces of meaning."
Student:	"Let's see: first of all, it's *more than one act or process*—that takes care of the two suffixes."
Student:	"And it's being *done again*, with the **re-** prefix."
Teacher:	"What is being done again?"
Student:	"The acts or processes of the verb **assign**."
Student:	"And we analyzed **assign** before—*to give an indication or mark to somebody, to give a task.*"

DISCUSS Why might **reassignments** be made? What decisions lead to **reassignments**? Lead students to discuss such causes as *errors*, *improvements*, or simple *mind-changing*.

DEMONSTRATE Give half of the class adhesive stickers saying Team A, the other half Team B to put on their foreheads. Then ask the class to find a classmate of the opposite team and make **reassignments**. They will be able to visualize actually *giving a mark or seal to someone again*.

Day 4

In Other Words
for **SIGN**

SIGN means
mark, meaning, indication

LESSON TIME

15 Minutes

OBJECTIVES

- **Understand** the meaning of the root **SIGN**

- **Reinforce** knowledge of the root **SIGN**

- **Understand** the meaning of words in the **SIGN** family

- **Apply** knowledge of words in the **SIGN** family

MATERIALS

- Student Activity Book
- **SIGN** Word Wall
- Dictionary *(print or on-line)*

In Other Words for **SIGN**

TEACH Have students turn to page 42 in their Student Activity Books. Explain that they are going to read a little story that uses some surprising and sometimes odd phrasing. The underlined words or phrases in the story are actually definitions or synonyms for words in the **SIGN** family. Then they will see sentences about the story, each containing a blank. Using context clues in the sentences, they will find a **SIGN** family word in the Word Bank at the bottom to fit in each blank. Have a student read aloud the opening sentence of the story that contains the first underlined phrase. Then say, "Let's look at the first numbered sentence with a blank to be filled in. Clues in the sentence tell us that we want a descriptive word, an adjective that

means *marked with importance,* describing what sort of detail it was. I see the word **significant** at the bottom of the page and that word fits all the clues. This word has two roots, **signi** and **fic**, and one suffix, **-ant**. These compound root words can be difficult, but we can ask ourselves what the parts add up to. One of the meanings for the **signi** part that seems to fit here is the idea of *meaning,* and another way to put this idea would be to say *most meaningful.* The **fic** part means *make* and the **-ant** part means *performing,* in the sense of *serving to.* The idea is that the detail being described in the sentence *served to make meaningful* and that's a good definition for the word **significant,** so let's write it in the blank for the first sentence."

COMPLETE This can be quite challenging, so allow students to work on this activity in small groups. Not every word in the Word Bank will be used.

DISCUSS After about 10 minutes, ask if there were any difficulties and share strategies they used that led to correct answers.

SAB
Pg 42

A Historical Connection

The detail most <u>marked with importance</u> about Morgan's family history was the fact that a distant relative had been one of the original <u>markers of his name</u> of the Declaration of Independence. When Morgan's teacher <u>marked off as a task</u> to the class to do a family history project, Morgan pleaded with his parents to make a trip to Washington, D.C., to view the document in person. They agreed that it would be a creative addition to the <u>marked task given him</u>.

After turning at the printed street <u>indications</u>, and traffic <u>markers</u>, the family arrived in front of the National Archives. This building is <u>marked down in purpose</u> as housing a collection of all the major papers of America's government. Lines of history buffs waiting to see the Declaration snaked around the building, but Morgan kept busy checking out the intricate <u>sketches marked down</u> all around the building's walls. Finally, the group with Morgan's family filed past the display case that contained the Declaration of Independence, and Morgan smiled as he read the <u>name markers</u> at the bottom of the document.

Picking up a brochure as he was leaving the building, Morgan said to his mother, "I'm **so** going to get an A."

<u>Fill in the blanks below using words from the "sign, signi" family.</u>

1. Morgan's ancestor was a <u>significant</u> contributor to American history.

2. That ancestor was a <u>signer</u> of the Declaration of Independence.

3. When the teacher <u>assigned</u> the project, Morgan realized he could use the Declaration of Independence as a research source.

4. The <u>assignment</u> that Morgan received from his teacher was to connect his family and history in some way.

5. Street and traffic <u>signals</u> led the family to the right place.

6. The National Archives is <u>designated</u> as a repository for America's historical papers.

7. Examining the <u>designs</u> on the building's walls helped Morgan pass the time in line.

8. The clear <u>signature</u> at the bottom of the Declaration was easy for Morgan to read.

<u>Not Used:</u>   designee   resign   redesign   signature

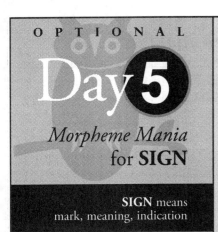
SIGN means
mark, meaning, indication

LESSON TIME

15 Minutes

OBJECTIVES

- **Build** words in the **SIGN** family

- **Apply** knowledge of synonyms and antonyms to **SIGN** words

Optional Morpheme Mania for **SIGN**

On page 43 of their Activity Books, students will see an optional vocabulary enrichment activity that they can work on in groups, time permitting. This activity makes a great review for the formal assessment on the next page.

All the affixes presented in the week's activities are provided at the top of the page on either side of the root of the week in all its forms. Students can write in up to 13 of the words they built during the week, possibly discovering additional ones.

Then students can brainstorm with each other to come up with antonyms and synonyms they may know. Starter examples are given with every Morpheme Mania in the Activity Book. Because antonyms and synonyms may require knowledge of roots which students have not yet studied, completion of this activity is not crucial. Simply remind students that they can at any time during the course of the year revisit any of their Morpheme Mania pages and add words, antonyms, and synonyms as their vocabulary grows.

Day 5 *Assessment*

Make and hand out copies.
The answer key is on page A-3.
The instructions are on page A-2.

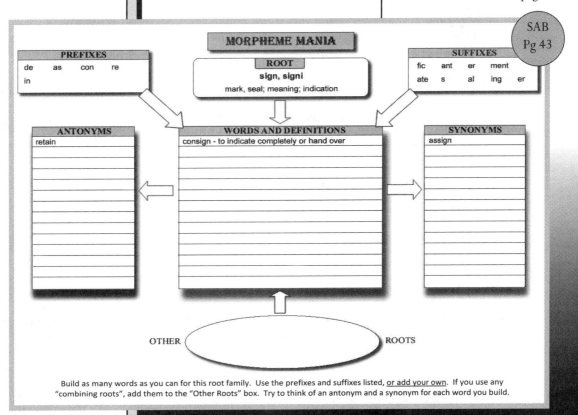

SAB
Pg 43

MORPHEME MANIA

PREFIXES			
de	as	con	re
in			

ROOT
sign, signi
mark, seal; meaning; indication

SUFFIXES			
fic	ant	er	ment
ate	s	al	ing	er

ANTONYMS
retain

WORDS AND DEFINITIONS
consign - to indicate completely or hand over

SYNONYMS
assign

OTHER   ROOTS

Build as many words as you can for this root family. Use the prefixes and suffixes listed, or add your own. If you use any "combining roots", add them to the "Other Roots" box. Try to think of an antonym and a synonym for each word you build.

assign to give a mark to; to give a task

assigned gave a mark or indication to; gave a task

assigning giving a mark or indication to; giving a task

assignment act or process of giving a mark to; a task

assignments acts or processes of giving a mark to; tasks

assigns gives a mark or indication to; gives a task

consign to indicate completely; to hand over or deliver

design to mark down; to sketch out a plan

designate to indicate; to name or appoint

designated indicated; named or appointed

designates indicates; names or appoints

designating indicating; naming or appointing

designation an act or process of indicating; a naming or appointment

designations acts or processes of indicating; names or appointments

designed marked down; sketched out a plan

designer a person who marks down; a person who sketches out a plan

designers people who mark down; people who sketch out plans

designing marking down; sketching out a plan

designs marks down; sketches out a plan

insignificance quality of making no marked importance; irrelevance

insignificancy quality of making no marked importance; irrelevancy

insignificant of no marked importance of something done; irrelevant

insignificantly in a manner of no marked importance of things done; irrelevantly

reassign to give a mark or indication to again; to give a task again

reassigned gave a mark or indication to again; gave a task again

reassigning giving a mark or indication to again; giving a task again

reassignment act or process of giving a mark to again; a task given again

reassignments acts or processes of giving a mark to again; tasks given again

reassigns gives a mark or indication to again; gives a task again

redesign to mark down again; to sketch out a new or different plan

redesigned marked down again; sketched out a new or different plan

redesigning marking down again; sketching out a new or different plan

redesigns marks down again; sketches out a new or different plan

resign to indicate back; to notify giving up a job or office

resignation an indication back; a notification of giving up a job or office

resignations indications back; notifications of giving up a job or office

resigned indicated back; notified giving up a job or office

resigning indicating back; notifying giving up a job or office

resigns indicates back; notifies giving up a job or office

sign a mark with meaning; omen

signal an indication; a non-verbal message

signaled made an indication; gave a non-verbal message

signaler a person who indicates; a person who gives a non-verbal message

signalers people who indicate; people who give non-verbal messages

signaling indicating; giving non-verbal messages

signals indications; non-verbal messages

signature a person's mark indicating who he or she is; a person's name as written by himself or herself

signatures people's marks indicating who they are; people's names as written by themselves

signed marked with meaning; communicated by hand language

signer a person who indicates; a person communicating by hand language

signers people who indicate; people communicating by hand language

significance a mark of something done; importance

significances marks of things done; importances

significant having a mark of something done; important

significantly in a manner having a mark of something done; importantly

signified caused to have a meaning; meant

signifies causes to have a meaning; means

signify to cause to have a meaning; to mean

signifying causing to have a meaning; meaning

signing making with meaning; communicating by hand language

signs marks that have meaning; omens

Check-Up for **SIGN**

Name _____

____ **1.** **SIGN** or **SIGNI** in words like **assign** and **significant** means:

    A to read

    B to speak

    C a mark or meaning

____ **2.** What is the meaning of the word **assign**?

    A to speak against

    B to give a meaning or purpose to

    C to read closely

____ **3.** What is the meaning of the word **insignificance**?

    A the result of too much reading

    B the process of speaking about

    C quality of having no marked importance

____ **4.** What is the meaning of the word **signaled**?

    A made an indication

    B read aloud

    C traveled

____ **5.** What is the meaning of the word **reassigns**?

    A speaks against

    B gives a mark or meaning again

    C reads carefully again

____ **6.** Which word means **marks down**?

    A designs

    B signifies

    C resignations

____ **7.** Which word means **people's marks indicating who they are**?

    A reassignments

    B insignificancies

    C signatures

____ **8.** Which word means **a person given a mark or purpose**?

    A designee

    B signaler

    C designation

____ **9.** The presidents **consigned** a new treaty with a handshake. The presidents:

    A will decide on the deal at a later date

    B decided not to go ahead with the deal

    C sealed the deal with each other

____ **10.** The expression on the leader's face **presignified** what he was about to say. This means:

    A his face was the opposite of what he was feeling

    B his face gave an indication ahead of his words

    C no one could expect what he was about to say

STA

meaning "to stand, stop"

OBJECTIVES

- **Understand** the meaning of the root **STA**
- **Build** words in the root **STA** family
- **Break Apart** words in the root **STA** family
- **Understand** the meaning of words in the **STA** family
- **Understand** the spelling principles applied to the root **STA**
- **Apply** knowledge of words in the **STA** family
- **Assess** and **Reinforce** knowledge of words in the **STA** family

MATERIALS

- Student Activity Books, pages 45-50
- Dictionary *(print or on-line)*
- A straw or paperclip *(optional)*

CROSS-CURRICULAR EXAMPLES

Science:
stasis, static

Social Studies:
circumstantial, instability, statistic

Language Arts:
statement, contrast, ecstatic

Math:
circumstance, constant, equidistant, statistics

---

stable
able to stand

station
a stop

Morpheme: **STA**
Allomorphs: **ST, STAS, STAT, STATE**

Over 700 words containing the morpheme **STA** or one of its allomorphs are current in English. During this unit, tell students to be alert for this root in their school texts, general reading, and oral language they hear. Some of the words they might encounter in their school subjects are listed on the left under Cross-Curricular Examples.

UNIT AT A GLANCE

Day **1**
Root Squares for **STA**

Day **2**
Magic Squares for **STA**

Day **3**
Stair Steps for **STA**

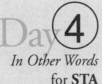
OPTIONAL
Day **4**
In Other Words for **STA**

Day **5**
Assessment or Morpheme Mania for **STA**

Each activity should take approximately **15 minutes**.

This root, with its many allomorphs, shows up in a huge array of words, and it is not always immediately recognizable.

When you hear the word **stat** in a hospital, you're hearing the shortened form of the Latin adverb **statim**, meaning *immediately, on the spot, instantly*.

Static primarily means *staying in one place*, or *being stationary*. **Stationary** charges of electricity that hover about cause the disturbing noise we call **static**.

Statues simply *stand*, don't they?

A bookseller or paper dealer who set up shop or a **station** (similar to a lemonade stand) was called a **stationer**, and the product was **stationery**. The difference between **stationary** and **stationery** can be seen by splitting the morphemes properly:

stat-ion-ary *relating to the act of standing still*

stat-ion-er-y *the activity or product of a* **stationer***, one operating a* **stand***)*

A **stage** is a period at which things seems to *stand consistent with each other*. It is also, of course, the area where performers **stand**. A **stagecoach** regularly passed from one station to another, as steps on a journey.

To be **still** is to be *standing*. To **stall** is to *stand still* and a **stall** is a *stand*. A **stallion** is *a male horse kept in a stall for breeding*.

One allomorph of this root, **stice**, appears in the word **solstice**, a time when the sun seems to *come to a stand* and then reverse its course.

Often the root takes on a meaning like *to be made to stand at a certain point*, thus *to stop or to stay at a certain level*. In fact, both words **stop** and **stay** belong to this root family. A **thermostat** causes the temperature *to stop or stay* at a certain point, and a **hemostat** causes blood flow to *stop*. A **rheostat** causes the flow of electricity *to stand* at a certain level.

Word Alert!

Most words with the letter sequences **s-t-a-s** or **s-t-a-t** do belong to this large root family. Ones that do not belong should be obvious. Words ending with the double suffix **at-ion** attached to roots that end in **s** will not belong because the morphemes split clearly: **infestation**, **crustation**, **manifestation**, etc.

Distaste and **pasta** are two other examples which morphemic-splitting will demonstrate to belong in other root families.

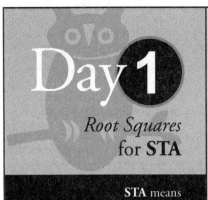

Day 1

Root Squares for **STA**

STA means to stand, stop

LESSON TIME

15 Minutes

OBJECTIVES

- **Understand** the meaning of the root **STA**
- **Build** words in the **STA** family
- **Understand** the meaning of words in the **STA** family
- **Understand** the spelling principles applied to the root **STA**

MATERIALS

- Student Activity Book
- **STA** Word Wall
- Dictionary *(print or on-line)*

DIFFERENTIATING INSTRUCTION

If you prefer easier or more difficult activities, use your personal account at www.dynamicliteracy.com to access novice or expert versions, along with ideas on using them.

Root Squares for STA

TEACH Have students turn to page 45 in their Activity Books. Say, "All of the prefixes and suffixes in the squares surrounding the shaded center are probably familiar, but if you have a question about any meaning, simply ask or look it up in the list inside the front and back cover of the activity book."

Call attention to the center box. Point out that the root **STA** has several different spellings, called *allomorphs*. Ask students to decide if one of the forms they see in the middle square can stand alone as a word. They will see that **state** is a word, and you can use that word to guide them to the meaning *to stand or to stop*. Discuss how a **state** is a political entity that *stands apart from others*. What do we do when we **state** an opinion or a fact?

Suggest that students continue their list with **stat** and then add **-ion** to build **station**. Invite students to explore how this word is related to the idea of *to stand or to stop*.

COMPLETE THE ACTIVITY

Have students follow the directions for the Root Squares activity for **STA** on page 45 to build words. If students have difficulty building words with the Root Squares, show them how by modeling the matrix approach found on the next page, taking one affix at a time and seeing if it will connect with any one of the allomorphs of the root.

DISCUSS After five minutes, have volunteers write some of their words on the board. Focus with the class on the words they have built and guide them in a discussion of how the meaning of the root is still *to stand or to stop*, even when prefixes and suffixes are added. Watch for target words that most easily demonstrate the meanings of *to stand or to stop*. If the word **contrast** is not present, ask the class, "Can anyone try to use the prefix **contra-**?" and then continue on to the target word discussion on the next page.

Root Squares

How many words can you make?

Start in any square. Your goal is to combine two or more word parts to make as many words in the 'st, sta, stas, stat, state' family as you can. Write each word and a definition you can think of for it in the space provided at the bottom of the page. Use the back of the page if you need to.

ion	circum	contra
ance	st, sta, stas, stat, state	ment
di	ant	ly

SAB Pg 45

Focus Word: **CONTRAST** → Write this word on the board.

TEACH

Lead with this:	"What do we do when we **compare** and **contrast** two things?"
Student:	"We examine them for how they are alike and how they are different."
Teacher:	"Good. We'll work with the word **compare** later, but let's look at the word **contrast**. It's a familiar word, but I think you'll be surprised to discover the true structure and meaning of the word. What do we see?"
Student:	"It looks like the prefix **con-** and the root **trast**, whatever that is."
Student:	"No—I see. It's the prefix **contra**-! But then only **st** is left, and that won't work."
Student:	"Yes it will—look, **st** is one of the spellings of this root."
Student:	"How can just the letters **st** have meaning?"
Teacher:	"Great question, but we see it here. Sometimes—not very often—a root morpheme can occur without a vowel. Now, what do we make of the meaning of the word **contrast**?"
Student:	"That's great—it's *to stand against*, to stand two things up against each other and take a look."

DISCUSS Ask if **contrast** is always a verb. Ask someone to give an example of a **contrast** (light and shadow in the room may provide a good example). A **contrast** in a painting or a **contrast** in story characters can make a good discussion here.

DEMONSTRATE Set any two objects up beside each other and let pairs of students list the differences they can see.

Root Squares Matrix

You can refer to this matrix to guide students in this activity. Students could build at least these 9 words. *It is not important how many words are built or whether non-dictionary words are coined*, so long as students understand the consistent meanings of the root and its affixes. Encourage discussion about the definitions of any words formed for the blank slots as well as for the attested words.

	inter-	circum-	contra-	di-
no suffix	state		contrast	
-ance		circumstance		distance
-ant				distant
-ion	station			
-ly	stately			
-ment	statement			
-ant + -ly				distantly

Day 2

Magic Squares
for **STA**

STA means
to stand, stop

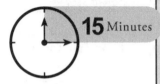

LESSON TIME

15 Minutes

OBJECTIVES

• **Understand** the meaning
of the root **STA**

• **Break Apart** words in the
STA family

• **Understand** the
meanings of words in
the **STA** family

MATERIALS

• Student Activity Book

• **STA** Word Wall

• Dictionary
(print or on-line)

• a straw or paper clip
(optional)

DIFFERENTIATING
INSTRUCTION

If you prefer easier or
more difficult activities,
use your personal account at
www.dynamicliteracy.com
to access novice or expert
versions, along with ideas
on using them.

Break Apart
Words with
STA

TEACH Have students turn to
the Magic Squares on page 46 in
their Student Activity Books.
Model a Think-Aloud strategy for
students: "I know that **STA**, and
the various spellings of this root,
mean *stand, stop*. I can use this
knowledge to find the definition of
a word with this as its root."

Direct students to word C,
statement. Say: "I know that the
suffix **-ment** means *result, process,*
or *act*. Definition #7 looks like a
result or act: *a stand; a specific
declaration*. I know that a
statement is a *delcaration*, so let's
write the number 7 in square D.

COMPLETE THE ACTIVITY

Ask students to use the same
strategy to find the correct
definitions for the other words.
Tell them to write the number
of the definition in the box that
matches the letter for the word.
Remind them that if all their
answers are correct, each row and
each column will add up to the
same Magic number.

DISCUSS After five minutes,
ask if there are any difficulties
about matching the words and
definitions. If there are, ask
volunteers to explain clues in the
definitions that will lead to the
correct choice of word. As
needed, follow the focus word
approach for **thermostat** that you
see modeled on the next page.

Add any new words to the
classroom **STA** Word Wall and
remind students to add these
words to the **STA**
Word Wall in their
Activity Books.

SAB
Pg 46

Magic Squares

Select the best answer for each of the words in the 'st, sta, stas, stat, state' family from the
numbered definitions. Put the number in the proper space in the Magic Square box. If the total
of the numbers is the same both across and down, you have found the magic number!

'st, sta, stas, stat, state' means to stand, stop

WORDS	DEFINITIONS
A. circumstances	1. time at which the sun seems to stand still
B. contrasted	2. stood one thing with another; compared one thing to another
C. statement	3. device to make temperature stand at a fixed point
D. stance	4. a specific stand; a person's point in view
E. stably	5. in a manner standing apart; far
F. equidistantly	6. in a manner able to stand; in a firm or unchanging manner
G. distantly	7. a stand; a specific declaration
H. stations	8. so as to stand at a balanced space away from
I. thermostat	9. things standing around; situations having a bearing on an event
	10. stands, as for trains, buses, and taxis

Magic Square Box

A. 9	B. 2	C. 7
D. 4	E. 6	F. 8
G. 5	H. 10	I. 3

Magic Number __18__

*** ANSWER KEY ***

Focus Word: **THERMOSTAT** ➞ Write this word on the board.

TEACH

Sample leading question:	"If it's too cold in the room, what can we do to the **thermostat**?"
Student:	"Turn it up!"
Student:	"I know. We're going to dig into the word **thermostat**."
Teacher:	"Right; let's do it."
Student:	"I see **stat**, *to stand*, but I thought a **thermostat** moved the temperature around."
Teacher:	"So do we agree that **thermo** means *heat*? Give some more examples of words you know using **therm** as *heat*."
Student:	"**Thermal** underwear keeps you warm."
Student:	"And **hypothermia** means *not being warm anymore*."
Teacher:	"All right, now let's take a look at **thermostat**. Does the **thermostat** *move the temperature around*?"
Student:	No, it makes the temperature *stay* at where you set it. I get it."
Student:	"Right—it *stops* the heat at a certain fixed point until you change it again."

DISCUSS Are there any other familiar words with the root **stat** used as a suffix? Some students may know of a **hemostat**, but there are others. Tools or instruments that stop or hold something steady have the suffix -**stat**. How can we find more -**stat** words? (Reverse dictionaries or on-line resources can help).

DEMONSTRATE Place a paper clip on a straw to show how an instrument called a **rheostat** works – it stops the flow (**rheo** means *flow or current*).

MINI-LESSON: the Combining Form **thermo**

The Greek word for heat is **thermos**, giving us over 100 scientific terms relating to heat or temperature.

Students will recognize these words to help them remember the meaning of this Combining Form:

thermos bottle: *a container that keeps liquids at a steady temperature*

hypothermia: *a condition of not having enough body heat*

Day 3

Stair Steps for STA

STA means to stand, stop

LESSON TIME

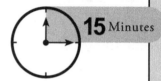

15 Minutes

OBJECTIVES

- **Understand** the meaning of the root **STA**

- **Apply** knowledge of the root **STA**

- **Break Apart** words in the **STA** family

- **Understand** the meaning of words in the **STA** family

- **Understand** the spelling principles applied to the root **STA**

MATERIALS

- Student Activity Book
- **STA** Word Wall

DIFFERENTIATING INSTRUCTION

If you prefer easier or more difficult activities, use your personal account at www.dynamicliteracy.com to access novice or expert versions, along with ideas on using them.

Apply Knowledge of STA

TEACH Have students turn to page 47 in their Student Activity Books. Explain that the boxes in front of and after the root indicate letters that spell out prefixes and suffixes. Students will spell out the correct prefixes and suffixes determined by clues in the definitions at the bottom of the page.

Have a volunteer read definition number one at the bottom of the page. Say, "The past tense clues in the definition indicate that the two-letter past tense suffix -**ed** will work. Let's write in the letters **e-d** for number one."

COMPLETE THE ACTIVITY Let students work in pairs (optionally) and tell them to use the same strategy to find the correct prefixes and suffixes for the words listed. These activities can be quite challenging!

DISCUSS After a few minutes, review the answers as a class. Ask if there were any difficulties. Listen to any problems and have volunteers solve the difficulties by explaining key clues in the given definitions. As needed, follow the focus word approach that you see modeled on the next page.

SAB Pg 47

Stair Steps

Fill in the missing letters of each 'st, sta, stas, stat, state' word by using the definitions below.

'st, sta, stas, stat, state' means to stand, stop

1.	s	t	a	t	e	d			
2.	i	n	s	t	a	n	t		
3.	d	i	s	t	a	n	c	e	
4.	c	o	n	t	r	a	s	t	s
5.	d	i	s	t	a	n	c	i	n	g
6.	c	o	n	t	r	a	s	t	i	n	g
7.	c	i	r	c	u	m	s	t	a	n	c	e
8.	e	q	u	i	d	i	s	t	a	n	c	e	s

1. took a stand; declared
2. standing in; immediate
3. the space between things standing apart
4. stands one thing with another; compares one thing to another
5. causing to stand apart; spacing apart
6. standing one thing with another; comparing one thing to another
7. a thing standing around; a situation having a bearing on an event
8. qualities of standing at a balances space away from

92

Focus Word: **DISTANCE** ➡ Write this word on the board.

TEACH

Sample leading question:	"Here's an interesting word we all know. What is **distance**?"
Student:	"It's how far it is between two points."
Student:	"How does that word split up into pieces?"
Teacher:	"Great question, and that's always what we want to do with words, isn't it?"
Student:	"Okay—I see **dis-**, and that means (consulting the inside cover of the Student Activity Book) *not or apart*, and some other things."
Student:	"**Stance** isn't one of the variations of our root."
Student:	"I'll bet it's the suffix -**ance**, like **importance**."
Student:	"Hey, but then only the letter **t** is left, and that doesn't mean anything."
Student:	"Wait a minute—**dis-** can also be **di-**. That's what it is. The -**s** on **dis-** drops because the next letter is also **s**."
Teacher:	Great, so now what is **distance**?"

DISCUSS Lead students to see that, based on its pieces of meaning, **distance** is *the action, result, or process of two things standing apart from each other.* Is **distance** always a noun?

DEMONSTRATE Have two students stand up next to each other and then ask them to **distance** themselves from one another. (They will stand apart).

MINI-LESSON: the Prefix **ec-** (goes with the *In Other Words* exercise)

The prefix **ec-** is from the Greek preposition meaning *outside of* or *away from.* It is much like its Latin cousin **ex-**. Relatively few words use this prefix, but they are important words with vivid etymologies which you can share with your students:

eccentric - *out of the center, odd*

eclectic - *picked out from a group, drawn as the best examples from different sources*

eclipse - *slipped away, hidden by something else larger or in front*

ecstatic - (the word seen in this exercise with the root **STA**), *standing outside, being outside yourself with joy*

STA means
to stand, stop

LESSON TIME

15 Minutes

OBJECTIVES

- **Understand** the meaning of the root **STA**

- **Reinforce** knowledge of the root **STA**

- **Understand** the meaning of words in the **STA** family

- **Apply** knowledge of words in the **STA** family

MATERIALS

- Student Activity Book

- **STA** Word Wall

- Dictionary *(print or on-line)*

In Other Words for **STA**

TEACH   There is a mini-lesson on the prefix **ec-** on page 93 if you need it (the word **ecstatic** is not used.) Have students turn to page 48 in their Student Activity Books. Explain that they are going to read a little story that uses some surprising and sometimes odd phrasing. The underlined words or phrases in the story are actually definitions or synonyms for words in the **STA** family. Then they will see sentences about the story, each containing a blank. Using context clues in the sentences, they will find a **STA** family word in the Word Bank at the bottom to fit in each blank. Have a student read aloud the opening sentence or sentences of the story that contain

the first underlined phrase. Then say, "Let's look at the first numbered sentence that contains a blank to be filled in. Clues in the sentence tell us that we want a naming word, a noun that is synonymous with *things standing around* and leading to the famous battle we call "Custer's Last Stand." I see the word **circumstances** at the bottom of the page and that word fits all the clues. The prefix **circum-** means *around*, the part following the root **st** is the suffix -**ance** plus the plural marker -**s**. Let's write **circumstances** in the blank for the first sentence."

COMPLETE THE ACTIVITY

This can be quite challenging, so allow students to work on this activity in small groups.   Not every word in the Word Bank will be used.

DISCUSS

After about 10 minutes, ask if there were any difficulties. Have volunteers explain strategies they used that led to correct answers.

SAB Pg 48

Custer's Last Stand

The Battle of the Little Bighorn, also known as Custer's Last Stand, took place on June 25-26, 1876 near the Little Bighorn River in Eastern Montana. The things standing around that led to this battle between the U.S. Cavalry and the Lakota and Northern Cheyenne Indians (Native Americans) were related to the fact that many Indians stood apart from their reservations. Their specific stand was that they should be free to live wherever they wanted. General Custer and other cavalry commanders sought to make the Indians home unchanging or standing thoroughly.

General Custer thought that if he could capture all of the Native Americans who had left the reservations and return them there, he could achieve a quality of being able to stand firm for the area. General Custer's own stands, or specific declarations, show that he thought the battle would be easy. However, when Custer's idea is stood with what actually took place, it is clear that he miscalculated the strength and resolve of the Native Americans.

The usual way the Cavalry fought, standing at a balanced space away from each other, didn't work, because there were so many Indians that the line of troops became not able to stand firm. Once this happened, the space standing between the Cavalrymen became too large and the battle was lost.

Fill in the blanks below using words from the "st, sta, stas, stat, state" family.

1. Many circumstances led to the Indian Wars and the Battle of the Little Bighorn.

2. Thousands of Native Americans distanced themselves from their reservations.

3. Many took the position, or stance, that they should be able to move freely about.

4. A constant place to live means standing in one place.

5. Stability, the quality of standing firm, is something every government seeks.

6. Custer's statements show that he underestimated his opponent.

7. Often, when ideas are compared or contrasted, new understandings emerge.

8. If three cavalrymen are standing equidistant to one another, they are all the same length apart.

9. Once the battle lines became unstable, Custer's strategy began to fail.

10. As soon as the distance between men became great enough, the battle was over.

Not Used: ecstatic   distantly

O P T I O N A L

Day 5

Morpheme Mania
for **STA**

STA means
to stand, stop

LESSON TIME

15 Minutes

OBJECTIVES

- **Build** words in the **STA** family
- **Apply** knowledge of synonyms and antonyms to **STA** words

Optional Morpheme Mania for **STA**

On page 49 of their Activity Books, students will see an optional vocabulary enrichment activity that they can work on in groups, time permitting. This activity makes a great review for the formal assessment on the next page.

All the affixes presented in the week's activities are provided at the top of the page on either side of the root of the week in all its forms. Students can write in up to 13 of the words they built during the week, possibly discovering additional ones.

Then students can brainstorm with each other to come up with antonyms and synonyms they may know. Starter examples are given with every Morpheme Mania in the Activity Book. Because antonyms and synonyms may require knowledge of roots which students have not yet studied, completion of this activity is not crucial. Simply remind students that they can at any time during the course of the year revisit any of their Morpheme Mania pages and add words, antonyms, and synonyms as their vocabulary grows.

Day 5 *Assessment*

Make and hand out copies.
The answer key is on page A-3.
The instructions are on page A-2.

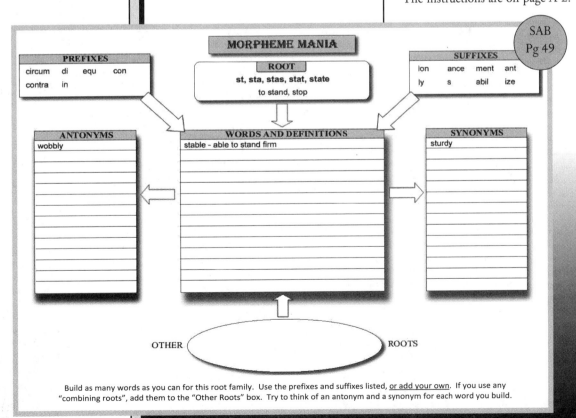

MORPHEME MANIA

PREFIXES

| circum | di | equ | con |
| contra | in | | |

ROOT

st, sta, stas, stat, state
to stand, stop

SUFFIXES

| ion | ance | ment | ant |
| ly | s | abil | ize |

SAB
Pg 49

ANTONYMS
wobbly

WORDS AND DEFINITIONS
stable - able to stand firm

SYNONYMS
sturdy

OTHER ROOTS

Build as many words as you can for this root family. Use the prefixes and suffixes listed, or add your own. If you use any "combining roots", add them to the "Other Roots" box. Try to think of an antonym and a synonym for each word you build.

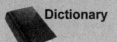

circumstance   a thing standing around; a situation having a bearing on an event

circumstances   things standing around; situations having a bearing on an event

constant   standing thoroughly; unchanging

constantly   in a manner standing thoroughly; in an unchanging manner

contrast   to stand one thing with another; to observe differences between

contrasted   stood one thing with another; observed differences between

contrasting   standing one thing with another; observing differences between

contrasts   stands one thing with another; observes differences between

distance   the space between things standing apart

distanced   caused to stand apart

distances   spaces between things standing apart

distancing   causing to stand apart; spacing apart

distant   standing apart; far

distantly   in a manner standing apart; far

ecstasies   states of standing outside oneself; states of intense joy

ecstasy   state of standing outside oneself; state of intense joy

ecstatic   standing outside oneself; intensely joyful

ecstatically   in a manner standing outside oneself; in an intensely joyful manner

equidistance   quality of standing at a balanced space away from

equidistances   qualities of standing at a balanced space away from

equidistant   standing at a balanced space away from

equidistantly   so as to stand at a balanced space away from

instance   something standing in; a single occasion or example

instances   things standing in; occasions or examples

instant   standing in; immediate

instantly   in a manner standing in; immediately

solstice   time at which the sun seems to stand still

solstices   times at which the sun seems to stand still

stabilities   qualities of being able to stand; qualities of firmness or steadiness

stability   quality of being able to stand; firmness or steadiness

stabilization   act or process of causing to stand; act or process of making firm or unchanging

stabilizations   acts or processes of causing to stand; acts or processes of making firm or unchanging

stabilize   to cause to stand; to make firm or unchanging

stabilized   caused to stand; made firm or unchanging

stabilizes   causes to stand; makes firm or unchanging

stabilizing   causing to stand; making firm or unchanging

stable   able to stand; firm or unchanging

stabled   caused to be able to stand; put into a sheltered place

stableness   quality of being able to stand; firmness or steadiness

stabler   better able to stand; firmer or more unchanging

stables   causes to be able to stand; puts into a sheltered place

stablest   best able to stand; firmest or most unchanging

stabling   causing to be able to stand; putting into a sheltered place

stably   in a manner able to stand; in a firm or unchanging manner

stance   a specific stand; a person's point in view

stances   specific stands; peoples' points of view

state   the condition at which things stand

stated   took a stand; declared

stately   standing grandly; having a dignified presence

statement   a stand; a specific declaration

statements   stands; specific declarations

states   conditions at which things stand; circumstances or conditions of things

stating   taking a stand; declaring

station   a stand, as for a train, bus, or taxi

stations   stands, as for trains, buses, and taxis

thermostat   device to make temperature stand at a fixed point

thermostats   devices to make temperature stand at a fixed point

unstability   condition of not standing firm; state of not having firmness or steadiness

unstable   not able to stand firm; changeable or not reliable

unstably   in a manner not able to stand firm; in a weak or changing manner

Check-Up for **STA**

Name _____

____ **1.** **ST** or **STAT** in words like **stance** and **station** means:

    A to ride

    B to stand or stop

    C to call or shout

____ **2.** What is the meaning of the word **unstable**?

    A taken for a ride

    B tending to shout

    C not likely to stay up

____ **3.** What is the meaning of the word **station**?

    A a stand for vehicles

    B the act of calling out

    C the process of riding

____ **4.** What is the meaning of the word **contrast**?

    A to stand one thing with another

    B to say something against another person

    C to travel far along with someone

____ **5.** If you have **distanced** yourself, you have:

    A written a note of reminder

    B taken a stand apart from something or someone

    C shown off your new clothing

____ **6.** Which word means **things standing around**?

    A equidistances

    B circumstances

    C ecstasies

____ **7.** Which word means **declarations taking a stand**?

    A stabilizations

    B instances

    C statements

____ **8.** Which word means **standing outside yourself**?

    A ecstatic

    B thermostatic

    C antistatic

____ **9.** The doctor reported a **stasis** of blood flow in Lorenzo. The doctor reported that:

    A he would check Lorenzo's blood flow later

    B Lorenzo was blood type O

    C there was a slowdown of Lorenzo's blood flow

____ **10.** What does a **humidistat** do about humidity, or air moisture? It:

    A increases the humidity

    B holds humidity at a certain point

    C causes humidity to fall

OBJECTIVES

- **Understand** the meaning of the root **ACT**
- **Build** words in the root **ACT** family
- **Break Apart** words in the root **ACT** family
- **Understand** the meaning of words in the **ACT** family
- **Understand** the spelling principles applied to the root **ACT**
- **Apply** knowledge of words in the **ACT** family
- **Assess** and **Reinforce** knowledge of words in the **ACT** family

MATERIALS

- Student Activity Books, pages 51-56
- Dictionary (print or on-line)
- Pencil

CROSS-CURRICULAR EXAMPLES

Science:
activate, agent, coagulate, react, photoactivity

Social Studies:
activist, reactionary, reenact

Language Arts:
actor, interact, agent, enact

Math:
actuality, actuary

ACT

meaning "to do; to perform; to cause to move"

action
something **done**

actor
a **performer**

agile
easily able to **move**

Morpheme: **ACT**
Allomorph: AG

Nearly 1800 words containing the morpheme **ACT** or its allomorph are current in English. During this unit, tell students to be alert for this root in their school texts, general reading, and oral language they hear. Some of the words they might encounter in their school subjects are listed on the left under Cross-Curricular Examples.

UNIT AT A GLANCE

Day 1 — *Root Squares* for **ACT**

Day 2 — *Magic Squares* for **ACT**

Day 3 — *Stair Steps* for **ACT**

OPTIONAL Day 4 — *In Other Words* for **ACT**

Day 5 — *Assessment or Morpheme Mania* for **ACT**

Each activity should take approximately **15 minutes**.

From this root comes the verb **exact**, as *to move out* or *bring about a punishment*. The adjective **exact** describes anything that has been carefully considered, as if *moved out* to its final details.

Active people tend to stay **agile** longer.

Two unchanged Latin words from this root are still commonly used in English: **agendum**, *a thing that must be done*, and its plural, **agenda**, *things that must be done*. The plural word **agenda** is evolving in some usages to be understood as a singular list, as, "The **agenda** for today's meeting is short."

The Greek word **agon** means *a gathering to perform athletic feats*, and **agonistic** is an English adjective that means *having to do with athletics*. The pain resulting from intense athletic endeavor was called **agony**, a word now applied to any deep or long-lasting struggle.

A **protagonist** is the lead **actor** or performer in a contest or drama. The second role is played by a **deuteragonist**.

To **antagonize** is *to provoke to act in a hostile way*.

A **pedagogue** (*child-mover*) led students to school in ancient Rome. The **demagogue** causes a mob of people *to act or move* in a certain direction. Both terms today have a pejorative, or negative, connotation.

Word Alert!

Words with the letter sequence **a-c-t** are not necessarily part of this root family. The words **pact** and **retract** can be shown by the "proof method" of morphemic splitting not to have the root **act**.

Wrong: **p—act**   Right: **pact**

Wrong: **retr—act**   Right: **re—tract**

Similarly, words with the letter sequence **a-g**, such as **page** and **cabbage**, can easily be shown not to belong to this root family

Day 1

Root Squares for ACT

ACT means to do; to perform; to cause to move

LESSON TIME

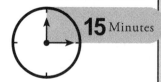

15 Minutes

OBJECTIVES

- **Understand** the meaning of the root **ACT**
- **Build** words in the **ACT** family
- **Understand** the meaning of words in the **ACT** family
- **Understand** the spelling principles applied to the root **ACT**

MATERIALS

- Student Activity Book
- **ACT** Word Wall
- Dictionary *(print or on-line)*
- pencil

DIFFERENTIATING INSTRUCTION

If you prefer easier or more difficult activities, use your personal account at www.dynamicliteracy.com to access novice or expert versions, along with ideas on using them.

Root Squares for ACT

TEACH Have students turn to page 51 in their Activity Books. Say, "All of the prefixes and suffixes in the squares surrounding the shaded center are familiar except one." Let's take a look at the prefix en- before we start." A Mini-Lesson for the prefix **en-** is provided on the next page. Access your account on the Dynamic Literacy website for help with other affixes that may need reviewing.

Then call attention to the center box. Point out that the root **ACT** has two different spellings, called allomorphs. Ask students to decide if one of the forms they see in the middle square can stand alone as a word. They will see that **act** is a word, and you can use that word to guide them to the meaning *to do; to perform; to cause to move*. Suggest

that students start their list with **act** and then add to that word the suffix -**or**, meaning *a person or device that does*, to build **actor**, meaning *a person who performs*.

COMPLETE THE ACTIVITY

Have students follow the directions to build words. If students have difficulty building words with the Root Squares, show them how by modeling the matrix approach found on the next page, taking one affix at a time and seeing if it will connect with any one of the allomorphs of the root.

DISCUSS After five minutes, have volunteers write some of their words on the board. Focus with the class on the words they have built and guide them in a discussion of how the meaning of the root is still *to do; to perform; to cause to move* even when prefixes and suffixes are added. Watch for target words that most easily demonstrate the meaning of *to do; to perform; to cause to move*. If the word **active** is not present, ask the class, "Can anyone try to use the suffix -**ive**?" and then continue on to the target word discussion on the next page.

Root Squares

How many words can you make?

Start in any square. Your goal is to combine two or more word parts to make as many words in the 'act, ag' family as you can. Write each word and a definition you can think of for it in the space provided at the bottom of the page. Use the back of the page if you need to.

ive	or	ate
re	act, ag	inter
en	ent	in

100

Day ① Extend the Learning

MINI-LESSON: the Prefix en-

The prefix **en-** is a variation (allomorph) of the prefix **in-**, meaning *in* or *into*. The prefix **en-** suggests *putting into or onto*, or *causing to be in a specific group*, as in the words **enthrone**, *to put onto a throne*, and **enslave**, *to cause to be in slavery*. Write any of these words up for your students, let them define the words, and then have them add the prefix **en-** to see what happens to the meanings.

able	camp	snare	shrine	list	noble	rich
force	gulf	courage	wrap	tangle	roll	joy
large	danger	dear	fold	circle	code	

Focus Word: **ACTIVE** ⟹ Write this word on the board.

TEACH

Lead with this:	"Who knows what it means to be an **active** participant in a game?"
Student:	"That's if you are actually playing in the game yourself."
Teacher:	"So how does the word **active** break apart?"
Student:	"Okay—it has our root, and it has a suffix **-ive**."
Teacher:	"Some other words with the suffix **-ive** include **creative**, **massive**, and **passive**. Can you tell what kind of words they are?
Student:	"They describe, so they're adjectives."
Teacher:	"Good. So tell me the deep meaning of the word **active**."
Student:	"Describing someone who is actually doing something."
Teacher:	"**Actually**? Is there any difference between the words **actual** and **active**?"
Student:	"Hey! An **active** participant is an **actual** participant!"

DISCUSS Let conversations such as this go as long as you deem productive. Lead students to see that, based on its pieces of meaning, **active** is a word that describes *a person or thing involved in doing or participating*. Lead the class in discussing what sorts of things besides game participants can be described as **active**. (**Active** ingredients, volcanoes, or duty, for example.) You could also use this opportunity to differentiate between **active** verbs and passive verbs.

DEMONSTRATE Hold up a pencil and say, "I am holding the pencil. What can we say is happening to the pencil? The pencil is what? (being held). I am doing something, so I am active. Is the pencil doing anything? No, it is having something done to it. That's the difference between an active verb like **holding**, and a passive verb like **being held**.

Root Squares Matrix
You can refer to this matrix to guide students in this activity. Students could build at least these 21 words. *It is not important how many words are built or whether non-dictionary words are coined*, so long as students understand the consistent meanings of the root and its affixes. Encourage discussion about the definitions of any words formed for the blank slots as well as for the attested words.

	no prefix	en-	in-	inter-	re-
no suffix	act	enact		interact	react
-ent	agent			interagent	
-ive	active		inactive	interactive	reactive
-or	actor	enactor			reactor
-iv(e) + ate	activate		inactivate		reactivate
-iv(e) + -at(e) + -or	activator		inactivator		reactivator
re-		reenact	reinactivate		

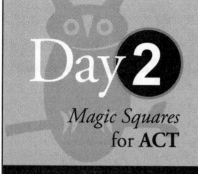

Day 2

Magic Squares
for **ACT**

ACT means
to do; to perform; to cause to move

LESSON TIME

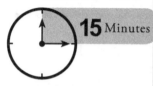

15 Minutes

OBJECTIVES

- **Understand** the meaning of the root **ACT**
- **Break Apart** words in the **ACT** family
- **Understand** the meanings of words in the **ACT** family

MATERIALS

- Student Activity Book
- **ACT** Word Wall
- Dictionary
  (print or on-line)

DIFFERENTIATING INSTRUCTION

If you prefer easier or more difficult activities, use your personal account at www.dynamicliteracy.com to access novice or expert versions, along with ideas on using them.

Break Apart Words with ACT

TEACH Have students turn to the Magic Squares on page 52 in their Student Activity Books. Model a Think-Aloud strategy for students: "I know that **ACT** and the alternate spelling of this root, **AG**, mean *to do, to perform, to cause to move.* I can use this knowledge to find the definition of a word with this as its root." Direct students to word **I**, **hyperactive**. Say, "I know that the prefix **hyper-** means more than normal and the suffix **-ive** means inclined to be. Definition #3 accounts for all these parts: *having excessive motion; overdoing.* Let's write the number **3** in square **I**.

Ask students to use the same strategy to find the correct definitions for the other words. Tell them to write the number of the definition in the box that matches the letter for the word. Remind them that if all their answers are correct, each row and each column will add up to the same Magic number.

DISCUSS After five minutes, ask if there are any difficulties about matching the words and definitions. If there are, ask volunteers to explain clues in the definitions that will lead to the correct choice of word. As needed, follow the focus word approach for **interactive** that you see modeled on the next page.

Add any new words to the classroom **ACT** Word Wall and remind students to add these words to the **ACT** Word Wall in their Activity Books.

**SAB
Pg 52**

Magic Squares

Select the best answer for each of the words in the 'act, ag' family from the numbered definitions. Put the number in the proper space in the Magic Square box. If the total of the numbers is the same both across and down, you have found the magic number!

'act, ag' means to do; to perform; to cause to move

WORDS	DEFINITIONS
A. activate	1. causing rays to move spontaneously; emitting nuclear particles
B. interactive	2. to set in motion
C. reactions	3. having excessive motion; overdoing
D. enacting	4. the state of not doing anything
E. inactivity	5. caused substances to move into one mass
F. agents	6. putting into motion; making into law
G. reactors	7. performances or movements in response to something
H. coagulated	8. forces that cause change or movement
I. hyperactive	9. serving to do or move between each other
	10. people or things that perform or move in response; machines causing nuclei to respond to stimuli

Magic Square Box

A. 2	B. 9	C. 7
D. 6	E. 4	F. 8
G. 10	H. 5	I. 3

Magic Number __18__

*** ANSWER KEY ***

Focus Word: **INTERACTIVE** → Write this word on the board.

TEACH

Sample leading question:	"I think we all know what **active** means. But what does it mean to be **interactive**?"
Student:	"That's when two things are doing the same thing, only back and forth between them."
Teacher:	"How about an example?"
Student:	"Some video games are described as **interactive**."
Student:	"Yes, it's like the game itself is a player, so if you do one thing, the game reacts in a certain way to you."
Teacher:	"So why is that called **interactive**?"
Student:	"It's between you and the game. **Inter-** must mean between, right?"
Student:	"Yes, like **intermission** or **international**."
Teacher:	"Any other examples of **interactive**?"
Student:	"People in general, in a community, are **interactive**. It's not like one person is **active** and everybody else just sits there. We **interact**."

DISCUSS Lead students to see that, based on its three pieces of meaning, **interactive** means *tending to perform or do something between participants.* Discuss what an **interactive** classroom is and the advantages of being a part of an **interactive** classroom.

DEMONSTRATE Let pairs of students ask each other their birthdates, and then that pair will trade that information with another pair and then another pair. Ask the class in what way they are being **interactive**.

MINI-LESSON: the Prefix **co-**

The prefix **co-** is a variation of the prefix **con-**, meaning *with or together.* Sometimes it is a hyphenated prefix, as in **co-workers** and **co-ed**, and sometimes it attaches directly onto a root, as **cohesion** and **cooperate**. The variation **co-** occurs before roots that begin with a vowel (**coagulate, coedit, coincidence, coordinate**) or with the letters **h** (**coheirs, cohorts**), **s** (**costar, cosponsor**), or **w** (**cowrite, cowinner**).

MINI-LESSON: the Prefix **hyper-**

The prefix **hyper-** comes from the Greek preposition that means *too much, over, or above.* About 400 English words, mostly scientific, use this prefix. Students may be familiar with one or more of these examples:

hyperactive: *overly active* **hypersensitive**: *too sensitive*
hypertense: *excessively tightened up* **hyperventilate**: *breathing too hard and fast*

The opposite of this prefix, **hypo-**, meaning *not enough, under, or below,* is sometimes confused with **hyper-**. One way to help distinguish between the two is to note that **hyper-** has five letters (more), and **hypo-** has four letters (fewer).

Day 3

Stair Steps for ACT

ACT means to do; to perform; to cause to move

LESSON TIME

15 Minutes

OBJECTIVES

- **Understand** the meaning of the root **ACT**

- **Apply** knowledge of the root **ACT**

- **Break Apart** words in the **ACT** family

- **Understand** the meaning of words in the **ACT** family

- **Understand** the spelling principles applied to the root **ACT**

MATERIALS

- Student Activity Book

- **ACT** Word Wall

DIFFERENTIATING INSTRUCTION

If you prefer easier or more difficult activities, use your personal account at www.dynamicliteracy.com to access novice or expert versions, along with ideas on using them.

Apply Knowledge of ACT

TEACH Have students turn to page 53 in their Student Activity Books. Explain that the boxes in front of and after the root indicate letters that spell out prefixes and suffixes. Students will spell out the correct prefixes and suffixes determined by clues in the definitions at the bottom of the page.

Have a volunteer read definition number one at the bottom of the page. Say, "The first two letters of the word we need in step one are an alternative spelling of **ACT**. But what word might begin with **AG** and end in a 3-letter suffix to give it

this definition? We know it will be a noun, a force. The meaning of the suffix **-ent**, *quality or state* would work and allow us to build **AGENT**. Our definition, *a force that causes change or movement*, confirms this suffix choice and the word."

COMPLETE THE ACTIVITY

Let students work in pairs (optionally) and tell them to use the same strategy to find the correct prefixes and suffixes for the words listed. These activities can be quite challenging!

DISCUSS After a few minutes, review the answers as a class. Ask if there were any difficulties. Listen to any problems and have volunteers solve the difficulties by explaining key clues in the given definitions. As needed, follow the focus word approach that you see modeled on the next page.

SAB Pg 53

Stair Steps

Fill in the missing letters of each 'act, ag' word by using the definitions below.
'act, ag' means to stand, stop

1.	a	g	e	n	t					
2.	a	c	t	o	r	s				
3.	e	n	a	c	t	e	d			
4.	i	n	a	c	t	i	o	n		
5.	c	o	a	g	u	l	a	t	e	
6.	a	c	t	i	v	i	t	i	e	s
7.	a	c	t	i	v	a	t	i	o	n	s
8.	i	n	t	e	r	a	c	t	i	o	n	s

1. a force that causes change or movement
2. people who perform or do; stage or film performers
3. put into motion; made into law
4. lack of performance or movement
5. to cause substances to move into one mass
6. movements; states of being in motion
7. processes or ways of setting things in motion
8. processes of doing or moving between each other

Focus Word: **INACTION** → Write this word on the board.

TEACH

Sample leading question:	"Let's focus on this word, **inaction**. What is the word saying to us?"
Student:	"I had a cousin wounded in action."
Student:	"That's not this word!"
Student:	"Just kidding—I know. When the **in-** is attached, it means *not*."
Teacher:	"So is **inaction** the *opposite* of **action**?"
Student:	"Sure—if you're doing something you're doing an **action**, but if you're not doing anything, you're…wait a minute. How can you do an **inaction**?"
Student:	"How about this: **action** is a thing, and so is **inaction**."
Teacher:	"Okay, before you go on, why do call them *things*?"
Student:	"Because the suffix **-ion** just means *a thing*, doesn't it?"
Teacher:	"In a way. It does mean a thing, since *a result or a process* is a thing. Let's check the inside back covers of our Student Activity Books to remind ourselves about the suffix -**ion**."
Student:	"Yes, *the result or outcome of an action or process*."
Teacher:	"So what is an **action** and what is an **inaction**?"
Student:	"An **action** is *the result of doing something*, and **inaction** is *the result of not doing something*."

DISCUSS Lead students to see that, based on its three pieces of meaning, **inaction** is a noun referring to *the lack of doing something*. Ask students if they can think of situations in which the word might arise. (**Inaction** of putting up a stop sign might lead to an accident, for example.)

DEMONSTRATE Divide the class into two halves. Inform one half that they will demonstrate **action**, and the other half will demonstrate **inaction** when you say, "Stand up!" What did the group demonstrating **action** do, and what did the group demonstrating **inaction** do?"

MINI-LESSON: the Suffix -iti

The suffix **-iti** is simply a spelling variant of **-ity**. Whenever any of the large number of words ending in **-ity** is made plural, the final **y** is changed to the letter **i** before the plural suffix is added.

MINI-LESSON: the Suffix -es

The plural suffix **-s** is regularly spelled **-es** whenever it is attached to a word ending in a vowel. Such will always be the case when a word with the suffix **-ity** is made plural. You can let your students practice that consistency with any of the following examples:

nationality	community	ability	possibility
nationalities	communities	abilities	possibilities

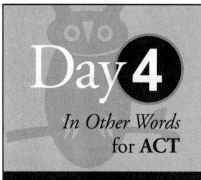

Day 4

In Other Words
for ACT

ACT means
to do; to perform; to cause to move

LESSON TIME

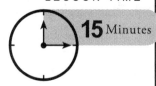

15 Minutes

OBJECTIVES

- **Understand** the meaning of the root **ACT**

- **Reinforce** knowledge of the root **ACT**

- **Understand** the meaning of words in the **ACT** family

- **Apply** knowledge of words in the **ACT** family

MATERIALS

- Student Activity Book

- **ACT** Word Wall

- Dictionary *(print or on-line)*

In Other Words for **ACT**

TEACH Have students turn to page 54 in their Student Activity Books. Explain that they are going to read a little story that uses some surprising and sometimes odd phrasing. The underlined words or phrases in the story are actually definitions or synonyms for words in the **ACT** family. Then they will see sentences about the story, each containing a blank. Using context clues in the sentences, they will find an **ACT** family word in the Word Bank at the bottom to fit in each blank. Have a student read aloud the opening sentence or sentences of the story that contain the first underlined phrase. Then say, "Let's look at the first numbered sentence that contains a blank to be filled in. Clues in the sentence tell us that we want a naming word, a noun that is synonymous with *performance* and the busy final one at the end of the year. I see the word **activity** at the bottom of the page and that word fits all the clues, especially since *to perform* is one of the meanings of the root **act**. The suffixes **-iv** and **-ity** together mean *inclined toward a state of*, in this case *doing or performing*. Let's write **activity** in the blank for the first sentence."

COMPLETE THE ACTIVITY
This can be quite challenging, so allow students to work on this activity in small groups. Not every word in the Word Bank will be used.

DISCUSS After about 10 minutes, ask if there were any difficulties. Have volunteers explain strategies they used that led to correct answers.

Class Play

SAB
Pg 54

The favorite <u>performance</u> of the students of Happydays School was always the end-of-the-year play. This year was special because the parents of the students in upper grades would be present. Zach was elected director, and his ideas for the play quickly began to <u>move together as a mass</u> in his brain. The big challenge, he thought, was getting as many students, in his homeroom as well as the other homerooms, to be <u>people to perform on stage</u>. He decided that instead of presenting one play, the class would do many short skits instead. Zach's principal <u>moved</u> favorably <u>in response</u> to the idea.

Zach put many of his classmates in charge of the skits that were historical events put on as <u>processes of causing to be done again</u>. The variety of skits and the number of roles that were required allowed students throughout the school to <u>perform among themselves</u>. No one was <u>not doing</u> anything during the rehearsals because there was so much to do.

On the night of the performance, Zach hopped around, <u>having excessive motion</u>. He was exhausted, but happy as he listened to applause from classmates and their parents.

<u>Fill in the blanks below using words from the "act, ag" family.</u>

1. The end-of-year play is a busy final <u>activity</u> at Happydays School.

2. The many ideas that Zach had for the play finally began to <u>coagulate</u> into a single thought.

3. Students in other classes were recruited to be <u>actors</u> in the skits.

4. The principal must have liked Zach's idea because she <u>reacted</u> to it well.

5. Zach's class play was a series of skits that were <u>reenactments</u> of historic events.

6. Students from all the classes <u>interacted</u> with each other during the skits.

7. With so much to do, there was not an <u>inactive</u> student at any rehearsal.

8. Because of all his scurrying around during the performance, audience members might have thought he was <u>hyperactive</u>.

<u>Not Used:</u>   interaction   enact   inaction   agilely

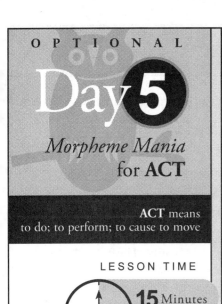

OPTIONAL

Day 5

Morpheme Mania
for **ACT**

ACT means
to do; to perform; to cause to move

LESSON TIME

15 Minutes

OBJECTIVES

- **Build** words in the **ACT** family

- **Apply** knowledge of synonyms and antonyms to **ACT** words

Optional Morpheme Mania for **ACT**

On page 55 of their Activity Books, students will see an optional vocabulary enrichment activity that they can work on in groups, time permitting. This activity makes a great review for the formal assessment on the next page.

All the affixes presented in the week's activities are provided at the top of the page on either side of the root of the week in all its forms. Students can write in up to 13 of the words they built during the week, possibly discovering additional ones.

Then students can brainstorm with each other to come up with antonyms and synonyms they may know. Starter examples are given with every Morpheme Mania in the Activity Book. Because antonyms and synonyms may require knowledge of roots which students have not yet studied, completion of this activity is not crucial. Simply remind students that they can at any time during the course of the year revisit any of their Morpheme Mania pages and add words, antonyms, and synonyms as their vocabulary grows.

Day 5 *Assessment*

Make and hand out copies.
The answer key is on page A-3.
The instructions are on page A-2.

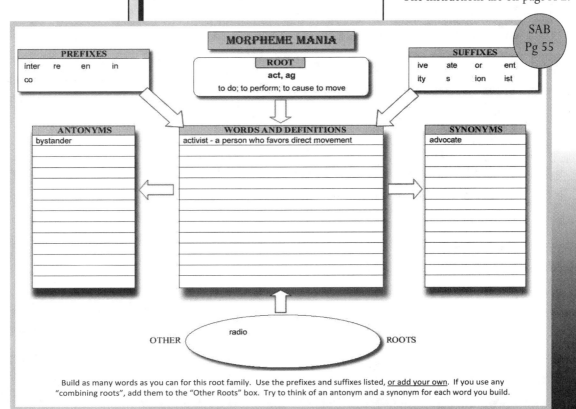

SAB
Pg 55

MORPHEME MANIA

PREFIXES			
inter	re	en	in
co			

ROOT
act, ag
to do; to perform; to cause to move

SUFFIXES			
ive	ate	or	ent
ity	s	ion	ist

ANTONYMS
bystander

WORDS AND DEFINITIONS
activist - a person who favors direct movement

SYNONYMS
advocate

OTHER   radio   ROOTS

Build as many words as you can for this root family. Use the prefixes and suffixes listed, <u>or add your own</u>. If you use any "combining roots", add them to the "Other Roots" box. Try to think of an antonym and a synonym for each word you build.

act to perform, to move, or to do
acted performed, moved, or did
acting performing, moving, or doing
action process of performing or doing; something done
actions processes of performing or doing; things done
activate to set in motion
activated set in motion
activates sets in motion
activating setting in motion
activation process or way of setting something in motion
activations processes or ways of setting things in motion
active busy, or in motion
activism direct movement or performance
activist a person who favors direct movement or performance
activists people who favor direct movement or performance
activities movements; states of being in motion
activity movement; state of being in motion
actor a person who performs or does; stage or film performer
actors people who perform or do; stage or film performers
acts performs, moves, or does
actual describing what is really done
actualities realities; things really happening or being done
actuality reality; a thing really happening or being done
actually in a manner done in fact or in reality
agent a force that causes change or movement
agents forces that cause change or movement
agile easily able to move
agilely in a manner of moving easily
agilities abilities to move easily
agility ability to move easily
coagulate to cause to move together into one mass
coagulated caused to move together into one mass
coagulates causes to move together into one mass
coagulating causing to move together into one mass

enact to put into motion; to make into law
enacted put into motion; made into law
enacting putting into motion; making into law
enacts puts into motion; makes into law
hyperactive having excessive motion; overdoing
inaction lack of performance or movement
inactive not doing anything
inactivity the state of not doing anything
interact to do, perform, or move between each other
interacted did, performed, or moved between each other
interacting doing, performing, or moving between each other
interaction process of doing or moving between each other
interactions processes of doing or moving between each other
interactive serving to do or move between each other
interacts does, performs, or moves between each other
radioactive causing rays to move spontaneously; emitting nuclear particles
radioactivity the condition of spontaneously making rays; emission of nuclear particles
react to perform or move in response to something
reacted performed or moved in response to something
reacting performing or moving in response to something
reaction a performance or movement in response to something
reactions performances or movements in response to something
reactive inclined to perform or move in response to something
reactor a person or thing that performs or moves in response; a machine causing nuclei to respond to stimuli
reactors people or things that perform or move in response; machines causing nuclei to respond to stimuli
reacts performs or moves in response to something

Check-Up for **ACT**

Name _____

____ **1.** **ACT** or **AG** in words like **active** and **agile** means:

A to look for

B to bring to mind

C to do

____ **2.** What is the meaning of the word **enact**?

A to look inward

B to put into motion

C not to remember well

____ **3.** What is the meaning of the word **interaction**?

A process of performing among things

B to be unable to bring to mind

C quality of moving away

____ **4.** What is the meaning of the word **reactor**?

A a process of recalling

B a person who is looking for something

C a device that does something in response

____ **5.** If you are **agile**, you are:

A able to find things easily

B easily able to move

C acting old for your age

____ **6.** Which word means **to move together in one mass**?

A coagulate

B agility

C radioactive

____ **7.** Which word means **moving too much**?

A proactive

B hyperactive

C reactive

____ **8.** Which word means **a device that stops a machine from doing something**?

A interactivity

B inactivator

C reactionary

____ **9.** An **agentive** morpheme or root tells us:

A what to look for

B how to remember something

C who or what does something

____ **10.** The **coagency** of wind and rain created the canyon. **Coagency** is:

A the process of working together

B not being able to work together

C a lack of working together

OBJECTIVES

- **Understand** the meaning of the root **PEL**
- **Build** words in the root **PEL** family
- **Break Apart** words in the root **PEL** family
- **Understand** the meaning of words in the **PEL** family
- **Understand** the spelling principles applied to the root **PEL**
- **Apply** knowledge of words in the **PEL** family
- **Assess** and **Reinforce** knowledge of words in the **PEL** family

MATERIALS

- Student Activity Books, pages 57-62
- Dictionary *(print or on-line)*
- an eraser

CROSS-CURRICULAR EXAMPLES

Science:
impulsion, pulsar

Social Studies:
pulse, expelled

Language Arts:
compelling, impulsive

Math:
propulsory, compulsation

PEL

meaning "to push, force, beat"

propel
to **push** forward

expulsion
an act of **forcing** out

pulse
a **beat**

Morpheme: **PEL**
Allomorphs: **PUL, PELL, PULS, PULSE**

About 600 words containing the morpheme **PEL** or one of its allomorphs are current in English. During this unit, tell students to be alert for this root in their school texts, general reading, and oral language they hear. Some of the words they might encounter in their school subjects are listed on the left under Cross-Curricular Examples

UNIT AT A GLANCE

Day 1
Root Squares for **PEL**

Day 2
Magic Squares for **PEL**

Day 3
Stair Steps for **PEL**

OPTIONAL
Day 4
In Other Words for **PEL**

Day 5
Assessment or Morpheme Mania for **PEL**

Each activity should take approximately **15 minutes**.

The existence of various spellings (called *allomorphs*, "other forms") for this root, as for so many others, is due to the changes in the principal parts of the original Latin verb: **pello, pellere, pepuli, pulsus**. Compare this feature in English, as with **ride, rode, ridden**, or **go, went, gone**.

One of the allomorphs of this root, **pulse**, can stand alone as a word (a free or unbound morpheme). The word **pulse** can be a noun (*feel my pulse*) or a verb (*to pulse*). In general, verbs will be derived from the allomorph **pel** (*to expel*), and nouns will be derived from the form **puls** (*expulsion*). There are, however, interesting exceptions: **repel** and **repulse** are both verbs.

Note with your students that the form **pel** will double its final **l** whenever a suffix beginning with a vowel is added (**repel** but **repellant**; **propel**, but **propeller**.) Remind students why this is so (the accent or stress of the words **repel** and **propel** is on the last syllable).

To **appeal** is literally *to push toward*. An **appellate** court is one that *attends to appeals*. Your **appellation** is originally what people call you when they appeal or plead to you, and it has come to mean, in general, *your name*.

This is an excellent root for exploring the effects of the prefixes. Let students list things that can be **expelled**; that can be **repelled**; that can be **compelled**; that can be **dispelled**; that can be **propelled**. Let them decide if some things can show up on more than one list. The words on any one list are called *collocations*.

The word **push**, with the internal **l** of the original root dropped—a common feature of French influence—belongs to this root family.

Word Alert!

Students will by now recognize that letter sequences in a word do not make morphemes. The sequence **p-e-l** as in the words **spell** or **pelvis**, and the sequence **p-u-l**, as in **population**, are not morphemes in this root family

Day 1

Root Squares for **PEL**

PEL means
to push, force, beat

LESSON TIME

15 Minutes

OBJECTIVES

- **Understand** the meaning of the root **PEL**

- **Build** words in the **PEL** family

- **Understand** the meaning of words in the **PEL** family

- **Understand** the spelling principles applied to the root **PEL**

MATERIALS

- Student Activity Book

- **PEL** Word Wall

- Dictionary *(print or on-line)*

- an eraser

DIFFERENTIATING INSTRUCTION

If you prefer easier or more difficult activities, use your personal account at www.dynamicliteracy.com to access novice or expert versions, along with ideas on using them.

Root Squares for PEL

TEACH Have students turn to page 57 in their Activity Books. Say, "All of the prefixes and suffixes in the squares surrounding the shaded center are probably familiar, but if you have questions about any of the meanings, simply ask or look them up inside the front and back cover of your activity book."

Call attention to the center box. Point out that the root **PEL** has several different spellings, called allomorphs. Ask students to decide if one of the forms they see in the middle square can stand alone as a word. Use **pulse** to guide them to the meaning *to push, force, or beat*. Explore how these meanings relate to **pulse**, and have them start their list with **pulse**. Suggest that students continue their list with **pel** and then add **ex-**, meaning *out of,*

or from, to build **expel**, meaning *to push out of or from*. Invite students to explore how this word is related to the idea of *to push, force, or beat*.

COMPLETE THE ACTIVITY

Have students follow the directions for the activity for **PEL** to build words. If students have difficulty building words with the Root Squares, show them how by modeling the matrix approach found on the next page, taking one affix at a time and seeing if it will connect with any one of the allomorphs of the root

DISCUSS After five minutes, have volunteers write some of their words on the board. Focus with the class on the words they have built and guide them in a discussion of how the meaning of the root is still *to push, force, or beat*, even when prefixes and suffixes are added. Watch for target words that most easily demonstrate the meanings of *to push, force, or beat*. If the word **propel** is not present, ask the class, "Can anyone try to use the prefix **pro-**?" and then continue on to the discussion on the next page.

SAB Pg 57

Root Squares

How many words can you make?

Start in any square. Your goal is to combine two or more word parts to make as many words in the 'pel, pul, pell, puls, pulse' family as you can. Write each word and a definition you can think of for it in the space provided at the bottom of the page. Use the back of the page if you need to.

com	ive	dis
ion	pel, pul, pell, puls, pulse	pro
ex	ent	re

Focus Word: **PROPEL** ⟶ Write this word on the board.

TEACH

Sample leading statement:	"Being in the right place at the right time just might **propel** you to become rich and famous. Let's look at this word, **propel**."
Student:	"I've heard of **propellers**, but not **propel**."
Teacher:	"Well, let's just work backwards then. What are **propellers**?"
Student:	"Spinning thingies on planes."
Teacher:	"What do the spinning thingies do for the plane?"
Student:	"Make it fly, I guess."
Student:	"Not just that—they make the plane *go forward*."
Teacher:	"Is there anything in the word that gives us information meaning *forward*?"
Student:	"Yes! The prefix **pro-** means *forward*, like in **progress** or **promote**."
Student:	"And **pel** is our root that means *push*. So **propel** is *push forward*."
Teacher:	"Good. The **propellers propel** the plane. "And let's go back to my original statement—how can being in the right spot **propel** somebody to fame?"
Student:	"That just means they get *pushed* into the limelight all of a sudden—it makes sense."

DISCUSS Lead students to see that, based on its pieces of meaning, **propel** means *push or force forward*. Some students might observe that **propellers** don't *push* a plane as much as they *pull*, and you can call attention to some other meanings of the root **pel**, including *to force*, as in *cause to go*.

DEMONSTRATE Put an eraser on the floor and ask a student to **propel** it somehow across the floor. (The student can use a foot or a yardstick or any other instrument.) Have the class observe that the eraser is being *pushed or forced forward*.

Root Squares Matrix

You can refer to this matrix to guide students in this activity. Students could build at least these 24 words. *It really doesn't matter how many they build* – the point is that they understand the consistent meanings of the root **PEL** and of its prefixes and suffixes.

	no prefix	com-	dis-	ex-	pro-	re-
no suffix	pulse			expulse		repulse
		compel	dispel	expel	propel	repel
-ent		compellent		expellent	propellent	repellent
-ion		compulsion		expulsion	propulsion	repulsion
-ive		compulsive		expulsive	propulsive	repulsive
re-		recompel	redispel	reexpel	repropel	

Words that students coin for empty slots are legitimate learning tools: have students who coin such words give appropriate definitions for them.

Day 2

Magic Squares
for **PEL**

PEL means
to push, force, beat

LESSON TIME

15 Minutes

OBJECTIVES

- **Understand** the meaning of the root **PEL**

- **Break Apart** words in the **PEL** family

- **Understand** the meanings of words in the **PEL** family

MATERIALS

- Student Activity Book

- **PEL** Word Wall

- Dictionary *(print or on-line)*

DIFFERENTIATING INSTRUCTION

If you prefer easier or more difficult activities, use your personal account at www.dynamicliteracy.com to access novice or expert versions, along with ideas on using them.

Break Apart Words with PEL

TEACH Have students turn to the Magic Squares on page 58 in their Student Activity Books. Model a Think-Aloud strategy for students: "I know that **PEL** and the several different spellings of this root mean *to push, force, or beat*. I can use this knowledge to find the definition of a word with this as its root." Direct students to word G, **pulsated**. Say, "I know that the suffix **-ate** means *to cause to become* and the suffix **-ed** is a *past tense marker*. (Of course, the final **e** on -ate drops before the **-ed** is added.) Looking for a definition that includes all these ideas, I see definition #5 is *pushed or beat; throbbed*. This ties in the meaning of **pulse** and since this definition accounts for all the parts of the

word, including two meanings of **PUL**, *push and beat*, we'll write the number 5 in square G.

COMPLETE THE ACTIVITY

Ask students to use the same strategy to find the correct definitions for the other words. Tell them to write the number of the definition in the box that matches the letter for the word. Remind them that if all their answers are correct, each row and each column will add up to the same Magic number.

DISCUSS After five minutes, ask if there are any difficulties about matching the words and definitions. If there are, ask volunteers to explain clues in the definitions that will lead to the correct choice of word. As needed, follow the focus word approach for expelled that you see modeled on the next page.

Add any new words to the classroom **PEL** Word Wall and remind students to add these words to the **PEL** Word Wall in their Activity Books.

SAB
Pg 58

Magic Squares

Select the best answer for each of the words in the 'pel, pul, pell, puls, pulse' family from the numbered definitions. Put the number in the proper space in the Magic Square box. If the total of the numbers is the same both across and down, you have found the magic number!

'pel, pul, pell, puls, pulse' means to push, force, beat

WORDS	DEFINITIONS
A. compellent	1. pushed or forced into
B. propellers	2. instruments that push forward
C. expulsion	3. pushed or forced out
D. repellents	4. substances that serve to push back; substances that act to drive back or keep away
E. dispelled	5. pushed or beat; throbbed
F. impulsive	6. pushed away; drove out
G. pulsated	7. the act or process of pushing or forcing out
H. repulsive	8. likely to drive or push into
I. expelled	9. tending to push together; tending to force
	10. likely to push back; offensive

Magic Square Box

A. 9	B. 2	C. 7
D. 4	E. 6	F. 8
G. 5	H. 10	I. 3

Magic Number __18__

*** ANSWER KEY ***

Focus Word: **EXPELLED** → Write this word on the board.

TEACH

Sample leading question:	"What happens to someone if he or she is **expelled** from a club or school?"
Student:	"They get kicked out."
Teacher:	"Do you mean somebody actually kicks that person?"
Student:	"No—they're told to get out."
Student:	"I see it—the prefix **ex-** means *out*, like an exit door."
Student:	"And the -**ed** suffix says it *happened in the past*."
Student:	"Or it could just describe the person, like an **expelled** member."
Teacher:	"Good. And where's the *kick* part?."
Student:	"That's our root **pel**, *push or force*."
Teacher:	"Why is the root spelled with a double **l**?"
Student:	"Because we accent that syllable that has the **l** in it."
Teacher:	"Would it also be spelled with double **l** if the suffix is -**ing**?"
Student:	"Yes, because both suffixes -**ed** and -**ing** start with a vowel."

DISCUSS Lead students to see that, based on its three pieces of meaning, **expelled** means *pushed or forced out*. Lead the class in discussing what sorts of things besides club or school members can be **expelled**. (Countries can be **expelled** from a world organization, traitors can be **expelled** from a country, a swallowed foreign object can be **expelled** from the body, cough medicine can be an **expellant** for cold congestion, etc.)

DEMONSTRATE Have students hold their hands in front of their mouths and have them **expel** their breath onto their hands and feel the air being forced out.

Day 3

Stair Steps
for **PEL**

LESSON TIME

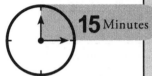

15 Minutes

OBJECTIVES

• **Understand** the meaning of the root **PEL**

• **Apply** knowledge of the root **PEL**

• **Break Apart** words in the **PEL** family

• **Understand** the meaning of words in the **PEL** family

• **Understand** the spelling principles applied to the root **PEL**

MATERIALS

• Student Activity Book

• **PEL** Word Wall

DIFFERENTIATING INSTRUCTION

If you prefer easier or more difficult activities, use your personal account at www.dynamicliteracy.com to access novice or expert versions, along with ideas on using them.

Apply Knowledge of PEL

TEACH Have students turn to page 59 in their Student Activity Books. Explain that the boxes in front of and after the root indicate letters that spell out prefixes and suffixes. Students will spell out the correct prefixes and suffixes determined by clues in the definitions at the bottom of the page.

Have a volunteer read definition number two at the bottom of the page. Say, "The first two letters of the word we need in step two are a prefix that means *back*. This is the common prefix **re-**. The final space will be filled with the *he, she, or it* verb marker, -**s**. The word we build will thus be **REPELS**."

COMPLETE THE ACTIVITY Let students work in pairs (optionally) and tell them to use the same strategy to find the correct prefixes and suffixes for the words listed. These activities can be quite challenging!

DISCUSS After a few minutes, review the answers as a class. Ask if there were any difficulties. Listen to any problems and have volunteers solve the difficulties by explaining key clues in the given definitions. As needed, follow the focus word approach that you see modeled on the next page.

SAB
Pg 59

Stair Steps

Fill in the missing letters of each 'pel, pul, pell, puls, pulse' word by using the definitions below.

'pel, pul, pell, puls, pulse' means to push, force, beat

1.	i	m	p	e	l			
2.	r	e	p	e	l	s		
3.	p	u	l	s	i	n	g	
4.	i	m	p	e	l	l	e	r
5.	r	e	p	e	l	l	e	n	t
6.	d	i	s	p	e	l	l	i	n	g
7.	p	r	o	p	u	l	s	i	o	n	s

1. to push or force into
2. pushes back; drives back or keeps away
3. pushing or beating; throbbing
4. a person or tool that pushes or forces into
5. serving or tending to push back; acting to drive back or tending to keep away
6. pushing away; driving out
7. acts or processes of pushing forward

Focus Word: **IMPEL** ⟶ Write this word on the board.

TEACH

Sample leading question:	"Let's take a look at this word, **impel**. What can anyone tell me about the word?"
Teacher:	"It has two morphemes, **im-** as a prefix and our root **pel**."
Student:	"So it means *not to push*?"
Student:	"The prefix **im-** could also mean *in* instead of *not*. Then it would mean *to push or force in*."
Teacher:	"Why is the prefix spelled **im-** instead of **in-**?"
Student:	"That's because it's easier to pronounce the letter **m** in front of a **p** than to pronounce the letter **n**."
Student:	"It's assimilation!"
Teacher:	"Good, now back to the meaning of the word. Is there any way to tell whether the prefix means *not* or *in*?"
Student:	< a deafening silence >
Teacher:	"I'll tell you. No, there is no way to tell unless you already know the meaning of the word. Sometimes tricky morphemes will do that. So how can we decide?"
Student:	"We can look it up. Or maybe a sentence that uses the word in a story might help."
Teacher:	"Let me give you a sentence. 'Hunger will **impel** the little child to beg for food.' Now can you tell what it means?"
Student:	"Yes, *forced the child on*, pushed him *into* it. I get it."

DISCUSS Lead students to see that, based on its pieces of meaning, **impel** means to *force* (something) *onto* somebody. Let the class experiment with a pattern such as, "Situation A **impelled** me to B," similar to the example about hunger and begging given in the dialogue box above. Help the class to see that the word is used in a formal and urgent sense to mean *force or require someone to do something*, or to *move that person to act in an urgent way.*

DEMONSTRATE **Impel** the door to open. Unless you have unusual powers, nothing will happen.* Gently **impel** a student to open the door. Action will occur.

*If you **are** able to impel the door to open using your mind, perhaps you missed your true calling!

Day 4

In Other Words for **PEL**

PEL means to push, force, beat

LESSON TIME

15 Minutes

OBJECTIVES

- **Understand** the meaning of the root **PEL**
- **Reinforce** knowledge of the root **PEL**
- **Understand** the meaning of words in the **PEL** family
- **Apply** knowledge of words in the **PEL** family

MATERIALS

- Student Activity Book
- **PEL** Word Wall
- Dictionary *(print or on-line)*

In Other Words for **PEL**

TEACH Have students turn to page 60 in their Student Activity Books. Explain that they are going to read a little story that uses some surprising and sometimes odd phrasing. The underlined words or phrases in the story are actually definitions or synonyms for words in the **PEL** family. Then they will see sentences about the story, each containing a blank.

Using context clues in the sentences, they will find a **PEL** family word in the Word Bank at the bottom to fit in each blank. Have a student read aloud the opening sentence or sentences of the story that contain the first underlined phrase. Then say, "Let's look at the first numbered sentence that contains a blank to be filled in. Clues in the sentence tell us that we want an action word, a verb that is synonymous with *to push or force* astronauts into the space program. I see the word **compel** at the bottom of the page and that word fits all the clues. The prefix **com-** has the meaning *thoroughly* and the sense we get of what happens to the astronauts is that they are *thoroughly* pushed into the space program, perhaps by forces not completely within their control. Let's write **compel** in the blank for the first sentence."

COMPLETE THE ACTIVITY

This can be quite challenging, so allow students to work on this activity in small groups. Not every word in the Word Bank will be used.

DISCUSS After about 10 minutes, ask if there were any difficulties. Have volunteers explain strategies they used that led to correct answers.

...3,2,1, Blastoff!

SAB Pg 60

Astronauts have different reasons that push or force them to train for a space expedition. Some may desire fame, some adventure, but many just have a forceful push to travel fast. Much training, though, is required before an astronaut is ready to be pushed forward into space.

Early flight training often comes at the stick of an airplane powered by instruments that push forward instead of by more advanced rockets. Math classes examining the process of pushing forward in jets are also required. People who want to become astronauts must master a flight simulator that mimics the weightless conditions that they will find in space.

All this training leads to the big moment when the clock beats or pushes down the seconds...3,2,1, and the spaceship is pushed out from Earth's atmosphere. The firing of the engines sends acts of pushing or throbbing of light through the small windows of the space capsule. A modern explorer to rival Christopher Columbus is launched.

Fill in the blanks below using words from the "pel, pul, pell, puls, pulse" family.

1. There are many reasons that compel astronauts to enter the space program.
2. Like other explorers, astronauts can have a compulsion to seek fame or speed.
3. Before he or she can be propelled into space, an astronaut must be trained.
4. Airplanes that move forward with propellers are less technically advanced than rockets.
5. The study of propulsion, forward motion, includes advanced mathematics.
6. The second-by-second pulses of the clock count the time down to the launch of the space ship.
7. A spaceship is expelled from Earth's atmosphere when it is launched.
8. Pulsations of light came through the windows from the engine firings.

Not Used: impelling   repel   repellent   repulsive

LESSON TIME

15 Minutes

OBJECTIVES

- **Build** words in the **PEL** family

- **Apply** knowledge of synonyms and antonyms to **PEL** words

Optional Morpheme Mania for **PEL**

On page 61 of their Activity Books, students will see a vocabulary enrichment activity that they can work on in groups as a culminating activity for this week instead of, or, time permitting, in addition to, the more formal assessment.

All the affixes presented in the week's activities are provided at the top of the page on either side of the root of the week in all its forms. Students can write in up to 13 of the words they built during the week, possibly discovering additional ones.

Then students can brainstorm with each other to come up with antonyms and synonyms they may know. Starter examples are given with every Morpheme Mania in the Activity Book. Because antonyms and synonyms may require knowledge of roots which students have not yet studied, completion of this activity is not crucial. Simply remind students that they can at any time during the course of the year revisit any of their Morpheme Mania pages and add words, antonyms, and synonyms as their vocabulary grows

Day 5 *Assessment*

Make and hand out copies.
The answer key is on page A-4.
The instructions are on page A-2.

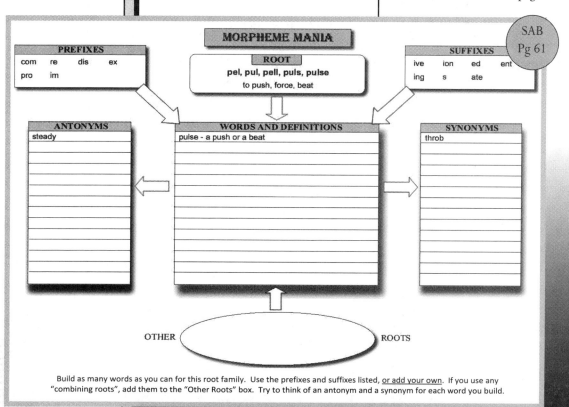

MORPHEME MANIA

SAB Pg 61

PREFIXES
| com | re | dis | ex |
| pro | im | | |

ROOT
pel, pul, pell, puls, pulse
to push, force, beat

SUFFIXES
| ive | ion | ed | ent |
| ing | s | ate | |

ANTONYMS
steady

WORDS AND DEFINITIONS
pulse - a push or a beat

SYNONYMS
throb

OTHER   ROOTS

Build as many words as you can for this root family. Use the prefixes and suffixes listed, <u>or add your own</u>. If you use any "combining roots", add them to the "Other Roots" box. Try to think of an antonym and a synonym for each word you build.

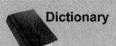

compel   to push together; to force
compelled   pushed together; forced
compellent   tending to push together; tending to force
compelling   pushing together; forcing
compels   pushes together; forces
dispel   to push away; to drive out
dispelled   pushed away; drove out
dispelling   pushing away; driving out
dispels   pushes away; drives out
expel   to push or force out
expellant   something that pushes or forces out
expellants   things that push or force out
expelled   pushed or forced out
expelling   pushing or forcing out
expels   pushes or forces out
expulsion   the act or process of pushing or forcing out
expulsions   acts or processes of pushing or forcing out
impel   to push or force into
impelled   pushed or forced into
impeller   a person or tool that pushes or forces into
impellers   people or tools that push or force into
impelling   pushing or forcing into
impels   pushes or forces into
impulse   a drive or push into; an urge
impulse   pushed or forced into
impulses   drives that push something into; urges
impulsion   act of driving or pushing into
impulsions   acts of driving or pushing into
impulsive   likely to drive or push into
propel   to push forward
propelled   pushed forward
propeller   instrument that pushes forward

propellers   instruments that push forward
propelling   pushing forward
propels   pushes forward
propulsion   act or process of pushing forward
propulsions   acts or processes of pushing forward
pulsate   to push or beat; to throb
pulsated   pushed or beat; throbbed
pulsates   pushes or beats; throbs
pulsating   pushing or beating; throbbing
pulsation   act of pushing or beating; act of throbbing
pulsations   acts of pushing or beating; acts of throbbing
pulse   a push or a beat
pulsed   pushed or beat; throbbed
pulses   acts of pushing or beating; acts of throbbing
pulsing   pushing or beating; throbbing
repel   to push back; to keep away
repellant   anything pushing or forcing back; anything keeping something away
repellants   things pushing or forcing back; things keeping away
repelled   pushed back; drove back or kept away
repellent   serving or tending to push back; acting to keep away
repellents   substances that serve to push back; substances that act to keep away
repelling   pushing back; keeping away
repellingly   in a manner pushing or forcing back
repels   pushes back; keeps away
repulse   to push away or back; to offend
repulsed   pushed away or back; offended
repulses   pushes or forces back; offends
repulsive   likely to push back; offensive

Check-Up for **PEL**

Name _____

____ **1.** **PEL** or **PUL** in words like **propel** and **expulsion** means:

   A to be strong

   B to be wrong

   C to push

____ **2.** What is the meaning of the word **repelling**?

   A being wrong again

   B acting strong

   C pushing back

____ **3.** If you consider something **repulsive**, you:

   A know that it will not hurt you

   B push it away from yourself

   C trust its strength

____ **4.** What is the meaning of the word **propeller**?

   A a device to help you push forward

   B someone in favor of strength

   C more incorrect

____ **5.** What are you doing if you **dispel** a rumor? You are:

   A spreading it

   B getting rid of it

   C learning more about it

____ **6.** Which word means **to force or drive into**?

   A compellent

   B impel

   C pulsation

____ **7.** Which word means **a process of beating**?

   A pulsation

   B repellant

   C impeller

____ **8.** Which word means **forced very much**?

   A expellant

   B compelled

   C propulsions

____ **9.** The discovery of gold proved **propulsive** for settling the West. The discovery:

   A stopped settlement

   B kept settlement from happening as fast

   C hurried up the settlement

____ **10.** Some Founders of the country believed in **compulsory** education.
This is education that is:

   A required for all

   B not wrong

   C provided only if you can afford it

OBJECTIVES

- **Understand** the meaning of the root **JUR**
- **Build** words in the root **JUR** family
- **Break Apart** words in the root **JUR** family
- **Understand** the meaning of words in the **JUR** family
- **Understand** the spelling principles applied to the root **JUR**
- **Apply** knowledge of words in the **JUR** family
- **Assess** and **Reinforce** knowledge of words in the **JUR** family

MATERIALS

- Student Activity Books, pages 63-68
- Dictionary *(print or on-line)*
- a picture and some tape *(optional)*

CROSS-CURRICULAR EXAMPLES

Science:
adjustment, injurious, readjust

Social Studies:
injustice, jurisdiction, perjury

Language Arts:
maladjusted, conjuration

Math:
justifiable, adjust, justify

JUR

meaning "law; right, true; to swear an oath"

jurisdiction
area of authority to enforce the **law**

just
right or fair

juror
a panelist serving to decide what is **right** or **true**

perjure
to **swear** a false **oath**

Morpheme: **JUR**
Allomorphs: **JURE, JURI, JURY, JURIS, JUS, JUST**

Nearly 200 words containing the morpheme **JUR** or one of its allomorphs are current in English. During this unit, tell students to be alert for this root in their school texts, general reading, and oral language they hear. Some of the words they might encounter in their school subjects are listed on the left under Cross-Curricular Examples.

UNIT AT A GLANCE

Day **1**
Root Squares
for **JUR**

Day **2**
Magic Squares
for **JUR**

Day **3**
Stair Steps
for **JUR**

OPTIONAL
Day **4**
In Other Words
for **JUR**

Day **5**
Assessment or Morpheme Mania
for **JUR**

Each activity should take approximately **15 minutes**.

Sometimes roots combine not just with prefixes and suffixes, but with other roots. The root **jur** combines with the root **dic**, meaning *to speak*, to generate a double root, **judic**. That double root is the source of such words as **judicious**, **prejudice**, **jurisdiction**, and even **judge**, the one who *speaks the law*.

Two variants, or allomorphs, of this root are free, unbound morphemes, standing independently as words: **jury** (an adjective and a noun), and **just** (an adjective and an adverb).

Allomorphs that have an **r** and those that have an **s** reflect a language phenomenon that appears in English with such pairs as **was** and **were**, and **lost** and **forlorn**.

Experimentation and experience will determine which forms go with which affixes. Sometimes different forms can occur with the same affix, as in the words **injure** and **injust**.

Note that the prefix **ad-** does not need to assimilate before the initial **j** of this root. That is because there is already a tendency for the **d** to be pronounced as a **j**. Listen for the **j** sound that occurs when we pronounce words like **draw** and **address**.

The prefix **per-** can have a negative connotation, meaning *thoroughly wrong*, as in words such as **perfidious**, **perdition**, and **perverse**. The word **perjury** means *the misuse or thorough violation of an oath or of what is right*.

Word Alert!

Nearly all words with the letter sequences **j-u-r** or **j-u-s** belong to this root family. The few exceptions include words like **jussive**, pertaining to *giving orders*, and **majuscule**, a word meaning *a capital letter*.

There is some debate about whether the word **adjust**, along with its companion words (**adjuster**, **adjustment**, etc.), belongs to this root family. Because its meaning, *to set toward what is right*, appears clearly to fit the meaning of this root, it is often listed as an example in the root family. It is possible that the word **adjust** actually comes from the prefix **ad-** plus another root, **juxta**, meaning *joined, near, or attached to*. Nevertheless, the word **adjust** can help students remember the meaning *right* or *true*.

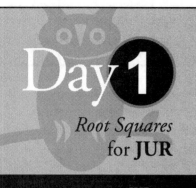

Day 1

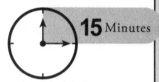

Root Squares for **JUR**

JUR means
law; right, true; to swear an oath

LESSON TIME
15 Minutes

OBJECTIVES

- **Understand** the meaning of the root **JUR**

- **Build** words in the **JUR** family

- **Understand** the meaning of words in the **JUR** family

- **Understand** the spelling principles applied to the root **JUR**

MATERIALS

- Student Activity Book
- **JUR** Word Wall
- Dictionary *(print or on-line)*

DIFFERENTIATING INSTRUCTION

If you prefer easier or more difficult activities, use your personal account at www.dynamicliteracy.com to access novice or expert versions, along with ideas on using them.

Root Squares for JUR

TEACH Have students turn to page 63 in their Activity Books. Say, "All of the prefixes and suffixes in the squares surrounding the shaded center are probably familiar except **-ice**, but if you have questions about any of the meanings, simply ask or look them up in the lists in your Activity Books." Conduct the Mini-Lesson on the suffix **-ice** as needed.

Call attention to the center box. Point out that the root **JUR** has quite a number of different spellings, called allomorphs. Ask students to decide if one of the forms they see in the middle square can stand alone as a word. They will see that both **jury** and **just** are words, and you can use these words to guide them to the meaning *law; right, true; to swear an oath.* Explore how these meanings relate to both **jury** and **just**. Suggest that students start their list with **just**

and then add **ad-**, meaning *toward,* to build **adjust**, meaning *to go toward right or true.* Invite students to explore how this word is related to the idea of *law, right, true.*

COMPLETE THE ACTIVITY

Have students follow the directions for the activity on page 63 to build words. If students have difficulty building words with the Root Squares, show them how by modeling the matrix approach found on the next page, taking one affix at a time and seeing if it will connect with any one of the allomorphs of the root.

DISCUSS After five minutes, have volunteers write some of their words on the board. Focus with the class on the words they have built and guide them in a discussion of how the meaning of the root is still *law, right, true; to swear an oath*, even when prefixes and suffixes are added. Watch for target words that most easily demonstrate the meanings of *law, right, true; to swear an oath.* If the word **juror** is not present, ask the class, "Can anyone try to use the suffix **-or**?" and then continue on to the target word discussion on the next page.

SAB Pg 63

Root Squares
How many words can you make?

Start in any square. Your goal is to combine two or more word parts to make as many words in the 'jur, jure, juri, jury, juris, jus, just' family as you can. Write each word and a definition you can think of for it in the space provided at the bottom of the page. Use the back of the page if you need to.

ment	ad	ed
ice	jur, jure, juri, jury, juris, jus, just	in
re	or	able

_____
_____
_____
_____
_____
_____
_____
_____

MINI-LESSON: the Suffix -ice

While not a large number of words make use of this suffix, -ice generates words that make an abstract noun meaning *quality, act, or condition.*

Illustrate this suffix through any of the following words:

cowardice	service	malice	avarice
practice	novice	injustice	justice

Focus Word: JUROR ⟶ Write this word on the board.

TEACH

Lead with this:	"Has anyone ever heard of the word **juror**?"
Student:	"Isn't that somebody on a **jury** in a court?"
Teacher:	"That's right. Let's dig into the word **juror** to see what i has to tell us."
Student:	"I see the suffix **-or**. That means it's *somebody who does something.*"
Teacher:	"Right, and now let's see what it is that a **juror** does."
Student:	"A **juror jures**!"
Teacher:	"That's right: the **juror jures**. But we have to dig into the meaning of this root."
Student:	"I don't think it always has to be in a courtroom. I've heard 'the **jurors** are still debating,' even when it's about a sport event decision or something."
Teacher:	"OK, so let's figure out what is meant by a **juror**. Just what is a **juror** doing?"
Student:	"The root means *law, right, or true, and to swear an oath.*"
Student:	"I get it—a **juror** is *a person who swears an oath to decide what the law is.*"
Student:	"And the **juror** has to decide what is *right or true.* That makes sense."

DISCUSS What is the difference between a **judge** and a **juror**? (They both make decisions, but about different matters; **judges** can act alone, while **jurors** are more likely to act as a group.)

DEMONSTRATE Ask the class to **judge** how many books are on a shelf in the room (or some such quantitative guess not readily clear). Would it be appropriate to call the ones guessing a number **jurors**? (A continued discussion can ensue.)

Root Squares Matrix
You can refer to this matrix to guide students in this activity. Students could build at least these 20 words. *It is not important how many words are built or whether non-dictionary words are coined*, so long as students understand the consistent meanings of the root and its affixes. Encourage discussion about the definitions of any words formed for the blank slots as well as for the attested words.

	no prefix	ad-	in-	re- + ad-	re- + in-
no suffix	jury				reinjure
	just	adjust	injury	readjust	
-able		adjustable	injurable	readjustable	
-ed		adjusted	injured	readjusted	reinjured
-ice	justice		injustice		
-ment		adjustment		readjustment	
-or	juror	adjustor		readjustor	

Day 2

Magic Squares
for **JUR**

JUR means
law; right, true; to swear an oath

LESSON TIME

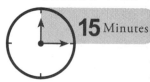

15 Minutes

OBJECTIVES

- **Understand** the meaning of the root **JUR**

- **Break Apart** words in the **JUR** family

- **Understand** the meanings of words in the **JUR** family

MATERIALS

- Student Activity Book

- **JUR** Word Wall

- Dictionary *(print or on-line)*

- a picture and some tape *(optional)*

DIFFERENTIATING INSTRUCTION

If you prefer easier or more difficult activities, use your personal account at www.dynamicliteracy.com to access novice or expert versions, along with ideas on using them.

Break Apart Words with JUR

TEACH Have students turn to the Magic Squares on page **64** in their Student Activity Books. Model a Think-Aloud strategy for students: "I know that **JUR** and the several different spellings of this root mean *law; right; true; to swear an oath*. I can use this knowledge to find the definition of a word with this as its root."

Direct students to word **H**, **perjuring**. Say, "I know one of the meanings of the prefix **per-** is *thoroughly* and the suffix **-ing** means *happening*. That leads me to definition 3, *making a thoroughly false oath*. Let's write the number 3 in square H."

COMPLETE THE ACTIVITY

Ask students to use the same strategy to find the correct definitions for the other words. Tell them to write the number of the definition in the box that matches the letter for the word. Remind them that if all their answers are correct, each row and each column will add up to the same Magic number.

DISCUSS After five minutes, ask if there are any difficulties about matching the words and definitions. If there are, ask volunteers to explain clues in the definitions that will lead to the correct choice of word. As needed, follow the focus word approach for **adjusted** that you see modeled on the next page.

Add any new words to the classroom **JUR** Word Wall and remind students to add these words to the **JUR** Word Wall in their Activity Books.

SAB Pg 64

Magic Squares

Select the best answer for each of the words in the 'jur, jure, juri, jury, juris, jus, just' family from the numbered definitions. Put the number in the proper space in the Magic Square box. If the total of the numbers is the same both across and down, you have found the magic number!

'jur, jure, juri, jury, juris, jus, just' means law; right; true; to swear an oath

WORDS	DEFINITIONS
A. adjusted	1. area of authority to state and enforce the law
B. unjustly	2. act of changing toward what is right; correction
C. adjustment	3. making a thoroughly false oath
D. injuries	4. deeds not right or lawful; harmful things
E. readjustable	5. did something not right or lawful; harmed again
F. conjurors	6. people who swear oaths together; people who call up a magic spirit
G. reinjured	7. in a manner not correct according to law
H. perjuring	8. able to be changed again toward what is right
I. injustices	9. changed toward what is right; corrected
	10. situations that are not right or lawful; acts of unfairness

Magic Square Box

A. 9	B. 7	C. 2
D. 4	E. 8	F. 6
G. 5	H. 3	I. 10

Magic Number 18

*** ANSWER KEY ***

Focus Word: **ADJUSTED** ⟶ Write this word on the board.

TEACH

Sample leading question:	"Sometimes when Daylight Savings time changes, it takes me a while to become **adjusted**. What is going on with the word **adjusted**?"
Student:	"That -**ed** suffix is an adjective, meaning *it has happened*."
Student:	"And the prefix **ad**- means (consulting the inside front cover of the Student Activity Book), *toward, to, in, for, or near*—that's too many meanings!"
Teacher:	"You've seen before that the meanings given for prefixes and suffixes are just general ideas about what they mean, right?"
Student:	"We know what **adjusted** means—*straightened out or corrected, or changed to be better*."
Teacher:	"Give some examples of those uses."
Student:	"**Adjust** the temperature, **adjust** the volume on the TV."
Teacher:	"All right, then from what we know about how to use the word, let's see if we can figure out what we're actually doing when we **adjust** the temperature or **adjust** the sound."
Student:	"We're making it comfortable or making it so we can hear."
Student:	"Ah—I have it. We're setting it to the point that is right!"
Teacher:	"How are you getting the meaning *to the point*?"
Student:	"That's the prefix **ad**-, which can mean all those definitions that are listed in the book—they all mean about the same thing, *going to a certain place*."
Teacher:	"And what about me becoming **adjusted** to the time?"

DISCUSS Lead the class to see how getting **adjusted** means *moving toward what a person judges to be right or true*. In what other contexts can the word **adjusted** be used? (getting eyes **adjusted** to the light after being in the dark, having a picture **adjusted** on the wall, having game scores **adjusted** after a dispute is settled, etc.)

DEMONSTRATE Give a student a picture with some tape on the back and have him or her **adjust** it on the wall. Ask another student to tilt that picture or make it crooked. Then ask another student to **readjust** it.

MINI-LESSON: the Prefix **per-**

The prefix **per-** is from the Latin prefix meaning *through* or *thoroughly*. It is used as a word in itself to mean *by way of, through the direction of*, or *according to*. We can say, "This letter is written **per** the boss," or "Addie drove 15 miles **per** hour."

The prefix **per-** appears rarely with free, unbound morphemes, but students may know some of the following words that clearly demonstrate the meaning "through" or "thoroughly":

perforated	permeate	pervasive	persist	perpetuate
permanent	perfected	perennial	percussion	percolate

The Latin phrases *per capita* ("by heads"), *per annum* ("by year"), and *per diem* ("by the day") are well known.

Day 3

Stair Steps
for **JUR**

JUR means
law; right, true; to swear an oath

LESSON TIME

15 Minutes

OBJECTIVES

- **Understand** the meaning of the root **JUR**

- **Apply** knowledge of the root **JUR**

- **Break Apart** words in the **JUR** family

- **Understand** the meaning of words in the **JUR** family

- **Understand** the spelling principles applied to the root **JUR**

MATERIALS

- Student Activity Book
- **JUR** Word Wall

DIFFERENTIATING INSTRUCTION

If you prefer easier or more difficult activities, use your personal account at www.dynamicliteracy.com to access novice or expert versions, along with ideas on using them.

Apply Knowledge of JUR

TEACH Have students turn to page 65 in their Student Activity Books. Explain that the boxes in front of and after the root indicate letters that spell out prefixes and suffixes. Students will spell out the correct prefixes and suffixes determined by clues in the definitions at the bottom of the page.

Have a volunteer read definition number one at the bottom of the page. Say, "We need a suffix with the meaning *a person who serves*. Who can recall which suffix adds that meaning to a root?" If no one answers correctly, say, "Think about words like **actor** or **visitor**. What does the suffix **-or** on **act** and **visit** add in meaning?" Then say, "So, if we add the suffix **-or**, we create a word with the meaning *one who*. Look again at definition one: *a person who serves to consider what is right*. Since one of the definitions of our root **JUR** is *right*, our word is **JUROR**."

COMPLETE THE ACTIVITY

Let students work in pairs (optionally) and tell them to use the same strategy to find the correct prefixes and suffixes for the words listed. These activities can be quite challenging!

DISCUSS After a few minutes, review the answers as a class. Ask if there were any difficulties. Listen to any problems and have volunteers solve the difficulties by explaining key clues in the given definitions. As needed, follow the focus word approach that you see modeled on the next page.

SAB
Pg 65

Stair Steps

Fill in the missing letters of each 'jur, jure, juri, jury, juris, jus, just' word by using the definitions b...
'jur, jure, juri, jury, juris, jus, just' means law, right, true; to swear an oath

1.	j	u	r	o	r				
2.	j	u	s	t	l	y			
3.	p	e	r	j	u	r	e		
4.	i	n	j	u	r	e	r	s	
5.	a	d	j	u	s	t	i	n	g
6.	i	n	j	u	s	t	i	c	e	s
7.	a	d	j	u	s	t	m	e	n	t	s
8.	r	e	a	d	j	u	s	t	m	e	n	t
9.	u	n	j	u	s	t	i	f	i	a	b	l	e

1. a person who serves to consider what is right; a panelist
2. in a manner correct according to law
3. to make a thoroughly false oath
4. people who do things not right or lawful; people who harm
5. changing toward what is right; correcting
6. situations that are not right or lawful; acts of unfairness
7. acts of changing toward what is right; corrections
8. act of changing again toward what is right
9. not able to be argued right and lawful; not defensible

128

Focus Word: **injurers** ⟶ Write this word on the board.

TEACH

Sample leading question:	"Here is a familiar enough word we all probably know, even though we may have never used it before. How many morphemes are in the word **injurers**?"
Student:	"Four. Besides the root, there is a prefix and there are two suffixes."
Teacher:	"So let's analyze the word **injurers**. What do we have?"
Teacher:	"Okay, the suffixes are easy—there are more than one people or things that do something."
Student:	"Right, and what they do is **injure**."
Teacher:	"Okay, and now what happens when we **injure**?
Student:	"We hurt somebody."
Student:	"There's that hard **in-** prefix again. Does it mean *not* or does it mean *in*?"
Student:	"Hmm. **Injure**. Well, since **injuring** is not a good thing, I think the **in-** means *not*."
Student:	"Sure, that makes sense. To **injure** is *to do something that is not right* for that other person or thing."
Teacher:	"So give us a good morphemic definition of the word **injurers**."
Student:	"It means *two or more people who do something not right to somebody else*."

DISCUSS Lead students to see that, based on its four pieces of meaning, **injurers** means just as the final student expressed in the dialogue box above.

DEMONSTRATE Show the class a binary morphemic splitting chart, dividing the word into two parts one step at a time until the meaningful pieces cannot be broken down any farther:

injurers
injurer + s
injur(e) + er
in + jur(e)

MINI-LESSON: the Suffix **-ifi**

The suffix **-ifi** is a spelling variant of the suffix **-ify**, meaning *to make or to form into*. According to the general rule, a final **y** is changed to the letter **i** before additional suffixes. The third-person singular morpheme **-s** is regularly spelled **-es** on verbs that end in a vowel, as this family does.

You can let your students practice that consistency with any of the following examples:

certify	**fortify**	**magnify**	**notify**	**testify**	**solidify**
certifies	**fortifies**	**magnifies**	**notifies**	**testifies**	**solidifies**

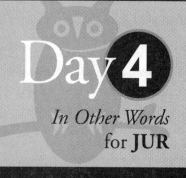

Day 4

In Other Words
for JUR

JUR means
law; right, true; to swear an oath

LESSON TIME

15 Minutes

OBJECTIVES

- **Understand** the meaning of the root **JUR**

- **Reinforce** knowledge of the root **JUR**

- **Understand** the meaning of words in the **JUR** family

- **Apply** knowledge of words in the **JUR** family

MATERIALS

- Student Activity Book

- **JUR** Word Wall

- Dictionary *(print or on-line)*

In Other Words for **JUR**

TEACH Have students turn to page 66 in their Student Activity Books. Explain that they are going to read a little story that uses some surprising and sometimes odd phrasing. The underlined words or phrases in the story are actually definitions or synonyms for words in the **JUR** family. Then they will see sentences about the story, each containing a blank. Using context clues in the sentences, they will find a **JUR** family word in the Word Bank at the bottom to fit in each blank.

Have a student read aloud the opening sentence or sentences of the story that contain the first underlined phrase. Then say, "Let's look at the first numbered sentence that contains a blank to be filled in. Clues in the sentence tell us that we want a naming word, a noun that means *fairness*, a concept that might arise in the context of a trial, in this case a mock trial. I see the word **justice** at the bottom of the page and that word fits all the clues. The root of that word is **just**, one of the spellings of **jur**, and the suffix **-ice** makes it a noun. Since the idea of what is *just* is often expressed as what is *fair*, let's write **justice** in the blank for the first sentence."

COMPLETE THE ACTIVITY

This can be quite challenging, so allow students to work on this activity in small groups. Not every word in the Word Bank will be used.

DISCUSS After about 10 minutes, ask if there were any difficulties. Have volunteers explain strategies they used that led to correct answers.

SAB
Pg 66

Mock Trial

For their project on <u>fairness</u>, the class decided to hold a mock trial of the Pied Piper of Hamelin. Officers of the court, lawyers for both sides, the Pied Piper, and <u>panel that serves to decide what is right</u> were chosen from the class.

Plaintiffs in the case were the townspeople of Hamelin who thought that the Piper's demand of payment was <u>not able to be argued as right and lawful</u>. They also argued that acts hurting the children as punishment for the town's non-payment were great <u>harmful deeds that are not right</u> to them. The deal with the Piper had to <u>be changed toward what is right</u>. The Piper, they argued, should have to restore the children to the town.

Defending himself, the Piper held that he had been treated <u>in a manner not correct in law</u> by the town's officials when they withheld payment for ridding the town of its rats. He further <u>argued to be right and lawful</u> his position by producing a contract signed by the city's mayor. Then each <u>person who considers what is right</u> retired to think about the case.

Who suffered the worse <u>harmful deed</u>: the Piper for non-payment, or the town for the kidnapping of the children? What would you decide?

<u>Fill in the blanks below using words from the "jur, jure, juri, jury, juris, jus, just" family.</u>

1. Everyone deserves <u>justice</u> and equal treatment.
2. The group that finally decides guilt or innocence is the <u>jury</u>.
3. Excessive demands and false arguments are <u>unjustifiable</u> in a court case.
4. The townspeople suffered many <u>injuries</u> by losing their children.
5. The people felt that the contract needed to be <u>adjusted</u> and altered.
6. The Piper felt that he had been <u>unjustly</u> treated by the people.
7. The Piper <u>justified</u> his actions since he had not been paid.
8. Each <u>juror</u> of the panel had to decide what was right.
9. Which side suffered the greater <u>injustice</u>?

<u>Not Used:</u> reinjures   adjusting   perjury

OPTIONAL

Day 5
Morpheme Mania
for **JUR**

JUR means
law; right, true; to swear an oath

LESSON TIME

15 Minutes

OBJECTIVES

- **Build** words in the **JUR** family

- **Apply** knowledge of synonyms and antonyms to **JUR** words

Optional Morpheme Mania for **JUR**

On page 67 of their Activity Books, students will see an optional vocabulary enrichment activity that they can work on in groups, time permitting. This activity makes a great review for the formal assessment on the next page.

All the affixes presented in the week's activities are provided at the top of the page on either side of the root of the week in all its forms. Students can write in up to 13 of the words they built during the week, possibly discovering additional ones.

Then students can brainstorm with each other to come up with antonyms and synonyms they may know. Starter examples are given with every Morpheme Mania in the Activity Book. Because antonyms and synonyms may require knowledge of roots which students have not yet studied, completion of this activity is not crucial. Simply remind students that they can at any time during the course of the year revisit any of their Morpheme Mania pages and add words, antonyms, and synonyms as their vocabulary grows.

Day 5 *Assessment*

Make and hand out copies.
The answer key is on page A-4.
The instructions are on page A-2.

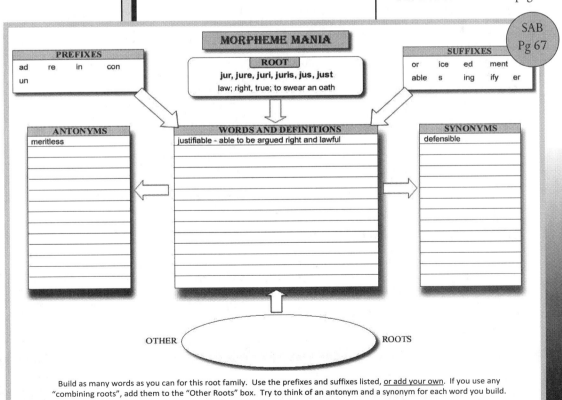

MORPHEME MANIA

PREFIXES			
ad	re	in	con
un			

ROOT
jur, jure, juri, juris, jus, just
law; right, true; to swear an oath

SUFFIXES			
or	ice	ed	ment
able	s	ing	ify	er

SAB
Pg 67

ANTONYMS
meritless

WORDS AND DEFINITIONS
justifiable - able to be argued right and lawful

SYNONYMS
defensible

OTHER ROOTS

Build as many words as you can for this root family. Use the prefixes and suffixes listed, or add your own. If you use any "combining roots", add them to the "Other Roots" box. Try to think of an antonym and a synonym for each word you build.

adjust to change toward what is right; to correct

adjustable able to be changed toward what is right; able to be corrected

adjusted changed toward what is right; corrected

adjuster a person who seeks to make right or correct

adjusters people who seek to make right or correct

adjusting changing toward what is right; correcting

adjustment act of changing toward what is right; correction

adjustments acts of changing toward what is right; corrections

adjusts changes toward what is right; corrects

conjurer a person who swears an oath with someone; person who calls up a magic spirit

conjurers people who swear oaths with others; people who call up a magic spirit

conjuror a person who swears an oath with someone; person who calls up a magic spirit

conjurors people who swear oaths together; people who call up a magic spirit

injure to do something not right or lawful; to harm

injured did something not right or lawful; harmed

injurer a person who does something not right or lawful; a person who harms

injurers people who do things not right or lawful; people who harm

injures does something not right or lawful; harms

injuries deeds not right or lawful; harmful things

injuring doing something not right or lawful; harming

injurious having the quality of not acting in the right way

injury a deed not right or lawful; something harmful

injust not right or lawful; unfair

injustice a situation that is not right or lawful; unfairness

injustices situations that are not right or lawful; acts of unfairness

juries groups of people sworn to consider what is right; deciding panels

jurisdiction area of authority to state and enforce the law

jurisdictions areas of authority to state and enforce the law

juror a person who serves to consider what is right; a panelist

jurors people who serve to judge what is right; panelists

jury a group of people sworn to consider what is right; a deciding panel

just right; correct according to law

justice a situation that is right or lawful; fairness

justices situations that are right or lawful; acts of fairness

justifiable able to be argued right and lawful; defensible

justifiably in a manner able to be argued right and lawful; defensibly

justified argued to be right and lawful; gave a good reason for

justifies argues to be right and lawful; gives a good reason for

justify to argue to be right or lawful; to give a good reason for

justly in a manner correct according to law

perjure to make a thoroughly false oath

perjured made a thoroughly false oath

perjures makes a thoroughly false oath

perjuring making a thoroughly false oath

perjury an act of making a thoroughly false oath

readjust to change again toward what is right

readjustable able to be changed again toward what is right

readjusted changed again toward what is right

readjusting changing again toward what is right

readjustment act of changing again toward what is right

readjustments acts of changing again toward what is right

readjusts changes again toward what is right

reinjure to do something again not right or lawful; to harm again

reinjured did something again not right or lawful; harmed again

reinjures does something not right or lawful; harms again

reinjuring doing something not right or lawful; harming again

unjust not right or correct according to law

unjustifiable not able to be argued right and lawful; not defensible

unjustifiably in a manner not able to be argued right and lawful; not defensibly

unjustly in a manner not correct according to law

Check-Up for **JUR**

Name _____

____ **1.** **JUR** or **JUS** in words like **injury** and **adjust** means:

   A to fall or stumble

   B to hurt

   C right or true

____ **2.** What is the meaning of the word **adjusts**?

   A causes to fall forward

   B changes toward what is right

   C hurts

____ **3.** What is the meaning of the word **conjurer**?

   A a person who swears an oath with someone

   B anything that causes you to stumble and fall

   C a result of being hurt

____ **4.** What is the meaning of the word **jurors**?

   A methods of falling safely

   B wounds or hurts

   C people selected to decide what is right

____ **5.** What is an **injustice**?

   A a situation that is not right or fair

   B a condition of stumbling

   C the process of putting fairness into a situation

____ **6.** Which word means **act of swearing something thoroughly false**?

   A perjury

   B injury

   C jury

____ **7.** Which word means **not able to be argued to be right**?

   A injustice

   B unjustifiable

   C perjuring

____ **8.** Which word means **people who change something back to being correct**?

   A perjurers

   B readjustors

   C injurers

____ **9.** The doctor discovered that Eric's arm was **maladjusted** after the cast was taken off. The arm:

   A hadn't been placed back correctly

   B was perfectly well

   C was broken again

____ **10.** Paula said she would **abjure** trusting Lena. Paula:

   A will now always trust Lena

   B will tell everyone that Lena can be trusted

   C swore off trusting Lena

133

GRAD
meaning "step; to go"

OBJECTIVES

- **Understand** the meaning of the root **GRAD**
- **Build** words in the root **GRAD** family
- **Break Apart** words in the root **GRAD** family
- **Understand** the meaning of words in the **GRAD** family
- **Understand** the spelling principles applied to the root **GRAD**
- **Apply** knowledge of words in the **GRAD** family
- **Assess** and **Reinforce** knowledge of words in the **GRAD** family

MATERIALS

- Student Activity Books, pages 69-74
- Dictionary *(print or on-line)*
- a ruler or yardstick *(optional)*
- copies of a simple maze *(optional)*

CROSS-CURRICULAR EXAMPLES

Science:
biodegradable, centigrade, graduated

Social Studies:
progress, congress, aggression

Language Arts:
digression, transgression

Math:
progression, gradual

gradual
in **steps**

progress
to go forward

Morpheme: **GRAD**
Allomorphs: **GRADE, GRESS**

Nearly 300 words containing the morpheme **GRAD** or one of its allomorphs are current in English. During this unit, tell students to be alert for this root in their school texts, general reading, and oral language they hear. Some of the words they might encounter in their school subjects are listed on the left under Cross-Curricular Examples.

UNIT AT A GLANCE

Day **1**
Root Squares
for **GRAD**

Day **2**
Magic Squares
for **GRAD**

Day **3**
Stair Steps
for **GRAD**

OPTIONAL
Day **4**
In Other Words
for **GRAD**

Day **5**
Assessment or Morpheme Mania
for **GRAD**

Each activity should take approximately **15 minutes**.

One free or unbound allomorph of this root can be used as a noun (*a grade*) or a verb (*to grade*). Another unbound form, the noun **grad**, is a shortening, or back-formation of the noun **graduate**.

The manner in which an animal walks gives such biological terms as **gravigrade**, *walking heavily*, as an elephant does; **plantigrade**, *walking on the full flat of the foot*, as we humans do; **pinnigrade**, *walking by means of flippers*, as seals or walruses do; and **digitigrade**, *walking on toes*, as cats and dogs can do. How do you think a creature described as **tardigrade** walks? (*in a slow manner*).

Of course, **centigrade** does not mean walking on a hundred feet, as a centipede might, but rather it means *divided into one hundred steps*.

As seen from the earth, some planets seem to move backward from their regular course. Such a movement is called **retrograde** motion.

Another allomorph of this root, **gred**, gives us the word **ingredient**, an item that has "stepped into" a compound to help create it or make it up.

Word Alert!

Only a very few words with the letter sequences **g-r-a-d** and **g-r-e-s-s** do not belong to this root family. While they are not words likely to come up in class, they are interesting and deserve notice.

Graddan is *parched grain* in Celtic English dialects.

The literary term **gradgrind** was coined from the materialistic, all-fact-and-no-fancy Dickensian character, Thomas Gradgrind. Dickens was famous for coining appropriate names, and it could be that he had in mind something playful like walking in a grind.

The word **ogress** is a *female ogre, or monster*. It is also a technical term for a dark black circle in heraldry, possibly stemming from the Latin deity of the dark underworld, Orcus.

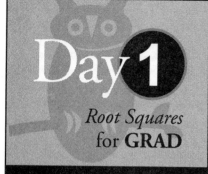

Day 1

Root Squares for GRAD

GRAD means *step; to go*

LESSON TIME

15 Minutes

OBJECTIVES

- **Understand** the meaning of the root **GRAD**

- **Build** words in the **GRAD** family

- **Understand** the meaning of words in the **GRAD** family

- **Understand** the spelling principles applied to the root **GRAD**

MATERIALS

- Student Activity Book
- **GRAD** Word Wall
- Dictionary *(print or on-line)*

DIFFERENTIATING INSTRUCTION

If you prefer easier or more difficult activities, use your personal account at www.dynamicliteracy.com to access novice or expert versions, along with ideas on using them.

Root Squares for GRAD

TEACH Have students turn to page 69 in their Activity Books. Note with your students that two new affixes occur: **ag-** and **-uate**, and refer to the Mini-Lessons found on the next page of this manual. Then call attention to the center box. Point out that the root **GRAD** has three different spellings, called allomorphs. Ask students to decide if one of the forms they see in the middle square can stand alone as a word.

They will see that **grade** is a word, and you can use that word to guide them to the meaning *step, or to go*. Explore how these meanings relate to **grade**. Each **grade** level in school is another *step* in a person's educational progress. Suggest that students continue their list with **gress** and then add the prefix **trans-**, meaning *across*, and the suffix **-ion**,

meaning *result or outcome*, to build **transgression**, meaning *the result or outcome of stepping across*. Invite students to explore how this word is related to the idea of *step, or to go*.

COMPLETE THE ACTIVITY

Have students follow the directions for the activity on page 69 to build words. If students have difficulty building words with the Root Squares, show them how by modeling the matrix approach found on the next page, taking one affix at a time and seeing if it will connect with any one of the allomorphs of the root.

DISCUSS After five minutes, have volunteers write some of their words on the board. Focus with the class on the words they have built and guide them in a discussion of how the meaning of the root is still *step, or to go*, even when prefixes and suffixes are added. Watch for target words that most easily demonstrate the meanings of *step, or to go*. If the word **progress** is not present, ask the class, "Can anyone try to use the prefix **pro-**?" and then continue on to the target word discussion on the next page.

Root Squares

How many words can you make?

Start in any square. Your goal is to combine two or more word parts to make as many words in the 'grad, grade, gress' family as you can. Write each word and a definition you can think of for it in the space provided at the bottom of the page. Use the back of the page if you need to.

trans	ive	ag
pro	grad, grade, gress	ion
di	uate	con

SAB Pg 69

MINI-LESSON: the Suffix -uate

The suffix **-ate**, meaning *to cause to become*, is spelled **-uate** when attached to a root ending in the letters **t**, **s**, or **d** (called dentals). This added letter **u** reflects a change in pronunciation called palatalization, a sound like **sh**, **zh**, **ch**, or **j**. Students can hear this change by comparing the following pairs of words:

| accent - accentuate | effect - effectuate | event - eventuate | habit - habituate |

The sound can also be heard in these familiar words: **punctuate, fluctuate, perpetuate, situate**

MINI-LESSON: the Prefix ag-

The prefix **ag-** is an assimilation of the prefix **ad-**, meaning *to or toward*. **Ad-** will become **ag-** before roots that begin with the letter **g**. Let students pronounce these unassimilated words, and they can detect why the assimilation occurs.

| adgravate | adgression | adgrieve | adgregate |

Focus Word: **PROGRESS** ⟶ Write this word on the board.

TEACH

Lead with this:	"Take a look at this word. First, would someone pronounce it for us?"
Student:	"**Prógress**." (pronouncing it with stress on the first syllable).
Student:	"**Progréss**." (pronouncing it with stress on the last syllable).
Teacher:	"Good. The word is pronounced two different ways. Do the different pronunciations make any difference in meaning?"
Student:	"One is a noun and one is a verb. **Prógress** is *improvement or getting ahead*, while **progréss** means *to improve or to get ahead.*"
Student:	"So they mean kind of the same thing, but they would be used in two different ways."
Teacher:	"Right—no matter where the accent or stress, the word still has the same structure of meaning, based on its morphemes. What are those morphemes?"
Student:	"The prefix **pro-** means *forward*."
Student:	"And the root means *step or go*. So *go forward* is what the word means."
Student:	"Or a *step forward.*"

DISCUSS Lead students to see that, based on its two pieces of meaning, **progress**, no matter which way it is pronounced, means *step forward*.

DEMONSTRATE Ask several students to **progréss** toward the door (or window or bookcase). As they are **progréssing**, ask them what they are making (**prógress**).

Root Squares Matrix
You can refer to this matrix to guide students in this activity. Students could build at least these 15 words. *It is not important how many words are built*, so long as students understand the meanings of the root and its affixes. Encourage discussion about the definitions of any words formed for the blank slots as well as for the attested words.

	no prefix	ag-	con-	di-	pro-	trans-
no suffix	grade		congress	digress	progress	transgress
-ion		aggression	congression	digression	progression	transgression
-ive		aggressive		digressive	progressive	transgressive
-uate	graduate					

Day 2

Magic Squares
for **GRAD**

GRAD means
step; to go

LESSON TIME

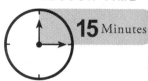

15 Minutes

OBJECTIVES

- **Understand** the meaning of the root **GRAD**
- **Break Apart** words in the **GRAD** family
- **Understand** the meanings of words in the **GRAD** family

MATERIALS

- Student Activity Book
- **GRAD** Word Wall
- Dictionary *(print or on-line)*
- A ruler or yardstick *(optional)*

DIFFERENTIATING INSTRUCTION

If you prefer easier or more difficult activities, use your personal account at www.dynamicliteracy.com to access novice or expert versions, along with ideas on using them.

Break Apart Words with **GRAD**

TEACH Have students turn to the Magic Squares on page 70 in their Student Activity Books. Model a Think-Aloud strategy for students: "I know that **GRAD** and the several different spellings of this root mean *step; to go*. I can use this knowledge to find the definition of a word with this as its root."

Direct students to word **C**, **progression**. Say, "I know one of the meanings of the prefix **pro-** is *forward* and the suffix **-ion** creates a noun meaning *result or outcome of an action or process*. All these ideas, including the idea of *to go*, are in definition **2**, *an act or process of going forward*. Let's write the number **2** in square **C**.

COMPLETE THE ACTIVITY

Ask students to use the same strategy to find the correct definitions for the other words. Tell them to write the number of the definition in the box that matches the letter for the word. Remind them that if all their answers are correct, each row and each column will add up to the same Magic number.

DISCUSS After five minutes, ask if there are any difficulties about matching the words and definitions. If there are, ask volunteers to explain clues in the definitions that will lead to the correct choice of word. As needed, follow the focus word approach for **gradual** that you see modeled on the next page.

Add any new words to the classroom **GRAD** Word Wall and remind students to add these words to the **GRAD** Word Wall in their Activity Books.

SAB
Pg 70

Magic Squares

Select the best answer for each of the words in the 'grad, grade, gress' family from the numbered definitions. Put the number in the proper space in the Magic Square box. If the total of the numbers is the same both across and down, you have found the magic number!

'grad, grade, gress' means step; to go

WORDS	DEFINITIONS
A. aggressions	1. stepping down; demeaning
B. transgressor	2. an act or process of going forward
C. progression	3. completing necessary steps; measuring in steps
D. digressed	4. went off apart; wandered or rambled
E. congressional	5. a measurement with 100 steps or degrees
F. regressed	6. stepped back; became worse
G. centigrade	7. a person who steps across or beyond; a person who does wrong
H. graduating	8. pertaining to a group that walks or goes together; relating to a council
I. gradual	9. acts of stepping toward; hostilities
	10. in steps; by slow movements

Magic Square Box

A. 9	B. 7	C. 2
D. 4	E. 8	F. 6
G. 5	H. 3	I. 10

Magic Number <u>18</u>

*** ANSWER KEY ***

138

MINI-LESSON: the Prefix cent-

This numerical prefix comes from the Latin word for *one hundred*, that is, **centum**. The **C** in Roman numerals, meaning 100, comes from the first letter of this word. Students will know that if they answer 90 out of 100 questions correctly, they earn ninety **percent**. Ask students if they know any of these:

What do we call a period of 100 years? (a **century**)   How old is a **centenarian**? (100 or more)

How many legs does a **centipede** have? (etymologically 100)   Why are pennies called **cents**? (100 in a dollar)

As a scientific prefix, **cent-** means not *one hundred* but *one hundredth*, as in **centimeter** (one-hundredth of a meter), **centiliter** (one-hundredth of a liter), etc.

MINI-LESSON: the Suffix -ual

The suffix **-ual** is a variation of **-al**, meaning *like or characterized by*. This variation reflects the pronunciation change called **palatalization** that is discussed above with the Mini-Lesson on **-uate**. Pronouncing the following words will show this pronunciation and spelling principle:

act	accent	reside	rite	use
actual	accentual	residual	ritual	usual

Not every root that ends in a dental sound requires the letter **u** before adding the suffix **-al**. There are many exceptions with familiar words, and the lack of the palatalized sound (**ch**, **j**, **sh**, or **zh**) is a clue that the suffix is spelled **-al** and not **-ual**: **accidental, pedal, nasal, coastal, tidal, appraisal, vital, societal, disposal, reversal.**

Focus Word: GRADUAL ➡ Write this word on the board.

TEACH

Sample leading question:	"I heard the weather forecaster announce that there would be a **gradual** rise in temperature this week. What does that mean?"
Student:	"It means it will be warmer and warmer every day."
Teacher:	"How much warmer will it be each day? A lot? Not much?"
Student:	"It will be slow or step-by-step, not all at once."
Teacher:	"Let's go see what that **-ual** suffix is on this root."
Student:	(Looking in the inside back cover of the Student Activity Book) "It's not here."
Student:	"Yes it is—it's back up there with **-al**. It's a variation of **-al**. *Characterized by.*"
Student:	"So, **gradual** means *characterized by steps*, or *moving by steps*."
Student:	"Why is the word pronounced like it has a **j** in it? You can say **grad-u-al**."
Student:	"Yes, but most people say it faster than that and the **d** sounds like a **j**: **gra-ju-al**."
Teacher:	"That's the effect of the letter **u**, and why the suffix **-ual** is listed along with the suffix **-al**. How would you pronounce **G-R-A-D-A-L**?"

DISCUSS Word play with pronunciation and morphemic variations is a worthwhile topic, so explore this as often as it happens. Lead students to see that **gradual** means like *steps*. You can introduce students to the language phenomenon called **palatalization** (see Mini-Lessons for **-uate** and **-ual** in this unit).

DEMONSTRATE Lay a ruler flat on a surface and ask what its slope is. (Zero). Hold the ruler straight up, perpendicular to the surface, and ask about the slope. Ask students how you should hold the ruler for it to have a **gradual** slope. Show them how to make the slope **gradually** steeper as you tilt it more.

Day 3

Stair Steps for GRAD

GRAD means step; to go

LESSON TIME

15 Minutes

OBJECTIVES

- **Understand** the meaning of the root **GRAD**
- **Apply** knowledge of the root **GRAD**
- **Break Apart** words in the **GRAD** family
- **Understand** the meaning of words in the **GRAD** family
- **Understand** the spelling principles applied to the root **GRAD**

MATERIALS

- Student Activity Book
- **GRAD** Word Wall
- copies of a simple drawn maze (optional)

DIFFERENTIATING INSTRUCTION

If you prefer easier or more difficult activities, use your personal account at www.dynamicliteracy.com to access novice or expert versions, along with ideas on using them.

Apply Knowledge of **GRAD**

TEACH Have students turn to page 71 in their Student Activity Books. Explain that the boxes in front of and after the root indicate letters that spell out prefixes and suffixes. Students will spell out the correct prefixes and suffixes determined by clues in the definitions at the bottom of the page.

Have a volunteer read definition number five at the bottom of the page. Say, "As we have seen before, the past tense of the definition will lead to the past tense marker at the end of the word we are building: the suffix **-ed**. We also need a prefix with

the meaning *forward or advance*. That would be the prefix **pro-**. Adding **-ed** and **pro-** here, we get **PROGRESSED**, the word with the meaning that goes with the definition *went forward* that we see for number five."

COMPLETE THE ACTIVITY

Let students work in pairs (optionally) and tell them to use the same strategy to find the correct prefixes and suffixes for the words listed. These activities can be quite challenging!

DISCUSS After a few minutes, review the answers as a class. Ask if there were any difficulties. Listen to any problems and have volunteers solve the difficulties by explaining key clues in the given definitions. As needed, follow the focus word approach that you see modeled on the next page.

SAB Pg 71

Stair Steps

Fill in the missing letters of each 'grad, grade, gress' word by using the definitions below.
'grad, grade, gress' means step; to go

1.	g	r	a	d	e	d				
2.	d	i	g	r	e	s	s			
3.	c	o	n	g	r	e	s	s		
4.	a	g	g	r	e	s	s	o	r	
5.	p	r	o	g	r	e	s	s	e	d
6.	d	i	g	r	e	s	s	i	o	n	s
7.	a	g	g	r	e	s	s	i	v	e	l	y
8.	p	r	o	g	r	e	s	s	i	v	e	l	y
9.	t	r	a	n	s	g	r	e	s	s	i	o	n	s

1. evaluated according to steps; assessed according to stages in a sequence
2. to go off apart; to wander or ramble
3. a group that walks or goes together; a council
4. anything that steps toward; a hostile person
5. went forward; advanced
6. acts of going apart; acts of wandering or rambling
7. in a manner stepping toward; in a hostile manner
8. in a manner moving forward in steps
9. acts of stepping across or beyond; violations

Focus Word: **DIGRESS** ⟶ Write this word on the board.

TEACH

Sample leading question:	"What happens if you **digress** from a topic?"
Student:	"That means you're talking about one thing and then you wind up talking about something not related."
Teacher:	"Do you mean to do it or does it just happen?"
Student:	"You could mean to do it. I've heard teachers say, 'Let's **digress** for a moment.'"
Teacher:	"Then maybe it's not entirely unrelated."
Student:	"I guess not, because a connection sometimes gets made. I love it when you suddenly realize that you're talking with friends about something completely different, and you say, 'How'd we get on that topic?' And then you try to make the connections back."
Student:	"Yes, and the connections are almost always there in some funny way."
Teacher:	"Yes, that is fun. And now back to the word itself—what's going on when you **digress**?"
Student:	"Let's look up **di**-. There it is with **dis**-, *not, apart, opposite of*, and so forth. *Not going*?"
Student:	"*Going apart.* You're going off the subject, apart from the main point."
Student:	"Yes, that's right. 'Let's **digress** for a moment,' means, '*let's talk about something else.*'"
Student:	"It also means *let's step apart from this line of thought.*'"

DISCUSS Lead students to see that, based on its pieces of meaning, **digress** means *to step apart*. If students ask if the word can be used other than for conversation or thought, you can use this opportunity to demonstrate language usage shift. There was a time in the English language when the word could mean literally *to step in another direction*, like off a path. Now that usage is called **archaic** or **obsolete**, but knowing that usage allows us to read older authors comfortably.

DEMONSTRATE Reproduce a simple maze for the class and let the students demonstrate a direct route through the maze and discuss the **digressions** that might occur.

Day 4

In Other Words
for **GRAD**

GRAD means
step; to go

LESSON TIME

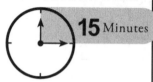

15 Minutes

OBJECTIVES

- **Understand** the meaning of the root **GRAD**
- **Reinforce** knowledge of the root **GRAD**
- **Understand** the meaning of words in the **GRAD** family
- **Apply** knowledge of words in the **GRAD** family

MATERIALS

- Student Activity Book
- **GRAD** Word Wall
- Dictionary *(print or on-line)*

In Other Words for **GRAD**

TEACH Have students turn to page 72 in their Student Activity Books. Explain that they are going to read a little story that uses some surprising and sometimes odd phrasing. The underlined words or phrases in the story are actually definitions or synonyms for words in the **GRAD** family. Then they will see sentences about the story, each containing a blank. Using context clues in the sentences, they will find a **GRAD** family word in the Word Bank at the bottom to fit in each blank. Have a student read aloud the opening sentence or sentences of the story that contain the first underlined phrase. Then say, "Let's look at the first numbered sentence that contains a

blank to be filled in. Clues in the sentence tell us that we want a naming word, a noun that means *a step across in violation of rules.* I see the word **transgression** at the bottom of the page. The prefix **trans-** takes care of the idea of *across* and the suffix **-ion** makes the word a noun. **Transgress** means *to step across,* which seems to be what happened in this story. So, let's write **transgression** in the blank for the first sentence."

COMPLETE THE ACTIVITY
This can be quite challenging, so allow students to work on this activity in small groups. Not every word in the Word Bank will be used.

DISCUSS After about 10 minutes, ask if there were any difficulties. Have volunteers explain strategies they used that led to correct answers.

SAB
Pg 72

Useless, Never-ending Work

King Sisyphus, who thought he was better and smarter than the gods of Greece, once managed to tie up Hades, the god of the underworld, so that nothing on earth would die. This <u>step across in violation</u> against gods and men halted the natural <u>stepping forward</u> of life and death. Even warriors, hacked to bits in battle, would not die, and <u>in slow-step manner</u> the earth became too crowded. Hades finally escaped from Sisyphus' trickery and ordered him to appear in the underworld for punishment.

However, Sisyphus had another trick up his sleeve. Planning in <u>step together</u> with his wife, Sisyphus arranged not to have an official funeral service. When he got to the underworld, he <u>stepped back</u> to childish behavior and begged Queen Persephone to allow him to go home for a proper burial. (Queen Persephone is in the underworld herself as a result of a trick, but we must not <u>step apart</u> from Sisyphus' story.)

Hades grows angry <u>in a manner moving forward</u> with Sisyphus and sentences him to eternal labor. Sisyphus' task is to roll a boulder up a steep hill, a task that he undertakes <u>in a hostile manner</u>, sweat popping from his brow. After he rolls the boulder to the top of the hill, it rolls back down the steep <u>slope</u>. Sisyphus has to start all over again and again forever.

<u>Fill in the blanks below using words from the "grad, grade, gress" family.</u>

1. Sisyphus made some serious <u>transgressions</u> against the rules of gods and men.
2. There is a natural <u>progression</u> in life as we are born, grow up, and pass from earth.
3. <u>Gradually</u> earth filled up with too many people.
4. Sisyphus' wife planned in <u>congress</u> with him to trick Hades again.
5. In order to sweet-talk the queen, Sisyphus <u>regressed</u> to the habits of a young child.
6. Telling Persephone's story would be to <u>digress</u> from the story of Sisyphus.
7. Hades' ill will toward Sisyphus piled up as he became <u>progressively</u> angrier.
8. Sisyphus pushes the boulder so <u>aggressively</u> that it becomes a tough workout.
9. The steep <u>grade</u> of the hill made Sisyphus' task even harder.

<u>Not Used:</u> degrading grader centigrade

Day 5

Morpheme Mania
for **GRAD**

GRAD means
step; to go

LESSON TIME

15 Minutes

OBJECTIVES

• **Build** words in the
GRAD family

• **Apply** knowledge of
synonyms and antonyms
to **GRAD** words

Optional
Morpheme Mania
for **GRAD**

On page 73 of their Activity
Books, students will see an
optional vocabulary enrichment
activity that they can work on in
groups, time permitting. This
activity makes a great review for
the formal assessment on the next
page.

All the affixes presented in the
week's activities are provided at
the top of the page on either side
of the root of the week in all its
forms. Students can write in up to
13 of the words they built during
the week, possibly discovering
additional ones.

Then students can brainstorm
with each other to come up with
antonyms and synonyms they may
know. Starter examples are given
with every Morpheme Mania
in the Activity Book. Because
antonyms and synonyms may
require knowledge of roots which
students have not yet studied,
completion of this activity is not
crucial. Simply remind students
that they can at any time during
the course of the year revisit any
of their Morpheme Mania pages
and add words, antonyms, and
synonyms as their vocabulary
grows.

Day 5 Assessment

Make and hand out copies.
The answer key is on page A-4.
The instructions are on page A-2.

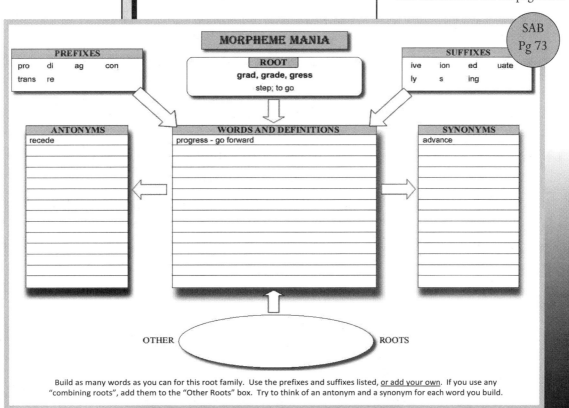

SAB
Pg 73

MORPHEME MANIA

PREFIXES

| pro | di | ag | con |
| trans | re | | |

ROOT

grad, grade, gress

step; to go

SUFFIXES

| ive | ion | ed | uate |
| ly | s | ing | |

ANTONYMS

recede

WORDS AND DEFINITIONS

progress - go forward

SYNONYMS

advance

OTHER   ROOTS

Build as many words as you can for this root family. Use the prefixes and suffixes listed, <u>or add your own</u>. If you use any
"combining roots", add them to the "Other Roots" box. Try to think of an antonym and a synonym for each word you build.

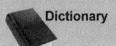

aggression an act of stepping toward; hostility

aggressions acts of stepping toward; hostilities

aggressive tending to step toward; hostile

aggressively in a manner stepping toward; in a hostile manner

aggressor anything that steps toward; a hostile person

aggressors things that step toward; hostile people

centigrade a measurement with 100 steps or degrees

congress a group that walks or goes together; a council

congresses groups that walk or go together; councils

congressional pertaining to a group that walks or goes together; relating to a council

degrade to step down; to demean

degraded stepped down; demeaned

degrades steps down; demeans

degrading stepping down; demeaning

digress to go off apart; to wander or ramble

digressed went off apart; wandered or rambled

digresses goes off apart; wanders or rambles

digressing going off apart; wandering or rambling

digression an act of going apart; act of wandering or rambling

digressions acts of going apart; acts of wandering or rambling

grad a person who has gone through steps; a person who has completed school

gradation the quality of having steps; a progression or sequence

gradations qualities of having steps; progressions or sequences

grade a step; a stage in a sequence

graded having steps; assessed according to stages in a sequence

grader a person who evaluates according to steps

graders people who evaluate according to steps

grades steps; stages in a sequence

grading evaluating according to steps

grads people who have gone through steps; people who have completed school

gradual in steps; by slow movements

gradually in a manner of steps; in a manner of slow movements

graduate to complete necessary steps; to measure in steps

graduated completed necessary steps; measured in steps

graduates completes necessary steps; measures in steps

graduating completing necessary steps; measuring in steps

graduation the process of moving to the next step

graduations processes of moving to the next step

progress to go forward; the benefits of moving forward

progressed went forward; advanced

progresses goes forward in steps; advances

progressing going forward; advancing

progression an act or process of going forward

progressional pertaining to the process of going forward

progressions acts or processes of going forward

progressive moving forward in steps

progressively in a manner moving forward in steps

regress to step back; to become worse

regressed stepped back; became worse

regresses steps back; becomes worse

regressing stepping back; becoming worse

transgress to step across or beyond; to violate

transgressed stepped across or beyond; violated

transgresses steps across or beyond; violates

transgressing stepping across or beyond; violating

transgression act of stepping across or beyond; a violation

transgressions acts of stepping across or beyond; violations

transgressor a person who steps across or beyond; a person who does wrong

transgressors people who step across or beyond; people who do wrong

Check-Up for **GRAD**

Name _____

____ **1.** **GRAD** or **GRESS** in words like **graduate** and **progress** means:

    A to demand

    B to throw

    C to step

____ **2.** What is the meaning of the word **regress**?

    A to ask for again

    B to go back

    C to toss away

____ **3.** What is the meaning of the word **digression**?

    A an act of going apart

    B the process of demanding strongly

    C a result of throwing in different directions

____ **4.** What is the meaning of the word **progress**?

    A to throw something back

    B to ask for a raises

    C movement forward

____ **5.** What is a **graduated** cylinder? A cylinder or glass tube that:

    A is full of liquid

    B throws out heat

    C indicates regular steps of measurement

____ **6.** Which word means **an act of stepping toward**?

    A aggression

    B aggressive

    C aggressor

____ **7.** Which word means **someone who steps across a boundary**?

    A congressional

    B transgressor

    C grader

____ **8.** Which word means **a result of putting down a step**?

    A degradation

    B retrogresses

    C centigrade

____ **9.** A building's **ingress** and **egress** are its:

    A height

    B doorways

    C location

____ **10.** A **gradation** from red to violet makes the rainbow. A **gradation** is:

    A water droplets thrown against clouds

    B brightness of colors

    C a series of steps

GRAPH

meaning "something written, drawn, or recorded; chart"

OBJECTIVES

- **Understand** the meaning of the root **GRAPH**
- **Build** words in the root **GRAPH** family
- **Break Apart** words in the root **GRAPH** family
- **Understand** the meaning of words in the **GRAPH** family
- **Understand** the spelling principles applied to the root **GRAPH**
- **Apply** knowledge of words in the **GRAPH** family
- **Assess** and **Reinforce** knowledge of words in the **GRAPH** family

MATERIALS

- Student Activity Books, pages 75-80
- Dictionary *(print or on-line)*

CROSS-CURRICULAR EXAMPLES

Science:
cardiograph, graphite, photography, thermography

Social Studies:
chronographer, demographics, geographic

Language Arts:
paragraph, biography, orthography, epigraphy, digraph

Math:
polygraphic, graphing

biography
a **writing** about a person's life

topography
the **drawing** of a region

graphics
detailed **recordings**

graph
chart

Morpheme: **GRAPH**
Allomorphs: **none**

Over 800 words containing the morpheme **GRAPH** are current in English. During this unit, tell students to be alert for this root in their school texts, general reading, and oral language they hear. Some of the words they might encounter in their school subjects are listed on the left under Cross-Curricular Examples.

UNIT AT A GLANCE

Day ① *Root Squares* for **GRAPH**

Day ② *Magic Squares* for **GRAPH**

Day ③ *Stair Steps* for **GRAPH**

OPTIONAL
Day ④ *In Other Words* for **GRAPH**

Day ⑤ *Assessment or Morpheme Mania* for **GRAPH**

Each activity should take approximately **15 minutes**.

Word Fun Facts

This root originally meant *to scratch*, a reference to how writing was first done (scratched onto clay tablets or waxed surfaces). Writing scratched onto walls is still called by the Italian form of this morpheme, **graffito**, with its plural **graffiti**.

The root **graph** is an unbound morpheme, standing alone as a word, either as a noun (a **graph**), an adjective (**graph** paper), or a verb (to **graph**). Any prefixes added to this root will generate this exact same variety of parts of speech, providing a good opportunity to observe student ability to manipulate the same words in different contexts and different parts of speech. Observe this ability by asking for sentences in a pattern such as, "We **telegraphed** (verb) the news in a **telegraph** (noun) from a **telegraph** (adjective) office."

A **paragraph**, literally, *written along side*, was once a distinctive mark (a forerunner of our modern "bullets") etched beside a text to set it off as its own unified section. The word then came to be that section itself, as it is used today.

This root combines with many others, particularly other Greek roots, such as **photo-**, **demo-**, **oceano-**, and **cinemato-**. Many of those combining roots will be recognizable to students, but trips to the dictionary are always to be encouraged.

Students should now know that a **morpheme** is a piece or form of a word that has meaning. A **phoneme** is a piece of a word that has sound. What is a **grapheme**? (a piece of a word that is *written*, a letter or accent mark).

Word Alert!

Every English word containing the letter sequence **g-r-a-p-h** belongs to this root family!

NOTE: These mini-lessons go with the Root Squares for GRAPH

MINI-LESSON: the Prefix **para-**

The prefix **para-** comes from the Greek preposition meaning *along side, beside*. Students may be familiar with occupations that indicate assistants to professionals:

paramedics **paralegals** **paratroopers** **paraprofessionals**

Parallel lines are those that stay *alongside* each other indefinitely.
Parasites are creatures that feed competitively *alongside* of others.
To **paraphrase** is to give a shortened version *alongside* a longer text.

Alert! Not every word beginning with **para-** is using this prefix. **Parasol** and **parachute**, for example, use the root **PAR**, presented later in this Manual.

MINI-LESSON: the Prefix **poly-**

The numerical prefix **poly-** is from a Greek word that means *several, many, or more than usual*. About 400 English words use this prefix, and more are added each year with advances in science and technology. Words most likely to be familiar with some students include the following: **polygon, polyglot, polygamy, polytheism, polytechnic.**

Henry VIII's wife Anne Boleyn and blues guitarist Hound Dog Taylor had six fingers (*dactyls*) on one of their hands, and they therefore had a condition called **polydactylism**.

Day 1

Root Squares for **GRAPH**

GRAPH means something written, drawn, or recorded; chart

LESSON TIME

15 Minutes

OBJECTIVES

- **Understand** the meaning of the root **GRAPH**

- **Build** words in the **GRAPH** family

- **Understand** the meaning of words in the **GRAPH** family

- **Understand** the spelling principles applied to the root **GRAPH**

MATERIALS

- Student Activity Book
- **GRAPH** Word Wall
- Dictionary *(print or on-line)*

DIFFERENTIATING INSTRUCTION

If you prefer easier or more difficult activities, use your personal account at www.dynamicliteracy.com to access novice or expert versions, along with ideas on using them.

Root Squares for GRAPH

TEACH Have students turn to page 75 in their Activity Books. Say, "Let's take a look at a few of the prefixes and suffixes with this activity." Refer to Mini-lessons or review references found on the next page of this manual as needed.

Then call attention to the center box. Point out that the root **GRAPH** has only this one spelling. Ask students to decide if **GRAPH** in the middle square can stand alone as a word. They will recognize that **graph** is a word, and you can use that word to guide them to the meaning *something written, drawn, or recorded; chart*. Have students start their word list with **graph**.

COMPLETE THE ACTIVITY

Have students follow the directions for the activity on page 75 to build words. If students have difficulty building words with the Root Squares, show them how by modeling the matrix approach found on the next page, taking one affix at a time and seeing if it will connect with the root.

DISCUSS After five minutes, have volunteers write some of their words on the board. Focus with the class on the words they have built and guide them in a discussion of how the meaning of the root is still something *written, drawn, or recorded; chart*, even when prefixes and suffixes are added. Watch for target words that most easily demonstrate the meanings of something *written, drawn, or recorded; chart*. If the word **graphic** is not present, ask the class, "Can anyone try to use the suffix **-ic**?" and then continue on to the focus word discussion on the next page.

SAB Pg 75

Root Squares

How many words can you make?

Start in any square. Your goal is to combine two or more word parts to make as many words in the 'graph' family as you can. Write each word and a definition you can think of for it in the space provided at the bottom of the page. Use the back of the page if you need to.

para	ic	auto
er	graph	poly
bio	tele	y

Day 1 Extend the Learning

MINI-LESSON Reminder

Mini-Lessons on the prefixes **auto-** and **tele-**, as well as on the suffixes -**ic**, and -**y**, were presented in *WordBuild Elements 1*, and can be accessed on the Dynamic Literacy website by using your personal account. Directions for creating your account can be found on the inside front cover of this Teachers Edition.

Focus Word: **GRAPHIC** ⟶ Write this word on the board.

TEACH

Lead with this:	"Has anyone ever heard of this word?"
Student:	"I thinks it's pictures and art in a book."
Student:	"It means detailed and clear."
Teacher:	"Good. Both definitions are right. Now let's find out why. What do we see in the word **graphic**?"
Student:	"The root we're working on and a suffix -**ic**."
Student:	"The root, meaning *anything written or drawn*, makes sense for both definitions. Let's see, the suffix means (consulting the inside back cover of the Student Activity Book) two things—it can be an adjective or a noun."
Student:	"That's why there are two definitions!"
Student:	"*Like* or *a thing characterized by*."
Student:	"So *detailed and clear* is a definition of **graphic** because that would mean *like something written down or drawn*."
Student:	"And art or pictures are *things drawn*."

DISCUSS Lead students to see that, based on its two pieces of meaning, **graphic**, whether it is used as an adjective or as a noun, means *like or characterized by something written or drawn*. Let students understand that a **graphic** makes things more **graphic**.

DEMONSTRATE Many good dictionaries have little pictures beside some words to help illustrate and clarify meanings. Find one and let the students determine how the **graphic** makes the meaning of the word more **graphic**.

Root Squares Matrix
You can refer to this matrix to guide students in this activity. Students could build at least these 23 words. ***It is not important how many words are built***, so long as students understand the meanings of the root and its affixes.

	no prefix	auto-	bio-	para-	poly-	tele-
no suffix	graph	autograph	biograph	paragraph	polygraph	telegraph
-er	grapher	autographer	biographer	paragrapher	polygrapher	telegrapher
-ic	graphic	autographic	biographic	paragraphic	polygraphic	telegraphic
-y	graphy	autography	biography		polygraphy	telegraphy

GRAPH means something written, drawn, or recorded; chart

LESSON TIME

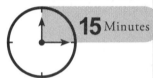

15 Minutes

OBJECTIVES

- **Understand** the meaning of the root **GRAPH**

- **Break Apart** words in the **GRAPH** family

- **Understand** the meanings of words in the **GRAPH** family

MATERIALS

- Student Activity Book

- **GRAPH** Word Wall

- Dictionary
  (print or on-line)

DIFFERENTIATING INSTRUCTION

If you prefer easier or more difficult activities, use your personal account at www.dynamicliteracy.com to access novice or expert versions, along with ideas on using them.

Break Apart Words with GRAPH

TEACH Have students turn to the Magic Squares on page 76 in their Student Activity Books. Model a Think-Aloud strategy for students: "I know that **GRAPH** means *written, drawn, or recorded; chart.* I can use this knowledge to find the definition of a word with this as its root."

Direct students to word F, **geography**. Say, "I see this as a compound root word, and the first half of this word, the root **GEO**, means *earth.* The suffix **-y** is *state, condition, or activity.* Definition 6 is *the drawing of the features of the earth.* Drawing is an *activity,* so that accounts for the suffix **-y**. Let's write the number 6 in square F."

COMPLETE THE ACTIVITY

Ask students to use the same strategy to find the correct definitions for the other words. Tell them to write the number of the definition in the box that matches the letter for the word. Remind them that if all their answers are correct, each row and each column will add up to the same Magic number.

DISCUSS After five minutes, ask if there are any difficulties about matching the words and definitions. If there are, ask volunteers to explain clues in the definitions that will lead to the correct choice of word. As needed, follow the focus word approach for **biography** that you see modeled on the next page.

Add any new words to the classroom **GRAPH** Word Wall and remind students to add these words to the **GRAPH** Word Wall in their Activity Books.

SAB Pg 76

Magic Squares

Select the best answer for each of the words in the 'graph' family from the numbered definitions. Put the number in the proper space in the Magic Square box. If the total of the numbers is the same both across and down, you have found the magic number!

'graph' means something written, drawn, or recorded; chart

WORDS	DEFINITIONS
A. autobiographic	1. the drawing of a region; the layout of the land
B. biography	2. indicating marks beside groups of written ideas; collections of sentences which concern a notion
C. paragraphs	3. related to writing about the earth
D. telegraphic	4. relating to a written message sent over a distance
E. polygraph	5. a person who records images on light sensitive paper; a person who takes pictures
F. geography	6. the drawing of the features of the earth
G. photographer	7. a writing about a person's life
H. geographic	8. a device that records many bits of data; a lie-detector
I. graphite	9. of a person's life story written by that person
	10. substance used for writing; pencil lead

Magic Square Box

A. 9	B. 7	C. 2
D. 4	E. 8	F. 6
G. 5	H. 3	I. 10

Magic Number __18__

*** ANSWER KEY ***

MINI-LESSON: the Combining Form **photo**

The root **photo** is from the Greek word for *light*. Over 300 English words, mostly biological and chemical, use the root as a prefix. As a shortening of the word **photograph**, the root has become a free, or unbound, morpheme in the form of the word **photo**.

Quite frequently, the prefix refers to **photography** itself, as in the following:

> **photogenic**, descriptive of people who are attractive in their pictures
> **photogeology**, analysis of earth's structures based on pictures
> **photocopy**, a reproduction of a picture

The prefix can refer literally to light, as in the following:

> **photophobia**, the fear or aversion to light
> **photosynthesis**, a chemical reaction in plants caused by sunlight
> **phototropic**, turning toward sunlight
> **photoactive**, responsive to light

Mini-Lessons on the Combining Forms **bio** and **geo** can be found on the Dynamic Literacy website.

Focus Word: **BIOGRAPHY** ⟶ Write this word on the board.

TEACH

Sample leading question:	"Here's a word we've all known since we started reading books. How many morphemes are in the word **biography**?"
Student:	"Easy—there are three."
Teacher:	"Good, and let's isolate and explain them."
Student:	"Our root, **graph**, is in the middle between a prefix and a suffix."
Student:	"The prefix has to do with *life and living things*, as in **biology**."
Student:	"And the suffix **-y** must mean *a thing*, a noun of some sort."
Teacher:	"Good, so putting the pieces together, what do we get?"
Student:	"A thing, I guess a book, written about a life."
Student:	"The list of suffixes says **-y** means *state, condition, or activity*. How is that a book?"
Student:	"A book is the activity of somebody writing."
Student:	"And the book is about somebody's life."

DISCUSS Let students talk about some **biographies** they have read and enjoyed.

DEMONSTRATE As an extended lesson, you can have students produce brief biographies about their parents, grandparents, or best friends.

Day 3

Stair Steps for GRAPH

GRAPH means something written, drawn, or recorded; chart

LESSON TIME

15 Minutes

OBJECTIVES

- **Understand** the meaning of the root **GRAPH**
- **Apply** knowledge of the root **GRAPH**
- **Break Apart** words in the **GRAPH** family
- **Understand** the meaning of words in the **GRAPH** family
- **Understand** the spelling principles applied to the root **GRAPH**

MATERIALS

- Student Activity Book
- **GRAPH** Word Wall

DIFFERENTIATING INSTRUCTION

If you prefer easier or more difficult activities, use your personal account at www.dynamicliteracy.com to access novice or expert versions, along with ideas on using them.

Apply Knowledge of GRAPH

TEACH   Have students turn to page 77 in their Student Activity Books.   Explain that the boxes in front of and after the root indicate letters that spell out prefixes and suffixes.   Students will spell out the correct prefixes and suffixes determined by clues in the definitions at the bottom of the page.

Have a volunteer read definition number five at the bottom of the page. Say, "Let's decide first what the singular of this word would be. The first three letters of this word are not a prefix, but are a common root that means life: **bio**-. *Something written about a*

life is a **BIOGRAPHY**. To make that word plural will involve more than simply adding -**s**. As so often happens, we'll need to change the -**y** to -**i** and add the letters -**es**. This will give us **BIOGRAPHIES**, the word with the meaning that matches the definition *writings about people's lives* that we see for stair step five."

COMPLETE THE ACTIVITY

Let students work in pairs (optionally) and tell them to use the same strategy to find the correct prefixes and suffixes for the words listed. These activities can be quite challenging!

DISCUSS   After a few minutes, review the answers as a class. Ask if there were any difficulties. Listen to any problems and have volunteers solve the difficulties by explaining key clues in the given definitions. As needed, follow the focus word approach that you see modeled on the next page.

SAB Pg 77

Stair Steps

Fill in the missing letters of each 'graph' word by using the definitions below.
'graph' means something written, drawn, or recorded; a chart

1. | g | r | a | p | h | e | d |
2. | g | r | a | p | h | i | c | s |
3. | p | a | r | a | g | r | a | p | h |
4. | p | o | l | y | g | r | a | p | h | s |
5. | b | i | o | g | r | a | p | h | i | e | s |
6. | t | e | l | e | g | r | a | p | h | i | n | g |
7. | p | h | o | t | o | g | r | a | p | h | e | r | s |
8. | b | i | o | g | r | a | p | h | i | c | a | l | l | y |

1. recorded; charted
2. detailed recordings; explicit representations
3. an indicating mark beside a written idea; a collection of sentences concerning a notion
4. devices that record many bits of data; lie-detectors
5. writings about people's lives
6. sending a written message over a distance
7. people who record images on light-sensitive paper; people who take pictures
8. in a manner related to the writing about a life

Day ③ Extend the Learning

MINI-LESSON: the Suffix -i

The suffix **-i** is the suffix **-y** changed when another suffix is added, as, for example, when a plural suffix is added. This spelling convention, as well as the **-es** plural, has been addressed with the partial suffixes **-iti** and **-ifi**, but it occurs with any word ending in the letter **y**. Let students practice this spelling convention with any of the following words:

baby - babies	**policy - policies**	**lady - ladies**
academy - academies	**pony - ponies**	**ruby - rubies**

MINI-LESSON: the Prefix ortho-

The prefix **ortho-** is from the Greek adjective meaning *correct, right, or true*. Over 100 English words use the prefix, the most familiar being:

orthodontics, the science of straightening teeth
orthopedics, the correction of skeletal problems in children
orthography, correct spelling (literally, correct writing)
orthodox, what is considered to be the correct and true line of belief or behavior

Focus Word: **TELEGRAPHING** ⟶ Write this word on the board.

TEACH

Sample leading question:	"Here's a big word we don't see too often anymore. But if we ever do see it somewhere, we'll be able to understand it, right?"
Student:	"There's our root **graph** in the middle."
Student:	"And the suffix **-ing**, which means *happening now*."
Student:	"That **-ing** can also mean *a thing, an act*."
Student:	"So it has something to do with *an act of writing or recording*."
Student:	"And the prefix **tele-** means *far off*."
Student:	"So writing far off? I don't get it."
Student:	"Oh, yes. There used to be a way of sending messages to far away with wires and buttons."
Student:	"You mean e-mail?"
Teacher:	"Yes—I guess you could call it early e-mail!"

DISCUSS Entering a message by keyboard in one location and having it appear in a distant location is a type of **telegraphing**. Some students may be able to explain to others how the process works.

DEMONSTRATE Find and share an encyclopedia article or an on-line site that has an illustration of an old **telegraph**.

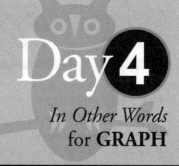

Day 4

In Other Words
for **GRAPH**

GRAPH means
something written, drawn, or
recorded; chart

LESSON TIME

15 Minutes

OBJECTIVES

- **Understand** the meaning of the root **GRAPH**

- **Reinforce** knowledge of the root **GRAPH**

- **Understand** the meaning of words in the **GRAPH** family

- **Apply** knowledge of words in the **GRAPH** family

MATERIALS

- Student Activity Book

- **GRAPH** Word Wall

- Dictionary
(print or on-line)

In Other Words for **GRAPH**

TEACH Have students turn to page 78 in their Student Activity Books. Explain that they are going to read a little story that uses some surprising and sometimes odd phrasing. The underlined words or phrases in the story are actually definitions or synonyms for words in the **GRAPH** family. Then they will see sentences about the story, each containing a blank. Using context clues in the sentences, they will find a **GRAPH** family word in the Word Bank at the bottom to fit in each blank. Have a student read aloud the opening sentence or sentences of the story that contain the first underlined phrase. Then say, "Let's look at the first numbered sentence that contains a blank to be filled in. Clues in the sentence tell us that we want a naming word, a noun that means *detailed recordings*. I see the word **graphics** at the bottom of the page. The suffix -**ic** makes this a noun, the -**s** marks the plural of **graphic**. The only detailed recordings a cave man could make would be something drawn, so let's write **graphics** in the blank for the first sentence."

COMPLETE THE ACTIVITY

This can be quite challenging, so allow students to work on this activity in small groups. Not every word in the Word Bank will be used.

DISCUSS After about 10 minutes, ask if there were any difficulties. Have volunteers explain strategies they used that led to correct answers.

SAB
Pg 78

It's About Writing

Ever since cavemen made <u>detailed recordings</u> on their walls to illustrate their lives, humans have been interested in the lives and endeavors of others. Many people agree that <u>writings about a person's life</u> and <u>writings about a person's life written by that very person</u> are the most interesting non-fiction to read. Where else can a reader find the juicy details of the <u>multi-charted lie-detector</u> results of a famous criminal, the inspirations behind the <u>light-image recordings</u> of Ansel Adams, or the life story of the inventor of the <u>device to send messages over a distance</u>?

In fact, one way to get to know yourself well is to write a story <u>relating to your life written by yourself</u>. Begin by <u>recording in chart form</u> the events of your life that have had an impact on your personality, including either photographs or your own drawings. Next, focus on a few of the most important and be <u>detailed in recording</u>. It doesn't matter whether you use keyboard or a pencil with <u>lead</u> to tell your story. Once you're famous you'll be glad you've already started to share your life with the world.

<u>Fill in the blanks below using words from the "graph" family.</u>

1. Cave paintings are considered the earliest <u>graphics</u> created by human beings.

2. <u>Biographies</u> are life stories written by someone other than themselves.

3. Writings by people about their very own life stories are called <u>autobiographies</u>.

4. Criminals fear <u>polygraphs</u> because they expose their many lies.

5. Ansel Adams' talent was taking black and white <u>photographs</u> of scenes in nature.

6. The <u>telegraph</u> conveys writing to places some distance from each other.

7. Most of the works by Dickens, reflecting his own life, are <u>autobiographical</u> in nature.

8. <u>Graphing</u> an outline of what they want to tell helps writers organize their big ideas.

9. A <u>graphic</u> description lets a reader actually see and feel a written event.

10. Writing pencils contain a carbon mineral called <u>graphite</u>.

<u>Not Used:</u> geography   orthography

154

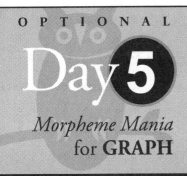

GRAPH means
something written, drawn, or
recorded; chart

LESSON TIME

15 Minutes

OBJECTIVES

• **Build** words in the
GRAPH family

• **Apply** knowledge of
synonyms and antonyms
to **GRAPH** words

Optional Morpheme Mania for **GRAPH**

On page 79 of their Activity Books, students will see an optional vocabulary enrichment activity that they can work on in groups, time permitting. This activity makes a great review for the formal assessment on the next page.

All the affixes presented in the week's activities are provided at the top of the page on either side of the root of the week in all its forms. Students can write in up to 13 of the words they built during the week, possibly discovering additional ones.

Then students can brainstorm with each other to come up with antonyms and synonyms they may know. Starter examples are given with every Morpheme Mania in the Activity Book. Because antonyms and synonyms may require knowledge of roots which students have not yet studied, completion of this activity is not crucial. Simply remind students that they can at any time during the course of the year revisit any of their Morpheme Mania pages and add words, antonyms, and synonyms as their vocabulary grows.

Day 5 *Assessment*

Make and hand out copies.
The answer key is on page A-4.
The instructions are on page A-2.

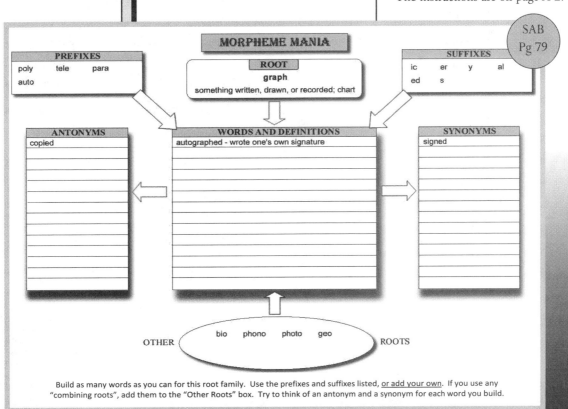

MORPHEME MANIA

PREFIXES		
poly	tele	para
auto		

ROOT
graph
something written, drawn, or recorded; chart

SUFFIXES			
ic	er	y	al
ed	s		

ANTONYMS
copied

WORDS AND DEFINITIONS
autographed - wrote one's own signature

SYNONYMS
signed

OTHER   bio phono photo geo   ROOTS

SAB
Pg 79

Build as many words as you can for this root family. Use the prefixes and suffixes listed, <u>or add your own</u>. If you use any "combining roots", add them to the "Other Roots" box. Try to think of an antonym and a synonym for each word you build.

autobiographer a person who writes his or her own life story

autobiographers people who write their own life stories

autobiographic of a person's life story written by that person

autobiographical of a person's life story written by that person

autobiographically in a way related to a self-written life story

autobiographies stories of peoples' lives written by those people

autobiography story of a person's life written by that person

autograph a person's self-written signature

autographed wrote one's own signature

autographing writing one's own signature

autographs people's own written signatures

biographer a person who writes the story of another's life

biographers people who write the stories of others' lives

biographic pertaining to the written story of a person's life

biographical related to a person's life story

biographically in a manner related to the writing about a life

biographies writings about people's lives

biography a writing about a person's life

demographic pertaining to records about a group of people

demographics the science of records about groups of people

geographer a person who writes about earth

geographers people who write about the earth

geographic related to writing about the earth

geographical related to writing about the earth

geography the drawing of the features of the earth

graph to record; a chart

graphed recorded; charted

grapheme a written unit; a written symbol that stands for one sound

graphemes written units; written symbols that stand for one sound

graphic detailed in recording; explicit

graphically in a manner detailed in recording; explicitly

graphics detailed recordings; explicit representations

graphing putting into form by drawing; charting

graphite substance used for writing; pencil lead

graphites substances used for writing; types of pencil lead

graphs written records; charts

orthography art or study of correct writing; proper spelling

paragraph an indicating mark beside a written idea; a collection of sentences concerning one idea

paragraphs indicating marks beside groups of written ideas; collections of sentences concerning one idea

phonograph a device for recording and reproducing sound

phonographs devices for recording and eproducing sound

photograph an image recorded on a light-sensitive surface; a picture

photographed recorded an image on a light-sensitive surface; took a picture

photographer a person who records images on light-sensitive surface; a person who takes pictures

photographers people who record images on light-sensitive surfaces; people who take pictures

photographic of an image recorded on light-sensitive surface; relating to a picture

photographically in a manner recorded on light-sensitive surface; in a manner relating to a picture

photographies arts of recording images on a light-sensitive surface; arts of taking pictures

photographing recording an image on a light-sensitive surface; taking pictures

photographs images recorded on light-sensitive surfaces; pictures

photography art of recording images on a light-sensitive surface; art of taking pictures

polygraph a device that records many bits of data; a lie-detector

polygraphs devices that record many bits of data; lie-detectors

telegraph a written message sent over a distance

telegraphed sent a written message over a distance

telegraphic relating to a written message sent over a distance

telegraphing sending a written message over a distance

telegraphs sends a written message over a distance

topography the drawing of a region; the layout of the land

Check-Up for **GRAPH**   Name _____

____ **1.** **GRAPH** in words like **biography** and **graphic** means:

    A run

    B chart or write

    C to seek or aim for

____ **2.** What is the meaning of the word **biography**?

    A to run for one's life

    B a writing about a life

    C to seek to live in another place

____ **3.** What is the meaning of the word **polygraphic**?

    A aiming at many targets at once

    B tending to run every day

    C relating to a chart that records many pieces of information

____ **4.** What is the meaning of the word **autograph**?

    A a signature personally written

    B a place to run privately

    C a person with full power

____ **5.** What is the meaning of the word **geographic**?

    A hunting for places on earth

    B how the earth spins

    C related to charting the earth

____ **6.** Which word means **getting information from far away**?

    A autobiographical

    B telegraphic

    C paragraphic

____ **7.** Which word means **correct writing**?

    A orthography

    B photography

    C telegraphy

____ **8.** Which word means **an indication sign or mark beside a written idea**?

    A polygraph

    B graphite

    C paragraph

____ **9.** The root **steno** means *narrow or tight*. **Stenography** is most closely related to:

    A seeking a job in tight times

    B running on a narrow road

    C writing in "shorthand"

____ **10.** The **demographics** of the area indicate a rise in average age. **Demographics** are:

    A charts about the people

    B lists of jobs in an area

    C game score cards

OBJECTIVES

- **Understand** the meaning of the root **LECT**
- **Build** words in the root **LECT** family
- **Break Apart** words in the root **LECT** family
- **Understand** the meaning of words in the **LECT** family
- **Understand** the spelling principles applied to the root **LECT**
- **Apply** knowledge of words in the **LECT** family
- **Assess** and **Reinforce** knowledge of words in the **LECT** family

MATERIALS

- Student Activity Books, pages 81–86
- Dictionary *(print or on-line)*

CROSS-CURRICULAR EXAMPLES

Science:
selection, selectivity

Social Studies:
collective, election, electoral

Language Arts:
eclectic, elegance, legible

Math:
collectively, inelegance, selector

LECT

meaning "to choose, read, gather, take from"

select
to **choose** apart

legible
able to be **read**

collect
to **gather** together

eclectic
taken from various sources

Morpheme: **LECT**
Allomorphs: **LEG, LEGE, LEGI, LIG**

Over 1000 words containing the morpheme **LECT** or one of its allomorphs are current in English. During this unit, tell students to be alert for this root in their school texts, general reading, and oral language they hear. Some of the words they might encounter in their school subjects are listed on the left under Cross-Curricular Examples.

UNIT AT A GLANCE

Day 1
Root Squares for **LECT**

Day 2
Magic Squares for **LECT**

Day 3
Stair Steps for **LECT**

OPTIONAL
Day 4
In Other Words for **LECT**

Day 5
Assessment or Morpheme Mania for **LECT**

Each activity should take approximately **15 minutes**.

People who can *choose and gather well from among (inter) what the world has to offer* are said to be **intelligent** (the prefix **inter-** has assimilated). Their power to make sound selections and to incorporate them into their minds is the **intellect**.

The variations (allomorphs) of this root are a result of the principal parts of the original Latin verb and of the phonetic changes that assimilation causes. You can help your students become better spellers if you let them know some phonetic tricks. Pronunciation can guide spelling. If the letter **g** in any words from this root family is "soft," sounding like a **j**, then the letters **e** or **i** will follow the **g**, as in **legible** and **college**. If the **g** sounds "hard," as in **ligament**, then the letters **a**, **o**, or **u** follow. This can help in deciding whether the suffix **-ent** or **-ant** is used: **diligent**, but **elegant**.

The two broad meanings of this morpheme, *gather* and *read*, may not seem related at first. If we visualize reading as an act of gathering up marks on a surface to make sense of them, we can see the connection.

A **legend** was originally something that must be read as an instructive example. On maps, the **legend** is the explanatory inset that must be read in order to understand symbols and scales on that map.

We usually think of a **lecture** as a speech, but the morphemic core of the word shows us that it was originally something being read to the audience. A **lectern** is a stand from which a **lecturer** reads.

School courses that you are not required to take but which you may choose are called **electives**.

To **collect** is of course to gather together (with the prefix **con-** assimilated). Notice the effect of adding the prefix **re-** to the word **collect**. What are we actually doing when we **recollect** something? *We are gathering it together again in our minds.* If you really wanted to **collect** something again, as to gather up spilled marbles, you would **re-collect** them.

Word Alert!

Another root, **leg**, meaning *law*, is possibly, but very remotely, related to this one meaning *to gather or read*. Law may originally have been a **collection** of rules. The root **leg** that means *law* will be presented as an individual root in its own right later. If the meanings of words such as **legal** and **legislate** are familiar, then it will be clear which root is the source. If the word is not familiar, a trip to the dictionary will be rewarding.

To add to the complication, the root **leg** meaning *law* can also mean *to tie or bind*, as in the words **ligature** or **ligament**. More will be said about this when this root is presented in a separate set of activities.

The anatomical limb, **leg**, comes from an Old Norse word for bone.

Words containing the letter sequence **l-e-c-t** do not necessarily belong to this root family. That will be obvious in such words as **deflect**, **inflect**, and **reflect**, a morphemic splitting proof method for which will show that the correct root there is **flect**.

The words **electron** and **electric** do not belong to this root family, but instead come from a Greek word meaning *bright and shining*.

Day 1

Root Squares
for **LECT**

LECT means
to choose, read, gather, take from

LESSON TIME

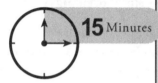

15 Minutes

OBJECTIVES

- **Understand** the meaning of the root **LECT**
- **Build** words in the **LECT** family
- **Understand** the meaning of words in the **LECT** family
- **Understand** the spelling principles applied to the root **LECT**

MATERIALS

- Student Activity Book
- **LECT** Word Wall
- Dictionary *(print or on-line)*

DIFFERENTIATING INSTRUCTION

If you prefer easier or more difficult activities, use your personal account at www.dynamicliteracy.com to access novice or expert versions, along with ideas on using them.

Root Squares for **LECT**

TEACH   Have students turn to page 81 in their Activity Books. Refer to Mini-Lessons on the prefixes **col-** and **se-** found on the next page of this manual. Then call attention to the center box. Point out that the root **LECT** has quite a number of different spellings, called allomorphs.

Ask students to decide if one of the forms they see in the middle square can stand alone as a word. They may suggest that **leg** is a word, but the ordinary meaning of that word is not in this family. Suggest that students start their list with **lect**, adding **se-**, meaning *apart, or away*, to build **select**, meaning *to take away from*. Invite students to explore how this word is related to the idea of *to choose, read, gather, or take from*.

COMPLETE THE ACTIVITY

Have students follow the directions for the Root Squares activity for **LECT** on page 81 to build words. If students have difficulty building words with the Root Squares, show them how by modeling the matrix approach found on the next page, taking one affix at a time and seeing if it will connect with any one of the allomorphs of the root.

DISCUSS   After five minutes, have volunteers write some of their words on the board. Focus with the class on the words they have built and guide them in a discussion of how the meaning of the root is still *to choose, read, gather, take from*, even when prefixes and suffixes are added. Watch for target words that most easily demonstrate the meanings of *to choose, read, gather, take from*. If the word **elect** is not present, ask the class, "Can anyone try to use the prefix **e-**?" and then continue on to the focus word discussion on the next page.

SAB Pg 81

Root Squares

How many words can you make?

Start in any square. Your goal is to combine two or more word parts to make as many words in the 'lect, leg, lege, legi, lig' family as you can. Write each word and a definition you can think of for it in the space provided at the bottom of the page. Use the back of the page if you need to.

e	ent	di
col	lect, leg, lege, legi, lig	ion
ure	ive	se

_____

_____

_____

_____

_____

_____

_____

_____

The prefix **col-** is an assimilation of **con-**, meaning *with* or *together*. The assimilation occurs before the letter **l**, as students can detect if you have them pronounce these unassimilated examples: **conlaborate, conlapse, conlision**.

MINI-LESSON: the Prefix **se-**

The prefix **se-** stems originally from the third-person pronoun base for *self*. Since the *self* is different from everybody else, the prefix came to mean *apart or away*, or *for oneself exclusively*. Those meanings can be detected in familiar words such as these:

secure - *away from care or worry*	**sever** - *to cut away*	**segregate** - *to move away from a group*
seduce -*to lead away from a correct path*	**secede** - *to move apart*	**separate** - *to arrange or organize apart*

Focus Word: ELECT ⟶ Write this word on the board.

TEACH

Lead with this:	"Every four years, we have an opportunity to **elect** a President. Let's see what that really means."
Student:	"I already see that one—*we pick one out*, **e-lect**."
Teacher:	"Great. Does everyone see that the word **elect** is an exact translation of the phrase **pick out**?"
Student:	"Why do we have so many words in English? Why can't we just say **pick out**?"
Student:	"That would sound silly—to **pick out** the president."
Student:	"It wouldn't sound silly if that's all we ever had in the language."
Student:	"But we have the word **elect**, so that's that."
Teacher:	"Does anyone remember why we have words like **elect** that are exact translations of phrases like **pick out**?"
Student:	"That invasion."
Student:	"Yes—1066 when the Normans conquered England and the language doubled."

DISCUSS It is fun to remind students every now and then why English is the way it is. You can refer to pages I-10 and I-11 in the Elements Level 1 Teacher Edition for a review of the Battle of Hastings.

Lead students to see that, based on its two pieces of meaning, **elect** means *to choose out or to take from*. Ask students to discuss other uses of the word they may have heard besides politically choosing a candidate (making any decision can be called **electing** to do something).

Root Squares Matrix
You can refer to this matrix to guide students in this activity. Students could build at least these 12 words. *It is not important how many words are built*, so long as students understand the meanings of the root and its affixes. Encourage discussion about the definitions of any words formed for the blank slots as well as for the attested words.

	no prefix	col-	di-	e-	se-
no suffix		college		elect	select
-ent			diligent		
-ion	legion	collection		election	selection
-ive		collective	elective		selective
-ure	lecture				

Day 2

Magic Squares
for **LECT**

LECT means
to choose, read, gather, take from

LESSON TIME

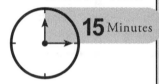

15 Minutes

OBJECTIVES

- **Understand** the meaning of the root **LECT**

- **Break Apart** words in the **LECT** family

- **Understand** the meanings of words in the **LECT** family

MATERIALS

- Student Activity Book
- **LECT** Word Wall
- Dictionary *(print or on-line)*

DIFFERENTIATING INSTRUCTION

If you prefer easier or more difficult activities, use your personal account at www.dynamicliteracy.com to access novice or expert versions, along with ideas on using them.

Break Apart Words with **LECT**

TEACH Have students turn to the Magic Squares on page 82 in their Student Activity Books. Model a Think-Aloud strategy for students: "I know that **LECT** means *to choose, read, gather, take from*. I can use this knowledge to find the definition of a word with this as its root."

Direct students to word B, **electives**. Say, "The prefix **e-** is a spelling for **ex-**, meaning *out of or from*. The suffix **-ive** means *inclined to be* and the **-s** makes the word a plural noun. Definition 9 is *courses chosen from a list*, which accounts for the idea of *choosing* in the definition of **LECT**. Let's write the number 9 in square B."

Ask students to use the same strategy to find the correct definitions for the other words. Tell them to write the number of the definition in the box that matches the letter for the word. Remind them that if all their answers are correct, each row and each column will add up to the same Magic number.

DISCUSS After five minutes, ask if there are any difficulties about matching the words and definitions. If there are, ask volunteers to explain clues in the definitions that will lead to the correct choice of word. As needed, follow the focus word approach for **legibly** that you see modeled on the next page.

Add any new words to the classroom **LECT** Word Wall and remind students to add these words to the **LECT** Word Wall in their Activity Books.

SAB
Pg 82

Magic Squares

Select the best answer for each of the words in the 'lect, leg, lege, legi, lig' family from the numbered definitions. Put the number in the proper space in the Magic Square box. If the total of the numbers is the same both across and down, you have found the magic number!

'lect, leg, lege, legi, lig' means to choose, read, gather, take from

WORDS	DEFINITIONS
A. collections	1. not able to be selected from; not fit or desirable
B. electives	2. things that have been gathered together; assemblies or compilations
C. diligently	3. in a manner able to be read
D. illegible	4. in a manner of choosing apart; in a manner carefully picking out
E. selectively	5. quality of being chosen from; refinement or beauty
F. lecturer	6. not able to be read
G. elector	7. in a manner of choosing apart; in a persevering manner
H. elegance	8. a person reading a chosen text; a person who explains or scolds
I. legibly	9. courses chosen from a list
	10. a person who chooses from; a person chosen to vote someone into office

Magic Square Box

A. 2	B. 9	C. 7
D. 6	E. 4	F. 8
G. 10	H. 5	I. 3

Magic Number __18__

*** ANSWER KEY ***

MINI-LESSON: the partial Suffixes -ib and -ibil

The suffix **-ible**, a variation of **-able**, easily recognizable as meaning *able or having the power*, takes on various spellings depending on other affixes that work with it. For example, **-ible** drops the final two letters when the adverb suffix **-ly** is added. Students can practice with that spelling and pronunciation principle with the following words:

possible – possibly	audible – audibly
terrible – terribly	visible – visibly

The partial suffix **-ibil** represents a pronunciation and spelling change for the suffix **-ible** whenever the additional suffix **-ity** is attached. Show students any of these pairs of words that illustrate the use of the suffix **-ibil**:

accessible – accessibility	legible – legibility
audible – audibility	divisible – divisibility
credible – credibility	eligible – eligibility
visible – visibility	

Focus Word: **LEGIBLY** ⟶ Write this word on the board.

TEACH

Sample leading question:	"Does anyone know why we should write or type **legibly**?"
Student:	"So people can read it."
Teacher:	"That's right, *so people can read it.* Now let's look at the word to see why it tells us *so people can read it.* First, how many morphemes do we see?"
Student:	"Two."
Student:	"No, there are three: our root and two suffixes!"
Student:	"Oh, right — **ibly** is two suffixes."
Student:	"**-ible** is the same as **-able**."
Teacher:	"So we have what morphemic definition?"
Student:	"*In a manner to be able to choose*—what's that got to do with reading?"
Student:	"Look—the root can mean *choose* or *read.* How can that be?"

DISCUSS If you have not done so, share with your students some of the Fun Facts on this root and lead them to see that reading is an act of gathering up letters, morphemes, and meaning. Lead students to see that, based on its three pieces of meaning, **legibly** means *in a manner so as to be able to be read.*

DEMONSTRATE Have a student write something on the board that cannot be read. Discuss why it can't be read (the letters cannot be picked out clearly). Then have another student write something **legibly**.

Day 3

Stair Steps for **LECT**

LECT means to choose, read, gather, take from

LESSON TIME

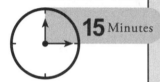

15 Minutes

OBJECTIVES

- **Understand** the meaning of the root **LECT**

- **Apply** knowledge of the root **LECT**

- **Break Apart** words in the **LECT** family

- **Understand** the meaning of words in the **LECT** family

- **Understand** the spelling principles applied to the root **LECT**

MATERIALS

- Student Activity Book
- **LECT** Word Wall

DIFFERENTIATING INSTRUCTION

If you prefer easier or more difficult activities, use your personal account at www.dynamicliteracy.com to access novice or expert versions, along with ideas on using them.

Apply Knowledge of LECT

TEACH Have students turn to page 83 in their Student Activity Books. Explain that the boxes in front of and after the root indicate letters that spell out prefixes and suffixes. Students will spell out the correct prefixes and suffixes determined by clues in the definitions at the bottom of the page.

Have a volunteer read definition number five at the bottom of the page. Say, "We can tell from this definition that the word we are building is a thing, a noun, so the ending 3-letter suffix is likely -**ion**. But what prefix would mean *together*? The prefix

con- has that meaning, though in this case we will need one of the assimilated forms to go with the first letter of our root **LECT**. We know the word **collect**, and if we add to it our choice of prefix, we will have **collection**. That fits and that's the choice."

COMPLETE THE ACTIVITY

Let students work in pairs (optionally) and tell them to use the same strategy to find the correct prefixes and suffixes for the words listed. These activities can be quite challenging!

DISCUSS After a few minutes, review the answers as a class. Ask if there were any difficulties. Listen to any problems and have volunteers solve the difficulties by explaining key clues in the given definitions. As needed, follow the focus word approach that you see modeled on the next page.

SAB Pg 83

Stair Steps

Fill in the missing letters of each 'lect, leg, lege, legi, lig' word by using the definitions below.

'lect, leg, lege, legi, lig' means to choose, read, gather, take from

1.	s	e	l	e	c	t				
2.	l	e	g	i	b	l	e			
3.	e	l	e	c	t	i	o	n		
4.	l	e	c	t	u	r	e	r	s	
5.	c	o	l	l	e	c	t	i	o	n
6.	s	e	l	e	c	t	i	v	e	l	y
7.	c	o	l	l	e	c	t	i	v	e	l	y
8.	i	n	e	l	i	g	i	b	i	l	i	t	y

1. to choose apart; to pick out
2. able to be read
3. the process of choosing from; act of voting into office
4. people reading chosen texts; people who explain or scold
5. that which has been gathered together; an assembly or compilation
6. in a manner of choosing apart; in a manner carefully picking out
7. in a manner of being gathered together; in a manner considered as one group
8. inability to be selected from; the lack of fitness or desirability

164

Focus Word: **SELECT** ➝ Write this word on the board.

TEACH

Sample leading question:	"Let's look at the word **select**. You know this word, because you do it every day. You **select** what to wear in the morning. What are you doing when you **select**?"
Student:	"You choose."
Teacher:	"So you have choices?"
Student:	"Yes. Say I have 7 pairs of socks and I take out the pair I want. That's **selecting**."
Student:	"Yes, you're taking one pair *apart or away* from the rest."
Student:	"I never thought of a **selection** that way. That's neat."
Student:	"I think it's fun seeing what words really mean deep down, especially words everybody already knows."
Teacher:	"And seeing what those words mean deep down helps you to figure out new words that you don't already know."
Student:	"But how is the word **select** different from **elect**?"

DISCUSS Let opportunities like this last question enrich your students' love of words. Lead students to see that, based on its two pieces of meaning, **select** means *to choose apart or gather out*. Ask students to think about any differences between **elect** and **select**. Do we **elect** from a bunch of socks? Do we **select** the President? Students will see that **selecting** a President means picking out one from a group of Presidents.

DEMONSTRATE Let students make lists on the board and sort them out according to what would best be **elected** and what **selected**. Some items might appear on both lists.

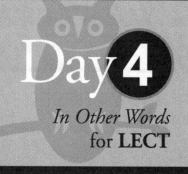

Day 4

In Other Words for **LECT**

LECT means to choose, read, gather, take from

LESSON TIME

15 Minutes

OBJECTIVES

- **Understand** the meaning of the root **LECT**
- **Reinforce** knowledge of the root **LECT**
- **Understand** the meaning of words in the **LECT** family
- **Apply** knowledge of words in the **LECT** family

MATERIALS

- Student Activity Book
- **LECT** Word Wall
- Dictionary *(print or on-line)*

In Other Words for **LECT**

TEACH Have students turn to page 84 in their Student Activity Books. Explain that they are going to read a little story that uses some surprising and sometimes odd phrasing. The underlined words or phrases in the story are actually definitions or synonyms for words in the **LECT** family. Then they will see sentences about the story, each containing a blank.

Using context clues in the sentences, they will find a **LECT** family word in the Word Bank at the bottom to fit in each blank. Have a student read aloud the opening sentence or sentences of the story that contain the first underlined phrase. Then say, "Let's look at the first numbered sentence that contains a blank to be filled in. Clues in the sentence tell us that we want a word that says how someone does something, an adverb that means *in a persevering manner*. I see the word **diligently** at the bottom of the page. The suffix -**ly** clues me to the adverb, a word *describing the manner of an action*. The prefix **di**- probably means *completely* in this case, as if the person were *studying completely*. That would be synonymous with the idea of **persevering**. Let's write **diligently** in the blank for the first sentence."

COMPLETE THE ACTIVITY
This can be quite challenging, so allow students to work on this activity in small groups. Not every word in the Word Bank will be used.

DISCUSS After about 10 minutes, ask if there were any difficulties. Have volunteers explain strategies they used that led to correct answers.

SAB Pg 84

The Job at the Museum

In the summer Merle could be found studying <u>in a persevering manner</u> the recent additions to the museum's <u>assembly of documents gathered together</u>. During the school year, Merle had taken a <u>chosen</u> class about old handwritten manuscripts, and he was eager to apply that knowledge to the <u>chosen quality</u> of the <u>items chosen apart</u> that the museum had bought.

Merle remembered that the <u>person reading to the class</u> stressed the importance of wearing white cotton gloves when handling documents to prevent making anything <u>unreadable</u> with oily fingerprints smudges. Merle soon had a reputation of being the most <u>persevering</u> of the museum aides and he was <u>chosen out</u> to guide a weekly tour to look at the prized manuscripts.

<u>Fill in the blanks below using words from the "lect, leg, lege, legi, lig" family.</u>

1. The eager student <u>diligently</u> studied over the manuscripts.
2. The museum's manuscript <u>collection</u> was quite large and valuable.
3. <u>Elective</u> classes are ones that students can choose.
4. The <u>elegance</u> and the beauty of the manuscripts attracted visitors.
5. Visitors could make <u>selections</u> about which rooms they wanted to see.
6. The <u>lecturer</u> of the class stressed care and cleanliness with the students.
7. We would not want the handwriting to become <u>illegible</u> by smudges.
8. Merle was considered a very <u>diligent</u> student.
9. He was <u>elected</u> to be a tour guide for the museum.

<u>Not Used:</u> legibility   collectively   legion

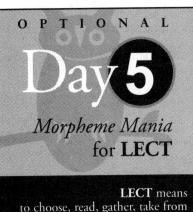

Day 5

Morpheme Mania
for **LECT**

LECT means
to choose, read, gather, take from

LESSON TIME

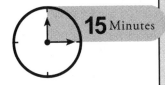

15 Minutes

OBJECTIVES

• **Build** words in the
LECT family

• **Apply** knowledge of
synonyms and antonyms
to **LECT** words

Optional
Morpheme Mania
for **LECT**

On page 85 of their Activity
Books, students will see an
optional vocabulary enrichment
activity that they can work on in
groups, time permitting. This
activity makes a great review for
the formal assessment on the next
page.

All the affixes presented in the
week's activities are provided at
the top of the page on either side
of the root of the week in all its
forms. Students can write in up to
13 of the words they built during
the week, possibly discovering
additional ones.

Then students can brainstorm
with each other to come up with
antonyms and synonyms they may
know. Starter examples are given
with every Morpheme Mania
in the Activity Book. Because
antonyms and synonyms may
require knowledge of roots which
students have not yet studied,
completion of this activity is not
crucial. Simply remind students
that they can at any time during
the course of the year revisit any
of their Morpheme Mania pages
and add words, antonyms, and
synonyms as their vocabulary
grows.

Day 5 *Assessment*

Make and hand out copies.
The answer key is on page A-4.
The instructions are on page A-2.

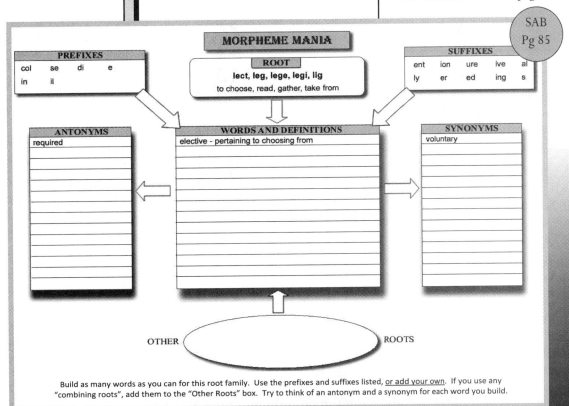

SAB
Pg 85

MORPHEME MANIA

PREFIXES			
col	se	di	e
in	il		

ROOT
lect, leg, lege, legi, lig
to choose, read, gather, take from

SUFFIXES				
ent	ion	ure	ive	al
ly	er	ed	ing	s

ANTONYMS
required

WORDS AND DEFINITIONS
elective - pertaining to choosing from

SYNONYMS
voluntary

OTHER   ROOTS

Build as many words as you can for this root family. Use the prefixes and suffixes listed, <u>or add your own</u>. If you use any
"combining roots", add them to the "Other Roots" box. Try to think of an antonym and a synonym for each word you build.

collect to gather together; to assemble or compile

collected gathered together; assembled or compiled

collectedly in a manner gathered together; in an assembled or compiled manner

collectibles items that are gathered together; things worth keeping

collecting gathering together; assembling or compiling

collection that which has been gathered together; an assembly or compilation

collections things that have been gathered together; assemblies or compilations

collective pertaining to what has been gathered together; considered as one group

collectively in a manner of being gathered together; in a manner considered as one group

collector a person who gathers items together

collectors people who gather items together

collects gathers together

diligence process of choosing apart and preferring; perseverance

diligent characterized by choosing apart and preferring; persevering

diligently in a manner of choosing apart and preferring; in a persevering manner

elect to choose from; to vote into office

elected chose from; voted into office

electing choosing from; voting into office

election the process of choosing from; act of voting into office

elections processes of choosing from; acts of voting into office

elective pertaining to choosing from; related to voting into office

electives courses chosen from a list

elector a person who chooses from; a person chosen to vote someone into office

electoral related to the process of choosing from; pertaining to voting into office

electorate a group who choose from; a body of voters

electorates groups who choose from; bodies of voters

electors people who choose from; people chosen to vote others into office

elects chooses from; votes into office

elegance quality of being chosen from; refinement or beauty

elegant chosen from; refined or beautiful

elegantly in a manner of choosing from; in a refined or beautiful manner

eligibility ability to be selected from; fitness and desirability

eligible able to be selected from; fit and desirable

eligibly in a manner able to be selected from; in a fit and desirable manner

illegible not able to be read

illegibly in a manner not able to be read

ineligibility inability to be selected from; the lack of fitness or desirability

ineligible not able to be selected from; not fit or desirable

ineligibly in a manner not able to be selected from; in a manner not fit or desirable

lecture to read from a chosen text; to explain or scold

lectured did a reading from a chosen text; explained or scolded

lecturer a person reading a chosen text; a person who explains or scolds

lecturers people reading chosen texts; people who explain or scold

lectures reads from a chosen text; explains or scolds

lecturing reading from a chosen text; explaining or scolding

legibility quality of being readable

legible able to be read

legibly in a manner able to be read

legion a large collected group

legions large collected groups

select to choose apart; to pick out

selected chose apart; picked out

selecting choosing apart; picking out

selection the process of choosing apart; something picked out

selections items chosen apart; things picked out

selective likely to choose apart; carefully picking out

selectively in a manner of choosing apart; in a manner carefully picking out

selects chooses apart; picks out

Check-Up for **LECT**   Name _____

____ **1.** **LECT, LEG, or LIG** in words like **collect**, **legible**, and **eligible** means:

    A gather or read

    B to step or go

    C a mark, seal, or meaning

____ **2.** What is the meaning of the word **collect**?

    A to go along with someone

    B to gather together

    C to put a seal on with

____ **3.** What is the meaning of the word **illegible**?

    A giving meaning to

    B a process of walking into

    C not able to be read

____ **4.** What is the meaning of the word **elegance**?

    A quality of being chosen out from

    B refusing to go anywhere

    C having no mark or meaning

____ **5.** What is the meaning of the word **selective**?

    A tending to give meaning to

    B unsure about where to step

    C likely to choose apart

____ **6.** Which word means **choosing out**?

    A electing

    B collecting

    C lecturing

____ **7.** Which word means **a person reading a chosen text**?

    A legibility

    B electorate

    C lecturer

____ **8.** Which word means **in a manner of choosing apart**?

    A diligently

    B selectivity

    C ineligibility

____ **9.** You are said to have **negligence** if you:

    A have a good sense of the meanings of words

    B go carefully into a situation

    C choose not to do something that you should do

____ **10.** The **lector** approached the stage. The **lector** was about to:

    A dance

    B read

    C sing

OBJECTIVES

- **Understand** the meaning of the root **EQU**
- **Build** words in the root **EQU** family
- **Break Apart** words in the root **EQU** family
- **Understand** the meaning of words in the **EQU** family
- **Understand** the spelling principles applied to the root **EQU**
- **Apply** knowledge of words in the **EQU** family
- **Assess** and **Reinforce** knowledge of words in the **EQU** family

MATERIALS

- Student Activity Books, pages 87-92
- Dictionary *(print or on-line)*

CROSS-CURRICULAR EXAMPLES

Science:
equalization, equative, equipotential

Social Studies:
egalitarian, equatorial, equitable

Language Arts:
equanimity, equivocate

Math:
equal, inequality, equidistant

EQU

meaning "fair, balanced"

equality
the state of being **fair** and balanced

equate
to make even or **balanced**

Morpheme: **EQU**
Allomorphs: **EQUI, EG**

About 600 words containing the morpheme **EQU** or one of its allomorphs are current in English. During this unit, tell students to be alert for this root in their school texts, general reading, and oral language they hear. Some of the words they might encounter in their school subjects are listed on the left under Cross-Curricular Examples.

UNIT AT A GLANCE

Day **1**
Root Squares
for **EQU**

Day **2**
Magic Squares
for **EQU**

Day **3**
Stair Steps
for **EQU**

OPTIONAL
Day **4**
In Other Words
for **EQU**

Day **5**
Assessment or Morpheme Mania
for **EQU**

Each activity should take approximately **15 minutes**.

Twice each year, there is an exact balance in minutes of daylight and minutes of nighttime. These two times are called **equinoxes**, *equal nights*.

The **equator** is the locus of points that divide the earth into two *balanced* halves between the North and South Poles.

Another root besides **equ**, also meaning *balanced*, combines to make the word **equilibrium**, literally *balanced balance*. This word has many applications. We speak of a person's inner ear **equilibrium**. **Equilibrium** (or lack of it) in air pressure affects the weather. The **equilibrium** in government between security and freedom is an issue. Incidentally, the second root in the word **equilibrium** is the origin of the abbreviation **lb.**, for *pound*, a basic weight measure.

The original Latin **equ** evolved into French as **eg**. An **egalitarian** believes in *equal* abilities, rights, and responsibilities for all people.

Word Alert!

The letter sequence **e-q-u** does not necessarily indicate the presence of this root. Words from the root **sequ**, meaning to follow, can be detected by the "proof" method of morphemic splitting. For example, the word **consequence** does not break into the morphemes **cons–equ–ence**. The word **frequently** is not divided as **fr–equ–ent–ly**.

The word **equip** comes from the Germanic word **ship**. To **equip** was simply to board, make ready, or load a ship.

Another Latin root looks exactly like this one but is not at all related. The root **equ** means horse, and it gives us words such as **equestrian** and **equerry**. It cannot be determined from merely looking at the word whether **equiform** means *shaped like a horse* or *having balanced shapes*.

Day 1

Root Squares for EQU

EQU means fair, balanced

LESSON TIME

15 Minutes

OBJECTIVES

- **Understand** the meaning of the root **EQU**
- **Build** words in the **EQU** family
- **Understand** the meaning of words in the **EQU** family
- **Understand** the spelling principles applied to the root **EQU**

MATERIALS

- Student Activity Book
- **EQU** Word Wall
- Dictionary *(print or on-line)*

DIFFERENTIATING INSTRUCTION

If you prefer easier or more difficult activities, use your personal account at www.dynamicliteracy.com to access novice or expert versions, along with ideas on using them.

Root Squares for EQU

TEACH Have students turn to page 87 in their Activity Books. Say, "All of the prefixes and suffixes in the squares surrounding the shaded center are probably familiar, except the Combining Form **later**." Refer to the Mini-Lesson found on the next page.

Call attention to the center box. Point out that the root **EQU** has three different spellings, called allomorphs. Ask students to decide if one of the forms they see in the middle square can stand alone as a word. Since none of these allomorphs is an independent word, each must have a prefix or a suffix to play a part in making a word. Suggest that students start their list with **equ** and then add the suffix **-al**, meaning *characterized by*, to build **equal**, meaning *characterized by being balanced.*

COMPLETE THE ACTIVITY

Have students follow the directions for the Root Squares activity for **EQU** on page 87 to build words. If students have difficulty building words with the Root Squares, show them how by modeling the matrix approach found on the next page, taking one affix at a time and seeing if it will connect with any one of the allomorphs of the root.

DISCUSS After five minutes, have volunteers write some of their words on the board. Focus with the class on the words they have built, and guide them in a discussion of how the meaning of the root is still *fair and balanced*, even when prefixes and suffixes are added. Watch for target words that most easily demonstrate the meanings of *fair and balanced*. If the word **equate** is not present, ask the class, "Can anyone try to use the suffix **-ate**?" and then continue on to the focus word discussion on the next page.

SAB Pg 87

Root Squares

How many words can you make?

Start in any square. Your goal is to combine two or more word parts to make as many words in the 'equ, equi, eg' family as you can. Write each word and a definition you can think of for it in the space provided at the bottom of the page. Use the back of the page if you need to.

in	ize	ad
al	equ, equi, eg	ate
ity	ion	later

MINI-LESSON: the Combining Form **later**

The Combining Form **later**, not to be confused with the comparative of the word **late**, is from the Latin word for *side*. A dozen or so words combine a prefix with the word **lateral**, meaning *having sides* or *relating to a side*, including:

bilateral, on two sides
trilateral, relating to three sides
unilateral, with everyone on the same side
multilateral, having many sides
quadrilateral, a figure with four sides

The word **collateral** refers to anything *sharing a side with* or *being alongside with*, as with **collateral** damage, damage that might accompany a storm, a war, or a financial collapse. As an economic term, **collateral** refers to *goods placed alongside others of equal worth.*

Focus Word: **EQUATE** ⟶ Write this word on the board.

TEACH

Lead with this:	"You might have heard somebody say to a friend's argument, 'That doesn't **equate**.' What does that mean?"
Student:	"It means it doesn't make any sense. It doesn't add up."
Teacher:	"And how does the word work to tell us that?"
Student:	"So it has a suffix -**ate**, *to cause to become*."
Student:	"*To cause to become balanced, or equal.*"
Teacher:	"Good, so when two things **equate**, they're the same, right?"
Student:	"Well, not exactly the same necessarily, but they *balance out*."
Teacher:	"Can anyone give us an example of two things that **equate**?"
Student:	"The number ten **equates** to five plus five. Hey—that's exactly what it means in math class when we write 5 + 5 = 10, and that's where the **equals** mark gets its name!"
Student:	"So there is a balance or an agreement between the amount five plus five and the amount we write as ten. Right?"

DISCUSS Lead students to see that, based on its two pieces of meaning, **equate** refers to *making balanced*. Ask pairs of students to write out two things that **equate** and check each other about it. Can the word be used in fields other than math? (an act or behavior can **equate** to a consequence. Studying hard can **equate** to good grades, for example).

DEMONSTRATE You can use this opportunity to demonstrate the commutative principle of math, which states that if A **equates** with B, then B **equates** with A. You can also demonstrate the transitive principle, which states that if A **equates** with B, and B **equates** with C, then A also **equates** with C.

Root Squares Matrix

You can refer to this matrix to guide students in this activity. Students could build at least these 12 words. *It is not important how many words are built*, so long as students understand the meanings of the root and its affixes. Encourage discussion about the definitions of any words formed for the blank slots as well as for the attested words.

	no prefix	ad-	in-	later-
-al	equal		inequal	equilateral
-ate	equate	adequate	inadequate	
-ity	equity		inequity	
-al + -ize	equalize			
-at(e) + -ion	equation	adequation		
-al + -iz(e) + -ation	equalization			

Day 2

Magic Squares for EQU

EQU means fair, balanced

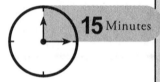
OBJECTIVES

- **Understand** the meaning of the root **EQU**

- **Break Apart** words in the **EQU** family

- **Understand** the meanings of words in the **EQU** family

MATERIALS

- Student Activity Book

- **EQU** Word Wall

- Dictionary *(print or on-line)*

DIFFERENTIATING INSTRUCTION

If you prefer easier or more difficult activities, use your personal account at www.dynamicliteracy.com to access novice or expert versions, along with ideas on using them.

Break Apart Words with EQU

TEACH Have students turn to the Magic Squares on page 88 in their Student Activity Books. Model a Think-Aloud strategy for students: "I know that **EQU** means *fair, balanced*. I can use this knowledge to find the definition of a word with this as its root." Direct students to word C, **equator**. Say: "I know that the suffix -**ate** means *to cause to become* and the suffix -**or** means *a person or device that does*. (Notice that the final **e** on -**ate** drops before the -**or** is added.) So, an **equator** is *a device that causes something to be fair and balanced*. The **equator** is an imaginary line running around the center of the earth at the point of **equal** distance from the North and South Poles,

or, as defined here in definition 7, *an imaginary line dividing earth into even halves*. Let's write the number 7 in square C."

COMPLETE THE ACTIVITY

Ask students to use the same strategy to find the correct definitions for the other words. Tell them to write the number of the definition in the box that matches the letter for the word. Remind them that if all their answers are correct, each row and each column will add up to the same Magic number.

DISCUSS After five minutes, ask if there are any difficulties about matching the words and definitions. If there are, ask volunteers to explain clues in the definitions that will lead to the correct choice of word. As needed, follow the focus word approach for **equity** that you see modeled on the next page.

SAB Pg 88 Add any new words to the classroom **EQU** Word Wall and remind students to add these words to the **EQU** Word Wall in their Activity Books.

Magic Squares

Select the best answer for each of the words in the 'equ, equi, eg' family from the numbered definitions. Put the number in the proper space in the Magic Square box. If the total of the numbers is the same both across and down, you have found the magic number!

'equ, equi, eg' means fair, balanced

WORDS	DEFINITIONS
A. adequately	1. the state of being unfair and unbalanced
B. equalization	2. the act of making balanced
C. equator	3. state of being balanced, just, or fair
D. inequities	4. conditions in which things are out of balance; acts of unfairness
E. equivalents	5. balanced-sided figures
F. equidistances	6. features of being even in worth
G. equilaterals	7. imaginary line dividing earth into even halves
H. unequaled	8. qualities of standing at a balanced space away from
I. equity	9. in a manner brought to balance or fairness; sufficiently
	10. not of the same fairness and balance; without a peer

Magic Square Box

A. 9	B. 2	C. 7
D. 4	E. 6	F. 8
G. 5	H. 10	I. 3

Magic Number _18_

*** ANSWER KEY ***

Focus Word: **EQUITY** ⟶ Write this word on the board.

TEACH

Sample leading question:	"Here's a word your parents may know of, but you may not have heard of it. Let's see if what we know about pieces of meaning can tell us anything about this word."
Student:	"Well, the root we're working on is in there, **equ**. If we take it away, we should see another meaningful piece."
Student:	"And that would be the suffix **-ity**, which shows up a lot."
Student:	"So is **equity** the same as **equality**? *A state of being fair or balanced?*"
Teacher:	"They can be used the same way, but **equity** also means the balance left on the value of your property after all the debts have been paid. Can someone try to explain that?"
Student:	"I know. My uncle has a car that cost $10,000. He's already paid half of it in car payments, so the balance remaining is $5000."
Student:	"So the **equity** of his car is $5000?"
Teacher:	"Yes, if the Uncle wanted to borrow some money and used his car to back up the loan, he could borrow the balanced value of the car, or $5000."
Student:	"So that's what they're talking about when my parents talk about the **equity** on their house?"
Student:	"Right—it's the balance of how much of the house is paid for."

DISCUSS Sometimes advanced vocabulary needs to be explained rather than simply deduced from what students already know. After a short exchange such as this, you can check for understanding by having students discuss the differences and similarities between **equity** and **equality**. **Equity** can be seen as a kind of **equality**.

DEMONSTRATE Using the Uncle's situation, write this on the board:

$10,000 minus $5000 still owed = (**equates** to) $5000.   [**Equity**]

$10,000 = (**equates** to) $5000 + $5000   [**Equality**]

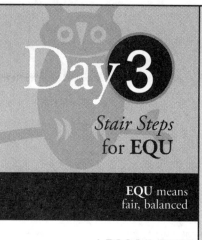
LESSON TIME

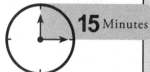

15 Minutes

OBJECTIVES

- **Understand** the meaning of the root **EQU**

- **Apply** knowledge of the root **EQU**

- **Break Apart** words in the **EQU** family

- **Understand** the meaning of words in the **EQU** family

- **Understand** the spelling principles applied to the root **EQU**

MATERIALS

- Student Activity Book
- **EQU** Word Wall

DIFFERENTIATING INSTRUCTION

If you prefer easier or more difficult activities, use your personal account at www.dynamicliteracy.com to access novice or expert versions, along with ideas on using them.

Apply Knowledge of EQU

TEACH Have students turn to page 89 in their Student Activity Books. Explain that the boxes in front of and after the root indicate letters that spell out prefixes and suffixes. Students will spell out the correct prefixes and suffixes determined by clues in the definitions at the bottom of the page.

Have a volunteer read definition number two at the bottom of the page. Say, "We can tell from the past tense words in this definition that the word we are building will have its past tense form, so the ending suffix is probably -**ed**. But we need another suffix to complete the word and make either a verb or an adjective. What suffix could go onto this root to create such a word? If we add -**al** we will have **EQUAL**, the kind of word we're looking for, and if we add -**ed** we get the word that fits: **EQUALED**. That does work, but there is another word we could build by the same reasoning and which has the same meaning. A synonym for **EQUAL** is **EQUATE** and adding the suffix -**ed** to that one while dropping the final **e**, we build **EQUATED** which is synonymous with **EQUALED** and fits just as well.

COMPLETE THE ACTIVITY

Let students work in pairs (optionally) and tell them to use the same strategy to find the correct prefixes and suffixes for the words listed. These activities can be quite challenging!

DISCUSS After a few minutes, review the answers. Ask if there were any difficulties. Listen to any problems and have volunteers solve the difficulties by explaining key clues in the given definitions.

SAB
Pg 89

Stair Steps

Fill in the missing letters of each 'equ, equi, eg' word by using the definitions below.
'equ, equi, eg' means fair; balanced

1.	e	q	u	a	l	s				
2.	e	q	u	a	t	e	d			
3.	e	q	u	a	l	i	z	e		
4.	e	q	u	a	t	i	o	n	s	
5.	i	n	a	d	e	q	u	a	t	e
6.	e	q	u	i	d	i	s	t	a	n	t
7.	i	n	e	q	u	a	l	i	t	i	e	s
8.	e	q	u	i	l	a	t	e	r	a	l	l	y

1. to make or be fair and balanced; is the same as
2. made even or balanced; showed similarities
3. to balance
4. balanced statements
5. not being brought to balance or fairness; not enough
6. standing at a balanced space away from
7. states of unfairness and imbalance
8. in a way having balanced sides

176

Focus Word: **EQUALIZE** ⟶ Write this word on the board.

TEACH

Sample leading question:	"Can someone explain what happens if you **equalize** something?"
Student:	"I guess you *balance* it. The suffix **-ize** means *to cause to be like*."
Teacher:	"Let's hear an example."
Student:	"I've heard the word when talking about how your ears pop when you go up a mountain. The pressure inside the ear makes a balance with the pressure outside the ear."
Teacher:	"Good. Let's hear another example."
Student:	"When I pour orange juice for me and my little sister, I try to **equalize** the amounts."
Teacher:	"What do the two amounts look like after you've **equalized** the juice?"
Student:	"They're the same. They're *balanced*, so that it's fair."

DISCUSS Let students discuss differences and similarities they may see between the words **equalize** and **equate**. Use the **collocation** method, that is, list things that can be **equated** and things that can be **equalized**.

DEMONSTRATE The temperature in Classroom A is 68 degrees. The temperature in Classroom B is 74 degrees. If I want to **equalize** them, what can I do? Would this be the same as **equating** the two temperatures? (**Equating** would mean figuring out some way that they are already balanced, as if to say they are both within a certain range.)

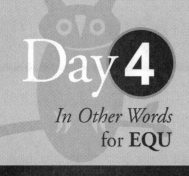

Day 4

In Other Words for **EQU**

EQU means fair, balanced

LESSON TIME

15 Minutes

OBJECTIVES

- **Understand** the meaning of the root **EQU**
- **Reinforce** knowledge of the root **EQU**
- **Understand** the meaning of words in the **EQU** family
- **Apply** knowledge of words in the **EQU** family

MATERIALS

- Student Activity Book
- **EQU** Word Wall
- Dictionary *(print or on-line)*

In Other Words for **EQU**

TEACH Have students turn to page 90 in their Student Activity Books. Explain that they are going to read a little story that uses some surprising and sometimes odd phrasing. The underlined words or phrases in the story are actually definitions or synonyms for words in the **EQU** family. Then they will see sentences about the story, each containing a blank. Using context clues in the sentences, they will find an **EQU** family word in the Word Bank at the bottom to fit in each blank.

Have a student read aloud the opening sentence or sentences of the story that contain the first underlined phrase. Then say, "Let's look at the first numbered sentence that contains a blank to be filled in. Clues in the sentence tell us that we want a naming word, a plural noun that is a synonym for states of being *unfair and unbalanced*. I see the word **inequalities** at the bottom of the page. The prefix **in-** meaning not added to **equalities** reflects the idea of *unfair and unbalanced*. Notice that the prefixes **in-** and **un-** both mean not. Let's write **inequalities** in the blank for the first sentence."

COMPLETE THE ACTIVITY

This can be quite challenging, so allow students to work on this activity in small groups. Not every word in the Word Bank will be used.

DISCUSS After about 10 minutes, ask if there were any difficulties. Have volunteers explain strategies they used that led to correct answers.

SAB Pg 90

Rosa Parks

When Rosa Parks wearily climbed the steps of the bus home from work, she did not realize that she was about to fuel a fight against <u>states of being unfair and unbalanced</u> between the races in Montgomery, Alabama. She wasn't thinking of the <u>unfairness</u> in treatment of blacks and whites; she wasn't thinking of the schools <u>not brought to balance or fairness</u> that black children attended in her city. She was simply tired and heading home. Her refusal to move to back of the bus to seats intended for blacks ignited a struggle for <u>fair and balanced</u> opportunities for all people regardless of race.

In the years since Parks' stand for <u>the state of being balanced and just</u>, laws have been passed and attitudes have changed which have begun to <u>balance</u> opportunities for everyone. More recent movements toward <u>a state of balance</u> among diverse groups, as well as attitudes treating all people <u>in a manner fair and balanced</u> are able to trace their history back to this woman.

<u>Fill in the blanks below using words from the "equ, equi, eg" family.</u>

1. Rosa Parks' actions illustrated one of many <u>inequalities</u> between blacks and whites.
2. The segregation of bus seats showed the <u>inequity</u> of the treatment of black and white riders of the bus.
3. In Montgomery, schools for black children were <u>inadequate</u> compared to schools for white children.
4. During this time in American history, the chances for every individual to succeed were not <u>equal</u>.
5. Laws were passed to assure that there was <u>equity</u> for all people.
6. Changes in laws and attitudes served to <u>equalize</u> the circumstances between the races.
7. Society is more secure when an <u>equilibrium</u> is found among diverse groups.
8. All people deserve to be treated <u>equitably</u> in their pursuits of life, liberty, and happiness.

<u>Not Used:</u> equalities   equate   equalization   equatorial

178

OPTIONAL

Day 5

Morpheme Mania
for **EQU**

EQU means
fair, balanced

LESSON TIME

15 Minutes

OBJECTIVES

- **Build** words in the **EQU** family

- **Apply** knowledge of synonyms and antonyms to **EQU** words

Optional Morpheme Mania for **EQU**

On page 91 of their Activity Books, students will see an optional vocabulary enrichment activity that they can work on in groups, time permitting. This activity makes a great review for the formal assessment on the next page.

All the affixes presented in the week's activities are provided at the top of the page on either side of the root of the week in all its forms. Students can write in up to 13 of the words they built during the week, possibly discovering additional ones.

Then students can brainstorm with each other to come up with antonyms and synonyms they may know. Starter examples are given with every Morpheme Mania in the Activity Book. Because antonyms and synonyms may require knowledge of roots which students have not yet studied, completion of this activity is not crucial. Simply remind students that they can at any time during the course of the year revisit any of their Morpheme Mania pages and add words, antonyms, and synonyms as their vocabulary grows.

Day 5 Assessment

Make and hand out copies.
The answer key is on page A-4.
The instructions are on page A-2.

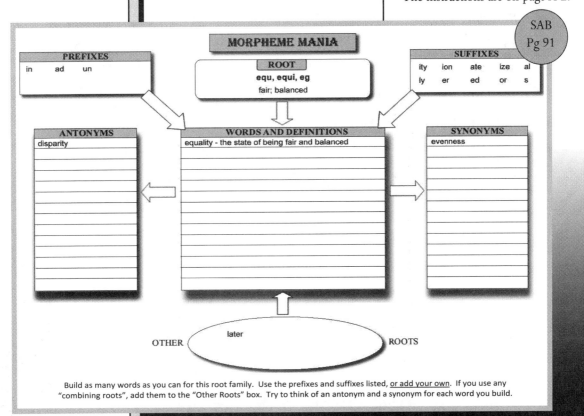

SAB
Pg 91

MORPHEME MANIA

PREFIXES		
in	ad	un

ROOT
equ, equi, eg
fair; balanced

SUFFIXES				
ity	ion	ate	ize	al
ly	er	ed	or	s

ANTONYMS
disparity

WORDS AND DEFINITIONS
equality - the state of being fair and balanced

SYNONYMS
evenness

OTHER   later   ROOTS

Build as many words as you can for this root family. Use the prefixes and suffixes listed, or add your own. If you use any "combining roots", add them to the "Other Roots" box. Try to think of an antonym and a synonym for each word you build.

adequacy state of being brought to balance or fairness; sufficiency

adequate brought to balance or fairness; enough or sufficient

adequately in a manner brought to balance or fairness; sufficiently

equal being fair and balanced; same

equaled made or was fair and balanced; was the same as

equaling making or being fair and balanced; being the same as

equalities states of being fair and balanced

equality the state of being fair and balanced

equalization the act of making balanced

equalizations acts of making balanced

equalize to balance

equalized balanced

equalizer a device that brings into balance or fairness

equalizers devices that bring into balance or fairness

equalizes balances

equalizing balancing

equally balanced to the same degree; in the same manner

equals makes or is fair and balanced; is the same as

equate to make even or balanced; to show similarities

equated made even or balanced; showed similarities

equates makes even or balanced; shows similarities

equating making even or balanced; showing similarities

equation a balanced statement

equations balanced statements

equator imaginary line dividing earth into even halves

equatorial pertaining to line dividing earth into even halves

equatorially in manner of a line dividing earth into even halves

equators imaginary lines dividing planets into even halves

equidistance quality of standing at a balanced space away from

equidistances qualities of standing at a balanced space away from

equidistant standing at a balanced space away from

equidistantly so as to stand at a balanced space away from

equilateral having balanced sides

equilaterally in a way of having balanced sides

equilaterals balanced-sided figures

equilibrium state of balance

equitable characterized by balance and fairness

equitably with balance and fairness

equity state of being balanced, just, or fair

equivalence quality of having balance in worth; sameness

equivalences qualities of having balance in worth

equivalencies qualities of having balance in worth

equivalency quality of having balance in worth; sameness

equivalent even in worth; same

equivalently in a manner being even in worth; so as to be the same

equivalents features of being even in worth; things that are the same

inadequacy state of not being brought to balance or fairness; insufficiency

inadequate not being brought to balance or fairness; not enough

inadequateness quality of not being brought to balance or fairness; insufficiency

inequalities states of unfairness and imbalance

inequality the state of being unfair and unbalanced

inequities conditions in which things are out of balance; acts of unfairness

inequity a condition in which something is out of balance; unfairness

unequal not fair and balanced; not the same

unequaled not of the same fairness and balance; without a peer

Check-Up for EQU

_____ **1.** EQU in words like **adequate** and **inequality** means:

    A fair or balanced

    B to give or offer

    C number

_____ **2.** What is the meaning of the word **inequity**?

    A an odd number

    B a condition of being out of balance

    C a process of giving in

_____ **3.** What is the meaning of the word **equation**?

    A the result of offering

    B the inability to count

    C a balanced statement

_____ **4.** What is the meaning of the word **adequate**?

    A brought to balance or fairness

    B not enough in number

    C to offer throughout

_____ **5.** The **equator**:

    A allows us to count the number of continents on earth

    B provides heat for the world

    C divides the world into balanced halves

_____ **6.** Which word means **standing at a balanced space away**?

    A equidistantly

    B equidistant

    C equidistance

_____ **7.** Which word means **a state of balance**?

    A equatorial

    B inequity

    C equilibrium

_____ **8.** Which word means **qualities of having balance in worth**?

    A adequately

    B equivalences

    C equalizer

_____ **9.** An **equably** cheerful person is happy:

    A only when doing arithmetic

    B none of the time

    C all the time

_____ **10.** At a time known as **equinox**, daytime is:

    A the same length as the night

    B much longer than the night

    C much shorter than the night

OBJECTIVES

- **Understand** the meaning of the root **PET**
- **Build** words in the root **PET** family
- **Break Apart** words in the root **PET** family
- **Understand** the meaning of words in the **PET** family
- **Understand** the spelling principles applied to the root **PET**
- **Apply** knowledge of words in the **PET** family
- **Assess** and **Reinforce** knowledge of words in the **PET** family

MATERIALS

- Student Activity Books, pages 93-98
- Dictionary *(print or on-line)*

CROSS-CURRICULAR EXAMPLES

Science:
centripetal, impetus

Social Studies:
competition, competitor

Language Arts:
impetuous, petulance

Math:
perpetual, repeating

PET

meaning "to seek, aim for; rush"

petition
a document that **seeks** something

repetitive
aiming for or seeking again

impetus
a **rush** into

Morpheme: **PET**
Allomorphs: **PEAT, PETE**

About 400 words containing the morpheme **PET** or one of its allomorphs are current in English. During this unit, tell students to be alert for this root in their school texts, general reading, and oral language they hear. Some of the words they might encounter in their school subjects are listed on the left under Cross-Curricular Examples.

UNIT AT A GLANCE

Day **1**
Root Squares
for **PET**

Day **2**
Magic Squares
for **PET**

Day **3**
Stair Steps
for **PET**

OPTIONAL
Day **4**
In Other Words
for **PET**

Day **5**
Assessment or Morpheme Mania
for **PET**

Each activity should take approximately **15 minutes**.

The basic sense of this root is *to rush*. A **petulant** person *flies off the handle*. The idea of flying as a type of rushing appears in the Greek form of this morpheme, which will be familiar to most students from their curiosity about dinosaurs: **pter-o-dactyl**, *flying with fingers, or feathered toes*.

Other directions of this root that pertain to flying and feathers involve the words **pen** (writing tool that was originally a feather) and **pennate** (also spelled **pinnate**), *possessing feathers*. The word **pinnacle**, meaning *topmost*, meant originally *a feather-shaped* spire at the top of a structure. A **panache** is a *decorative tuft of feathers* on a helmet, and, from that, the strut or swagger that a person so-helmeted often assumed.

As amazing as it may seem, the words **hippopotamus**, *horse of the river*, and **Mesopotamia**, *area between rivers*, contain this root. The Greek word **potamos**, *river*, means *rushing water*.

Word Alert!

Some common words that appear to have this morpheme are deceptive:

> The word **petal** comes from a Greek verb meaning *to spread*.
>
> The word **petunia** comes from a French word referring to *tobacco*.
>
> A **petticoat** is a small (as in **petty**) coat.
>
> **Petroleum** is *oil from the rocks*.

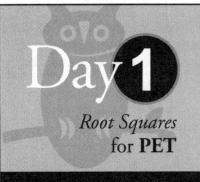

Day 1

Root Squares for PET

PET means to seek, aim for; rush

LESSON TIME

15 Minutes

OBJECTIVES

- **Understand** the meaning of the root **PET**
- **Build** words in the **PET** family
- **Understand** the meaning of words in the **PET** family
- **Understand** the spelling principles applied to the root **PET**

MATERIALS

- Student Activity Book
- **PET** Word Wall
- Dictionary *(print or on-line)*

DIFFERENTIATING INSTRUCTION

If you prefer easier or more difficult activities, use your personal account at www.dynamicliteracy.com to access novice or expert versions, along with ideas on using them.

Root Squares for PET

TEACH Have students turn to page 93 in their Activity Books. Say, "All of the prefixes and suffixes except one in the squares surrounding the center are probably familiar, but if you have questions about any of the meanings, look them up in your activity book." A Mini-Lesson on the only completely new suffix, -**uous**, is provided on the next page of this Manual.

Call attention to the center box. Point out that the root **PET** has three different spellings. Ask students to decide if one of the forms they see in the middle square can stand alone as a word. Though each of the spellings may look like words, none actually is related to this family. The words **pet** and **peat**, and the name **Pete** come from other roots. In the cases here, each allomorph must have a prefix or a suffix to make a word. Suggest that students start their list with **peat** and then add the prefix **re-**, meaning *again*, to build **repeat**, meaning *to do or try again*. Explore how this word is related to the idea of *to seek, or aim for*, or *to rush*.

COMPLETE THE ACTIVITY

Have students follow the directions to build words. If students have difficulty building words with the Root Squares, show them how by modeling the matrix approach found on the next page, taking one affix at a time and seeing if it will connect with any one of the allomorphs of the root.

DISCUSS After five minutes, have volunteers write some of their words on the board. Guide the class in a discussion of how the meaning of the root is still *to seek, or aim for, or to rush*, even when prefixes and suffixes are added. Watch for target words that most easily demonstrate the meanings of *to seek, or aim for, or to rush*. If the word **compete** is not present, ask the class, "Can anyone try to use the prefix **com-**?" and then continue on to the focus word discussion on the next page.

SAB Pg 93

Root Squares

How many words can you make?

Start in any square. Your goal is to combine two or more word parts to make as many words in the 'pet, peat, pete' family as you can. Write each word and a definition you can think of for it in the space provided at the bottom of the page. Use the back of the page if you need to.

im	uate	com
it	pet, peat, pete	re
per	ion	uous

_____
_____
_____
_____
_____
_____
_____
_____
_____
_____
_____

MINI-LESSON: the Suffix -uous

The suffix **-uous** is a variation of **-ous**, meaning *full of or possessing qualities of.* The letter **u** in some situations belongs to the root stem, and in other situations, it serves to cause *palatalization* (a sound of **ch**, **j**, **zh**, or **sh**) with a dental sound (**t**, **d**, or **s**). The **-uous** form occurs in about 50 English words, the most familiar being the following:

ambiguous	**conspicuous**	**continuous**	**strenuous**
superfluous	**tenuous**	**vacuous**	

Palatalization can be heard in these familiar words:

arduous	**contemptuous**	**tumultuous**	**sensuous**	**assiduous**
sumptuous	**virtuous**	**deciduous**	**tempestuous**	**voluptuous**

Focus Word: COMPETE ⟹ Write this word on the board.

TEACH

Lead with this:	"Here is a word we see a lot, in sports, school, business—everywhere. What does it mean?"
Student:	"It means to try to win."
Student:	"It means you're trying to get ahead of somebody else."
Teacher:	"Good, and, as usual, let's look at the word to see what it tells us."
Student:	"There's our root, and that means *to seek or aim for,* and *to rush.*"
Student:	"And the prefix is **com-**, meaning *with or together.*"
Teacher:	"Why is it spelled **com-**?"
Students:	"ASSIMILATION!"
Teacher:	"And so what do the pieces of the word **compete** add up to meaning?"
Student:	"*To seek or aim for together.* Ah, I see. It's two or more people *seeking* or *aiming* for the same goal together."

DISCUSS Lead students to see that, based on its two pieces of meaning, **compete** refers *to seeking or aiming for something along with others.* Students can discuss that a common goal has to be established, and then individuals or teams work out ways to achieve that goal. A sample leading discussion question is, "Are rules required?" Another approach could be to ask, "Can the word **compete** be used with non-living things?"

DEMONSTRATE Let students interested in and knowledgeable about automobiles explain in what ways two different types of cars can or cannot **compete**. Let students demonstrate how two types of shoes can or cannot **compete** in walking, running, or playing sports.

Root Squares Matrix

You can refer to this matrix to guide students in this activity. Students could build at least these 9 words. *It is not important how many words are built*, so long as students understand the meanings of the root and its affixes. Encourage discussion about the definitions of any words formed for the blank slots as well as for the attested words.

	no prefix	com-	im-	per-	re-
no suffix		compete			repeat
-itive		competitive			repetitive
-uate				perpetuate	
-uous			impetuous		
-ition	petition	competition			repetition

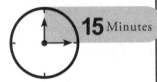

LESSON TIME

15 Minutes

OBJECTIVES

- **Understand** the meaning of the root **PET**
- **Break Apart** words in the **PET** family
- **Understand** the meanings of words in the **PET** family

MATERIALS

- Student Activity Book
- **PET** Word Wall
- Dictionary *(print or on-line)*

DIFFERENTIATING INSTRUCTION

If you prefer easier or more difficult activities, use your personal account at www.dynamicliteracy.com to access novice or expert versions, along with ideas on using them.

Break Apart Words with **PET**

TEACH Have students turn to the Magic Squares on page 94 in their Student Activity Books. Model a Think-Aloud strategy for students: "I know that **PET** means *to seek, aim for; rush*. I can use this knowledge to find the definition of a word with this as its root." Direct students to word C, **appetizer**. Say, "This is a common word, and I know it is something that causes me to want to eat, but let's look at the parts of the word to see how it means that. The prefix **ap-** in front of the root, **pet**, is an assimilation of **ad-**, meaning *toward*. I know that the suffix **-ize** means *to cause to be like* and the suffix **-er** means *a person or device that does*. (Notice that the final **e** on **-ize** drops before the **-er** is added.) Look at

definition 2, *something that causes a seeking toward; something to whet the taste*. That accounts for all the parts, and then some, so let's write the number 2 in square C."

COMPLETE THE ACTIVITY

Ask students to use the same strategy to find the correct definitions for the other words. Tell them to write the number of the definition in the box that matches the letter for the word. Remind them that if all their answers are correct, each row and each column will add up to the same Magic number.

DISCUSS After five minutes, ask if there are any difficulties about matching the words and definitions. If there are, ask volunteers to explain clues in the definitions that will lead to the correct choice of word. As needed, follow the focus word approach for **competence** that you see modeled on the next page. Add any new words to the classroom **PET** Word Wall and remind students to add these words to the **PET** Word Wall in their Activity Books.

SAB Pg 94

Magic Squares

Select the best answer for each of the words in the 'pet, peat, pete' family from the numbered definitions. Put the number in the proper space in the Magic Square box. If the total of the numbers is the same both across and down, you have found the magic number!

'pet, peat, pete' means to seek, aim for; rush

WORDS	DEFINITIONS
A. repetitions	1. likely to seek a goal along with others
B. petitioners	2. something that causes a seeking toward; something to whet the taste
C. appetizer	3. aimed to make something last throughout; eternalized
D. repeatedly	4. so as to have aimed for or sought again; over and over
E. competence	5. seeking to last thoroughly; ever-lasting
F. impetuously	6. in a manner rushing onto; in an impulsive and uncontrolled manner
G. perpetual	7. people who seek something
H. perpetuated	8. the ability to seek a goal along with others
I. petition	9. acts of aiming for or seeking again; acts of saying or doing again
	10. a document that seeks something

Magic Square Box

A. 9	B. 7	C. 2
D. 4	E. 8	F. 6
G. 5	H. 3	I. 10

Magic Number __18__

*** ANSWER KEY ***

Focus Word: **COMPETENCE** → Write this word on the board.

TEACH

Sample leading question:	"This word pops up a lot. Let's see if we can figure out how it works."
Student:	"I see the word **compete** in there."
Student:	"But -**nce** doesn't make a suffix, I don't think."
Teacher:	"So what could be going on in the spelling of this word?"
Student:	"I know—it's **compete** with the last **e** dropped, so the suffix is -**ence**."
Student:	"So does it mean the act of **competing**, like **competition**?"
Teacher:	"It can be used like that, but more recently, it has another twist."
Student:	"I think it means *the ability or desire* to **compete**, because there's the word **competent**, which means you can **compete**."
Teacher:	"And what was the deep meaning of **compete**?"
Student:	"*To seek or aim for along with others.*"
Student:	"So **competence** is the *condition of actually seeking or aiming along with others.*"

DISCUSS Lead students to see that, based on its three pieces of meaning, **competence** refers to *the act or condition of seeking or aiming for something along with others*, with an added element of desiring to be able to do that.

DEMONSTRATE Have small groups of students share discussing the areas in which they feel they have **competence**. Encourage the idea that not only ability determines **competence**, but desire to **compete** as well.

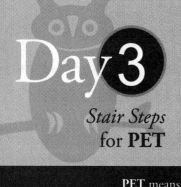

Day 3

Stair Steps
for **PET**

PET means
to seek, aim for; rush

LESSON TIME

15 Minutes

OBJECTIVES

- **Understand** the meaning of the root **PET**
- **Apply** knowledge of the root **PET**
- **Break Apart** words in the **PET** family
- **Understand** the meaning of words in the **PET** family
- **Understand** the spelling principles applied to the root **PET**

MATERIALS

- Student Activity Book
- **PET** Word Wall

DIFFERENTIATING INSTRUCTION

If you prefer easier or more difficult activities, use your personal account at www.dynamicliteracy.com to access novice or expert versions, along with ideas on using them.

Apply Knowledge of PET

TEACH Have students turn to page 95 in their Student Activity Books. Explain that the boxes in front of and after the root indicate letters that spell out prefixes and suffixes. Students will spell out the correct prefixes and suffixes determined by clues in the definitions at the bottom of the page.

Have a volunteer read definition number three at the bottom of the page. Say, "The first thing we notice in this definition is the plural—*people or tools*. The suffix that means *person or thing that does* is one we have seen previously, -**er**. What prefix do you recall that means *again*? It

also means *back* or *against*. The prefix **re**- has that meaning, and that would give us **repeaters**."

COMPLETE THE ACTIVITY

Let students work in pairs (optionally) and tell them to use the same strategy to find the correct prefixes and suffixes for the words listed. These activities can be quite challenging!

DISCUSS After a few minutes, review the answers as a class. Ask if there were any difficulties. Listen to any problems and have volunteers solve the difficulties by explaining key clues in the given definitions. As needed, follow the focus word approach that you see modeled on the next page.

SAB
Pg 95

Stair Steps

Fill in the missing letters of each 'pet, peat, pete' word by using the definitions below.
'pet, peat, pete' means to seek; aim for; rush

1. | r | e | p | e | a | t |
2. | a | p | p | e | t | i | t | e |
3. | r | e | p | e | a | t | e | r | s |
4. | p | e | t | i | t | i | o | n | e | r |
5. | p | e | r | p | e | t | u | a | t | e | d |
6. | p | e | r | p | e | t | u | a | t | i | n | g |
7. | c | o | m | p | e | t | i | t | i | v | e | l | y |
8. | r | e | p | e | t | i | t | i | v | e | n | e | s | s |

1. to aim for or seek again; to say or do again
2. process of seeking toward; something hungered or yearned for
3. people or tools that aim for or seek again
4. a person who seeks something
5. aimed to make something last throughout; eternalized
6. aiming to make something last throughout; eternalizing
7. in a manner likely to seek goals along with others
8. quality of aiming for or seeking again; quality of being done again and again

MINI-LESSON: the Suffix -ness

The native noun-forming English suffix -**ness**, meaning *state, condition, or quality*, usually appears with roots of native English, as you can demonstrate to your students. Put any of these words on the board and have students define them. Then have students add the suffix -**ness** to see how nouns emerge:

fair	neat	calm	good	kind	weak	mean
dark	gentle	dull	cold	wide	bald	late
open	numb	helpful	mad	full	blind	well
fit	weak	damp	bold	ripe	sick	strange

The suffix -**ness** has become a standard noun-formation for many Latin-based words, especially those adjectives ending in the suffixes -**ous** and -**ate**. Alongside nouns such as **courtesy** and **accuracy** have arisen **courteousness** and **accurateness**. Here we see language evolution in action. Other examples include:

viciousness   **spaciousness**   **luxuriousness**   **elaborateness**   **courageousness**   **anxiousness**

MINI-LESSON: the partial Suffix -enc

The suffix -**ence**, indicating *a quality or state*, will drop its final **e** when the suffix -**y** is attached as well. Note the words **residence** and **residency**. More significantly and less obviously, the adjective-forming suffix -**ent**, meaning *doing or behaving*, will be spelled -**enc**- when the suffix -**y** is attached. Students can hear the loss of the **t** sound in the following pairs of words:

frequent – frequency	agent – agency
decent – decency	urgent – urgency

Focus Word: **REPEAT** ⟶ Write this word on the board.

TEACH

Sample leading question:	"Now I'm sure everyone knows what this word means."
Student:	*"Do it again, say it again."*
Student:	"But the pieces mean *to seek or aim for again*. What is being aimed for again when you **repeat** something?"
Teacher:	"Class?"
Student:	"I guess you're *aiming* for a better result, you want somebody to hear you better, or you want do something again because you like it."
Student:	"I guess so, but that seems a stretch."
Teacher:	"Yes, I agree. Sometimes words have gone through so much of a change that it is difficult to see how the morphemes have their original meanings anymore."
Student:	"No, I think you're still *aiming again at something*, so I get it."

DISCUSS Let pairs of students discuss situations in which **repeating** is indeed *seeking or aiming at something again*. Let them share their conclusions with the whole class. For example, **repeating** a specific exercise, like sit-ups, seeks to stretch the muscles again for greater benefits. A sample focused discussion topic can be to ask, "Is **repeating** always aiming for the better?"

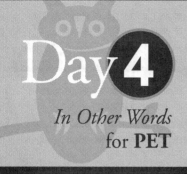

Day 4

In Other Words for PET

PET means to seek, aim for; rush

LESSON TIME

15 Minutes

OBJECTIVES

- **Understand** the meaning of the root **PET**
- **Reinforce** knowledge of the root **PET**
- **Understand** the meaning of words in the **PET** family
- **Apply** knowledge of words in the **PET** family

MATERIALS

- Student Activity Book
- **PET** Word Wall
- Dictionary *(print or on-line)*

In Other Words for **PET**

TEACH Have students turn to page 96 in their Student Activity Books. Explain that they are going to read a little story that uses some surprising and sometimes odd phrasing. The underlined words or phrases in the story are actually definitions or synonyms for words in the **PET** family. Then they will see sentences about the story, each containing a blank.

Using context clues in the sentences, they will find a **PET** family word in the Word Bank at the bottom to fit in each blank. Have a student read aloud the opening sentence or sentences of the story that contain the first underlined phrase. Then say, "Let's look at the first numbered sentence that contains a blank to be filled in. Clues in the sentence tell us that we want a describing word, an adjective that is a synonym for **rushed** and which could modify **decision**. I see the word **impetuous** at the bottom of the page. The prefix **im-** is a form of **in-** meaning *in* and the suffix **-uous** makes the word mean *full of*. That's the idea, *full of rush*, since rush is one of the meanings we have for the root **pet**. Let's write **impetuous** in the blank for the first sentence."

COMPLETE THE ACTIVITY

This can be quite challenging, so allow students to work on this activity in small groups. Not every word in the Word Bank will be used.

DISCUSS After about 10 minutes, ask if there were any difficulties. Have volunteers explain strategies they used that led to correct answers.

SAB Pg 96

Champion Gymnast

Christa's decision to train as a gymnast was not a <u>rushed</u> one. For a long time her idol had been Mary Lou Retton, who <u>sought along with others</u> in the Olympics in 1984, winning the women's gold medal in the All Around. Christa, also born in West Virginia, wanted <u>thoroughly to seek to make everlasting</u> the championship ways of Retton in her own gymnastics career. As her skills grew <u>in a manner likely to seek goals along with others</u>, so did Christa's <u>yearning to seek toward</u> winning. She was dedicated to her sport and did not mind the <u>quality of being done again and again</u> that practice sessions seemed to have. She knew that in order to learn a new skill in floor exercise, she had to <u>aim for and seek again</u> her routines many times.

One afternoon at the end of a long practice, Christa was stopped by a group of young girls <u>seeking in documentary form</u> her autograph. She felt just like a star.

<u>Fill in the blanks below using words from the "pet, peat, pete" family</u>.

1. Christa thought about her decision a long time and did not make a(n) <u>impetuous</u> decision to be a gymnast.
2. Mary Lou Retton <u>competed</u> against women from all over the world in the 1984 Olympics.
3. Becoming a champion gymnast was Christa's way to <u>perpetuate</u> the fame of other Olympians born in West Virginia.
4. Both Christa and Mary Lou worked <u>competitively</u> to be at the top of their abilities.
5. With a strong <u>appetite</u> for winning, Christa could almost taste her success.
6. To learn the basics, Christa endured the endless <u>repetitiveness</u> of practice sessions.
7. In order to perfect the dismount of her floor exercise, Christa had to <u>repeat</u> it many times.
8. Christa was proud of her hard work when she saw the group of girls <u>petitioning</u> for her autograph.

<u>Not Used:</u> incompetency   appetizer   competitor   repeatedly

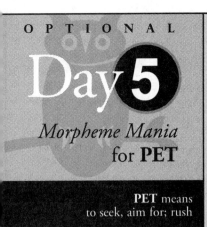
LESSON TIME

15 Minutes

OBJECTIVES

• **Build** words in the **PET** family

• **Apply** knowledge of synonyms and antonyms to **PET** words

Optional Morpheme Mania for **PET**

On page 97 of their Activity Books, students will see an optional vocabulary enrichment activity that they can work on in groups, time permitting. This activity makes a great review for the formal assessment on the next page.

All the affixes presented in the week's activities are provided at the top of the page on either side of the root of the week in all its forms. Students can write in up to 13 of the words they built during the week, possibly discovering additional ones.

Then students can brainstorm with each other to come up with antonyms and synonyms they may know. Starter examples are given with every Morpheme Mania in the Activity Book. Because antonyms and synonyms may require knowledge of roots which students have not yet studied, completion of this activity is not crucial. Simply remind students that they can at any time during the course of the year revisit any of their Morpheme Mania pages and add words, antonyms, and synonyms as their vocabulary grows.

Day 5 *Assessment*

Make and hand out copies.
The answer key is on page A-4.
The instructions are on page A-2.

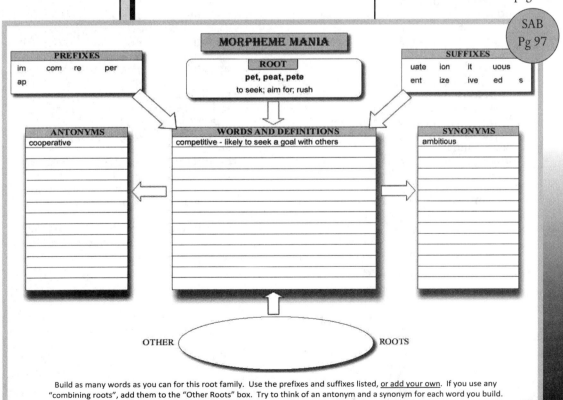

SAB Pg 97

MORPHEME MANIA

PREFIXES			
im	com	re	per
ap			

ROOT
pet, peat, pete
to seek; aim for; rush

SUFFIXES			
uate	ion	it	uous
ent	ize	ive	ed	s

ANTONYMS
cooperative

WORDS AND DEFINITIONS
competitive - likely to seek a goal with others

SYNONYMS
ambitious

OTHER — ROOTS

Build as many words as you can for this root family. Use the prefixes and suffixes listed, <u>or add your own</u>. If you use any "combining roots", add them to the "Other Roots" box. Try to think of an antonym and a synonym for each word you build.

appetite process of seeking toward; something hungered or yearned for

appetites processes of seeking toward; things hungered or yearned for

appetizer something that causes a seeking toward; something to whet the taste

appetizers things that cause a seeking toward; things that whet the taste

appetizing causing a seeking toward; whetting the taste

compete to seek the same thing with someone else

competed sought the same thing with someone else

competence the ability to seek a goal along with others

competency quality of seeking a goal along with others

competent able to seek a goal along with others

competes seeks the same thing with someone else

competing seeking the same thing with someone else

competition act of seeking the same thing with someone else

competitions acts of seeking the same thing with someone else

competitive likely to seek a goal along with others

competitively in a manner likely to seek goals along with others

competitiveness quality of seeking a goal along with others

competitor a person seeking a goal along with others

competitors people seeking a goal along with others

impetuous rushing onto; impulsive and uncontrolled

impetuously in a manner rushing onto; in an impulsive and uncontrolled manner

impetus a rush onto; momentum

impetuses acts of rushing onto; states of momentum

incompetence inability to seek a goal along with others; lack of qualification or skill

incompetencies qualities of not seeking a goal along with others; states of lacking qualification or skill

incompetency quality of not seeking a goal along with others; lack of qualification or skill

incompetent not able to seek a goal along with others; not qualified or skillful

perpetual seeking to last thoroughly; ever-lasting

perpetually in a manner seeking to last thoroughly; ever-lastingly

perpetuate to aim to make something last throughout; to eternalize

perpetuated aimed to make something last throughout; eternalized

perpetuates aims to make something last throughout; eternalizes

perpetuating aiming to make something last throughout; eternalizing

perpetuation act of aiming to make last throughout; act or process of eternalizing

perpetuity an aim to make something last throughout; eternity

petition a document that seeks something

petitioner a person who seeks something

petitioners people who seek something

petitions documents that seek something

repeat to aim for or seek again; to say or do again

repeated aimed for or sought again; said or did again

repeatedly so as to have aimed for or sought again; over and over

repeater a person or tool that aims for or seeks again

repeaters people or tools that aim for or seek again

repeats aims for or seeks again; says or does again

repetition the act of aiming for or seeking again; the act of saying or doing again

repetitions acts of aiming for or seeking again; acts of saying or doing again

repetitious aiming for or seeking again; over and over again

repetitiously in a manner aiming for or seeking again; in a manner over and over

repetitiousness quality of aiming for or seeking again; quality of being done over and over

repetitive aiming for or seeking again; done over and over

repetitively in a manner aiming for or seeking again; in a manner done over and over

repetitiveness quality of aiming for or seeking again; quality of being done again and again

Check-Up for **PET**

Name _____

_____ **1.** **PET** or **PEAT** in words like **appetite** and **repeat** means:

    A to arrange or put in order

    B to eat

    C to seek or aim for

_____ **2.** What is the meaning of the word **compete**?

    A to arrange in a specific order

    B to prepare food for eating

    C to aim for the same goal along with others

_____ **3.** What is the meaning of the word **appetizer**?

    A anything that causes a seeking toward

    B something that makes you eat less

    C a person who arranges food attractively on a tray

_____ **4.** What is the meaning of the word **impetus**?

    A a lack of arrangement

    B a rush or drive into

    C not able to seek a goal

_____ **5.** **Repetitious** means:

    A putting back in order

    B aiming for or seeking again and again

    C divides the world into balanced halves

_____ **6.** Which word means **aimed to make something last throughout time**?

    A competed

    B perpetuated

    C incompetence

_____ **7.** Which word means **people who seek something**?

    A petitioners

    B competitions

    C appetites

_____ **8.** Which word means **a quality of not seeking a goal along with others**?

    A noncompetitive

    B incompetency

    C impetuously

_____ **9.** The **petulant** salesclerk asked me what I wanted. The salesclerk:

    A practically attacked me

    B had a pleasant smile

    C was eating lunch

_____ **10.** **Centripetal** forces:

    A keep things away from the center

    B do not like being in the center

    C move toward the center

OBJECTIVES

- **Understand** the meaning of the root **FUND**

- **Build** words in the root **FUND** family

- **Break Apart** words in the root **FUND** family

- **Understand** the meaning of words in the **FUND** family

- **Understand** the spelling principles applied to the root **FUND**

- **Apply** knowledge of words in the **FUND** family

- **Assess** and **Reinforce** knowledge of words in the **FUND** family

MATERIALS

- Student Activity Books, pages 99-104

- Dictionary
  (print or on-line)

CROSS-CURRICULAR EXAMPLES

Science:
affuse, diffused, fusile, transfusion

Social Studies:
confusion, foundries

Language Arts:
suffusedly, effusive

Math:
diffusive, interfuse

FUND

meaning "to melt, pour, or blend"

fusion
act of **melting** and pouring together

infusion
act of **pouring** into

confuse
to **blend** together

Morpheme: **FUND**
Allomorphs: **FUS, FUSE, FOUND**

Nearly 400 words containing the morpheme **FUND** or one of its allomorphs are current in English. During this unit, tell students to be alert for this root in their school texts, general reading, and oral language they hear. Some of the words they might encounter in their school subjects are listed on the left under Cross-Curricular Examples.

UNIT AT A GLANCE

Day **1**
Root Squares
for **FUND**

Day **2**
Magic Squares
for **FUND**

Day **3**
Stair Steps
for **FUND**

OPTIONAL
Day **4**
In Other Words
for **FUND**

Day **5**
Assessment or Morpheme Mania
for **FUND**

Each activity should take approximately **15 minutes**.

If you are given a **refund**, there is literally a *pouring back* of what you had originally given.

The **fuse** in the electric box is named because it *melts* during an overload in order to break a circuit of current.

A **foundry** is a place where metals are *melted* and cast into shapes, or **founded**. (not to be confused with the idea of *built* or *established*—see below).

If you have ever dined on **fondue**, you will now recognize why this *melted* blend of cheeses, chocolates, or other delicacies is so named.

A **funnel** is used to make *pouring* a liquid neater and more direct.

Useless things are called **futile**, a word coming from a Latin adjective that meant *easily poured out or gotten rid of.*

Word Alert!

The **fuse** that allows you to light fireworks is not from this root but from a word that means "rod-shaped."

The words **found** (to establish or the past tense of find), **funds** (as in money), and **fundamental** (basic) are built on a similar-looking Latin root meaning *bottom or ground*. Words can be misleading: the word **fund** has to do with money and property (bottom land originally), and it would seem logical that to **refund** means to give money or property back. However, as seen above, to **refund** does belong to the root meaning *to pour*.

The word **fuss** is possibly a slurring of the word **force** (just as the word **cuss** comes from **curse**).

Resistance is **futile**!

Day 1

FUND means
to melt, pour, or blend

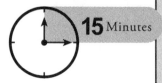

LESSON TIME

15 Minutes

OBJECTIVES

- **Understand** the meaning of the root **FUND**

- **Build** words in the **FUND** family

- **Understand** the meaning of words in the **FUND** family

- **Understand** the spelling principles applied to the root **FUND**

MATERIALS

- Student Activity Book

- **FUND** Word Wall

- Dictionary *(print or on-line)*

DIFFERENTIATING INSTRUCTION

If you prefer easier or more difficult activities, use your personal account at www.dynamicliteracy.com to access novice or expert versions, along with ideas on using them.

Root Squares for FUND

TEACH Have students turn to page 99 in their Activity Books. Say, "All of the prefixes and suffixes in the squares surrounding the shaded center are probably familiar, but if you have questions about any of the meanings, simply ask or look them up in the list inside the front and back cover of the activity book. "

Call attention to the center box. Point out that the root **FUND** has a number of different spellings, called allomorphs. Ask students to decide if any of the forms they see in the middle square can stand alone as a word. They may suggest that three of the spellings they see are words–**fund**, **fuse**, and **found**. Share information from the Word Stories above to explain how these words do or do not belong to this family. Suggest that students start their list with **fuse** and then add **in**-, meaning *in or into*, to build **infuse**, meaning *to pour into*. Invite students to explore how this word is related to the idea of *melt, pour, or blend*.

COMPLETE THE ACTIVITY

Have students follow the directions for the Root Squares activity for **FUND** on page 99 to build words. If students have difficulty building words with the Root Squares, show them how by modeling the matrix approach found on the next page, taking one affix at a time and seeing if it will connect with any one of the allomorphs of the root.

DISCUSS After five minutes, have volunteers write some of their words on the board. Focus with the class on the words they have built and guide them in a discussion of how the meaning of the root is still *melt, pour, or blend*, even when prefixes and suffixes are added. Watch for target words that most easily demonstrate the meanings of *melt, pour, or blend*. If the word **confuse** is not present, ask the class, "Can anyone try to use the prefix **con**- ?" and then continue on to the focus word discussion on the next page.

SAB Pg 99

Root Squares

How many words can you make?

Start in any square. Your goal is to combine two or more word parts to make as many words in the 'fund, fus, fuse, found' family as you can. Write each word and a definition you can think of for it in the space provided at the bottom of the page. Use the back of the page if you need to.

pro	con	ness
ion	fund, fus, fuse, found	dif
trans	in	ef

_____

_____

_____

_____

_____

_____

_____

_____

Day ① Extend the Learning

Focus Word: **CONFUSE** ⟶ Write this word on the board.

TEACH

Lead with this:	"Did you ever really think what you do when you **confuse** someone?"
Student:	"You mix them up. If I'm **confused**, I'm all mixed up."
Teacher:	"And how does the word work to tell us that?"
Student:	"The prefix **con-** is there on our root."
Student:	"But the root means *to melt or pour or blend*."
Student:	"Sure–to *blend* things, you *pour them together*."
Student:	"But what gets *poured together* when you **confuse** somebody?"
Student:	"Different ideas or just different stuff in general that doesn't quite make sense."
Student:	"Oh, right–it doesn't have to be actually blending, like paint colors."
Teacher:	"Right. We call that a *figurative* meaning rather than a *literal* meaning."
Student:	"I can see how being **confused** about stuff is like having swirls of different colors of paint all poured together—hey, *poured together*!"

DISCUSS Lead students to see that, based on its two pieces of meaning, **confuse** means *to pour or blend together*.

DEMONSTRATE Imagine a scenario with your class in which a cup half filled with orange juice is poured into a cup half filled with a cola soft drink. Then half of that mixture is poured back into the now empty cup. Ask the class to explain both literally and figuratively how the drinks are **confused**.

Root Squares Matrix
You can refer to this matrix to guide students in this activity. Students could build at least these 19 words. ***It is not important how many words are built***, so long as students understand the meanings of the root and its affixes. Encourage discussion about the definitions of any words formed for the blank slots as well as for the attested words.

	no prefix	con-	dif-	ef-	in-	pro-	trans-
no suffix	found	confound					
no suffix	fuse	confuse	diffuse	effuse	infuse	profuse	transfuse
-ion	fusion	confusion	diffusion	effusion	infusion	profusion	transfusion
-ness			diffuseness	effuseness		profuseness	

Day 2

Magic Squares for **FUND**

FUND means to melt, pour, or blend

LESSON TIME

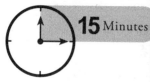

15 Minutes

OBJECTIVES

- **Understand** the meaning of the root **FUND**

- **Break Apart** words in the **FUND** family

- **Understand** the meanings of words in the **FUND** family

MATERIALS

- Student Activity Book

- **FUND** Word Wall

- Dictionary *(print or on-line)*

DIFFERENTIATING INSTRUCTION

If you prefer easier or more difficult activities, use your personal account at www.dynamicliteracy.com to access novice or expert versions, along with ideas on using them.

Break Apart Words with **FUND**

TEACH Have students turn to the Magic Squares on page 100 in their Student Activity Books. Model a Think-Aloud strategy for students: "I know that **FUND** means *to melt, pour, or blend*. I can use this knowledge to find the definition of a word with this as its root."

Direct students to word I, **fusions**. Say, "I know that the **-ion** and the **-s** create a plural noun, *a thing or an act, something one does*. Look at definition 1, *acts of melting and pouring together*. That sums up the parts, so let's write the number 1 in square I."

COMPLETE THE ACTIVITY

Ask students to use the same strategy to find the correct definitions for the other words. Tell them to write the number of the definition in the box that matches the letter for the word. Remind them that if all their answers are correct, each row and each column will add up to the same Magic number.

DISCUSS After five minutes, ask if there are any difficulties about matching the words and definitions. If there are, ask volunteers to explain clues in the definitions that will lead to the correct choice of word. As needed, follow the focus word approach for **infused** that you see modeled on the next page.

Add any new words to the classroom **FUND** Word Wall and remind students to add these words to the **FUND** Word Wall in their Activity Books.

SAB Pg 100

Magic Squares

Select the best answer for each of the words in the 'fund, fus, fuse, found' family from the numbered definitions. Put the number in the proper space in the Magic Square box. If the total of the numbers is the same both across and down, you have found the magic number!

'fund, fus, fuse, found' means to melt, pour, or blend

WORDS		DEFINITIONS
A. transfusing	1.	acts of melting and pouring together
B. refused	2.	acts or processes of being blended together; states of perplexity or bewilderment
C. profusely	3.	pouring across; carrying over or penetrating
D. confounding	4.	pouring together; baffling or ruining
E. confusions	5.	in a manner pouring forth; abundantly
F. diffusion	6.	poured into; instilled or permeated
G. effusions	7.	poured back; rejected or was unwilling to accept
H. infused	8.	out-pourings
I. fusions	9.	act of pouring or melting apart; act of scattering or making widespread

Magic Square Box

A. 3	B. 7	C. 5
D. 4	E. 2	F. 9
G. 8	H. 6	I. 1

Magic Number 15

*** ANSWER KEY ***

Focus Word: **INFUSED** ➡ Write this word on the board.

TEACH	
Sample leading question:	"Here's a word we don't see very often. But because we know how to understand words, we can probably figure out what it means and how to use it, just by looking at the morphemes. Let's try."
Student:	"It's like solving a puzzle or a math problem."
Teacher:	"Great—here we go. How many pieces of meaning do we see?"
Teacher:	"Three! A prefix, a root, and a suffix."
Student:	"That's the suffix -**ed**, making a dropped **e** on the root."
Student:	"There's that **in-** prefix, though, that can mean either *in* or *not*."
Teacher:	"So it's either *not poured* or *poured in*."
Student:	"We would see the word in a context that would probably (smiling) **unconfuse** us about which prefix it is."
Student:	"I'm betting it means *in* rather than *not*."
Teacher:	"Do you have any evidence to back you up?"
Student:	"It's just that all the other prefixes that go with this word seem to be a place: *back, across, forward, out.* I just think it's *in*."
Teacher:	"Great word investigating, class. Let me give you a sentence using the word and then you'll see how good you were even without context: I want to **infuse** a love of words into my students."
Student:	"I was right—*pour into!*"

DISCUSS Lead students to see that, based on its three pieces of meaning, **infused** means *poured or blended into*. Ask small groups to think of situations in which this word might be used.

DEMONSTRATE Turn off the room light and then turn it back on, showing how light **infuses** the room, or spreads throughout.

Day 3

Stair Steps for FUND

FUND means to melt, pour, or blend

LESSON TIME

15 Minutes

OBJECTIVES

- **Understand** the meaning of the root **FUND**

- **Apply** knowledge of the root **FUND**

- **Break Apart** words in the **FUND** family

- **Understand** the meaning of words in the **FUND** family

- **Understand** the spelling principles applied to the root **FUND**

MATERIALS

- Student Activity Book
- **FUND** Word Wall

DIFFERENTIATING INSTRUCTION

If you prefer easier or more difficult activities, use your personal account at www.dynamicliteracy.com to access novice or expert versions, along with ideas on using them.

Apply Knowledge of FUND

TEACH Have students turn to page 101 in their Student Activity Books. Explain that the boxes in front of and after the root indicate letters that spell out prefixes and suffixes. Students will spell out the correct prefixes and suffixes determined by clues in the definitions at the bottom of the page.

Have a volunteer read definition number three at the bottom of the page. Say, "What prefix do you recall that means *back* that also means *again or against*? The familiar and common prefix **re-** has all those meanings and would fit in the two blank spaces in front of **FUS** (an allomorph

of **FUND**) on step three of this puzzle. The suffix would need to be one that means *act of*. Looking down our list of suffixes, we see that **-al** means *action or process* and adding that to the end would give us **refusal**. That fits our definition perfectly, so we'll go with it for the third step of this Stair Steps exercise."

COMPLETE THE ACTIVITY

Let students work in pairs (optionally) and tell them to use the same strategy to find the correct prefixes and suffixes for the words listed. These activities can be quite challenging!

DISCUSS After a few minutes, review the answers as a class. Ask if there were any difficulties. Listen to any problems and have volunteers solve the difficulties by explaining key clues in the given definitions. As needed, follow the focus word approach that you see modeled on the next page.

SAB Pg 101

Stair Steps

Fill in the missing letters of each 'fund, fus, fuse, found' word by using the definitions below.
'fund, fus, fuse, found' means to melt, pour, or blend

1.	f	u	s	e	d				
2.	f	u	s	i	o	n			
3.	r	e	f	u	s	a	l		
4.	c	o	n	f	u	s	e	d	
5.	i	n	f	u	s	i	o	n	s
6.	c	o	n	f	o	u	n	d	e	d
7.	p	r	o	f	u	s	e	n	e	s	s
8.	t	r	a	n	s	f	u	s	i	o	n	s

1. melted and poured together
2. act of melting and pouring together
3. act of pouring back; act of rejecting or not accepting
4. blended together; perplexed or bewildered
5. acts of pouring into; acts of instilling or permeating
6. poured together; baffled or ruined
7. condition of pouring forth; abundance
8. acts of pouring across; processes of carrying over or penetrating

200

Focus Word: **INFUSIONS** ⟶ Write this word on the board.

TEACH

Sample leading question:	"Let's take a look at another hard word. But words aren't hard anymore, are they, you word masters!"
Student:	"They used to be hard, but now we know how to start figuring them out."
Teacher:	"Let's start by figuring out how many and what morphemes are here in the word **infusions**."
Student:	"There are four morphemes! It's a plural, and it's a noun, because of the two suffixes **-s** and **-ion**."
Student:	"And we already figured out that **infuse** means *to pour in*."
Student:	"So this one means *more than one act of pouring in*."
Teacher:	"That's great—see how fast you were able to do that? Now, try using it in a sentence."

DISCUSS Lead students to see that, based on its four pieces of meaning, **infusions** means *acts or processes of pouring or blending in*. Let small groups experiment with how they think the word might appear in a sentence. Groups can share their best examples.

Day 4

In Other Words for FUND

FUND means to melt, pour, or blend

LESSON TIME

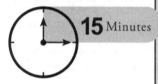

15 Minutes

OBJECTIVES

- **Understand** the meaning of the root **FUND**
- **Reinforce** knowledge of the root **FUND**
- **Understand** the meaning of words in the **FUND** family
- **Apply** knowledge of words in the **FUND** family

MATERIALS

- Student Activity Book
- **FUND** Word Wall
- Dictionary *(print or on-line)*

In Other Words for **FUND**

TEACH Have students turn to page 102 in their Student Activity Books. Explain that they are going to read a little story that uses some surprising and sometimes odd phrasing. The underlined words or phrases in the story are actually definitions or synonyms for words in the **FUND** family. Then they will see sentences about the story, each containing a blank.

Using context clues in the sentences, they will find a **FUND** family word in the Word Bank at the bottom to fit in each blank. Have a student read aloud the opening sentence or sentences of the story that contain the first underlined phrase. Then say, "Let's look at the first numbered sentence that contains a blank to be filled in. Clues in the sentence tell us that we want a naming word, a noun that is a synonym for *the act of melting and pouring together and blending ingredients*. I see the word **fusion** at the bottom of the page. The suffix **-ion** marks the word as a noun, and since *to blend* is one of the meanings of the root, we can confirm the choice. Let's write **fusion** in the blank for the first sentence."

COMPLETE THE ACTIVITY

This can be quite challenging, so allow students to work on this activity in small groups. Not every word in the Word Bank will be used.

DISCUSS After about 10 minutes, ask if there were any difficulties. Have volunteers explain strategies they used that led to correct answers.

In Other Words...

SAB Pg 102

All Together Now....

The latest thing in music, food, and dance is the <u>act of melting and pouring together</u>. When it comes to food, people used to be afraid <u>to blend together</u> ingredients from different countries. Now, chefs <u>pour forth abundantly</u> such combinations. Herbs and spices that were once <u>poured apart</u> are now <u>poured into</u> one another. It is now common to <u>pour across</u> Caribbean meats with African spices. Such <u>out-pourings</u> are generally well received.

Music is another area where such <u>acts of melting and pouring</u> together are taking place. The influences of musicians from Asia, Europe, and the Americas have provided an <u>act of pouring into</u> music the cultures of many countries.

Was this explanation <u>blending together in a manner perplexing or bewildering</u> to you?

<u>Fill in the blanks below using words from the "fund, fus, fuse, found" family.</u>

1. The new style of blending ingredients is called <u>fusion.</u>
2. Chefs used to be afraid to <u>confuse</u> ingredients.
3. Now, chefs blend foods from different countries <u>profusely</u>.
4. Many <u>diffuse</u> ingredients are used with regularity.
5. The result is meals <u>infused</u> with many flavors.
6. In the cooking process chefs <u>transfuse</u> meats with a variety of spices.
7. Such out-pourings, or <u>effusions</u> of flavor are often well received.
8. Music is another area where <u>fusions</u> take place.
9. The <u>infusion</u> of one sound into another creates new and interesting music.
10. If this explanation was <u>confusing</u> to you, you need to study this root a little harder!

<u>Not Used:</u>   profusion   confounded

202

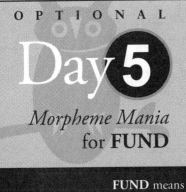

OPTIONAL

Day 5

Morpheme Mania
for **FUND**

FUND means
to melt, pour, or blend

LESSON TIME

15 Minutes

OBJECTIVES

- **Build** words in the **FUND** family

- **Apply** knowledge of synonyms and antonyms to **FUND** words

Optional Morpheme Mania for **FUND**

On page 103 of their Activity Books, students will see an optional vocabulary enrichment activity that they can work on in groups, time permitting. This activity makes a great review for the formal assessment on the next page.

All the affixes presented in the week's activities are provided at the top of the page on either side of the root of the week in all its forms. Students can write in up to 13 of the words they built during the week, possibly discovering additional ones.

Then students can brainstorm with each other to come up with antonyms and synonyms they may know. Starter examples are given with every Morpheme Mania in the Activity Book. Because antonyms and synonyms may require knowledge of roots which students have not yet studied, completion of this activity is not crucial. Simply remind students that they can at any time during the course of the year revisit any of their Morpheme Mania pages and add words, antonyms, and synonyms as their vocabulary grows.

Day 5 *Assessment*

Make and hand out copies.
The answer key is on page A-4.
The instructions are on page A-2.

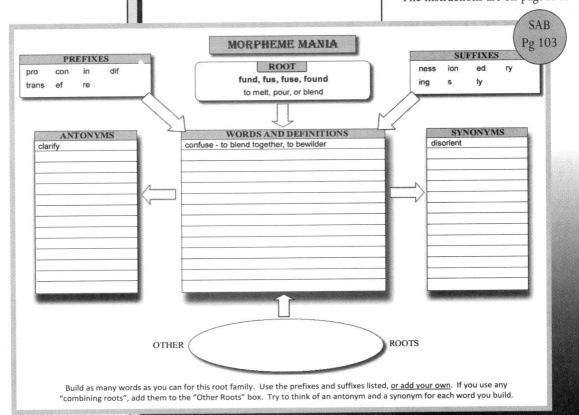

SAB
Pg 103

MORPHEME MANIA

PREFIXES			
pro	con	in	dif
trans	ef	re	

ROOT
fund, fus, fuse, found
to melt, pour, or blend

SUFFIXES			
ness	ion	ed	ry
ing	s	ly	

ANTONYMS
clarify

WORDS AND DEFINITIONS
confuse - to blend together, to bewilder

SYNONYMS
disorient

OTHER ROOTS

Build as many words as you can for this root family. Use the prefixes and suffixes listed, <u>or add your own</u>. If you use any "combining roots", add them to the "Other Roots" box. Try to think of an antonym and a synonym for each word you build.

confounded poured together; baffled or ruined

confounding pouring together; baffling or ruining

confounds pours together; baffles or ruins

confuse to blend together; to perplex or bewilder

confused blended together; perplexed or bewildered

confuses blends together; perplexes or bewilders

confusing blending together; perplexing or bewildering

confusingly in a manner blending together; in a perplexing or bewildering manner

confusion act or process of being blended together; perplexity or bewilderment

confusions acts or processes of being blended together; states of perplexity or bewilderment

diffuse to melt or pour apart; to scatter or make widespread

diffused melted or poured apart; scattered or made widespread

diffuses melts or pours apart; scatters or makes widespread

diffusing melting or pouring apart; scattering or making widespread

diffusion act of melting or pouring apart; act of scattering or making widespread

diffusions acts of melting or pouring apart; acts of scattering or making widespread

effusions out-pourings

effusive characterized by being excessively poured out

foundries places where metal is melted and poured into molds

foundry place where metal is melted and poured into molds

fuse to melt and pour together

fused melted and poured together

fuses melts and pours together

fusion act of melting and pouring together

fusions acts of melting and pouring together

infuse to pour into; to instill or permeate

infused poured into; instilled or permeated

infuses pours into; instills or permeates

infusing pouring into; instilling or permeating

infusion act of pouring into; act of instilling or permeating

infusions acts of pouring into; acts of instilling or permeating

profuse poured forth; abundant

profusely in a manner pouring forth; abundantly

profuseness condition of pouring forth; abundance

profusion act or process of pouring forth; abundance

profusions acts or processes of pouring forth; abundances

refund to pour back; to pay back money or merchandise

refunded poured back; paid back money or merchandise

refunding pouring back; paying back money or merchandise

refunds pours back; pays back money or merchandise

refusal act of pouring back; act of rejecting or not accepting

refuse to pour back; to reject or be unwilling to accept

refused poured back; rejected or was unwilling to accept

refuses pours back; rejects or is unwilling to accept

refusing pouring back; rejecting or being unwilling to accept

transfuse to pour across; to carry over or penetrate

transfused poured across; carried over or penetrated

transfuse a person or instrument that pours across; a person or device that carries over or penetrates

transfuses pours across; carries over or penetrates

transfusing pouring across; carrying over or penetrating

transfusion the act of pouring across; process of carrying over or penetrating

transfusions acts of pouring across; processes of carrying over or penetrating

Check-Up for **FUND**

Name _____

____ **1.** **FUND**, **FUS**, or **FOUND** in words like **refund**, **infusion**, and **confound** means:

    A to see

    B to pour

    C to pay

____ **2.** What is the meaning of the word **diffuse**?

    A poured in different directions

    B does not pay

    C sees in several ways

____ **3.** What is the meaning of the word **infusion**?

    A result of not being paid

    B quality of not being able to see

    C act or process of pouring into

____ **4.** What is the meaning of the word **confound**?

    A to overpay

    B to pour together and mix up

    C to see clearly with another person

____ **5.** If you are **effusive** with your praise, what do you do?

    A people can't see you give it

    B you don't pay it out

    C you give it out fully

____ **6.** Which word means **a lot or poured forth**?

    A profuse

    B transfusion

    C refusal

____ **7.** Which word means **a place where metals are melted and poured into molds**?

    A profusely

    B diffusion

    C foundry

____ **8.** Which word means **pours across**?

    A transfusers

    B transfuses

    C transfusions

____ **9.** The doctor **perfused** the patient's heart with a salt solution. The doctor:

    A took the blood out of the heart

    B put a layer of the solution outside the heart

    C spread the solution throughout the heart

____ **10.** Her nice attitude **suffuses** everything she does. Her attitude:

    A pours up through

    B contradicts

    C messes up

OBJECTIVES

- **Understand** the meaning of the root **METER**
- **Build** words in the root **METER** family
- **Break Apart** words in the root **METER** family
- **Understand** the meaning of words in the **METER** family
- **Understand** the spelling principles applied to the root **METER**
- **Apply** knowledge of words in the **METER** family
- **Assess** and **Reinforce** knowledge of words in the **METER** family

MATERIALS

- Student Activity Books, pages 105-110
- Dictionary *(print or on-line)*

CROSS-CURRICULAR EXAMPLES

Science:
barometer, centimeter, metric

Social Studies:
geochronometrist, odometer

Language Arts:
meter, pentameter, hexameter

Math:
diameter, perimeter, geometry

METER

meaning "measure"

perimeter
the **measure** around

Morpheme: **METER**
Allomorph: **METR**

Over 700 words containing the morpheme **METER** or its allomorph are current in English. During this unit, tell students to be alert for this root in their school texts, general reading, and oral language they hear. Some of the words they might encounter in their school subjects are listed on the left under Cross-Curricular Examples.

UNIT AT A GLANCE

Day **1**
Root Squares
for **METER**

Day **2**
Magic Squares
for **METER**

Day **3**
Stair Steps
for **METER**

OPTIONAL

Day **4**
In Other Words
for **METER**

Day **5**
Assessment or Morpheme Mania
for **METER**

Each activity should take approximately **15 minutes**.

The unbound, free form of this root, **meter**, is a noun used to mean *a basic unit of measure in the metric system*. In bio-scientific terminology, there are hundreds of words for which **meter** is used as a suffix for whatever is being measured (**thermometer**, *heat*; **barometer**, *heaviness*; **odometer**, the *road*). **Meter** is also used as a suffix for how far something measures (**kilometer**, a thousand units; **millimeter**, one-thousandth of a unit.)

Traditional poetry lines have **meter**, that is, there is *a measured pattern*. Poetic **meters** are measured using such terms as **monometer**, **dimeter**, **trimeter**, **tetrameter**, and, most familiar to English speakers, **pentameter**, all named using Greek numbers.

Advertisers, amateur sociologists, and politicos have come up with such terms as **health-o-meter, stress-o-meter**, **green-o-meter**, and many more. You and your students can play with this suffixed morpheme to illustrate and observe the process of word-creation.

To **mete** is *to measure out*, as justice or land areas.

Word Alert!

While all English words with the letter sequence **m-e-t-e-r** belong to this root family, a few with the sequence **m-e-t-r** come from another source.

The Greek word for *mother*, **meter**, gives English such words as **metropolitan** (*mother city*) and **metronymic** (*pertaining to a mother-based naming system*).

NOTE: These mini-lessons go with the Root Squares for METER

MINI-LESSON: the Prefix **a-**

This prefix **a-**, unlike one of the assimilated form of the prefix **ad-**, is from a Greek prefix that means *not or without*. When the negating prefix **a-** is attached to a root that begins with a vowel, it is spelled **an-**. Thus we see that it is related to the Germanic negative prefix **un-** and to the Latin negating prefix **in-**. The following words help illustrate this Greek prefix:

moral – amoral	esthesia – anesthesia, lack of feeling	theistic – atheistic
archy – anarchy, without rule	sexual – asexual	typical – atypical

MINI-LESSON: the Prefix **milli-**

The numerical prefix **milli-** or **mill-** comes from the Latin word for *one thousand*: **mille**. The **M** in Roman numerals, meaning 1000, comes from the first letter of this word. Ask students these questions:

How many years make up a **millennium**? (1000)   How many feet does a **millipede** have?   (Etymologically 1000, but, like the word 100, the word 1000 is often used for exaggeration ("I've told you a thousand times…").

The word **million** is derived from this root, meaning *a thousand thousands*.

In most scientific terminology, the prefix means not *a thousand*, but *a thousandth*, as in **millimeter**, **milliliter**, or **millisecond**.

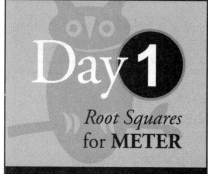

METER means
measure

LESSON TIME

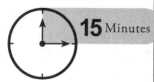

15 Minutes

OBJECTIVES

- **Understand** the meaning of the root **METER**
- **Build** words in the **METER** family
- **Understand** the meaning of words in the **METER** family
- **Understand** the spelling principles applied to the root **METER**

MATERIALS

- Student Activity Book
- **METER** Word Wall
- Dictionary *(print or on-line)*

DIFFERENTIATING INSTRUCTION

If you prefer easier or more difficult activities, use your personal account at www.dynamicliteracy.com to access novice or expert versions, along with ideas on using them.

Root Squares for METER

TEACH Mini-Lessons for the new prefixes applicable to this activity are found on the previous and next page. Then have students turn to page 105 in their Activity Books. Call attention to the center box. Point out that the root **METER** has two different spellings, called allomorphs. Ask students to decide if one of the forms they see in the middle square can stand alone as a word. They will see that **meter** is a word, and you can use that word to guide them to the meaning *to measure*. Suggest that students start their list with **meter** and then add to that word the prefix **peri-**, meaning around, to build another word, **perimeter**, meaning *the measure around*. Invite students to explore how this word is related to the idea of *measure*. Say, "All of the prefixes and suffixes in the squares surrounding the shaded center are now familiar, but if you have questions about any of the meanings, simply ask or look it up in the list inside the front and back cover of the activity book."

COMPLETE THE ACTIVITY

Have students follow the directions for the activity to build words. If students have difficulty building words with the Root Squares, show them how by modeling the matrix approach found on the next page, taking one affix at a time and seeing if it will connect with any one of the allomorphs of the root.

DISCUSS After five minutes, have volunteers write some of their words on the board. Focus with the class on the words they have built and guide them in a discussion of how the meaning of the root is still *measure* even when prefixes and suffixes are added. Watch for target words that most easily demonstrate the meaning of measure. If the word **metric** is not present, ask the class, "Can anyone try to use the suffix **-ic**?" and then continue on to the focus word discussion on the next page.

Root Squares

How many words can you make?

Start in any square. Your goal is to combine two or more word parts to make as many words in the 'meter, metr' family as you can. Write each word and a definition you can think of for it in the space provided at the bottom of the page. Use the back of the page if you need to.

a	ic	sym
y	meter, metr	dia
al	peri	milli

SAB
Pg 105

208

MINI-LESSON: the Prefix peri-

The prefix **peri-** comes from the Greek preposition meaning *around or in the vicinity of*. Ask students if they know what the **perimeter** of a lawn or room is (*the measure all around the outside*).

The **pericardium** is a membrane that surrounds the heart. Ask students if they know what their **peripheral** vision is (*the vision on the sides*, outside of the direct line of sight). The dentist who cares for the areas surrounding the teeth, the gums, is a **periodontist**. The word **period** means *around the journey* and refers to a complete thought.

MINI-LESSON: the Prefix sym-

The prefix **sym-** is an assimilation of the prefix **syn-**, meaning *with or together*, occurring before the letters **b**, **m**, or **p** (representing labial sounds). As you have done before, let students pronounce these unassimilated forms of words they will know, and they will detect why assimilation occurs: **synbol**, **synmetrical**, **synpathy**, **synphony**, **synptom**.

Focus Word: **METRIC** ⟶ Write this word on the board.

TEACH

Lead with this:	"Who can tell us anything about the **metric** system?"
Student:	"It's a way of measuring."
Student:	"It uses tens as a way to measure."
Student:	"It's based on a meter instead of a yardstick—that must be why it's called **metric**."
Student:	"But it's for other stuff than just distance—it's for weight, too."
Teacher:	"That's right. Let's take a close look. What do we see?"
Student:	"Our root, meaning *measure*, and a suffix **-ic** that we had before, meaning (consulting the inside back cover Student Activity Book) *like or belonging to*."
Student:	"So what is the **metric** system?"
Student:	"It just means *having to do with measure*! Is that all?"

DISCUSS While there are other measuring systems, the **metric** system calls itself *the measuring system*. Ask if any students know how to use any parts of the **metric** system, and discuss advantages or disadvantages of the system in comparison with other systems. Why is ten a standard gradation in the **metric** system (it is our number system in general and therefore easy to use).

DEMONSTRATE There is a **metric** system that everyone uses even in the United States–the money system. Let the class show how the dollar is a ten-based system like everything else in the **metric** world.

Root Squares Matrix
You can refer to this matrix to guide students in this activity. Students could build at least these 14 words. *It is not important how many words are built*, so long as students understand the meanings of the root and its affixes.

Encourage discussion about the definitions of any words formed for the blank slots as well as for the attested words.

	no prefix	dia-	milli-	peri-	sym-	a- + sym-
no suffix	meter	diameter	millimeter	perimeter		
-al		diametral				
-ic	metric				symmetric	asymmetric
-y					symmetry	asymmetry
-ic + -al	metrical	diametrical			symmetrical	asymmetrical

Day 2

Magic Squares
for **METER**

METER means measure

LESSON TIME

15 Minutes

OBJECTIVES

- **Understand** the meaning of the root **METER**
- **Break Apart** words in the **METER** family
- **Understand** the meanings of words in the **METER** family

MATERIALS

- Student Activity Book
- **METER** Word Wall
- Dictionary *(print or on-line)*

DIFFERENTIATING INSTRUCTION

If you prefer easier or more difficult activities, use your personal account at www.dynamicliteracy.com to access novice or expert versions, along with ideas on using them.

Break Apart Words with **METER**

TEACH Have students turn to the Magic Squares on page 106 in their Student Activity Books. Model a Think-Aloud strategy for students: "I know that **METER** means measure. I can use this knowledge to find the definition of a word with this as its root."

Direct students to word A, **thermometers**. Say, "I see this as a compound root word, and the meaning of the first half of this word, the root **THERMO**, as in **Thermos**, the trademark for a vacuum bottle, is *heat*. I know that the **-s** creates a plural noun. Look at definition 3, *devices for measuring heat*. That sums up the parts, so let's write the number 3 in square A."

SAB Pg 106

COMPLETE THE ACTIVITY

Ask students to use the same strategy to find the correct definitions for the other words. Tell them to write the number of the definition in the box that matches the letter for the word. Remind them that if all their answers are correct, each row and each column will add up to the same Magic number.

DISCUSS After five minutes, ask if there are any difficulties about matching the words and definitions. If there are, ask volunteers to explain clues in the definitions that will lead to the correct choice of word. As needed, follow the focus word approach for **geometry** that you see modeled on the next page.

Add any new words to the classroom **METER** Word Wall and remind students to add these words to the **METER** Word Wall in their Activity Books.

Magic Squares

Select the best answer for each of the words in the 'meter, metr' family from the numbered definitions. Put the number in the proper space in the Magic Square box. If the total of the numbers is the same both across and down, you have found the magic number!

'meter, metr' means measure

WORDS	DEFINITIONS
A. thermometers	1. related to measure through; exactly opposite or contrary
B. symmetrical	2. multiples of 1/1000 of a basic measure of length
C. speedometer	3. devices for measuring heat
D. perimeter	4. measurements around; lengths of boundaries around closed figures
E. millimeters	5. device for measuring velocity
F. metrical	6. in a manner not measuring with; in an uneven or out of proportion manner
G. geometry	7. measuring with; even or in proportion
H. asymmetrically	8. science of measuring the earth; math dealing with area, space, and volume
I. diametrical	9. relating to a system of measurement; relating to units of ten

Magic Square Box

A. 3	B. 7	C. 5
D. 4	E. 2	F. 9
G. 8	H. 6	I. 1

Magic Number **15**

*** ANSWER KEY ***

Day ② Extend the Learning

| **MINI-LESSON:** | the Combining Form **speedo** |

While this root seems obvious in English, it actually comes from an old root meaning *thriving, success, or hope.* The **sp** in the root of that word is the same partial morpheme as found in the words **despair** and **prosperous.** Occasionally we still hear the blessing, **Godspeed**, which was also the name of one of the first English ships to come to the American New World in 1607.

The root now is mostly used to refer to quickness.

Focus Word: GEOMETRY ⟶ Write this word on the board.

TEACH

Sample leading question:	"Has anyone ever heard of a type of mathematics called **geometry**?"
Student:	"My sister studies that and loves it. But what is it?"
Student:	"I think it figures out areas and stuff."
Student:	"Let's take a look at the word, as usual!"
Student:	"There are three morphemes. The root, the suffix –**y**, *an activity*, and the prefix **geo**-. What was that?"
Student:	"It meant *earth*–we had it before with the root **graph**–remember **geography**?"
Teacher:	"Great! Now what do we get for the word **geometry**?"
Student:	"*Earth measuring?* Isn't that **astronomy** or something in science?"
Teacher:	"Think about things we might want to measure on the earth."
Student:	"Distance!" "Areas!"
Teacher:	"Right. **Geometry** is a way of figuring out how *far* something is, or how *big*, and also things like *angles* and *volumes*. It all started with ancient farmers' need to measure their land, or *earth*!"

DISCUSS Let small groups think of reasons why land needs to be measured, and have them share those reasons with the full class. See if anyone knows how to find out how big a square piece of land is.

DEMONSTRATE If someone knows, let him or her show the class how to figure out the area of a square. If not, draw a three-by-three square grid on the board and let the class count how many squares are in the grid. Explain that measuring this square is one basic part of **geometry**.

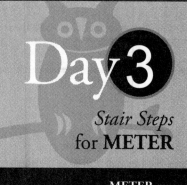

Day 3

Stair Steps for METER

METER means measure

LESSON TIME

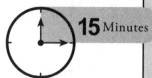

15 Minutes

OBJECTIVES

- **Understand** the meaning of the root **METER**
- **Apply** knowledge of the root **METER**
- **Break Apart** words in the **METER** family
- **Understand** the meaning of words in the **METER** family
- **Understand** the spelling principles applied to the root **METER**

MATERIALS

- Student Activity Book
- **METER** Word Wall

DIFFERENTIATING INSTRUCTION

If you prefer easier or more difficult activities, use your personal account at www.dynamicliteracy.com to access novice or expert versions, along with ideas on using them.

Apply Knowledge of METER

TEACH Have students turn to page 107 in their Student Activity Books. Explain that the boxes in front of and after the root indicate letters that spell out prefixes and suffixes. Students will spell out the correct prefixes and suffixes determined by clues in the definitions at the bottom of the page.

Have a volunteer read definition number four at the bottom of the page. Say, "The first part of the word we are looking for must mean *around*. This is not one of the more common prefixes, but it's a very useful one you'll see in some math classes. Looking down the list of prefixes, you'll confirm that **peri-** is the one with the meaning *around*. You may know what a **periscope** does–it allows one to *see around*. So, the word **perimeter** would have the meaning we are after, *the measure around*. That will fit exactly in the fourth step of this Stair Steps exercise."

COMPLETE THE ACTIVITY

Let students work in pairs (optionally) and tell them to use the same strategy to find the correct prefixes and suffixes for the words listed. These activities can be quite challenging!

DISCUSS After a few minutes, review the answers as a class. Ask if there were any difficulties. Listen to any problems and have volunteers solve the difficulties by explaining key clues in the given definitions. As needed, follow the focus word approach that you see modeled on the next page.

SAB Pg 107

Stair Steps

Fill in the missing letters of each 'meter, metr' word by using the definitions below.
'meter, metr' means measure

1.	m	e	t	r	i	c				
2.	m	e	t	e	r	e	d			
3.	d	i	a	m	e	t	e	r		
4.	p	e	r	i	m	e	t	e	r	
5.	a	s	y	m	m	e	t	r	i	c
6.	m	i	l	l	i	m	e	t	e	r	s
7.	s	p	e	e	d	o	m	e	t	e	r	s
8.	d	i	a	m	e	t	r	i	c	a	l	l	y
9.	a	s	y	m	m	e	t	r	i	c	a	l	l	y

1. relating to a system of measurement; a method of measurement using units of ten
2. measured
3. the measure through; the distance through the centerpoint of a circle
4. the measure around; the length of the boundary around a closed figure
5. not measuring with; uneven or out of proportion
6. multiples of 1/1000 of a basic measure of length
7. devices for measuring velocity
8. so as to measure through; in a manner being exactly opposite or contrary
9. in a manner not measuring with; in an uneven or out of proportion manner

MINI-LESSON: the Prefix **baro-**

The prefix **baro-** comes from the Greek word for *heavy*, and it is used with a small but important collection of scientific words dealing mostly with atmospherics or physiology. Often it refers specifically to air pressure, as it does with the familiar word **barometer**, *a device that measures the heaviness*, or pressure, of the atmosphere.

MINI-LESSON: the Combining Form **opt**

The Combining Form **opt** comes from the Greek word for *eye, seeing, or vision*. Some words students may be familiar with include:

optic, as in optic nerve, the nerve in the eye
optical, as in optical illusion, a picture that tricks the vision
optician, an expert at making visual lenses

Information for reviewing the suffix **-ist** can be accessed on the Dynamic Literacy website, if needed.

Focus Word: **DIAMETER** ⟶ Write this word on the board.

TEACH

Sample leading question:	"Take a look at this word. A basketball hoop has a **diameter**, and the earth has a **diameter**. Does anyone know what that is?"
Student:	"Yes, it's how big it is."
Teacher:	"In what way is it how big it is?"
Student:	"Well, I see the **meter** part. I forget what **dia-** means."
Student:	"Here it is in the list of prefixes. **Dia**, *across or through*."
Student:	"I know—it's *how far across the hoop ring is*, or *how far it is through the earth*."
Student:	"So it's a *measure through*. Does it have to be through a circle?"
Teacher:	"It usually means that, but let's see what a dictionary says."
Student:	"(Consulting a dictionary) It says *the thickness of anything at its farthest point*."
Teacher:	"So *measure through* is all it means."

DEMONSTRATE Let a student draw a circle on the board and demonstrate its **diameter**.

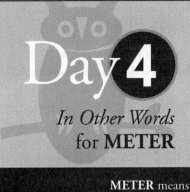

Day 4

In Other Words for METER

METER means measure

LESSON TIME

15 Minutes

OBJECTIVES

- **Understand** the meaning of the root **METER**
- **Reinforce** knowledge of the root **METER**
- **Understand** the meaning of words in the **METER** family
- **Apply** knowledge of words in the **METER** family

MATERIALS

- Student Activity Book
- **METER** Word Wall
- Dictionary *(print or on-line)*

In Other Words for **METER**

TEACH Have students turn to page 108 in their Student Activity Books. Explain that they are going to read a little story that uses some surprising and sometimes odd phrasing. The underlined words or phrases in the story are actually definitions or synonyms for words in the **METER** family. Then they will see sentences about the story, each containing a blank.

Using context clues in the sentences, they will find a **METER** family word in the Word Bank at the bottom to fit in each blank. Have a student read aloud the opening sentence or sentences of the story that contain the first underlined phrase. Then say, "Let's look at the first numbered sentence that contains a blank to be filled in. Clues in the sentence tell us that we want a naming word, a noun that means *a device for measuring heat.* I see the word **thermometer** at the bottom of the page. The first part of that word, **therm**, is the leading root in this compound root word. It means **heat**. Since the second part of the word is **meter**, meaning *measure*, that has to be what we are looking for. Let's write **thermometer** in the blank for the first sentence."

COMPLETE THE ACTIVITY

This can be quite challenging, so allow students to work on this activity in small groups. Not every word in the Word Bank will be used.

DISCUSS After about 10 minutes, ask if there were any difficulties. Have volunteers explain strategies they used that led to correct answers.

SAB Pg 108

Measurement All Around Us

Note for a moment all the things in your day that are measured:

- Before you decide how you'll dress for the day, you might check the temperature on the <u>device for measuring heat.</u> You calculate the <u>measure all the way around</u> of a big-screen TV to see if it will fit on your bedroom wall.
- You could read on the carton whether a gallon of milk is in standard measure or <u>a system of measurement using units of ten.</u> Your favorite music has patterned rhythmic <u>measures.</u>
- You use <u>math measuring area, space, and volume</u> when you play pool. Is the <u>measure through the middle</u> of a paper towel tube large enough to accommodate a ping-pong ball?
- Your home's electricity use is mechanically <u>measured</u> so that you can pay the bill.
- You'll get a ticket if you don't watch the <u>device for measuring speed</u> in the car.
- You can even describe a sculpture as <u>measured with even proportion</u> or <u>not measured with even proportion</u>, depending on how the parts are arranged.

<u>Fill in the blanks below using words from the "meter, metr" family.</u>

1. Local weathermen use a <u>thermometer</u> to report the day's high temperature.

2. Adding up the lengths of all the sides gives you a figure's <u>perimeter.</u>

3. In contrast to standard measure used in the U.S., most Europeans take measurements using the <u>metric</u> system that is based on tens.

4. The <u>meter</u> of music or poetry is its pattern of rhythm.

5. Good pool players study the <u>geometry</u> of the shot to hit at correct angles.

6. The <u>diameter</u> of a circle divides it into two equal parts.

7. The amount of electricity and water have been <u>metered</u> outside your house.

8. A <u>speedometer</u> measures the speed of a moving vehicle.

9. A mirror image, something exactly the same on both sides is described as <u>symmetrical</u>, while a figure that is not the same on both sides is called <u>asymmetric.</u>

<u>Not Used:</u> barometer optometrist

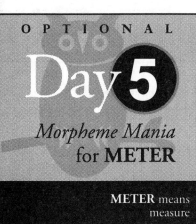

OPTIONAL

Day 5

Morpheme Mania
for **METER**

METER means
measure

LESSON TIME

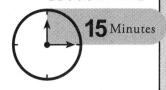

15 Minutes

OBJECTIVES

• **Build** words in the
  METER family

• **Apply** knowledge of
  synonyms and antonyms
  to **METER** words

Optional Morpheme Mania for **METER**

On page 109 of their Activity Books, students will see an optional vocabulary enrichment activity that they can work on in groups, time permitting. This activity makes a great review for the formal assessment on the next page.

All the affixes presented in the week's activities are provided at the top of the page on either side of the root of the week in all its forms. Students can write in up to 13 of the words they built during the week, possibly discovering additional ones.

Then students can brainstorm with each other to come up with antonyms and synonyms they may know. Starter examples are given with every Morpheme Mania in the Activity Book. Because antonyms and synonyms may require knowledge of roots which students have not yet studied, completion of this activity is not crucial. Simply remind students that they can at any time during the course of the year revisit any of their Morpheme Mania pages and add words, antonyms, and synonyms as their vocabulary grows.

Day 5 Assessment

Make and hand out copies.
The answer key is on page A-4.
The instructions are on page A-2.

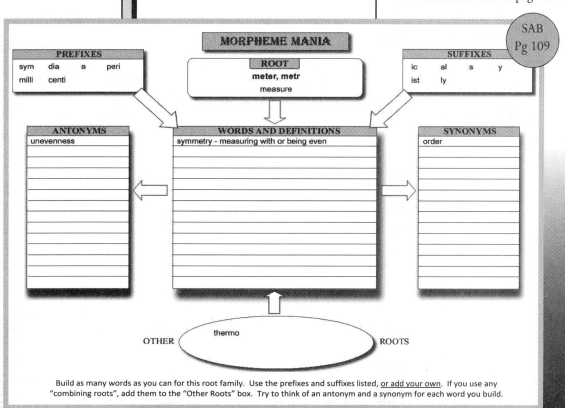

MORPHEME MANIA

SAB
Pg 109

PREFIXES			
sym	dia	a	peri
milli	centi		

ROOT
meter, metr
measure

SUFFIXES			
ic	al	s	y
ist	ly		

ANTONYMS
unevenness

WORDS AND DEFINITIONS
symmetry - measuring with or being even

SYNONYMS
order

OTHER   thermo   ROOTS

Build as many words as you can for this root family. Use the prefixes and suffixes listed, <u>or add your own</u>. If you use any "combining roots", add them to the "Other Roots" box. Try to think of an antonym and a synonym for each word you build.

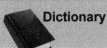
asymmetric not measuring with; uneven or out of proportion

asymmetrical not measuring with; uneven or out of proportion

asymmetrically in a manner not measuring with; in an uneven or out of proportion manner

asymmetries qualities of not measuring with; qualities of being uneven or out of proportion

asymmetry quality of not measuring with; quality of being uneven or out of proportion

barometer an instrument for measuring atmospheric pressure

barometers instruments for measuring atmospheric pressure

barometric related to the measure of atmospheric pressure

centimeter 1/100 of a basic measure of length

centimeters multiples of 1/100 of a basic measure of length

decimeter 1/10 of a basic measure of length

decimeters multiples of 1/10 of a basic measure of length

diameter the measure through; the distance through the centerpoint of a circle

diameters measures through; distances through the centerpoints of circles

diametric related to measure through; exactly opposite or contrary

diametrical related to measure through; exactly opposite or contrary

diametrically so as to measure through; in a manner being exactly opposite or contrary

geometric relating to measuring the earth; relating to area, space, and volume

geometrical relating to measuring the earth; relating to area, space, and volume

geometrist a person who measures the earth; a person who measures area, space, and volume

geometrists people who measure the earth; people who measure area, space, and volume

geometry science of measuring the earth; math dealing with area, space, and volume

meter a basic measure of length; any device that measures

metered measured

meters basic units of measure; devices that measure

metric relating to a system of measurement; a method of measurement using units of ten

metrical relating to a system of measurement; relating to units of ten

metrics measuring systems; systems based on ten

millimeter 1/1000 of a basic measure of length

millimeters multiples of 1/1000 of a basic measure of length

odometer a device that measures road distance

odometers devices that measure road distance

optometrical pertaining to measuring the eyes; relating to assessing vision

optometrist a person who measures the eyes; a specialist in assessing vision

optometrists people who measure the eyes; specialists in assessing vision

optometry the practice of measuring the eyes; the practice of assessing vision

pedometer device for measuring distance covered on foot

pedometers devices for measuring distance covered on foot

pentameter a line of verse of five measured, regular beats

perimeter the measure around; the length of the boundary around a closed figure

perimeters measurements around; lengths of boundaries around closed figures

perimetry act or process of measuring around; outer limits

speedometer device for measuring velocity

speedometers devices for measuring velocity

symmetric measuring with; even or in proportion

symmetrical measuring with; even or in proportion

symmetrically in a manner measuring with; in an even or proportional manner

symmetries qualities of measuring with; qualities of being even or in proportion

symmetry quality of measuring with; quality of being even or in proportion

thermometer device for measuring heat

thermometers devices for measuring heat

Check-Up for **METER**   Name _____

____ **1.** **METER** or **METR** in words like **diameter** and **metric** means:

    A decide

    B draw

    C measure

____ **2.** What is the meaning of the word **diameter**?

    A a drawing of a circle

    B to decide on size

    C a measure through

____ **3.** What is the meaning of the word **asymmetric**?

    A drawn straight

    B not measuring with

    C deciding with

____ **4.** What is the meaning of the word **perimeter**?

    A a measure around

    B a decision about something

    C to draw a line through

____ **5.** What does a **thermometer** do to temperature?

    A decides what it should be

    B measures it

    C fixes it at a certain level

____ **6.** Which word means **a person who measures eyesight**?

    A optometrist

    B optometry

    C optimist

____ **7.** Which word means **the science of measuring the earth**?

    A geomancy

    B geometrical

    C geometry

____ **8.** Which word means **one-tenth of a basic measure of length**?

    A decimeter

    B decibel

    C decade

____ **9.** To measure how well someone was breathing, you would use a:

    A respirational

    B respirometer

    C meter stick

____ **10.** A **metronome** serves to do what for a person practicing a piece of music?

    A decide which instrument to use

    B provide a quiet place

    C measure time and rhythm

PART

meaning "side; piece; make a division"

OBJECTIVES

- **Understand** the meaning of the root **PART**
- **Build** words in the root **PART** family
- **Break Apart** words in the root **PART** family
- **Understand** the meaning of words in the **PART** family
- **Understand** the spelling principles applied to the root **PART**
- **Apply** knowledge of words in the **PART** family
- **Assess** and **Reinforce** knowledge of words in the **PART** family

MATERIALS

- Student Activity Books, pages 111-116
- Dictionary *(print or on-line)*

CROSS-CURRICULAR EXAMPLES

Science:
particulars, impartial

Social Studies:
party, departmentalize, nonpartisan

Language Arts:
impartiality, counterpart

Math:
part, partitive

apart
to the **side**

impart
to put a **piece** into

departure
act of **making a division** from

Morpheme: **PART**
Allomorph: **PARTI**

About 200 words containing the morpheme **PART** or its allomorph are current in English. During this unit, tell students to be alert for this root in their school texts, general reading, and oral language they hear. Some of the words they might encounter in their school subjects are listed on the left under Cross-Curricular Examples.

UNIT AT A GLANCE

Day ① *Root Squares* for **PART**

Day ② *Magic Squares* for **PART**

Day ③ *Stair Steps* for **PART**

OPTIONAL
Day ④ *In Other Words* for **PART**

Day ⑤ *Assessment or Morpheme Mania* for **PART**

Each activity should take approximately **15 minutes**.

The basic idea of this morpheme has to do with *making divisions* so that there are clear distinctions. Something may break into its **parts**. A **partition** is a wall or curtain that sets a room off into a *different, clearly defined area*. When you take **part** in a project, you are an individual helping the whole group.

A **particle** is *a small individual piece of a larger article*, and a **particular** is *a small individual element of an issue or event*. If you are **particular** about what you eat, you make fine distinctions and separate what is okay from what is not okay.

A shortened form of **particle** is **parcel**, *a unit*. From **parcel** comes the word **passel**, *an endearing bunch of similar items*.

In grammar, there are words called **participles**, *words which take two distinct roles or parts*. They are like verbs in some ways, but they are actually adjectives. In the sentence, "The searching child found the hidden toy," the words *searching* and *hidden* are **participles** because they have roles as both action words and descriptive words.

Continuing in the field of grammar, the **parts** of speech are the categorical pieces of syntax that join to make sense: nouns, pronouns, verbs, adjectives, adverbs, prepositions, conjunctions, and interjections.

To divide and analyze a sentence into its pieces, we **parse** the sentence, labeling each type of word and usage.

Partake is a shortening of **part-take** (*to take part*).

Word Alert!

Several families of words with the letter sequence **p-a-r-t** do not belong to this morpheme family.

The **Parthenon** in Athens is named from a Greek word for *virgin*. **Parthenogenesis** is *reproduction by females only*.

The bird name **partridge** comes from a Greek root meaning *to make noise*.

Words such as **parturition**, *the act of giving birth*, and **postpartum**, *after birth*, come from a root meaning *to break off from*, as *to pare*.

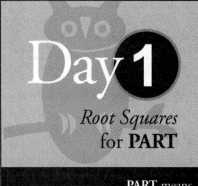

Day 1

Root Squares
for **PART**

PART means
side; piece; make a division

LESSON TIME

15 Minutes

OBJECTIVES

- **Understand** the meaning of the root **PART**

- **Build** words in the **PART** family

- **Understand** the meaning of words in the **PART** family

- **Understand** the spelling principles applied to the root **PART**

MATERIALS

- Student Activity Book
- **PART** Word Wall
- Dictionary *(print or on-line)*

DIFFERENTIATING INSTRUCTION

If you prefer easier or more difficult activities, use your personal account at www.dynamicliteracy.com to access novice or expert versions, along with ideas on using them.

Root Squares for PART

TEACH Have students turn to page 111 in their Activity Books. Say, "The only new affix here is the prefix **counter**-." Refer to the Mini-Lesson on the next page of this manual as needed. Then call attention to the center box. Point out that the root **PART** has two different spellings, called allomorphs.

Ask students to decide if one of the forms they see in the middle square can stand alone as a word. They will see that **part** is a word, and you can use that word to guide them to the meaning *side; piece; make a division.* Suggest that students continue their list with **part** and then add to that word the prefix **a**-, meaning *from or away*, to build **apart**, meaning *to the side or not together with the rest.* Invite students to explore how this word is related to the idea of *side; piece; make a division.*

Have students follow the directions for the Root Squares activity for **PART** on page 111 to build words. If students have difficulty building words with the Root Squares, show them how by modeling the matrix approach found on the next page, taking one affix at a time and seeing if it will connect with any one of the allomorphs of the root.

DISCUSS After five minutes, have volunteers write some of their words on the board. Focus with the class on the words they have built and guide them in a discussion of how the meaning of the root is still *side; piece; make a division* even when prefixes and suffixes are added. Watch for target words that most easily demonstrate the meaning of *side; piece; make a division.* If the word **impart** is not present, ask the class, "Can anyone try to use the prefix **im**-?" and then continue on to the target word discussion on the next page

SAB
Pg 111

Root Squares

How many words can you make?

Start in any square. Your goal is to combine two or more word parts to make as many words in the 'part, parti' family as you can. Write each word and a definition you can think of for it in the space provided at the bottom of the page. Use the back of the page if you need to.

a	com	counter
ure	part, parti	im
ment	ial	de

_____

_____

_____

_____

_____

_____

_____

_____

_____

220

MINI-LESSON: the Prefix **counter-**

The prefix **counter-** is a variation of the prefix **contra-**, a Latin preposition and adverb meaning *against, in opposition to, or in balance with*. The form **counter-**, however, is far more prevalent, with nearly 400 examples. A Mini-Lesson for the allomorph **contra-** is included with material on the root **DIC** in the Level I Manual, and it can also be accessed on the Dynamic Literacy website.

Put any of these words on the board for the students. Have students define ones they know, and then have them add the prefix **counter-**. Discuss with them the new meanings (*in opposition*, *against*, *balanced*, etc.):

act	argue	attack	balance	bid	blow	charge
claim	measure	current	effort	view	intuitive	demonstration
offensive	play	part	raid	proposal	revolution	suggestion

Focus Word: **IMPART** ⟶ Write this word on the board.

TEACH

Lead with this:	"Let's focus on this word, impart. What is the word saying to us?"
Student:	"Okay. If the root part means just what it looks like, *a part or piece*, then the word could mean *not a piece*. I'm really doubting that."
Student:	"And if **in-** means *in or into*, then the word means *a piece into*. What would that mean?"
Student:	"This is one that needs more context for us to figure out."
Teacher:	"The rich woman said she would **impart** some of her fortune to her cats."
Student:	"Give?"
Teacher:	"Play with the meanings of the prefix and root."
Student:	"Give the cats a piece of her fortune?"
Teacher:	"That's good, and notice an additional meaning of the root: *make a division*."
Student:	"Yes—she's splitting up her money into pieces."

DISCUSS Lead students to see that, based on its pieces of meaning, **impart** is a verb meaning *to put a piece of something onto another person or thing, to give*. You can **impart** other examples of how this word can be used, such as to **impart** the details of a story, to **impart** seriousness to a situation, to **impart** purpose to a plan, and to **impart** knowledge.

Root Squares Matrix

You can refer to this matrix to guide students in this activity. Students could build at least these 13 words. *It is not important how many words are built*, so long as students understand the meanings of the root and its affixes. Encourage discussion about the definitions of any words formed for the blank slots as well as for the attested words.

	no prefix	a-	com-	counter-	de-	im-
no suffix	part	apart	compart	counterpart	depart	impart
-al	partial					impartial
-ment		apartment	compartment		department	impartment
-ure					departure	

Day 2

Magic Squares
for **PART**

PART means
side; piece; make a division

LESSON TIME

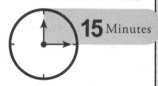

15 Minutes

OBJECTIVES

- **Understand** the meaning of the root **PART**

- **Break Apart** words in the **PART** family

- **Understand** the meanings of words in the **PART** family

MATERIALS

- Student Activity Book

- **PART** Word Wall

- Dictionary
  (print or on-line)

DIFFERENTIATING INSTRUCTION

If you prefer easier or more difficult activities, use your personal account at www.dynamicliteracy.com to access novice or expert versions, along with ideas on using them.

Break Apart Words with **PART**

TEACH Have students turn to the Magic Squares on page 112 in their Student Activity Books. Model a Think-Aloud strategy for students: "I know that **PART** means *side; portion; make a division.* It's one of those words that can as easily be a noun as a verb, as often a thing as an action. I can use all this knowledge to find the definition of a word with **PART** or **PARTI** as its root."

Direct students to word B, **counterpart**. Say, "I know the prefix of this word, **counter-**, means *against.* Look at definition 5, *a portion opposite; a mirror image.* That captures the idea, so let's write the number 5 in square B."

SAB Pg 112

COMPLETE THE ACTIVITY

Ask students to use the same strategy to find the correct definitions for the other words. Tell them to write the number of the definition in the box that matches the letter for the word. Remind them that if all their answers are correct, each row and each column will add up to the same Magic number.

DISCUSS After five minutes, ask if there are any difficulties about matching the words and definitions. If there are, ask volunteers to explain clues in the definitions that will lead to the correct choice of word. As needed, follow the focus word approach for **departure** that you see modeled on the next page.

Add any new words to the classroom **PART** Word Wall and remind students to add these words to the **PART** Word Wall in their Activity Books.

Magic Squares

Select the best answer for each of the words in the 'part, parti' family from the numbered definitions. Put the number in the proper space in the Magic Square box. If the total of the numbers is the same both across and down, you have found the magic number!

'part, parti' means side; portion; make a division

WORDS	DEFINITIONS
A. partitioned	1. act of making a division from; a going away
B. counterpart	2. quality of not taking a side; neutrality
C. apartment	3. divided into portions or sides; put a wall between
D. imparting	4. putting a portion into; bestowing ownership to a segment of something
E. participants	5. a portion opposite; a mirror image
F. impartiality	6. involving only one side or portion; incompletely
G. departments	7. a room to the side of the main dwelling
H. departure	8. portions divided off from the whole; distinct subdivisions
I. partially	9. people who share a portion, side, or role

Magic Square Box

A. 3	B. 5	C. 7
D. 4	E. 9	F. 2
G. 8	H. 1	I. 6

Magic Number __15__

*** ANSWER KEY ***

Day ② Extend the Learning

The Combining Form cip

The Combining Form **cip** is an allomorph of the root **CAP**, meaning *take or hold*. That root is featured in the Elements Level 1 Manual, pages 100-109, and activities for it can also be accessed on the Dynamic Literacy website.

Focus Word: **DEPARTURE** ⟶ Write this word on the board.

TEACH

Sample leading question:	"You're at the train station and the announcer says, '**Departure** will be in five minutes.' What does the announcer mean?"
Student:	"The train will leave in five minutes."
Teacher:	"Let's work with the pieces of meaning. This one should be easy, since we know what a **departure** is."
Student:	"Three morphemes: a prefix, a root, and a suffix."
Teacher:	"What do those pieces mean?"
Student:	"**De-** is *away from, remove.* **Part** is *a piece or a division.* We had **-ure** a while back. Let's see: (reading from the inside back cover of the Student Activity Book) *act of, process, function.*"
Student:	"So **departure** is *the act of making a division away from*—how does that work?"
Student:	"I get it—think of a **division** made between you and whatever you're leaving."
Teacher:	"Yes, like leaving a piece of space between."

DISCUSS Lead students to see that, based on its three pieces of meaning, **departure** is a noun referring to *an act of making a division or going off to the side away from something.*

DEMONSTRATE Stand two students side-by-side. Ask one student to make a **departure** from the other, and let the class visualize the division, the portion of space being created.

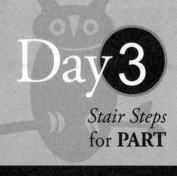

Day 3

Stair Steps
for **PART**

PART means
side; piece; make a division

LESSON TIME

15 Minutes

OBJECTIVES

- **Understand** the meaning of the root **PART**

- **Apply** knowledge of the root **PART**

- **Break Apart** words in the **PART** family

- **Understand** the meaning of words in the **PART** family

- **Understand** the spelling principles applied to the root **PART**

MATERIALS

- Student Activity Book
- **PART** Word Wall

DIFFERENTIATING INSTRUCTION

If you prefer easier or more difficult activities, use your personal account at www.dynamicliteracy.com to access novice or expert versions, along with ideas on using them.

Apply Knowledge of **PART**

TEACH Have students turn to page 113 in their Student Activity Books. Explain that the boxes in front of and after the root indicate letters that spell out prefixes and suffixes. Students will spell out the correct prefixes and suffixes determined by clues in the definitions at the bottom of the page.

Have a volunteer read definition number five at the bottom of the page. Say, "The suffix we need is the one on two words in the definition; look carefully and you'll see -**ing** used in both parts of the definition. The prefix will be one meaning *from*. Think of a

synonym for leaving or for making a division from. Try the concept **removing**. Now look for a prefix with that meaning and you'll find it in the definition of **de-**. That gives us the word **DEPARTING** for this step, the word you see fits the definition exactly."

COMPLETE THE ACTIVITY

Let students work in pairs (optionally) and tell them to use the same strategy to find the correct prefixes and suffixes for the words listed. These activities can be quite challenging!

DISCUSS After a few minutes, review the answers as a class. Ask if there were any difficulties. Listen to any problems and have volunteers solve the difficulties by explaining key clues in the given definitions. As needed, follow the focus word approach that you see modeled on the next page.

SAB Pg 113

Stair Steps

Fill in the missing letters of each 'part, parti' word by using the definitions below.
'part, parti' means side; piece; make a division

1.	a	p	a	r	t						
2.	i	m	p	a	r	t					
3.	p	a	r	t	i	a	l				
4.	i	m	p	a	r	t	e	d			
5.	d	e	p	a	r	t	i	n	g		
6.	a	p	a	r	t	m	e	n	t	s	
7.	c	o	m	p	a	r	t	m	e	n	t
8.	c	o	u	n	t	e	r	p	a	r	t	s
9.	p	a	r	t	i	c	i	p	a	t	i	o	n

1. to the side; not together with the rest
2. to put a piece into; to grant or bestow
3. referring to a piece; incomplete
4. put a piece into; granted or bestowed
5. making a division from; leaving
6. rooms to the side of the main dwelling
7. an area divided off thoroughly; a box or cubbyhole
8. models on the opposite side; mirror images
9. act of taking a side or role

Focus Word: APART → Write this word on the board.

TEACH

Sample leading question:	"Let's try this familiar word. We'll apply what we know about the word to what we can figure out about its pieces of meaning."
Student:	"When you're **apart**, you're not there, you're off somewhere else."
Student:	"You can pull things **apart**."
Student:	"And that's different from not wanting **a part** of something."
Teacher:	"Let's think about how it is different."
Student:	"What does that prefix **a**- mean here? *Not, without*?"
Student:	"Look at the spellings of the prefix **ad**-. One of them is just **a**-."
Student:	"Yes, that's it–*to the side*. When you're **apart**, you're *off to the side*."
Student:	"And if you tear something **apart**, you put both pieces *off to the side*."
Teacher:	"And how is the phrase **a part** different from the word **apart**?"
Student:	"No prefix in the phrase!"

DISCUSS Lead students to see that, based on its two pieces of meaning, **apart** is an adverb meaning *to the side*.

DEMONSTRATE Place two objects next to each other, Move one away, and let the class guess how far **apart** the objects now are.

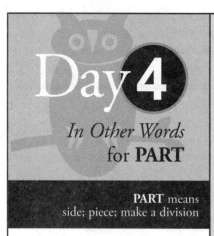

Day 4

In Other Words
for **PART**

PART means
side; piece; make a division

LESSON TIME

15 Minutes

OBJECTIVES

- **Understand** the meaning of the root **PART**
- **Reinforce** knowledge of the root **PART**
- **Understand** the meaning of words in the **PART** family
- **Apply** knowledge of words in the **PART** family

MATERIALS

- Student Activity Book
- **PART** Word Wall
- Dictionary *(print or on-line)*

In Other Words for **PART**

TEACH Have students turn to page 114 in their Student Activity Books. Explain that they are going to read a little story that uses some surprising and sometimes odd phrasing. The underlined words or phrases in the story are actually definitions or synonyms for words in the **PART** family. Then they will see sentences about the story, each containing a blank.

Using context clues in the sentences, they will find a **PART** family word in the Word Bank at the bottom to fit in each blank. Have a student read aloud the opening sentence or sentences of the story that contain the first underlined phrase. Then say, "Let's look at the first numbered sentence that contains a blank to be filled in. Clues in the sentence tell us that we want a naming word, a plural noun that means *mirror images of some people that are "top spellers."* There are three plural nouns at the bottom of the page. I see that the word **counterparts** is a choice. The prefix **counter-** means *against*, and since this seems to be a story about a spelling contest, one team, or part of the gathering, against another, we can go with **counterparts**. Let's write **counterparts** in the blank for the first sentence."

COMPLETE THE ACTIVITY

This can be quite challenging, so allow students to work on this activity in small groups. Not every word in the Word Bank will be used.

DISCUSS After about 10 minutes, ask if there were any difficulties. Have volunteers explain strategies they used that led to correct answers.

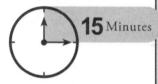

The Big Spell-Off

SAB
Pg 114

The top spellers from Canada and their United States <u>mirror images</u> were about to be <u>people who take a role</u> in the North American English Spell-Off. The <u>act of taking a role</u> in this contest was a great honor. A judge and word-caller <u>not taking a side</u> were the officials from Mexico.

The spelling coaches <u>bestowed</u> some last-minute instructions and advice, and then sat <u>to the side</u> away from the spellers. A <u>dividing wall</u> was placed between every competitor so they wouldn't distract each other. One of the prizes was a <u>piece of</u> payment for college expenses.

After an hour of tight competition, the winning word was *compartmentalized*. The winner won <u>in one way</u> because of knowing the six morphemes in the winning word.

<u>Fill in the blanks below using words from the "part, parti" family.</u>

1. The Canadian spellers greeted their American <u>counterparts</u> at the opening ceremony.
2. All of the <u>participants</u> of the Spell-Off were champions from their schools.
3. <u>Participation</u> in such a major event was a great honor.
4. The judge and caller were <u>impartial</u> and showed favor to neither group.
5. The coaches <u>imparted</u> some last-minute advice to their spellers.
6. Then the coaches sat <u>apart</u> from the spellers.
7. For better concentration, a <u>partition</u> was put between every contestant.
8. <u>Partial</u> payment for future college costs was one of the prizes.
9. The winning student got the word right <u>partly</u> by knowing morphemes.

<u>Not Used:</u>   departments   impartially   compartmentalized

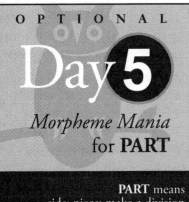

PART means
side; piece; make a division

LESSON TIME

15 Minutes

OBJECTIVES

- **Build** words in the **PART** family

- **Apply** knowledge of synonyms and antonyms to **PART** words

Optional Morpheme Mania for **PART**

On page 115 of their Activity Books, students will see an optional vocabulary enrichment activity that they can work on in groups, time permitting. This activity makes a great review for the formal assessment on the next page.

All the affixes presented in the week's activities are provided at the top of the page on either side of the root of the week in all its forms. Students can write in up to 13 of the words they built during the week, possibly discovering additional ones.

Then students can brainstorm with each other to come up with antonyms and synonyms they may know. Starter examples are given with every Morpheme Mania in the Activity Book. Because antonyms and synonyms may require knowledge of roots which students have not yet studied, completion of this activity is not crucial. Simply remind students that they can at any time during the course of the year revisit any of their Morpheme Mania pages and add words, antonyms, and synonyms as their vocabulary grows.

Day 5 Assessment

Make and hand out copies.
The answer key is on page A-5.
The instructions are on page A-2.

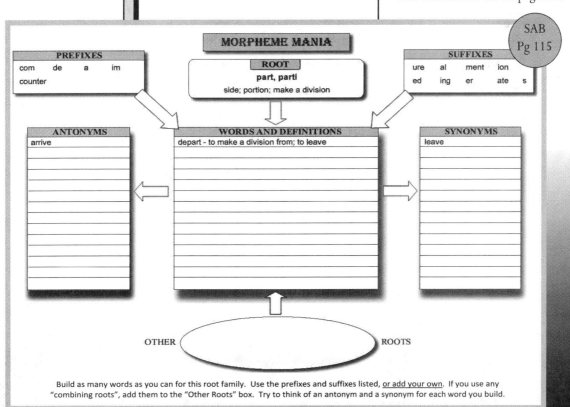

SAB
Pg 115

MORPHEME MANIA

PREFIXES			
com	de	a	im
counter			

ROOT
part, parti
side; portion; make a division

SUFFIXES			
ure	al	ment	ion
ed	ing	er	ate	s

ANTONYMS
arrive

WORDS AND DEFINITIONS
depart - to make a division from; to leave

SYNONYMS
leave

OTHER ( ) ROOTS

Build as many words as you can for this root family. Use the prefixes and suffixes listed, <u>or add your own</u>. If you use any "combining roots", add them to the "Other Roots" box. Try to think of an antonym and a synonym for each word you build.

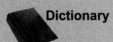
apart   to the side; not together with the rest

apartment   a room to the side of the main dwelling

apartments   rooms to the side of the main dwelling

compartment   an area divided off thoroughly; a box or cubbyhole

compartments   areas divided off thoroughly; boxes or cubbyholes

counterpart   a model on the opposite side; a mirror image

counterparts   models on the opposite side; mirror images

depart   to make a division from; to leave

departed   made a division from; left

departing   making a division from; leaving

department   an area divided off from the whole; a distinct subdivision

departments   areas divided off from the whole; distinct subdivisions

departs   makes a division from; leaves

departure   act of making a division from; a going away

departures   acts of making a division from; acts of going away

impart   to put a piece into; to grant or bestow

imparted   put a piece into; granted or bestowed

imparter   a person who puts a piece into; a person who grants or bestows

imparters   people who put a piece into; people who grant or bestow

impartial   not taking a side; neutral

impartiality   quality of not taking a side; neutrality

impartially   in a manner not taking a side; in a neutral manner

impartialness   quality of not taking a side; neutrality

imparting   putting a piece into; bestowing ownership to a segment of something

part   a side or role; to divide; to leave

parted   divided; left

partial   referring to a piece; incomplete

partially   involving only one piece or side; incompletely

partials   pieces

participant   a person who shares a side or role

participants   people who share a side or role

participate   to take a side or role

participated   took a side or role

participates   takes a side or role

participating   taking a side or role

participation   act of taking a side or role

participator   a person taking a side or role

participators   people taking sides or roles

particularly   in a manner pertaining to a small, specific piece

particulars   small, specific pieces

particulate   to reduce to a small, specific piece

parties   people who have sides or roles in a situation; festivities

parting   siding; dividing; leaving

partition   act of dividing into sides or sections; a wall

partitioned   divided into sides or sections; put a wall between

partitioning   dividing into sides or sections; putting a wall between

partitions   divides into sides or sections; puts a wall between

partly   in a manner pertaining to a side or division; not completely

parts   sides; divides; leaves

party   a person who has a side or role; festivity

Check-Up for **PART**

Name _____

_____ 1. **PART** or **PARTI** in words like **apart** and **partial** means:

    A to place or put

    B side or piece

    C to push

_____ 2. What is the meaning of the word **apart**?

    A putting together again

    B pushed into

    C to the side

_____ 3. What is the meaning of the word **partial**?

    A to put down

    B pushing upward

    C referring to a piece

_____ 4. What is the meaning of the word **departure**?

    A act of making a division away from

    B to push down the stairs

    C process of asking for help

_____ 5. When you are **impartial**, you:

    A push your friends into action

    B put your support into two causes

    C do not take a side

_____ 6. Which word means **a model on the opposite side**?

    A counterpart

    B imparter

    C partially

_____ 7. Which word means **small, specific pieces**?

    A particulars

    B imparts

    C departments

_____ 8. Which word means **a room to the side of a main dwelling**?

    A participant

    B apartment

    C party

_____ 9. The announcer at the contest was clearly **nonpartisan**. The announcer:

    A wasn't able to be heard

    B did not take sides

    C had definite ideas about who should win

_____ 10. A **tripartite** alliance:

    A is made up of three sides

    B has attacked three countries

    C lasts three years

OBJECTIVES

- **Understand** the meaning of the root **LAT**
- **Build** words in the root **LAT** family
- **Break Apart** words in the root **LAT** family
- **Understand** the meaning of words in the **LAT** family
- **Understand** the spelling principles applied to the root **LAT**
- **Apply** knowledge of words in the **LAT** family
- **Assess** and **Reinforce** knowledge of words in the **LAT** family

MATERIALS

- Student Activity Books, pages 117-122
- Dictionary *(print or on-line)*

CROSS-CURRICULAR EXAMPLES

Science:
dilate, relativity, relational

Social Studies:
correlate, legislate

Language Arts:
translate, superlative, correlative

Math:
relative, correlation

LAT

meaning "to bring"

legislate
to **bring** into law

Morpheme: **LAT**
Allomorph: **LATE**

About 600 words containing the morpheme **LAT** or its allomorph are current in English. During this unit, tell students to be alert for this root in their school texts, general reading, and oral language they hear. Some of the words they might encounter in their school subjects are listed on the left under Cross-Curricular Examples.

UNIT AT A GLANCE

Day 1
Root Squares
for **LAT**

Day 2
Magic Squares
for **LAT**

Day 3
Stair Steps
for **LAT**

OPTIONAL
Day 4
In Other Words
for **LAT**

Day 5
Assessment or Morpheme Mania
for **LAT**

Each activity should take approximately **15 minutes**.

This morpheme is actually connected with the root **fer**. **Lat** is the past tense root of the Latin verb root **fer**, meaning *bring or carry*. Compare **went** as the odd past tense of the English word **go**. If you *carry something across from one place to another*, you **transfer** it. If you *carry one language across to another form*, you **translate** it. In fact, the word **translate** means, in some contexts, the same as **transfer**: a quarrel that starts out between two people can be **translated** over a whole crowd a people. To be taken out of one environment and placed into another can be called **translation** in formal, literary English.

The connection between the roots **fer** and **lat** appears also in the words **refer** and **relate**. If you **refer** a friend to the librarian, you *bring* the librarian and your friend together into a relationship. A **relative** pronoun, such as *who* or *which*, **refers** to some other noun in the sentence. A **prelate** in a church is technically one who is **preferred**, originally *brought in* before the others in a procession.

To **relate** a story is to *bring it back* to tell someone, and to **relate** two things to one another is to *bring them into comparison* so that you can see their relationship. The relationship between two things can then determine their **relativity**. The day can be **relatively** hot (compared to other days) or the soup can be **relatively** cold (compared to other soups).

Word Alert!

Another root **lat** looks exactly like this one but means *wide*, as in the word **latitude**. The word **dilate** means *widened apart*, though it can also be thought of as *brought apart*, and is so used in these activities.

The word **late** comes from a Germanic root that meant *slow or lazy*.

Many English words end with the suffix -**ate**. The root **lat** can be misidentified if that suffix -**ate** is attached to a root ending in the letter **l**, as with words such as **consulate** or **violate**.

The word **chocolate** comes not from this root but from South American Indian for *bitter water*.

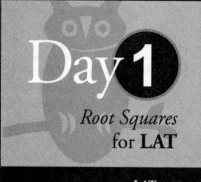

Day 1

Root Squares
for **LAT**

LAT means
to bring

LESSON TIME

15 Minutes

OBJECTIVES

- **Understand** the meaning of the root **LAT**

- **Build** words in the **LAT** family

- **Understand** the meaning of words in the **LAT** family

- **Understand** the spelling principles applied to the root **LAT**

MATERIALS

- Student Activity Book

- **LAT** Word Wall

- Dictionary *(print or on-line)*

DIFFERENTIATING INSTRUCTION

If you prefer easier or more difficult activities, use your personal account at www.dynamicliteracy.com to access novice or expert versions, along with ideas on using them.

Root Squares for LAT

TEACH Have students turn to page 117 in their Activity Books. All the affixes in the outside boxes should be familiar except perhaps **cor-**, an assimilation of **con-**, meaning with or together. Discuss that prefix and any other affixes if necessary. Then call attention to the center box.

Point out that the root **LAT** has two different spellings, called allomorphs. Ask students to decide if one of the forms they see in the middle square can stand alone as a word. They will see that **late** is a word, but explain that it is not in the **LAT** family. This activity is challenging, so suggest a starter word such as **translate**.

COMPLETE THE ACTIVITY
Have students follow the directions for the Root Squares activity for **LAT** on page 117 to build words. If students have difficulty building words with the Root Squares, show them how by modeling the matrix approach found on the next page, taking one affix at a time and seeing if it will connect with any one of the allomorphs of the root.

DISCUSS After five minutes, have volunteers write some of their words on the board. Focus with the class on the words they have built and guide them in a discussion of how the meaning of the root is still *bring* even when prefixes and suffixes are added.

Watch for target words that most easily demonstrate the meaning of *bring*. If the word **relate** is not present, ask the class, "Can anyone try to use the prefix **re**-?" and then continue on to the target word discussion on the next page.

SAB
Pg 117

Root Squares

How many words can you make?

Start in any square. Your goal is to combine two or more word parts to make as many words in the 'lat, late' family as you can. Write each word and a definition you can think of for it in the space provided at the bottom of the page. Use the back of the page if you need to.

cor	re	or
ing	lat, late	ive
trans	ed	e

Before the letter **r**, the prefix **con**, meaning *with or together*, and sometimes *completely*, assimilates to **cor-**. Have students try to pronounce the following, and they will sense why this assimilation occurs:

conrect   **conrelate**   **conrespond**   **conrosion**   **conrupt**

Focus Word: **RELATE** ⟶ Write this word on the board.

TEACH

Lead with this:	"If I **relate** a story to you, do you know what I do?"
Student:	"Do you show how it fits us, or **relates** to us?"
Teacher:	"Well, that is one use of the word, and we will get to that, but this usage is much clearer in meaning."
Student:	"Let's see, to **relate** a story. Does it mean *tell* a story?"
Teacher:	"Yes, in a way. As always, let's look at the word."
Student:	"Our new root is there, **late**, meaning *bring*. And **re-** is a prefix that means *again or back*. *Bring back, bring again?*"
Student:	"Is it a story that somebody else told and you're telling it to somebody else?"
Student:	"You're bringing it back again to tell others. I get that. But how does that **relate** to the other meaning?"
Student:	"You just said **relate**. I already get it. It means how something can be *brought back to match or fit something else!*"

DISCUSS Lead students to see that, based on its two pieces of meaning, **relate** means very literally, *to bring back*. This morphemic definition fits the usages both of retelling a story and of making a connection.

DEMONSTRATE Draw a simple family tree diagram like this on the board. Cousins **relate** because their line can be brought back to a common grandfather and grandmother.

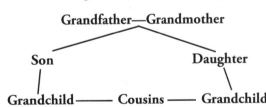

Root Squares Matrix

You can refer to this matrix to guide students in this activity. Students could build at least these 18 words. *It is not important how many words are built*, so long as students understand the meanings of the root and its affixes. Encourage discussion about the definitions of any words formed for the blank slots as well as for the attested words.

	cor- + re-	e-	re-	trans-
no suffix	correlate	elate	relate	translate
-ed	correlated	elated	related	translated
-ing	correlating	elating	relating	translating
-ive	correlative	elative	relative	translative
-or			relator	translator

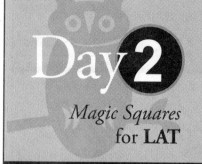

Day 2

Magic Squares for **LAT**

LAT means to bring

LESSON TIME

15 Minutes

OBJECTIVES

- **Understand** the meaning of the root **LAT**
- **Break Apart** words in the **LAT** family
- **Understand** the meanings of words in the **LAT** family

MATERIALS

- Student Activity Book
- **LAT** Word Wall
- Dictionary *(print or on-line)*

DIFFERENTIATING INSTRUCTION

If you prefer easier or more difficult activities, use your personal account at www.dynamicliteracy.com to access novice or expert versions, along with ideas on using them.

Break Apart Words with **LAT**

TEACH Have students turn to the Magic Squares on page 118 in their Student Activity Books. Model a Think-Aloud strategy for students: "I know that **LAT** means *to bring*. I can use this knowledge to find the definition of a word with **LAT** or **LATE** as its root."

Direct students to word G, **correlation**. Say, "I know the prefix of this word, **cor-**, is an assimilation of **con-** and means *together*. The additional prefix on this root, **re-**, means *back*. The suffix **-ion** makes the word a noun. Look at definition 3, *act of bringing back together; quality of meshing or being similar*. This definition includes all the parts, so let's write the number 3 in square G."

COMPLETE THE ACTIVITY
Ask students to use the same strategy to find the correct definitions for the other words. Tell them to write the number of the definition in the box that matches the letter for the word. Remind them that if all their answers are correct, each row and each column will add up to the same Magic number.

DISCUSS After five minutes, ask if there are any difficulties about matching the words and definitions. If there are, ask volunteers to explain clues in the definitions that will lead to the correct choice of word. As needed, follow the focus word approach for **translating** that you see modeled on the next page.

Add any new words to the classroom **LAT** Word Wall and remind students to add these words to the **LAT** Word Wall in their Activity Books.

SAB Pg 118

Magic Squares

Select the best answer for each of the words in the 'lat, late' family from the numbered definitions. Put the number in the proper space in the Magic Square box. If the total of the numbers is the same both across and down, you have found the magic number!

'lat, late' means to bring

WORDS
A. translators
B. superlatively
C. relatively
D. relations
E. elating
F. dilated
G. correlation
H. translating
I. legislate

DEFINITIONS
1. a person who brings across; a person who puts works into a different language
2. in a manner brought above; so as to be the best in the category
3. act of bringing back together; quality of meshing or being similar
4. brought apart; widened or expanded
5. to bring into law; to enact law
6. bringing out; making very happy
7. people who bring across; people who put works into a different language
8. acts of bringing back; acts of telling stories or of fitting in
9. in a manner that brings back; with respect to being compared
10. bringing across; putting into a different language

Magic Square Box

A. 7	B. 2	C. 9
D. 8	E. 6	F. 4
G. 3	H. 10	I. 5

Magic Number **18**

*** ANSWER KEY ***

The Combining Form **legis**

The Combining Form **legis** means *law*, and it is discussed in full later in this Elements Level 2 Manual.

Activities for teaching the prefix **super-** appear in the WordBuild Foundations Level 1 Teacher Edition, pages 133-139, and they can be accessed on the Dynamic Literacy website.

Focus Word: **TRANSLATING** ⟶ Write this word on the board.

TEACH

Sample leading question:	"Does anyone know what **translating** is?"
Student:	"Telling what somebody meant."
Student:	"My older brother has **translating** to do for Spanish homework all the time."
Student:	"Putting foreign words into English."
Teacher:	"Can it also be putting English into another language?"
Student:	"Yes—it's just putting one way of saying something over into another way of saying something."
Student:	"I get it—you're *bringing it across*! **Trans-lat-ing**!"
Student:	"And it doesn't have to be foreign languages—it's bringing across meaning to somebody who might not understand."

DISCUSS Lead students to see that, based on its three pieces of meaning, **translating** simply means *the act of bringing across*. Specifically, of course, it refers to bringing meaning across from one style or language into another. Decoding morphemic meanings is a kind of **translating**.

DEMONSTRATE Take the Latinate word **translate** and **translate** it into its Germanic equivalent:

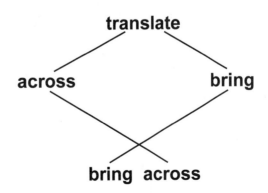

Day 3

Stair Steps
for **LAT**

LESSON TIME

15 Minutes

OBJECTIVES

- **Understand** the meaning of the root **LAT**

- **Apply** knowledge of the root **LAT**

- **Break Apart** words in the **LAT** family

- **Understand** the meaning of words in the **LAT** family

- **Understand** the spelling principles applied to the root **LAT**

MATERIALS

- Student Activity Book
- **LAT** Word Wall

DIFFERENTIATING INSTRUCTION

If you prefer easier or more difficult activities, use your personal account at www.dynamicliteracy.com to access novice or expert versions, along with ideas on using them.

Apply Knowledge of **LAT**

TEACH Have students turn to page 119 in their Student Activity Books. Explain that the boxes in front of and after the root indicate letters that spell out prefixes and suffixes. Students will spell out the correct prefixes and suffixes determined by clues in the definitions at the bottom of the page.

Have a volunteer read definition number five at the bottom of the page. Say, "We need only a prefix for this word, a prefix that means *across*. The put into a different language part of the definition serves as an extra hint. Can you think of a prefix

with the meaning we are looking for? Looking down the list, you'll see **trans-** has the meaning *across*. Think of other words with this prefix. (There are many: e.g., **transatlantic; transfusion; transgress; transplant; transport**.) So, the word we will build for step five in this Stair Steps is **TRANSLATE**."

COMPLETE THE ACTIVITY

Let students work in pairs (optionally) and tell them to use the same strategy to find the correct prefixes and suffixes for the words listed. These activities can be quite challenging!

DISCUSS After a few minutes, review the answers as a class. Ask if there were any difficulties. Listen to any problems and have volunteers solve the difficulties by explaining key clues in the given definitions. As needed, follow the focus word approach that you see modeled on the next page.

SAB
Pg 119

Stair Steps

Fill in the missing letters of each 'lat, late' word by using the definitions below.
'lat, late' means to bring

1.	e	l	a	t	e				
2.	r	e	l	a	t	e			
3.	e	l	a	t	i	n	g		
4.	e	l	a	t	i	o	n	s	
5.	t	r	a	n	s	l	a	t	e
6.	r	e	l	a	t	i	v	e	l	y
7.	c	o	r	r	e	l	a	t	i	o	n
8.	t	r	a	n	s	l	a	t	i	o	n	s
9.	s	u	p	e	r	l	a	t	i	v	e	l	y

1. to bring out; to make very happy
2. to bring back; to tell a story or to fit in
3. bringing out; making very happy
4. acts of being brought out; states of being very happy
5. to bring across; to put into a different language
6. in a manner that brings back; with respect to being compared
7. act of bringing back together; quality of meshing or being similar
8. acts or processes of bringing across; works put into a different language
9. in a manner brought above; so as to be the best in the category

Focus Word: **CORRELATION** ⟶ Write this word on the board.

Sample leading question:	"Can anyone give us an example of a **correlation** between two things?"
Student:	"Yes—eating too much Halloween candy will make you sick."
Student:	"Not paying attention in school leads to bad grades."
Student:	"The farther away an object, the smaller it looks."
Teacher:	"Good, and what is it about the word **correlation** that makes these examples all good ones?"
Student:	"That's easy—they *relate together with each other*."
Teacher:	"And what was **relate**?"
Student:	"*Bring back*—maybe come back to each other in some way."
Student:	"Or you can take them back to some connection."

DISCUSS Lead students to see that, based on its four pieces of meaning, **correlation** is *an act of bringing things back together again in some connection*. Discuss a difference between **relation** and **correlation**. Fixed, unchanging connections, such as cousins, share a **relationship**, but variables, like changing seasons, loudness, water depths, etc., cause **correlationships**.

DEMONSTRATE Write this chart on the board. One **correlation** between the numbers in Column A with those in Column B is that as the number in the first column grows by just one, the amount in the second column leaps in quantities greater and greater. See if anyone can figure out what the missing number should be. (25)

Column A	Column B
1	2
2	4
3	9
4	16
5	?

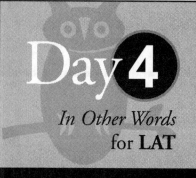

Day 4

In Other Words
for **LAT**

LAT means
to bring

LESSON TIME

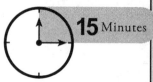

15 Minutes

OBJECTIVES

- **Understand** the meaning of the root **LAT**

- **Reinforce** knowledge of the root **LAT**

- **Understand** the meaning of words in the **LAT** family

- **Apply** knowledge of words in the **LAT** family

MATERIALS

- Student Activity Book

- **LAT** Word Wall

- Dictionary *(print or on-line)*

In Other Words for **LAT**

TEACH Have students turn to page 120 in their Student Activity Books. Explain that they are going to read a little story that uses some surprising and sometimes odd phrasing. The underlined words or phrases in the story are actually definitions or synonyms for words in the **LAT** family. Then they will see sentences about the story, each containing a blank.

Using context clues in the sentences, they will find a **LAT** family word in the Word Bank at the bottom to fit in each blank. Have a student read aloud the opening sentence or sentences of the story that contain the first underlined phrase.

Then say, "Let's look at the first numbered sentence that contains a blank to be filled in. Clues in the sentence tell us that we want an action word, a verb that is a synonym for *are brought apart.* Let's explore the word **dilated**, something that is said to happen to our eyes. One thing a doctor might do to your eyes during a check-up is **dilate** them. The root **LAT** refers to *bringing*, the **-ed** suffix takes care of the past tense *brought*, but what about the idea of **apart**? Check the meaning of the prefix **di-** and you'll see that *apart* is one of its meanings. Let's write **dilated** in the blank for the first sentence."

COMPLETE THE ACTIVITY

This can be quite challenging, so allow students to work on this activity in small groups. Not every word in the Word Bank will be used.

DISCUSS

After about 10 minutes, ask if there were any difficulties. Have volunteers explain strategies they used that led to correct answers.

SAB
Pg 120

Einstein

The eyes of most of us are <u>brought apart</u> with wonder and amazement about two ideas that Albert Einstein figured out. One is the theory of <u>comparison</u>. One simple way to understand that is to think of yourself walking forward at three miles per hour on a bus that is moving 50 miles per hour. <u>Brought</u> back in comparison to the ground, you are actually walking 53 miles per hour.

Einstein's famous formula, e=mc², <u>is brought across</u> into the words "energy equals mass times the speed of light squared." This means that energy, mass, and light <u>are brought back together</u> in a comparison. Although this opened the way to develop nuclear weapons, Einstein was always interested in national <u>law-bringing</u> against such weapons.

If you've ever thought you weren't as smart as somebody else, you might be <u>brought out of yourself with happiness</u> to know that Einstein, with an intellect most <u>brought above in comparison</u> of all time, was considered dull by some of his early teachers. A story is <u>brought back</u> that this genius failed some of his subjects in school.

It just goes to show that there is not necessarily a <u>quality of being brought back together</u> between early performance and later achievement.

<u>Fill in the blanks below using words from the "lat, late" family.</u>

1. When the pupils of our eyes get large, they are said to have <u>dilated</u>.

2. The theory of <u>relativity</u> involves a comparison among place, time, and speed.

3. The <u>relative</u> speeds of two objects is figured out by adding or subtracting them.

4. The famous formula e=mc² <u>translates</u> into nine simple words.

5. Energy, mass, and light <u>correlate</u> with each other.

6. Some nations have enacted <u>legislation</u> that outlaws nuclear weapons.

7. Many of us are <u>elated</u> to learn that a weak start doesn't mean a weak finish.

8. Einstein's intellect is one of the most <u>superlative</u> that the world has ever known.

9. A story has been <u>related</u> that the genius was weak at some school subjects.

10. Sometimes there is no <u>correlation</u> between two events.

<u>Not Used:</u>   legislator   translator

238

OPTIONAL

Day 5

Morpheme Mania
for **LAT**

LAT means
to bring

LESSON TIME

15 Minutes

OBJECTIVES

• **Build** words in the
LAT family

• **Apply** knowledge of
synonyms and antonyms
to **LAT** words

Optional Morpheme Mania for **LAT**

On page 121 of their Activity Books, students will see an optional vocabulary enrichment activity that they can work on in groups, time permitting. This activity makes a great review for the formal assessment on the next page.

All the affixes presented in the week's activities are provided at the top of the page on either side of the root of the week in all its forms. Students can write in up to 13 of the words they built during the week, possibly discovering additional ones.

Then students can brainstorm with each other to come up with antonyms and synonyms they may know. Starter examples are given with every Morpheme Mania in the Activity Book. Because antonyms and synonyms may require knowledge of roots which students have not yet studied, completion of this activity is not crucial. Simply remind students that they can at any time during the course of the year revisit any of their Morpheme Mania pages and add words, antonyms, and synonyms as their vocabulary grows.

Day 5 Assessment

Make and hand out copies.
The answer key is on page A-5.
The instructions are on page A-2.

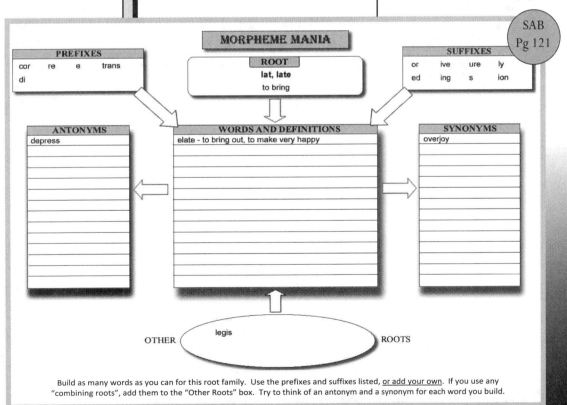

SAB
Pg 121

MORPHEME MANIA

PREFIXES	
cor	re	e	trans
di			

ROOT
lat, late
to bring

SUFFIXES	
or	ive	ure	ly
ed	ing	s	ion

ANTONYMS
depress

WORDS AND DEFINITIONS
elate - to bring out, to make very happy

SYNONYMS
overjoy

OTHER   legis   ROOTS

Build as many words as you can for this root family. Use the prefixes and suffixes listed, or add your own. If you use any
"combining roots", add them to the "Other Roots" box. Try to think of an antonym and a synonym for each word you build.

239

correlate to bring back together; to mesh or be similar

correlated brought back together; meshed or was similar

correlates brings back together; meshes or is similar

correlating bringing back together; meshing or being similar

correlation act of bringing back together; quality of meshing or being similar

correlations acts of bringing back together; qualities of meshing or being similar

dilate to bring apart; to widen or expand

dilated brought apart; widened or expanded

dilates brings apart; widens or expands

dilating bringing apart; widening or expanding

elate to bring out; to make very happy

elated brought out; made very happy

elates brings out; makes very happy

elating bringing out; making very happy

elation the act of being brought out; state of being very happy

elations acts of being brought out; states of being very happy

legislate to bring into law; to enact

legislated brought into law; enacted

legislates brings into law; enacts

legislating bringing into law; enacting

legislation act or process of bringing into law

legislations acts or processes of bringing into law

legislative related to bringing into law

legislatively in a manner related to bringing into law

legislator a person who brings into law

legislators people who bring into law

legislature a group that brings into law

legislatures groups that bring into law

relate to bring back; to tell a story or to fit in

related brought back; told a story or fit in

relates brings back; tells a story or fits in

relating bringing back; telling a story or fitting in

relation the act of bringing back; the telling of a story or a fitting in

relations acts of bringing back; acts of telling stories or of fitting in

relative a person brought back; a person with a family connection

relatively in a manner that brings back; with respect to being compared

relatives people brought back; people with a family connection

relativity quality of being brought back; quality determined by being compared

superlative anything brought above; the best of the category

superlatively in a manner brought above; so as to be the best in the category

superlatives things brought above; things that are the best in their categories

translate to bring across; to put into a different language

translated brought across; put into a different language

translates brings across; puts into a different language

translating bringing across; putting into a different language

translation act or process of bringing across; a work put into a different language

translations acts or processes of bringing across; works put into a different language

translator a person who brings across; a person who puts works into a different language

translators people who bring across; people who put works into a different language

translator pertaining to being brought across; related to putting into a different language

Check-Up for **LAT**

Name _____

____ **1.** **LAT** in words like **elated** and **translate** meanss:

    A to bring

    B to read

    C to measure

____ **2.** What is the meaning of the word **elated**?

    A read later

    B brought out

    C measured from

____ **3.** What is the meaning of the word **legislating**?

    A measuring the law

    B reading the law

    C bringing into law

____ **4.** What is the meaning of the word **dilated**?

    A brought apart

    B read twice

    C measured across

____ **5.** Two things that are **correlated** are:

    A measured inaccurately

    B brought back together

    C divided

____ **6.** Which word means **brings across**?

    A relates

    B elates

    C translates

____ **7.** Which word means **anything brought above**?

    A superlative

    B illative

    C translative

____ **8.** Which word means **the act of bringing back**?

    A correlative

    B relation

    C legislation

____ **9.** The speaker **prolated** each word as he ended his talk.
Each word was:

    A read from notes

    B brought forth or stressed

    C not able to be heard

____ **10.** We wanted to **collate** the two versions of the story.
We wanted to:

    A measure how long each was

    B read them at different times

    C bring them together for a comparison

OBJECTIVES

- **Understand** the meaning of the root **VOL**
- **Build** words in the root **VOL** family
- **Break Apart** words in the root **VOL** family
- **Understand** the meaning of words in the **VOL** family
- **Understand** the spelling principles applied to the root **VOL**
- **Apply** knowledge of words in the **VOL** family
- **Assess** and **Reinforce** knowledge of words in the **VOL** family

MATERIALS

- Student Activity Books, pages 123-128
- Dictionary *(print or on-line)*

CROSS-CURRICULAR EXAMPLES

Science:
revolve, convolution

Social Studies:
revolt, counterrevolution

Language Arts:
revolution, involvement

Math:
circumvolute, revolutions

VOL

meaning "to roll, turn, coil, fold"

revolve
to **roll** again

circumvolute
to roll or **turn** around a central point

involve
to **coil** or roll in

convolute
to **fold** intricately together

Morpheme: **VOL**
Allomorph: **VOLT, VOLV, VOLVE, VOLUT, VOLUTE**

About 200 words containing the morpheme **VOL** or one of its allomorphs are current in English. During this unit, tell students to be alert for this root in their school texts, general reading, and oral language they hear. Some of the words they might encounter in their school subjects are listed on the left under Cross-Curricular Examples.

UNIT AT A GLANCE

Day ① Root Squares for **VOL**

Day ② Magic Squares for **VOL**

Day ③ Stair Steps for **VOL**

OPTIONAL
Day ④ In Other Words for **VOL**

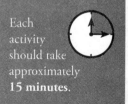

Day ⑤ Assessment or Morpheme Mania for **VOL**

Each activity should take approximately **15 minutes**.

Time and processes are imagined as *unrolling*. To observe an ongoing process over time is to watch its **evolution**. Character and personality **evolve** over time, as does language.

An important direction this morpheme takes in word-building is related to books. As is often the case, history is embedded in words, and in the word **volume**, meaning a book, we see the nature of original books. Reading material was originally *unrolled* from a scroll in a continuous sheet rather than turned on separate pages. Since scrolled works tended to be quite large, the word **volume** came also to refer to *size*. Thus in science and geometry classes we study **volume** as *the size of a space*. We speak of the **volume** of traffic or the **volume** of sales.

As a unit of size, the word **volume** also came to be a measure of *loudness*. We turn down or up the **volume** of the television sound.

A horse's **volt** is a *circular movement*, and a swordsman's **volt** is *a turn aside to avoid a cut*.

The word **valley** is related to this root, in the sense that valleys emerge as mountains seem to *roll* in patterns.

Word Alert!

The word **volt**, as in electricity, is from a person's name, Alessandro Volta. Words that stem from people's names are called *eponyms*.

The word **volcano** comes from the Roman deity of fire, *Vulcan*.

Words such as **voluntary**, **volition**, and **volunteer** stem from a similar-looking root meaning *to wish or will*.

Another similar-looking root refers to flying. A **volatile** person "flies" off into rages, and a **volley** is a flight of things thrown or shot.

The letter sequence **v-o-l** does not necessarily indicate the presence of the root meaning *roll or turn*. The word **frivolous**, for example, is from a Latin source meaning *crumbling*.

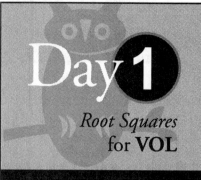

Day 1

Root Squares for VOL

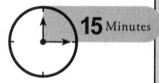

VOL means
to roll, turn, coil, fold

LESSON TIME

15 Minutes

OBJECTIVES

- **Understand** the meaning of the root **VOL**

- **Build** words in the **VOL** family

- **Understand** the meaning of words in the **VOL** family

- **Understand** the spelling principles applied to the root **VOL**

MATERIALS

- Student Activity Book
- **VOL** Word Wall
- Dictionary *(print or on-line)*

DIFFERENTIATING INSTRUCTION

If you prefer easier or more difficult activities, use your personal account at www.dynamicliteracy.com to access novice or expert versions, along with ideas on using them.

Root Squares for VOL

TEACH Have students turn to page 123 in their Activity Books. Say, "All of the prefixes and suffixes in the squares surrounding the shaded center are probably familiar, but if you have questions about any of them, simply look them up in the list in your activity book."

Call attention to the center box. Point out that the root **VOL** has a number of different spellings, called allomorphs. Ask students to decide if any of the forms they see in the middle square can stand alone as a word. They will see that **volt** is a word, but they may associate it only with something to do with electricity. But there is another word spelled and pronounced the same way, meaning *the movement of a horse going sideways and turning around a central point*. It is also a

defensive move in fencing. Though these uses of **volt** are not likely ever to have been seen by students, their discussion will lead to the idea of *to turn*. Suggest that students start their list with **volt**, even though it may be unfamiliar.

COMPLETE THE ACTIVITY

Have students follow the directions to build words. If students have difficulty building words with the Root Squares, show them how by modeling the matrix approach found on the next page, taking one affix at a time and seeing if it will connect with any one of the allomorphs of the root.

DISCUSS After five minutes, have volunteers write some of their words on the board. Focus with the class on the words they have built and guide them in a discussion of how the meaning of the root is still *roll, turn, coil, or fold*, even when prefixes and suffixes are added. Watch for target words that most easily demonstrate the meanings of *roll, turn, coil, or fold*. If the word **revolve** is not present, ask the class, "Can anyone try to use the prefix **re**-?" and then continue on to the target word discussion on the next page.

SAB Pg 123

Root Squares

How many words can you make?

Start in any square. Your goal is to combine two or more word parts to make as many words in the 'vol, volt, volv, volve, volut, volute' family as you can. Write each word and a definition you can think of for it in the space provided at the bottom of the page. Use the back of the page if you need to.

con	ize	re
ary	vol, volt, volv, volve, volut, volute	ist
e	ion	counter

_____
_____
_____
_____
_____
_____
_____
_____
_____

Focus Word: **REVOLVE** ➡ Write this word on the board.

TEACH

Lead with this:	"What do we mean when we say the planets **revolve** around the sun?"
Student:	"They go *around* it."
Student:	"They *turn* around it."
Teacher:	"Is that the same as **rotate**?"
Student:	"No—**rotate** means *goes around on itself*, and **revolve** means *travels around a big circle*."
Student:	"So what happens when, say, the Earth **revolves** all the way around the sun?"
Student:	"A year is up!"
Student:	"And it starts all over again, so I guess that's why the word has the prefix **re-**, *again or back*."

DISCUSS Encourage students to see a word like **revolve** in terms of its two morphemic parts: *to roll again*. What things besides planets **revolve**? What does it mean to say somebody's life **revolves** around music, or money, or any such thing?

DEMONSTRATE Let one student play the sun, and have two or three others **revolve** around that student. As a contrast, have a student **rotate** and **revolve** at the same time. Slow down! This could cause dizziness!

Root Squares Matrix

You can refer to this matrix to guide students in this activity. Students could build at least these 17 words. *It is not important how many words are built*, so long as students understand the meanings of the root and its affixes. Encourage discussion about the definitions of any words formed for the blank slots as well as for the attested words.

	no prefix	con-	counter- + re-	e-	re-
no suffix		convolve		evolve	revolve
	volute	convolute		evolute	
-ion		convolution	counterrevolution	evolution	revolution
-ion + -ary			counterrevolutionary	evolutionary	revolutionary
-ion + -ist			counterrevolutionist	evolutionist	revolutionist
-ion + -ize					revolutionize

Day 2

Magic Squares for VOL

VOL means
to roll, turn, coil, fold

LESSON TIME

15 Minutes

OBJECTIVES

- **Understand** the meaning of the root **VOL**
- **Break Apart** words in the **VOL** family
- **Understand** the meanings of words in the **VOL** family

MATERIALS

- Student Activity Book
- **VOL** Word Wall
- Dictionary *(print or on-line)*

DIFFERENTIATING INSTRUCTION

If you prefer easier or more difficult activities, use your personal account at www.dynamicliteracy.com to access novice or expert versions, along with ideas on using them.

Break Apart Words with VOL

TEACH Have students turn to the Magic Squares on page 124 in their Student Activity Books. Model a Think-Aloud strategy for students: "I know that **VOL** means to roll, coil, turn, or fold. I can use this knowledge to find the definition of a word with **VOL** or one of its allomorphs as its root."

Direct students to word A, revolving. Say, "I know the prefix of this word, **re-**, means *again*. The suffix *-ing* means *going on, happening*. I'll watch for that suffix in the definition, though I notice there are several definitions with that feature. Look at definition 9, *rolling again; circling around a set point*. This definition includes both the parts we're looking for,

plus a meaning of **VOL**, so let's write the number 9 in square A."

COMPLETE THE ACTIVITY
Ask students to use the same strategy to find the correct definitions for the other words. Tell them to write the number of the definition in the box that matches the letter for the word. Remind them that if all their answers are correct, each row and each column will add up to the same Magic number.

DISCUSS After five minutes, ask if there are any difficulties about matching the words and definitions. If there are, ask volunteers to explain clues in the definitions that will lead to the correct choice of word. As needed, follow the focus word approach for **evolved** that you see modeled on the next page.

Add any new words to the classroom **VOL** Word Wall and remind students to add these words to the **VOL** Word Wall in their Activity Books.

SAB Pg 124

Magic Squares

Select the best answer for each of the words in the 'vol, volt, volv, volve, volut, volute' family from the numbered definitions. Put the number in the proper space in the Magic Square box. If the total of the numbers is the same both across and down, you have found the magic number!

'vol, volt, volv, volve, volut, volute' means to roll, turn, coil, or fold

WORDS	DEFINITIONS
A. revolving	1. qualities of being coiled or rolled in; qualities of being drawn in or a part of
B. revolutionizing	2. rolling back; rising up against forcefully
C. revolters	3. rolling back the old for new
D. involvements	4. able to roll again; able to circle around a set point
E. evolved	5. people who roll back; people who rise up against forcefully
F. devolving	6. people against overturning the old for the new
G. convoluted	7. aiming to roll back the old for the new
H. counterrevolutionists	8. rolled out; developed
I. revolvable	9. rolling again; circling around a set point
	10. a person who believes in a rolling out; a person who believes in a gradual progression
	11. rolled together, complicated; mixed up and intricate
	12. rolling down; passing down to

Magic Square Box

A. 9	B. 7	C. 5
D. 1	E. 8	F. 12
G. 11	H. 6	I. 4

Magic Number __21__

*** ANSWER KEY ***

Day ② Extend the Learning

Focus Word: **EVOLVED** ⟶ Write this word on the board.

TEACH

Sample leading question:	"If something has **evolved** over time, what has happened? Take a look at the word and tell me how many morphemes are there."
Student:	"There are three. A prefix, a root, and a suffix."
Student:	"The root is **volv**, the suffix is -**ed**, and the prefix is **e-**."
Teacher:	"What is the prefix **e-**?"
Student:	"That's the same as **ex-**, just simplified."
Student:	"Good, so what do we have as a meaning for **evolved**?"
Student:	"*Rolled out, turned out, folded out?*"
Student:	"Yes, like figured out over time, or came into being gradually. My interest in words has **evolved** over the last year!"

DISCUSS Encourage students to see a word like **evolved** in terms of its morphemic parts: *rolled out*. What things besides interests and skills **evolve**? (Ideas, works of art, personalities, geological shapes, physical shapes, languages, etc.)

DEMONSTRATE You can illustrate how the word *father* **evolved**, showing the gradual changes in the word over time:

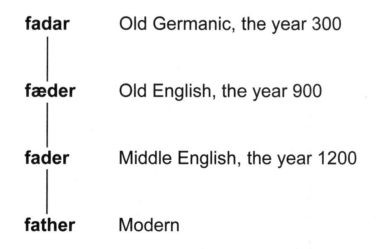

fadar   Old Germanic, the year 300

fæder   Old English, the year 900

fader   Middle English, the year 1200

father   Modern

247

Day 3

Stair Steps for VOL

VOL means to roll, turn, coil, fold

LESSON TIME

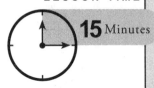

15 Minutes

OBJECTIVES

- **Understand** the meaning of the root **VOL**

- **Apply** knowledge of the root **VOL**

- **Break Apart** words in the **VOL** family

- **Understand** the meaning of words in the **VOL** family

- **Understand** the spelling principles applied to the root **VOL**

MATERIALS

- Student Activity Book
- **VOL** Word Wall

DIFFERENTIATING INSTRUCTION

If you prefer easier or more difficult activities, use your personal account at www.dynamicliteracy.com to access novice or expert versions, along with ideas on using them.

Apply Knowledge of VOL

TEACH Have students turn to page 125 in their Student Activity Books. Explain that the boxes in front of and after the root indicate letters that spell out prefixes and suffixes. Students will spell out the correct prefixes and suffixes determined by clues in the definitions at the bottom of the page.

Have a volunteer read definition number one at the bottom of the page. Say, "Notice that there are lots of spellings of this root, one of them being **VOLVE** that we see in step one of this Stair Steps exercise. Once again, we need only a prefix for this word,

a one-letter prefix that means *out*. The actual prefix is **ex-**, but in this case it takes its assimilated form, **e-** (dropping the x-) to make it easier to pronounce in front of the first sound of the root **volve**. That gives us the word **evolve**, with the meaning *to roll out*."

COMPLETE THE ACTIVITY

Let students work in pairs (optionally) and tell them to use the same strategy to find the correct prefixes and suffixes for the words listed. These activities can be quite challenging!

DISCUSS After a few minutes, review the answers as a class. Ask if there were any difficulties. Listen to any problems and have volunteers solve the difficulties by explaining key clues in the given definitions. As needed, follow the focus word approach that you see modeled on the next page.

SAB
Pg 125

Stair Steps

Fill in the missing letters of each 'vol, volt, volv, volve, volut, volute' word by using the definitions below.

'vol, volt, volv, volve, volut, volute' means to roll, turn, coil, or fold

1.	e	v	o	l	v	e			
2.	r	e	v	o	l	v	e		
3.	i	n	v	o	l	v	e	s	
4.	e	v	o	l	u	t	i	o	n
5.	r	e	v	o	l	v	a	b	l	e
6.	i	n	v	o	l	v	e	m	e	n	t
7.	e	v	o	l	u	t	i	o	n	a	r	y
8.	r	e	v	o	l	u	t	i	o	n	i	s	t
9.	r	e	v	o	l	u	t	i	o	n	i	z	e	d

1. to roll out; to develop
2. to roll again; to circle around a set point
3. coils or rolls in; concerns or includes
4. act or process of rolling out; a gradual maturing or progress
5. able to roll again; able to circle around a set point
6. quality of being coiled or rolled in; quality of being drawn in or a part of
7. marked by rolling out; marked by gradually maturing or progressing
8. a person aiming to roll back the old for the new
9. aimed to roll back the old for the new

Focus Word: **INVOLVES** ➞ Write this word on the board.

TEACH

Sample leading question:	"Success **involves** a lot of good, hard work. Let's take a look at the word **involves**. What do we see?"
Student:	"Three pieces—a prefix, a root, and a suffix."
Student:	"The root **volve** and the suffix -**s**—easy. But there's that **in-** again."
Teacher:	"I'll bet you can detect what the **in-** means here."
Student:	"It must be *in*, like a place."
Teacher:	"So what does **involves** mean literally?"
Student:	"*Rolls in, turns in, folds in.* How does that work?"
Student:	"It's like you add ingredients in, you *fold* them in."
Student:	"So to say somebody is **involved** in an accident, the accident folded them in, made them a part of it. I get it."

DISCUSS Encourage students to see a word like **involves** in terms of the meanings of its pieces, *rolls or folds in,* or *enfolds*. What other uses of **involved** can the class determine (complicated, twisted, hard to understand).

DEMONSTRATE Find a picture on-line of a Rube Goldberg contraption and show the class how **involved** it is, turned in and on itself in complicated twists and turns.

Day 4

In Other Words
for **VOL**

VOL means
to roll, turn, coil, fold

LESSON TIME

15 Minutes

OBJECTIVES

- **Understand** the meaning of the root **VOL**

- **Reinforce** knowledge of the root **VOL**

- **Understand** the meaning of words in the **VOL** family

- **Apply** knowledge of words in the **VOL** family

MATERIALS

- Student Activity Book

- **VOL** Word Wall

- Dictionary
(print or on-line)

In Other Words for **VOL**

TEACH Have students turn to page 126 in their Student Activity Books. Explain that they are going to read a little story that uses some surprising and sometimes odd phrasing. The underlined words or phrases in the story are actually definitions or synonyms for words in the **VOL** family. Then they will see sentences about the story, each containing a blank.

Using context clues in the sentences, they will find a **VOL** family word in the Word Bank at the bottom to fit in each blank. Have a student read aloud the opening sentence or sentences of the story that contain the first underlined phrase. Then say, "Let's look at the first numbered sentence that contains a blank to be filled in. Clues in the sentence tell us that we want an action word, a verb that is a synonym for *rolls out and develops*. There is one word among the choices we have that seems to be the form of verb we are looking for, one ending in the suffix **-s**. Let's explore the word **evolves**. The single-letter prefix **e-** is a form of the prefix **ex-**, so that would indicate *out*. So we have *rolls out* along with the implication *develops*. That seems to explain the word we need, so let's write **evolves** in the blank for the first sentence."

COMPLETE THE ACTIVITY

This can be quite challenging, so allow students to work on this activity in small groups. Not every word in the Word Bank will be used.

DISCUSS

After about 10 minutes, ask if there were any difficulties. Have volunteers explain strategies they used that led to correct answers.

SAB Pg 126

Sorry, Pluto.....

Scientific theory constantly <u>rolls out and develops</u> as more information is learned. Recently, scientists declared that our solar system was one planet short of the nine that science books taught. This was enough to cause a <u>forceful rise up against</u> the decision in classrooms across the country. What was the reasoning behind "deplaneting" the smallest and most remote of the bodies that <u>roll around the set point</u> of our sun? Did the reasoning <u>concern</u> the planet's orbit? Was it that Pluto's <u>act or process of rolling around</u> was erratic? Did the planet's rocks <u>pass</u> down into wispy clouds and disappear?

This last step in Pluto's <u>gradual progress</u> from planet, originally discovered in 1930, to "dwarf planet" occurred in August, 2006. Scientists agreed that one major characteristic of a planet was that it sweeps smaller objects clean from the region immediately around it. Since Pluto occupies a region that contains a lot of other small objects in its space, it cannot be a planet.

Of course there are dissenters who say Pluto **is** a planet. Is there a <u>movement against overthrowing the old for the new</u> on the horizon?

<u>Fill in the blanks below using words from the "vol, volt, volv, volve, volut" family.</u>

1. Scientific ideas change over time and theory <u>evolves</u> as more information is gathered and analyzed.

2. Some classrooms that were obviously fans of the small planet staged a <u>revolt</u> in their science classrooms to protest the decision.

3. Pluto does <u>revolve</u> around the sun just as other planets do.

4. Pluto's removal as a planet did not <u>involve</u> trouble with its orbit around the sun.

5. There was no dispute about Pluto's <u>revolution</u> on its axis.

6. The solid material comprising Pluto's mass did not <u>devolve</u> into gaseous clouds.

7. Pluto's <u>evolution</u> from planet to dwarf planet took over seventy years.

8. There are scientists who disagree with booting Pluto from the list of planets; their <u>counterrevolution</u> may have it reinstated in the years to come.

<u>Not Used:</u>   convoluted   involvement   revolutionist   revolver

O P T I O N A L

Day 5

Morpheme Mania
for **VOL**

VOL means
to roll, turn, coil, fold

LESSON TIME

15 Minutes

OBJECTIVES

- **Build** words in the **VOL** family

- **Apply** knowledge of synonyms and antonyms to **VOL** words

Optional Morpheme Mania for **VOL**

On page 127 of their Activity Books, students will see an optional vocabulary enrichment activity that they can work on in groups, time permitting. This activity makes a great review for the formal assessment on the next page.

All the affixes presented in the week's activities are provided at the top of the page on either side of the root of the week in all its forms. Students can write in up to 13 of the words they built during the week, possibly discovering additional ones.

Then students can brainstorm with each other to come up with antonyms and synonyms they may know. Starter examples are given with every Morpheme Mania in the Activity Book. Because antonyms and synonyms may require knowledge of roots which students have not yet studied, completion of this activity is not crucial. Simply remind students that they can at any time during the course of the year revisit any of their Morpheme Mania pages and add words, antonyms, and synonyms as their vocabulary grows.

Day 5 *Assessment*

Make and hand out copies.
The answer key is on page A-5.
The instructions are on page A-2.

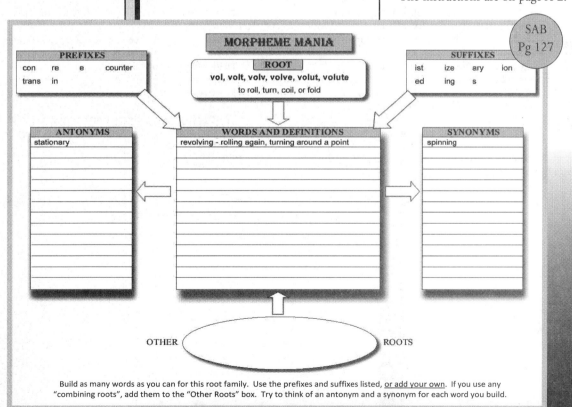

MORPHEME MANIA

SAB Pg 127

PREFIXES

| con | re | e | counter |
| trans | in | | |

ROOT
vol, volt, volv, volve, volut, volute
to roll, turn, coil, or fold

SUFFIXES

| ist | ize | ary | ion |
| ed | ing | s | |

ANTONYMS
stationary

WORDS AND DEFINITIONS
revolving - rolling again, turning around a point

SYNONYMS
spinning

OTHER   ROOTS

Build as many words as you can for this root family. Use the prefixes and suffixes listed, <u>or add your own</u>. If you use any "combining roots", add them to the "Other Roots" box. Try to think of an antonym and a synonym for each word you build.

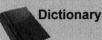
convoluted rolled together; complicated; mixed up and intricate

convolution part that is rolled together or coiled; anything mixed up or intricate

counterrevolution a movement against overturning the old for the new

counterrevolutionary a g a i n s t overturning the old for the new

counterrevolutionist a person against overturning the old for the new

counterrevolutionists people against overturning the old for the new

counterrevolutions movements against overturning the old for the new

devolve to roll down; to pass down to

devolved rolled down; passed down to

devolves rolls down; passes down to

devolving rolling down; passing down to

evolution act or process of rolling out; a gradual maturing or progress

evolutional pertaining to rolling out; maturing or progressing

evolutionary marked by rolling out; marked by gradually maturing or progressing

evolutionist a person who believes in a rolling out; a person who believes in a gradual progression

evolve to roll out; to develop

evolved rolled out; developed

evolves rolls out; develops

evolving rolling out; developing

involve to coil or roll in; to concern or include

involved coiled or rolled in; complicated

involvement quality of being coiled or rolled in; quality of being drawn in or a part of

involvements qualities of being coiled or rolled in; qualities of being drawn in or a part of

involves coils or rolls in; concerns or includes

involving coiling or rolling in; concerning or including

revolt to roll back; to rise up against forcefully

revolted rolled back; rose up against forcefully

revolter a person who rolls back; a person who rises up against forcefully

revolters people who roll back; people who rise up against forcefully

revolting rolling back; rising up against forcefully

revolts rolls back; rises up against forcefully

revolution an act to roll back the old for the new

revolutionaries people who roll back the old for the new

revolutionary rolling back the old for the new

revolutionist a person aiming to roll back the old for the new

revolutionists people aiming to roll back the old for the new

revolutionize to aim to roll back the old for the new

revolutionized aimed to roll back the old for the new

revolutionizes aims to roll back the old for the new

revolutionizing aiming to roll back the old for the new

revolutions acts to roll back the old for the new

revolvable able to roll again; able circle around a set point

revolve to roll again; to circle around a set point

revolved rolled again; circled around a set point

revolver a device that rolls again; a gun with a rotating barrel

revolvers devices that roll again; guns with rotating barrels

revolves rolls again; circles around a set point

revolving rolling again; circling around a set point

volute a rolled or spiraled formation; having curves

Check-Up for **VOL**

Name _____

____ **1.** **VOLT**, **VOLV**, or **VOLUT** in words like **revolt**, **involve**, and **revolution** means:

    A to break

    B to demand

    C to roll

____ **2.** What is the meaning of the word **convoluted**?

    A rolled or folded together

    B not breakable

    C helping to build in or arrange

____ **3.** What is the meaning of the word **devolve**?

    A to break away

    B to roll down

    C to demand against

____ **4.** What is the meaning of the word **involvement**?

    A the act of being folded in

    B the process of keeping something from breaking

    C the quality of demanding nicely

____ **5.** A **revolutionist** is a:

    A process of turning

    B device for breaking down boxes

    C person aiming to roll back the old for the new

____ **6.** Which word means **rolled or coiled**?

    A volute

    B revolver

    C convolution

____ **7.** Which word means **likely to turn again**?

    A revolutionize

    B revolvable

    C evolution

____ **8.** Which word means **relating to rolling out**?

    A counterrevolutionist

    B evolutionary

    C revolters

____ **9.** Which type of columns have the **circumvolutions** at the top? The columns:

    A with the coils going around

    B that look like an orange broken open

    C that are completely plain

____ **10.** The homeless person was in an **involuted** position on the bench. The person:

    A was lying stretched out

    B was standing straight up

    C sat as if coiled inward

OBJECTIVES

- **Understand** the meaning of the root **STRU**

- **Build** words in the root **STRU** family

- **Break Apart** words in the root **STRU** family

- **Understand** the meaning of words in the **STRU** family

- **Understand** the spelling principles applied to the root **STRU**

- **Apply** knowledge of words in the **STRU** family

- **Assess** and **Reinforce** knowledge of words in the **STRU** family

MATERIALS

- Student Activity Books, pages 129-134

- Dictionary *(print or on-line)*

- A deck of playing cards *(optional)*

CROSS-CURRICULAR EXAMPLES

Science:
instrument, structuration

Social Studies:
destruction, infrastructure, reconstruction

Language Arts:
construed, unstructured

Math:
construe, construct, superstruct

STRU

meaning "to build, arrange, pile up"

instructive
serving to **build** into

construct
to build or **arrange** together

obstruct
pile up against

Morpheme: **STRU**
Allomorphs: **STRUE, STRUCT**

About 200 words containing the morpheme **STRU** or one of its allomorphs are current in English. During this unit, tell students to be alert for this root in their school texts, general reading, and oral language they hear. Some of the words they might encounter in their school subjects are listed on the left under Cross-Curricular Examples

UNIT AT A GLANCE

Day **1**
Root Squares
for **STRU**

Day **2**
Magic Squares
for **STRU**

Day **3**
Stair Steps
for **STRU**

OPTIONAL
Day **4**
In Other Words
for **STRU**

Day **5**
Assessment or Morpheme Mania
for **STRU**

Each activity should take approximately **15 minutes.**

Two variations, or allomorphs, of this root join with the prefix **con-** to form the words **construct** and **construe**. To **construct** is *to arrange materials together and built them into a unity*. To **construe** has more to do with *interpreting what is already built or created*. We **construe** what someone has said. We **construe** a sentence by analyzing, or parsing, its parts. Have a student **construct** an interesting sentence on the board and then you and the rest of the class **construe** it.

There are certain sounds in the English language called **obstruents**, a word meaning *built up in the way*, like an **obstruction**. Sounds made by blocking air temporarily with our speech organs (lips, teeth, tongue) are called **obstruents**. Let students play with the sounds made by letters **b**, **p**, **k**, hard **g**, **t**, and **d** to observe how the speech organs block the sound before releasing it.

It is easy to see the morphemic meaning of **destruction**, the *opposite or undoing of* **construction**, but less obvious is the word **destroy**, which evolved through the French characteristic of dropping consonants.

The word **industry** is the most recent evolution of the prefix **endo-**, meaning *within*, attached to the root **stru**. Industry is *building or arranging within*.

Word Alert!

The letter sequence **s-t-r-u** does not guarantee the presence of this root. The "proof method" of proper morphemic splitting is always a worthwhile activity to revisit. Let students experiment with isolating the morphemes in any of these words:

awestruck

distrust

mistruth

strut

Remember, when any one morpheme is correctly isolated, whatever remains will also be one or more morphemes. Thus, the word **strut** cannot contain the morpheme **stru**, because the final **t** that would remain has no meaning in that word.

The adjective **struthious** means *like an ostrich*.

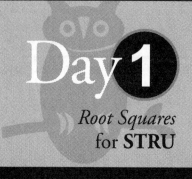

Day 1

Root Squares for **STRU**

STRU means
to build, arrange, pile up

LESSON TIME

15 Minutes

OBJECTIVES

- **Understand** the meaning of the root **STRU**

- **Build** words in the **STRU** family

- **Understand** the meaning of words in the **STRU** family

- **Understand** the spelling principles applied to the root **STRU**

MATERIALS

- Student Activity Book
- **STRU** Word Wall
- Dictionary *(print or on-line)*

DIFFERENTIATING INSTRUCTION

If you prefer easier or more difficult activities, use your personal account at www.dynamicliteracy.com to access novice or expert versions, along with ideas on using them.

Root Squares for STRU

TEACH A Mini-Lesson for the prefix **infra-** is provided on the next page. Then have students turn to page 129 in their Activity Books. Say, "All of the prefixes and suffixes in the squares surrounding the shaded center are now familiar, but if you have questions about any of the meanings, simply ask or look them up in the list inside the front or back covers of the activity book."

Call attention to the center box. Point out that the root **STRU** has three different spellings, called allomorphs. Ask students to decide if any of the forms they see in the middle square can stand alone as a word. Since none of the forms can stand as a word, each must have a prefix or a suffix attached to it to build an independent word. Suggest that students start their list with **struct**, adding the prefix

con-, meaning *together*, to build **construct**, meaning *to build or arrange together*. Invite students to explore how this word is related to the idea of *build; arrange; pile up*.

COMPLETE THE ACTIVITY

Have students follow the directions to build words. If students have difficulty building words with the Root Squares, show them how by modeling the matrix approach found on the next page, taking one affix at a time and seeing if it will connect with any one of the allomorphs of the root.

DISCUSS After five minutes, have volunteers write some of their words on the board. Focus with the class on the words they have built and guide them in a discussion of how the meaning of the root is still *build; arrange; pile up*, even when prefixes and suffixes are added. Watch for target words that most easily demonstrate the meanings of *build; arrange; pile up*. If the word **structure** is not present, ask the class, "Can anyone try to use the suffix **-ure**?" and then continue on to the target word discussion on the next page.

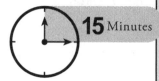

SAB Pg 129

Root Squares

How many words can you make?

Start in any square. Your goal is to combine two or more word parts to make as many words in the 'stru, strue, struct' family as you can. Write each word and a definition you can think of for it in the space provided at the bottom of the page. Use the back of the page if you need to.

un	de	ive
infra	stru, strue, struct	con
ure	or	ob

256

MINI-LESSON: the Prefix **infra-**

The prefix **infra-** is from a Latin preposition and adverb meaning *beneath or after*. **Infra-** can mean literally *underneath*, as in **infrapose** (*to place below*), or *included within*, as **infraterritorial** (*inside an area*). Sometimes we see it as an actual word in texts, indicating that something more will be said about a topic later (afterwards or below in the text).

About 30 words associated with physics, geology, or anatomy use this prefix. Here are some of the words that most easily demonstrate the effect of the prefix **infra-**:

> **infrasonic**, below heard sound—compare supersonic
> **infraglacial**, located deep down under a glacier
> **infraorbital**, situated within or inside an orbit

Focus Word: **STRUCTURE** → Write this word on the board.

TEACH

Lead with this:	"Here's a fairly familiar word. Take a look."
Student:	"It's a building."
Student:	"It's also a word for how something is arranged."
Teacher:	"What pieces of meaning do we see in the word?"
Student:	"The root we're working on, **struct**, and the suffix **-ure**, *an act or process*."
Teacher:	"Is the word **structure** a noun, or is it a verb?"
Student:	(Looking at the inside back cover of the Activity Book) "It can be either one."
Teacher:	"Yes, you can **structure** something, or arrange it a certain way, and you can call a building like a sky-scraper or a barn a **structure**."
Student:	"So you could **structure** a **structure**!"
Student:	"Yes, you can build a building!"
Teacher:	"Those two examples have a special name. They're called *cognate direct objects,* when the verb and the thing receiving the action of the verb have the same morpheme."

DISCUSS Name some famous **structures**. What things can have **structure** besides buildings? (bone structure, sentences structure, muscles, etc.)

DEMONSTRATE You can demonstrate a sentence structure with a diagram:

(subject) **sentences** | (verb) **have** — (direct objects) **subjects** / **a n d** / **verbs**

Root Squares Matrix
You can refer to this matrix to guide students in this activity. Students could build at least these 13 words.

It is not important how many words are built, so long as students understand the meanings of the root and its affixes.

	no prefix	con-	de-	infra-	ob-	un-
no suffix		construct	destruct		obstruct	
		construe				
-ive		constructive	destructive		obstructive	unconstructive
-or			destructor		obstructor	
-ure	structure	constructure		infrastructure		

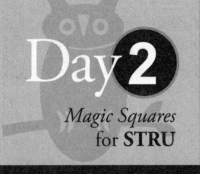

Day 2

Magic Squares
for **STRU**

STRU means
to build, arrange, pile up

LESSON TIME

15 Minutes

OBJECTIVES

- **Understand** the meaning of the root **STRU**
- **Break Apart** words in the **STRU** family
- **Understand** the meanings of words in the **STRU** family

MATERIALS

- Student Activity Book
- **STRU** Word Wall
- Dictionary *(print or on-line)*
- A deck of playing cards *(optional)*

DIFFERENTIATING INSTRUCTION

If you prefer easier or more difficult activities, use your personal account at www.dynamicliteracy.com to access novice or expert versions, along with ideas on using them.

Break Apart Words with STRU

TEACH Have students turn to the Magic Squares on page 130 in their Student Activity Books. Model a Think-Aloud strategy for students: "I know that **STRU** means *to build, arrange, pile up.* I can use this knowledge to find the definition of a word with **STRU** or one of its allomorphs as its root."

Direct students to word D, **instructors**. Say, "I know the prefix on this word, the **in-**, can mean *in* or *into,* or *not.* The suffixes **-or** and **-s** together mean *people or devices that do something.* Look at definition 6, *people who build into; teachers.* This definition includes a meaning for all the parts we're looking for, and confirms the meaning for **in-**, so let's write the number 6 in square D."

COMPLETE THE ACTIVITY Ask students to use the same strategy to find the correct definitions for the other words. Tell them to write the number of the definition in the box that matches the letter for the word. Remind them that if all their answers are correct, each row and each column will add up to the same Magic number.

DISCUSS After five minutes, ask if there are any difficulties about matching the words and definitions. If there are, ask volunteers to explain clues in the definitions that will lead to the correct choice of word. As needed, follow the focus word approach for **constructions** that you see modeled on the next page.

Add any new words to the classroom **STRU** Word Wall and remind students to add these words to the **STRU** Word Wall in their Activity Books.

SAB Pg 130

Magic Squares

Select the best answer for each of the words in the 'stru, strue, struce' family from the numbered definitions. Put the number in the proper space in the Magic Square box. If the total of the numbers is the same both across and down, you have found the magic number!

'stru, strue, struct' means to build, arrange; pile up

WORDS	DEFINITIONS
A. constructions	1. helping to build in or arrange; aiding to develop or achieve
B. indestructibly	2. things built or arranged together; things made
C. constructively	3. built or arranged together again; made again
D. instructors	4. parts of buildings within; internal frameworks of buildings
E. infrastructures	5. in a manner related to the basic arrangement of
F. destructive	6. people who build into; teachers
G. unobstructed	7. in a manner serving to build or arrange together; helpfully
H. structurally	8. causing to be unbuilt or disarranged; resulting in ruin or broken parts
I. reconstructed	9. so as not to be capable of being unbuilt or disarranged; in a way not capable of being broken apart
	10. with nothing piled up against; not blocked

Magic Square Box

A. 2	B. 9	C. 7
D. 6	E. 4	F. 8
G. 10	H. 5	I. 3

Magic Number <u>18</u>

*** ANSWER KEY ***

Focus Word: **CONSTRUCTIONS** ⟶ Write this word on the board.

TEACH

Sample leading question:	"What is the difference between **structures** and **constructions**?"
Student:	"I think a **structure** is a finished product, and **construction** is going on, like at a **construction** site."
Student:	"That sounds right. I guess you want us to look at the word **constructions**."
Teacher:	"You're right!"
Student:	"Well, we have a prefix **con-**, *together*—that already makes sense—build together, because a **construction** has parts."
Student:	"And two suffixes: **-ion** and **-s**."
Student:	"And the root, four pieces of meaning."
Student:	"So it's *more than one act of building together*."
Student:	"It must be the *way or process that things are put together*."
Student:	"You can **construct** a **construction**! What is that called again?"
Teacher:	"A **cognate direct object**."

DISCUSS **Construction** is a common word, but why hasn't the word **struction** made it into dictionaries? (Perhaps it will eventually—words are "real" as long as they carry meaning. Students might also suggest that the act of building requires putting pieces together.) What things can be called **constructions** besides buildings? (arguments, geometric figures, sentences, gardens, etc.)

DEMONSTRATE Have students **construct** "houses" out of cards. Have them note that they are arranging pieces together into **constructions**.

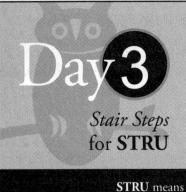

Day 3

Stair Steps
for **STRU**

STRU means
to build, arrange, pile up

LESSON TIME

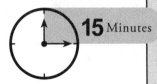

15 Minutes

OBJECTIVES

- **Understand** the meaning of the root **STRU**

- **Apply** knowledge of the root **STRU**

- **Break Apart** words in the **STRU** family

- **Understand** the meaning of words in the **STRU** family

- **Understand** the spelling principles applied to the root **STRU**

MATERIALS

- Student Activity Book

- **STRU** Word Wall

DIFFERENTIATING INSTRUCTION

If you prefer easier or more difficult activities, use your personal account at www.dynamicliteracy.com to access novice or expert versions, along with ideas on using them.

Apply Knowledge of STRU

TEACH Have students turn to page 131 in their Student Activity Books. Explain that the boxes in front of and after the root indicate letters that spell out prefixes and suffixes. Students will spell out the correct prefixes and suffixes determined by clues in the definitions at the bottom of the page.

Have a volunteer read definition number one at the bottom of the page. Say, "Notice that there are three spellings of this root, one of them being **STRUCT** that we see in step one of this Stair Steps exercise. Again we need only a prefix for this word, this time a two-letter prefix that means *against*. That's one of the meanings of **re-** but there's no such word **restruct**, is there? Keep looking and you'll find the prefix **ob-** with the meaning *against*. The word **OBSTRUCT** is familiar and it fits the definition we are looking at, so let's write **OB** in those first two blanks in step one of this Stair Steps."

COMPLETE THE ACTIVITY

Let students work in pairs (optionally) and tell them to use the same strategy to find the correct prefixes and suffixes for the words listed. These activities can be quite challenging!

DISCUSS After a few minutes, review the answers as a class. Ask if there were any difficulties. Listen to any problems and have volunteers solve the difficulties by explaining key clues in the given definitions. As needed, follow the focus word approach that you see modeled on the next page.

SAB
Pg 131

Stair Steps

Fill in the missing letters of each 'stru, strue, struct' word by using the definitions below.
'stru, strue, struct' means to build; arrange; pile up

1.	o	b	s	t	r	u	c	t			
2.	i	n	s	t	r	u	c	t	s		
3.	s	t	r	u	c	t	u	r	a	l	
4.	r	e	c	o	n	s	t	r	u	c	t
5.	o	b	s	t	r	u	c	t	i	o	n	s
6.	i	n	s	t	r	u	c	t	i	v	e	l	y
7.	r	e	c	o	n	s	t	r	u	c	t	i	n	g

1. to pile up against; to block
2. builds into; teaches
3. related to the basic arrangement of
4. to build or arrange together again; to make again
5. things piled up against; things that block
6. in a manner serving to build into; in a manner serving to teach
7. building or arranging together again; making again

260

Focus Word: **INSTRUCTS** → Write this word on the board.

Sample leading question:	"The sentence at the top of the activity instructs us to fill in the missing letters. Now just what does the word **instructs** mean?"
Student:	"It has that same root we've been working on, meaning *to build*. I'm not sure how that works, since **instructs** means *teaches or shows*."
Student:	"I don't see how building works here, either."
Teacher:	"Remember when we have had some words that don't mean what they say in a literal sense, but in a figurative way, like an image?"
Student:	"Well, I guess something is being *built* in our minds—an *idea* or a *plan* maybe?"
Student:	"Or it shows us how to arrange the activity?"
Student:	"How about NOT to build? You never know with that **in-** prefix!"
Student:	"No, I'm pretty sure that **in-** means *in, to build in*, like inside our heads."
Student:	"Yes—**instruction** is training or education, so it goes *inside*."
Student:	"I see—it's what's *built in or arranged inside our minds*."

DISCUSS Have students see that **instructs** and associated words have to do with *building a structure inside the mind for future reference*, as if to equip. Refer to the word **built-in** to make the concept even clearer.

Day 4

STRU means
to build, arrange, pile up

LESSON TIME

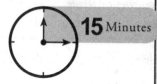

15 Minutes

OBJECTIVES

- **Understand** the meaning of the root **STRU**
- **Reinforce** knowledge of the root **STRU**
- **Understand** the meaning of words in the **STRU** family
- **Apply** knowledge of words in the **STRU** family

MATERIALS

- Student Activity Book
- **STRU** Word Wall
- Dictionary *(print or on-line)*

In Other Words for **STRU**

TEACH Have students turn to page 132 in their Student Activity Books. Explain that they are going to read a little story that uses some surprising and sometimes odd phrasing. The underlined words or phrases in the story are actually definitions or synonyms for words in the **STRU** family. Then they will see sentences about the story, each containing a blank.

Using context clues in the sentences, they will find a **STRU** family word in the Word Bank at the bottom to fit in each blank. Have a student read aloud the opening sentence or sentences of the story that contain the first underlined phrase. Then say, "Let's look at the first numbered sentence that contains a blank to be filled in. Clues in the sentence tell us that we want a describing word, an adjective that is a synonym for *building and making* and which could modify business. What is the business of building and making? I see the word **construction** at the bottom of the page. The prefix **con-** would give us *together, or with*. One always builds and makes with something. This word is a likely choice, so let's write **construction** in the blank for the first sentence."

COMPLETE THE ACTIVITY

This can be quite challenging, so allow students to work on this activity in small groups. Not every word in the Word Bank will be used.

DISCUSS After about 10 minutes, ask if there were any difficulties. Have volunteers explain strategies they used that led to correct answers.

SAB
Pg 132

Building a Birdhouse

Molly decided to build a birdhouse for her 4-H project. Because her uncle was in the <u>building and making</u> business, she had tools. She also had a book <u>for the process of teaching</u> her and blueprints showing measurements for the wood pieces <u>related to the basic arrangement</u> that she needed.

Molly worked quickly to assemble the pieces, but the roof wouldn't fit correctly on top of the birdhouse. She had to <u>undo what had been built together</u> at the front of the house and decided to watch a video <u>serving to build know-how</u>, hoping it would help fix the problem. The video warned to make sure that the entrance to the birdhouse had no <u>things piled up against it</u>, so that the birds could enter.

Later, Molly <u>arranged in her mind</u> that her project was a success when she heard chirping coming from the little house. When she presented the project to her 4-H club, Molly offered to <u>put know-how into</u> anyone wanting to learn about making birdhouses.

<u>Fill in the blanks below using words from the "stru, strue, struct" family.</u>

1. The idea to build a birdhouse was obvious to Molly because her uncle was in the <u>construction</u> business.

2. Assembling the pieces without an <u>instruction</u> booklet would be difficult.

3. Walls, floor and roof make up the <u>structural</u> pieces for the birdhouse project.

4. When she made a mistake Molly had to <u>deconstruct</u> part of the building and repair it.

5. Watching an <u>instructive</u> video before starting may have helped Molly arrange the pieces correctly the first time.

6. Without <u>obstructions</u> at the door of the birdhouse, birds could enter and leave easily.

7. Molly <u>construed</u> that birds had moved into the house when she heard them chirping.

8. She did such a good job that she could <u>instruct</u> other students in her club on making a birdhouse.

<u>Not Used:</u> destructive instrumentally   obstruct   structured

OPTIONAL

Day 5

Morpheme Mania
for **STRU**

STRU means
to build, arrange, pile up

LESSON TIME

15 Minutes

OBJECTIVES

- **Build** words in the
  STRU family

- **Apply** knowledge of
  synonyms and antonyms
  to **STRU** words

Optional Morpheme Mania for **STRU**

On page 133 of their Activity Book, students will see an optional vocabulary enrichment activity that they can work on in groups, time permitting. This activity makes a great review for the formal assessment on the next page.

All the affixes presented in the week's activities are provided at the top of the page on either side of the root of the week in all its forms. Students can write in up to 13 of the words they built during the week, possibly discovering additional ones.

Then students can brainstorm with each other to come up with antonyms and synonyms they may know. Starter examples are given with every Morpheme Mania in the Activity Book. Because antonyms and synonyms may require knowledge of roots which students have not yet studied, completion of this activity is not crucial. Simply remind students that they can at any time during the course of the year revisit any of their Morpheme Mania pages and add words, antonyms, and synonyms as their vocabulary grows.

Day 5 *Assessment*

Make and hand out copies.
The answer key is on page A-5.
The instructions are on page A-2.

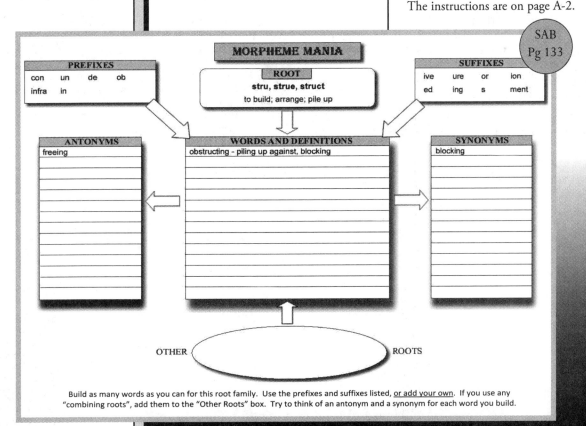

SAB
Pg 133

MORPHEME MANIA

PREFIXES			
con	un	de	ob
infra	in		

ROOT
stru, strue, struct
to build; arrange; pile up

SUFFIXES			
ive	ure	or	ion
ed	ing	s	ment

ANTONYMS
freeing

WORDS AND DEFINITIONS
obstructing - piling up against, blocking

SYNONYMS
blocking

OTHER ⬭ ROOTS

Build as many words as you can for this root family. Use the prefixes and suffixes listed, <u>or add your own</u>. If you use any "combining roots", add them to the "Other Roots" box. Try to think of an antonym and a synonym for each word you build.

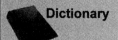
construct   to build or arrange together; to make

constructed   built or arranged together; made

constructing   building or arranging together; making

construction   anything built or arranged together; something made

constructions   things built or arranged together; things made

constructive   serving to build or arrange together; helpful

constructively   in a manner serving to build or arrange together; helpfully

constructs   builds or arranges together; makes

destruction   act of unbuilding or disarranging; ruin

destructive   causing to be unbuilt or disarranged; resulting in ruin or broken parts

indestructible   not capable of being unbuilt or torn down

indestructibly   so as not to be capable of being unbuilt or torn down

infrastructure   part of a building within; the internal framework of a building

infrastructures   parts of buildings within; internal frameworks of buildings

instruct   to build into; to teach

instructed   built into; taught

instructing   building into; teaching

instruction   act or process of building into; anything taught

instructional   related to building into; relating to teaching

instructions   things serving to build into; things taught

instructive   serving to build into; serving to teach

instructively   in a manner serving to build into; so as to teach

instructor   a person who builds into; teacher

instructors   people who build into; teachers

instructs   builds into; teaches

instrument   device by which something is built in or arranged; a tool or device

instrumental   helping to build in or arrange; aiding to develop or achieve

instrumentally   so as to help build in or arrange; so as to aid development or achievement

instrumentation   process by which something is built in or arranged

instruments   devices by which things are built in or arranged; tools or devices

obstruct   to pile up against; to block

obstructed   piled up against; blocked

obstructing   piling up against; blocking

obstruction   anything piled up against; something that blocks

obstructions   things piled up against; things that block

obstructs   piles up against; blocks

reconstruct   to build or arrange together again

reconstructed   built or arranged together again

reconstructing   building or arranging together again

reconstruction   anything built or arranged together again

reconstructs   builds or arranges together again

structural   related to the basic arrangement of

structurally   in a manner related to the basic arrangement of

structure   something made up of parts

structured   having been made up of parts

structures   things made up of parts

structuring   making up of parts; arranging

unobstructed   with nothing piled up against; not blocked

Check-Up for **STRU**

____ **1.** **STRU** or **STRUCT** in words like **construe** and **construct** means:

   A to break

   B to build

   C to divide

____ **2.** What is the meaning of the word **instrumental**?

   A likely to divide into

   B not breakable

   C helping to build in or arrange

____ **3.** What is the meaning of the word **constructive**?

   A to break with

   B serving to arrange together

   C to divide along lines

____ **4.** What is the meaning of the word **destruction**?

   A the act of unbuilding

   B the process of building again

   C the process of sending away

____ **5.** The way that something is **structured** is the way it is:

   A able to be broken

   B arranged

   C divided

____ **6.** Which word means **to tear down what was put together**?

   A unobstructed

   B deconstruct

   C infrastructure

____ **7.** Which word means **piled up in the way**?

   A obstructive

   B indestructibly

   C reconstructing

____ **8.** Which word means **built together again**?

   A unconstructive

   B instrumentally

   C reconstructed

____ **9.** We couldn't find the mistake, so we had to **reconstrue** the whole plan. We had to:

   A arrange it all together again

   B stop completely

   C take a break

____ **10.** The movie monster's **indestructibility** allowed "The Return of…" type films. The monster:

   A ate people

   B did not have a name

   C wouldn't die

OBJECTIVES

- **Understand** the meaning of the root **SPIR**
- **Build** words in the root **SPIR** family
- **Break Apart** words in the root **SPIR** family
- **Understand** the meaning of words in the **SPIR** family
- **Understand** the spelling principles applied to the root **SPIR**
- **Apply** knowledge of words in the **SPIR** family
- **Assess** and **Reinforce** knowledge of words in the **SPIR** family

MATERIALS

- Student Activity Books, pages 135-140
- Dictionary *(print or on-line)*

CROSS-CURRICULAR EXAMPLES

Science:
perspiration, respire, transpire

Social Studies:
conspiracy, expiration

Language Arts:
aspirate, inspiration

Math:
spirometry, spirographic

SPIR

meaning "to breathe; to whisper; essence"

expires
breathes out

conspire
to **whisper** together

spirit
essence

Morpheme: **SPIR**
Allomorphs: **SPIRE, SPIRO, PIR, PIRE**

About 400 words containing the morpheme **SPIR** or one of its allomorphs are current in English. During this unit, tell students to be alert for this root in their school texts, general reading, and oral language they hear. Some of the words they might encounter in their school subjects are listed on the left under Cross-Curricular Examples.

UNIT AT A GLANCE

Day **1**
Root Squares for **SPIR**

Day **2**
Magic Squares for **SPIR**

Day **3**
Stair Steps for **SPIR**

OPTIONAL
Day **4**
In Other Words for **SPIR**

Day **5**
Assessment or Morpheme Mania for **SPIR**

Each activity should take approximately **15 minutes**.

This morpheme has a basic sense of *breath* or *force of life*. This is quite easy to see in a word like **respiration**, *the process of breathing in and back out again and again.*

Breathing, especially when exaggerated or strengthened, has a connotation of *yearning or desire* (we pant after something). Such a connotation appears in the word **aspire**. When we **aspire** for great things, we literally *breathe toward them*, our life force is aimed at them.

Breathing, if not exaggerated or strengthened, can be thought of as *whispering*. When people *whisper together*, they are said to be **conspiring**.

A life force without body but thought of as nothing but breath or air is a **spirit**. Ask students what it means to have school **spirit**. What is the **spirit** of the law?

The language phenomenon of reversing letters and sounds is called *metathesis*. For example, nearly all English words ending in -**le**, such as **example**, **people**, and **nimble**, are spelled the way they were once pronounced, but now the letters are reversed according to pronunciation (we say them as if spelled **exampel**, **peopel**, and **nimbel**. Metathesis is at work with the root **spir** to produce the word **sprite**, a creature with light, fleeting characteristic like *breath*.

To **aspirate** is to pronounce the "breathing" sound **h** at the beginning of a word, such as to pronounce the **h** in **herb** or **history**, as opposed to the pronunciations /erb/ or /istory/.

When the prefix **ex-** is attached to this root, the initial **s** is dropped because it seems already to be accounted for by the pronunciation of ex- (/eks/).

Word Alert!

Words relating to **spire** and **spiral** do not belong to this root family. Instead they come from a root meaning *sharp point*.

The **Spirea** plant, with a name from the root for *sharp point*, is the source of the acid that is used to make **aspirin**.

Day 1

Root Squares
for **SPIR**

SPIR means
to breathe; to whisper; essence

LESSON TIME

15 Minutes

OBJECTIVES

- **Understand** the meaning of the root **SPIR**
- **Build** words in the **SPIR** family
- **Understand** the meaning of words in the **SPIR** family
- **Understand** the spelling principles applied to the root **SPIR**

MATERIALS

- Student Activity Book
- **SPIR** Word Wall
- Dictionary *(print or on-line)*

DIFFERENTIATING INSTRUCTION

If you prefer easier or more difficult activities, use your personal account at www.dynamicliteracy.com to access novice or expert versions, along with ideas on using them.

Root Squares for SPIR

TEACH Have students turn to page 135 in their Activity Books. Say, "All of the prefixes and suffixes in the squares surrounding the shaded center are familiar, but if you have questions about any of the meanings, simply ask or look them up in the list inside the front and back cover of the activity book."

Call attention to the center box. Point out that the root **SPIR** has several different spellings, called allomorphs. Ask students to decide if any of the forms they see in the middle square can stand alone as a word. They may recognize **spire**, but that word, meaning *tapering blade or steeple* is not in this family. This family contains words that have something to do with *to breathe; to whisper; essence*. Since none of the forms of **SPIR** can stand as a word bearing that meaning, each must have a prefix or a suffix attached to it to build an independent word. Suggest that students start their list with **spire** and then add to that word the prefix **ex-**, meaning *out*, to build **expire**, meaning *to breathe out*, or *to run out of time, come to the end*. Invite students to explore how this word is related to the idea of *to breathe; to whisper; essence*.

COMPLETE THE ACTIVITY

Have students follow the directions to build words. If students have difficulty building words with the Root Squares, show them how by modeling the matrix approach found on the next page, taking one affix at a time and seeing if it will connect with any one of the allomorphs of the root.

DISCUSS After five minutes, have volunteers write some of their words on the board. Watch for target words that most easily demonstrate the meanings of *to breathe; to whisper; essence*. If the word **inspire**

SAB
Pg 135

is not present, ask the class, "Can anyone try to use the prefix **in-**?" and then continue on to the target word discussion on the next page.

Root Squares

How many words can you make?

Start in any square. Your goal is to combine two or more word parts to make as many words in the 'spir, spire, spiro, pir, pire' family as you can. Write each word and a definition you can think of for it in the space provided at the bottom of the page. Use the back of the page if you need to.

re	ed	per
ex	spir, spire, spiro, pir, pire	in
a	ant	ion

Focus Word: **INSPIRE** ⟶ Write this word on the board.

TEACH

Lead with this:	"Certain people, certain books, and certain pieces of music are able to **inspire** us. What does that mean?"
Student:	"It means to make us feel good."
Student:	"Or make us want to do good things."
Teacher:	"As always, let's take a closer look at the word."
Student:	"Not **in-** again!"
Teacher:	"It's okay—you've done a great job figuring it out after all these times. Let's go."
Student:	"The root means *breathe* or *whisper*. Breathe in? That can't be right."
Student:	"I bet it's one of those meanings that is not literal. Think about it. When you're **inspired**, something goes inside you. What?"
Student:	"What is an *essence*? That's one of the meanings given for the root."
Teacher:	"An *essence* is a general quality or feeling you get, a sense you feel."
Student:	"That's it—that's what goes in you, and that's why *breath* is also a definition, like air."

DISCUSS Students in small groups can discuss who or what has served to **inspire** them. What were they **inspired** to do as a result of those **inspirations**?

Root Squares Matrix You can refer to this matrix to guide students in this activity. Students could build at least these 16 words. ***It is not important how many words are built***, so long as students understand the meanings of the root and its affixes.

	a-	ex-	in-	per-	re-
no suffix	aspire	expire	inspire	perspire	respire
-ant	aspirant				
-ed	aspired	expired	inspired	perspired	respired
-ate + -ion	aspiration	expiration	inspiration	perspiration	respiration

Day 2

Magic Squares
for **SPIR**

SPIR means
to breathe; to whisper; essence

LESSON TIME

15 Minutes

OBJECTIVES

- **Understand** the meaning of the root **SPIR**

- **Break Apart** words in the **SPIR** family

- **Understand** the meanings of words in the **SPIR** family

MATERIALS

- Student Activity Book

- **SPIR** Word Wall

- Dictionary
  (print or on-line)

DIFFERENTIATING INSTRUCTION

If you prefer easier or more difficult activities, use your personal account at www.dynamicliteracy.com to access novice or expert versions, along with ideas on using them.

Break Apart Words with SPIR

TEACH Have students turn to the Magic Squares on page 136 in their Student Activity Books. Model a Think-Aloud strategy for students: "I know that **SPIR** means *to breathe; to whisper; essence*. I can use this knowledge to find the definition of a word with **SPIR** or one of its allomorphs as its root."

Direct students to word I, **respiration**. Say, "I know the prefix on this word, **re-**, can mean *again, back,* or *against*. The suffix **-at** is **-ate** with the **e** dropped, and adds the meaning of *acted upon*; the suffix **-ion** makes the word a noun, *a thing or an act one performs*. Look at definition 6, *the process of breathing again; the act of breathing in and out*. This definition includes a meaning for all the parts we're looking for, so let's write the number 6 in square I."

COMPLETE THE ACTIVITY
Ask students to use the same strategy to find the correct definitions for the other words. Tell them to write the number of the definition in the box that matches the letter for the word. Remind them that if all their answers are correct, each row and each column will add up to the same Magic number.

DISCUSS After five minutes, ask if there are any difficulties about matching the words and definitions. If there are, ask volunteers to explain clues in the definitions that will lead to the correct choice of word. As needed, follow the focus word approach for **expiration** that you see modeled on the next page.

Add any new words to the classroom **SPIR** Word Wall and remind students to add these words to the **SPIR** Word Wall in their Activity Books.

SAB Pg 136

Magic Squares

Select the best answer for each of the words in the 'spir, spire, spiro, pir, pire' family from the numbered definitions. Put the number in the proper space in the Magic Square box. If the total of the numbers is the same both across and down, you have found the magic number!

'spir, spire, spiro, pir, pire' means to breathe; to whisper; essence

WORDS	DEFINITIONS
A. aspirations	1. serving to breathe into; relating to motivation and encouragement
B. transpired	2. people whispering with others; people secretly plotting
C. spiritually	3. acts or processes of breathing toward; desires for high goals
D. perspiring	4. breathing through; sweating
E. aspirants	5. breathed through; gave off vapor or occurred
F. conspirators	6. the process of breathing again; the act of breathing in and out
G. expiration	7. so as to pertain to the breath of life; so as to relate to the animating force of life
H. inspirational	8. an act of breathing out; an end
I. respiration	9. people breathing toward; people desiring high goals

Magic Square Box

A. 3	B. 5	C. 7
D. 4	E. 9	F. 2
G. 8	H. 1	I. 6

Magic Number **15**

*** ANSWER KEY ***

Focus Word: **EXPIRATION** ⟶ Write this word on the board.

TEACH

Sample leading question:	"My driver's license has an **expiration** date on it. Does anyone know what that means?"
Student:	"It's on a loaf of bread, too."
Student:	"And medicine bottles."
Teacher:	"Yes, and what does it mean?"
Student:	It's an act, a noun, because of that double suffix **-ation**."
Student:	"It has a prefix **ex-**, *out*."
Student:	"*A breathing out*? I don't see that."
Student:	"Well, to **expire** is to die, *to breathe your last*."
Student:	"So an **expiration** is *a death*. How can your license or bread die?"
Student:	"It must be another one of those non-literal meanings. It means *ends* or *isn't any good any more after a certain date*."

DISCUSS Lead students to see that the word **expiration** is made up of four morphemes whose meanings add up to *an act of causing to breathe out*, a metaphor for *ending*. Groups of students can list other things that can have an **expiration**.

LESSON TIME

15 Minutes

OBJECTIVES

- **Understand** the meaning of the root **SPIR**

- **Apply** knowledge of the root **SPIR**

- **Break Apart** words in the **SPIR** family

- **Understand** the meaning of words in the **SPIR** family

- **Understand** the spelling principles applied to the root **SPIR**

MATERIALS

- Student Activity Book

- **SPIR** Word Wall

DIFFERENTIATING INSTRUCTION

If you prefer easier or more difficult activities, use your personal account at www.dynamicliteracy.com to access novice or expert versions, along with ideas on using them.

Apply Knowledge of **SPIR**

TEACH Have students turn to page 137 in their Student Activity Books. Explain that the boxes in front of and after the root indicate letters that spell out prefixes and suffixes. Students will spell out the correct prefixes and suffixes determined by clues in the definitions at the bottom of the page.

Have a volunteer read definition number one at the bottom of the page. Say, "Notice that there are a number of spellings of this root, one of them being **SPIRE** that we see in step one of this Stair Steps exercise. We are looking for a prefix for this word,

a two-letter prefix that means *out* or *out of*. We can see in our list of prefixes that **ex-** has that meaning, so we'll write **EX** in the first two blanks in step one of this Stair Steps. That will complete the word **expire**."

COMPLETE THE ACTIVITY

Let students work in pairs (optionally) and tell them to use the same strategy to find the correct prefixes and suffixes for the words listed. These activities can be quite challenging!

DISCUSS After a few minutes, review the answers as a class. Ask if there were any difficulties. Listen to any problems and have volunteers solve the difficulties by explaining key clues in the given definitions. As needed, follow the focus word approach that you see modeled on the next page.

SAB Pg 137

Stair Steps

Fill in the missing letters of each 'spir, spire, spiro, pir, pire' word by using the definitions below:
'spir, spire, spiro, pir, pire' means to breathe; to whisper; essence

1.	e	x	p	i	r	e				
2.	i	n	s	p	i	r	e			
3.	a	s	p	i	r	i	n	g		
4.	c	o	n	s	p	i	r	e	s	
5.	e	x	p	i	r	a	t	i	o	n
6.	i	n	s	p	i	r	a	t	i	o	n
7.	p	e	r	s	p	i	r	a	t	i	o	n
8.	t	r	a	n	s	p	i	r	a	t	i	o	n

1. to breathe out; to run out of time or end
2. to breathe into; to motivate and encourage
3. breathing toward; desiring a high goal
4. whispers together; secretly plots together
5. act of breathing out; an end
6. act of breathing into; motivation and encouragement
7. act of breathing through; sweat
8. the act of breathing through; process of giving off vapor

Day ③ Extend the Learning

Focus Word: **ASPIRING** ⟶ Write this word on the board.

TEACH

Sample leading question:	"Do you know what you are if you are an **aspiring** artist or writer? "
Student:	"Isn't that what you want to be when you grow up?"
Student:	"**Aspiring** artist—that makes it an adjective."
Teacher:	"Do you remember what an adjective with **-ing** is called?"
Student:	"A gerund?"
Student:	"I think that's the noun. Isn't it a participle?"
Student:	"That's right, a present participle."
Teacher:	"Great. Now, what's going on with this present participle?"
Student:	"Take away the root, and you have a prefix **a-**. What's that?"
Student:	"That means *not*, like we had in **asymmetrical**."
Student:	(Consulting the inside front cover of the Student Activity Book) "But wait a minute—two other prefixes look like that—both **ab-** and **ad-**, *away from* and *toward*. How can anybody tell?"
Student:	"Think about it—**aspiring** writer—that's where you want to go *to*, not *away*, and it can't mean *not*. So it must be the prefix **ad-**, **adspiring**."
Student:	"I know—assimilation! But what's this breathing part?"
Student:	"It's where your spirit wants to go, your being—your *essence*, that's it!"

DISCUSS Students in small groups can discuss what roles they are **aspiring** to.

273

Day 4

In Other Words
for **SPIR**

SPIR means
to breathe; to whisper; essence

LESSON TIME

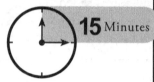

15 Minutes

OBJECTIVES

- **Understand** the meaning of the root **SPIR**

- **Reinforce** knowledge of the root **SPIR**

- **Understand** the meaning of words in the **SPIR** family

- **Apply** knowledge of words in the **SPIR** family

MATERIALS

- Student Activity Book

- **SPIR** Word Wall

- Dictionary
(print or on-line)

In Other Words for **SPIR**

TEACH Have students turn to page 138 in their Student Activity Books. Explain that they are going to read a little story that uses some surprising and sometimes odd phrasing. The underlined words or phrases in the story are actually definitions or synonyms for words in the **SPIR** family. Then they will see sentences about the story, each containing a blank.

Using context clues in the sentences, they will find a **SPIR** family word in the Word Bank at the bottom to fit in each blank. Have a student read aloud the opening sentence or sentences of the story that contain the first underlined phrase. Then say, "Let's look at the first numbered sentence that contains a blank to be filled in. Clues in the sentence tell us that we want an action word, a verb that is a synonym for *secretly plotted with others*. I see the word **conspired** at the bottom of the page. The prefix **con**- would give us *together, or with*. If this action was done in secret, there was probably a lot of whispering among those involved. This would make **conspired** the choice, so let's write that word in the blank for the first sentence."

COMPLETE THE ACTIVITY

This can be quite challenging, so allow students to work on this activity in small groups. Not every word in the Word Bank will be used.

DISCUSS After about 10 minutes, ask if there were any difficulties. Have volunteers explain strategies they used that led to correct answers.

*SAB
Pg 138*

Juno Tries to Ruin Hercules

Juno, the Queen of Mt. Olympus, hated Hercules and <u>secretly plotted</u> with others to drive Hercules crazy. She brought it about that Hercules fell into a fit of insanity and unknowingly killed his own children. When Hercules snapped out of his insanity, he saw what had <u>happened</u> and lost all the <u>liveliness and animation</u> from his body.

Hercules <u>breathed toward the high goal</u> to be forgiven for his crimes. <u>Breathed into</u> by a sense of purpose, he became a slave to a king and offered to accomplish whatever tasks might be given to him.

The first task was to squeeze a lion to death. <u>Sweat</u> poured from his body as he wrestled the lion. The rate of his <u>breathing in and out again</u> had tripled. Finally the lion <u>breathed out</u> its last and Hercules was the victor.

Eleven more tasks would <u>occur</u> before it was all over, but finally Hercules was cleansed <u>in a manner relating to his breath</u> of life and sat with the gods on Mt. Olympus.

<u>Fill in the blanks below using words from the "spir, spire, spiro, pir, pire" family.</u>

1. Juno and other enemies of Hercules <u>conspired</u> to bring about his downfall.

2. Hercules was horrified to learn what had <u>transpired</u> while he was in a fit.

3. It was as if his <u>spirit</u> left his body.

4. Hercules <u>aspired</u> toward a high goal.

5. A sense of purpose <u>inspired</u> Hercules to live and become a better person.

6. The <u>perspiration</u> poured from Hercules' body as he wrestled.

7. His <u>respiration</u> rate tripled.

8. Even more exhausted than Hercules, the lion finally <u>expired</u> its last breath.

9. Twelve tasks in all would <u>transpire</u> before the ordeal of Hercules was over.

10. The labors cleansed Hercules <u>spiritually</u> and he had a new outlook.

<u>Not Used:</u>   aspirations   conspiracy

274

OPTIONAL

Day 5

Morpheme Mania
for **SPIR**

SPIR means
to breathe; to whisper; essence

LESSON TIME

15 Minutes

OBJECTIVES

- **Build** words in the **SPIR** family

- **Apply** knowledge of synonyms and antonyms to **SPIR** words

Optional Morpheme Mania for **SPIR**

On page 139 of their Activity Book, students will see an optional vocabulary enrichment activity that they can work on in groups, time permitting. This activity makes a great review for the formal assessment on the next page.

All the affixes presented in the week's activities are provided at the top of the page on either side of the root of the week in all its forms. Students can write in up to 13 of the words they built during the week, possibly discovering additional ones.

Then students can brainstorm with each other to come up with antonyms and synonyms they may know. Starter examples are given with every Morpheme Mania in the Activity Book. Because antonyms and synonyms may require knowledge of roots which students have not yet studied, completion of this activity is not crucial. Simply remind students that they can at any time during the course of the year revisit any of their Morpheme Mania pages and add words, antonyms, and synonyms as their vocabulary grows.

Day 5 *Assessment*

Make and hand out copies.
The answer key is on page A-5.
The instructions are on page A-2.

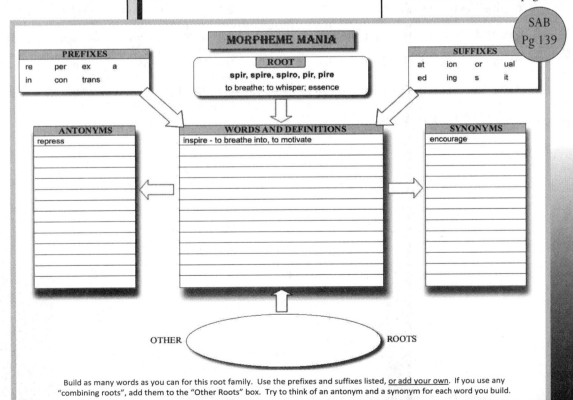

SAB
Pg 139

MORPHEME MANIA

PREFIXES			
re	per	ex	a
in	con	trans	

ROOT
spir, spire, spiro, pir, pire
to breathe; to whisper; essence

SUFFIXES			
at	ion	or	ual
ed	ing	s	it

ANTONYMS
repress

WORDS AND DEFINITIONS
inspire - to breathe into, to motivate

SYNONYMS
encourage

OTHER ROOTS

Build as many words as you can for this root family. Use the prefixes and suffixes listed, *or add your own*. If you use any "combining roots", add them to the "Other Roots" box. Try to think of an antonym and a synonym for each word you build.

aspirant a person breathing toward; a person desiring a high goal

aspirants people breathing toward; people desiring high goals

aspiration act or process of breathing toward; the desire for a high goal

aspirations acts or processes of breathing toward; desires for high goals

aspire to breathe toward; to desire a high goal

aspired breathed toward; desired a high goal

aspires breathes toward; desires a high goal

aspiring breathing toward; desiring a high goal

conspiracies groups whispering together; secret plots

conspiracy a group whispering together; a secret plot

conspirator a person whispering with another; a person secretly plotting

conspirators people whispering with others; people secretly plotting

conspire to whisper together; to plot secretly

conspired whispered together; secretly plotted together

conspires whispers together; secretly plots together

conspiring whispering together; secretly plotting together

expiration act of breathing out; an end

expirations acts of breathing out; ends

expire to breathe out; to run out of time or end

expired breathed out; ran out of time or ended

expires breathes out; runs out of time or ends

expiring breathing out; running out of time or ending

inspiration act of breathing into; motivation and encouragement

inspirational serving to breathe into; relating to motivation and encouragement

inspirations acts of breathing into; motivations and encouragements

inspire to breathe into; to motivate and encourage

inspired breathed into; motivated and encouraged

inspires breathes into; motivates and encourages

inspiring breathing into; motivating and encouraging

perspiration act of breathing through; sweat

perspire to breathe through; to sweat

perspired breathed through; sweated

perspires breathes through; sweats

perspiring breathing through; sweating

respiration the process of breathing again; the act of breathing in and out

spirit breath; liveliness or animation

spirited having breath; lively or animated

spiritedly in a manner having breath; in a lively or animated manner

spirits breaths; animating forces

spiritual pertaining to the breath; relating to the animating forces of life

spiritually so as to pertain to the breath of life; so as to relate to the animating force of life

transpiration the act of breathing through; process of giving off vapor

transpirations acts of breathing through; processes of giving off vapor

transpire to breathe through; to give off vapor or to occur

transpired breathed through; gave off vapor or occurred

transpires breathes through; gives off vapor or occurs

transpiring breathing through; giving off vapor or occurring

Check-Up for **SPIR**

Name _____

____ **1.** SPIR or PIR in words like **inspire** and **expire** means:

    A to pile up

    B to want

    C to breathe

____ **2.** What is the meaning of the word **inspire**?

    A not to want

    B to breathe into

    C to pile up onto

____ **3.** What is the meaning of the word **expire**?

    A to breathe out

    B to want very much

    C to pull down

____ **4.** What is the meaning of the word **respiration**?

    A to build up again

    B the quality of wanting something back

    C the process of breathing over and over

____ **5.** **Conspirators** :

    A whisper among themselves

    B try to build barriers

    C don't want to be together

____ **6.** Which word means **acts of breathing toward** a goal?

    A perspirations

    B aspirations

    C transpirations

____ **7.** Which word means **breathing through**?

    A expiring

    B conspiring

    C perspiring

____ **8.** Which word means **having breath**?

    A spirited

    B uninspired

    C expiration

____ **9.** The students were **dispirited**. They:

    A were eager to keep on playing

    B had lost the breath of joy

    C won many awards

____ **10.** The machine's **expirator** serves to:

    A turn it on

    B let water in

    C send out air

OBJECTIVES

- **Understand** the meaning of the root **MAN**
- **Build** words in the root **MAN** family
- **Break Apart** words in the root **MAN** family
- **Understand** the meaning of words in the **MAN** family
- **Understand** the spelling principles applied to the root **MAN**
- **Apply** knowledge of words in the **MAN** family
- **Assess** and **Reinforce** knowledge of words in the **MAN** family

MATERIALS

- Student Activity Books, pages 141-146
- Dictionary *(print or on-line)*

CROSS-CURRICULAR EXAMPLES

Science:
management, bimanual

Social Studies:
emancipation, manufacture, micromanage

Language Arts:
mannerism, manuscript

Math:
manipulate, unmanageable

MAN
meaning "hand"

> **manual**
> done by **hand**

Morpheme: **MAN**
Allomorphs: **MANN, MANU**

About 400 words containing the morpheme **MAN** or one of its allomorphs are current in English. During this unit, tell students to be alert for this root in their school texts, general reading, and oral language they hear. Some of the words they might encounter in their school subjects are listed on the left under Cross-Curricular Examples.

UNIT AT A GLANCE

Day **1**
Root Squares
for **MAN**

Day **2**
Magic Squares
for **MAN**

Day **3**
Stair Steps
for **MAN**

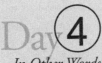

OPTIONAL
Day **4**
In Other Words
for **MAN**

Day **5**
Assessment or Morpheme Mania
for **MAN**

Each activity should take approximately **15 minutes**.

The hand is often used as a rich image of helpfulness (give someone a hand, on hand, be handy, lift a hand) or the method in which something is done (firsthand, heavy-handed, handwritten. The Latin word for hand, **manus**, likewise lent itself to many usages and idioms.

Manner is the way of handling a situation or deed.

With the French word for work, **oeuvre**, this root appears in English in the word **maneuver**, originally meaning *handiwork*, now extended to any skillful movement, whether in wrestling, chess, military tactics, policy, getting ahead in business, and so on.

From the word **maneuver** comes the word **manure**, originally working the field with the hands. Notice the ubiquitous dropping of internal consonants characteristic of English words of French origin.

A writ of **mandamus** hands over a legal responsibility to a person or corporation.

Something **manifest**, or clear, is etymologically anything grasped *by hand*.

In music, the expression **mano sinistra** indicates that the left hand is to be used (as on the piano).

The pasta **manicotti** is from the Italian for *hand covering, or sleeve*.

Word Alert!

A family of words in English with the letter sequence **m-a-n** belongs to a root pertaining to the **mind**, as **mania** and the many words ending in -**mancy**, meaning *a type of fortunetelling or worship*.

The word **man** itself is related to the root for *mind*. Etymologically, **man** is the *creature with a mind*.

The estate called a **manor** is from the root meaning *to remain or stay*. Unlike a movable residence or a temporary house, the **manor** is a permanent homestead.

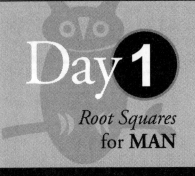

Day 1

Root Squares for MAN

MAN means hand

LESSON TIME

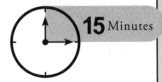

15 Minutes

OBJECTIVES

- **Understand** the meaning of the root **MAN**

- **Build** words in the **MAN** family

- **Understand** the meaning of words in the **MAN** family

- **Understand** the spelling principles applied to the root **MAN**

MATERIALS

- Student Activity Book
- **MAN** Word Wall
- Dictionary *(print or on-line)*

DIFFERENTIATING INSTRUCTION

If you prefer easier or more difficult activities, use your personal account at www.dynamicliteracy.com to access novice or expert versions, along with ideas on using them.

Root Squares for MAN

TEACH Have students turn to page 141 in their Activity Books. Say, "Let's look at the suffixes and prefixes in the outside boxes and make sure we know what they mean." Use the Mini-Lessons or references on the next page of this manual if needed. Then call attention to the center box. Point out that the root **MAN** has three different spellings, called allomorphs. Ask students to decide if any of the forms they see in the middle square can stand alone as a word. They may recognize **man**, but that word, meaning member of the human species is not in this family. All words of this family relate to the idea of *hand*. Since none of the three forms of **MAN** can stand as a word with that meaning, each must have a prefix or a suffix attached to it to build an independent word.

Suggest that students start their list with **manu** and then add to that word another root, **script**, meaning *to write*, to build the compound root word **manuscript**, meaning *something written by hand*. Invite students to explore how this word is related to the idea of *hand*.

COMPLETE THE ACTIVITY

Have students follow the directions for the activity to build words. If students have difficulty building words with the Root Squares, show them how by modeling the matrix approach found on the next page, taking one affix at a time and seeing if it will connect with any one of the allomorphs of the root.

DISCUSS After five minutes, have volunteers write some of their words on the board. Watch for target words that most easily demonstrate the meaning of *hand*. If the word **manage** is not present, ask the class, "Can anyone try to use the suffix -**age**?" and then continue on to the target word discussion on the next page.

SAB Pg 141

Root Squares

How many words can you make?

Start in any square. Your goal is to combine two or more word parts to make as many words in the 'man, mann, manu' family as you can. Write each word and a definition you can think of for it in the space provided at the bottom of the page. Use the back of the page if you need to.

age	mis	fact
ment	man, mann, manu	ure
er	script	able

MINI-LESSON: the Suffix -age

The suffix -**age** regularly makes collective nouns, such as **wordage, luggage, breakage, usage, dosage, leakage, peerage**, and hundreds of others, with new applications coined annually. Surprising to see, it comes from a simplification and French or Italian pronunciation of a Latin noun-forming suffix, -**aticum**. Only rarely does it serve as a verb, but it does so prominently with the root **man**, *hand*: to **manage**. Other examples of verb usage include **package, disparage**, and **damage**.

MINI-LESSON: the Prefix mis-

The prefix **mis**-, not to be confused with the root allomorph meaning *send*, appears on hundreds of English words to mean *badly or wrong*. Write up some of these words, and have students add the prefix **mis**-. Then discuss how the prefix affects the meanings:

lead	step	file	use	state	understand
address	word	label	play	locate	behave

Focus Word: MANAGE ⟶ Write this word on the board.

TEACH

Lead with this:	"Let's talk about this familiar word, **manage**. What do you know about its meaning?"
Student:	"It can mean *to run a store*."
Student:	"It can mean *to get along*, as in 'I'll **manage**.'"
Student:	"It can mean *was able to*, like I **managed** to get an A."
Student:	"It's a verb and it has something to do with *hand*, I'll bet."
Student:	"Oh, I get it, to *handle*!"
Student:	"Yes, or to put your *hand* to something."
Student:	"That one is pretty easy to see."

DISCUSS Lead students to see that, based on its two pieces of meaning, **manage** means *to do something by hand*. **Handle** and **manage** are great examples of the doublet nature of English, one word from native English set against a synonym, actually a translation, of a word from Latin.

Root Squares Matrix

You can refer to this matrix to guide students in this activity. Students could build at least these 11 words. ***It is not important how many words are built***, so long as students understand the meanings of the root and its affixes.

	no prefix	fact	mis-	script
no suffix				manuscript
-able	manage			
-age	manner		mismanage	
-er				
-ment	manure			
-ure		manufacture		
-ur(e) + -er		manufacturer		
-ag(e) + -er	manager			
-age + -ment	management		mismanagement	
-age + -able	manageable			

Day 2

Magic Squares
for **MAN**

MAN means hand

LESSON TIME

15 Minutes

OBJECTIVES

- **Understand** the meaning of the root **MAN**

- **Break Apart** words in the **MAN** family

- **Understand** the meanings of words in the **MAN** family

MATERIALS

- Student Activity Book

- **MAN** Word Wall

- Dictionary *(print or on-line)*

DIFFERENTIATING INSTRUCTION

If you prefer easier or more difficult activities, use your personal account at www.dynamicliteracy.com to access novice or expert versions, along with ideas on using them.

Break Apart Words with **MAN**

TEACH Have students turn to the Magic Squares on page 142 in their Student Activity Books. Model a Think-Aloud strategy for students: "I know that **MAN** means *hand*. It's similar to the common Spanish word, *mano*. I can use this knowledge to find the definition of a word with **MAN** or one of its allomorphs as its root."

Direct students to word I, **managers**. Say, "I know the suffix -**ag** has the meaning of *to do*; the suffixes -**er** plus -**s** mean *people or things that do*. Do what? Look at definition 6, *people who handle; people who deal with or control*. That accounts for the meanings of the parts we're looking for, so let's write the number 6 in square I."

Ask students to use the same strategy to find the correct definitions for the other words. Tell them to write the number of the definition in the box that matches the letter for the word. Remind them that if all their answers are correct, each row and each column will add up to the same Magic number.

DISCUSS After five minutes, ask if there are any difficulties about matching the words and definitions. If there are, ask volunteers to explain clues in the definitions that will lead to the correct choice of word. As needed, follow the focus word approach for **manually** that you see modeled on the next page.

Add any new words to the classroom **MAN** Word Wall and remind students to add these words to the **MAN** Word Wall in their Activity Books.

SAB Pg 142

Magic Squares

Select the best answer for each of the words in the 'man, mann, manu' family from the numbered definitions. Put the number in the proper space in the Magic Square box. If the total of the numbers is the same both across and down, you have found the magic number!

'man, mann, manu' means hand

WORDS	DEFINITIONS
A. emancipating	1. a document written by hand
B. manageable	2. act of taking from the hand; act of liberation from a master
C. mannerly	3. uncontrollable, not able to be handled; unable to deal with
D. manuscript	4. handles in a bad way
E. manufacturers	5. handleable; able to be dealt with or controlled
F. manually	6. people who handle; people who deal with or control
G. unmannered	7. having ways of handling things; polite
H. mismanages	8. in a manner done by hand
I. managers	9. taking from the hand; liberating from a master
	10. not made by hand; not produced or created
	11. marked by a way of not handling something; without a specific method or style
	12. people who make products by hand (or machine)

Magic Square Box

A. 9	B. 5	C. 7
D. 1	E. 12	F. 8
G. 11	H. 4	I. 6

Magic Number __21__

*** ANSWER KEY ***

Focus Word: **MANUALLY** ⟶ Write this word on the board.

TEACH

Sample leading question:	"If you turn on a television **manually**, what do you do?"
Student:	"Can you actually do that?"
Student:	"Sure—my grandmother has an old television set with knobs and buttons all over it."
Student:	"Wow. I guess you use your hand to turn the knobs or push the buttons."
Teacher:	"And why do you guess that you use your hand?"
Student:	"The root **man**!"
Student:	"Oh, and I see the word **manual**, like **manual** labor, *working by hand*."
Teacher:	"And what does the suffix **-ly** do to the adjective **manual**?"
Student:	"It makes an adverb, how something is done."

DISCUSS Lead students to see that, based on its three pieces of meaning, **manually** means *in a manner characterized by the hand*, or *so as to be done by hand*.

DEMONSTRATE If you have equipment in your classroom that can be turned on or off both by remote control and **manually**, show the distinction to your class. They may point out that you need to use your hand for the remote control as well, but you can counter with the observation that you are using the remote control **manually**, but that the device in question is not touched by hand.

LESSON TIME

15 Minutes

OBJECTIVES

- **Understand** the meaning of the root **MAN**

- **Apply** knowledge of the root **MAN**

- **Break Apart** words in the **MAN** family

- **Understand** the meaning of words in the **MAN** family

- **Understand** the spelling principles applied to the root **MAN**

MATERIALS

- Student Activity Book
- **MAN** Word Wall

DIFFERENTIATING INSTRUCTION

If you prefer easier or more difficult activities, use your personal account at www.dynamicliteracy.com to access novice or expert versions, along with ideas on using them.

Apply Knowledge of **MAN**

TEACH Have students turn to page 143 in their Student Activity Books. Explain that the boxes in front of and after the root indicate letters that spell out prefixes and suffixes. Students will spell out the correct prefixes and suffixes determined by clues in the definitions at the bottom of the page.

Have a volunteer read definition number four at the bottom of the page. Say, "We are looking for a prefix and a suffix. What three-letter suffix might come after the root **MAN** to describe the action of *handling*? Looking down our list, we see **-age** means

to do. Adding that suffix will give us the word **manage**, which would mean *to handle*. What prefix might give us the idea of *bad*? That is precisely the meaning of the prefix **mis-**, and by adding those three letters we get **MISMANAGE**, which fits the spaces on step four and fits the definition we have for the word."

COMPLETE THE ACTIVITY

Let students work in pairs (optionally) and tell them to use the same strategy to find the correct prefixes and suffixes for the words listed. These activities can be quite challenging!

DISCUSS After a few minutes, review the answers as a class. Ask if there were any difficulties. Listen to any problems and have volunteers solve the difficulties by explaining key clues in the given definitions. As needed, follow the focus word approach that you see modeled on the next page.

SAB Pg 143

Stair Steps

Fill in the missing letters of each 'man, mann, manu' word by using the definitions below.
'man, mann, manu' means hand

1.	m	a	n	u	a	l			
2.	m	a	n	n	e	r	s		
3.	m	a	n	a	g	e	r	s	
4.	m	i	s	m	a	n	a	g	e
5.	m	a	n	a	g	e	r	i	a	l
6.	m	a	n	u	s	c	r	i	p	t	s
7.	m	a	n	u	f	a	c	t	u	r	e	r
8.	m	i	s	m	a	n	a	g	e	m	e	n	t

1. related to hands; done by hand
2. ways of handling things; socially accepted habits
3. people who handle; people who deal with or control
4. to handle in a bad way
5. pertaining to handling; related to dealing with or controlling
6. documents written by hand
7. a person who makes products by hand (or machine)
8. quality of handling in a bad way

Focus Word: **MANUFACTURER** ⟶ Write this word on the board.

TEACH

Sample leading question:	"Who can tell us what this word means?"
Student:	"It's a company that **manufactures**."
Teacher:	"How can you tell it's a company that does that?"
Student:	"Well, a company or a person—it has the suffix **-er**, *a person who does something*."
Teacher:	"Good, and what else do we see?"
Student:	"The root for *hand* is there, and the root that means *make or do*."
Student:	"So it's somebody who *makes things by hand?*"
Student:	"I don't think that's right—**manufacturing** is by machine, not by hand."
Student:	"Maybe it's to operate the machines by hand."

DISCUSS Discuss with students how history is embedded in words by looking at the morphological meaning of the word **manufacturer**, *someone who makes (things) by hand*. You can also use this word to point out how meanings change over time, even to a point almost opposite what they originally were. We think of a **manufacturer** as a producer of goods not *by hand* but *by machine*.

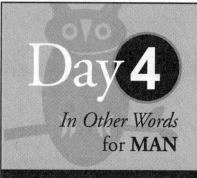

Day 4

In Other Words for MAN

MAN means hand

LESSON TIME

15 Minutes

OBJECTIVES

- **Understand** the meaning of the root **MAN**

- **Reinforce** knowledge of the root **MAN**

- **Understand** the meaning of words in the **MAN** family

- **Apply** knowledge of words in the **MAN** family

MATERIALS

- Student Activity Book

- **MAN** Word Wall

- Dictionary
  (print or on-line)

In Other Words for **MAN**

TEACH Have students turn to page 144 in their Student Activity Books. Explain that they are going to read a little story that uses some surprising and sometimes odd phrasing. The underlined words or phrases in the story are actually definitions or synonyms for words in the **MAN** family. Then they will see sentences about the story, each containing a blank.

Using context clues in the sentences, they will find a **MAN** family word in the Word Bank at the bottom to fit in each blank. Have a student read aloud the opening sentence or sentences of the story that contain the first underlined phrase. Then say, "Let's look at the first numbered sentence that contains a blank to be filled in. Clues in the sentence tell us that we want an action word, a verb that is a synonym for *handled*. I see the word **managed** at the bottom of the page. The word **managed** would be a perfect synonym, so let's write that word in the blank for the first sentence."

COMPLETE THE ACTIVITY

This can be quite challenging, so allow students to work on this activity in small groups. Not every word in the Word Bank will be used.

DISCUSS After about 10 minutes, ask if there were any difficulties. Have volunteers explain strategies they used that led to correct answers.

SAB
Pg 144

Farmer, Writer, and Friend to Raiders

Snorri of Iceland <u>handled</u> his little sheep farm well. He had <u>liberated and taken out from his hand</u> the indentured servant he once had and did all the <u>hand</u> labor himself. He and his wife Bergthora also made a living by the <u>hand-making</u> of sheepskins used for writing. Bergthora was an excellent <u>handler</u> of the estate. Many of their neighbors had <u>badly handled</u> their lands and had become <u>impolite</u>, roving Vikings.

Sometimes when former neighbors came back from a raid, they would stay with Snorri and Bergthora, and they would tell about their adventures. Snorri would put these stories in form <u>written by hand</u>, and these <u>documents written by hand</u> became sources of some famous sagas.

<u>Fill in the blanks below using words from the "man, mann, manu" family.</u>

1. Snorri owned and <u>managed</u> a little sheep farm in Iceland.

2. He did all the work himself because he had <u>emancipated</u> his farmhand.

3. Gathering grass, milking sheep, cutting wool, and other <u>manual</u> labor kept him busy and tired.

4. Income was also gained by the <u>manufacture</u> of sheepskin for writing.

5. Bergthora was an excellent <u>manager</u> of the estate.

6. Other Icelanders had <u>mismanaged</u> their lands and failed as farmers.

7. They turned from farming and took up a life as wild, <u>unmannerly</u> Vikings.

8. Using his sheepskins, Snorri wrote out some stories in <u>manuscript</u> form.

9. His <u>manuscripts</u> are still known for the great stories they tell.

<u>Not Used:</u> emancipated manure manually

OPTIONAL

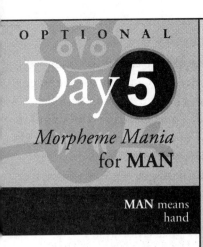

Day 5

Morpheme Mania
for **MAN**

MAN means
hand

LESSON TIME

15 Minutes

OBJECTIVES

• **Build** words in the **MAN** family

• **Apply** knowledge of synonyms and antonyms to **MAN** words

Optional Morpheme Mania for **MAN**

On page 145 of their Activity Book, students will see an optional vocabulary enrichment activity that they can work on in groups, time permitting. This activity makes a great review for the formal assessment on the next page.

All the affixes presented in the week's activities are provided at the top of the page on either side of the root of the week in all its forms. Students can write in up to 13 of the words they built during the week, possibly discovering additional ones.

Then students can brainstorm with each other to come up with antonyms and synonyms they may know. Starter examples are given with every Morpheme Mania in the Activity Book. Because antonyms and synonyms may require knowledge of roots which students have not yet studied, completion of this activity is not crucial. Simply remind students that they can at any time during the course of the year revisit any of their Morpheme Mania pages and add words, antonyms, and synonyms as their vocabulary grows.

Day 5 *Assessment*

Make and hand out copies.
The answer key is on page A-5.
The instructions are on page A-2.

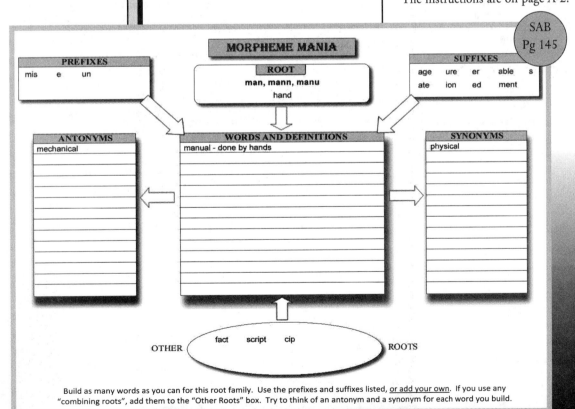

emancipate   to take from the hand; to liberate from a master

emancipated   took from the hand; liberated from a master

emancipates   takes from the hand; liberates from a master

emancipating   taking from the hand; liberating from a master

emancipation   act of taking from the hand; act of liberation from a master

emancipations   acts of taking from the hand; acts of liberation from a master

emancipator   a person who takes from the hand; a liberator

emancipators   people who take from the hand; liberators

manage   to handle; to deal with or control

manageable   handleable; able to be dealt with or controlled

manageably   so as to be handleable; in a manner dealing with or controlling

managed   handled; dealt with or controlled

management   act or process of handling; process of dealing with or controlling

manager   a person who handles; a person who deal with or controls

managerial   pertaining to handling; related to dealing with or controlling

managers   people who handle; people who deal with or control

manages   handles; deals with or controls

managing   handling; dealing with or controlling

manner   a way of handling something; method or style

mannered   marked by a way of handling something; having a specific method or style

mannerly   having ways of handling things; polite

manners   ways of handling things; socially accepted habits

manual   related to hands; done by hand

manually   in a manner done by hand

manufacture   to make products by hand (or machine)

manufactured   made products by hand (or machine)

manufacturer   a person who makes products by hand (or machine)

manufacturers   people who make products by hand (or machine)

manufactures   makes products by hand (or machine)

manufacturing   making products by hand (or machine)

manure   substance worked by hand; animal waste used to enrich soil

manured   worked by hand; spread animal waste to enrich soil

manuring   working by hand; spreading animal waste to enrich soil

manuscript   a document written by hand

manuscripts   documents written by hand

mismanage   to handle in a bad way

mismanaged   handled in a bad way

mismanagement   quality of handling in a bad way

mismanages   handles in a bad way

mismanaging   handling in a bad way

unmanageable   uncontrollable, not able to be handled; unable to deal with

unmanageably   uncontrollably; in a manner not able to be handled; in a way unable to deal with or control

unmannered   marked by a way of not handling something; without a specific method or style

unmannerly   pertaining to a way of not handling something; impolite

unmanufactured   not made by hand; not produced or created

unmanured   not worked by hand; without animal waste to enrich soil

Check-Up for **MAN**

Name _____

____ 1. **MAN** in words like **manners**, **manuscript** and **manage** means:

    A mind

    B hand

    C measure

____ 2. What is the meaning of the word **manual**?

    A a book showing how to measure something

    B using the mind

    C done by hand

____ 3. What is the meaning of the word **managerial**?

    A having to do with handling

    B able to be brought to mind

    C knowing how to measure

____ 4. What is the meaning of the word **emancipation**?

    A act of taking from the hand

    B to bring up in the mind

    C stretching out

____ 5. A **manner** is:

    A a type of measurement

    B someone who brings ideas to mind

    C a way of handling a situation

____ 6. Which word means **in a way not able to be handled**?

    A emancipator

    B mismanages

    C unmanageably

____ 7. Which word means **made by hand**?

    A manufactured

    B manuscripted

    C mismanaged

____ 8. Which word means **the quality of handling in the wrong way**?

    A unmannerly

    B mismanagement

    C unmanured

____ 9. The musicians used **manualism** with their technicians. The musicians:

    A communicated by hand

    B made off-key noises

    C measured each sound carefully

____ 10. The machine must be operated **bimanually**. It must:

    A be started after each use

    B be used with two hands

    C be checked often

OBJECTIVES

- **Understand** the meaning of the root **MEM**
- **Build** words in the root **MEM** family
- **Break Apart** words in the root **MEM** family
- **Understand** the meaning of words in the **MEM** family
- **Understand** the spelling principles applied to the root **MEM**
- **Apply** knowledge of words in the **MEM** family
- **Assess** and **Reinforce** knowledge of words in the **MEM** family

MATERIALS

- Student Activity Books, pages 147-152
- Dictionary *(print or on-line)*

CROSS-CURRICULAR EXAMPLES

Science:
mentation, dementia

Social Studies:
commentator, memorial

Language Arts:
commemorate, memento

Math:
mentor, commentational

MEM
meaning "mind"

mental
related to the **mind**

Morpheme: **MEM**
Allomorphs: **MENT**

Over 700 words containing the morpheme **MEM** or its allomorph are current in English. During this unit, tell students to be alert for this root in their school texts, general reading, and oral language they hear. Some of the words they might encounter in their school subjects are listed on the left under Cross-Curricular Examples.

UNIT AT A GLANCE

Day ①
Root Squares
for **MEM**

Day ②
Magic Squares
for **MEM**

Day ③
Stair Steps
for **MEM**

OPTIONAL
Day ④
In Other Words
for **MEM**

Day ⑤
Assessment or Morpheme Mania
for **MEM**

Each activity should take approximately **15 minutes**.

The word **memento** is an unaltered ancient Latin word. The suffix -**nto** is a Latin morpheme meaning *do this in the future!* The Latin imperative verb, or command, has become an English noun meaning *a keepsake or continuous reminder of something from the past.*

Another unaltered ancient Latin word still in English is **memorandum**. Now an English noun, the word was originally an adjective meaning *must be remembered.* A shortened form of **memorandum** is the word **memo**.

In Romance languages, that is, those evolving directly from the language of the Romans, the root allomorphs **ment** or **mente** are regularly used to make adverbs. For example, the word **secretly** in Spanish, Italian, and French, is **secretamente**, **segretamente**, and **secretement**, respectively, all literally meaning *with a secret mind or intention.*

The two consonants of this root appear together in English words of Greek origin. A **mnemonic** device helps you remember something. The condition of not being able to remember is **amnesia**. To pay no mind to a bad thing someone has done is to offer **amnesty**.

Mimir in Norse mythology carries this root in his name. He was the source of mindful wisdom and remembrance.

Homer's character **Mentor** lends his name to English as a trusted adviser or coach, but the etymological base of the original name itself is almost certainly this root.

Word Alert!

The common English suffix -**ment**, as in **fragment**, **adornment**, **accomplishment**, and many others, is not related to the root meaning *mind*. Instead, it refers to a generic noun substance or thing.

Words relating to **member** and **membrane** come from a root meaning *tissue or material.*

Day 1

*Root Squares
for MEM*

MEM means
mind

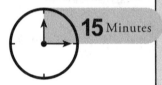

15 Minutes

OBJECTIVES

- **Understand** the meaning of the root **MEM**

- **Build** words in the **MEM** family

- **Understand** the meaning of words in the **MEM** family

- **Understand** the spelling principles applied to the root **MEM**

MATERIALS

- Student Activity Book
- **MEM** Word Wall
- Dictionary *(print or on-line)*

DIFFERENTIATING INSTRUCTION

If you prefer easier or more difficult activities, use your personal account at www.dynamicliteracy.com to access novice or expert versions, along with ideas on using them.

Root Squares for MEM

TEACH Have students turn to page 147 in their Activity Books. Say, "All of the prefixes and suffixes in the squares surrounding the shaded center are probably familiar, but if you have questions about any of the meanings, simply ask or look them up in the list inside the front and back cover of the activity book." Call attention to the center box. Point out that the root **MEM** has two spellings. Ask students to decide if either spelling they see in the middle square can stand alone as a word. Since these spellings are not independent words, either one must have a prefix or a suffix to play a part in making a word. Ask students to put one of the word parts they see in the surrounding squares onto the root **MEM** or **MENT**. If they need help, ask them to add the prefix **com-** in order to build **comment**, a word they may recognize, and you can use that word to guide them to the meaning mind. Since the prefix **com-** means *together*, when we **comment** on something, *we bring it to mind together*.

COMPLETE THE ACTIVITY

Have students use the pieces provided to build words. If students have difficulty building words with the Root Squares, show them how by modeling the matrix approach found on the next page, taking one affix at a time and seeing if it will connect with any one of the allomorphs of the root.

DISCUSS After five minutes, have volunteers write some of their words on the board. Focus with the class on the words they have built and guide them in a discussion of how the meaning of the root is still *mind*, even when prefixes and suffixes are added. Watch for target words that demonstrate the meanings of *mind*.

If the word **mental** is not present, ask, "Can anyone try to use the suffix **-al**?" and then continue on to the target word discussion on the next page.

SAB
Pg 147

Root Squares

How many words can you make?

Start in any square. Your goal is to combine two or more word parts to make as many words in the 'mem, ment' family as you can. Write each word and a definition you can think of for it in the space provided at the bottom of the page. Use the back of the page if you need to.

de	ed	ize
or	mem, ment	y
al	ity	com

_____
_____
_____
_____
_____
_____
_____
_____
_____

Focus Word: **MENTAL** ⟶ Write this word on the board.

TEACH

Lead with this:	"Who can tell us what **mental** ability is?"
Student:	"It's how smart you are."
Student:	"Isn't it also how some people can *do things with their minds*?"
Student:	"*Mind*—that's it. It just means something to do with the *mind*."
Student:	"That's right—see the suffix? What is that?"
Student:	"The suffix is **-al**, *characterized by*."
Student:	"So if you take a **mental** note, you jot it down in your *mind*."

DISCUSS Students can think of other phrases besides *mental note* that occur regularly in their experience (*mental health*, *mental relaxation*, etc.)

DEMONSTRATE Ask students to make a note physically by writing down the word **mental**. Then ask them to make the same note **mentally**.

Root Squares Matrix

You can refer to this matrix to guide students in this activity. Students could build at least these 7 words. *It is not important how many words are built*, so long as students understand the meanings of the root and its affixes.

	no prefix	com	de-
no suffix		comment	
-al			
-ed		commented	demented
-ity			
-ize			
-or	mentor		
-y			
-or + -ize	memorize		
-or + -y	memory		
-or + -iz(e) + -ed	memorized		

Day 2

Magic Squares
for **MEM**

MEM means
mind

LESSON TIME

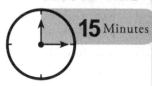

15 Minutes

OBJECTIVES

- **Understand** the meaning of the root **MEM**

- **Break Apart** words in the **MEM** family

- **Understand** the meanings of words in the **MEM** family

MATERIALS

- Student Activity Book

- **MAN** Word Wall

- Dictionary *(print or on-line)*

DIFFERENTIATING INSTRUCTION

If you prefer easier or more difficult activities, use your personal account at www.dynamicliteracy.com to access novice or expert versions, along with ideas on using them.

Break Apart Words with **MEM**

TEACH Have students turn to the Magic Squares on page 148 in their Student Activity Books. Model a Think-Aloud strategy for students: "I know that **MEM** means *mind*. I can use this knowledge to find the definition of a word with **MEM** or **MENT** as its root."

Direct students to word B, **mentionable**. Say, "I know the suffix -**ion** makes the word a noun, *a thing or an act one performs*. The second suffix, -**able** adds the meaning *having the power*. Look at definition 7, *able to be brought to mind; able to be said briefly and informally*. That accounts for the meanings of the parts we're looking

for, so let's write the number 7 in square B."

COMPLETE THE ACTIVITY

Ask students to use the same strategy to find the correct definitions for the other words. Tell them to write the number of the definition in the box that matches the letter for the word. Remind them that if all their answers are correct, each row and each column will add up to the same Magic number.

After five minutes, ask if there are any difficulties about matching the words and definitions. If there are, ask volunteers to explain clues in the definitions that will lead to the correct choice of word. As needed, follow the focus word approach for **mentor** that you see modeled on the next page.

Add any new words to the classroom **MEM** Word Wall and remind students to add these words to the **MEM** Word Wall in their Activity Books.

SAB
Pg 148

Magic Squares

Select the best answer for each of the words in the 'mem, ment' family from the numbered definitions. Put the number in the proper space in the Magic Square box. If the total of the numbers is the same both across and down, you have found the magic number!

'mem, ment' means mind

WORDS	DEFINITIONS
A. mentor	1. frame of mind; sum of intellectual power
B. mentionable	2. writing or voicing a note to call to mind
C. memorizations	3. a person who guides thinking; a person who counsels a student
D. commemorations	4. acts of bringing something to mind with others
E. commenting	5. acts of committing data to the mind
F. dementia	6. people who write or voice notes to call to mind
G. memorializing	7. able to be brought to mind; able to be said briefly and informally
H. commentators	8. keeping in the mind across time
I. mentality	9. state of being out of one's mind; craziness

Magic Square Box

A. 3	B. 7	C. 5
D. 4	E. 2	F. 9
G. 8	H. 6	I. 1

Magic Number <u>15</u>

*** ANSWER KEY ***

MINI-LESSON: the Suffix -ia

The suffix -**ia** is an unchanged holdover from the original Greek and Latin. Many abstract nouns in the Classical languages ended with this suffix, and it is often retained in English to name, among other things, conditions, disorders, or biological groups.

Some terms that may be familiar to students to illustrate this suffix include:

phobia	tibia	encyclopedia	hypothermia	neuralgia
anemia	mania	insomnia	myopia	utopia
amnesia	inertia	anorexia	dyslexia	wisteria

Focus Word: MENTOR ⟶ Write this word on the board.

TEACH

Sample leading question:	"Can anyone tell us what a **mentor** is?"
Student:	"Let's see—*someone who uses the mind.*"
Teacher:	"That's good—you see the morphemes in there correctly."
Student:	"Is it just somebody who is smart or uses common sense?"
Student:	"I've heard **mentor** used as somebody's tutor or coach."
Teacher:	"That's right—there is a famous character in Homer's *Odyssey* named **Mentor**, and he is the teacher of Odysseus' son."
Student:	"So do people's names have morphemes in them, too?"
Teacher:	"Yes. Names are words, too, and they have meaning. See if you can find out what your name means and in what language."

DISCUSS Why would an author call a character **Mentor**? What characteristic is the author trying to get across by that name?

DEMONSTRATE Have students who know the morphemic meaning of their names share them with the class.

LESSON TIME

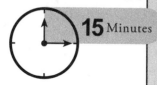

15 Minutes

OBJECTIVES

- **Understand** the meaning of the root **MEM**

- **Apply** knowledge of the root **MEM**

- **Break Apart** words in the **MEM** family

- **Understand** the meaning of words in the **MEM** family

- **Understand** the spelling principles applied to the root **MEM**

MATERIALS

- Student Activity Book
- **MEM** Word Wall

DIFFERENTIATING INSTRUCTION

If you prefer easier or more difficult activities, use your personal account at www.dynamicliteracy.com to access novice or expert versions, along with ideas on using them.

Apply Knowledge of MEM

TEACH Have students turn to page 149 in their Student Activity Books. Explain that the boxes in front of and after the root indicate letters that spell out prefixes and suffixes. Students will spell out the correct prefixes and suffixes determined by clues in the definitions at the bottom of the page.

Have a volunteer read definition number three at the bottom of the page. Say, "We are looking for a prefix and a suffix. What two-letter suffix might come after the root **MENT** to describe *a person*, and what two-letter prefix might indicate *being out of or*

away from your mind? Someone crazy might be called **demented**, so let's write in the prefix **de-** and the suffix **-ed** on step 3."

COMPLETE THE ACTIVITY

Let students work in pairs (optionally) and tell them to use the same strategy to find the correct prefixes and suffixes for the words listed. These activities can be quite challenging!

DISCUSS After a few minutes, review the answers as a class. Ask if there were any difficulties. Listen to any problems and have volunteers solve the difficulties by explaining key clues in the given definitions. As needed, follow the focus word approach that you see modeled on the next page.

SAB Pg 149

Stair Steps

Fill in the missing letters of each 'mem, ment' word by using the definitions below.
'mem, ment' means mind

1.	m	e	n	t	a	l
2.	m	e	n	t	o	r	s
3.	d	e	m	e	n	t	e	d
4.	m	e	m	o	r	i	z	e	s
5.	m	e	n	t	i	o	n	i	n	g
6.	m	e	m	o	r	i	a	l	i	z	e
7.	c	o	m	m	e	n	t	a	t	o	r	s
8.	m	e	m	o	r	i	a	l	i	z	i	n	g
9.	c	o	m	m	e	m	o	r	a	t	i	o	n	s

1. related to the mind
2. people who guide thinking; people who counsel students
3. out of one's mind; crazy
4. commits to the mind in order to recall
5. bringing to mind; saying briefly and informally
6. to keep in the mind across time
7. people who write or voice notes to call to mind
8. keeping in the mind across time
9. acts of bringing something to mind with others

Day ③ Extend the Learning

Focus Word: **MEMORIZE** ⟶ Write this word on the board.

TEACH

Sample leading question:	"How many of you find it easy to **memorize** things?"
Student:	"Oh, oh. What do we have to **memorize**?"
Teacher:	"Nothing in particular—right now!"
Student:	"It's easy to **memorize** things that are fun and have a rhythm."
Student:	"I have a feeling we're supposed to take a look at the word."
Student:	"Okay—I see the suffix -**ize**. That's a verb ending, *to cause to be like, or to make something into.*"
Student:	"So to **memorize** is *to cause something to be like the mind*?"
Student:	"Well, it causes something to be **mental**, *familiar in the mind*, maybe."
Student:	"What is that -**or** doing in there? Is that *a person who does*?"
Teacher:	"The suffix -**or** can also just be *an activity or a condition.*"
Student:	"Oh, yes, like in **valor** and **color** we saw before."

DISCUSS Let students share techniques they use to **memorize** information.

DEMONSTRATE If anyone knows a valuable or enjoyable **mnemonic** device to aid **memorization**, have him or her share it. The well-known Roy G. Biv for the rainbow colors is an example.

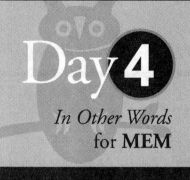
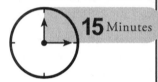
OBJECTIVES

- **Understand** the meaning of the root **MEM**
- **Reinforce** knowledge of the root **MEM**
- **Understand** the meaning of words in the **MEM** family
- **Apply** knowledge of words in the **MEM** family

MATERIALS

- Student Activity Book
- **MEM** Word Wall
- Dictionary *(print or on-line)*

In Other Words for **MEM**

TEACH   Have students turn to page 150 in their Student Activity Books. Explain that they are going to read a little story that uses some surprising and sometimes odd phrasing. The underlined words or phrases in the story are actually definitions or synonyms for words in the **MEM** family. Then they will see sentences about the story, each containing a blank.

Using context clues in the sentences, they will find a **MEM** family word in the Word Bank at the bottom to fit in each blank. Have a student read aloud the opening sentence or sentences of the story that contain the first underlined phrase. Then say, "Let's look at the first numbered sentence that contains a blank to be filled in. Clues in the sentence tell us that we want an action word, a verb that is a synonym for *bring to mind*. I see the word **commemorate** at the bottom of the page. The prefix **com-** and the suffix **-ate** are clues. These parts combine to yield the meaning *to cause to come together* and so to **commemorate** would be *to cause something to come together in the mind*, or, we might say, *to bring to mind*. Let's write **commemorate** in the blank for the first sentence."

COMPLETE THE ACTIVITY

This can be quite challenging, so allow students to work on this activity in small groups.   Not every word in the Word Bank will be used.

DISCUSS   After about 10 minutes, ask if there were any difficulties. Have volunteers explain strategies they used that led to correct answers.

SAB
Pg 150

The Wall

Washington, D.C. is a city of monuments that <u>bring to mind</u> people and events that have shaped the country. Of these <u>things meant to keep others in mind</u> none is so frequently visited as the one in <u>mind recall</u> of those who lost their lives during the Vietnam War. What is perhaps so <u>worthy of keeping in mind</u> about this wall of 58,256 names is the silence of the visitors as they walk around. Below the names, mourners have placed <u>objects to aid memory</u> to honor the people listed on the seventy-four polished black granite slabs.

Beginning with the names of those who went originally as <u>people who guide thinking</u> or military advisers from the late 1950's, the list stretches out almost 247 feet to include the names of all killed or missing in action in the years of fighting. Standing at one end of the wall or the other gives the observer an image <u>related to the mind</u> of the sheer number of military men and women that the list represents.

<u>Fill in the blanks below using words from the "mem, ment" family.</u>

1. Monuments <u>commemorate</u> important people and events in any country's history.

2. <u>Memorials</u> are often dedicated to fallen soldiers or leaders.

3. The Wall is dedicated to the <u>memory</u> of Vietnam Veterans.

4. The <u>memorable</u> effect of the silence of the observers will always linger with you.

5. <u>Mementos</u> or keepsakes help the survivors to honor the fallen soldiers.

6. The first names listed are of military advisers or <u>mentors</u> from the 1950's.

7. Viewing the list of names gives an observer a <u>mental</u> image of multitudes that the Wall represents.

<u>Not Used:</u>   memorized   mentality   commentary
            mention   memorization

298

O P T I O N A L

Day 5

Morpheme Mania
for **MEM**

MEM means
mind

OBJECTIVES

- **Build** words in the **MEM** family

- **Apply** knowledge of synonyms and antonyms to **MEM** words

Optional Morpheme Mania for **MEM**

On page 151 of their Activity Book, students will see an optional vocabulary enrichment activity that they can work on in groups, time permitting. This activity makes a great review for the formal assessment on the next page.

All the affixes presented in the week's activities are provided at the top of the page on either side of the root of the week in all its forms. Students can write in up to 13 of the words they built during the week, possibly discovering additional ones.

Then students can brainstorm with each other to come up with antonyms and synonyms they may know. Starter examples are given with every Morpheme Mania in the Activity Book. Because antonyms and synonyms may require knowledge of roots which students have not yet studied, completion of this activity is not crucial. Simply remind students that they can at any time during the course of the year revisit any of their Morpheme Mania pages and add words, antonyms, and synonyms as their vocabulary grows.

Day 5 *Assessment*

Make and hand out copies.
The answer key is on page A-5.
The instructions are on page A-2.

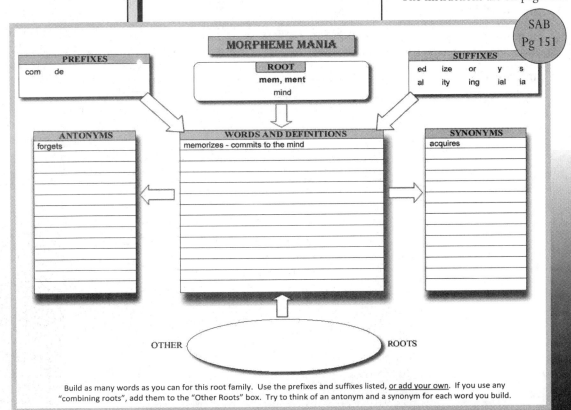

SAB
Pg 151

MORPHEME MANIA

PREFIXES	
com	de

ROOT
mem, ment
mind

SUFFIXES				
ed	ize	or	y	s
al	ity	ing	ial	ia

ANTONYMS
forgets

WORDS AND DEFINITIONS
memorizes - commits to the mind

SYNONYMS
acquires

OTHER ROOTS

Build as many words as you can for this root family. Use the prefixes and suffixes listed, <u>or add your own</u>. If you use any "combining roots", add them to the "Other Roots" box. Try to think of an antonym and a synonym for each word you build.

commemorate   to bring something to mind with others

commemorated   brought something to mind with others

commemorates   brings something to mind with others

commemorating   bringing something to mind with others

commemoration   an act of bringing something to mind with others

commemorations   acts of bringing something to mind with others

commemorative   serving to bring to mind with others

comment   a written or voiced note to call to mind

commentaries   discussions of things called to mind

commentary   a discussion of something called to mind

commentator   a person who writes or voices notes to call to mind

commentators   people who write or voice notes to call to mind

commented   wrote or voiced a note to call to mind

commenting   writing or voicing a note to call to mind

comments   written or voiced notes to call to mind

demented   out of one's mind; crazy

dementia   state of being out of one's mind; craziness

memorable   worthy of keeping in mind

memorably   in a manner worthy of keeping in mind

memorial   a thing meant to keep in the mind; a monument to someone or something

memorialize   to keep in the mind across time

memorialized   kept in the mind across time

memorializes   keeps in the mind across time

memorializing   keeping in the mind across time

memorials   things meant to keep in the mind across time; monuments to someone or something

memories   things retained and recalled in the mind

memorization   act of committing data to the mind

memorizations   acts of committing data to the mind

memorize   to commit to the mind in order to recall

memorized   committed to the mind in order to recall

memorizes   commits to the mind in order to recall

memorizing   committing to the mind in order to recall

memory   the ability to retain and recall in the mind

mental   related to the mind

mentality   frame of mind; sum of intellectual power

mentally   in a manner related to the mind

mention   to bring to mind; to say briefly and informally

mentionable   able to be brought to mind; able to be said briefly and informally

mentioned   brought to mind; said briefly and informally

mentioning   bringing to mind; saying briefly and informally

mentions   brings to mind; says briefly and informally

mentor   a person who guides thinking; a person who counsels a student

mentors   people who guide thinking; people who counsel students

Check-Up for **MEM**

Name _____

____ **1.** **MEM** or **MENT** in words like **memorial** and **mentality** means:
  A mind
  B measure
  C death

____ **2.** What is the meaning of the word **commemorate**?
  A to announce that someone has died
  B to measure a distance
  C to bring something to mind

____ **3.** What is the meaning of the word **mentionable**?
  A likely to be measured
  B able to be brought to mind
  C not heard

____ **4.** What is the meaning of the word **demented**?
  A out of the mind
  B did not measure right
  C pretending to be dead

____ **5.** A **memento** serves to help:
  A read faster
  B measure accurately
  C recall something

____ **6.** Which word means **acts of committing data to mind**?
  A mentioning
  B memorizations
  C commentators

____ **7.** Which word means **to keep in mind across time**?
  A memorialize
  B commemoration
  C memorable

____ **8.** Which word means **related to the mind**?
  A commentators
  B mentality
  C mental

____ **9.** The president's remarks were **immemorable**.
The remarks were:
  A not likely to be brought to mind
  B long
  C published after he died

____ **10.** Children's **mentation** while figuring out a new toy is fun to watch:
  A long-lasting happiness
  B activity in the mind
  C boredom

OBJECTIVES

- **Understand** the meaning of the root **CLAIM**
- **Build** words in the root **CLAIM** family
- **Break Apart** words in the root **CLAIM** family
- **Understand** the meaning of words in the **CLAIM** family
- **Understand** the spelling principles applied to the root **CLAIM**
- **Apply** knowledge of words in the **CLAIM** family
- **Assess** and **Reinforce** knowledge of words in the **CLAIM** family

MATERIALS

- Student Activity Books, pages 153-158
- Dictionary *(print or on-line)*

CROSS-CURRICULAR EXAMPLES

Science:
   nomenclature

Social Studies:
   acclamation, claimant, proclamation

Language Arts:
   exclamation, declamatory

Math:
   disclaimant

CLAIM

meaning "to demand, call for; shout"

claimed
demanded or asked for

nomenclature
a system to **call** things by name

proclamation
acts or processes of **shouting** forth

Morpheme: **CLAIM**
Allomorphs: **CLAM, CLAT**

Over 100 words containing the morpheme **CLAIM** or one of its allomorphs are current in English. During this unit, tell students to be alert for this root in their school texts, general reading, and oral language they hear. Some of the words they might encounter in their school subjects are listed on the left under Cross-Curricular Examples..

UNIT AT A GLANCE

Day 1
Root Squares
for **CLAIM**

Day 2
Magic Squares
for **CLAIM**

Day 3
Stair Steps
for **CLAIM**

OPTIONAL
Day 4
In Other Words
for **CLAIM**

Day 5
Assessment or Morpheme Mania
for **CLAIM**

Each activity should take approximately **15 minutes.**

The allomorph **clat** appears only with the Latin word for name, **nomen**. The process of calling living things by a universally-accepted name is **nomenclature**. Usually two words of Latin or Greek origin make up the name, so the system is called *binomial nomenclature*. It was begun by the French Bauhin brothers in the early 17th century and perfected by the Swede, Carl Linnaeus, in the 18th century.

The word **council** is made up etymologically of the root for *call* and the prefix **con-**, together. A **council** is *a body of advisers called together.*

The word **calendar** contains this root meaning to **call**. A Roman priest would, every month, officially call out the important days upcoming, so that people could adjust their schedules.

Word Alert!

There is a family of words with a root similar to this, but meaning *heat*. Such words include **calorie**, *a unit of heat*, and **caldron**, *a kettle for heating liquid*.

The name of the mollusk **clam** stems from a root meaning *compact mass or clump*. The word **clamp** belongs in that family of words as well.

The adjective **clammy** does not stem from the mollusk, but instead from a related word meaning *clay or glue*.

Day 1

Root Squares
for **CLAIM**

CLAIM means
to demand, call for; shout

LESSON TIME

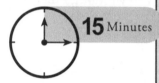

15 Minutes

OBJECTIVES

- **Understand** the meaning of the root **CLAIM**

- **Build** words in the **CLAIM** family

- **Understand** the meaning of words in the **CLAIM** family

- **Understand** the spelling principles applied to the root **CLAIM**

MATERIALS

- Student Activity Book
- **CLAIM** Word Wall
- Dictionary *(print or on-line)*

DIFFERENTIATING INSTRUCTION

If you prefer easier or more difficult activities, use your personal account at www.dynamicliteracy.com to access novice or expert versions, along with ideas on using them.

Root Squares for CLAIM

TEACH Have students turn to page 153 in their Activity Books. Say, "All of the prefixes and suffixes in the squares surrounding the shaded center are probably familiar, but if you have questions about any of the meanings, simply ask or look them up in the list inside the front and back cover of the activity book."

Call attention to the center box. Point out that the root **CLAIM** has three different spellings, called allomorphs. Ask students to decide if any of the forms they see in the middle square can stand alone as a word. They may recognize both **claim** and **clam** as words, though the second of these spellings is not an independent word in this family. The other word, **claim**, is in fact a member of this family, all words of which have to do with *demand, call out for, shout*. Suggest that students

start their list with **claim** and then continue the list by adding to that word the prefix **re-**, meaning *again*. Invite students to explore how this word is related to the idea of *demand, call out for, shout*.

COMPLETE THE ACTIVITY

Have students use the pieces provided to build words. If students have difficulty building words with the Root Squares, show them how by modeling the matrix approach found on the next page, taking one affix at a time and seeing if it will connect with any one of the allomorphs of the root.

DISCUSS After five minutes, have volunteers write some of their words on the board. Focus with the class on the words they have built and guide them in a discussion of how the meaning of the root is still *demand, call out for, shout*, even when prefixes and suffixes are added. Watch for target words that most easily demonstrate the meanings of *demand, call out for, shout*. If the word **exclaim** is not present, ask the class, "Can anyone try to use the prefix **ex-**?" and then continue on to the target word discussion on the next page.

SAB
Pg 153

Root Squares

How many words can you make?

Start in any square. Your goal is to combine two or more word parts to make as many words in the 'claim, clam, clat' family as you can. Write each word and a definition you can think of for it in the space provided at the bottom of the page. Use the back of the page if you need to.

re	at	ac
ory	claim, clam, clat	ed
pro	ion	ex

Focus Word: **EXCLAIM** ⟶ Write this word on the board.

TEACH

Lead with this:	"What do you do if you **exclaim** something?"
Student:	"You shout it out!"
Teacher:	"Are you sure? Is that what the word means?"
Student:	*(Thinking a moment)* "Yes—that's it exactly—look at the pieces—I really wasn't even thinking about the pieces at first."
Teacher:	"You naturally knew both the native English and the borrowed English: **exclaim** and *shout out*."
Student:	"That's a really good example of the Norman invasion thing."
Student:	"That one was really easy!"

DISCUSS Let students discuss situations in which **exclaim** would be the correct term rather than **said** or **asked**.

DEMONSTRATE Write this sentence on the board and have students punctuate it as a sentence according to whether it should be *said*, *asked*, or *exclaimed*:

The quick brown fox jumped over the lazy dog

See if students know the name of the symbol **!**, the **exclamation** point.

Root Squares Matrix

You can refer to this matrix to guide students in this activity. Students could build at least these 16 words. *It is not important how many words are built*, so long as students understand the meanings of the root and its affixes.

	no prefix	ac-	ex-	pro-	re-
no suffix	claim	acclaim	exclaim	proclaim	reclaim
-at(e) + ion		acclamation	exclamation	proclamation	reclamation
-ed	claimed	acclaimed	exclaimed	proclaimed	reclaimed
-at(e) + -ory			exclamatory	proclamatory	

Day 2

Magic Squares
for **CLAIM**

CLAIM means
to demand, call for; shout

LESSON TIME

15 Minutes

OBJECTIVES

- **Understand** the meaning of the root **CLAIM**
- **Break Apart** words in the **CLAIM** family
- **Understand** the meanings of words in the **CLAIM** family

MATERIALS

- Student Activity Book
- **CLAIM** Word Wall
- Dictionary
  (print or on-line)

DIFFERENTIATING INSTRUCTION

If you prefer easier or more difficult activities, use your personal account at www.dynamicliteracy.com to access novice or expert versions, along with ideas on using them.

Break Apart Words with **CLAIM**

TEACH Have students turn to the Magic Squares on page 154 in their Student Activity Books. Model a Think-Aloud strategy for students: "I know that **CLAIM** means *to demand; call out for; shout.* I can use this knowledge to find the definition of a word with **CLAIM** or one of its allomorphs as its root."

Direct students to word A, **unclaimed**. Say, "I know the prefix **un-** means *not*; the suffix **-ed** means either *having been* or *made to become* or *did*. Look at definition 3, *not called for; not taken into ownership.* That includes all the meanings of the parts, so let's write the number 3 in square A."

COMPLETE THE ACTIVITY

Ask students to use the same strategy to find the correct definitions for the other words. Tell them to write the number of the definition in the box that matches the letter for the word. Remind them that if all their answers are correct, each row and each column will add up to the same Magic number.

DISCUSS After five minutes, ask if there are any difficulties about matching the words and definitions.   If there are, ask volunteers to explain clues in the definitions that will lead to the correct choice of word.   As needed, follow the focus word approach for **proclaimed** that you see modeled on the next page.

Add any new words to the classroom **CLAIM** Word Wall and remind students to add these words to the **CLAIM** Word Wall in their Activity Books.

SAB Pg 154

Magic Squares

Select the best answer for each of the words in the 'claim, clam, clat' family from the numbered definitions. Put the number in the proper space in the Magic Square box. If the total of the numbers is the same both across and down, you have found the magic number!

'claim, clam, clat' means to demand; call out for; shout

WORDS	DEFINITIONS
A. unclaimed	1. an act or process of shouting forth; an official declaration
B. reclaimable	2. tending to be shouted out; spoken out with sudden or strong emotion
C. proclaimed	3. not called for; not taken into ownership
D. nomenclature	4. a system to call things by name
E. exclamatory	5. shouted forth; declared officially
F. disclaimers	6. the act of shouting toward; the act or process of praising
G. clamorously	7. able to be demanded or asked for again; able to be taken back in ownership
H. acclamation	8. in a manner full of loud shouting; noisily
I. proclamation	9. statements that call out denial; renunciations or acts of disownment

Magic Square Box

A. 3	B. 7	C. 5
D. 4	E. 2	F. 9
G. 8	H. 6	I. 1

Magic Number 15

*** ANSWER KEY ***

MINI-LESSON: the Combining Form **nomen**

The Latin word for *name* is **nomen**, and the word continues to appear in English in connection with the root allomorph **CLAT**. The scientific process of giving every living thing a Latin or Greek name is called **binomial nomenclature**, literally *a two-name name calling*. A side project that your students will enjoy is having them find the scientific name of a favorite plant or animal, research what the two-term name means, and give a report to the rest of the class.

Focus Word: **PROCLAIMED** ⟶ Write this word on the board.

TEACH

Sample leading question:	"If something is **proclaimed**, what is happening?"
Student:	"Let's see, there's the root for *shout*."
Student:	"And the suffix **-ed**, *happened already*."
Student:	"And **pro-** means *for or forward*."
Student:	"So what does all that add up to?"
Student:	*"Shouted out for, shouted out forward."*
Teacher:	"Can you give an example of how the word might be used? For example, how is it different from **exclaimed**?"
Student:	"I think of it as a special announcement, like something a king or queen might do. Or a president."
Teacher:	"Good. Can anybody think of a word that would name the thing that has been **proclaimed**?"
Student:	"A **proclamation**!"
Teacher:	"Does anyone know of any famous **proclamations**?"
Student:	"The *Emancipation Proclamation*!"

DISCUSS Why would a formal document be called a **proclamation**? Why the *shout* part, and why the *forward* part?

DEMONSTRATE Have a student demonstrate how something might be **proclaimed**, by pretending to be an authority who is announcing some new rule.

Day 3

Stair Steps
for **CLAIM**

CLAIM means
to demand, call for; shout

LESSON TIME

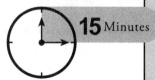

15 Minutes

OBJECTIVES

- **Understand** the meaning of the root **CLAIM**

- **Apply** knowledge of the root **CLAIM**

- **Break Apart** words in the **CLAIM** family

- **Understand** the meaning of words in the **CLAIM** family

- **Understand** the spelling principles applied to the root **CLAIM**

MATERIALS

- Student Activity Book
- **CLAIM** Word Wall

DIFFERENTIATING INSTRUCTION

If you prefer easier or more difficult activities, use your personal account at www.dynamicliteracy.com to access novice or expert versions, along with ideas on using them.

Apply Knowledge of **CLAIM**

TEACH Have students turn to page 155 in their Student Activity Books. Explain that the boxes in front of and after the root indicate letters that spell out prefixes and suffixes. Students will spell out the correct prefixes and suffixes determined by clues in the definitions at the bottom of the page.

Have a volunteer read definition number two at the bottom of the page. Say, "Since the meaning of the root **CLAIM** is *shout* that we see in this definition, we are looking for a prefix with the meaning *out* that we see in the words of the definition: *to*

shout out; to speak out. That is the meaning of the prefix **ex-** and if we add that to **CLAIM** we will have **EXCLAIM**. Let's write the letters **EX** in the two blank spaces on step two of this Stair Steps exercise."

COMPLETE THE ACTIVITY

Let students work in pairs (optionally) and tell them to use the same strategy to find the correct prefixes and suffixes for the words listed. These activities can be quite challenging!

DISCUSS After a few minutes, review the answers as a class. Ask if there were any difficulties. Listen to any problems and have volunteers solve the difficulties by explaining key clues in the given definitions. As needed, follow the focus word approach that you see modeled on the next page.

SAB Pg 155

Stair Steps

Fill in the missing letters of each 'claim, clam, clat' word by using the definitions below
'claim, clam, clat' means mind

1.	c	l	a	i	m	s			
2.	e	x	c	l	a	i	m		
3.	c	l	a	i	m	i	n	g	
4.	r	e	c	l	a	i	m	e	d
5.	d	i	s	c	l	a	i	m	e	r
6.	a	c	c	l	a	m	a	t	i	o	n
7.	e	x	c	l	a	m	a	t	i	o	n	s
8.	p	r	o	c	l	a	m	a	t	i	o	n	s

1. demands or asks for; states ownership
2. to shout out; to speak out with sudden or strong emotion
3. demanding or asking for; stating ownership
4. demanded or asked for again; took back in ownership
5. a denial or giving up demanding; a renunciation of disownment
6. the act of shouting toward; the act or process of praising
7. acts or processes of shouting out; sudden or emotionally strong statements
8. acts or processes of shouting forth; official declarations

308

Focus Word: **RECLAIMED** → Write this word on the board.

TEACH

Sample leading question:	"I read that the people in the Netherlands, where Holland is, **reclaimed** their land from the sea. What do you suppose that means?"
Student:	"Shouted back? Shouted again?"
Student:	"Well, let's start from **claimed** *back* or **claimed** *again*. We know it's *back* or *again* because of the prefix **re-**."
Student:	"And **claim** means *shout*, so how does that work?"
Student:	"Well, look, **claim** can mean *demand*. They *demanded* the land back."
Student:	"From what? Did someone take it?"
Student:	"I guess—doesn't the sea flood the place? Or maybe it flooded once and they drained it."
Teacher:	"Oh, I see, they *demanded* it back really means they *got* it back."

DISCUSS Let groups of students think of other situations in which something was **reclaimed**, keeping in mind that the word means *demanded back*. Let them share what was lost, who took it, and whether it was gotten back.

Day 4

In Other Words
for **CLAIM**

CLAIM means
to demand, call for; shout

LESSON TIME

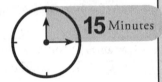

15 Minutes

OBJECTIVES

- **Understand** the meaning of the root **CLAIM**

- **Reinforce** knowledge of the root **CLAIM**

- **Understand** the meaning of words in the **CLAIM** family

- **Apply** knowledge of words in the **CLAIM** family

MATERIALS

- Student Activity Book
- **CLAIM** Word Wall
- Dictionary *(print or on-line)*

In Other Words for **CLAIM**

TEACH Have students turn to page 156 in their Student Activity Books. Explain that they are going to read a little story that uses some surprising and sometimes odd phrasing. The underlined words or phrases in the story are actually definitions or synonyms for words in the **CLAIM** family. Then they will see sentences about the story, each containing a blank.

Using context clues in the sentences, they will find a **CLAIM** family word in the Word Bank at the bottom to fit in each blank. Have a student read aloud the opening sentence or sentences of the story that contain the first underlined phrase. Then say, "Let's look at the first numbered sentence that contains a blank to be filled in. Clues in the sentence tell us that we want an action word, a verb that is a synonym for *shout forth*. I see the word **proclaim** at the bottom of the page. The prefix **pro-** means *forward* and that is another way to say *forth*. The idea of *shout forth* makes **proclaim** a good choice, so let's write **proclaim** in the blank for the first sentence."

COMPLETE THE ACTIVITY

This can be quite challenging, so allow students to work on this activity in small groups. Not every word in the Word Bank will be used.

DISCUSS After about 10 minutes, ask if there were any difficulties. Have volunteers explain strategies they used that led to correct answers.

SAB
Pg 156

Rock Concert

"It's the Frogs! The Frogs at the arena," Betsy squealed when she heard the radio announcer <u>shout forth</u> the weekend's entertainment. "I've always wanted to see them perform live," she <u>shouted out</u>. "Pleeeese, Mom, may I go? PLEASE...." she <u>shouted noisily</u>. "They're so great. They <u>are praised</u> internationally. It says so in my fan magazine. I can't miss a group that famous. What if they never tour here again, huh?"

"I thought you might like to go to the concert," Betsy's mother said smiling as she handed her an envelope. "Wow, Mom!" Betsy's <u>act of shouting out</u> could be heard next door at the neighbor's house. "TWO tickets! I'll call Jill."

"Wait a minute, Betts. I'm going with you. How can I miss the famous Frogs with such an interesting <u>system of being named</u>?" her mother asked. "Besides, the <u>denial</u> on the ticket reads that no one under eighteen will be admitted without an adult."

"Oh," Betsy mumbled. "But maybe Jill can get a seat that has <u>not been called for</u>."

<u>Fill in the blanks below using words from the "claim, clam, clat" family.</u>

1. Betsy heard the announcer <u>proclaim</u> the Frogs' appearance in her town.

2. "What an opportunity!" the excited girl <u>exclaimed</u> when she heard the news.

3. Begging her mother, Betsy <u>clamored</u> for tickets to see the group.

4. The Frogs are <u>acclaimed</u> all over the world.

5. Neighbors knew Betsy won her mom over when they heard her <u>exclamation</u> of joy.

6. Her Mom thought the <u>nomenclature</u> of rock groups was interesting.

7. An age-limit <u>disclaimer</u> appeared on the concert ticket stub.

8. There might be some <u>unclaimed</u> seats so that others could attend.

<u>Not Used:</u>

clamorous   exclaimer   acclaiming   reclaiming

310

OPTIONAL

Day 5

Morpheme Mania
for **CLAIM**

CLAIM means
to demand, call for; shout

LESSON TIME

15 Minutes

OBJECTIVES

• **Build** words in the **CLAIM** family

• **Apply** knowledge of synonyms and antonyms to **CLAIM** words

Optional Morpheme Mania for **CLAIM**

On page 157 of their Activity Book, students will see an optional vocabulary enrichment activity that they can work on in groups, time permitting. This activity makes a great review for the formal assessment on the next page.

All the affixes presented in the week's activities are provided at the top of the page on either side of the root of the week in all its forms. Students can write in up to 13 of the words they built during the week, possibly discovering additional ones.

Then students can brainstorm with each other to come up with antonyms and synonyms they may know. Starter examples are given with every Morpheme Mania in the Activity Book. Because antonyms and synonyms may require knowledge of roots which students have not yet studied, completion of this activity is not crucial. Simply remind students that they can at any time during the course of the year revisit any of their Morpheme Mania pages and add words, antonyms, and synonyms as their vocabulary grows.

Day 5 Assessment

Make and hand out copies.
The answer key is on page A-5.
The instructions are on page A-2.

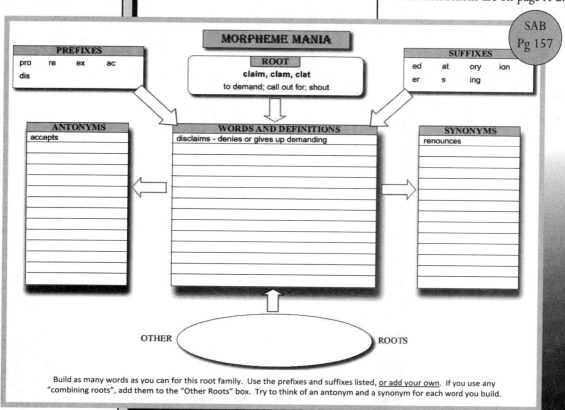

SAB
Pg 157

MORPHEME MANIA

PREFIXES

| pro | re | ex | ac |
| dis | | | |

ROOT
claim, clam, clat
to demand; call out for; shout

SUFFIXES

| ed | at | ory | ion |
| er | s | ing | |

ANTONYMS
accepts

WORDS AND DEFINITIONS
disclaims - denies or gives up demanding

SYNONYMS
renounces

OTHER ROOTS

Build as many words as you can for this root family. Use the prefixes and suffixes listed, <u>or add your own</u>. If you use any "combining roots", add them to the "Other Roots" box. Try to think of an antonym and a synonym for each word you build.

acclaim to shout toward; to praise

acclaimed shouted toward; praised

acclaiming shouting toward; praising

acclaims shouts toward; praises

acclamation the act of shouting toward; the act or process of praising

acclamations acts of shouting toward; acts or processes of praising

claim to demand or ask for; to state ownership

claimed demanded or asked for; stated ownership

claiming demanding or asking for; stating ownership

claims demands or asks for; states ownership

clamor a loud shout; noise

clamored shouted out loudly; was noisy

clamoring shouting out loudly; being noisy

clamorous full of loud shouting; noisy

clamorously in a manner full of loud shouting; noisily

clamors shouts out loudly; is noisy

disclaim to deny or give up demanding; disown or renounce

disclaimed denied or gave up demanding; disowned or renounced

disclaimer a denial or giving up demanding; a renunciation or disownment

disclaimers statements that call out denial; renunciations or acts of disownment

disclaiming denying or giving up demanding; disowning or renouncing

disclaims denies or gives up demanding; disowns or renounces

exclaim to shout out; to speak out with sudden or strong emotion

exclaimed shouted out; spoke out with sudden or strong emotion

exclaimer a person who shouts out; a person who speaks out with sudden or strong emotion

exclaimers people who shout out; people who speak out with sudden or strong emotion

exclaiming shouting out; speaking out with sudden or strong emotion

exclaims shouts out; speaks out with sudden or strong emotion

exclamation act or process of shouting out; a sudden or emotionally strong statement

exclamations acts or processes of shouting out; sudden or emotionally strong statements

exclamatory tending to be shouted out; spoken out with sudden or strong emotion

nomenclature a system to call things by name

proclaim to shout forth; to declare officially

proclaimed shouted forth; declared officially

proclaiming shouting forth; declaring officially

proclaims shouts forth; declares officially

proclamation an act or process of shouting forth; an official declaration

proclamations acts or processes of shouting forth; official declarations

reclaim to demand or ask for again; to take back in ownership

reclaimable able to be demanded or asked for again; able to be taken back in ownership

reclaimed demanded or asked for again; took back in ownership

reclaiming demanding or asking for again; taking back in ownership

reclaims demands or asks for again; takes back in ownership

unclaimed not called for; not taken into ownership

Check-Up for **CLAIM**   Name _____

____ **1.** **CLAIM**, **CLAM**, or **CLAT** in words like **exclaim**, **clamor**, and **nomenclature** means:

   A to buy

   B to shout

   C to be in charge

____ **2.** What is the meaning of the word **clamor**?

   A a lot of noise

   B a person in charge

   C the process of buying

____ **3.** What is the meaning of the word **claimer**?

   A more able to buy

   B more in charge than anyone else

   C a person demanding ownership

____ **4.** What is the meaning of the word **proclaim**?

   A to shout forth

   B to be in favor of buying

   C to put in charge

____ **5.** **Reclaimable** land is land that:

   A is the chief growing area

   B cannot be bought

   C can be called back into use

____ **6.** Which word means **a shouting out**?

   A clamorously

   B exclaimer

   C exclamation

____ **7.** Which word means **a statement that gives up a demand**?

   A proclamation

   B disclaimer

   C clamorous

____ **8.** Which word means **shouting toward**?

   A acclaiming

   B exclaimer

   C nomenclature

____ **9.** A **clamant** crowd was waiting at the gates. The crowd was:

   A silent

   B buying tickets

   C demanding information

____ **10.** A modern **nomenclaturist** uses Latin and Greek to:

   A buy products such as olives

   B call new species by a name

   C prove that he or she is in charge

LEG

meaning "law; bind in purpose"

OBJECTIVES

- **Understand** the meaning of the root **LEG**
- **Build** words in the root **LEG** family
- **Break Apart** words in the root **LEG** family
- **Understand** the meaning of words in the **LEG** family
- **Understand** the spelling principles applied to the root **LEG**
- **Apply** knowledge of words in the **LEG** family
- **Assess** and **Reinforce** knowledge of words in the **LEG** family

MATERIALS

- Student Activity Books, pages 159-164
- Dictionary *(print or on-line)*

CROSS-CURRICULAR EXAMPLES

Science:
allege

Social Studies:
legal, legislature, delegate

Language Arts:
privileges

Math:
relegations

legislated
brought into **law**

college
a group **bound** together to a **purpose**

Morpheme: **LEG**
Allomorphs: **LEGE, LEGIS**

Over 200 words containing the morpheme **LEG** or one of its allomorphs are current in English. During this unit, tell students to be alert for this root in their school texts, general reading, and oral language they hear. Some of the words they might encounter in their school subjects are listed on the left under Cross-Curricular Examples.

UNIT AT A GLANCE

Day ①
Root Squares for **LEG**

Day ②
Magic Squares for **LEG**

Day ③
Stair Steps for **LEG**

OPTIONAL
Day ④
In Other Words for **LEG**

Day ⑤
Assessment or Morpheme Mania for **LEG**

Each activity should take approximately **15 minutes**.

Cognates are separate words that evolve from an identical source. The word **legal** preserves the original Latin spelling of the morpheme. As French continued to evolve from Latin, it tended to drop or soften consonants, and the word **loyal** came into being. Thus, **legal** and **loyal** are cognates, even though their meanings have diverged.

It is possible that the root **lect**, *to choose, gather, or read*, and the root **leg**, *law, bind in purpose*, are themselves cognates from a much older common source. The root for **law** may pertain to something that is read, or perhaps a collection of rules gathered together. Another similar-looking morpheme, **leg** or **lig**, *to tie or bind*, is almost certainly another cognate. The root **log**, *word, study, or reason*, is also a cognate with these roots.

The word **legitimate** is similar to **legal**, but it has a broader scope to mean *genuine, real,* or *reasonable*, as a *legitimate argument*, a *legitimate complaint*, or a *legitimate van Gogh painting*.

Laws or rights granted in favor of certain private individuals, as opposed to the entire population, are called **privileges**.

Many words belong to this family through a secondary meaning of this morpheme, not *law*, but something like *bound by law, or assigned*. Thus, a **legate** is *someone sent to perform an official task*, like an ambassador. **Colleagues** are *people chosen to carry out the same task*, and a **college** is made up of *people bound together for the same purpose*, as the *electoral college* or the *college of cardinals*.

Legacy is originally that which you have been *assigned to do*, or, in formal legal terms, what you have been *given or ordered*. Now we think of **legacy** as what you leave behind from among the things that you have accumulated in your career.

A **sacrilege** is the *gathering up* of something holy and taking it away.

Legumes are vegetables *gathered* as food.

Word Alert!

The word **leg** is a fundamental Germanic root for the *lower limb*.

Allegro and **allegretto**, musical terms meaning *lively*, stem from the Latin word for *quick and happy*.

An **allegory** is literally *another way of speaking*, related to the Greek word for public place, **agora**.

Day 1

Root Squares for LEG

LEG means
law; bind in purpose

LESSON TIME

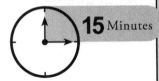

15 Minutes

OBJECTIVES

• **Understand** the meaning of the root **LEG**

• **Build** words in the **LEG** family

• **Understand** the meaning of words in the **LEG** family

• **Understand** the spelling principles applied to the root **LEG**

MATERIALS

• Student Activity Book

• **LEG** Word Wall

• Dictionary *(print or on-line)*

DIFFERENTIATING INSTRUCTION

If you prefer easier or more difficult activities, use your personal account at www.dynamicliteracy.com to access novice or expert versions, along with ideas on using them.

Root Squares for LEG

TEACH Have students turn to page 159 in their Activity Books. Say, "One of the pieces in the outside boxes is a root we have studied. Can you spot it and do you remember what it means?" Remind students of the root **late**, meaning *to bring*, and refer to previous activities if necessary. "There is a new suffix, too, -**acy**, so let's take a look." Use the Mini-Lesson found on the next page of this manual.

Then call attention to the center box. Point out that the root **LEG** has three different spellings, called allomorphs. Ask students to decide if any of the forms they see in the middle square can stand alone as a word. They will recognize **leg** as a word, though this spelling of the root is not an independent word in this family. (Refer to discussion of the root **lect**.) Suggest that students start their list with **leg**, adding the suffix -**acy**, meaning *having the quality of*, and thus creating the word **legacy**. Invite students to explore how this word is related to the idea of *law; bind in purpose*. A **legacy** is a *legal gift*.

COMPLETE THE ACTIVITY

Have students use the pieces provided to build words. If students have difficulty building words with the Root Squares, show them how by modeling the matrix approach found on the next page, taking one affix at a time and seeing if it will connect with any one of the allomorphs of the root.

DISCUSS After five minutes, have volunteers write some of their words on the board. Focus with the class on the words they have built and guide them in a discussion of how the meaning of the root is still *law; bind in purpose*, even when prefixes and suffixes are added. Watch for target words that most easily demonstrate the meanings of *law; bind in purpose*. If the word **legal** is not present, ask the class, "Can anyone try to use the suffix -**al**?" and then continue on to the target word discussion on the next page.

Root Squares

How many words can you make?

Start in any square. Your goal is to combine two or more word parts to make as many words in the 'leg, lege, legis' family as you can. Write each word and a definition you can think of for it in the space provided at the bottom of the page. Use the back of the page if you need to.

al	ize	ate
il	leg, lege, legis	late
ive	ion	acy

SAB Pg 159

_____

_____

_____

_____

_____

_____

_____

MINI-LESSON: the Suffix -acy

The suffix -**acy**, meaning *an act, process, or quality*, comes from a softening in sound of the Latin and Greek noun-forming ending -**tia** (similar to the suffix -**ia** discussed as a Mini-Lesson with the root **MEM** in this Manual).   Note with your students how nouns are made out of these words that end in -**ate** or -**at** (the **t** becomes a **c**):

accurate – accuracy	confederate – confederacy	illiterate – literacy
candidate – candidacy	diplomat – diplomacy	delicate – delicacy
immediate – immediacy	pirate – piracy	private – privacy

Focus Word: **LEGAL** ⟶ Write this word on the board.

TEACH

Lead with this:	"What does this word, **legal**, mean?"
Student:	"Does it have something to do with your legs?"
Student:	"Silly!"
Student:	"I'm just kidding, but why doesn't it have to do with legs?"
Teacher:	"That's really a good question. The reason is that suffixes and prefixes that come from Latin tend to attach only to Latin roots, and not to native English roots."
Student:	"And -**al** must be from Latin, right?"
Teacher:	"So if not legs, what does the word **legal** have to do with?"
Student:	"It's what you are allowed to do, it's what's *related to the law*."
Student:	"Right, exactly. Take a look at the pieces of the word."

DISCUSS Guide students to see the morphemes in the word **legal** adding up to *pertaining to the law*.

Root Squares Matrix

You can refer to this matrix to guide students in this activity. Students could build at least these 13 words. *It is not important how many words are built*, so long as students understand the meanings of the root and its affixes.

	no prefix	al-	il-	late
no suffix		allege		legislate
-al	legal		illegal	
-acy	legacy			
-ate	legate			
-ion				legislation
-at(e) + -ion	legation	allegation		
-ive	legative			legislative
-al + -ize	legalize		illegalize	

Day 2

Magic Squares for **LEG**

LEG means law; bind in purpose

LESSON TIME

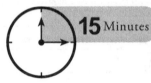

15 Minutes

OBJECTIVES

- **Understand** the meaning of the root **LEG**

- **Break Apart** words in the **LEG** family

- **Understand** the meanings of words in the **LEG** family

MATERIALS

- Student Activity Book

- **LEG** Word Wall

- Dictionary *(print or on-line)*

DIFFERENTIATING INSTRUCTION

If you prefer easier or more difficult activities, use your personal account at www.dynamicliteracy.com to access novice or expert versions, along with ideas on using them.

Break Apart Words with **LEG**

TEACH Have students turn to the Magic Squares on page 160 in their Student Activity Books. Model a Think-Aloud strategy for students: "I know that **LEG** means *law; bind in purpose*. I can use this knowledge to find the definition of a word with **LEG** or one of its allomorphs as its root."

Direct students to word I, **legislator**. Say, "This is a compound root word, though it may not at first look like one. That second part, the **lat**, is the root meaning *to bring*. The suffix **-or** means *a person or device that does*. Look at definition 11, *a person who brings into law; a person who enacts laws*. That reflects the meanings of

the second root and the suffix, so let's write the number 11 in square I."

COMPLETE THE ACTIVITY

Ask students to use the same strategy to find the correct definitions for the other words. Tell them to write the number of the definition in the box that matches the letter for the word. Remind them that if all their answers are correct, each row and each column will add up to the same Magic number.

DISCUSS After five minutes, ask if there are any difficulties about matching the words and definitions. If there are, ask volunteers to explain clues in the definitions that will lead to the correct choice of word. As needed, follow the focus word approach for **illegally** that you see modeled on the next page.

SAB Pg 160

Add any new words to the classroom **LEG** Word Wall and remind students to add these words to the **LEG** Word Wall in their Activity Books.

Magic Squares

Select the best answer for each of the words in the 'leg, lege, legis' family from the numbered definitions. Put the number in the proper space in the Magic Square box. If the total of the numbers is the same both across and down, you have found the magic number!

'leg, lege, legis' means law; bind in purpose

WORDS	DEFINITIONS
A. allegedly	1. making lawful
B. colleges	2. acts of depriving things of their holy character; acts of desecrating things of their holiness
C. delegated	
D. illegally	3. a group sent away bound to a purpose; a group entrusted with an appointment
E. legacies	
F. legalizing	4. laws or rights belonging to individuals; unique benefits or honors
G. legislating	5. groups bound together to a purpose; institutions of higher learning
H. privileges	6. bringing into law; enacting law
I. legislator	7. in a manner addressing the law; so as to accuse without legal evidence
	8. in a manner that is not lawful
	9. sent away bound to a purpose; entrusted with an appointment
	10. a statement toward the law; a claim without legal evidence
	11. a person who brings into law; a person who enacts laws
	12. legal gifts of personal property by will; things inherited

Magic Square Box

A. 7	B. 5	C. 9
D. 8	E. 12	F. 1
G. 6	H. 4	I. 11

Magic Number __21__

*** ANSWER KEY ***

Focus Word: **ILLEGALLY** ⟶ Write this word on the board.

TEACH

Sample leading question:	"I saw a guy U-turn **illegally** the other day. Let's look at the word **illegally**."
Student:	"That one is pretty easy."
Teacher:	"How many morphemes and what are they?"
Student:	"Three"
Student:	"Four!"
Student:	"Take the root out and you have a prefix and two suffixes."
Student:	"That **il**- is *not*."
Student:	"The -**ly** makes an adverb out of the adjective **legal**."
Teacher:	"So, let's hear it defined according to its pieces of meaning."
Student:	*"In a manner that is not according to the law."*

DISCUSS Lead students to see that the meaning of the word **illegally** can easily be determined by adding up the meanings of the word's four pieces.

Day 3

Stair Steps for **LEG**

LEG means law; bind in purpose

LESSON TIME

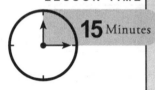

15 Minutes

OBJECTIVES

- **Understand** the meaning of the root **LEG**

- **Apply** knowledge of the root **LEG**

- **Break Apart** words in the **LEG** family

- **Understand** the meaning of words in the **LEG** family

- **Understand** the spelling principles applied to the root **LEG**

MATERIALS

- Student Activity Book

- **LEG** Word Wall

DIFFERENTIATING INSTRUCTION

If you prefer easier or more difficult activities, use your personal account at www.dynamicliteracy.com to access novice or expert versions, along with ideas on using them.

Apply Knowledge of **LEG**

TEACH Have students turn to page 161 in their Student Activity Books. Explain that the boxes in front of and after the root indicate letters that spell out prefixes and suffixes. Students will spell out the correct prefixes and suffixes determined by clues in the definitions at the bottom of the page.

Have a volunteer read definition number three at the bottom of the page. Say, "What word would mean *lawful*? If we add the suffix -**al** after the root **LEG** we have **LEGAL**. How would we turn that into its opposite, add the idea of *not*? Note that one of

the spellings, or allomorphs, of the prefix **in-**, meaning *not*, is **il-**. In front of the first letter of **LEGAL** that assimilation makes the word **INLEGAL** easier to pronounce as **ILLEGAL**. Write the prefix **IL-** in front of the word we've built on step three and you'll have all the blanks filled in to fit the definition we started from, *not lawful*."

COMPLETE THE ACTIVITY

Let students work in pairs (optionally) and tell them to use the same strategy to find the correct prefixes and suffixes for the words listed. These activities can be quite challenging!

DISCUSS After a few minutes, review the answers as a class. Ask if there were any difficulties. Listen to any problems and have volunteers solve the difficulties by explaining key clues in the given definitions. As needed, follow the focus word approach that you see modeled on the next page.

SAB Pg 161

Stair Steps

Fill in the missing letters of each 'leg, lege, legis' word by using the definitions below.
'leg, lege, legis' means mind

1.	l	e	g	a	l				
2.	a	l	l	e	g	e			
3.	i	l	l	e	g	a	l		
4.	l	e	g	a	l	i	z	e	
5.	i	l	l	e	g	a	l	l	y
6.	a	l	l	e	g	a	t	i	o	n
7.	l	e	g	i	s	l	a	t	u	r	e
8.	l	e	g	i	s	l	a	t	i	o	n	s

1. lawful
2. to address the law; to accuse without legal evidence
3. not lawful
4. to make lawful
5. in a manner that is not lawful
6. a statement toward the law; a claim without legal evidence
7. a group that brings into law; a body that enacts laws
8. acts or processes of bringing into law; enactments of law

Day 3 Extend the Learning

MINI-LESSON: the Combining Form **privi**

The Combining Form **privi** derives from a Latin word meaning *individual* or *of one's own*. It shows its meaning clearly in words like **private** and **privacy**. To **deprive** someone is to take away something individually important to that person.

Focus Word: **LEGALIZE** → Write this word on the board.

Sample leading question:	"Here's a good word to figure out. What do we see?"
Student:	"That suffix **-ize** means *to make*."
Student:	"To *make legal*, so to make it so it's related to the law."
Student:	"This keeps getting easier and easier."
Student:	"Give us some harder ones!"
Teacher:	"You are getting so good, there aren't many hard ones left!"

DISCUSS Lead students to see that the meaning of the word **legalize** is the sum of the meanings of its three morphemes.

Day 4

In Other Words
for **LEG**

LEG means
law; bind in purpose

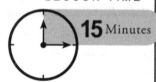

LESSON TIME

15 Minutes

OBJECTIVES

- **Understand** the meaning of the root **LEG**

- **Reinforce** knowledge of the root **LEG**

- **Understand** the meaning of words in the **LEG** family

- **Apply** knowledge of words in the **LEG** family

MATERIALS

- Student Activity Book

- **LEG** Word Wall

- Dictionary *(print or on-line)*

In Other Words for **LEG**

TEACH Have students turn to page 162 in their Student Activity Books. Explain that they are going to read a little story that uses some surprising and sometimes odd phrasing. The underlined words or phrases in the story are actually definitions or synonyms for words in the **LEG** family. Then they will see sentences about the story, each containing a blank.

Using context clues in the sentences, they will find a **LEG** family word in the Word Bank at the bottom to fit in each blank. Have a student read aloud the opening sentence or sentences of the story that contain the first underlined phrase. Then say, "Let's look at the first numbered sentence

that contains a blank to be filled in. Clues in the sentence tell us that we want a naming word, a plural noun that is a synonym for *claims made without evidence.* I see the word **allegations** at the bottom of the page. This word has three suffixes that follow the root **leg**. These are -**at**, meaning *to cause to become*; -**ion**, which changes the word to a noun, and -**s**, the plural marker. The prefix **al**- is a form of **ad**- meaning *toward or to*. I know the word **allege** means *to claim*, as in *to accuse, with unproven evidence.* This word, **allegations**, is the noun form of that idea. Let's write **allegations** in the blank for the first sentence."

COMPLETE THE ACTIVITY

This can be quite challenging, so allow students to work on this activity in small groups. Not every word in the Word Bank will be used.

DISCUSS

After about 10 minutes, ask if there were any difficulties. Have volunteers explain strategies they used that led to correct answers.

In Other Words...

SAB
Pg 162

Being President

Becoming and being president is a tough job. While you're running for office, all sorts of ugly <u>claims made without evidence</u> are brought up against you and dirty tricks done to you. Your enemies might <u>make accusations</u> that you once got a speeding ticket or said bad words.

You have to win over most of the <u>people entrusted with an appointment</u> at the nominating convention. You need to be careful about which contributions are <u>lawful</u> and which ones are <u>not lawful</u>. Even if you persuade a majority of the people to vote for you, you still have to be elected by the electoral <u>group bound together for a purpose</u>.

If after all that, you do get elected, then you have to start worrying about keeping your power of executive <u>rights belonging to you individually</u> and planning your <u>lawful gift to be left behind</u> once you leave the position. You have to compromise with <u>law makers</u> who are there to check and balance you, and you have to try to get your favorite policies <u>brought into law</u>. It's hard work!

<u>Fill in the blanks below using words from the "leg, lege, legis" family.</u>

1. There have been serious <u>allegations</u> against some candidates.

2. One candidate was <u>alleged</u> to have insulted vegetarians by eating a burger.

3. States send <u>delegates</u> to a national convention which will nominate someone.

4. The size of contributions must stay within <u>legal</u> limits; otherwise, <u>illegal</u> contributions can ruin a candidate.

5. The electoral <u>college</u> makes the ultimate decision about who wins.

6. Each branch of government has specific rights and <u>privileges</u>.

7. Presidents think about the <u>legacy</u> that they will leave behind.

8. Members of the Senate and House, called <u>legislators</u>, are meant to serve as a check on the president's power.

9. Presidents hope to have policies <u>legislated</u> which suit them.

<u>Not Used:</u> legislators   illegality   sacrilege

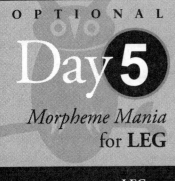

OPTIONAL

Day 5

Morpheme Mania
for **LEG**

LEG means
law; bind in purpose

LESSON TIME

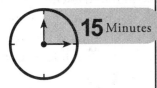

15 Minutes

OBJECTIVES

- **Build** words in the **LEG** family
- **Apply** knowledge of synonyms and antonyms to **LEG** words

Optional Morpheme Mania for **LEG**

On page 163 of their Activity Book, students will see an optional vocabulary enrichment activity that they can work on in groups, time permitting. This activity makes a great review for the formal assessment on the next page.

All the affixes presented in the week's activities are provided at the top of the page on either side of the root of the week in all its forms. Students can write in up to 13 of the words they built during the week, possibly discovering additional ones.

Then students can brainstorm with each other to come up with antonyms and synonyms they may know. Starter examples are given with every Morpheme Mania in the Activity Book. Because antonyms and synonyms may require knowledge of roots which students have not yet studied, completion of this activity is not crucial. Simply remind students that they can at any time during the course of the year revisit any of their Morpheme Mania pages and add words, antonyms, and synonyms as their vocabulary grows.

Day 5 *Assessment*

Make and hand out copies.
The answer key is on page A-5.
The instructions are on page A-2.

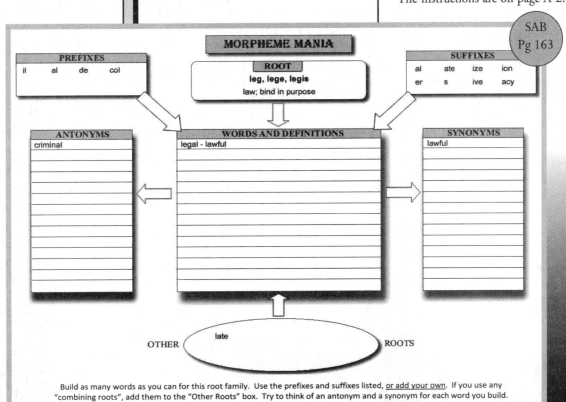

SAB
Pg 163

MORPHEME MANIA

PREFIXES			
il	al	de	col

ROOT
leg, lege, legis
law; bind in purpose

SUFFIXES			
al	ate	ize	ion
er	s	ive	acy

ANTONYMS
criminal

WORDS AND DEFINITIONS
legal - lawful

SYNONYMS
lawful

OTHER   late   ROOTS

Build as many words as you can for this root family. Use the prefixes and suffixes listed, <u>or add your own</u>. If you use any "combining roots", add them to the "Other Roots" box. Try to think of an antonym and a synonym for each word you build.

allegation a statement toward the law; a claim without legal evidence

allegations statements toward the law; claims without legal evidence

allege to address the law; to accuse without legal evidence

alleged addressed the law; accused without legal evidence

allegedly in a manner addressing the law; so as to accuse without legal evidence

alleges addresses the law; accuses without legal evidence

alleging addressing the law; accusing without legal evidence

college a group bound together to a purpose; an institution of higher learning

colleges groups bound together to a purpose; institutions of higher learning

delegate to send away bound to a purpose; to entrust with a specific job

delegated sent away bound to a purpose; entrusted with a specific job

delegates sends away bound to a purpose; entrusts with a specific job

delegating sending away bound to a purpose; entrusting with a specific job

delegation a group sent away bound to a purpose; a group entrusted with a specific job

delegations groups sent away bound to a purpose; groups entrusted with specific jobs

illegal not lawful

illegally in a manner that is not lawful

legacies legal gifts of personal property by will; things inherited

legacy a legal gift of personal property by will; a thing inherited

legal lawful

legality a point of law; observance of the law

legalize to make lawful

legalized made lawful

legalizes makes lawful

legalizing making lawful

legally in a manner conforming to the law

legation a team bound by law to represent a group

legations teams bound by law to represent a group

legislate to bring into law; to enact

legislated brought into law; enacted

legislates brings into law; enacts

legislating bringing into law; enacting

legislation act or process of bringing into law

legislations acts or processes of bringing into law

legislative related to bringing into law

legislator a person who brings laws

legislators people who bring laws

legislature a group that brings laws

legislatures groups that bring laws

privilege a law or right belonging to an individual; a unique benefit or honor

privileged descriptive of a person with an individual law or right; having unique benefits or honors

privileges laws or rights belonging to individuals; unique benefits or honors

privileging granting a special law or right to an individual; granting a unique benefit or honor

Check-Up for **LEG**

_____ 1. **LEG** or **LEGIS** in words like **legal**, **legislate** means:

    A standard

    B arm or leg

    C law

_____ 2. What is the meaning of the word **legislative**?

    A following the standard procedure

    B pertaining to making into law

    C standing on one's own feet

_____ 3. What is the meaning of the word **legalize**?

    A to make lawful

    B standardization

    C putting in standard form

_____ 4. What is the meaning of the word **delegates**? People:

    A sent out chosen for a purpose

    B who follow standards

    C have lost an arm or a leg

_____ 5. To **allege** a crime is to:

    A address it to the law

    B be opposed to it

    C decide whether to do it or not

_____ 6. Which word means **a group bound together to a purpose**?

    A illegality

    B college

    C delegate

_____ 7. Which word means **a law or right belonging to an individual**?

    A legislatorship

    B legacy

    C privilege

_____ 8. Which word means **a state of not being lawful**?

    A illegally

    B illegalize

    C illegality

_____ 9. A **legalist** would most likely:

    A obey every law

    B not care about some standards

    C not be bound in purpose to anything or anyone

_____ 10. The school offered a course on **medicolegal** issues.
The course is about:

    A standards of behavior

    B law and medical procedures

    C medical problems with the arms and legs

OBJECTIVES

- **Understand** the meaning of the root **LOC**
- **Build** words in the root **LOC** family
- **Break Apart** words in the root **LOC** family
- **Understand** the meaning of words in the **LOC** family
- **Understand** the spelling principles applied to the root **LOC**
- **Apply** knowledge of words in the **LOC** family
- **Assess** and **Reinforce** knowledge of words in the **LOC** family

MATERIALS

- Student Activity Books, pages 165-170
- Dictionary *(print or on-line)*

CROSS-CURRICULAR EXAMPLES

Science:

translocate, locale

Social Studies:

dislocate, misallocation

Language Arts:

locative, local color

Math:

locus of points, locate

LOC

meaning "place"

localize

to put into or find at a specific **place**

Morpheme: **LOC**
Allomorphs: **none**

Over 200 words containing the morpheme **LOC** are current in English. During this unit, tell students to be alert for this root in their school texts, general reading, and oral language they hear. Some of the words they might encounter in their school subjects are listed on the left under Cross-Curricular Examples.

UNIT AT A GLANCE

Day 1
Root Squares
for **LOC**

Day 2
Magic Squares
for **LOC**

Day 3
Stair Steps
for **LOC**

OPTIONAL
Day 4
In Other Words
for **LOC**

Day 5
Assessment or Morpheme Mania
for **LOC**

Each activity should take approximately **15 minutes**.

This is a fairly simple root morpheme for seeing etymological meanings, since words like **locate** and **location** will be familiar to most students. A word like **dislocate** may be familiar to your active athletic students who have ever **dislocated** a shoulder or knee.

The word **locomotion** refers to *an ability to move from a place*, the **o** in the word probably not a connector vowel but rather a grammatical form indicating *place from which*. You may wish to discuss with students the linguistic process called **back-formation**, the coinage of a shorter word from a longer word. A verb **locomote** has appeared in the English language since the end of the nineteenth century.

The English noun **locale** is a formation derived from the French adjective meaning **local**, *belonging to a specific place*.

The characteristic dropping of internal or final consonants in words of French origin appears in the word **lieu**, *place*, as **in lieu of**.

The Latin word for place, **locus**, appears in many useful English phrases, particularly in law and bibliography. The *locus criminis* is where the crime takes place. *In loco parentis*, in place of a parent, is the legal term for a temporary guardian. *In loco citato*, in the place (already) cited, is a short-cut to bibliographical referencing.

Word Alert!

As is most often the case, the letter sequence **l-o-c** does not necessarily indicate the presence of the morpheme meaning *place*.

The Spanish slang word for crazy, **loco**, likely stems from the medieval Arabic influence on the Spanish language. The Arabic word for foolish is **lawqa**.

The two words **lock**, as a *piece of hair* or as a *fastening*, have Germanic bases unrelated to the root meaning *place*.

The word **elocution** comes from the root meaning *speak*, as in the words **colloquial** and **loquacious**.

The word **velocity** is from the Latin word **velox**, meaning *swift*.

The word **locust** comes from the same source as the word **leg**, perhaps because of the shape of a locust or because of its jumping ability.

Day 1

Root Squares
for **LOC**

LOC means
place

LESSON TIME

15 Minutes

OBJECTIVES

- **Understand** the meaning of the root **LOC**

- **Build** words in the **LOC** family

- **Understand** the meaning of words in the **LOC** family

- **Understand** the spelling principles applied to the root **LOC**

MATERIALS

- Student Activity Book
- **LOC** Word Wall
- Dictionary *(print or on-line)*

DIFFERENTIATING INSTRUCTION

If you prefer easier or more difficult activities, use your personal account at www.dynamicliteracy.com to access novice or expert versions, along with ideas on using them.

Root Squares for **LOC**

TEACH Have students turn to page 165 in their Activity Books. Say, "All of the prefixes and suffixes in the squares surrounding the shaded center are probably familiar, but if you have questions about any of the meanings, simply ask or look them up in the list inside the front and back cover of the activity book."

Call attention to the center box. Point out that the root **LOC** has only this one spelling. Ask students to decide if the form they see in the middle square can stand alone as a word. Since **loc** is not a word, it must have a prefix or a suffix added to it for it to play a part in making a word. Suggest that students start their list with **loc**, add the suffix **-al**, meaning *characterized by*, and build the word **local**, meaning *characterized by a place*. Invite

students to explore how this word is related to the idea of place.

COMPLETE THE ACTIVITY

Have students follow the directions for the Root Squares activity for **LOC** on page 165 to build words. If students have difficulty building words with the Root Squares, show them how by modeling the matrix approach found on the next page, taking one affix at a time and seeing if it will connect with any one of the allomorphs of the root.

DISCUSS After five minutes, have volunteers write some of their words on the board. Focus with the class on the words they have built and guide them in a discussion of how the meaning of the root is still *place*, even when prefixes and suffixes are added. Watch for target words that most easily demonstrate the meanings of *place*.

If the word **locate** is not present, ask the class, "Can anyone try to use the suffix **-ate**?" and then continue on to the target word discussion on the next page.

SAB Pg 165

Root Squares

How many words can you make?

Start in any square. Your goal is to combine two or more word parts to make as many words in the 'loc' family as you can. Write each word and a definition you can think of for it in the space provided at the bottom of the page. Use the back of the page if you need to.

al	ity	dis
mis	loc	re
ize	or	ate

_____
_____
_____
_____
_____
_____
_____
_____
_____

Focus Word: **LOCATE** → Write this word on the board.

TEACH

Lead with this:	"Let's take a close look at this familiar word, **locate**. We'll learn something about the suffix -**ate**."
Student:	"If you **locate** something, you find out where it is."
Student:	"But the suffix -**ate** means *to cause to become or to make into*, so the word looks like it would mean *to make into a place*."
Student:	"That's not what **locate** means."
Teacher:	"Listen to this sentence: 'My ancestors **located** in Ohio.' Have you ever heard something like that?"
Student:	"No, but that would make sense out of making a *place*, like making a home."
Teacher:	"If you check a dictionary, you'll see that *making a place* is a primary definition of the word. Words can evolve or change and be used in additional ways over time, but we can almost always make sense out of the morphemes and the usage."
Student:	"I guess when you find something, you establish its *place*—that makes sense."
Student:	"Yes, you don't put it there yourself, but in a way you give the thing a *place* so that it can be found."

DISCUSS Lead students to see that words are living and changing all the time, as long as they continue to be used in new situations. This shift and swirl of meanings is what makes discussions about words an interesting human interaction.

DEMONSTRATE You can use the word **locate** to explain the difference between **transitive** verbs and **intransitive** verbs. To **locate** something, that is, to find it, illustrates a transitive use of the verb, or a verb that has a direct object. To **locate** in a place, that is, to settle there, illustrates an intransitive use of the verb, with no direct object. Tell some students to **locate** (make their place) near the door. Then have other students **locate** (find) them (direct object).

Root Squares Matrix

You can refer to this matrix to guide students in this activity. Students could build at least these 12 words. *It is not important how many words are built*, so long as students understand the meanings of the root and its affixes.

	no prefix	al-	dis-	mis-	re-
-al	local				
-ate	locate	allocate	dislocate	mislocate	relocate
-al + -ity	locality				
-al + -ize	localize				
-at(e) + -or	locator	allocator	dislocator		relocator

Day 2

Magic Squares
for **LOC**

LOC means
place

LESSON TIME

15 Minutes

OBJECTIVES

- **Understand** the meaning of the root **LOC**
- **Break Apart** words in the **LOC** family
- **Understand** the meanings of words in the **LOC** family

MATERIALS

- Student Activity Book
- **LOC** Word Wall
- Dictionary *(print or on-line)*

DIFFERENTIATING INSTRUCTION

If you prefer easier or more difficult activities, use your personal account at www.dynamicliteracy.com to access novice or expert versions, along with ideas on using them.

Break Apart Words with **LOC**

TEACH Have students turn to the Magic Squares on page 166 in their Student Activity Books. Model a Think-Aloud strategy for students: "I know that **LOC** means place. I can use this knowledge to find the definition of a word with **LOC** as its root."

Direct students to word D, **locators**. Say, "This word has three suffixes. The suffix -**at** is -**ate** with the **e** dropped, and adds the meaning of *acted upon*; the suffix -**or** means *a person or device that does*; the suffix -**s** makes this word mean more than one. Look at definition 1, *people or tools that find places*. That reflects the meanings of the root and the suffixes, so let's

write the number 1 in square D."

COMPLETE THE ACTIVITY

Ask students to use the same strategy to find the correct definitions for the other words. Tell them to write the number of the definition in the box that matches the letter for the word. Remind them that if all their answers are correct, each row and each column will add up to the same Magic number.

DISCUSS After five minutes, ask if there are any difficulties about matching the words and definitions. If there are, ask volunteers to explain clues in the definitions that will lead to the correct choice of word. As needed, follow the focus word approach for **relocate** that you see modeled on the next page.

Add any new words to the classroom **LOC** Word Wall and remind students to add these words to the **LOC** Word Wall in their Activity Books.

SAB
Pg 166

Magic Squares

Select the best answer for each of the words in the 'loc' family from the numbered definitions. [P]? the number in the proper space in the Magic Square box. If the total of the numbers is the same both across and down, you have found the magic number!

'loc' means place

WORDS	DEFINITIONS
A. allocation	1. people or tools that build places
B. dislocations	2. to place toward; to set aside or distribute
C. localities	3. found in a certain place
D. locators	4. places apart; moves out of usual or proper place
E. misallocated	5. acts or processes of placing apart; movements out of the usual or proper place
F. localizing	
G. relocate	6. acts of placing things toward badly; poor jobs setting aside or distributing
H. dislocates	7. specific places
I. misallocations	8. putting into or finding at a specific place
	9. act of placing things toward; act of setting aside or distributing
	10. finding in a place again; moving to a new place
	11. to find in a place again; to move to a new place
	12. placed things toward badly; did a poor job setting aside or distributing

Magic Square Box

A. 9	B. 5	C. 7
D. 1	E. 12	F. 8
G. 11	H. 4	I. 6

Magic Number __21__

*** ANSWER KEY ***

Focus Word: **RELOCATE** ⟶ Write this word on the board.

TEACH

Sample leading question:	"This word will give us another chance to look at the suffix **-ate** and what shifts of meaning it can have."
Student:	"It's just the same as **locate**, only you do it *again*."
Student:	"So can you say, 'My ancestors in Ohio **relocated** to Indiana'?"
Student:	"Yes—I've heard that, even though I never thought about the word **located** as settling down."
Student:	"And if you find something, lose it again, and then find it again, that would be to **relocate**, right"?"
Student:	"How can you tell which meaning a word like that has?"
Student:	"Context?"
Teacher:	"And when using words like this in your conversation or writing, be sure that the meaning you want is clear. Words, as you know, can be a bit tricky at times."

DISCUSS Carry on with a discussion of **transitive** versus **intransitive** verbs. Remember, transitive verbs are those used with a *direct object* (to find the place of an object again), while the intransitive usage does *not have a direct object* (to settle, to move into a place).

DEMONSTRATE Ask a student to go stand in a certain place in the room (to **locate**). Then have that student take his or her place in another part of the room (to **relocate**). Have a student **locate** a pencil (find in what place there is a pencil). Let the class demonstrate how **relocating** the pencil can be acted out (someone can hide that pencil, requiring it be **relocated**, *refound*).

Day 3

Stair Steps
for **LOC**

LOC means
place

LESSON TIME

15 Minutes

OBJECTIVES

- **Understand** the meaning of the root **LOC**

- **Apply** knowledge of the root **LOC**

- **Break Apart** words in the **LOC** family

- **Understand** the meaning of words in the **LOC** family

- **Understand** the spelling principles applied to the root **LOC**

MATERIALS

- Student Activity Book
- **LOC** Word Wall

DIFFERENTIATING INSTRUCTION

If you prefer easier or more difficult activities, use your personal account at www.dynamicliteracy.com to access novice or expert versions, along with ideas on using them.

Apply Knowledge of LOC

TEACH Have students turn to page 167 in their Student Activity Books. Explain that the boxes in front of and after the root indicate letters that spell out prefixes and suffixes. Students will spell out the correct prefixes and suffixes determined by clues in the definitions at the bottom of the page.

Have a volunteer read definition number one at the bottom of the page. Say, "We need a suffix to add to the root we see in step one that will add the meaning of *a particular*. There is no suffix in our list with that precise definition, but look at

the adjective definition of the suffix -**al**. See how *characterized by* would fit? If something is **LOCAL** it is *characterized by a place*. That's the word we need for step one of this Stair Steps puzzle. Often you will need to think beyond the information given to figure out how a word and a definition go together."

COMPLETE THE ACTIVITY

Let students work in pairs (optionally) and tell them to use the same strategy to find the correct prefixes and suffixes for the words listed. These activities can be quite challenging!

DISCUSS After a few minutes, review the answers as a class. Ask if there were any difficulties. Listen to any problems and have volunteers solve the difficulties by explaining key clues in the given definitions. As needed, follow the focus word approach that you see modeled on the next page.

SAB Pg 167

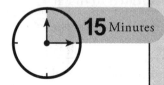

Stair Steps

Fill in the missing letters of each 'loc' word by using the definitions below.
'loc' means place

1.	l	o	c	a	l					
2.	l	o	c	a	t	e				
3.	l	o	c	a	t	o	r			
4.	l	o	c	a	l	i	z	e		
5.	r	e	l	o	c	a	t	e	d	
6.	l	o	c	a	l	i	z	i	n	g
7.	a	l	l	o	c	a	t	i	o	n	s
8.	d	i	s	l	o	c	a	t	i	o	n	s
9.	m	i	s	a	l	l	o	c	a	t	i	n	g

1. of a particular place
2. to find in a place
3. a person or tool that finds places
4. to put into or find at a specific place
5. found in a place again; moved to a new place
6. putting into or finding at a specific place
7. acts of placing things toward; acts of setting aside or distributing
8. acts or processes of placing things apart; movements out of the usual or proper place
9. placing things toward badly; doing a poor job setting aside or distributing

Focus Word: **DISLOCATIONS** → Write this word on the board.

TEACH

Sample leading question:	"Athletes suffered some **dislocations** during sports season. What does that mean?"
Student:	"It looks like it means they moved away or didn't know where they were!"
Student:	"No, it means they got things out of joint."
Teacher:	"Explain how that works, based on the pieces of the word."
Student:	"Okay, starting easy, it's more than one of whatever it is because of the suffix -**s**."
Student:	"And it's *an act or process of locating* because of the suffix -**ion**."
Student:	"And the -**at** is really -**ate** with **e** dropped."
Teacher:	"Why did the **e** drop?"
Student:	"Because of the suffix -**ion**, which starts with a vowel."
Student:	"And, finally, the prefix **dis**- means *not or apart, or opposite*."
Student:	"I look at it first as **locations**, *places*, and then add the **dis**- to get the meaning *out of places*!"
Teacher:	"So give me an example of **dislocations**."
Student:	"If your shoulder and your knee get knocked out of place, you'd have two **dislocations**!"

DISCUSS Lead students to see that the meaning of the word **dislocations** is the sum of the meanings of its five pieces

DEMONSTRATE Let a student illustrate a ball and socket bone structure on the board and show the class what a **dislocation** would look like.

Day 4

In Other Words for **LOC**

LOC means place

LESSON TIME

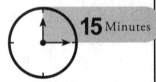

15 Minutes

OBJECTIVES

- **Understand** the meaning of the root **LOC**
- **Reinforce** knowledge of the root **LOC**
- **Understand** the meaning of words in the **LOC** family
- **Apply** knowledge of words in the **LOC** family

MATERIALS

- Student Activity Book
- **LOC** Word Wall
- Dictionary *(print or on-line)*

In Other Words for **LOC**

TEACH Have students turn to page 168 in their Student Activity Books. Explain that they are going to read a little story that uses some surprising and sometimes odd phrasing. The underlined words or phrases in the story are actually definitions or synonyms for words in the **LOC** family. Then they will see sentences about the story, each containing a blank.

Using context clues in the sentences, they will find a **LOC** family word in the Word Bank at the bottom to fit in each blank. Have a student read aloud the opening sentence or sentences of the story that contain the first underlined phrase. Then say, "Let's look at the first numbered sentence that contains a blank to be filled in. Clues in the sentence tell us that we want an action word, a verb that is a synonym for *move to a new place*. I see the word **relocate** at the bottom of the page. The prefix **re-** means *again*. What happens if someone has to **relocate**? What if I asked you to **relocate** your desk? (The answer should be *move*.) Let's write **relocate** in the blank space in the first sentence."

COMPLETE THE ACTIVITY This can be quite challenging, so allow students to work on this activity in small groups. Not every word in the Word Bank will be used.

DISCUSS After about 10 minutes, ask if there were any difficulties. Have volunteers explain strategies they used that led to correct answers.

SAB Pg 168

Moving Day

Jan's father earned a promotion in his job and the family had to <u>move to a new place</u>. The company <u>set aside for distribution</u> some money for the move but the responsibility of researching the new <u>specific places in a region</u> fell to Jan. She wrote a letter to the Chamber of Commerce in her new city and they sent her information on significant historic sites <u>as related to the place</u> and maps <u>of the specific place</u> so that she could <u>find in that place</u> her new street and house.

Once the moving truck was packed, Jan and her family piled into the SUV for the trip to her new house. Using directions and a map she had gotten from a website, she was able to find the <u>place</u> easily. Once the <u>act of moving to a new place</u> was completed, Jan happily settled into her new environment.

<u>Fill in the blanks below using words from the "loc" family.</u>

1. Jan's family had to <u>relocate</u> to a new city because her father had been promoted.

2. The company <u>allocated</u> money for the family's move.

3. Finding your way around in new <u>localities</u> might be difficult without maps.

4. Historical sites that were <u>locally</u> significant interested Jan.

5. Jan requested <u>local</u> maps of her new town to learn her new surroundings.

6. Before she could <u>locate</u> her new house, Jan had to find the new street on the map.

7. Jan found the exact <u>location</u> of her new house on a web-map.

8. With so much information about her new town, Jan's <u>relocation</u> to a new environment went smoothly.

<u>Not Used:</u> misallocating   locators   misallocation   dislocate

---

334

OPTIONAL

Day 5

Morpheme Mania
for **LOC**

LOC means
place

LESSON TIME

15 Minutes

OBJECTIVES

- **Build** words in the **LOC** family
- **Apply** knowledge of synonyms and antonyms to **LOC** words

Optional Morpheme Mania for **LOC**

On page 169 of their Activity Book, students will see an optional vocabulary enrichment activity that they can work on in groups, time permitting. This activity makes a great review for the formal assessment on the next page.

All the affixes presented in the week's activities are provided at the top of the page on either side of the root of the week in all its forms. Students can write in up to 13 of the words they built during the week, possibly discovering additional ones.

Then students can brainstorm with each other to come up with antonyms and synonyms they may know. Starter examples are given with every Morpheme Mania in the Activity Book. Because antonyms and synonyms may require knowledge of roots which students have not yet studied, completion of this activity is not crucial. Simply remind students that they can at any time during the course of the year revisit any of their Morpheme Mania pages and add words, antonyms, and synonyms as their vocabulary grows.

Day 5 *Assessment*

Make and hand out copies.
The answer key is on page A-6.
The instructions are on page A-2.

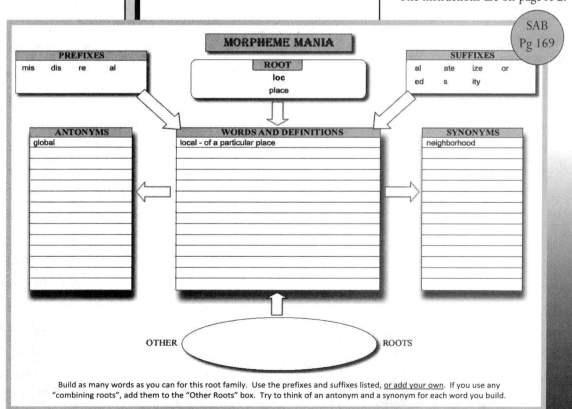

SAB
Pg 169

MORPHEME MANIA

PREFIXES
mis   dis   re   al

ROOT
loc
place

SUFFIXES
al   ate   ize   or
ed   s   ity

ANTONYMS
global

WORDS AND DEFINITIONS
local - of a particular place

SYNONYMS
neighborhood

OTHER   ROOTS

Build as many words as you can for this root family. Use the prefixes and suffixes listed, <u>or add your own</u>. If you use any "combining roots", add them to the "Other Roots" box. Try to think of an antonym and a synonym for each word you build.

allocate to place toward; to set aside or distribute

allocated placed toward; set aside or distributed

allocates places toward; sets aside or distributes

allocating placing toward; setting aside or distributing

allocation act of placing things toward; act of setting aside or distributing

allocations acts of placing things toward; acts of setting aside or distributing

dislocate to place apart; to move out of the usual or proper place

dislocated placed apart; moved out of the usual or proper place

dislocates places apart; moves out of usual or proper place

dislocating placing apart; moving out of the usual or proper place

dislocation act or process of placing apart; a movement out of the usual or proper place

dislocations acts or processes of placing apart; movements out of the usual or proper place

local of a particular place

locale a place

locales places

localities specific places

locality a specific place

localize to put into or find at a specific place

localized put into or found at a specific place

localizes puts into or finds at a specific place

localizing putting into or finding at a specific place

locally in a specific place

locals people native to a particular place

locate to find in a place

located found in a certain place

locates finds in a certain place

locating finding in a certain place

location a particular place

locations particular places

locator a person or tool that finds places

locators people or tools that find places

locus a collection of places; the center of an activity

misallocate to place things toward badly; to do a poor job setting aside or distributing

misallocated placed things toward badly; did a poor job setting aside or distributing

misallocates places things toward badly; does a poor job setting aside or distributing

misallocating placing things toward badly; doing a poor job setting aside or distributing

misallocation act of placing things toward badly; a poor job setting aside or distributing

misallocations acts of placing things toward badly; poor jobs setting aside or distributing

relocate to find in a place again; to move to a new place

relocated found in a place again; moved to a new place

relocates finds in a place again; moves to a new place

relocating finding in a place again; moving to a new place

relocation act of finding in a place again; act of moving to a new place

relocations acts of finding in a place again; acts of moving to a new place

Check-Up for **LOC**

Name _____

_____ **1.** **LOC** in words like **mislocate** or **localize** means:

    A speak

    B lose

    C place

_____ **2.** What is the meaning of the word **localize**?

    A to put into a specific place

    B to speak about several topics

    C to lose the temper

_____ **3.** What is the meaning of the word **allocate**?

    A to speak to

    B to take away

    C to put in place for a definite purpose

_____ **4.** What is the meaning of the word **locally**?

    A so as to lose

    B in a particular place

    C speaking in a specific way

_____ **5.** To **dislocate** something is to:

    A speak badly about

    B find it again after being lost

    C get it out of place

_____ **6.** Which word means **the process of going to a new place**?

    A allocate

    B relocation

    C locality

_____ **7.** Which word means **badly placed for a certain purpose**?

    A misallocated

    B dislocator

    C localizing

_____ **8.** Which word means **a device that puts something in a place**?

    A localization

    B relocation

    C locator

_____ **9.** Grandfather wrote a **locodescriptive** story. The story mostly described the:

    A area

    B time

    C weather

_____ **10.** We set the machine to **collocate** the pages. What did the machine do to the pages?

    A color-print

    B put them together in order

    C make sure words were spelled right

OBJECTIVES

- **Understand** the meaning of the root **SERV**
- **Build** words in the root **SERV** family
- **Break Apart** words in the root **SERV** family
- **Understand** the meaning of words in the **SERV** family
- **Understand** the spelling principles applied to the root **SERV**
- **Apply** knowledge of words in the **SERV** family
- **Assess** and **Reinforce** knowledge of words in the **SERV** family

MATERIALS

- Student Activity Books, pages 171-176
- Dictionary *(print or on-line)*

CROSS-CURRICULAR EXAMPLES

Science:
conservation, observable

Social Studies:
conservative, observance

Language Arts:
reservation, reserved

Math:
unobserved, observability

SERV

meaning "to save or protect"

reserve
to **save** or keep back

conserve
to save or **protect** thoroughly

Morpheme: **SERV**
Allomorphs: **SERVE**

About 250 words containing the morpheme **SERV** or its allomorph are current in English. During this unit, tell students to be alert for this root in their school texts, general reading, and oral language they hear. Some of the words they might encounter in their school subjects are listed on the left under Cross-Curricular Examples.

UNIT AT A GLANCE

Day **1**
Root Squares
for **SERV**

Day **2**
Magic Squares
for **SERV**

Day **3**
Stair Steps
for **SERV**

OPTIONAL

Day **4**
In Other Words
for **SERV**

Day **5**
*Assessment or
Morpheme Mania*
for **SERV**

Each activity should take approximately **15 minutes**.

338

An **observatory** might not seem to be an obvious place for stars to be *saved or protected*, but there they are being *watched over*, as if protected. The basic meaning of the verb to **observe** is *to watch over so as to protect or keep*, understood clearly in phrases such as, to **observe** a holiday or to be kept under **observation**.

Similarly, a **conservatory** of music or the arts, is a place where those arts are *nurtured and protected*.

Word Alert!

It is important to point out to students (or let them discover on their own) that the free, unbound morpheme **serve** is not from this root family, as odd as that may seem. Only with prefixes will this root appear with its meaning of *save or protect*.

Instead, the word **serve**, *to be of use to*, and its whole family of associated words, such as **servant**, **servile**, and **servitude**, come from a root meaning *to be of use* or *a slave*. The origin of the root for **slave** is not fully known, but it may be Etruscan. The meanings of familiar words will make it clear which morpheme is the source, but students (and teachers!) will need to consult a dictionary for less familiar words.

The word **deserve** also stems from the root meaning *to be of use*, with the prefix **de-** either in its intensive role (very much of use) or its sense of *coming down*, as if the reward that is **deserved** is laid down upon the recipient.

Only rarely does the letter sequence **s-e-r-v** have nothing to do with either the roots meaning *save or protect*, or *be of use; slave*. A **serval** is a type of wildcat. **Servian** is an adjective used to describe either the reign of Rome's sixth king or the culture of Serbia.

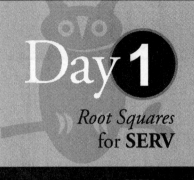

Day 1

Root Squares for SERV

SERV means to save or protect

LESSON TIME

15 Minutes

OBJECTIVES

- **Understand** the meaning of the root **SERV**
- **Build** words in the **SERV** family
- **Understand** the meaning of words in the **SERV** family
- **Understand** the spelling principles applied to the root **SERV**

MATERIALS

- Student Activity Book
- **SERV** Word Wall
- Dictionary *(print or on-line)*

DIFFERENTIATING INSTRUCTION

If you prefer easier or more difficult activities, use your personal account at www.dynamicliteracy.com to access novice or expert versions, along with ideas on using them.

Root Squares for SERV

TEACH Have students turn to page 171 in their Activity Books. Say, "All of the prefixes and suffixes in the squares surrounding the shaded center are probably familiar, but if you have questions about any of the meanings, simply ask or look them up in the list inside the front and back cover of the activity book."

Call attention to the center box. Ask students to decide if one of the forms they see in the middle square can stand alone as a word. They will see that **serve** is a word, though it is not in the **SERV** family. Consult a good dictionary to prove that **serve**, as an independent word, is related to the idea of *to be of use*. Suggest that students start their list with **serve**, adding the prefix **con-**, meaning *thoroughly*, to build **conserve**, meaning *to save thoroughly*. Use this

word to guide students to the idea of *save or protect*. You might in this discussion mention how students might build the word **conservation**, *the idea of saving or protecting thoroughly*.

COMPLETE THE ACTIVITY

Have students follow the directions for the activity to build words. If students have difficulty building words with the Root Squares, show them how by modeling the matrix approach found on the next page, taking one affix at a time and seeing if it will connect with any one of the allomorphs of the root.

DISCUSS After five minutes, have volunteers write some of their words on the board. Focus with the class on the words they have built and guide them in a discussion of how the meaning of the root is still *save or protect* even when prefixes and suffixes are added. Watch for target words that most easily demonstrate the meaning of *save or protect*. If the word **reserve** is not present, ask the class, "Can anyone try to use the prefix **re-**?" and then continue on to the target word discussion on the next page.

Root Squares

How many words can you make?

Start in any square. Your goal is to combine two or more word parts to make as many words in the 'serv, serve' family as you can. Write each word and a definition you can think of for it in the space provided at the bottom of the page. Use the back of the page if you need to.

at	ion	con
re	serv, serve	ory
pre	ist	ob

SAB Pg 171

Focus Word: **RESERVE** ➡ Write this word on the board.

TEACH

Lead with this:	"I think when we look closely at this word, we're going to make some interesting discoveries."
Student:	"It looks pretty easy to me. You can **serve** a tennis ball and then you can do it again to **reserve** it."
Student:	"Or **serve** somebody some food and then do it again."
Teacher:	"Listen carefully to how you're pronouncing that word. Do you hear the **s** sound that you're saying?"
Student:	"Sure—is there any other way?"
Teacher:	"I know—say it with a **z** sound, like when we say, 'I **reserve** the right to remain silent.'"
Student:	"Oh, I see. That is tricky. So what gives?"
Student:	"**Serving** food or tennis balls and then **reserving** them doesn't belong to this root!"
Student:	"But **reserving** rights—or how about a **reservation** at a restaurant—those words have the root that means *save* or *protect*."
Student:	"Is there a way to tell which meaning is meant?"
Teacher:	"Aside from context, I think it is customary to spell the word that means *give again* as **re-serve**."

DISCUSS See if students can think of any other situations like this. **Resign** (give up) and **re-sign** (put another signature on); **reside** (live) and **re-side** (put on new house siding); **research** (study) and **re-search** (look for again); **resort** (vacation home or decide on) and **re-sort** (arrange again in piles); **resent** (dislike) and **re-sent** (mailed again) are similar examples.

Root Squares Matrix

You can refer to this matrix to guide students in this activity. Students could build at least these 15 words. *It is not important how many words are built*, so long as students understand the meanings of the root and its affixes.

	con-	ob-	pre-	re-
no suffix	conserve	observe	preserve	reserve
-ist				reservist
-at + -ory		observatory	preservatory	reservatory
-at + -ion	conservation	observation	preservation	reservation
-at + -ion + -ist	conservationist		preservationist	reservationist

Day 2

Magic Squares for SERV

SERV means to save or protect

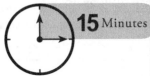
OBJECTIVES

- **Understand** the meaning of the root **SERV**

- **Break Apart** words in the **SERV** family

- **Understand** the meanings of words in the **SERV** family

MATERIALS

- Student Activity Book

- **SERV** Word Wall

- Dictionary *(print or on-line)*

DIFFERENTIATING INSTRUCTION

If you prefer easier or more difficult activities, use your personal account at www.dynamicliteracy.com to access novice or expert versions, along with ideas on using them.

Break Apart Words with SERV

Have students turn to the Magic Squares on page 172 in their Student Activity Books. Model a Think-Aloud strategy for students: "I know that **SERV** means *to save or protect*. I can use this knowledge to find the definition of a word with **SERV** or **SERVE** as its root."

Direct students to word G, **reserves**. Say: "This word has a prefix, **re-** meaning *again, back, or against* and a suffix -**s** that either makes this word mean *more than one* or makes it mean *he, she, or it does*. Look at definition 5, *saves or keeps back*. That reflects the meanings of the root, **SERVE**, the prefix, **re-**, and the second of the suffix -**s** meanings, so let's write the number 5 in square G."

COMPLETE THE ACTIVITY

Ask students to use the same strategy to find the correct definitions for the other words. Tell them to write the number of the definition in the box that matches the letter for the word. Remind them that if all their answers are correct, each row and each column will add up to the same Magic number.

DISCUSS After five minutes, ask if there are any difficulties about matching the words and definitions. If there are, ask volunteers to explain clues in the definitions that will lead to the correct choice of word. As needed, follow the focus word approach for preserver that you see modeled on the next page.

Add any new words to the classroom **SERV** Word Wall and remind students to add these words to the **SERV** Word Wall in their Activity Books.

SAB Pg 172

Magic Squares

Select the best answer for each of the words in the 'serv, serve' family from the numbered definitions. Put the number in the proper space in the Magic Square box. If the total of the numbers is the same both across and down, you have found the magic number!

'serv, serve' means to save or protect

WORDS	DEFINITIONS
A. conservationists	1. tending to watch over or keep safe
B. observational	2. related to watching over or keeping safe
C. reservations	3. people who watch over or keep safe; people who notice
D. preserver	4. a person who protects or saves thoroughly
E. observatory	5. saves or keeps back
F. conservatively	6. place for watching over or keeping safe; a planetarium
G. reserves	7. acts of saving or keeping back; hesitations
H. preservatives	8. in a manner that saves or protects thoroughly
I. observers	9. people who act to save or protect thoroughly
	10. substances serving to protect or save thoroughly

Magic Square Box

A. 9	B. 2	C. 7
D. 4	E. 6	F. 8
G. 5	H. 10	I. 3

Magic Number __18__

*** ANSWER KEY ***

Focus Word: **PRESERVER** ⟶ Write this word on the board.

TEACH

Sample leading question:	"What's a life **preserver**?"
Student:	"A vest you wear when you're on a boat."
Student:	"It's something that **preserves** your life!"
Teacher:	"We're going to see some interesting things about this word's pieces."
Student:	"Hey, look, just like with **reserve** and **re-serve**. This word could mean *a person who gives something ahead of time*, a **pre-server**."
Student:	"I don't think there's any such word as that."
Student:	"Sure there is—I just said it and defined it."
Student:	"But the thing called a life **preserver** actually has the root meaning *to save*. What's that prefix mean, *though*? *Before*?"
Student:	"I guess the life **preserver** is going to protect you ahead of time in case some disaster hits."
Teacher:	"That sounds good. But sometimes prefixes like this simply mean *very much* or *thoroughly, out in front* like *foremost* or *most importantly*."
Student:	"I think I see the connection between *out in front* and *very much*."

DISCUSS Several prefixes have shades of meaning more relating to *very much* rather than their original literal meaning. The prefixes **con-**, **dis-**, and **per-** sometimes have this meaning of *very much* as well as their literal meaning of *with*, *apart*, and *through*. Occasionally, other prefixes, such as **ex-**, **in-**, and **ob-** also have shades of meaning that relate to *very much*. Such prefix usages are called **intensifiers**.

DEMONSTRATE The phrase **firm up** and the word **confirm** are examples of an intensifier usage. Consult a dictionary with your class to look at the word **perform**. You will see that this word does not mean *form through*, but *to finish thoroughly*.

Day 3

Stair Steps for SERV

SERV means to save or protect

LESSON TIME

15 Minutes

OBJECTIVES

- **Understand** the meaning of the root **SERV**

- **Apply** knowledge of the root **SERV**

- **Break Apart** words in the **SERV** family

- **Understand** the meaning of words in the **SERV** family

- **Understand** the spelling principles applied to the root **SERV**

MATERIALS

- Student Activity Book
- **SERV** Word Wall

DIFFERENTIATING INSTRUCTION

If you prefer easier or more difficult activities, use your personal account at www.dynamicliteracy.com to access novice or expert versions, along with ideas on using them.

Apply Knowledge of SERV

TEACH Have students turn to page 173 in their Student Activity Books. Explain that the boxes in front of and after the root indicate letters that spell out prefixes and suffixes. Students will spell out the correct prefixes and suffixes determined by clues in the definitions at the bottom of the page.

Have a volunteer read definitions number one and number two at the bottom of the page. Say, "We usually complete only one step together, but the first two of these provide such a nice contrast between two prefixes. The first one is one we have seen often,

meaning *back*. By adding **re-** to this root, we get **RESERVE**, with the meaning *to save or keep back*. Now look at the second definition, *to protect or save thoroughly*. Sometimes, as we have seen before, a prefix is used as an *intensifier*."

COMPLETE THE ACTIVITY
Let students work in pairs (optionally) and tell them to use the same strategy to find the correct prefixes and suffixes for the words listed. These activities can be quite challenging!

DISCUSS After a few minutes, review the answers as a class. Ask if there were any difficulties. Listen to any problems and have volunteers solve the difficulties by explaining key clues in the given definitions. As needed, follow the focus word approach that you see modeled on the next page.

SAB Pg 173

Stair Steps

Fill in the missing letters of each 'serv, serve' word by using the definitions below.
'serv, serve' means to save or protect

1.	r	e	s	e	r	v	e		
2.	p	r	e	s	e	r	v	e	
3.	r	e	s	e	r	v	i	n	g
4.	c	o	n	s	e	r	v	i	n	g
5.	o	b	s	e	r	v	a	t	i	o	n
6.	r	e	s	e	r	v	a	t	i	o	n	s
7.	o	b	s	e	r	v	a	t	o	r	i	e	s
8.	c	o	n	s	e	r	v	a	t	i	v	e	l	y

1. to save or keep back
2. to protect or save thoroughly
3. saving or keeping back
4. saving or protecting thoroughly
5. an act of watching over or keeping safe
6. acts of saving or keeping back; hesitations
7. places for watching over or keeping safe; planetaria
8. in a manner that saves or protects thoroughly

MINI-LESSON: the Suffix -ori

The partial suffix **-ori** is a spelling variation of **-ory**, meaning *relating to*. Here is an opportunity to reinforce the spelling principle of changing a final **y** to the letter **i** before adding another prefix. Show students any of these word pairs:

memory – **memories**   **factory** – **factories**   **story** – **stories**

Focus Word: **CONSERVING** ⟶ Write this word on the board.

TEACH

Sample leading question:	"If you are **conserving** your energy, what are you doing?"
Student:	"*Not wearing yourself out.*"
Student:	"*Saving it together?*"
Student:	I'll bet that's an example of that *very much* meaning for **con-**."
Teacher:	"I agree—an ***intensifier***."
Student:	"So you're saving your energy *very much* for later use."
Student:	"I see what **conservation** really means now, too."
Student:	"Yes—*saving very much.*"

DISCUSS Let small groups discuss usages in which **conserving** is going on. Examples are **conserving** paper, **conserving** fuel, or **conserving** rivers.

Day 4

In Other Words
for **SERV**

SERV means
to save or protect

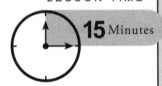
OBJECTIVES

- **Understand** the meaning of the root **SERV**

- **Reinforce** knowledge of the root **SERV**

- **Understand** the meaning of words in the **SERV** family

- **Apply** knowledge of words in the **SERV** family

MATERIALS

- Student Activity Book
- **SERV** Word Wall
- Dictionary *(print or on-line)*

In Other Words for **SERV**

TEACH Have students turn to page 174 in their Student Activity Books. Explain that they are going to read a little story that uses some surprising and sometimes odd phrasing. The underlined words or phrases in the story are actually definitions or synonyms for words in the **SERV** family. Then they will see sentences about the story, each containing a blank.

Using context clues in the sentences, they will find a **SERV** family word in the Word Bank at the bottom to fit in each blank. Have a student read aloud the opening sentence or sentences of the story that contain the first underlined phrase. Then say, "Let's look at the first numbered sentence that contains a blank to be filled in. Clues in the sentence tell us that we want a describing word, an adjective that is a synonym for *who kept himself back* and which could modify an *old man*. I see the word **reserved** at the bottom of the page. The prefix **re-** means *back*, and the suffix **-ed** can mean *characterized by*. That all seems to fit, so let's write **reserved** in the blank for the first sentence."

COMPLETE THE ACTIVITY
This can be quite challenging, so allow students to work on this activity in small groups. Not every word in the Word Bank will be used.

DISCUSS After about 10 minutes, ask if there were any difficulties. Have volunteers explain strategies they used that led to correct answers.

SAB
Pg 174

Lorenzo the Champion of Trees

   Uncle Lorenzo was a good old character <u>who kept himself back</u> and who hardly ever said a word, except when it came to <u>the act of thoroughly protecting</u> natural resources, especially trees, or <u>the act of keeping as before</u> famous battlefields. He was an ardent <u>person who believed in thoroughly saving</u> and a <u>person believing in keeping as before</u>. He had no <u>acts of hesitation</u> about arguing with folks over the slow disappearance of trees and of open space, but on other issues, he <u>thoroughly saved</u> his energy. He kept an eye <u>tending to watch out</u> on land developers who weren't interested in <u>keeping safe</u> the land.
   Throughout his hundred and one years, he always <u>kept</u> Arbor Day in honor of trees and Memorial Day in honor of soldiers.

<u>Fill in the blanks below using words from the "serv, serve" family.</u>

1. Lorenzo was a quiet, <u>reserved</u> old man.

2. However, he was vocal when it came to the <u>conservation</u> of natural resources.

3. He was also very interested in the <u>preservation</u> and upkeep of famous battle sites.

4. Lorenzo was an early <u>conservationist</u> and <u>preservationist</u> who inspired many to hold onto nature and history.

5. He had no <u>reservations</u> about making his anti-development viewpoints known.

6. On most other issues, though, he <u>conserved</u> his energy and kept quiet.

7. Lorenzo was a very <u>observant</u> reader about land deals and new developments.

8. He knew that developers were not interested in <u>preserving</u> nature.

9. All his life Lorenzo <u>observed</u> two holidays with special honor.

<u>Not Used:</u>   reserved   observances

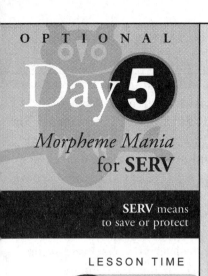

Day 5

Morpheme Mania
for **SERV**

SERV means
to save or protect

LESSON TIME

15 Minutes

OBJECTIVES

• **Build** words in the
SERV family

• **Apply** knowledge of
synonyms and antonyms
to **SERV** words

Optional Morpheme Mania for **SERV**

On page 175 of their Activity Book, students will see an optional vocabulary enrichment activity that they can work on in groups, time permitting. This activity makes a great review for the formal assessment on the next page.

All the affixes presented in the week's activities are provided at the top of the page on either side of the root of the week in all its forms. Students can write in up to 13 of the words they built during the week, possibly discovering additional ones.

Then students can brainstorm with each other to come up with antonyms and synonyms they may know. Starter examples are given with every Morpheme Mania in the Activity Book. Because antonyms and synonyms may require knowledge of roots which students have not yet studied, completion of this activity is not crucial. Simply remind students that they can at any time during the course of the year revisit any of their Morpheme Mania pages and add words, antonyms, and synonyms as their vocabulary grows.

Day 5 *Assessment*

Make and hand out copies.
The answer key is on page A-6.
The instructions are on page A-2.

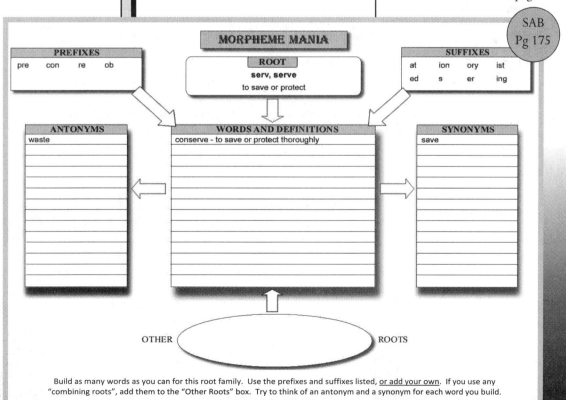

SAB
Pg 175

MORPHEME MANIA

PREFIXES
| pre | con | re | ob |

ROOT
serv, serve
to save or protect

SUFFIXES
| at | ion | ory | ist |
| ed | s | er | ing |

ANTONYMS
waste

WORDS AND DEFINITIONS
conserve - to save or protect thoroughly

SYNONYMS
save

OTHER   ROOTS

Build as many words as you can for this root family. Use the prefixes and suffixes listed, or add your own. If you use any "combining roots", add them to the "Other Roots" box. Try to think of an antonym and a synonym for each word you build.

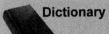
conservation act of saving or protecting thoroughly

conservationist a person who acts to save or protect thoroughly

conservationists people who act to save or protect thoroughly

conservatism belief in saving or protecting thoroughly

conservative tending to save or protect thoroughly

conservatively in a manner that saves or protects thoroughly

conservatives people who tend to save or protect thoroughly

conserve to save or to protect thoroughly

conserved saved or protected thoroughly

conserves saves or protects thoroughly

conserving saving or protecting thoroughly

observance the act of watching over or keeping safe

observances acts of watching over or keeping safe

observant tending to watch over or keep safe

observation an act of watching over or keeping safe

observational related to watching over or keeping safe

observations acts of watching over or keeping safe

observatories places for watching over or keeping safe; planetaria

observatory place for watching over or keeping safe; a planetarium

observe to watch over or keep safe; to notice

observed watched over or kept safe; noticed

observer a person who watches over or keeps safe; a person who notices

observers people who watch over or keep safe; people who notice

observes watches over or keeps safe; notices

observing watching over or keeping safe; noticing

preservation act of protecting or saving thoroughly

preservationist a person dedicated to protecting or saving thoroughly

preservationists people dedicated to protecting or saving thoroughly

preservations acts of protecting or saving thoroughly

preservative serving to protect or save thoroughly

preservatives substances serving to protect or save thoroughly

preserve to protect or save thoroughly

preserved protected or saved thoroughly

preserver a person who protects or saves thoroughly

preservers people who protect or save thoroughly

preserves protects or saves thoroughly

preserving protecting or saving thoroughly

reservation act of saving or keeping back; a hesitation

reservations acts of saving or keeping back; hesitations

reserve to save or keep back

reserved saved or kept back

reserves saves or keeps back

reserving saving or keeping back

Check-Up for **SERV**

____ **1.** **SERV** in words like **preserve**, **reservist**, and **conservation** means:

   A to save or keep

   B to offer food

   C to fight

____ **2.** What is the meaning of the word **reservists**?

   A the process or result of fighting

   B people who don't want to fight

   C people held back for future use

____ **3.** What is the meaning of the word **preservation**?

   A a person who puts food in containers for future use

   B the process of arranging to save

   C relating to fighting for rights

____ **4.** What is the meaning of the word **conserving**?

   A providing food for a group

   B tending to hold together what exists

   C fighting for a cause

____ **5.** To **observe** a holiday is to:

   A hold to its purpose

   B be against it

   C eat during it

____ **6.** Which word means **tending to watch over or keep safe**?

   A observant

   B observation

   C observatory

____ **7.** Which word means **serving to keep safe**?

   A reserves

   B conservationist

   C preservative

____ **8.** Which word means **a person who watches over to protect**?

   A preserving

   B observer

   C reservation

____ **9.** The **unobservant** child was walking along the road. The child:

   A wasn't keeping watch

   B was offering help to a friend

   C didn't like having to walk

____ **10.** Sandy had **reservations** about going to the party. Sandy was:

   A thinking about what food to take

   B very excited

   C holding back

OBJECTIVES

- **Understand** the meaning of the root **CAPIT**
- **Build** words in the root **CAPIT** family
- **Break Apart** words in the root **CAPIT** family
- **Understand** the meaning of words in the **CAPIT** family
- **Understand** the spelling principles applied to the root **CAPIT**
- **Apply** knowledge of words in the **CAPIT** family
- **Assess** and **Reinforce** knowledge of words in the **CAPIT** family

MATERIALS

- Student Activity Books, pages 177-182
- Dictionary *(print or on-line)*

CROSS-CURRICULAR EXAMPLES

Science:
   precipitate, biceps, triceps

Social Studies:
   capitulate, capitalism, capitation

Language Arts:
   capitals, recapitulate

Math:
   principle, capital

CAPIT

meaning "head, chief, wealth"

decapitate
to cut the **head** off

principle
main idea or **chief** concept

capitalist
a person whose focus is on **wealth**

Morpheme: **CAPIT**
Allomorphs: **CEP, CIP, CIPIT**

Over 500 words containing the morpheme **CAPIT** or one of its allomorph are current in English. During this unit, tell students to be alert for this root in their school texts, general reading, and oral language they hear. Some of the words they might encounter in their school subjects are listed on the left under Cross-Curricular Examples.

UNIT AT A GLANCE

Day **1**
Root Squares
for **CAPIT**

Day **2**
Magic Squares
for **CAPIT**

Day **3**
Stair Steps
for **CAPIT**

OPTIONAL
Day **4**
In Other Words
for **CAPIT**

Day **5**
Assessment or Morpheme Mania
for **CAPIT**

Each activity should take approximately **15 minutes**.

Our head as a body part gives rise to many idioms: *the head of the class, the head of a government, heads of cattle*. Likewise, the Latin word for head, **caput**, produces many channels of metaphorical meaning. The root can be used literally for the actual physical feature of the head: the scientific word **capitate** means *possessing a head*. Figuratively, the head is thought of as the center of intellect and consciousness, so the root came to mean *main or most important*, as in a **capital** city, or a **capital** idea. A capital letter is *the one made big*. **Capital** crime and punishment are *major*.

Students may wonder why the main city is a **capital**, but the main building is a **capitol**. The building word derives from the name of the highest of the seven hills of Rome, the **Capitoline**, site of a major temple to Jupiter, the chief Roman god.

Capitulate as an adjective means *having a little head*, but as a verb it means *to surrender or give in*. The history of the meaning goes as follows: in long documents, headings (or main points) were written for various sections of the work for organization and easy retrieval. The headings were called **capitula**, little heads. This word evolved into our word **chapter**. Certain war documents, called documents of surrender, led the word **capitula** to its narrow meaning of *surrender* during the 17th century.

To **recapitulate**, however, is not *to surrender again*, but *to repeat the main, head points said or written earlier*.

Capital as a word referring to *wealth* derives from the phrases **capital** goods or **capital** assets, with the adjective taking over as a noun.

Another direction this morpheme's meaning takes relates to *steepness* or *suddenness*, with the connection to head seen in the English **headlong**, *rushing or plunging*. A **precipice** is *a steep cliff*. Rain and snow falling headlong is called **precipitation**.

The words **biceps**, **triceps**, and **quadriceps** are actually singular in form, the **s** being part of a variation in the spelling of this root. By a process of language evolution called <u>**back-formation**</u>, however, the **s** has become thought to be a plural marker for the supposed words **bicep**, **tricep**, and **quadricep**, and it is so treated in this program. These muscles are so-named because of the number of places they originate from or are attached to.

Word Alert!

The words **principle** and **principal** come from the root that means *to hold or take*. A **principle** is *a foremost or major idea taken on or believed*. **Principal** is a word that means *taking first place*.

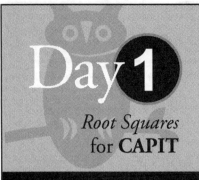

Day 1

Root Squares
for **CAPIT**

CAPIT means
head, chief, wealth

LESSON TIME

15 Minutes

OBJECTIVES

- **Understand** the meaning of the root **CAPIT**
- **Build** words in the **CAPIT** family
- **Understand** the meaning of words in the **CAPIT** family
- **Understand** the spelling principles applied to the root **CAPIT**

MATERIALS

- Student Activity Book
- **CAPIT** Word Wall
- Dictionary *(print or on-line)*

DIFFERENTIATING INSTRUCTION

If you prefer easier or more difficult activities, use your personal account at www.dynamicliteracy.com to access novice or expert versions, along with ideas on using them.

Root Squares for **CAPIT**

TEACH Have students turn to page 177 in their Activity Books. Say, "All of the prefixes and suffixes in the squares surrounding the shaded center are familiar, except **tri-** and **-ism**, so let's take a look at those." Tell students that **tri-** means *three*, as in **triangle** and **triceratops**. Refer to the Mini-Lesson for **-ism** on the next page.

Then call attention to the center box. Point out that the root **CAPIT** has several different spellings, called allomorphs. Ask students to decide if one of the forms they see in the middle square can stand alone as a word. Since none of these forms can stand as an independent word, they all will need a prefix or suffix attached if they are to become part of a word. Suggest that students start their list with **cep**, adding

the prefix **tri-**, meaning *three*, to build **tricep**, meaning *three-headed*. Students will recognize it as the name of a muscle, and you can share the Fun Facts above to explain the name.

COMPLETE THE ACTIVITY
Have students follow the directions to build words. If students have difficulty building words with the Root Squares, show them how by modeling the matrix approach found on the next page, taking one affix at a time and seeing if it will connect with any one of the allomorphs of the root.

DISCUSS After five minutes, have volunteers write some of their words on the board. Focus with the class on the words they have built and guide them in a discussion of how the meaning of the root is still *head, chief, wealth* even when prefixes and suffixes are added. Watch for target words that most easily demonstrate the meaning of *head; chief, wealth*. If the word **capital** is not present, ask the class, "Can anyone try to use the suffix **-al**?" and then continue on to the target word discussion on the next page.

Root Squares

How many words can you make?

Start in any square. Your goal is to combine two or more word parts to make as many words in the 'capit, cep, cip, cipit' family as you can. Write each word and a definition you can think of for it in the space provided at the bottom of the page. Use the back of the page if you need to.

de	al	tri
pre	capit, cep, cip, cipit	ate
ism	ize	ion

SAB
Pg 177

MINI-LESSON: the Suffix -ism

The suffix **-ism** is ultimately from the Greek noun-forming suffix **-ismos**. The suffix refers to *an act or practice*. Two related suffixes are often associated with **-ism**: **-ist**, indicating *the person who performs the act or process*, and **-ize**, the verb-forming suffix meaning *to cause to be like*. For example, **terrorism** is the practice of **terrorizing**, carried out by **terrorists**. An **individualist** enjoys **individualism**, preferring things to be **individualized**.

Over 800 words with the suffix **-ism** are in current use in English, with more coined all the time. Write up any of these words on the board and have students define the ones they know. Then have them add the suffix **-ism** and define the newly made nouns (the *act or process of* whatever it is attached to):

federal	material	sceptic	industrial	classic	human	tour
journal	imperial	ideal	magnet	defeat	cynic	creation

Dropped **e**: favorite   active   extreme   cube

Focus Word: **CAPITAL** ⟶ Write this word on the board.

TEACH

Lead with this:	"How many of you know the **capital** city of every state?"
Students:	"I do! I do."
Teacher:	"Great—now what is a state **capital**?"
Student:	"It's where the governor lives."
Student:	"It's the main city."
Teacher:	"I get it—it's the HEAD city."
Student:	"What about a **capital** letter?"
Student:	"Yes—see, it's like the *head* letter."

DISCUSS The word **capital** has many usages. You can let groups list more usages or you can share some of the Fun Facts with your class. One usage involves the tops of columns, and you can use this opportunity to teach or review the three main **capital** types: Doric, Ionic, and Corinthian.

DEMONSTRATE Ask a student who may know the **capital** types to draw them on the board and explain why they are called **capitals** (they are the top, or head, of a column.

Root Squares Matrix

You can refer to this matrix to guide students in this activity. Students could build at least these 15 words. *It is not important how many words are built*, so long as students understand the meanings of the root and its affixes.

	no prefix	de-	pre-	tri-
no suffix				tricep
-al	capital		precipital	tricipital
-ate	capitates	decapitate	precipitate	tricapitate
-al + -ism	capitalism			
-al + -ize	capitalize	decapitalize		
-at(e) + -ion	capitation	decapitation	precipitation	
-alize + -ation	capitalization			

Day 2

Magic Squares
for **CAPIT**

CAPIT means
head, chief, wealth

LESSON TIME

15 Minutes

OBJECTIVES

- **Understand** the meaning of the root **CAPIT**

- **Break Apart** words in the **CAPIT** family

- **Understand** the meanings of words in the **CAPIT** family

MATERIALS

- Student Activity Book
- **CAPIT** Word Wall
- Dictionary
  (print or on-line)

DIFFERENTIATING INSTRUCTION

If you prefer easier or more difficult activities, use your personal account at www.dynamicliteracy.com to access novice or expert versions, along with ideas on using them.

Break Apart Words with **CAPIT**

Have students turn to the Magic Squares on page 178 in their Student Activity Books. Model a Think-Aloud strategy for students: "I know that **CAPIT** means *head; chief; wealth*. I can use this knowledge to find the definition of a word with **CAPIT** or one of its allomorphs as its root."

Direct students to word I, **biceps**. Say, "This word has the prefix, **bi-** meaning *two,* and a suffix -**s** that makes the word mean *more than one.* Look at definition 6, *things two-headed; muscles with two masses.* That reflects the meanings of the root, **CEP**, the prefix, **bi-**, and the suffix -**s**, so let's write the number 6 in square I."

COMPLETE THE ACTIVITY

Ask students to use the same strategy to find the correct definitions for the other words. Tell them to write the number of the definition in the box that matches the letter for the word. Remind them that if all their answers are correct, each row and each column will add up to the same Magic number.

DISCUSS After five minutes, ask if there are any difficulties about matching the words and definitions. If there are, ask volunteers to explain clues in the definitions that will lead to the correct choice of word. As needed, follow the focus word approach for **decapitates** that you see modeled on the next page.

Add any new words to the classroom **CAPIT** Word Wall and remind students to add these words to the **CAPIT** Word Wall in their Activity Books.

SAB Pg 178

MINI-LESSON: the Prefix bi-

The numerical prefix **bi-** comes from a Latin prefix meaning *two*. To **bisect** is to cut into *two*. A **biweekly** paycheck is paid out every *two* weeks. A **bilingual** person is fluent in *two* languages. **Bipedal** creatures walk on *two* feet.

Usage is becoming blurred, however, as a word like **biquarterly** can mean *twice* a quarter as well as every *half* year. The word **bimonthly**, along with **semimonthly**, is beginning to mean *twice* a month by some writers and readers. **Biweekly** appears in modern English meaning both every *two* weeks and *twice* a week.

For the most part, however, the prefix is not ambiguous, as seen in words like **bicycle** or **biracial**. Write some of these words up for your students, and discuss how the meaning *two* operates in the words they may know or research:

bicameral	bicarbonate	bicentennial	bifocals
binoculars	bigamy	bilabial	bilateral

Focus Word: **DECAPITATES** ⟶ Write this word on the board.

TEACH

Sample leading question:	"In museums about the French revolution, we can see a machine that **decapitates**. Does anyone know what that machine can do?"
Student:	"How about tear columns down?"
Teacher:	"That's a good guess, but it's worse than that. Let's study the word. What do we see?"
Student:	"Okay—the suffix **-s** just makes it a *he, she, or it* verb, like *does it*."
Student:	"Right, the suffix **-ate** makes it a verb."
Student:	"Oh, no! I get it—it takes people's **heads** off!"
Student:	"Oh, that's right, that blade that came down fast while somebody was placed at the bottom."
Student:	"I know what it was called—a guillotine!"

DISCUSS Lead students to see that the meaning of **decapitates** is the sum of the meanings of its four morphemes.

Day 3

Stair Steps for CAPIT

CAPIT means head, chief, wealth

LESSON TIME

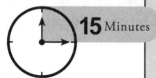

15 Minutes

OBJECTIVES

- **Understand** the meaning of the root **CAPIT**

- **Apply** knowledge of the root **CAPIT**

- **Break Apart** words in the **CAPIT** family

- **Understand** the meaning of words in the **CAPIT** family

- **Understand** the spelling principles applied to the root **CAPIT**

MATERIALS

- Student Activity Book
- **CAPIT** Word Wall

DIFFERENTIATING INSTRUCTION

If you prefer easier or more difficult activities, use your personal account at www.dynamicliteracy.com to access novice or expert versions, along with ideas on using them.

Apply Knowledge of **CAPIT**

TEACH Have students turn to page 179 in their Student Activity Books. Explain that the boxes in front of and after the root indicate letters that spell out prefixes and suffixes. Students will spell out the correct prefixes and suffixes determined by clues in the definitions at the bottom of the page.

Have a volunteer read definition number five at the bottom of the page. Say, "Think about the suffix that is attached to words to make them refer to belief systems, words you know that end in **-ism**, words like **communism**, **feminism**, **spiritualism**, etc. What kind of **-ism** is the word that matches

definition five? If you add the suffix **-al** to the root we see in step five, you get **CAPITAL**, the word we'd build in step two of this Stair Steps exercise. You can see in our list that suffix means *characterized by*. So, another definition for our word would be *a system characterized by belief in wealth*. That's **CAPITALISM**. If we fill in the blanks on step five with these two suffixes, we'll build that word to fit the definition we are given."

COMPLETE THE ACTIVITY

Let students work in pairs (optionally) and tell them to use the same strategy to find the correct prefixes and suffixes for the words listed. These activities can be quite challenging!

DISCUSS After a few minutes, review the answers as a class. Ask if there were any difficulties. Listen to any problems and have volunteers solve the difficulties by explaining key clues in the given definitions. As needed, follow the focus word approach that you see modeled on the next page.

SAB Pg 179

Stair Steps

Fill in the missing letters of each 'capit, cep, cip, cipit' word by using the definitions below.
'capit, cep, cip, cipit' means head; chief; wealth

1.	t	r	i	c	e	p			
2.	c	a	p	i	t	a	l		
3.	c	a	p	i	t	a	l	s	
4.	p	r	i	n	c	i	p	a	l
5.	c	a	p	i	t	a	l	i	s	m
6.	p	r	i	n	c	i	p	a	l	l	y
7.	d	e	c	a	p	i	t	a	t	i	o	n
8.	p	r	e	c	i	p	i	t	a	t	i	o	n
9.	c	a	p	i	t	a	l	i	z	a	t	i	o	n

1. something three-headed; a three massed muscle at the back of the arm
2. the head seat of government; wealth; upper-case letter
3. the head seats of government; upper-case letters
4. the head of or first among; major item; the person in charge
5. belief based on wealth, originally heads of cattle; economic system advocating a free flow of wealth
6. mainly or chiefly
7. the act of cutting off the head
8. falling head-first; falling, as rain or snow from the sky
9. act of making the head letter of a word big; act of making an upper-case letter

Day ③ Extend the Learning

Focus Word: **TRICEP** ➝ Write this word on the board.

TEACH

Sample leading question:	"Who knows where there's a muscle called a **tricep**?"
Student:	"It's in the back of the arm."
Teacher:	"I wonder why it's called a **tricep**?"
Student:	"*Three heads*? That's weird."
Student:	"I think it's attached at three points."
Student:	"Why heads?"
Teacher:	"I'm not sure. Let's see if we can find a picture that will show us."

DISCUSS AND DEMONSTRATE Find a chart that illustrates muscles and determine the three heads that name the muscle **triceps**. Inform students that the muscle is properly called **triceps**, but through **back-formation** (see Fun Facts above), the supposed plural **triceps** was "singularized" to **tricep**.

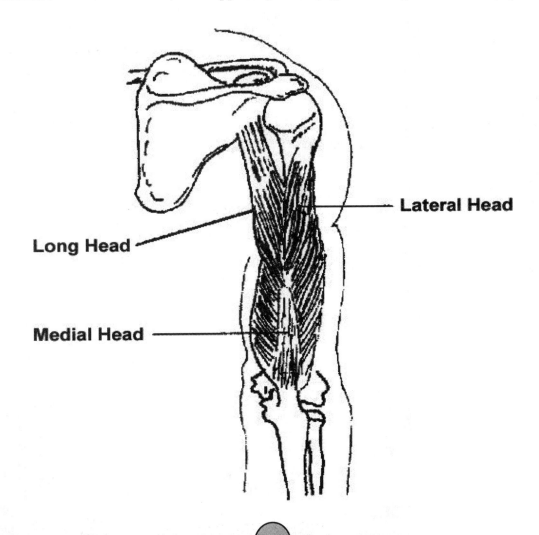

Lateral Head

Long Head

Medial Head

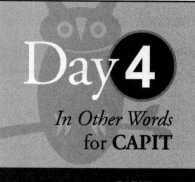

Day 4

In Other Words for **CAPIT**

CAPIT means head, chief, wealth

LESSON TIME

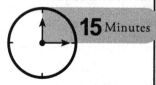

15 Minutes

OBJECTIVES

- **Understand** the meaning of the root **CAPIT**
- **Reinforce** knowledge of the root **CAPIT**
- **Understand** the meaning of words in the **CAPIT** family
- **Apply** knowledge of words in the **CAPIT** family

MATERIALS

- Student Activity Book
- **CAPIT** Word Wall
- Dictionary *(print or on-line)*

In Other Words for **CAPIT**

TEACH Have students turn to page 180 in their Student Activity Books. Explain that they are going to read a little story that uses some surprising and sometimes odd phrasing. The underlined words or phrases in the story are actually definitions or synonyms for words in the **CAPIT** family. Then they will see sentences about the story, each containing a blank.

Using context clues in the sentences, they will find a **CAPIT** family word in the Word Bank at the bottom to fit in each blank. Have a student read aloud the opening sentence or sentences of the story that contain the first underlined phrase. Then say, "Let's look at the first numbered sentence that contains a blank to be filled in. Clues in the sentence tell us that we want a describing word, an adjective that is a synonym for *main city* and which could modify city. I see the word **capital** at the bottom of the page. The suffix -**al** means *characterized by*. Wouldn't a city that was the main city in a state be called the **capital**? That all seems to fit, so let's write **capital** in the blank for the first sentence."

COMPLETE THE ACTIVITY

This can be quite challenging, so allow students to work on this activity in small groups. Not every word in the Word Bank will be used.

DISCUSS After about 10 minutes, ask if there were any difficulties. Have volunteers explain strategies they used that led to correct answers.

SAB
Pg 180

The Peasants Stage a Revolution

The starving peasants stormed into the country's <u>main city</u> and <u>chiefly</u> demanded that the cruel queen come to speak to them. She simply laughed at their demand and refused <u>to bow her head in defeat</u>. The <u>chief head</u> of the rebels stood up, flexed his <u>two-headed arm muscles</u>, and demanded that they <u>cut the head off</u> of the queen.

There was a hush for a moment, but then the leader <u>called out the main points again</u> and reminded them of their misery. His words caused a noisy riot to <u>fall head-first</u>, and the peasants rushed <u>head-long</u> into the palace, held a quick trial, and <u>cut off her head</u> and the heads of many of her attendants.

<u>Fill in the blanks below using words from the "capit, cep, cip, cipit" family.</u>

1. The queen resided in the <u>capital</u> city of her country.
2. The people wanted foremost and <u>principally</u> that the queen speak to them.
3. The proud queen refused to <u>capitulate</u> to their demand.
4. The <u>principal</u> leader of the rebellion was good at urging on the crowd.
5. The flexing of his <u>biceps</u> became a symbol of power for the people.
6. The bold call to <u>decapitate</u> the queen caused shock at first in the mob.
7. The leader <u>recapitulated</u> the reasons they had come and pulled the mob out of their silence.
8. His reminders of their misery <u>precipitated</u> a loud riot.
9. The peasants ran boldly and <u>precipitously</u> into the palace.
10. In a short while, the queen and many others were <u>decapitated</u>.

<u>Not Used:</u>   capitalizing   capitalism

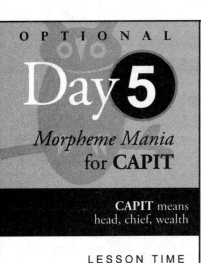

O P T I O N A L

Day 5

Morpheme Mania
for **CAPIT**

CAPIT means
head, chief, wealth

LESSON TIME

15 Minutes

OBJECTIVES

- **Build** words in the **CAPIT** family

- **Apply** knowledge of synonyms and antonyms to **CAPIT** words

Optional Morpheme Mania for **CAPIT**

On page 181 of their Activity Book, students will see an optional vocabulary enrichment activity that they can work on in groups, time permitting. This activity makes a great review for the formal assessment on the next page.

All the affixes presented in the week's activities are provided at the top of the page on either side of the root of the week in all its forms. Students can write in up to 13 of the words they built during the week, possibly discovering additional ones.

Then students can brainstorm with each other to come up with antonyms and synonyms they may know. Starter examples are given with every Morpheme Mania in the Activity Book. Because antonyms and synonyms may require knowledge of roots which students have not yet studied, completion of this activity is not crucial. Simply remind students that they can at any time during the course of the year revisit any of their Morpheme Mania pages and add words, antonyms, and synonyms as their vocabulary grows.

Day 5 Assessment

Make and hand out copies.
The answer key is on page A-6.
The instructions are on page A-2.

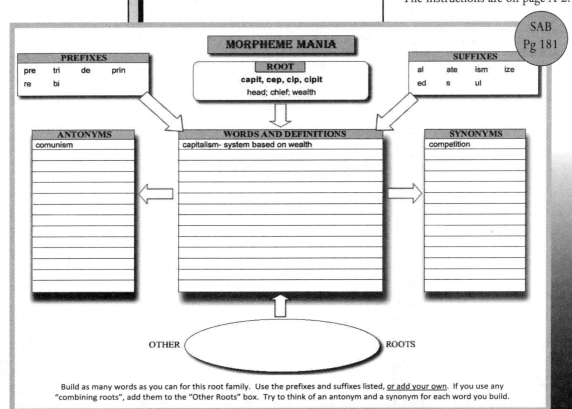

SAB
Pg 181

MORPHEME MANIA

PREFIXES			
pre	tri	de	prin
re	bi		

ROOT

capit, cep, cip, cipit

head; chief; wealth

SUFFIXES			
al	ate	ism	ize
ed	s	ul	

ANTONYMS
comunism

WORDS AND DEFINITIONS

capitalism- system based on wealth

SYNONYMS
competition

OTHER ⬭ ROOTS

Build as many words as you can for this root family. Use the prefixes and suffixes listed, <u>or add your own</u>. If you use any "combining roots", add them to the "Other Roots" box. Try to think of an antonym and a synonym for each word you build.

bicep   something two-headed; a muscle with two masses

biceps   things two-headed; muscles with two masses

capital   first-rate or head; wealth; upper-case letter

capitalism   belief based on wealth, originally heads of cattle; economic system advocating a free flow of wealth

capitalist   a person whose focus is on wealth

capitalists   people whose focus is on wealth

capitalization   act of making the head letter of a word big; act of making an upper-case letter

capitalizations   acts of making the head letter of a word big; acts of making an upper-case letter

capitalize   to make the head or first letter of a word big; to make an upper-case letter

capitalized   made the head or first letter of a word big; made an upper-case letter

capitalizes   makes the head or first letter of a word big; makes an upper-case letter

capitalizing   making the head or first letter of a word big; making an upper-case letter

capitals   the head seats of government; upper-case letters

capitulate   to bow one's head in defeat; to give up or surrender

capitulated   bowed one's head in defeat; gave up or surrendered

capitulates   bows the head in defeat; gives up or surrenders

capitulating   bowing one's head in defeat; giving up or surrendering

capitulation   the act of bowing one's head in defeat; the act giving up or surrendering

capitulations   acts of bowing one's head in defeat; acts of giving up or surrendering

decapitate   to cut off the head

decapitated   cut off the head

decapitates   cuts off the head

decapitating   cutting off the head

decapitation   the act of cutting off the head

precipitate   to fall head-first; to fall, as rain or snow

precipitated   fell head-first; fell, as rain or snow

precipitates falls head-first; falls as rain or snow

precipitating   falling head-first; falling, as rain or snow

precipitation   act or process of falling head-first; a type of weather falling from the sky

precipitations   acts or processes of falling head-first; types of weather falling from the sky

recapitulate   to tell the head or main points again

recapitulated   told the head or main points again

recapitulates   tells the head or main points again

recapitulation   the act of telling the head or main points again

recapitulations   acts of telling the head or main points again

tricep   something three-headed; a three-massed muscle at the back of the arm

triceps   things three-headed; three-massed muscles at the backs of the arms

Check-Up for **CAPIT**   Name _____

____ **1.** **CAPIT**, **CEP**, or **CIPIT** in words like **capital**, **biceps**, and **tricipital** means:

    A to take or keep

    B head or chief

    C to demand or call out for

____ **2.** What is the meaning of the word **capital**?

    A first-rate or main

    B the process of taking and keeping

    C relating to calling forth

____ **3.** What is the meaning of the word **capitulate**?

    A people concerned with wealth

    B a small letter

    C to bow the head in defeat

____ **4.** What is the meaning of the word **recapitulation**?

    A the act of telling the main points again

    B to give in again

    C relating to keeping important papers

____ **5.** What is the meaning of the word **precipitate**?

    A to keep to the left

    B to fall head-first

    C the act of calling forth

____ **6.** Which word means **to take away the head**?

    A decapitate

    B principate

    C recapitulate

____ **7.** Which word means **to make wealth from**?

    A capitalization

    B capitalize

    C capitalist

____ **8.** Which word means **three-headed**?

    A tricipital

    B tricyclics

    C trichologist

____ **9.** The Roundhead Party became the **decapitators** of King Charles. The Roundheads:

    A called for King Charles to keep the law

    B made King Charles the head of the government

    C cut off the head of King Charles

____ **10.** Bones described as **sincipital** and **occipital** are found in the:

    A finger

    B foot

    C head

GENER

meaning "family, creation, birth, sort"

OBJECTIVES

- **Understand** the meaning of the root **GENER**
- **Build** words in the root **GENER** family
- **Break Apart** words in the root **GENER** family
- **Understand** the meaning of words in the **GENER** family
- **Understand** the spelling principles applied to the root **GENER**
- **Apply** knowledge of words in the **GENER** family
- **Assess** and **Reinforce** knowledge of words in the **GENER** family

MATERIALS

- Student Activity Books, pages 183-188
- Dictionary *(print or on-line)*

CROSS-CURRICULAR EXAMPLES

Science:
   regenerate, genera, degenerate

Social Studies:
   generation, general

Language Arts:
   generalize, generosity

Math:
   generalities, generically

genera
families or sorts

generators
devices or people that **create**

generation
the process of giving **birth** to

generic
of the same **sort**

Morpheme: **GENER**
Allomorphs: **none**

Over 100 words containing the morpheme **GENER** are current in English. During this unit, tell students to be alert for this root in their school texts, general reading, and oral language they hear. Some of the words they might encounter in their school subjects are listed on the left under Cross-Curricular Examples.

UNIT AT A GLANCE

Day ① *Root Squares* for **GENER**

Day ② *Magic Squares* for **GENER**

Day ③ *Stair Steps* for **GENER**

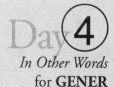
OPTIONAL
Day ④ *In Other Words* for **GENER**

Day ⑤ *Assessment or Morpheme Mania* for **GENER**

Each activity should take approximately **15 minutes**.

Word Fun Facts

This morpheme is a rich and prolific variation of a root meaning *birth or beginning*, as in **gene**, **genus**, and **genesis**.

The military title **general** comes from a Latin phrase, *dux generalis* or *caput generalis*, an overall leader. The phrase was shortened simply to its adjective, which came to be used as a noun in the context of, "Washington was the **general** of the army."

A **general** purpose vehicle was called a G.P. From the letters G.P. evolved the word Jeep.

A **genus** is a class of things that are similar in origin. The plural of **genus** is **genera**, just as the plural of **opus** is **opera**.

Anything **generic** is considered *a basic member of a large family or sort*, rather than something specific.

Students exploring this morpheme will come upon words like **generous** and **generosity**. These words originally had to do with *being of good and noble birth*. Along with being of noble birth came an obligation to care about others less fortunate.

Word Alert!

No alerts! All words in English with the letter sequence **g-e-n-e-r** belong to this root family.

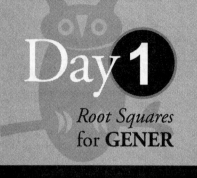

Day 1

Root Squares for **GENER**

GENER means
family, creation, birth, sort

LESSON TIME

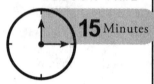

15 Minutes

OBJECTIVES

- **Understand** the meaning of the root **GENER**

- **Build** words in the **GENER** family

- **Understand** the meaning of words in the **GENER** family

- **Understand** the spelling principles applied to the root **GENER**

MATERIALS

- Student Activity Book

- **GENER** Word Wall

- Dictionary *(print or on-line)*

DIFFERENTIATING INSTRUCTION

If you prefer easier or more difficult activities, use your personal account at www.dynamicliteracy.com to access novice or expert versions, along with ideas on using them.

Root Squares for **GENER**

TEACH Have students turn to page 183 in their Activity Books. Say, "All of the prefixes and suffixes in the squares surrounding the shaded center are probably familiar, but if you have questions about any of the meanings, simply ask or look them up in the list inside the front and back cover of the activity book."

Call attention to the center box. Point out that the root **GENER** has only one spelling, which does not stand alone as a word. It will always need a prefix or suffix attached in order to become part of a word. Suggest that students start their list with **gener**, adding the suffix **-al**, meaning *characterized by*, to build **general**, meaning *characterized as being of a sort*. Use this word to guide students to the idea of *family, creation, birth, or sort*.

Root Squares

How many words can you make?

Start in any square. Your goal is to combine two or more word parts to make as many words in the 'gener' family as you can. Write each word and a definition you can think of for it in the space provided at the bottom of the page. Use the back of the page if you need to.

ate	al	de
ic	**gener**	ize
re	ion	ous

_____
_____
_____
_____
_____
_____
_____
_____
_____
_____

COMPLETE THE ACTIVITY

Have students follow the directions for the Root Squares activity for **GENER** on page 183 to build words. If students have difficulty building words with the Root Squares, show them how by modeling the matrix approach found on the next page, taking one affix at a time and seeing if it will connect with any one of the allomorphs of the root.

DISCUSS After five minutes, have volunteers write some of their words on the board. Focus with the class on the words they have built and guide them in a discussion of how the meaning of the root is still *family, creation, birth, sort*, even when prefixes and suffixes are added.

Watch for target words that most easily demonstrate the meaning of *family, creation, birth, sort*. If the word **generic** is not present, ask the class, "Can anyone try to use the suffix **-ic**?" and then continue on to the target word discussion on the next page.

SAB
Pg 183

Focus Word: **GENERIC** ➡ Write this word on the board.

TEACH

Lead with this:	"What are you buying if you get the **generic** brand of a product?"
Students:	"It's not a famous brand name."
Teacher:	"It's just plain old."
Student:	"It's usually cheaper."
Teacher:	"All right, now let's see why all those observations are good ones."
Student:	"The root **gener** is there, and a suffix **-ic**."
Student:	"And that suffix means *like or belonging to*."
Student:	"So *like a family, like a sort?*"
Student:	"Yes—nothing individual or special, just plain old, as somebody said."

DISCUSS Let students in small groups think of what items appear in a **generic** form. (prescription medicines, cola, bread, etc.) Lead students to see that **generic** is technically the opposite of **specific** (some students may know the terms **genus** and **species**).

DEMONSTRATE Find a picture on the internet of a **generic** dog or cat, and then a picture of a very specialized breed.

Root Squares Matrix

You can refer to this matrix to guide students in this activity. Students could build at least these 12 words. ***It is not important how many words are built***, so long as students understand the meanings of the root and its affixes. Encourage discussion about the definitions of any words formed for the blank slots as well as for the attested words.

	no prefix	de-	re-
-al	general		
-ate	generate	degenerate	regenerate
-ic	generic		
-at(e) + -ion	generation	degeneration	regeneration
-ous	generous	degenerous	
-al + -ize	generalize		
-al + -iz(e) + -at(e) + -ion	generalization		

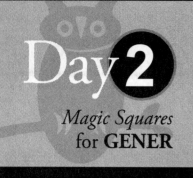

Day 2

Magic Squares
for **GENER**

GENER means
family, creation, birth, sort

LESSON TIME

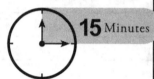

15 Minutes

OBJECTIVES

- **Understand** the meaning of the root **GENER**

- **Break Apart** words in the **GENER** family

- **Understand** the meanings of words in the **GENER** family

MATERIALS

- Student Activity Book
- **GENER** Word Wall
- Dictionary
  (print or on-line)

DIFFERENTIATING INSTRUCTION

If you prefer easier or more difficult activities, use your personal account at www.dynamicliteracy.com to access novice or expert versions, along with ideas on using them.

Break Apart Words with **GENER**

Have students turn to the Magic Squares on page 184 in their Student Activity Books. Model a Think-Aloud strategy for students: "I know that **GENER** means *family, creation, birth, sort.* I can use this knowledge to find the definition of a word with **GENER** as its root."

Direct students to word I, **regenerate**. Say, "This word has a prefix, **re-** meaning *again, back or against* and a suffix **-ate** that means *to cause to become.* Look at definition 3, *to produce one of the same sort again.* That reflects the meanings of the root, **GENER**, the prefix, **re-**, meaning *again*, and the suffix **-ate**, which we can take to

mean *to produce.* So let's write the number 3 in square I."

COMPLETE THE ACTIVITY

Ask students to use the same strategy to find the correct definitions for the other words. Tell them to write the number of the definition in the box that matches the letter for the word. Remind them that if all their answers are correct, each row and each column will add up to the same Magic number.

DISCUSS After five minutes, ask if there are any difficulties about matching the words and definitions. If there are, ask volunteers to explain clues in the definitions that will lead to the correct choice of word. As needed, follow the focus word approach for **generator** that you see modeled on the next page.

Add any new words to the classroom **GENER** Word Wall and remind students to add these words to the **GENER** Word Wall in their Activity Books.

SAB Pg 184

Magic Squares

Select the best answer for each of the words in the 'gener' family from the numbered definitions. Put the number in the proper space in the Magic Square box. If the total of the numbers is the same both across and down, you have found the magic number!

'gener' means family, creation, birth, or sort

WORDS	DEFINITIONS
A. degenerating	1. process of declining into a less desirable sort; act or process of deteriorating
B. generality	
C. generational	2. statement involving most members of a group; a commonality
D. regeneration	3. to produce one of the same sort again
E. generator	4. act or process of producing one of the same sort again
F. generosity	5. of the same sort; without a brand name
G. generic	6. a device or person that creates
H. generous	7. belonging by birth to one group
I. regenerate	8. quality of being of good family or breeding; quality of giving to others freely
	9. declining into a less desirable sort; deteriorating
	10. of good family or breeding; giving freely

Magic Square Box

A. 9	B. 2	C. 7
D. 4	E. 6	F. 8
G. 5	H. 10	I. 3

Magic Number __18__

*** ANSWER KEY ***

MINI-LESSON: the Suffix -os

The partial suffix **-os** is a variation of **-ous**. When an additional suffix is attached after the suffix **-ous**, the pronunciation and spelling are altered. Let students experiment with any of the following pairs of words, noticing the effects on pronunciation and spelling of the final suffix **-ity**:

curious	religious	virtuous	sensuous	strenuous
curiosity	religiosity	virtuosity	sensuosity	strenuosity

MINI-LESSON: the Suffix -a

The suffix **-a** is a plural marker that was the way Latin made the plural of words that end in **-um**. Words in modern scientific English that end in the morpheme **-um** are mostly unchanged Latin words, and their technical plurals end in the suffix **-a**. As the English language continues to change, the standard English plural suffix **-s** is beginning to be seen alongside the more historical **-a**.

agendum, something that needs to be done
agenda, things that need to be done

memorandum, something that needs to be remembered
memoranda, things that need to be remembered

curriculum, the plan of a course
curricula, plans for courses

one **bacterium**
two **bacteria**

Focus Word: GENERATOR ⟶ Write this word on the board.

TEACH

Sample leading statement:	"This word can be used in many ways and in lots of topics. Let's see what it means deep down."
Student:	"It has three pieces of meaning!"
Student:	"The root is there, **gener**, and that leaves **-ate** with the **e** dropped and **-or**."
Teacher:	"Why does the **e** of **-ate** drop?"
Student:	"Because the suffix attached to it starts with a vowel."
Teacher:	"Good. Now, what do **-ate** and **-or** mean?"
Student:	"The **-or** ending is *a thing or person that does some action*."
Student:	"And the action being done here is **generating**—a **generator generates**."
Student:	"And the **-ate** means *cause to become*."
Student:	"So the word means a thing or person that causes something to become a type of something? A family?"
Student:	"How about just *creates or gives birth*?"
Student:	"Sure, that will work."

DISCUSS After they have been led to see the meanings of the pieces of the word **generator**, let students discuss applications of the word in their experience. Mechanically-inclined students will bring up a car **generator**, and some students may have heard of hospital- or home-**generators** of electricity.

Day 3

Stair Steps for GENER

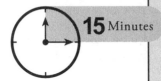

GENER means
family, creation, birth, sort

LESSON TIME

15 Minutes

OBJECTIVES

- **Understand** the meaning of the root **GENER**

- **Apply** knowledge of the root **GENER**

- **Break Apart** words in the **GENER** family

- **Understand** the meaning of words in the **GENER** family

- **Understand** the spelling principles applied to the root **GENER**

MATERIALS

- Student Activity Book
- **GENER** Word Wall

DIFFERENTIATING INSTRUCTION

If you prefer easier or more difficult activities, use your personal account at www.dynamicliteracy.com to access novice or expert versions, along with ideas on using them.

Apply Knowledge of GENER

TEACH Have students turn to page 185 in their Student Activity Books. Explain that the boxes in front of and after the root indicate letters that spell out prefixes and suffixes. Students will spell out the correct prefixes and suffixes determined by clues in the definitions at the bottom of the page.

Have a volunteer read definition number two at the bottom of the page. Say, "To build this word will require a suffix making a verb with the meaning *to produce one of the same.* Look at the three-letter suffix **-ate** and think about its definition *to cause to become.* If we attach that suffix to the root

we are shown, we get **GENERATE**. That fits our definition quite well, so write in the letters **a-t-e** on step two."

COMPLETE THE ACTIVITY
Let students work in pairs (optionally) and tell them to use the same strategy to find the correct prefixes and suffixes for the words listed. These activities can be quite challenging!

DISCUSS After a few minutes, review the answers as a class. Ask if there were any difficulties. Listen to any problems and have volunteers solve the difficulties by explaining key clues in the given definitions. As needed, follow the focus word approach that you see modeled on the next page.

SAB
Pg 185

Stair Steps

Fill in the missing letters of each 'gener' word by using the definitions below.
'gener' means family, creation, birth, or sort

1.	g	e	n	e	r	a	l			
2.	g	e	n	e	r	a	t	e		
3.	g	e	n	e	r	a	l	l	y	
4.	g	e	n	e	r	o	u	s	l	y
5.	r	e	g	e	n	e	r	a	t	e	d
6.	g	e	n	e	r	a	l	i	z	i	n	g
7.	d	e	g	e	n	e	r	a	t	i	o	n	s
8.	g	e	n	e	r	a	l	i	z	a	t	i	o	n

1. relating to many members of a group or family
2. to produce one of the same sort
3. in a manner relating to many members of a group; as a rule
4. as from of "good" family or breeding; in a manner giving freely
5. produced one of the same sort again
6. simplifying into one group or sort
7. processes of declining into a less desirable sort; acts or processes of deteriorating
8. an act of simplifying into one group or sort

Focus Word: **GENERAL** ➡ Write this word on the board.

TEACH

Sample leading question:	"Take a look at this word. What's going on here?"
Student:	"The root we're working on and the suffix **-al**."
Teacher:	"So that means…?"
Student:	*"Like or relating to?"*
Teacher:	"Yes, that's fine. *Characterized by, having the nature of,* anything of that sort."
Student:	"How is **general** different from **generic**?"
Teacher:	"Well, that's a good discussion question for the class. Let's do it."

DISCUSS   Let groups of students list situations in which they think the word **generic** would be appropriate, and those in which **general** would fit. For example, an officer called a **generic** would not be appropriate.

Definitely not a **generic General**!

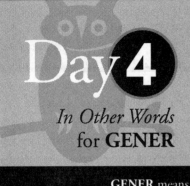

Day 4

In Other Words
for **GENER**

GENER means
family, creation, birth, sort

LESSON TIME

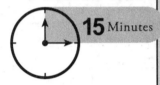

15 Minutes

OBJECTIVES

- **Understand** the meaning of the root **GENER**

- **Reinforce** knowledge of the root **GENER**

- **Understand** the meaning of words in the **GENER** family

- **Apply** knowledge of words in the **GENER** family

MATERIALS

- Student Activity Book

- **GENER** Word Wall

- Dictionary *(print or on-line)*

In Other Words for **GENER**

TEACH Have students turn to page 186 in their Student Activity Books. Explain that they are going to read a little story that uses some surprising and sometimes odd phrasing. The underlined words or phrases in the story are actually definitions or synonyms for words in the **GENER** family. Then they will see sentences about the story, each containing a blank. Using context clues in the sentences, they will find a **GENER** family word in the Word Bank at the bottom to fit in each blank. Have a student read aloud the opening sentence or sentences of the story that contain the first underlined phrase. Then say, "Let's look at the first numbered sentence that contains a blank to be filled in. Clues in the sentence tell us that we want a naming word, a noun that is a synonym for *group born in the same era*. I see the word **generation** at the bottom of the page. The suffix -**at** is a form of -**ate** which would be the ending of **generate**, a verb meaning *to create*, and the suffix -**ion** makes the word a noun, meaning *that which is created*. That's the sense of *group born in the same era*, so let's write **generation** in the blank for the first sentence."

COMPLETE THE ACTIVITY

This can be quite challenging, so allow students to work on this activity in small groups. Not every word in the Word Bank will be used.

DISCUSS After about 10 minutes, ask if there were any difficulties. Have volunteers explain strategies they used that led to correct answers.

SAB
Pg 186

Nothing Really New

Every new group born in the same era seems to go through the same process. We are in our early years as a rule under the guidance of parents, but at some point in childhood we try to be different from them. The search for something new produces a sense that the previous values belonging by birth to one group are too old-fashioned. The parents see this as a process of declining to a less desirable sort, with unfamiliar sorts of music, clothing, and even language.

In time, the new takes the place of the old, and the same cycle begins all over. A new group is born and the search for the new and shocking is produced again. The new and shocking then becomes the standard of the same sort. Do you think it's too much of an act of simplifying into one sort to say that all the groups born in the same era have more in common with each other than they have differences?

Fill in the blanks below using words from the "gener" family.

1. It appears that every <u>generation</u> goes through the same experiences.

2. <u>Generally</u> speaking, young people try to be different from their parents.

3. Peer pressure <u>generates</u> a search for new values.

4. The <u>generational</u> values seem old-fashioned to newcomers.

5. Parents often consider new values a <u>degeneration</u> from what theirs are.

6. The new types or <u>genera</u> of music, clothes, and language may disturb parents.

7. This cycle is <u>regenerated</u> over and over.

8. <u>Generic</u> standards last for just a short while.

9. It may not be too much of a <u>generalization</u> to say that all groups are the same.

10. All <u>generations</u> seem to have at least one common experience.

<u>Not Used:</u>   generosity   generalists

OPTIONAL

Day 5

Morpheme Mania
for **GENER**

GENER means
family, creation, birth, sort

LESSON TIME

15 Minutes

OBJECTIVES

- **Build** words in the **GENER** family

- **Apply** knowledge of synonyms and antonyms to **GENER** words

Optional Morpheme Mania for **GENER**

On page 187 of their Activity Book, students will see an optional vocabulary enrichment activity that they can work on in groups, time permitting. This activity makes a great review for the formal assessment on the next page.

All the affixes presented in the week's activities are provided at the top of the page on either side of the root of the week in all its forms. Students can write in up to 13 of the words they built during the week, possibly discovering additional ones.

Then students can brainstorm with each other to come up with antonyms and synonyms they may know. Starter examples are given with every Morpheme Mania in the Activity Book. Because antonyms and synonyms may require knowledge of roots which students have not yet studied, completion of this activity is not crucial. Simply remind students that they can at any time during the course of the year revisit any of their Morpheme Mania pages and add words, antonyms, and synonyms as their vocabulary grows.

Day 5 *Assessment*

Make and hand out copies.
The answer key is on page A-6.
The instructions are on page A-2.

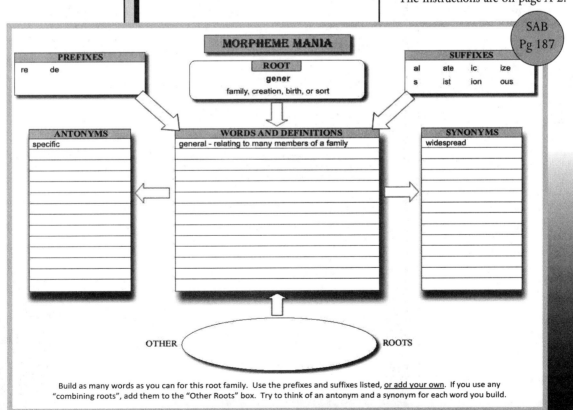

SAB
Pg 187

MORPHEME MANIA

PREFIXES			
re	de		

ROOT
gener
family, creation, birth, or sort

SUFFIXES			
al	ate	ic	ize
s	ist	ion	ous

ANTONYMS
specific

WORDS AND DEFINITIONS
general - relating to many members of a family

SYNONYMS
widespread

OTHER   ROOTS

Build as many words as you can for this root family. Use the prefixes and suffixes listed, <u>or add your own</u>. If you use any "combining roots", add them to the "Other Roots" box. Try to think of an antonym and a synonym for each word you build.

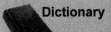

degenerate to decline into a less desirable sort; to deteriorate

degenerated declined into a less desirable sort; deteriorated

degenerately so as to decline into a less desirable sort; in a deteriorating manner

degenerates declines into a less desirable sort; deteriorates

degenerating declining into a less desirable sort; deteriorating

degeneration process of declining into a less desirable sort; act or process of deteriorating

degenerations processes of declining into a less desirable sort; acts or processes of deteriorating

genera families or sorts; groups

general relating to many members of a group or family

generalist a person with broad knowledge of many groups

generalists people with broad knowledge of many groups

generalities statements involving most members of groups

generality statement involving most members of a group; a commonality

generalization an act of simplifying into one group or sort

generalizations acts of simplifying into one group or sort

generalize to simplify into one group or sort

generalized simplified into one group or sort

generalizes simplifies into one group or sort

generalizing simplifying into one group or sort

generally in a manner relating to many members of a group; as a rule

generate to produce one of the same sort

generated produced one of the same sort

generates produces one of the same sort

generating producing one of the same sort

generation the process of creating or giving birth to

generational belonging by birth to one group

generations groups born in the same era

generator a device or person that creates

generators devices or people that create

generic of the same sort; without a brand name

generical of the same sort; without a brand name

generically in a manner being of the same sort

generosities qualities of being of good family or breeding; qualities of giving to others freely

generosity quality of being of good family or breeding; quality of giving to others freely

generous of good family or breeding; giving freely

generously as from of good family or breeding; in a manner giving freely

regenerate to produce one of the same sort again

regenerated produced one of the same sort again

regenerates produces one of the same sort again

regenerating producing one of the same sort again

regeneration act or process of producing one of the same sort again

Check-Up for **GENER**   Name _____

_____ **1.** **GENER** in words like **generic** and **generation** means:

   A step or go

   B chart

   C family or sort

_____ **2.** What is the meaning of the word **generic**?

   A with a passageway charted

   B to be born

   C of the same sort

_____ **3.** What is the meaning of the word **generation**?

   A a group born in the same era

   B the act of planning a chart

   C the process of moving across the country

_____ **4.** What is the meaning of the word **generalize**?

   A to chart the progress of

   B to simplify into one group

   C to go from one place to another

_____ **5.** What is the meaning of the word **genera**?

   A to make new charts

   B kind and respectful

   C familes or groups

_____ **6.** Which word means **to decline to a less desirable sort**?

   A degenerate

   B nongeneric

   C degenerous

_____ **7.** Which word means **to produce one of the same sort again**?

   A regenerative

   B regenerate

   C regenerator

_____ **8.** Which word means **relating to many members of a group or family**?

   A general

   B generality

   C generalist

_____ **9.** Dancing in Greece is **transgenerational**. That means:

   A only a small group still dances

   B dancing has died out and no one does it anymore

   C older and younger members of the group dance together

_____ **10.** Someone with a **neurodegenerative** condition has nerves that are:

   A powerful and strong

   B not working as well as they once did

   C able to make new ones

OBJECTIVES

- **Understand** the meaning of the root **FLEX**

- **Build** words in the root **FLEX** family

- **Break Apart** words in the root **FLEX** family

- **Understand** the meaning of words in the **FLEX** family

- **Understand** the spelling principles applied to the root **FLEX**

- **Apply** knowledge of words in the **FLEX** family

- **Assess** and **Reinforce** knowledge of words in the **FLEX** family

MATERIALS

- Student Activity Books, pages 189-194

- Dictionary *(print or on-line)*

- (optional) a mirror, magnifying glass, aluminum foil, or some shiny surface

- (optional) a pencil and a piece of pipe cleaner

CROSS-CURRICULAR EXAMPLES

Science:
  reflection, deflector, flexors

Social Studies:
  flexibility

Language Arts:
  inflection, unreflective, reflectively

Math:
  flection, reflex

FLEX

meaning "to bend, turn, change direction"

flexes
bends

reflect
to bend or **turn** back

deflect
to bend away or **change direction**

Morpheme: **FLEX**
Allomorphs: **FLECT**

Over 100 words containing the morpheme **FLEX** or its allomorph are current in English. During this unit, tell students to be alert for this root in their school texts, general reading, and oral language they hear. Some of the words they might encounter in their school subjects are listed on the left under Cross-Curricular Examples.

UNIT AT A GLANCE

Day ①
Root Squares
for **FLEX**

Day ②
Magic Squares
for **FLEX**

Day ③
Stair Steps
for **FLEX**

OPTIONAL
Day ④
In Other Words
for **FLEX**

Day ⑤
Assessment or Morpheme Mania
for **FLEX**

Each activity should take approximately **15 minutes**.

The two allomorphs of this root are often interchangeable. Both **flexion** and **flection** occur as spellings of the same word, as do **reflexion** and **reflection**. The **flect** spellings are considered more standard in American English.

The word **inflection** can be used to mean stress or accent on a syllable, as to say the **inflection** is on the middle syllable in the word **infléction**. **Inflection** can determine meaning, as when we say **recórd** with the stress on the second syllable as opposed to saying it with the stress on the first syllable. Two distinct words emerge by bending or turning the pronunciation of the word.

Inflection can also refer to the *upward bend* of our voices when we ask a question. It is also a term for the listing of variations (changes or "bendings") that a word undergoes as it is used in different situations. These variations are extremely relevant to a study in morphemes, as some suffixes are actually indications of **inflection**, or change in usage. The **-s** for the *he, she, or it* form of verbs, for example, indicates an **inflection**, as do the **-ed** and **-ing** suffixes.

See if anyone in your class will **genuflect**, and if not, show your students the act with a curtsy, a courteous *bending of the knee*. Then let students derive the etymological meaning of the word **genuflect** from what they see.

This root provides a good opportunity to demonstrate to students the <u>**reflexive**</u> pronoun. Guide students to recognize reflexive pronouns by saying, "I see ___ in the mirror. You see ___ in the mirror. Bill sees ___ in the mirror. Cindy sees ___ in the mirror. Kelvin and Rona see ___ in the mirror. We see ___ in the mirror." These **-self** and **-selves** words are **reflexive** pronouns, in that they are objects renaming and *reflecting back* to the subject. If nothing is being **reflected**, then **reflexive** pronouns should not be used. For example, "Ron and myself went to town," is a misuse of the **reflexive**.

Word Alert!

No alerts. All English words with the letters sequences **f-l-e-x** or **f-l-e-c-t** belong to this root family.

Day 1

Root Squares for FLEX

FLEX means
to bend, turn, change direction

LESSON TIME

15 Minutes

OBJECTIVES

- **Understand** the meaning of the root **FLEX**

- **Build** words in the **FLEX** family

- **Understand** the meaning of words in the **FLEX** family

- **Understand** the spelling principles applied to the root **FLEX**

MATERIALS

- Student Activity Book

- **FLEX** Word Wall

- Dictionary *(print or on-line)*

- A mirror or magnifying glass or some shiny surface

DIFFERENTIATING INSTRUCTION

If you prefer easier or more difficult activities, use your personal account at www.dynamicliteracy.com to access novice or expert versions, along with ideas on using them.

Root Squares for FLEX

TEACH Have students turn to page 189 in their Activity Books. Say, "All of the prefixes and suffixes in the squares surrounding the shaded center are probably familiar, but if you have questions about any of the meanings, simply ask or look them up in the list inside the front and back cover of the activity book." Call attention to the center box. Point out that the root **FLEX** has two different spellings, called allomorphs. Ask students to decide if one of the forms they see in the middle square can stand alone as a word. They will see that **flex** is a word, and you can use that word to guide them to the meaning *bend, turn, or change direction.* Suggest that students start their list with **flex** and then continue their lists by adding to that word the suffix **-or**, meaning *person or device that does*, to

build **flexor**, meaning *one that serves to bend a limb or part.* Invite students to explore how this word is related to the idea of *bend, turn, or change direction.*

COMPLETE THE ACTIVITY

Have students follow the directions to build words. If students have difficulty building words with the Root Squares, show them how by modeling the matrix approach found on the next page, taking one affix at a time and seeing if it will connect with any one of the allomorphs of the root

DISCUSS After five minutes, have volunteers write some of their words on the board. Focus with the class on the words they have built and guide them in a discussion of how the meaning of the root is still *bend, turn, or change direction* even when prefixes and suffixes are added. Watch for target words that most easily demonstrate the meaning of *bend, turn, or change direction.* If the word **reflect** is not present, ask the class, "Can anyone try to use the prefix **re**-?" and then continue on to the target word discussion on the next page.

SAB
Pg 189

Root Squares

How many words can you make?

Start in any square. Your goal is to combine two or more word parts to make as many words in the 'flex, flect' family as you can. Write each word and a definition you can think of for it in the space provided at the bottom of the page. Use the back of the page if you need to.

ity	or	ive
de	flex, flect	in
re	ed	ibil

Focus Word: **REFLECT** ➡ Write this word on the board.

TEACH

Lead with this:	"Who can tell us what light rays do when they **reflect**?"
Student:	"They shine off something into your eyes."
Student:	"They give an image, like in a mirror."
Teacher:	"Right—let's get a better understanding of the word by looking at its pieces closely."
Student:	"There's the root spelled **flect**, and the prefix **re-**."
Student:	"So it means *bend again, turn again*."
Student:	"Try *bend back, turn back*."
Student:	"Yes, that's it—the light *bends or turns back*."

DISCUSS Let students discuss situations they know about in which the word **reflect** can be used. For example, they may bring up the idea of a person's behavior **reflecting** upon friends or family.

DEMONSTRATE Using a mirror, magnifying glass, sheet of aluminum foil, or any other shiny surface, show how beams from a light source **reflect** to wherever you aim them.

Root Squares Matrix

You can refer to this matrix to guide students in this activity. Students could build at least these 19 words. *It is not important how many words are built*, so long as students understand the meanings of the root and its affixes. Encourage discussion about the definitions of any words formed for the blank slots as well as for the attested words.

	no prefix	de-	in-	re-
-no suffix	flex		inflex	reflex
		deflect	inflect	reflect
-ed	flexed	deflected	inflected	reflected
			inflexed	reflexed
-ibil + -ity	flexibility		inflexibility	
-ive	flexive		inflexive	reflexive
				reflective
-iv(e) + -ity				reflectivity

Day 2

Magic Squares
for **FLEX**

FLEX means
to bend, turn, change direction

LESSON TIME

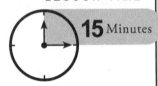

15 Minutes

OBJECTIVES

- **Understand** the meaning of the root **FLEX**

- **Break Apart** words in the **FLEX** family

- **Understand** the meanings of words in the **FLEX** family

MATERIALS

- Student Activity Book

- **FLEX** Word Wall

- Dictionary *(print or on-line)*

- (optional) a pencil and a piece of pipe cleaner

DIFFERENTIATING INSTRUCTION

If you prefer easier or more difficult activities, use your personal account at www.dynamicliteracy.com to access novice or expert versions, along with ideas on using them.

Break Apart Words with FLEX

Have students turn to the Magic Squares on page 190 in their Student Activity Books. Model a Think-Aloud strategy for students: "I know that **FLEX** means *to bend, turn,* or *change direction.* I can use this knowledge to find the definition of a word with **FLEX** or **FLECT** as its root."

Direct students to word G, **reflector**. Say, "This word has a prefix, **re-** meaning *again, back,* or *against* and a suffix **-or** that means *a person or device that does.* Look at definition 6, *a surface that bends or turns back; something that directs back light.* That "reflects" the meanings of the root, **FLECT**, the prefix, **re-**, meaning *back,* and the

suffix **-or**, *a device that does,* so let's write the number 6 in square G."

COMPLETE THE ACTIVITY

Ask students to use the same strategy to find the correct definitions for the other words. Tell them to write the number of the definition in the box that matches the letter for the word. Remind them that if all their answers are correct, each row and each column will add up to the same Magic number.

DISCUSS After five minutes, ask if there are any difficulties about matching the words and definitions. If there are, ask volunteers to explain clues in the definitions that will lead to the correct choice of word. As needed, follow the focus word approach for **flexibly** that you see modeled on the next page.

Add any new words to the classroom **FLEX** Word Wall and remind students to add these words to the **FLEX** Word Wall in their Activity Books.

SAB Pg 190

Magic Squares

Select the best answer for each of the words in the 'flex, flect' family from the numbered definitions. Put the number in the proper space in the Magic Square box. If the total of the numbers is the same both across and down, you have found the magic number!

'flex, flect' means to bend, turn, or change direction

WORDS	DEFINITIONS
A. deflected	1. quality of not being able to bend or change; rigidity
B. flex	2. related to bending or turning into; related to changing words into their other forms
C. flexibly	3. in a manner able to bend
D. inflectional	4. things bent or turned back; acts of glancing back at or pondering
E. reflexive	5. to bend; to bend a joint or contract a muscle
F. reflections	6. a surface that bends or turns back; something that directs back light
G. reflector	7. bent away; redirected
H. inflexibility	8. in a manner bent or turned back; so as to glance back at or ponder
I. reflectedly	9. turned back on itself; responded instinctively on itself

Magic Square Box

A. 7	B. 5	C. 3
D. 2	E. 9	F. 4
G. 6	H. 1	I. 8

Magic Number **15**

*** ANSWER KEY ***

Day ② Extend the Learning

Focus Word: **FLEXIBLY** ⟶ Write this word on the board.

TEACH

Sample leading question:	"Let's take a close look at this word, **flexibly**. How many morphemes?"
Student:	"Three—it has the **-ly** adverb suffix for the adjective **flexible**."
Student:	"Right, and **flexible** is made up of two pieces, our root and the suffix **-ible**, which is the same as **-able**."
Student:	"So if **flexible** means *able to bend or turn*, then **flexibly** means *in a manner of being able to bend or turn*."
Teacher:	"Great, and how might this word be used?"
Student:	"You could say pole-vaulters have to twist their bodies **flexibly**."
Student:	"Or people who can change their minds or see other viewpoints act **flexibly**."

DISCUSS Lead students to see that meaning of the word **flexibly** is the sum of the meanings of its morphemic pieces, *in a manner so as to be able to bend or change direction.*

DEMONSTRATE Hold up a pencil and demonstrate that it is not able to bend. Then hold up a piece of pipe cleaner and demonstrate that it can be moved **flexibly** as you bend and turn it into different directions.

Day 3

Stair Steps for **FLEX**

FLEX means to bend, turn, change direction

LESSON TIME

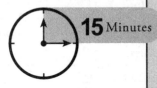

15 Minutes

OBJECTIVES

- **Understand** the meaning of the root **FLEX**

- **Apply** knowledge of the root **FLEX**

- **Break Apart** words in the **FLEX** family

- **Understand** the meaning of words in the **FLEX** family

- **Understand** the spelling principles applied to the root **FLEX**

MATERIALS

- Student Activity Book

- **FLEX** Word Wall

- (optional) a mirror, magnifying glass, aluminum foil, or some shiny surface

DIFFERENTIATING INSTRUCTION

If you prefer easier or more difficult activities, use your personal account at www.dynamicliteracy.com to access novice or expert versions, along with ideas on using them.

Apply Knowledge of **FLEX**

TEACH Have students turn to page 191 in their Student Activity Books. Explain that the boxes in front of and after the root indicate letters that spell out prefixes and suffixes. Students will spell out the correct prefixes and suffixes determined by clues in the definitions at the bottom of the page.

Have a volunteer read definition number three at the bottom of the page. Say, "Using the clues in the definition we are given, we can see that to build this word will require a two-letter prefix with the meaning *back* and a suffix indicating plural. The prefix **re**- will take care of the *back* and the plural will need to be -**es** rather than the simple -**s** because of the sound of the final letter **x** in **FLEX**. Try pronouncing the plural with each of these suffixes and observe the difference in the two endings. So what we have built is **REFLEXES**.

COMPLETE THE ACTIVITY

Let students work in pairs (optionally) and tell them to use the same strategy to find the correct prefixes and suffixes for the words listed. These activities can be quite challenging!

DISCUSS After a few minutes, review the answers as a class. Ask if there were any difficulties. Listen to any problems and have volunteers solve the difficulties by explaining key clues in the given definitions. As needed, follow the focus word approach that you see modeled on the next page.

SAB
Pg 191

Stair Steps

Fill in the missing letters of each 'flex, flect' word by using the definitions below.
'flex, flect' means head; chief; wealth

1. | f | l | e | x | e | d |
2. | r | e | f | l | e | c | t |
3. | r | e | f | l | e | x | e | s |
4. | r | e | f | l | e | x | i | v | e |
5. | d | e | f | l | e | c | t | o | r | s |
6. | f | l | e | x | i | b | i | l | i | t | y |
7. | i | n | f | l | e | c | t | i | o | n | a | l |
8. | f | l | e | x | i | b | i | l | i | t | i | e | s |
9. | i | n | f | l | e | c | t | i | o | n | a | l | l | y |

1. bent; bent a joint or tensed a muscle
2. to bend or turn back; to glance back at or ponder
3. acts of bending or turning back; acts of instinctively responding
4. turned back on itself; responded instinctively on itself
5. things that cause to bend away
6. quality of being able to bend
7. related to bending or turning into; related to changing words into their other forms
8. qualities of being able to bend
9. so as to bend or change into; so as to change words into their other forms

Focus Word: **DEFLECTORS** ⟶ Write this word on the board.

TEACH

Sample leading question:	"Look at this word, **deflectors**. How many morphemes?"
Student:	"Four!"
Student:	"It's a plural of a noun, **deflector**."
Student:	"And a deflector is somebody or something that **deflects**."
Teacher:	"It's great that you work out these words by looking at the last morphemes first."
Student:	"And **deflect** must mean *turn in reverse* or *down* or *away*."
Student:	"So where would you ever use a word like that?"
Student:	"I'll bet it's something that might keep you from being hit."
Student:	"Yes—it *turns away* something that might be thrown at you."
Student:	"Would a sun visor on a car be a **deflector**?"
Student:	"Sure—that's a good example."

DISCUSS Lead students to see that meaning of the word **deflectors** is the sum of the meanings of its morphemic pieces, *more than one device or person that bends or changes direction.*

DEMONSTRATE If you use a shiny surface to **reflect** light rays, have a student place a piece of paper in the way of the **reflection** to see the use of a **deflector**.

Day 4

In Other Words
for **FLEX**

FLEX means
to bend, turn, change direction

LESSON TIME

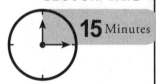

15 Minutes

OBJECTIVES

- **Understand** the meaning of the root **FLEX**

- **Reinforce** knowledge of the root **FLEX**

- **Understand** the meaning of words in the **FLEX** family

- **Apply** knowledge of words in the **FLEX** family

MATERIALS

- Student Activity Book

- **FLEX** Word Wall

- Dictionary *(print or on-line)*

In Other Words for **FLEX**

TEACH Have students turn to page 192 in their Student Activity Books. Explain that they are going to read a little story that uses some surprising and sometimes odd phrasing. The underlined words or phrases in the story are actually definitions or synonyms for words in the **FLEX** family. Then they will see sentences about the story, each containing a blank.

Using context clues in the sentences, they will find a **FLEX** family word in the Word Bank at the bottom to fit in each blank. Have a student read aloud the opening sentence or sentences of the story that contain the first underlined phrase. Then say, "Let's look at the first numbered sentence that contains a blank to be filled in. Clues in the sentence tell us that we want an action word, a verb that is a synonym for *glance back*. I see the word **reflect** at the bottom of the page. The root **flect** does not mean *glance* but it does mean *turn*. *To glance* might imply *to turn*. Let's write **reflect** in the blank space in the first sentence."

COMPLETE THE ACTIVITY

This can be quite challenging, so allow students to work on this activity in small groups. Not every word in the Word Bank will be used.

DISCUSS After about 10 minutes, ask if there were any difficulties. Have volunteers explain strategies they used that led to correct answers.

SAB
Pg 192

"Kneesworthy" Advice

Take care of your knees! Your knees take care of you. Just <u>glance back</u> for a moment on how much stress your knees take each day, with every step you take, especially if you are a runner. To keep your knees healthy, be sure to <u>bend</u> them often, so that they stay <u>bendable</u>.

Actually, what <u>bends</u> the knee or any joint is a muscle called a <u>thing that bends</u>. By exercising such muscles you avoid <u>the quality of not being able to bend</u> and pain in the joints. Check the <u>instinctive bending response</u> in your knees with a tap; good <u>quality of being able to bend</u> in your knees helps you run from a dangerous situation. If you run in the evenings, be sure to wear <u>things that bend light back</u> on your clothing so you can <u>redirect</u> traffic away from you.

<u>Fill in the blanks below using words from the "flex, flect" family.</u>

1. We should often <u>reflect</u> on how to maintain healthy bones and muscles.
2. You should <u>flex</u> your knees and elbows often to keep them limber.
3. <u>Flexible</u> joints tend to be pain-free.
4. A specific muscle <u>flexes</u> each joint.
5. A muscle that helps bend a joint is called a <u>flexor</u>.
6. <u>Inflexibility</u> in a joint causes swelling and pain.
7. Healthy knees have an automatic kicking <u>reflex</u> when they are tapped.
8. Joint <u>flexibility</u> can save your life.
9. Wear <u>reflectors</u> if you are walking or running after dark.
10. You want to be able to <u>deflect</u> traffic away from you.

<u>Not Used:</u>   reflections   reflexive

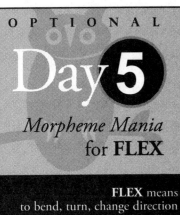

Day 5

Morpheme Mania
for **FLEX**

FLEX means
to bend, turn, change direction

LESSON TIME

15 Minutes

OBJECTIVES

- **Build** words in the
  FLEX family

- **Apply** knowledge of
  synonyms and antonyms
  to **FLEX** words

Optional Morpheme Mania for **FLEX**

On page 193 of their Activity Book, students will see an optional vocabulary enrichment activity that they can work on in groups, time permitting. This activity makes a great review for the formal assessment on the next page.

All the affixes presented in the week's activities are provided at the top of the page on either side of the root of the week in all its forms. Students can write in up to 13 of the words they built during the week, possibly discovering additional ones.

Then students can brainstorm with each other to come up with antonyms and synonyms they may know. Starter examples are given with every Morpheme Mania in the Activity Book. Because antonyms and synonyms may require knowledge of roots which students have not yet studied, completion of this activity is not crucial. Simply remind students that they can at any time during the course of the year revisit any of their Morpheme Mania pages and add words, antonyms, and synonyms as their vocabulary grows.

Day 5 *Assessment*

Make and hand out copies.
The answer key is on page A-6.
The instructions are on page A-2.

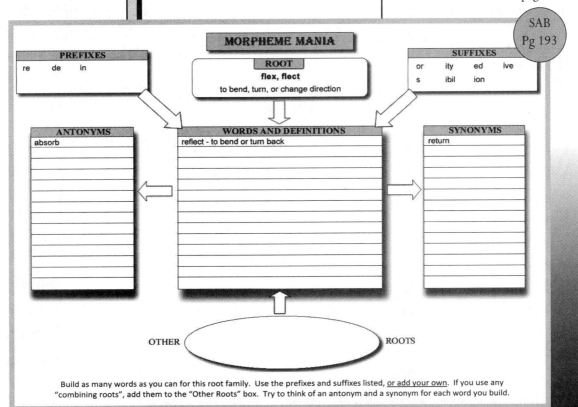

SAB
Pg 193

MORPHEME MANIA

PREFIXES		
re	de	in

ROOT
flex, flect
to bend, turn, or change direction

SUFFIXES			
or	ity	ed	ive
s	ibil	ion	

ANTONYMS
absorb

WORDS AND DEFINITIONS
reflect - to bend or turn back

SYNONYMS
return

OTHER ◯ ROOTS

Build as many words as you can for this root family. Use the prefixes and suffixes listed, <u>or add your own</u>. If you use any "combining roots", add them to the "Other Roots" box. Try to think of an antonym and a synonym for each word you build.

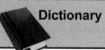
deflect   to bend away; to redirect

deflected   bent away; redirected

deflecting   bending away; redirecting

deflection   a bending away; an act of redirecting

deflections   acts of bending away; acts of redirecting

deflector   anything that causes to bend away

deflectors   things that cause to bend away

deflects   bends away; redirects

deflexed   bent away; directed downward at a steep angle

flex   to bend; to bend a joint or contract a muscle

flexed   bent; bent a joint or tensed a muscle

flexes   bends; bends a joint or tenses a muscle

flexibilities   qualities of being able to bend

flexibility   quality of being able to bend

flexible   bendable; responsive to change

flexibly   in a manner able to bend

flexing   bending; bending a joint or tensing a muscle

inflection   the act or bending into; the changing of tone or word form

inflectional   related to bending into; related to changing tone or word form

inflectionally   so as to bend into; so as to change tone or word form

inflections   acts of bending into; acts of changing tone or word form

inflexibilities   qualities of not being able to bend or change; qualities of rigidity

inflexibility   quality of not being able to bend or change; rigidity

inflexible   not easily bent or changed; rigid

inflexibleness   quality of not being able to bend or change; rigidity

inflexibly   in a manner not easily bent or changed; rigidly

reflect   to bend or turn back; to bounce light images; to think about

reflected   bent or turned back; bounced light images; thought about

reflectedly   in a manner bent or turned back; so as to bounce light images

reflectedness   quality of having been bent or turned back; quality of bouncing light images

reflecting   bending or turning back; bouncing light images; thinking about

reflection   something bent or turned back; a light image bounced back; something thought back upon

reflections   things bent or turned back; light images bounced back; things thought back upon

reflective   relating to bending or turning back; serving to bounce light images; serving to think again

reflector   a surface that bends or turns back; something that directs back light

reflectors   surfaces that bend or turn back; things that direct back light

reflects   bends or turns back; glances back at or ponders

reflex   a bending or turning back; an instinctive response

reflexes   acts of bending or turning back; acts of instinctively responding

reflexive   tending to bend or turn back; acting upon itself

Check-Up for **FLEX**

Name _____

____ 1. **FLEX** or **FLECT** in words like **flexible** and **reflect** means:

A to throw

B to make or do

C to bend

____ 2. What is the meaning of the word **inflexive**?

A to make a shape

B tending to curve inward

C relating to making paper

____ 3. What is the meaning of the word **flexor**?

A a person who throws things

B a building

C something that allows or causes bending

____ 4. What is the meaning of the word **reflexed**?

A made again

B tossed again

C bent back

____ 5. What is the meaning of the word **flexibility**?

A quality of being able to change direction

B the right to own property

C process of throwing large objects

____ 6. Which word means **to change direction away from**?

A deflection

B deflect

C deflector

____ 7. Which word means **things that bend light back**?

A inflections

B reflectors

C inflexes

____ 8. Which word means **relating to a change in words**?

A reflexivity

B inflectional

C deflected

____ 9. Sam blurted out the information **unreflectingly**. Sam:

A didn't turn back in his mind what the information might mean

B had thought long and hard about the information

C was asking for more details

____ 10. A **circumflexed** sound:

A seems to curve around

B is thrown up from below

C seems thrown from far away

OBJECTIVES

- **Understand** the meaning of the root **SECT**

- **Build** words in the root **SECT** family

- **Break Apart** words in the root **SECT** family

- **Understand** the meaning of words in the **SECT** family

- **Understand** the spelling principles applied to the root **SECT**

- **Apply** knowledge of words in the **SECT** family

- **Assess** and **Reinforce** knowledge of words in the **SECT** family

MATERIALS

- Student Activity Books, pages 195-200

- Dictionary *(print or on-line)*

CROSS-CURRICULAR EXAMPLES

Science:
dissect, insect

Social Studies:
sector, sectionalist

Language Arts:
sectionalism, segments

Math:
segment, bisect, trisect, secant, intersect

SECT

meaning "to cut, divide"

dissects
cuts apart

bisect
to cut or **divide** into two halves

Morpheme: **SECT**
Allomorphs: **SECTI, SEC, SEG**

Nearly 500 words containing the morpheme **SECT** or one of its allomorphs are current in English. During this unit, tell students to be alert for this root in their school texts, general reading, and oral language they hear. Some of the words they might encounter in their school subjects are listed on the left under Cross-Curricular Examples.

U N I T   A T   A   G L A N C E

Day **1**
Root Squares
for **SECT**

Day **2**
Magic Squares
for **SECT**

Day **3**
Stair Steps
for **SECT**

OPTIONAL
Day **4**
In Other Words
for **SECT**

Day **5**
*Assessment or
Morpheme Mania*
for **SECT**

Each activity should take approximately **15 minutes**.

The word **section** was initially, like most **-ion** words, *the act of cutting*, as a physician may perform a **section**. Then the word was applied to the part that was cut off. Finally the idea of cutting became figurative, as when we talk about a *section of the country*. The word can now also be used as a verb, as to **section** off an area of a room.

The allomorph **seg** of this root will occur only with the suffix **-ment**. Let students play with the difficulty of pronouncing **sectment**.

Segment, like **section**, can be used as a verb, with very similar meaning. Let students discuss what distinctions, if any, they feel exist between the words **segment** and **section** or **segmental** and **sectional**.

Morphemic awareness of how the word **dissect** is built will promote good spelling, as students see the root **sect** prefixed by **dis-**, meaning *apart*.

Morphemic awareness is also enlightening when we consider the word **insect**, bug. Looking closely, we see the morpheme for *cut* and the prefix meaning *in*. *Cut in?* Exactly: the bodies of these creatures have indented **segments**. These two Latin-based morphemes are an exact translation of the Greek **in-cut: en-tom**, which is the source of the word that means *the study of insects*, **entomology**.

The word **sickle** and **scythe**, two types of cutting tools, carry a trace of this morpheme.

Word Alert!

Be careful with words like **sect** and **sectarian**. While it may seem reasonable that a **sect** is a **section** of a group or an off-shoot of a larger body of believers, **sect** is another of those tricky words in the study of morphemes. **Sect** and **sectarian** come from a Latin root meaning *to follow*, as in **secondary** and **sequence**. As always, a reliable etymological dictionary can settle morphemic puzzles such as this.

The word **segregate** might be thought to contain an allomorph of the root meaning *cut*. Try a "proof-method" morphemic splitting experiment to see that **seg** is not a morpheme in the word.

segregate: WRONG   **seg**, cut | **reg**, right | **ate**, to cause to become

                RIGHT   **se**, apart | **greg**, flock | **ate**, to cause to become

Day 1

Root Squares
for **SECT**

SECT means
to cut, divide

LESSON TIME

15 Minutes

OBJECTIVES

- **Understand** the meaning of the root **SECT**

- **Build** words in the **SECT** family

- **Understand** the meaning of words in the **SECT** family

- **Understand** the spelling principles applied to the root **SECT**

MATERIALS

- Student Activity Book

- **SECT** Word Wall

- Dictionary *(print or on-line)*

DIFFERENTIATING INSTRUCTION

If you prefer easier or more difficult activities, use your personal account at www.dynamicliteracy.com to access novice or expert versions, along with ideas on using them.

Root Squares for SECT

TEACH Have students turn to page 195 in their Activity Books. Say, "All of the prefixes and suffixes in the squares surrounding the shaded center are probably familiar, but if you have questions about any of the meanings, simply ask or look them up in the list inside the front and back cover of the activity book."

Call attention to the center box. Point out that the root **SECT** has several different spellings, called allomorphs. Ask students to decide if one of the forms they see in the middle square can stand alone as a word. They may see that **sect** is a word, and if so you can point out that as an independent word, **sect** does not belong in this family. Instead, it is related to the root **sequi**, meaning *to follow*. (We see this in **sequence** and **segue**; a **sect** is

a following.) Suggest that students start their list with **sect**, adding the prefix **bi-**, meaning *two*, to build **bisect**, meaning *to cut in two*. Invite students to explore how this word is related to the idea of *to cut or divide*.

COMPLETE THE ACTIVITY

Have students follow the directions to build words. If students have difficulty building words with the Root Squares, show them how by modeling the matrix approach found on the next page, taking one affix at a time and seeing if it will connect with any one of the allomorphs of the root.

DISCUSS After five minutes, have volunteers write some of their words on the board. Focus with the class on the words they have built and guide them in a discussion of how the meaning of the root is still *to cut or divide* even when prefixes and suffixes are added. Watch for target words that most easily demonstrate

the meaning of *to cut or divide*. If the word **intersect** is not present, ask the class, "Can anyone try to use the prefix **inter-**?" and then continue on to the target word discussion on the next page.

Root Squares

How many words can you make?

Start in any square. Your goal is to combine two or more word parts to make as many words in the 'sect, secti, sec, seg' family as you can. Write each word and a definition you can think of for it in the space provided at the bottom of the page. Use the back of the page if you need to.

bi	or	dis
inter	sect, secti, sec, seg	in
ion	ment	al

SAB Pg 195

Focus Word: **INTERSECT** ⟶ Write this word on the board.

TEACH

Lead with this:	"What do two roads do if they **intersect**?"
Student:	"They meet."
Student:	"They come together."
Student:	"Come on. We'll figure it out in the word itself."
Teacher:	"Right. Let's look at the pieces of meaning in the word."
Student:	"I see a prefix **inter-**, like in **interfere** or **international**."
Student:	"And the root **sect**. Hey, the word meets *cut in between*! I see it."
Student:	"So it's not just meet or come together, but actually cut through each other. I see it, too."

DISCUSS Let students discuss situations they know about in which the word **intersect** can be used.

DEMONSTRATE Have a student draw for the class two lines that **intersect**. Demonstrate a Venn diagram in which two circles **intersect** and overlap.

Root Squares Matrix

You can refer to this matrix to guide students in this activity. Students could build at least these 17 words. *It is not important how many words are built*, so long as students understand the meanings of the root and its affixes. Encourage discussion about the definitions of any words formed for the blank slots as well as for the attested words.

	no prefix	bi-	dis-	in-	inter-
no suffix		bisect	dissect	insect	intersect
-or	sector	bisector	dissector		
-ion	section	bisection	dissection	insection	intersection
-ion + -al	sectional	bisectional	dissectional		intersectional
-ment	segment				

Day 2

Magic Squares for SECT

SECT means to cut, divide

LESSON TIME

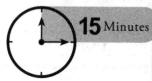

15 Minutes

OBJECTIVES

- **Understand** the meaning of the root **SECT**
- **Break Apart** words in the **SECT** family
- **Understand** the meanings of words in the **SECT** family

MATERIALS

- Student Activity Book
- **SECT** Word Wall
- Dictionary *(print or on-line)*

DIFFERENTIATING INSTRUCTION

If you prefer easier or more difficult activities, use your personal account at www.dynamicliteracy.com to access novice or expert versions, along with ideas on using them.

Break Apart Words with SECT

Have students turn to the Magic Squares on page 196 in their Student Activity Books. Model a Think-Aloud strategy for students: "I know that **SECT** means *to cut or divide*. I can use this knowledge to find the definition of a word with **SECT** or one of its allomorphs as its root."

Direct students to word C, **insects**. Say, "This word has a prefix, **in-** meaning either *in, into* or *not*, and a suffix **-s** that means plural. Look at definition 7, *animals whose body shapes are cut inward; bugs*. That's surely a definition of a plural, and the word **inward** suggests the meaning of the prefix **in-** is *in, into*. The meaning of the root, **SECT**,

is in the word *cut*, which is how insect bodies look. We'll write the number 7 in square C."

COMPLETE THE ACTIVITY

Ask students to use the same strategy to find the correct definitions for the other words. Tell them to write the number of the definition in the box that matches the letter for the word. Remind them that if all their answers are correct, each row and each column will add up to the same Magic number.

DISCUSS After five minutes, ask if there are any difficulties about matching the words and definitions. If there are, ask volunteers to explain clues in the definitions that will lead to the correct choice of word. As needed, follow the focus word approach for **bisected** that you see modeled on the next page.

Add any new words to the classroom **SECT** Word Wall and remind students to add these words to the **SECT** Word Wall in their Activity Books.

SAB Pg 196

Magic Squares

Select the best answer for each of the words in the 'sect, secti, sec, seg' family from the numbered definitions. Put the number in the proper space in the Magic Square box. If the total of the numbers is the same both across and down, you have found the magic number!

'sect, secti, sec, seg' means to cut, divide

WORDS	DEFINITIONS
A. bisected	1. agent that kills animals with incut bodies; agent that exterminates bugs
B. dissecting	2. cutting apart; analyzing
C. insects	3. relating to places cut into by each other; pertaining to a crossroad
D. intersected	4. cut in between; crossed
E. sectarian	5. pieces cut off from other things
F. sectionalism	6. a person belonging to a group cut apart from a larger group, a member of a cult
G. segments	7. animals whose body shapes are cut inward; bugs
H. sections	8. preference for a small area cut from a larger area; a partiality for some particular place
I. intersectional	9. cut into two halves
	10. pieces cut from the whole; segments

Magic Square Box

A. 9	B. 2	C. 7
D. 4	E. 6	F. 8
G. 5	H. 10	I. 3

Magic Number __18__

*** ANSWER KEY ***

MINI-LESSON: the Combining Form **cid**

The Combining Form **cid** is a root meaning *to cut or kill*. It can also mean *to fall*, as if cut off (as in the word **deciduous**, describing trees whose leaves *fall*). This root is featured in Elements Level 3, but it can be introduced here in connection with the familiar word **insecticide**. There are several dozens of words with this Combining Form used as a suffix to name a product or substance that kills other substances. Put some of these words on the board for your students and see if they can figure out what the product does:

algicide	bactericide	fungicide	germicide
herbicide	larvicide	pesticide	rodenticide

Focus Word: **BISECTED** → Write this word on the board.

TEACH

Sample leading question:	"If something is **bisected**, what happened to it?"
Student:	"It got opened up and examined."
Student:	"No, that's **dissected**."
Student:	"Oh, right. Let's see, what does this word tell us?"
Student:	"I see our root, **sect**, *to cut*."
Student:	"And the prefix **bi-**, like in **bicycle**, means *two*."
Student:	"So there you go, *cut in two*."
Student:	"Do the two pieces have to be equal?"
Teacher:	"You know, I always thought so, but I'm not sure. Let's check to see what a dictionary says."

DISCUSS Let students discuss situations they know about in which the word **bisect** can be used. Angles can be **bisected** (into two equal parts), highways can **bisect** railroads (cross), roads can **bisect** (fork).

DEMONSTRATE Draw a right angle (corner or 90 degree) and ask a student to **bisect** it (by drawing a diagonal halfway between the legs of the angle).

Day 3

Stair Steps for **SECT**

SECT means to cut, divide

LESSON TIME

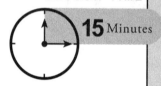

15 Minutes

OBJECTIVES

- **Understand** the meaning of the root **SECT**

- **Apply** knowledge of the root **SECT**

- **Break Apart** words in the **SECT** family

- **Understand** the meaning of words in the **SECT** family

- **Understand** the spelling principles applied to the root **SECT**

MATERIALS

- Student Activity Book
- **SECT** Word Wall

DIFFERENTIATING INSTRUCTION

If you prefer easier or more difficult activities, use your personal account at www.dynamicliteracy.com to access novice or expert versions, along with ideas on using them.

Apply Knowledge of SECT

TEACH Have students turn to page 197 in their Student Activity Books. Explain that the boxes in front of and after the root indicate letters that spell out prefixes and suffixes. Students will spell out the correct prefixes and suffixes determined by clues in the definitions at the bottom of the page.

Have a volunteer read definition number two at the bottom of the page. Say, "The **s** on the end of **cut** in the definition tells us we need that same suffix on the word we are building, so we'll write the suffix **-s** in the last blank on step two. The prefix needs to have the meaning of the two in the definition. What do you call a wheeled vehicle with two wheels? (A bicycle) So, we want our word to begin with the letters **bi-**, the prefix that means *two*. That will give us the word **BISECTS**."

COMPLETE THE ACTIVITY

Let students work in pairs (optionally) and tell them to use the same strategy to find the correct prefixes and suffixes for the words listed. These activities can be quite challenging!

DISCUSS After a few minutes, review the answers as a class. Ask if there were any difficulties. Listen to any problems and have volunteers solve the difficulties by explaining key clues in the given definitions. As needed, follow the focus word approach that you see modeled on the next page.

SAB Pg 197

Stair Steps

Fill in the missing letters of each 'sect, secti, sec, seg' word by using the definitions below
'sect, secti, sec, seg' means to cut; divide

1.	s	e	c	t	o	r				
2.	b	i	s	e	c	t	s			
3.	s	e	g	m	e	n	t	s		
4.	b	i	s	e	c	t	o	r	s	
5.	i	n	t	e	r	s	e	c	t	s
6.	d	i	s	s	e	c	t	i	o	n	s
7.	i	n	s	e	c	t	i	c	i	d	e	s
8.	s	e	c	t	i	o	n	a	l	i	s	t	s
9.	i	n	t	e	r	s	e	c	t	i	o	n	a	l

1. an area cut from a bigger area; a precinct
2. cuts into two parts
3. pieces cut off from other things
4. instruments that cut into halves
5. cuts in between; crosses
6. acts of cutting apart; separations acts of analysis
7. agents that kill animals with incut bodies; bug poisons
8. people who prefer small areas cut from larger areas; people partial to local interests and customs
9. relating to places cut into by each other; pertaining to a crossroad

Focus Word: **SEGMENTS** ⟶ Write this word on the board.

TEACH

Sample leading question:	"If I've seen only **segments** of a particular movie, what have I seen?"
Student:	"You've just seen clips of it."
Teacher:	"I like that—*clips*. What are *clips*?"
Student:	"Clips are *cuts*, like getting your hair clipped."
Teacher:	"So **segments** are *cuts* of the movie?"
Student:	"Well, pieces of the movie instead of the whole thing."
Student:	"Right—a **segment** is *a piece* or *a part*."
Teacher:	"And how do you get *a piece* or *a part*?"
Student:	"You *cut* it from the whole."
Student:	"But not necessarily for real."

DISCUSS   Lead students to see that **segments** are pieces *cut* from a whole in a figurative sense. Show them that the word can also be used as a verb, to **segment**, *to cut into pieces*. Let students discuss any differences they sense between the words **segments** and **sections**.

DEMONSTRATE   A line **segment** is that part of a line which can be drawn, if a line is defined as an infinite path of points in a row. Draw a line **segment** on the board, and then ask a student to **section** that line **segment** off into three pieces.

··········_____|_____|_____··········

Day 4

In Other Words for SECT

SECT means to cut, divide

LESSON TIME

15 Minutes

OBJECTIVES

- **Understand** the meaning of the root **SECT**
- **Reinforce** knowledge of the root **SECT**
- **Understand** the meaning of words in the **SECT** family
- **Apply** knowledge of words in the **SECT** family

MATERIALS

- Student Activity Book
- **SECT** Word Wall
- Dictionary *(print or on-line)*

In Other Words for **SECT**

TEACH Have students turn to page 198 in their Student Activity Books. Explain that they are going to read a little story that uses some surprising and sometimes odd phrasing. The underlined words or phrases in the story are actually definitions or synonyms for words in the **SECT** family. Then they will see sentences about the story, each containing a blank.

Using context clues in the sentences, they will find a **SECT** family word in the Word Bank at the bottom to fit in each blank. Have a student read aloud the opening sentence or sentences of the story that contain the first underlined phrase. Then say, "Let's look at the first numbered sentence that contains a blank to be filled in. Clues in that sentence tell us that we want a naming word, a plural noun meaning *people who believed in cutting off an area*. I see the word **sectionalists** at the bottom of the page. The root **sect** means *to cut*. What meaning do those suffixes add? The **-al** gives us the idea of *describing as in sections*. The **-ists** would indicate *people who*. That seems to be it, so let's write **sectionalists** in the blank space in the first sentence."

COMPLETE THE ACTIVITY

This can be quite challenging, so allow students to work on this activity in small groups. Not every word in the Word Bank will be used.

DISCUSS After about 10 minutes, ask if there were any difficulties. Have volunteers explain strategies they used that led to correct answers.

SAB Pg 198

The Father of Entomology

William Kirby, an English minister, was opposed to Thomas Paine and other people who believed in cutting off an area from the British Empire. He did not want to see America cut as a smaller area from England, but the American Revolution settled that debate.

Yet William Kirby is more famous for something else. Open a science book and turn to the part cut off from the rest concerning biology, where you might find something about him. He is known for his studies of the little animals with bodies that seem cut inward, especially bees. In bees he believed that he saw the point at which religion and nature cut into each other. He did not approve of poisonous agents that kill these in-cut creatures, but he nevertheless advanced our knowledge by cutting apart their bodies and discovering their three pieces that seem cut.

After the acts of cutting apart and analyzing, Kirby drew pictures and wrote studies that became, in 1815, the first popular book on the subject in English.

Fill in the blanks below using words from the "sect, secti, sec, seg" family.

1. Thomas Paine and many American colonists were sectionalists; they wanted America to break off from the larger Empire.
2. The broken and segmented Empire bothered William Kirby, but he turned his attention to new things.
3. You may learn about William Kirby in the biology section of a science book.
4. He studied insects such as bees.
5. He believed that bees were an example of the intersection of Nature and religious teachings.
6. He did not approve of using poisonous insecticides.
7. Kirby is famous for dissecting bees and examining their bodies.
8. The bodies of bees and animals like them have three segments.
9. From his dissections Kirby compiled an important and popular study on Entomology.

Not Used: bisects   sectors   sectional

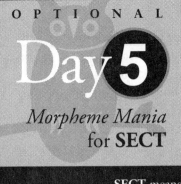

OPTIONAL

Day 5

Morpheme Mania
for **SECT**

SECT means
to cut, divide

LESSON TIME

15 Minutes

OBJECTIVES

- **Build** words in the **SECT** family

- **Apply** knowledge of synonyms and antonyms to **SECT** words

Optional Morpheme Mania for **SECT**

On page 199 of their Activity Book, students will see an optional vocabulary enrichment activity that they can work on in groups, time permitting. This activity makes a great review for the formal assessment on the next page.

All the affixes presented in the week's activities are provided at the top of the page on either side of the root of the week in all its forms. Students can write in up to 13 of the words they built during the week, possibly discovering additional ones.

Then students can brainstorm with each other to come up with antonyms and synonyms they may know. Starter examples are given with every Morpheme Mania in the Activity Book. Because antonyms and synonyms may require knowledge of roots which students have not yet studied, completion of this activity is not crucial. Simply remind students that they can at any time during the course of the year revisit any of their Morpheme Mania pages and add words, antonyms, and synonyms as their vocabulary grows.

Day 5 *Assessment*

Make and hand out copies.
The answer key is on page A-6.
The instructions are on page A-2.

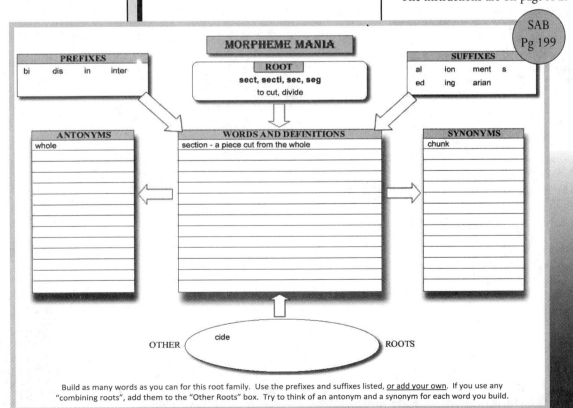

SAB
Pg 199

MORPHEME MANIA

PREFIXES			
bi	dis	in	inter

ROOT
sect, secti, sec, seg
to cut, divide

SUFFIXES			
al	ion	ment	s
ed	ing	arian	

ANTONYMS
whole

WORDS AND DEFINITIONS
section - a piece cut from the whole

SYNONYMS
chunk

OTHER   cide   ROOTS

Build as many words as you can for this root family. Use the prefixes and suffixes listed, <u>or add your own</u>. If you use any "combining roots", add them to the "Other Roots" box. Try to think of an antonym and a synonym for each word you build.

bisect to cut into two halves
bisected cut into two halves
bisecting cutting into two halves
bisector instrument that cuts into halves
bisectors instruments that cut into halves
bisects cuts into two parts
dissect to cut apart; to analyze
dissected cut apart; analyzed
dissecting cutting apart; analyzing
dissection act of cutting apart; analysis
dissections acts of cutting apart; separations acts of analysis
dissects cuts apart; analyzes
insect animal whose body shape is cut inward; a bug
insecticide agent that kills animals with incut bodies; bug poison
insecticides agents that kill animals with incut bodies; bug poisons
insects animals whose body shapes are cut inward; bugs
intersect to cut in between; to cross
intersectant cutting in between; crossing
intersected cut in between; crossed
intersecting cutting in between; crossing
intersection act of cutting in between; a crossroad
intersectional relating to places cut into by each other; pertaining to a crossroad

intersections acts of cutting in between; crossroads
intersects cuts in between; crosses
section piece cut from the whole; a specific area
sectional related to a piece cut from the whole; related to a specific area
sectionalism preference for a small area cut from a larger area; a partiality for some particular place
sectionalist a person who prefers a small area cut from larger area; a person partial to local interests and customs
sectionalists people who prefer small areas cut from larger areas; people partial to local interests and customs
sectionals pieces cut from a whole; segments
sections pieces cut from the whole; specific areas
sector an area cut from a bigger area; a precinct
sectors areas cut from bigger areas; precincts
segment a piece cut off from something else
segments pieces cut off from other things

Check-Up for **SECT**

Name _____

_____ **1.** **SECT** or **SEG** in words like **section** and **segment** means:

A place

B to cut

C to save or protect

_____ **2.** What is the meaning of the word **bisect**?

A to kill bugs

B to divide into two

C to save well

_____ **3.** What is the meaning of the word **intersection**?

A the arrangement of things that are protected

B a point where lines cut into each other

C places used for storage

_____ **4.** What is the meaning of the word **segmented**?

A followed closely

B protected carefully

C cut into pieces

_____ **5.** What is the meaning of the word **sections**?

A stores for later use

B places in a safe location

C divides off into pieces

_____ **6.** Which word means **divided into two**?

A bisected

B bisection

C bisects

_____ **7.** Which word means **the process of cutting apart**?

A bisectional

B insecticide

C dissection

_____ **8.** Which word means **people interested in specific divisions or areas of a country**?

A segments

B sectionalists

C bisectors

_____ **9.** What is **sectility**?

A the quality of being cut easily

B the process of being quiet

C the condition of protecting certain plants and animals

_____ **10.** A vein of iron ore **transected** the layers of rock.
The vein of iron ore:

A cut across the layers of rock

B completely colored the layers of rock

C was located under the layers of rock

OBJECTIVES

- **Understand** the meaning of the root **PAR**
- **Build** words in the root **PAR** family
- **Break Apart** words in the root **PAR** family
- **Understand** the meaning of words in the **PAR** family
- **Understand** the spelling principles applied to the root **PAR**
- **Apply** knowledge of words in the **PAR** family
- **Assess** and **Reinforce** knowledge of words in the **PAR** family

MATERIALS

- Student Activity Books, pages 201-206
- Dictionary *(print or on-line)*
- (optional) playing cards or sheets of colored paper

CROSS-CURRICULAR EXAMPLES

Science:
apparatus, preparatory

Social Studies:
reparations, separatist

Language Arts:
parade, separate

Math:
inseparable, disparate

PAR

meaning "arrange, order"

repair
arrange back into proper order

preparation
act of putting in **order** or arranging beforehand

Morpheme: **PAR**
Allomorphs: **PARE, PAIR**

About 300 words containing the morpheme **PAR** or one of its allomorphs are current in English. During this unit, tell students to be alert for this root in their school texts, general reading, and oral language they hear. Some of the words they might encounter in their school subjects are listed on the left under Cross-Curricular Examples.

UNIT AT A GLANCE

Day **1**
Root Squares
for **PAR**

Day **2**
Magic Squares
for **PAR**

Day **3**
Stair Steps
for **PAR**

OPTIONAL
Day **4**
In Other Words
for **PAR**

Day **5**
Assessment or Morpheme Mania
for **PAR**

Each activity should take approximately **15 minutes**.

The word **separate** and its many associated words, such as **separation** and **inseparable**, belong to this root family, with a meaning of *arranged apart*. With a phonetic alteration from **p** to **v**, the word **sever** emerges, also meaning *arranged apart* or *trimmed away*.

The word **prepare** offers a clear example of one of the meanings of this morpheme, with its idea of *getting ready* or *arranging ahead of time*. The word **apparatus** takes on a clear meaning as well when we see that its morphemes add up to *arranged or ordered for* (a task).

The word **pare**, meaning *to put in order or arrange by trimming off*, provides another related meaning of this complex morpheme. As a metaphor, reproduction can be seen as a trimming off, or cutting away from the original, a part taken from the whole. Thus, this morpheme appears in a family of words referring to giving birth, as with **parent**, *one giving birth*, or **biparous**, *giving birth to two young at a time*, and **oviparous**, *reproducing with eggs*.

To **repair** is *to arrange back what was trimmed or broken off*.

Another direction this morpheme takes is that of *arranging or putting in order for a show*, as in the word **parade**.

A political unit that is arranged and put in order uses this morpheme with an altered vowel: **empire**, and the person who so arranges or orders it is an **emperor**, who has **imperial** power. People who like to arrange things and order others to do so are described as **imperious**.

Selecting which allomorph, **pare** or **pair** goes with which affix will be problematic with students, so assure them that only experience and observation, plus trips to a current dictionary, will settle the issue. English has **prepare**, but **repair**. Along with **repair** are both **repairable** and **reparable**, though pronunciation can help with the spelling difference of those last two examples.

Word Alert!

The apparent free, unbound allomorphs of this root, **par** and **pair,** are not examples of words that come from this root. Instead, both words belong to a root family meaning *equal*.

The verb **impair** comes from yet another entirely different source, meaning *to make worse*. These morphemic similarities but meaning differences add to the fun of studying the English language

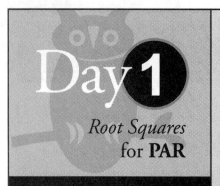
PAR means
arrange, order

LESSON TIME

15 Minutes

OBJECTIVES

- **Understand** the meaning of the root **PAR**

- **Build** words in the **PAR** family

- **Understand** the meaning of words in the **PAR** family

- **Understand** the spelling principles applied to the root **PAR**

MATERIALS

- Student Activity Book
- **PAR** Word Wall
- Dictionary *(print or on-line)*

DIFFERENTIATING INSTRUCTION

If you prefer easier or more difficult activities, use your personal account at www.dynamicliteracy.com to access novice or expert versions, along with ideas on using them.

Root Squares for PAR

TEACH Have students turn to page 201 in their Activity Books. Say, "All of the prefixes and suffixes in the squares surrounding the shaded center are probably familiar, but if you have questions about any of the meanings, look them up in your activity book." Call attention to the center box. Point out that the root **PAR** has several different spellings, called allomorphs. Ask students to decide if one of the forms they see in the middle square can stand alone as a word. All three forms are stand-alone words, but only one of these is in the **PAR** family, having to do with a *arrange, order*. That word is **pare**, meaning *to arrange for better appearance*. You can use this word to lead students to the idea of *arrange, order*. Suggest that students start their list with **pare**, and then move on to **pair**,

with the prefix **re**-, meaning *back*, to build **repair**, meaning *to arrange back in proper order*. Invite students to explore how this word is related to the idea of *arrange, order*.

COMPLETE THE ACTIVITY

Have students follow the directions to build words. If students have difficulty building words with the Root Squares, show them how by modeling the matrix approach found on the next page, taking one affix at a time and seeing if it will connect with any one of the allomorphs of the root.

DISCUSS After five minutes, have volunteers write some of their words on the board. Focus with the class on the words they have built and guide them in a discussion of how the meaning of the root is still *arrange, order,* even when prefixes and suffixes are added. Watch for target words that most easily demonstrate the meaning of *arrange, order*. If the word **prepare** is not present, ask the class, "Can anyone try to use the prefix **pre**-?" and then continue on to the target word discussion on the next page.

SAB Pg 201

Root Squares

How many words can you make?

Start in any square. Your goal is to combine two or more word parts to make as many words in the 'par, pare, pair' family as you can. Write each word and a definition you can think of for it in the space provided at the bottom of the page. Use the back of the page if you need to.

ir	ate	pre
able	par, pare, pair	ion
se	ory	re

_____
_____
_____
_____
_____
_____
_____
_____
_____

Focus Word: **PREPARE** ➡️ Write this word on the board.

TEACH

Lead with this:	"Did you ever stop to think what you do when you **prepare** for something?"
Student:	"You get ready for it."
Teacher:	"You plan it."
Student:	"Or, it could just mean you make it, like **prepare** dinner."
Teacher:	"You know what we have to do now."
Student:	"Yes, look at the word!"
Student:	"This one should be pretty easy. It has the prefix **pre**-, which means *before* or *ahead of time.*"
Student:	"And there's our root, which means *arrange* or *order.*"
Student:	"Okay, I get it. You *arrange for something ahead of time*, like planning it out."

DISCUSS Let students discuss situations they know about in which the word **prepare** can be used. You can **prepare** a speech, a way, a patient, a person for bad news, or you can **prepare** for a storm, a test, *etc.* Small groups can also list things to think about in **preparing** for a trip to the beach (or mountains, or grocery store).

DEMONSTRATE Take a volunteer group who has **prepared** for some specific thing and let that group show how arranging or ordering is part of what they have done.

Root Squares Matrix

You can refer to this matrix to guide students in this activity. Students could build at least these 19 words. *It is not important how many words are built*, so long as students understand the meanings of the root and its affixes. Encourage discussion about the definitions of any words formed for the blank slots as well as for the attested words.

	no prefix	ir- + re-	pre-	re-	se-
no suffix	pare	irrepair	prepare	repair	
-able	pareable	irrepairable	prepareable	repairable	
		irreparable		reparable	separable
-ate			preparate		separate
-at(e) + -ion			preparation	reparation	separation
-at(e) + -ory			preparatory	reparatory	separatory

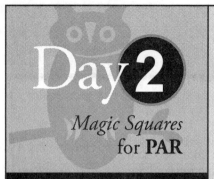

Day 2

Magic Squares
for **PAR**

PAR means
arrange, order

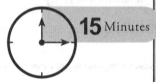

LESSON TIME

15 Minutes

OBJECTIVES

- **Understand** the meaning of the root **PAR**

- **Break Apart** words in the **PAR** family

- **Understand** the meanings of words in the **PAR** family

MATERIALS

- Student Activity Book
- **PAR** Word Wall
- Dictionary *(print or on-line)*
- (optional) playing cards or sheets of colored paper

DIFFERENTIATING INSTRUCTION

If you prefer easier or more difficult activities, use your personal account at www.dynamicliteracy.com to access novice or expert versions, along with ideas on using them.

Break Apart Words with PAR

Have students turn to the Magic Squares on page 202 in their Student Activity Books. Model a Think-Aloud strategy for students: "I know that **PAR** means *arrange, order*. I can use this knowledge to find the definition of a word with **PAR** or one of its allomorphs as its root." Direct students to word A, **inseparable**. Say, "This word has a prefix, **in-** meaning *in, into* or *not*, a second prefix, **se-** meaning *apart*, and a suffix -**able** that means *having the power*. Look at definition 9, *not able to be arranged or moved apart*. We can read this as *not able to be arranged apart or moved apart*. That suggests the meaning of the prefix **in-** is *not* and the word **apart** accounts for the meaning of

the second prefix. The meaning of the suffix is literal: **able**. The root, **PAR**, is defined by the word *arranged*. We'll write the number 9 in square A."

COMPLETE THE ACTIVITY

Ask students to use the same strategy to find the correct definitions for the other words. Tell them to write the number of the definition in the box that matches the letter for the word. Remind them that if all their answers are correct, each row and each column will add up to the same Magic number.

DISCUSS After five minutes, ask if there are any difficulties about matching the words and definitions. If there are, ask volunteers to explain clues in the definitions that will lead to the correct choice of word. As needed, follow the focus word approach for **separated** that you see modeled on the next page.

SAB
Pg 202

Add any new words to the classroom **PAR** Word Wall and remind students to add these words to the **PAR** Word Wall in their Activity Books.

Magic Squares

Select the best answer for each of the words in the 'par, pare, pair' family from the numbered definitions. Put the number in the proper space in the Magic Square box. If the total of the numbers is the same both across and down, you have found the magic number!

'par, pare, pair' means arrange, order, command

WORDS	DEFINITIONS
A. inseparable	1. in a manner arranged or ordered apart; in a manner done apart from another
B. paraded	2. clothing arranged or laid out for an occasion
C. unseparated	3. arranged or trimmed for better appearance; cut into small pieces
D. separately	4. not able to be mended back into proper order
E. preparations	5. moved forward in a formal arrangement for show; processed along in a line
F. repairable	6. object arranged for preparing to do a task; a device for a particular purpose
G. preparatory	7. not arranged or ordered apart; together, not parted
H. irreparable	8. able to be arranged back into proper order; fixable
I. apparatus	9. not able to be arranged or moved apart
	10. not having arranged things beforehand; not ready
	11. tending to arrange a situation beforehand; serving to get things ready
	12. acts of putting in order or arranging beforehand; things done to get ready

Magic Square Box

A. 9	B. 5	C. 7
D. 1	E. 12	F. 8
G. 11	H. 4	I. 6

Magic Number _21_

*** ANSWER KEY ***

The suffix **-ade** is a dialectical variation of the suffix **-ate**. It primarily means *an action*, but it can also mean *to do the action*, that is, it is used to make nouns that can also be used as verbs. Show your students the following words and discuss the difference between the words as nouns and as verbs:

> **masquerade**, from mask
> **marinade**, from a word for liquid
> **blockade**, from block (as noun or verb)
> **promenade**, from a word for going forward

Focus Word: **SEPARATED** ➡ Write this word on the board.

TEACH

Sample leading question:	"Have you ever gotten **separated** from your friends in a crowd? What literally happened when you became **separated**?"
Student:	"You lost them. Or they lost you."
Student:	"You went the wrong way. Or they did."
Student:	"This looks like a tough one to figure out. It has three morphemes."
Student:	"No, four! Look: take the root out and you have a prefix and two suffixes."
Student:	"Okay, I see **separate** and the past tense **-ed**."
Student:	"And in **separate**, there is a suffix **-ate** on the root."
Student:	"That means *to make or cause to become*."
Student:	"There's no word **separ**, so break that down to our root and a prefix **se-**. I forget what **se-** means."
Student:	"It says in our activity book that it means *apart or away*—that makes sense."
Student:	"*To cause to be apart or away*. What about the root? Is that the same as the root **part**?"
Teacher:	"What do you think, class?"
Student:	"I guess you're in a situation that can be thought of as *arranged apart*, or *set apart* in some way."

DISCUSS Lead students to see that the meaning of the word **separated** is the sum of the meanings of its pieces, *caused to be arranged apart*.

DEMONSTRATE Have playing cards or colored pieces of paper **separated** into two or more piles and show let the class show how and why the piles are arranged apart.

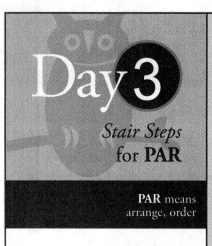

LESSON TIME

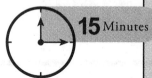

15 Minutes

OBJECTIVES

- **Understand** the meaning of the root **PAR**

- **Apply** knowledge of the root **PAR**

- **Break Apart** words in the **PAR** family

- **Understand** the meaning of words in the **PAR** family

- **Understand** the spelling principles applied to the root **PAR**

MATERIALS

- Student Activity Book
- **PAR** Word Wall

DIFFERENTIATING INSTRUCTION

If you prefer easier or more difficult activities, use your personal account at www.dynamicliteracy.com to access novice or expert versions, along with ideas on using them.

Apply Knowledge of **PAR**

TEACH Have students turn to page 203 in their Student Activity Books. Explain that the boxes in front of and after the root indicate letters that spell out prefixes and suffixes. Students will spell out the correct prefixes and suffixes determined by clues in the definitions at the bottom of the page.

Have a volunteer read definition number nine at the bottom of the page. Say, "This very long word is built of a number of affixes, each of which is probably familiar to you. For example, what prefix means *beforehand*? Looking at the list we have we see that **pre-** has this meaning. Now we need a few suffixes. One is going to be the plural marker **-s** which we know because of the plural words in the definition. What suffix have we seen before with the meaning *act or thing*? Let's try **-ion**. That leaves one more part to add, two letters that mean *to do something*. The suffix **-ate** would do that for us, after we drop the final **e** before the **-ion**. The word we then have is **PREPARATIONS**."

COMPLETE THE ACTIVITY

Let students work in pairs (optionally) and tell them to use the same strategy to find the correct prefixes and suffixes for the words listed. These activities can be quite challenging!

DISCUSS After a few minutes, review the answers as a class. Ask if there were any difficulties. Listen to any problems and have volunteers solve the difficulties by explaining key clues in the given definitions. As needed, follow the focus word approach that you see modeled on the next page.

SAB
Pg 203

Stair Steps

Fill in the missing letters of each 'par, pare, pair' word by using the definitions below.
'par, pare, pair' means arrange, order, command

#										
1.	r	e	p	a	i	r				
2.	p	a	r	a	d	e	d			
3.	p	r	e	p	a	r	e			
4.	s	e	p	a	r	a	t	e		
5.	r	e	p	a	i	r	i	n	g	
6.	s	e	p	a	r	a	t	e	s	
7.	s	e	p	a	r	a	t	i	o	n
8.	i	r	r	e	p	a	r	a	b	l	e
9.	p	r	e	p	a	r	a	t	i	o	n	s

1. to arrange back into proper order; to fix
2. moved forward in a formal arrangement for show; processed along in a line
3. to arrange beforehand; to get ready
4. to arrange or order apart; to divide or distinguish
5. arranging back into proper order; fixing
6. arranges or orders apart
7. act of arranging or ordering apart; act of dividing or distinguishing
8. not able to be arranged back into proper order; beyond remedy
9. acts of putting in order or arranging beforehand; things done to get ready

Focus Word: **REPAIR** ⟶ Write this word on the board.

TEACH

Sample leading question:	"I need to take my television to the **repair** shop. What are they going to do to my broken television?"
Student:	"They're going to fix it."
Student:	"Well, they're going to do something to it *again*."
Student:	"Right—there's the prefix **re-**, *again*."
Student:	"They're going to make it work again."
Student:	"Not work, but *arrange it again or put it back in order*."
Student:	"Hey, that's right, it's *out of order* now, and they will *re-order* it. *Wow!*"

DISCUSS   Lead students to see that the word **repair** means *to put something back in order*. Let students discuss situations they know about in which the word **repair** can be used.

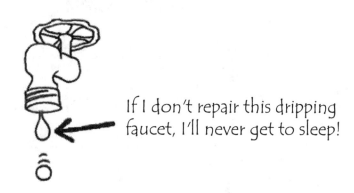

If I don't repair this dripping faucet, I'll never get to sleep!

ô

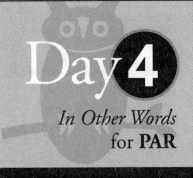

Day 4

In Other Words
for **PAR**

PAR means
arrange, order

LESSON TIME

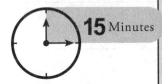

15 Minutes

OBJECTIVES

- **Understand** the meaning of the root **PAR**

- **Reinforce** knowledge of the root **PAR**

- **Understand** the meaning of words in the **PAR** family

- **Apply** knowledge of words in the **PAR** family

MATERIALS

- Student Activity Book

- **PAR** Word Wall

- Dictionary *(print or on-line)*

In Other Words for **PAR**

TEACH Have students turn to page 204 in their Student Activity Books. Explain that they are going to read a little story that uses some surprising and sometimes odd phrasing. The underlined words or phrases in the story are actually definitions or synonyms for words in the **PAR** family. Then they will see sentences about the story, each containing a blank.

Using context clues in the sentences, they will find a **PAR** family word in the Word Bank at the bottom to fit in each blank. Have a student read aloud the opening sentence or sentences of the story that contain the first underlined phrase. Then say, "Let's look at the first numbered sentence that contains a blank to be filled in. Clues in that sentence tell us that we want a naming word, a noun meaning *the process of getting ready*. I see the word **preparation** at the bottom of the page. We recognize **prepare** in that word, meaning *get ready* and the suffix **-ion** makes the word a noun. Let's write **preparation** in the blank space in the first sentence."

COMPLETE THE ACTIVITY

This can be quite challenging, so allow students to work on this activity in small groups. Not every word in the Word Bank will be used.

DISCUSS After about 10 minutes, ask if there were any difficulties. Have volunteers explain strategies they used that led to correct answers.

SAB
Pg 204

Some Advice on Career Choices

The <u>process of getting ready</u> for a future choice of career doesn't mean you have to decide early what you'd like to do for a living. The good <u>person who arranges beforehand</u> for the future makes plans with diversity in mind. Try not to <u>arrange</u> yourself <u>apart</u> from opportunities to learn new things, whether it's learning <u>to arrange back into shape</u> faulty machinery, to design <u>clothing arranged for occasions</u>, or to stock scientific <u>devices for particular purposes</u>. Such <u>act of arranging yourself apart</u> leads to harm <u>not able to be put back in proper order</u> to your flexibility and job-holding potential.

Take as many classes <u>serving to get things ready</u> as you can in school. That way you will be happily <u>ready</u> to follow a variety of interests.

<u>Fill in the blanks below using words from the "par, pare, pair" family.</u>

1. <u>Preparation</u> for future careers doesn't mean making final decisions now.
2. A person who is a good <u>preparer</u> for the future thinks about diversity.
3. Don't <u>separate</u> yourself from offered opportunities.
4. There will always be broken machinery to <u>repair</u>.
5. People are always interested in nice wearing <u>apparel</u>.
6. Science labs need certain <u>apparatus</u> to carry out experiments.
7. <u>Separation</u> from opportunity leads to inflexibility.
8. Inflexibility can bring <u>irreparable</u> harm to your attraction to employers.
9. A variety of <u>preparatory</u> classes taken in school will provide future choices.
10. You will find yourself happily <u>prepared</u> for your chosen career.

<u>Not Used:</u>   parade   unprepared

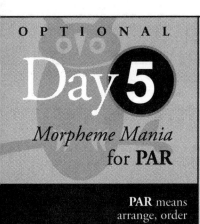

OPTIONAL

Day 5

Morpheme Mania
for **PAR**

PAR means
arrange, order

LESSON TIME

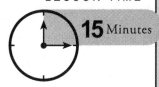

15 Minutes

OBJECTIVES

- **Build** words in the **PAR** family

- **Apply** knowledge of synonyms and antonyms to **PAR** words

Optional Morpheme Mania for **PAR**

On page 205 of their Activity Book, students will see an optional vocabulary enrichment activity that they can work on in groups, time permitting. This activity makes a great review for the formal assessment on the next page.

All the affixes presented in the week's activities are provided at the top of the page on either side of the root of the week in all its forms. Students can write in up to 13 of the words they built during the week, possibly discovering additional ones.

Then students can brainstorm with each other to come up with antonyms and synonyms they may know. Starter examples are given with every Morpheme Mania in the Activity Book. Because antonyms and synonyms may require knowledge of roots which students have not yet studied, completion of this activity is not crucial. Simply remind students that they can at any time during the course of the year revisit any of their Morpheme Mania pages and add words, antonyms, and synonyms as their vocabulary grows.

Day 5 *Assessment*

Make and hand out copies.
The answer key is on page A-6.
The instructions are on page A-2.

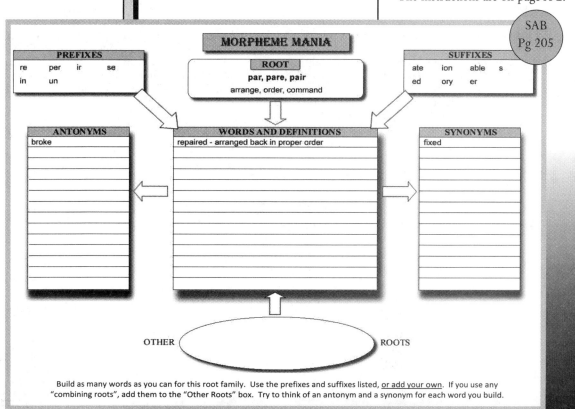

SAB
Pg 205

MORPHEME MANIA

PREFIXES			
re	per	ir	se
in	un		

ROOT
par, pare, pair
arrange, order, command

SUFFIXES			
ate	ion	able	s
ed	ory	er	

ANTONYMS
broke

WORDS AND DEFINITIONS
repaired - arranged back in proper order

SYNONYMS
fixed

OTHER ◯ ROOTS

Build as many words as you can for this root family. Use the prefixes and suffixes listed, <u>or add your own</u>. If you use any "combining roots", add them to the "Other Roots" box. Try to think of an antonym and a synonym for each word you build.

407

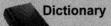
apparatus   object arranged for preparing to do a task; a device for a particular purpose

apparel   clothing arranged or laid out for an occasion

inseparable   not able to be arranged or moved apart

irreparable   not able to be arranged back into proper order; beyond remedy

parade   a formal arrangement for show; a procession of people moving along in a line

paraded   moved forward in a formal arrangement for show; processed along in a line

parades   formal arrangements for show; processions of people moving along in a line

parading   moving forward in a formal arrangement for show; processing along in a line

pare   to arrange for better appearance; to trim

pared   arranged for better appearance; trimmed

pares   arranges for better appearance; trims

paring   arranging for better appearance; trimming

preparation   act of putting in order or arranging beforehand; process of getting ready

preparations   acts of putting in order or arranging beforehand; things done to get ready

preparatory   tending to arrange a situation beforehand; serving to get things ready

prepare   to arrange beforehand; to get ready

prepared   arranged beforehand; got ready

preparedness   quality of being arranged beforehand; quality of being ready

preparer   a person who arranges beforehand; person who gets things ready

preparers   people who arrange beforehand; people who get things ready

prepares   arranges beforehand; gets ready

preparing   arranging beforehand; getting ready

repair   to arrange back into proper order; fix

repairable   able to be arranged back into proper order; fixable

repaired   arranged back into proper order; fixed

repairer   a person who arranges back into proper order; a person who fixes things

repairers   people who arrange back into proper order; people who fix things

repairing   arranging back into proper order; fixing

repairs   arranges back into proper order; fixes

separate   to arrange or order apart; to divide or distinguish

separated   arranged or ordered apart; divided or distinguished

separately   in a manner arranged or ordered apart; in a manner divided or distinguished

separateness   state of being arranged or ordered apart; condition of being divided or distinguished

separates   arranges or orders apart; divides or distinguishes

separating   arranging or ordering apart; dividing or distinguishing

separation   act of arranging or ordering apart; act of dividing or distinguishing

separations   acts of arranging or ordering apart; acts of dividing or distinguishing

unprepared   not having arranged things beforehand; not ready

unseparated   not arranged or ordered apart; together, not divided or distinguished

Check-Up for **PAR**

Name _____

____ 1. **PAR** or **PAIR** in words like **separate** and **repair** means:

  A arrange or order

  B to push or beat

  C to change

____ 2. What is the meaning of the word **inseparable**?

  A to keep from being pushed

  B not able to be set apart

  C able to be changed

____ 3. What is the meaning of the word **reparation**?

  A not to get ready

  B to push or beat again

  C an act of arranging or ordering back the way something was

____ 4. What is the meaning of the word **pare**?

  A to arrange or trim

  B not to change

  C a push or a beat

____ 5. What is the meaning of the word **irrepair**?

  A a state of not being ordered or arranged properly

  B to change back to the way something was

  C not to beat or push

____ 6. Which word means **not arranged apart**?

  A unprepared

  B unseparated

  C reparable

____ 7. Which word means **material arranged out to help with special tasks**?

  A reparatory

  B paraded

  C apparatus

____ 8. Which word means **serving to arrange ahead of time**?

  A preparatory

  B reparation

  C apparel

____ 9. **Comparability** has to do with:

  A giving short speeches

  B arranging and looking at things side-by-side

  C setting out on planned trips

____ 10. Juan and Amahl have **disparate** personalities. They:

  A do not worry about anything

  B behave exactly the same

  C are different

OBJECTIVES

- **Understand** the meaning of the root **VIA**
- **Build** words in the root **VIA** family
- **Break Apart** words in the root **VIA** family
- **Understand** the meaning of words in the **VIA** family
- **Understand** the spelling principles applied to the root **VIA**
- **Apply** knowledge of words in the **VIA** family
- **Assess** and **Reinforce** knowledge of words in the **VIA** family

MATERIALS

- Student Activity Books, pages 207-212
- Dictionary *(print or on-line)*

CROSS-CURRICULAR EXAMPLES

Science:
deviation, conveyer, deviated, impervious, viaduct

Social Studies:
via, obviate, conveyance, convoy, envoy, voyage

Language Arts:
convey, obvious, devious, trivia

Math:
deviate, previous

VIA

meaning "road, passageway, trip; to pass"

| **deviate** |
| to go off from the **road** |

| **viaduct** |
| **passageway** leading over a road |

| **voyage** |
| a **trip** |

| **convey** |
| **to pass** along with |

Morpheme: **VIA**
Allomorphs: **VI, VEY, VOY**

About 250 words containing the morpheme **VIA** or one of its allomorphs are current in English. During this unit, tell students to be alert for this root in their school texts, general reading, and oral language they hear. Some of the words they might encounter in their school subjects are listed on the left under Cross-Curricular Examples.

UNIT AT A GLANCE

Day ① ** *Root Squares* for **VIA

Day ② ** *Magic Squares* for **VIA

Day ③ ** *Stair Steps* for **VIA

OPTIONAL Day ④ ** *In Other Words* for **VIA

Day ⑤ ** *Assessment or Morpheme Mania* for **VIA

Each activity should take approximately **15 minutes**.

The Latin word for road or route, **via**, is still used in English as an anatomical passage (such as a vein) and as a preposition meaning *by way of*, as in we traveled to California **via** the Panama canal, or the teacher helped us enjoy our studies **via** humor.

One of the most surprising applications of this morpheme is the word **trivia**, literally *three roads*. Embedded in the word is some fascinating history of education. Elementary instruction consisted of studies in three subjects, or paths: grammar, rhetoric, and logic, together called the **trivium**. These being the three primary, basal roads to knowledge, the adjective **trivial** came to mean commonplace or ordinary. By a linguistic process called degeneration, **trivia** and **trivial** came to mean unimportant, quite the reverse of the original intent of the word. Note that **trivia** is the plural of the Latin word **trivium**.

There was also a **quadrivium**, the four-path study of arithmetic, astronomy, geometry, and music, which followed the **trivium**. Together the **trivium** and the **quadrivium** constituted the *Seven Liberal Arts*.

The distance or difference in value between what is expected and what actually results is called a **deviation**. For example, if you are using a directional compass near a magnet, you may need to account for a reading that is "off the path."

A group moving along together so as to protect or help each other is a **convoy**. If you go on vacation with neighbors, for example, but in separate vehicles, you may want to **convoy** so that you don't become separated or lost.

The words **vehicle**, **vector**, and **wagon** also contain vestiges of this root.

Word Alert!

The word **viable** would seem to be a good example of this morpheme, but instead it comes from a similar-looking morpheme meaning *life*, as in **vitamin** or **revive**. **Viable** means *capable of growing or sustaining life*.

On airmail envelopes we may see the French phrase **par avion**, meaning *by flight*, coming from the root for *birds* (**avian** or **aviary**).

As usual, words containing the letter sequence **v-i-a** are not necessarily illustrations of the root meaning *road or passageway*. For example, the **v-i-a** in words such as **abbreviate** and **jovial** cannot be isolated as the morpheme **via,** as the proof method of morphemic splitting will show:

> **ab**, *toward* + **brevi**, *short* + **ate**, *to cause to become*
>
> NOT ab + bre + via + te
>
> **jov**, *Jupiter* + **ial**, *characterized by*
>
> NOT jo + via + al

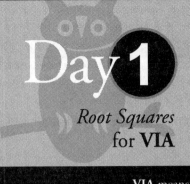

Day 1

Root Squares for VIA

VIA means
road, passageway, trip; to pass

LESSON TIME

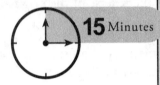

15 Minutes

OBJECTIVES

- **Understand** the meaning of the root **VIA**

- **Build** words in the **VIA** family

- **Understand** the meaning of words in the **VIA** family

- **Understand** the spelling principles applied to the root **VIA**

MATERIALS

- Student Activity Book
- **VIA** Word Wall
- Dictionary *(print or on-line)*

DIFFERENTIATING INSTRUCTION

If you prefer easier or more difficult activities, use your personal account at www.dynamicliteracy.com to access novice or expert versions, along with ideas on using them.

Root Squares for VIA

TEACH Have students turn to page 207 in their Activity Books. Say, "All of the prefixes and suffixes in the squares surrounding the shaded center are probably familiar, but if you have questions about any of the meanings, simply ask or look them up in the list inside the front and back cover of the activity book."

Call attention to the center box. Point out that the root **VIA** has several different spellings, called allomorphs. Ask students to decide if one of the forms they see in the middle square can stand alone as a word. They may recognize the word **via**, meaning *a route passing through*. You can use this word to lead students to the idea of *road, passageway, trip; to pass*. Suggest that students start their list with voy and then add to that word the prefix **con-**, meaning *together*, to build **convoy**, meaning *a group taking a trip together*. Explore how this word is related to the idea of *road, passageway, trip; to pass*.

COMPLETE THE ACTIVITY

Have students follow the directions to build words. If students have difficulty building words with the Root Squares, show them how by modeling the matrix approach found on the next page, taking one affix at a time and seeing if it will connect with any one of the allomorphs of the root.

DISCUSS After five minutes, have volunteers write some of their words on the board. Focus with the class on the words they have built and guide them in a discussion of how the meaning of the root is still *road, passageway, trip; to pass* even when prefixes and suffixes are added. Watch for target words that most easily demonstrate the meaning of *road, passageway, trip; to pass*. If the word **voyage** is not present, ask the class, "Can anyone try to use the suffix **-age**?" and then continue on to the target word discussion on the next page.

SAB Pg 207

Root Squares

How many words can you make?

Start in any square. Your goal is to combine two or more word parts to make as many words in the 'via, vi, vey, voy' family as you can. Write each word and a definition you can think of for it in the space provided at the bottom of the page. Use the back of the page if you need to.

de	age	ob
pre	via, vi, vey, voy	con
ate	per	ous

_____
_____
_____
_____
_____
_____
_____
_____

Focus Word: **VOYAGE** → Write this word on the board.

TEACH

Lead with this:	"What's happening if you're on a **voyage**?"
Student:	"You're on a trip."
Student:	"I think you're on the ocean."
Teacher:	"Those sound like good answers. Let's look at the pieces of meaning in the word."
Student:	"I see a suffix -**age**, but I'm not sure what that means. Have we studied that?"
Student:	"We had it with **manage**, but I don't think that's it."
Student:	"It says here in the suffix list that it can be a noun that means *a result, place,* or *action.*"
Student:	"**Voy** means *a road or a trip*, so **voyage** is just *the action of taking a trip.*"
Student:	"Doesn't it mean a trip on the sea?"
Teacher:	"I'm not sure—let's see if it's a sea trip or any trip."

DISCUSS Consult a dictionary with your class and discover the varieties of usage of the word. It can also be used as a verb, to **voyage**.

Root Squares Matrix

You can refer to this matrix to guide students in this activity. Students could build at least these 10 words. *It is not important how many words are built*, so long as students understand the meanings of the root and its affixes. Encourage discussion about the definitions of any words formed for the blank slots as well as for the attested words.

	no prefix	con-	de-	ob-	per-	pre-
no suffix	via	convoy				
		convey				
-age	voyage					
-ate			deviate	obviate		
-ous			devious	obvious	pervious	previous

Day 2

Magic Squares
for **VIA**

VIA means
road, passageway, trip; to pass

LESSON TIME

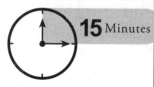

15 Minutes

OBJECTIVES

- **Understand** the meaning of the root **VIA**

- **Break Apart** words in the **VIA** family

- **Understand** the meanings of words in the **VIA** family

MATERIALS

- Student Activity Book

- **VIA** Word Wall

- Dictionary *(print or on-line)*

DIFFERENTIATING INSTRUCTION

If you prefer easier or more difficult activities, use your personal account at www.dynamicliteracy.com to access novice or expert versions, along with ideas on using them.

Break Apart Words with **VIA**

Have students turn to the Magic Squares on page 208 in their Student Activity Books. Model a Think-Aloud strategy for students: "I know that **VIA** means *road, passageway, trip; to pass*. I can use this knowledge to find the definition of a word with **VIA** or one of its allomorphs as its root."

Direct students to word D, **conveys**. Say: "This word has a prefix, **con-** meaning *together, with or thoroughly*, and a suffix **-s** that means either *plural* or *he, she, or it does*. Look at definition 2, *passes along with; makes known*. We can see from this that the suffix -s must be the marker for *he, she, or it does*. The word *with* is the prefix **con-**,

and the root, **VIA**, is defined by the word **passes**. We'll write the number 2 in square D."

COMPLETE THE ACTIVITY

Ask students to use the same strategy to find the correct definitions for the other words. Tell them to write the number of the definition in the box that matches the letter for the word. Remind them that if all their answers are correct, each row and each column will add up to the same Magic number.

DISCUSS After five minutes, ask if there are any difficulties about matching the words and definitions. If there are, ask volunteers to explain clues in the definitions that will lead to the correct choice of word. As needed, follow the focus word approach for **deviating** that you see modeled on the next page.

Add any new words to the classroom **VIA** Word Wall and remind students to add these words to the **VIA** Word Wall in their Activity Books.

SAB
Pg 208

Magic Squares

Select the best answer for each of the words in the 'via, vi, vey, voy' family from the numbered definitions. Put the number in the proper space in the Magic Square box. If the total of the numbers is the same both across and down, you have found the magic number!

'via, vi, vey, voy' means road, passageway, trip; to pass

WORDS	DEFINITIONS
A. conveyable	1. a person sent on a diplomatic trip
B. deviating	2. passes along with; makes known
C. deviously	3. a group of vehicles traveling together on a trip
D. conveys	4. in a manner being on the same passage but earlier; before
E. impervious	5. going on a trip
F. obviously	6. in a manner acting off from the road; in a meandering or scheming manner
G. voyaged	7. quality of being in the way of; quality of being evident
H. obviousness	8. going off from the road; straying from
I. voyaging	9. not allowing passage through; resistant to
	10. able to be passed along with; able to be made known
	11. related to the three basic roads of knowledge; related to something of small importance
	12. went on a trip
	13. in a manner in the way of; evidently

Magic Square Box

A. 10	B. 8	C. 6
D. 2	E. 9	F. 13
G. 12	H. 7	I. 5

Magic Number **24**

*** ANSWER KEY ***

Focus Word: **DEVIATING** —→ Write this word on the board.

TEACH

Sample leading question:	"Here's a word you might not have seen before, but with all our word skills, I'll bet we can figure it out."
Student:	"Okay, let's go. I see the suffix -**ing**, *happening now*. Something is **deviating** now."
Student:	"Or -**ing** can mean a noun that is *an act*. The act of **deviating**."
Student:	"And I see the prefix **de-**, which means *away or down from*."
Teacher:	"There's out root, **via**. But what's that **t** doing there?"
Student:	"I have it—there is a suffix -**ate** in this word, but the **e** on -**ate** drops because of the -**ing**."
Student:	"So the root spelling is not **via** but just **vi**."
Student:	"Now what do we have?"
Student:	"*Being on a road away?* I don't know what that is."
Student:	"Wait—**deviate**. That means *to go your own way* or something like that."
Teacher:	"And if you go your own way, what have you done as far as everyone else is doing?"
Student:	"I'll bet it's going off the regular path of everybody else, so *away-road*, being on an *off-road*."
Student:	"But not literally. Like being an individual."

DISCUSS You can use this opportunity to discuss the concept of **connotation**, or usage with "feeling" that a word has. Words can be negative in connotation, or positive in connotation. In a negative connotation, **deviating** can mean *going away from the accepted norm*. In a positive connotation, the word can mean *being adventurous*.

Day 3

Stair Steps
for **VIA**

VIA means
road, passageway, trip; to pass

LESSON TIME

15 Minutes

OBJECTIVES

- **Understand** the meaning of the root **VIA**

- **Apply** knowledge of the root **VIA**

- **Break Apart** words in the **VIA** family

- **Understand** the meaning of words in the **VIA** family

- **Understand** the spelling principles applied to the root **VIA**

MATERIALS

- Student Activity Book
- **VIA** Word Wall

DIFFERENTIATING INSTRUCTION

If you prefer easier or more difficult activities, use your personal account at www.dynamicliteracy.com to access novice or expert versions, along with ideas on using them.

Apply Knowledge of **VIA**

TEACH Have students turn to page 209 in their Student Activity Books. Explain that the boxes in front of and after the root indicate letters that spell out prefixes and suffixes. Students will spell out the correct prefixes and suffixes determined by clues in the definitions at the bottom of the page.

Have a volunteer read definition number eight at the bottom of the page. Say, "This step in the Stair Steps puzzle is yet another challenger. The acts of is familiar to us from other words we've built. The word we're building looks as if it ends in **-ions**. As we saw in **PREPARATIONS**, the suffix **-ate**, with the **e** dropped

before the **-ion**, will give us the idea of doing something. But what would we add to **VIATIONS** to get the ideas of *going off or straying from*? Looking at our list of two-letter prefixes, we see **de-** gets at that idea with its definition *make opposite, reverse, remove*. With that prefix added to what we have built to this point, we get **DEVIATIONS**. That fits the space and the definition very well."

COMPLETE THE ACTIVITY

Let students work in pairs (optionally) and tell them to use the same strategy to find the correct prefixes and suffixes for the words listed. These activities can be quite challenging!

DISCUSS After a few minutes, review the answers as a class. Ask if there were any difficulties. Listen to any problems and have volunteers solve the difficulties by explaining key clues in the given definitions. As needed, follow the focus word approach that you see modeled on the next page.

SAB Pg 209

Stair Steps

Fill in the missing letters of each 'via, vi, vey, voy' word by using the definitions below.
'via, vi, vey, voy' means road, passageway, trip; to pass

1. | c | o | n | v | e | y |
2. | v | o | y | a | g | e |
3. | o | b | v | i | o | u | s |
4. | p | r | e | v | i | o | u | s |
5. | v | o | y | a | g | e | r | s |
6. | o | b | v | i | o | u | s | l | y |
7. | c | o | n | v | e | y | a | n | c | e |
8. | d | e | v | i | a | t | i | o | n | s |
9. | c | o | n | v | e | y | a | n | c | e | s |

1. to pass along with; to make known
2. a trip
3. in the way of; evident
4. on the same passage at an earlier time; earlier
5. people who go on trips
6. in a manner in the way of; evidently
7. a means to pass along with; act of making known
8. acts of going off from the road; acts of straying from
9. various means to pass along with; acts of making known

Focus Word: **CONVEY** → Write this word on the board.

TEACH

Sample leading question:	"You might hear somebody say, 'Please **convey** my regards to your grandfather.' What's meant by that?"
Student:	"It sounds like it means *give or tell*. Give a greeting. Tell him hello."
Student:	"What does that have to do with a road or trip?"
Student:	"It seems that the person you're talking to is going to go see his grandfather, so he's going on a trip in a way."
Student:	"Right, and he's going to take this message *with* him. The prefix **con**-!"
Student:	"Yes, he's *taking a message with him on the trip*."
Student:	"And he'll share the message with the person he's gone to see."
Teacher:	"You word investigators are super."

DISCUSS Let groups of students discuss ways the word **convey** might be used. They may know of factory devices called **conveyor** belts, such as those at a car-wash. Lead students to see that the word means *to take along with from one place to another.* Facial or bodily expressions can **convey** meaning, or get meanings *across*.

DEMONSTRATE Let students list a few emotions, such as happiness, sadness, disappointment, surprise, *etc.*, and let them act out how the face could **convey** those emotions.

Day 4

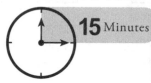

In Other Words for **VIA**

VIA means
road, passageway, trip; to pass

LESSON TIME

15 Minutes

OBJECTIVES

- **Understand** the meaning of the root **VIA**

- **Reinforce** knowledge of the root **VIA**

- **Understand** the meaning of words in the **VIA** family

- **Apply** knowledge of words in the **VIA** family

MATERIALS

- Student Activity Book

- **VIA** Word Wall

- Dictionary *(print or on-line)*

In Other Words for **VIA**

TEACH Have students turn to page 210 in their Student Activity Books. Explain that they are going to read a little story that uses some surprising and sometimes odd phrasing. The underlined words or phrases in the story are actually definitions or synonyms for words in the **VIA** family. Then they will see sentences about the story, each containing a blank.

Using context clues in the sentences, they will find a **VIA** family word in the Word Bank at the bottom to fit in each blank. Have a student read aloud the opening sentence or sentences of the story that contain the first underlined phrase. Then say, "Let's look at the first numbered sentence that contains a blank to be filled in. Clues in that sentence tell us that we want a naming word, a noun meaning *a trip*. I see the word **voyage** at the bottom of the page. The root of this word is **voy**, a form of via, meaning *trip*, and the suffix **-age** indicates an action. The word means *the act of taking a trip*. Let's write **voyage** in the blank space in the first sentence."

COMPLETE THE ACTIVITY
This can be quite challenging, so allow students to work on this activity in small groups. Not every word in the Word Bank will be used.

DISCUSS After about 10 minutes, ask if there were any difficulties. Have volunteers explain strategies they used that led to correct answers.

SAB
Pg 210

Caesar Blocks Swiss Plans

Caesar had just returned from a sea <u>trip</u> when he learned that the Swiss wanted to move as a group from their mountainous homeland to the coast <u>by way of</u> Roman territory. The Swiss sent <u>a person on the trip</u> to ask Caesar if that would be allowed.

Caesar <u>passed news along</u> to the Swiss messenger that he would decide about the issue soon.

In reality, Caesar was acting rather <u>off the road and scheming</u>. He remembered that <u>on the same passage at an earlier time</u> there had been trouble with these same people.

With astonishing speed, Caesar marched an army with a big <u>group of vehicles traveling together</u> through the mountains toward the Swiss. He then ordered that a wall <u>which would not allow passage through</u> be built.

Then Caesar told the Swiss that he would not <u>go off the path</u> of Roman tradition by allowing them to pass through their property. He had <u>schemingly</u> bought time to be able to block the Swiss plan.

<u>Fill in the blanks below using words from the "via, vi, vey, voy" family.</u>

1. At the beginning of this story, Caesar had just returned from a <u>voyage</u>.

2. He learned that the Swiss were heading toward the seacoast <u>via</u> Roman territory.

3. The Swiss sent an <u>envoy</u> to ask Caesar's permission.

4. Caesar <u>conveyed</u> to him the message that he would think about it for a while.

5. Yet Caesar was being <u>devious</u> with his message.

6. He recalled that <u>previously</u> he had had trouble in this area.

7. He therefore gathered a big army with wagons and horses and quickly moved this <u>convoy</u> toward the area.

8. When he got there, he ordered an <u>impervious</u> barrier to be built to stop the Swiss.

9. It was only then that Caesar sent word to the Swiss that he would not <u>deviate</u> from Roman tradition by allowing the Swiss to enter Roman land.

10. Caesar had <u>deviously</u> stalled for time and was able to prevent the Swiss from moving.

<u>Not Used:</u>   conveyances   deviation

418

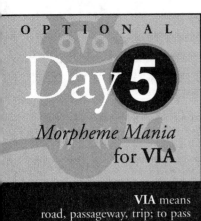

O P T I O N A L

Day 5

Morpheme Mania
for **VIA**

VIA means
road, passageway, trip; to pass

LESSON TIME

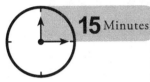

15 Minutes

OBJECTIVES

- **Build** words in the **VIA** family

- **Apply** knowledge of synonyms and antonyms to **VIA** words

Optional Morpheme Mania for **VIA**

On page 211 of their Activity Book, students will see an optional vocabulary enrichment activity that they can work on in groups, time permitting. This activity makes a great review for the formal assessment on the next page.

All the affixes presented in the week's activities are provided at the top of the page on either side of the root of the week in all its forms. Students can write in up to 13 of the words they built during the week, possibly discovering additional ones.

Then students can brainstorm with each other to come up with antonyms and synonyms they may know. Starter examples are given with every Morpheme Mania in the Activity Book. Because antonyms and synonyms may require knowledge of roots which students have not yet studied, completion of this activity is not crucial. Simply remind students that they can at any time during the course of the year revisit any of their Morpheme Mania pages and add words, antonyms, and synonyms as their vocabulary grows.

Day 5 *Assessment*

Make and hand out copies.
The answer key is on page A-6.
The instructions are on page A-2.

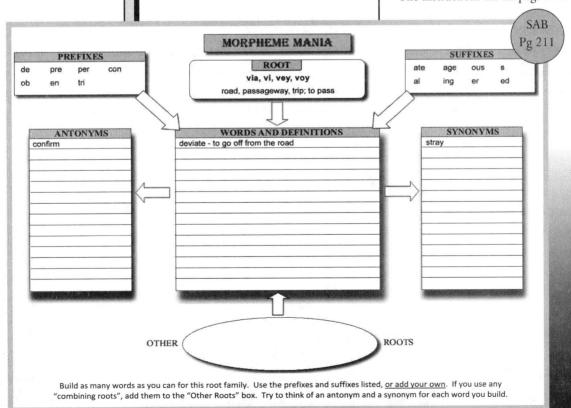

SAB
Pg 211

PREFIXES			
de	pre	per	con
ob	en	tri	

MORPHEME MANIA

ROOT
via, vi, vey, voy
road, passageway, trip; to pass

SUFFIXES			
ate	age	ous	s
al	ing	er	ed

ANTONYMS
confirm

WORDS AND DEFINITIONS
deviate - to go off from the road

SYNONYMS
stray

OTHER ⟨ ⟩ ROOTS

Build as many words as you can for this root family. Use the prefixes and suffixes listed, or add your own. If you use any "combining roots", add them to the "Other Roots" box. Try to think of an antonym and a synonym for each word you build.

convey to pass along with; to make known

conveyable able to be passed along with; able to be made known

conveyance a means to pass along with; act of making known

conveyances various means to pass along with; acts of making known

conveyed passed along with; made known

conveyer a person or device that passes along with; a passageway belt

conveyers people or devices to pass along with; passageway belts

conveying passing along with; making known

conveys passes along with; makes known

convoy a group of vehicles traveling together on a trip

convoys groups of vehicles traveling together on a trip

deviate to go off from the road; to stray from

deviated went off from the road; strayed from

deviates goes off from the road; strays from

deviating going off from the road; straying from

deviation an act of going off from the road; an act of straying from

deviations acts of going off from the road; acts of straying from

devious located away from the road; roundabout or tricky

deviously in a manner being from the road; in a roundabout or tricky manner

envoy a person sent on a diplomatic trip

envoys people sent on diplomatic trips

impervious not allowing passage through; resistant to

obvious in the way of; evident

obviously in a manner being in the way of; evidently

obviousness quality of being in the way of; quality of being evident

previous on the same passage at an earlier time; earlier

previously in a manner being on the same passage but earlier; before

trivia the three basic roads to knowledge; something of small importance

trivial related to the three basic roads to knowledge; related to something of small importance

via by way of

viaduct passageway leading over a road

viaducts passageways leading over roads

voyage a trip

voyaged went on a trip

voyager a person who goes on a trip

voyagers people who go on trips

voyages trips

voyaging going on a trip

Check-Up for **VIA**

____ 1. **VIA**, **VEY** or **VOY** in words like **viaduct**, **conveyance**, and **voyage** means:

    A road or trip

    B wish

    C bend or turn

____ 2. What is the meaning of the word **deviate**?

    A to wish

    B to develop

    C to go down the wrong path

____ 3. What is the meaning of the word **obvious**?

    A wants very much

    B difficult to turn

    C being right in one's path

____ 4. What is the meaning of the word **via**?

    A good-bye

    B by way of

    C far from

____ 5. What is the meaning of the word **conveyance**?

    A a method of passing along information or goods

    B wishing to have the same things as other people

    C an act of kindness

____ 6. Which word means **traveling**?

    A convoy

    B voyagers

    C voyaging

____ 7. Which word means **not having a passageway through**?

    A previously

    B impervious

    C conveyed

____ 8. Which word means **to stand in the way of**?

    A obviousness

    B conveyable

    C obviate

____ 9. If a river is **deviable**, it:

    A can be moved from its course

    B has no turns in it

    C is not clean enough to swim in

____ 10. To **reconvey** a message is to:

    A keep it back from someone

    B pass it along again

    C put false information in it

OBJECTIVES

- **Understand** the meaning of the root **HER**
- **Build** words in the root **HER** family
- **Break Apart** words in the root **HER** family
- **Understand** the meaning of words in the **HER** family
- **Understand** the spelling principles applied to the root **HER**
- **Apply** knowledge of words in the **HER** family
- **Assess** and **Reinforce** knowledge of words in the **HER** family

MATERIALS

- Student Activity Books, pages 213-218
- Dictionary (*print or on-line*)
- several pencils and adhesive tape (optional)

CROSS-CURRICULAR EXAMPLES

Science:
cohesion, cohere

Social Studies:
adherent, inherent

Language Arts:
coherent, incoherency

Math:
equicohesion, cohere

HER

meaning "to stick or cling"

cohesive
tending to **stick** together

adheres
sticks or **clings** to

Morpheme: **HER**
Allomorphs: **HERE, HES**

About 100 words containing the morpheme **HER** or one of its allomorphs are current in English. During this unit, tell students to be alert for this root in their school texts, general reading, and oral language they hear. Some of the words they might encounter in their school subjects are listed on the left under Cross-Curricular Examples.

UNIT AT A GLANCE

Day **1**
Root Squares
for **HER**

Day **2**
Magic Squares
for **HER**

Day **3**
Stair Steps
for **HER**

OPTIONAL
Day **4**
In Other Words
for **HER**

Day **5**
Assessment or Morpheme Mania
for **HER**

Each activity should take approximately **15 minutes**.

Knowing the deep etymological meanings of roots adds a layer of appreciation for words. Guide students to observe the metaphor of *sticking* or *clinging* in such words as **hesitate**, **hesitation**, and **unhesitatingly**.

The switch between **s** and **r** that occurs in the allomorphs of this root is a common linguistic occurrence. We see it in the English words **was** and **were**. Either allomorph of this root for *stick* can go with some of the same affixes, so we can learn specific vocabulary only with experimentation and experience. For example, we have both **cohere** and **cohesion**.

The difference between literal or concrete meanings and figurative or abstract meanings can be illustrated through this root. Students will almost certainly have heard of **adhesive** tape, tape that literally **adheres** to surfaces. See if students understand what it means to **adhere** to rules, or to be an **adherent** of some political or social belief. You can also discuss **inherent** rights or **inherent** characteristics.

Word Alert!

As usual, the letter sequences **h-e-r** and **h-e-s** do not automatically indicate the presence of the root meaning *to stick*. Words such as **father**, **these**, **parentheses**, and **decipher** can make enjoyable proof-method morphemic splitting exercises.

The word **heresy** and its related **heretical** come from a Greek root meaning *to attack or take away*.

The word **heredity** is from a root meaning *left behind*, as an **heir**.

LESSON TIME

15 Minutes

OBJECTIVES

- **Understand** the meaning of the root **HER**

- **Build** words in the **HER** family

- **Understand** the meaning of words in the **HER** family

- **Understand** the spelling principles applied to the root **HER**

MATERIALS

- Student Activity Book

- **HER** Word Wall

- Dictionary *(print or on-line)*

- several pencils and adhesive tape (optional)

DIFFERENTIATING INSTRUCTION

If you prefer easier or more difficult activities, use your personal account at www.dynamicliteracy.com to access novice or expert versions, along with ideas on using them.

Root Squares for HER

TEACH Have students turn to page 213 in their Activity Books. Say, "All of the prefixes and suffixes in the squares surrounding the shaded center are probably familiar, but if you have questions about any of the meanings, simply ask or look them up in the list inside the front and back cover of the activity book."

Call attention to the center box. Point out that the root **HER** has several different spellings, called allomorphs. Ask students to decide if one of the forms they see in the middle square can stand alone as a word. They may recognize the words **her** and **here**, but you should point out that these do not belong to this family. Suggest that students start their list with **here** and then add to that word the prefix **co-**, meaning *together*, to build **cohere**, meaning *to stick together*. Invite

students to explore how this word is related to the idea of *to stick or cling*.

COMPLETE THE ACTIVITY

Have students follow the directions to build words. If students have difficulty building words with the Root Squares, show them how by modeling the matrix approach found on the next page, taking one affix at a time and seeing if it will connect with any one of the allomorphs of the root.

DISCUSS After five minutes, have volunteers write some of their words on the board. Focus with the class on the words they have built and guide them in a discussion of how the meaning of the root is still *to stick or cling* even when prefixes and suffixes are added.

Watch for target words that most easily demonstrate the meaning of *to stick or cling*. If the word adhere is not present, ask the class, "Can anyone try to use the prefix **ad-**?" and then continue on to the target word discussion on the next page.

SAB
Pg 213

Root Squares

How many words can you make?

Start in any square. Your goal is to combine two or more word parts to make as many words in the 'her, here, hes' family as you can. Write each word and a definition you can think of for it in the space provided at the bottom of the page. Use the back of the page if you need to.

ive	ion	in
ent	her, here, hes	co
ad	ence	ly

Focus Word: **ADHERE** ⟶ Write this word on the board.

TEACH

Lead with this:	"What does it mean to **adhere** to a certain belief?"
Student:	"You believe in it."
Student:	"You belong to a certain religion."
Teacher:	"Good, and let's look at the word to see what it tells us about itself."
Student:	"I see. It means *to stick*, like tape."
Teacher:	"What does the part **ad-** mean?"
Student:	"*To* or *toward*."
Student:	"Hey, like saying '*Stick to your beliefs!*'"

DISCUSS Encourage students to see a word like **adhere** in terms of its two morphemic parts: *to stick to*. Let small groups discuss principles or ideas they **adhere** to.

DEMONSTRATE Lay out some pencils in columns, and then place over them all a strip of **adhesive** tape. Lift and ask the class what the pencils are doing to the tape. (They are **adhering**.)

Root Squares Matrix

You can refer to this matrix to guide students in this activity. Students could build at least these 19 words. *It is not important how many words are built*, so long as students understand the meanings of the root and its affixes. Encourage discussion about the definitions of any words formed for the blank slots as well as for the attested words.

	ad-	co-	in-
no suffix	adhere	cohere	inhere
-ence	adherence	coherence	inherence
-ent	adherent	coherent	inherent
-ion	adhesion	cohesion	inhesion
-ive	adhesive	cohesive	
-ion	adherently	coherently	inherently
-ive	adhesively	cohesively	

Day 2

Magic Squares
for **HER**

HER means
to stick or cling

LESSON TIME

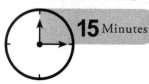

15 Minutes

OBJECTIVES

• **Understand** the meaning of the root **HER**

• **Break Apart** words in the **HER** family

• **Understand** the meanings of words in the **HER** family

MATERIALS

• Student Activity Book

• **HER** Word Wall

• Dictionary
(print or on-line)

DIFFERENTIATING INSTRUCTION

If you prefer easier or more difficult activities, use your personal account at www.dynamicliteracy.com to access novice or expert versions, along with ideas on using them.

Break Apart Words with **HER**

Have students turn to the Magic Squares on page 214 in their Student Activity Books. Model a Think-Aloud strategy for students: "I know that **HER** means *to stick or cling*. I can use this knowledge to find the definition of a word with **HER** or one of its allomorphs as its root."

Direct students to word A, **adhere**. Say, "This word has only a prefix, **ad-** meaning *toward; to; in, for; near*. Look at definition 7, *to stick to or cling to*. The root, **HERE**, is defined by the words *stick* and *cling*. We'll write the number 7 in square A."

Ask students to use the same strategy to find the correct definitions for the other words. Tell them to write the number of the definition in the box that matches the letter for the word. Remind them that if all their answers are correct, each row and each column will add up to the same Magic number.

DISCUSS After five minutes, ask if there are any difficulties about matching the words and definitions. If there are, ask volunteers to explain clues in the definitions that will lead to the correct choice of word. As needed, follow the focus word approach for **inherent** that you see modeled on the next page.

Add any new words to the classroom **HER** Word Wall and remind students to add these words to the **HER** Word Wall in their Activity Books.

SAB Pg 214

Magic Squares

Select the best answer for each of the words in the 'her, here, hes' family from the numbered definitions. Put the number in the proper space in the Magic Square box. If the total of the numbers is the same both across and down, you have found the magic number!

'her, here, hes' means to stick or cling

WORDS		DEFINITIONS
A.	adhere	1. not tending to cling; not slow or reluctant to act
B.	cohesions	2. things that stick to other things; types of glue or tape
C.	adhesives	3. having the quality of sticking within; intrinsic or inborn
D.	incohesive	4. state of not sticking together; quality of lacking sense or logic
E.	incoherence	5. quality of sticking or clinging to
F.	hesitantly	6. in a clinging manner; in a manner slow or reluctant to act
G.	inherent	7. to stick to or cling to
H.	adherence	8. tending not to stick together
I.	coherences	9. processes of sticking together
		10. processes or acts of sticking together

Magic Square Box

A.	B.	C.
7	9	2
D.	**E.**	**F.**
8	4	6
G.	**H.**	**I.**
3	5	10

Magic Number __18__

*** ANSWER KEY ***

Focus Word: **INHERENT** ➜ Write this word on the board.

TEACH

Sample leading question:	"You may have heard in the belief that certain human rights are **inherent**. Who can tell us what that means?"
Student:	"Yes, I've heard of that—like life, liberty and the pursuit of happiness, isn't it?"
Student:	"Or that all men are created equal."
Student:	"And women!"
Teacher:	"Good, and what is it about those rights that lets us call them **inherent**?"
Student:	"I know—we'll find out by looking closely at the word."
Student:	"*Not* and *stick*."
Student:	"How about *in* and *stick*? They belong in each of us and can't be taken away."

DISCUSS Encourage students to see a word like **inherent** in terms of its morphemic parts: *sticking in.* Let small groups discuss their individual natural, **inherent** physical features, such as eye and hair color.

DEMONSTRATE While the word **inherent** is still on the board, isolate each of the pieces to show the **inherent** meaning of the word!

Day 3

Stair Steps
for HER

HER means
to stick or cling

LESSON TIME

15 Minutes

OBJECTIVES

- **Understand** the meaning of the root **HER**

- **Apply** knowledge of the root **HER**

- **Break Apart** words in the **HER** family

- **Understand** the meaning of words in the **HER** family

- **Understand** the spelling principles applied to the root **HER**

MATERIALS

- Student Activity Book
- **HER** Word Wall

DIFFERENTIATING INSTRUCTION

If you prefer easier or more difficult activities, use your personal account at www.dynamicliteracy.com to access novice or expert versions, along with ideas on using them.

Apply Knowledge of HER

TEACH Have students turn to page 215 in their Student Activity Books. Explain that the boxes in front of and after the root indicate letters that spell out prefixes and suffixes. Students will spell out the correct prefixes and suffixes determined by clues in the definitions at the bottom of the page.

Have a volunteer read definition number three at the bottom of the page. Say, "This two-word definition provides minimal clues, but we can use it to solve the puzzle of which word fits in step three. The suffix will be -**ing** as we see in the first word of the definition, *sticking* together.

The prefixed idea of *together* is one of the spellings of the prefix **con-**, defined in our list as *together, with*. The prefix is spelled **co-**, with which we get **COHERING**."

COMPLETE THE ACTIVITY

Let students work in pairs (optionally) and tell them to use the same strategy to find the correct prefixes and suffixes for the words listed. These activities can be quite challenging!

DISCUSS After a few minutes, review the answers as a class. Ask if there were any difficulties. Listen to any problems and have volunteers solve the difficulties by explaining key clues in the given definitions. As needed, follow the focus word approach that you see modeled on the next page.

SAB
Pg 215

Stair Steps

Fill in the missing letters of each 'her, here, hes' word by using the definitions below.
'her, here, hes' means to stick or cling

1.	c	o	h	e	r	e			
2.	a	d	h	e	r	e	d		
3.	c	o	h	e	r	i	n	g	
4.	a	d	h	e	r	e	n	t	s
5.	c	o	h	e	r	e	n	t	l	y
6.	h	e	s	i	t	a	t	i	o	n	s
7.	i	n	c	o	h	e	r	e	n	t	l	y
8.	i	n	c	o	h	e	r	e	n	c	i	e	s

1. to stick together; to fit together
2. stuck to or clung to
3. sticking together
4. people who stick to a cause or belief; supporters or advocates
5. in the manner of sticking together; logically and sensibly
6. conditions of clinging; states of being slow or reluctant to act
7. in a manner not sticking together; so as to lack sense or logic
8. states of not sticking together; qualities of lacking sense or logic

428

Day ③ Extend the Learning

Focus Word: **COHERE** ⟶ Write this word on the board.

TEACH

Sample leading question:	"What if you told somebody that their argument did not **cohere**? What would you mean?"
Student:	"That's easy: '*stick together*.' But what does that mean?"
Student:	"I think it means that the points they're trying to make don't fit together or follow."
Student:	"Oh, okay. I've heard of **coherent** and **incoherent**, *making sense* and *not making sense*, but I never knew of the verb **to cohere**."
Teacher:	"Great—you're continuing to see how morphemic families of words work!"

DISCUSS   Encourage students to see a word like **cohere** in terms of its two morphemic parts: *to stick together*. Let groups discuss how the following things can **cohere**: room decoration (example target answer: matching colors and styles); mud pies (target answer: with wetness).

DEMONSTRATE   Put these two sentences on the board and ask students if they see some ways to make them **cohere**:

> It was sunny today. We couldn't have a picnic.

Possible ways:

> It was sunny today, but we still couldn't have a picnic.

> Although it was sunny today, we couldn't have a picnic.

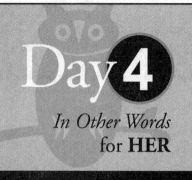

Day 4

In Other Words for **HER**

HER means to stick or cling

LESSON TIME

15 Minutes

OBJECTIVES

• **Understand** the meaning of the root **HER**

• **Reinforce** knowledge of the root **HER**

• **Understand** the meaning of words in the **HER** family

• **Apply** knowledge of words in the **HER** family

MATERIALS

• Student Activity Book

• **HER** Word Wall

• Dictionary *(print or on-line)*

In Other Words for **HER**

TEACH Have students turn to page 216 in their Student Activity Books. Explain that they are going to read a little story that uses some surprising and sometimes odd phrasing. The underlined words or phrases in the story are actually definitions or synonyms for words in the **HER** family. Then they will see sentences about the story, each containing a blank.

Using context clues in the sentences, they will find a **HER** family word in the Word Bank at the bottom to fit in each blank. Have a student read aloud the opening sentence or sentences of the story that contain the first underlined phrase. Then say, "Let's look at the first numbered sentence that contains a blank to be filled in. Clues in that sentence tell us that we want a naming word, a noun meaning *a substance to stick to other things*. I see the word **adhesive** at the bottom of the page. The root of the word is **HES**, a form of **HER**. The suffix **-ive** means *that which performs or serves to*. The prefix **ad-** means *toward or to*. Let's write **adhesive** in the blank space in the first sentence."

COMPLETE THE ACTIVITY
This can be quite challenging, so allow students to work on this activity in small groups. Not every word in the Word Bank will be used.

DISCUSS After about 10 minutes, ask if there were any difficulties. Have volunteers explain strategies they used that led to correct answers.

SAB Pg 216

The Failure That Wasn't

Sometimes a failure turns out to be a success. A man named Spencer was trying in 1970 to invent a super-strong <u>substance to stick to other things</u>. However, he came up with a substance that would <u>stick to things</u> all right, but did not have a permanent <u>state of sticking together</u>. He was <u>slow</u> to tell anyone about his failure, but he did tell his friend Art, hoping that there might be some usefulness <u>sticking within</u> about the product.

Four years later, Art was having trouble keeping up with all the passages he wanted to refer to in a book, since his bookmarkers kept falling out. He remembered Spencer's weak glue, was <u>not slow</u> about rubbing some of it on the markers, and the *Post-It®* note was invented!

Just remember, the next time something seems <u>in an inborn manner</u> <u>making no sense or logic</u>, it may turn out to be a brilliant discovery.

<u>Fill in the blanks below using words from the "her, here, hes" family.</u>

1. Spencer was trying to develop a super-strong <u>adhesive</u>.

2. What he found did indeed <u>adhere</u> to things.

3. However, its quality of <u>adherence</u> was weak and temporary.

4. People are <u>hesitant</u> to tell others about their mistakes or failures.

5. Many things that seem useless have some <u>inherent</u> value.

6. With inspiration, Art was <u>unhesitant</u> to try the new product in a new way.

7. The failure was actually not <u>inherently</u> a failure after all.

8. Things that make no sense or are <u>incoherent</u> are often brilliant.

<u>Not Used:</u>   cohesion   hesitation   incoherently   hesitated

430

OPTIONAL

Day 5

Morpheme Mania
for **HER**

HER means
to stick or cling

LESSON TIME

15 Minutes

OBJECTIVES

- **Build** words in the **HER** family

- **Apply** knowledge of synonyms and antonyms to **HER** words

Optional Morpheme Mania for **HER**

On page 217 of their Activity Book, students will see an optional vocabulary enrichment activity that they can work on in groups, time permitting. This activity makes a great review for the formal assessment on the next page.

All the affixes presented in the week's activities are provided at the top of the page on either side of the root of the week in all its forms. Students can write in up to 13 of the words they built during the week, possibly discovering additional ones.

Then students can brainstorm with each other to come up with antonyms and synonyms they may know. Starter examples are given with every Morpheme Mania in the Activity Book. Because antonyms and synonyms may require knowledge of roots which students have not yet studied, completion of this activity is not crucial. Simply remind students that they can at any time during the course of the year revisit any of their Morpheme Mania pages and add words, antonyms, and synonyms as their vocabulary grows.

Day 5 *Assessment*

Make and hand out copies.
The answer key is on page A-6.
The instructions are on page A-2.

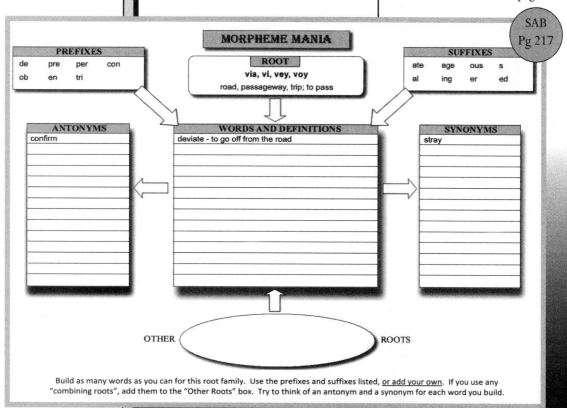

SAB Pg 217

MORPHEME MANIA

PREFIXES			
de	pre	per	con
ob	en	tri	

ROOT
via, vi, vey, voy
road, passageway, trip; to pass

SUFFIXES			
ate	age	ous	s
al	ing	er	ed

ANTONYMS
confirm

WORDS AND DEFINITIONS
deviate - to go off from the road

SYNONYMS
stray

OTHER ROOTS

Build as many words as you can for this root family. Use the prefixes and suffixes listed, _or add your own_. If you use any "combining roots", add them to the "Other Roots" box. Try to think of an antonym and a synonym for each word you build.

adhere to stick to or cling to

adhered stuck to or clung to

adherence quality of sticking or clinging to; faithful attachment or obedience to

adherent a person sticking or clinging to; a supporter or advocate

adherents people sticking or clinging to; supporters or advocates

adheres sticks to or clings to

adhering sticking to or clinging to

adhesive something that sticks to another thing; glue or tape

adhesives things that stick to other things; types of glue or tape

cohere to stick together; to fit together; to make sense

cohered stuck together; fit together; made sense

coherence process or act of sticking together; clarity and sense

coherences processes or acts of sticking together; qualities of clarity and sense

coherent having the quality of sticking together; logical and sensible

coherently in the manner of sticking together; logically and sensibly

coheres sticks together

cohering sticking together

cohesion process of sticking together

cohesions processes of sticking together

cohesive tending to stick together

hesitance act of clinging; slowness or reluctance to act

hesitances acts of clinging; acts of being slow or reluctant to act

hesitant tending to cling; tending be slow or reluctant to act

hesitantly in a clinging manner; in a manner slow or reluctant to act

hesitate to cling; to be slow or reluctant to act

hesitated clung; was slow or reluctant to act

hesitates clings; is slow or reluctant to act

hesitating clinging; being slow or reluctant to act

hesitation condition of clinging; slowness or reluctance to act

hesitations conditions of clinging; states of being slow or reluctant to act

incoherence state of not sticking together; quality of lacking sense or logic

incoherencies states of not sticking together; qualities of lacking sense or logic

incoherent not sticking together; lacking sense or logic

incoherently in a manner not sticking together; so as to lack sense or logic

incohesive tending not to stick together

inherent having the quality of sticking within; relevant or inborn

inherently in the manner of sticking within; in a relevant or inborn manner

unhesitant not tending to cling; not slow or reluctant to act

Check-Up for **HER**

Name _____

____ **1.** **HER** or **HES** in words like **adhere** and **cohesion** means:

   A place

   B stick

   C person

____ **2.** What is the meaning of the word **cohere**?

   A to invite a person

   B locating something

   C to cling together

____ **3.** What is the meaning of the word **hesitate**?

   A to act as if stuck

   B to remove

   C to imitate a person

____ **4.** What is the meaning of the word **incohesive**?

   A being found in no place

   B not sticking together

   C not liking people

____ **5.** What is the meaning of the word **adherent**?

   A tending to stick to something

   B to cling to a place

   C listening badly

____ **6.** Which word means **not holding back**?

   A hesitantly

   B incoherent

   C unhesitant

____ **7.** Which word means **the quality of belonging inside**?

   A cohere

   B inhesion

   C adhesively

____ **8.** Which word means **quality of not being connected**?

   A incoherence

   B hesitated

   C inherent

____ **9.** JoJo is an **adhesional** kind of person. JoJo:

   A made enough money to buy a car

   B has lived in many different places

   C always seems to be hanging around

____ **10.** The **incoherency** of the speaker left the listeners:

   A wondering what the topic of the speech was

   B excited about joining the new club

   C with clear ideas about the new plan

Check-Up for **HER**

Appendix

A

Assessments

EACH ROOT

MID-TERM

COMPREHENSIVE (PRE/POST TEST)

Instructions for Individual Root Unit Assessments

For every root unit, there is a quick 10-question assessment designed to give you and your students immediate "feed-back," reinforcement, summative grades, and extended learning. Each of these tests has the same design:

Question 1 checks simple knowledge about the root's meaning.

Questions 2-5 are applications, asking students to decode a word by selecting a definition that deconstructs the word into its morphemic meanings.

Questions 6 through 8 do the reverse by giving a definition, and students construct the appropriate word.

Questions 2 through 8 address words that are likely to have been covered in the unit's work.

Questions 9 and 10 on each test offer students a chance to demonstrate their ability to decode words that they may not ever have seen before, but which illustrate the target root and familiar affixes. This part of each assessment provides an insight into comprehension and how well students are growing as independent readers with valuable lifetime skills.

If you discover that some of your students need more help with a specific root unit, you will find on the website, using your teacher account, additional "novice" activities to offer them.

Weekly Assessment ANSWER KEYS

Assessment 1: FORM

1. **C** - arrangement
2. **B** - having one shape
3. **C** - an act of crossing shapes
4. **A** - a process of taking on a shape with something else
5. **C** - serving to put into good arrangement
6. **A** - malformed
7. **B** - formative
8. **C** - oviform
9. **B** - liked things to be arranged his way
10. **A** - arranged it in a new way

Assessment 2: PON

1. **A** - to place or put
2. **B** - to put together
3. **C** - to put down
4. **A** - put forth
5. **C** - an act of putting a burden on someone
6. **B** - repository
7. **A** - opposition
8. **C** - postponement
9. **B** - put his money in many different places
10. **B** - switched the letters

Assessment 3: QUEST

1. **A** - to seek
2. **B** - a search into
3. **C** - tending to look for and gain for oneself
4. **C** - needing to be sought after and gotten
5. **A** - tending to look into matters a lot
6. **B** - conquer
7. **A** - reacquire
8. **A** - requisitioners
9. **B** - needed before you can study algebra
10. **C** - asked for information from his friends

Assessment 4: VAL

1. **B** - strength or worth
2. **C** - to take worth away from
3. **A** - having balanced strength
4. **A** - feeling that two differing things both have worth
5. **B** - so as not to have any worth
6. **B** - validated
7. **A** - prevalent
8. **C** - valor
9. **C** - lost worth in people's eyes
10. **B** - gather strength together

Assessment 5: PORT

1. **A** - to carry
2. **B** - brought in
3. **C** - able to be carried
4. **A** - to bring back
5. **B** - so as to carry or hold up
6. **C** - porter
7. **B** - retransport
8. **A** - exportation
9. **C** - letting themselves be carried with fun in all directions
10. **C** - how people carried themselves and behaved

Assessment 6: JECT

1. **C** - to throw
2. **A** - to throw back
3. **B** - a device to throw light forward
4. **A** - something thrown in between
5. **C** - threw up a barrier
6. **A** - trajectory
7. **B** - dejected
8. **B** - conjecture
9. **C** - as if thrown off a bus
10. **B** - thrown all over the place

Assessment 7: SIGN

1. **C** - a mark or meaning
2. **B** - to give a meaning or purpose to
3. **C** - quality of having no marked importance
4. **A** - made an indication
5. **B** - gives a mark or meaning again
6. **A** - designs
7. **C** - signatures
8. **A** - designee
9. **C** - sealed the deal with each other
10. **B** - his face gave an indication ahead of his words

Assessment 8: STA

1. **B** - to stand or stop
2. **C** - not likely to stay up
3. **A** - a stand for vehicles
4. **A** - to stand one thing with another
5. **B** - taken a stand apart from something or someone
6. **B** - circumstances
7. **C** - statements
8. **A** - ecstatic
9. **C** - there was a slowdown of Lorenzo's blood flow
10. **B** - holds humidity at a certain point

Assessment 9: ACT

1. **C** - to do
2. **B** - to put into motion
3. **A** - process of performing among things
4. **C** - a device that does something in response
5. **B** - easily able to move
6. **A** - coagulate
7. **B** - hyperactive
8. **B** - inactivator
9. **C** - who or what does something
10. **A** - the process of working together

Weekly Assessment ANSWER KEYS

Assessment 10: PUL

1. **C** - to push
2. **C** - pushing back
3. **B** - push it away from yourself
4. **A** - a device to help you push forward
5. **B** - getting rid of it
6. **B** - impel
7. **A** - pulsation
8. **B** - compelled
9. **C** - hurried up the settlement
10. **A** - required for all

Assessment 11: JUR

1. **C** - right or true
2. **B** - changes toward what is right
3. **A** - a person who swears an oath with someone
4. **C** - people selected to decide what is right
5. **A** - a situation that is not right or fair
6. **A** - perjury
7. **B** - unjustifiable
8. **B** - readjustors
9. **A** - hadn't been placed back correctly
10. **C** - swore off trusting Lena

Assessment 12: GRAD

1. **C** - to step
2. **B** - to go back
3. **A** - an act of going apart
4. **C** - movement forward
5. **C** - indicates regular steps of measurement
6. **A** - aggression
7. **B** - transgressor
8. **A** - degradation
9. **B** - doorways
10. **C** - a series of steps

Assessment 13: GRAPH

1. **B** - chart or write
2. **B** - a writing about a life
3. **C** - relating to a chart that records many pieces of information
4. **A** - a signature personally written
5. **C** - related to charting the earth
6. **B** - telegraphic
7. **A** - orthography
8. **C** - paragraph
9. **C** - writing in "shorthand"
10. **A** - charts about the people

Assessment 14: LECT

1. **A** - gather or read
2. **B** - to gather together
3. **C** - not able to be read
4. **A** - quality of being chosen out from
5. **C** - likely to choose apart
6. **A** - electing
7. **C** - lecturer
8. **A** - diligently
9. **C** - choose not to do something that you should do
10. **B** - read

Assessment 15: EQU

1. **A** - fair or balanced
2. **B** - a condition of being out of balance
3. **C** - a balanced statement
4. **A** - brought to balance or fairness
5. **C** - divides the world into balanced halves
6. **B** - equidistant
7. **C** - equilibrium
8. **B** - equivalences
9. **C** - all the time
10. **A** - the same length as the night

Assessment 16: PET

1. **C** - to seek or aim for
2. **C** - to aim for the same goal along with others
3. **A** - anything that causes a seeking toward
4. **B** - a rush or drive into
5. **B** - aiming for or seeking again and again
6. **B** - perpetuated
7. **A** - petitioners
8. **B** - incompetency
9. **A** - practically attacked me
10. **C** - move toward the center

Assessment 17: FUND

1. **B** - to pour
2. **A** - poured in different directions
3. **C** - act or process of pouring into
4. **B** - to pour together and mix up
5. **C** - you give it out fully
6. **A** - profuse
7. **C** - foundry
8. **B** - transfuses
9. **C** - spread the solution throughout the heart
10. **A** - pours up through

Assessment 18: METER

1. **C** - measure
2. **C** - a measure through
3. **B** - not measuring with
4. **A** - a measure around
5. **B** - measures it
6. **A** - optometrist
7. **C** - geometry
8. **A** - decimeter
9. **B** - respirometer
10. **C** - measure time and rhythm

Weekly Assessment ANSWER KEYS

Assessment 19: PART

1. **B** - side or piece
2. **C** - to the side
3. **C** - referring to a piece
4. **A** - act of making a division away from
5. **C** - push your friends to action
6. **A** - counterpart
7. **A** - particulars
8. **B** - apartment
9. **B** - did not take sides
10. **A** - is made up of three sides

Assessment 20: LAT

1. **A** - to bring
2. **B** - brought out
3. **C** - bringing into law
4. **A** - brought apart
5. **B** - brought back together
6. **C** - translates
7. **A** - superlative
8. **B** - relation
9. **B** - brought forth or stressed
10. **C** - bring them together for a comparison

Assessment 21: VOL

1. **C** - to roll
2. **A** - rolled or folded together
3. **B** - to roll down
4. **A** - the act of being folded in
5. **C** - person aiming to roll back the old for the new
6. **A** - volute
7. **B** - revolvable
8. **B** - evolutionary
9. **A** - with the coils going around
10. **C** - sat as if coiled inward

Assessment 22: STRU

1. **B** - to build
2. **C** - helping to build in or arrange
3. **B** - serving to arrange together
4. **A** - the act of unbuilding
5. **B** - arranged
6. **B** - deconstruct
7. **A** - obstructive
8. **C** - reconstructed
9. **A** - arrange it all together again
10. **C** - wouldn't die

Assessment 23: SPIR

1. **C** - to breathe
2. **B** - to breathe into
3. **A** - to breathe out
4. **C** - the process of breathing over and over
5. **A** - whisper among themselves
6. **B** - aspirations
7. **C** - perspiring
8. **A** - spirited
9. **B** - had lost the breath of joy
10. **C** - send out air

Assessment 24: MAN

1. **B** - hand
2. **C** - done by hand
3. **A** - having to do with handling
4. **A** - act of taking from the hand
5. **C** - a way of handling a situation
6. **C** - unmanageably
7. **A** - manufactured
8. **B** - mismanagement
9. **A** - communicated by hand
10. **B** - be used with two hands

Assessment 25: MEM

1. **A** - mind
2. **C** - to bring something to mind
3. **B** - able to be brought to mind
4. **A** - out of the mind
5. **C** - recall something
6. **B** - memorizations
7. **A** - memorialize
8. **C** - mental
9. **A** - not likely to be brought to mind
10. **B** - activity in the mind

Assessment 26: CLAIM

1. **B** - to shout
2. **A** - a lot of noise
3. **C** - a person demanding ownership
4. **A** - to shout forth
5. **C** - can be called back into use
6. **C** - exclamation
7. **B** - disclaimer
8. **A** - acclaiming
9. **C** - demanding information
10. **B** - call new species by a name

Assessment 27: LEG

1. **C** - law
2. **B** - pertaining to making into law
3. **A** - to make lawful
4. **A** - sent out chosen for a purpose
5. **A** - address it to the law
6. **B** - college
7. **C** - privilege
8. **C** - illegality
9. **A** - obey every law
10. **B** - law and medical procedures

Weekly Assessment ANSWER KEYS

Assessment 28: LOC

1. **C** - place
2. **A** - to put into a specific place
3. **C** - to put in place for a definite purpose
4. **B** - in a particular place
5. **C** - get it out of place
6. **B** - relocation
7. **A** - misallocated
8. **C** - locator
9. **A** - area
10. **B** - put them together in order

Assessment 29: SERV

1. **A** - to save or keep
2. **C** - people held back for future use
3. **B** - the process of arranging to save
4. **B** - tending to hold together what exists
5. **A** - hold to its purpose
6. **A** - observant
7. **C** - preservative
8. **B** - observer
9. **A** - wasn't keeping watch
10. **C** - holding back

Assessment 30: CAPIT

1. **B** - head or chief
2. **A** - first-rate or main
3. **C** - to bow the head in defeat
4. **A** - the act of telling the main points again
5. **B** - to fall head-first
6. **A** - decapitate
7. **B** - capitalize
8. **A** - tricipital
9. **C** - cut off the head of King Charles
10. **C** - head

Assessment 31: GENER

1. **C** - family or sort
2. **C** - of the same sort
3. **A** - a group born in the same era
4. **B** - to simplify into one group
5. **C** - familes or groups
6. **A** - degenerate
7. **B** - regenerate
8. **A** - general
9. **C** - older and younger members of the group dance together
10. **B** - not working as well as they once did

Assessment 32: FLEX

1. **C** - to bend
2. **B** - tending to curve inward
3. **C** - something that allows or causes bending
4. **C** - bent back
5. **A** - quality of being able to change direction
6. **B** - deflect
7. **B** - reflectors
8. **B** - inflectional
9. **A** - didn't turn back in his mind what the information might mean
10. **A** - seems to curve around

Assessment 33: SECT

1. **B** - to cut
2. **B** - to divide into two
3. **B** - a point where lines cut into each other
4. **C** - cut into pieces
5. **C** - divides off into pieces
6. **A** - bisected
7. **C** - dissection
8. **B** - sectionalists
9. **A** - the quality of being cut easily
10. **A** - cut across the layers of rock

Assessment 34: PAR

1. **A** - arrange or order
2. **B** - not able to be set apart
3. **C** - an act of arranging or ordering back the way something was
4. **A** - to arrange or trim
5. **A** - a state of not being ordered or arranged properly
6. **B** - unseparated
7. **C** - apparatus
8. **A** - preparatory
9. **B** - arranging and looking at things side-by-side
10. **C** - are different

Assessment 35: VIA

1. **A** - road or trip
2. **C** - to go down the wrong path
3. **C** - being right in one's path
4. **B** - by way of
5. **A** - a method of passing along information or goods
6. **C** - voyaging
7. **B** - impervious
8. **C** - obviate
9. **A** - can be moved from its course
10. **B** - pass it along again

Assessment 36: HER

1. **B** - stick
2. **C** - to cling together
3. **A** - to act as if stuck
4. **B** - not sticking together
5. **A** - tending to stick to something
6. **C** - unhesitant
7. **B** - inhesion
8. **A** - incoherence
9. **C** - always seems to be hanging around
10. **A** - wondering what the topic of the speech was

DON'T FORGET THE COMPREHENSIVE (POST) TEST ON PAGE A-13

Mid-Term Assessment

A twenty-four question assessment is available for your use as a mid-point test of only the first eighteen roots in the program. After you have covered the first eighteen roots, that is, through the root **METER**, administer this assessment to measure students' morphological skills at that point.

The test is structured so that each root up to this point is evaluated in two ways:

First, students' knowledge of words that they are likely to have met in the course of the unit is assessed.

Secondly, morphological problem-solving skills are assessed, based on words that students may not ever have seen, yet which apply knowledge that they have acquired.

You could use the scores of this test as a summative record for each student, or, alternatively, as a formative assessment designed to promote student success. You may discover, for example, that some students need more challenging activities, and that others need remediation.

You can differentiate your instruction by logging onto the dynamicliteracy.com website using your personal account.

Appendix A

Part I. Write in the letter of the word that is best defined:

____ **1.** to move across to another shape
- **A** transform
- **B** formation
- **C** formalize
- **D** informative

____ **2.** tending to seek into
- **A** inquisitive
- **B** inquisition
- **C** inquire
- **D** required

____ **3.** standing apart at a balanced space
- **A** perimeter
- **B** instance
- **C** equidistant
- **D** metrical

____ **4.** to make a thoroughly false oath
- **A** readjustable
- **B** juror
- **C** jury
- **D** perjure

____ **5.** to choose apart
- **A** devalue
- **B** select
- **C** repetition
- **D** propose

____ **6.** sending a written message over a distance
- **A** paragraphing
- **B** teleport
- **C** equivalent
- **D** telegraphing

____ **7.** to put upon
- **A** inquest
- **B** import
- **C** impose
- **D** inject

____ **8.** caused to move together
- **A** compel
- **B** collector
- **C** coagulated
- **D** composition

Part II. Write in the letter of the word that best defines each root.

____ **9. FOUND** or **FUS** in words like **confound** and **transfusion** means:

A to fight

B to run or hurry

C to be ill

D to melt, pour, or blend

____ **10. PET** or **PEAT** in words like **petition** and **repeatedly** means:

A to speak

B to seek or aim for

C to do or perform

D chart

____ **11. GRAD** or **GRESS** in words like **graduate** and **progress** means:

A to step or go

B law, right, or true

C to choose or read

D fair or balanced

____ **12. PEL** or **PULS** in words like **expelled** and **impulsion** means:

A to carry or bring

B to put or place

C to push or beat

D to seek or rush

____ **13. STA** or **STAT** in words like **stable** and **thermostat** means:

A to build

B to stand or stop

C mark, seal, or meaning

D strength or health

____ **14. JECT** in words like **project** and **subjected** means:

A measure

B shape or appearance

C to swear an oath

D to throw

____ **15. PORT** in words like **exported** and **portable** means:

A side or portion

B to carry or bring

C to push or force

D to arrange or order

____ **16. VAL** or **VAIL** in words like **valiant** and **prevailing** means:

A strength or worth

B to blend or melt

C road or passageway

D to save or protect

Appendix A

Part III. Write in the letter of the correct word explanation.

_____ **17.** Ben Franklin was a **signatory** to both the Declaration of Independence and the Constitution.

A He refused to give his okay to either document.

B He believed that both documents should be improved.

C He agreed with both documents.

D He did not agree with either document.

_____ **18.** The windows on either side of the door were **asymmetrical**.
The windows:

A were broken

B were as large as the door

C were exactly the same size

D did not have the same measurement

_____ **19.** Darryl had a **compulsion** to talk. Darryl:

A learned to talk at a late age

B could not talk

C wanted to, but did not talk

D felt forced to talk

_____ **20.** The Court **validated** the Senate's law. The Court :

A changed the law

B had nothing to say about the law

C gave strength to the law

D stopped the law from being enforced

Part IV. Write in the letter of the correct word explanation.

_____ **21.** An **affusion** of oil and vinegar finished the salad.
Oil and vinegar were:

A poured onto the salad

B set apart for later use

C removed from the salad

D not used on the salad

_____ **22.** The **ejecta** of the volcano caused little concern to the farmers.
Ejecta refers to:

A material thrown out

B slight heat

C small size

D nearness

_____ **23.** Louis had the right of **ingress** to the rare book room. Louis could:

A see the room from where he sat

B go into the room

C stop people from using the room

D stake books out of the room

_____ **24.** Edna owned a **portative** keyboard. This means that:

A Edna had several other keyboards as well

B Edna could carry the keyboard to different places

C the keyboard was too heavy to move

D the keyboard was old and in bad shape

_____ correct out of 24

ANSWER KEY

1. **A** - transform
2. **A** - inquisitive
3. **C** - equidistant
4. **D** - perjure
5. **B** - select
6. **D** - telegraphing
7. **C** - impose
8. **C** - coagulated
9. **D** - to melt, pour, or blend
10. **B** - to seek or aim for
11. **A** - to step or go
12. **C** - to push or beat
13. **B** - to stand or stop
14. **D** - to throw
15. **B** - to carry or bring
16. **A** - strength or worth
17. **C** - He agreed with both documents
18. **D** - did not have the same measurement
19. **D** - felt forced to talk
20. **C** - gave strength to the law
21. **A** - poured onto the salad
22. **A** - material thrown out
23. **B** - go into the room
24. **B** - Edna could carry the keyboard to different places

Comprehensive Pre/Post Assessment

A 36-question test covering all 36 roots of the Level II Elements program begins on the next page. The test is designed to assess knowledge of each individual root and specific affixes that work with the root. You could administer this test at the very beginning of the term, record the results on the score sheet below, in the pre-test column, and keep the tests in a safe place until the end of the year. You could let your students know how they did without going over the answers. Scores would not be expected to be high, and the "grades" would not be included in summative assessment scores.

Some teachers may want to give this same test at some mid-point to see how improvement is going, or to make formative changes in instruction as needed. Scores will be up, but since only half of the roots will have been covered, summative assessment scores would again not be counted. Interestingly, however, you are likely to see a good improvement even on the decoding of words that have not yet been covered.

Most importantly you will want to re-administer the test after all the roots have been covered in instruction. You will see dramatic improvement in your students' ability to decode and analyze words, and you can now go over the tests with the class so students can see how far they have come. It is likely that you and your students would enjoy "counting" these scores.

Student Name or ID	Pre-Test	Post-Test	Student Name or ID	Pre-Test	Post-Test

WordBuild Elements Level 2
Full Course Assessment, 36 Roots   Name _____

Part I. Write in the letter of the word that is best defined:

____ **1.** a movement across to another shape
  A reformative
  B transformation
  C uniformity
  D malform

____ **2.** to send a written message over a distance
  A paragraphed
  B telegraph
  C equivalency
  D teleporting

____ **3.** in a manner tending to seek into or ask
  A inquisitively
  B questionable
  C inquisitor
  D acquiring

____ **4.** quality of not taking a side
  A departmental
  B partitioned
  C counterpart
  D impartiality

____ **5.** took worth away from
  A valedictory
  B prevailed
  C devalued
  D reevaluated

____ **6.** capable of being carried from beneath
  A superimposable
  B supportable
  C understated
  D suppositional

____ **7.** not arranged or ordered apart
  A inseparable
  B irreparable
  C separating
  D unseparated

____ **8.** people who swear oaths together
  A conjurors
  B injurers
  C justifiers
  D rejoinders

____ **9.** able to be read
  A scripture
  B biographical
  C legible
  D nominative

____ **10.** figures with balanced sides
  A collaterals
  B unilaterals
  C equilaterals
  D contralateral

____ **11.** out-pourings
  A effusions
  B reconstructions
  C destructions
  D progenerative

____ **12.** measurements around
  A ambivalencies
  B perimeters
  C interdepartmentals
  D retrogrades

Appendix A

Part II. Write in the letter of the word that best defines each root.

____ **13.** SECT or SEG in words like **section** and **segment** means:
  A mark, seal, or meaning
  B to build or arrange
  C to cut or divide
  D chart

____ **14.** CAPIT or CIP in words like **capital** and **incipient** means:
  A to demand or call out
  B head or chief
  C to ask or seek
  D mind

____ **15.** LAT in words like **translate** and **legislate** means:
  A read
  B to save or protect
  C road or passageway
  D to bring

____ **16.** JECT in words like **inject** and **rejected** means:
  A to throw
  B to carry
  C family or creation
  D to stick or cling

____ **17.** PEL or PULS in words like **repelled** and **propulsion** means:
  A to push or beat
  B shape or appearance
  C to do or perform
  D law or right

____ **18.** SPIR or PIR in words like **inspire** and **expire** means:
  A step or go
  B to breathe
  C to choose or read
  D fair or balanced

____ **19.** VOLV or VOLUT in words like **involve** and **convoluted** means:
  A to melt or pour
  B measure
  C side or division
  D to roll or turn

____ **20.** STA or STAT in words like **stability** and **static** means:
  A to bend or change
  B to arrange or order
  C to stand or stop
  D a mark or meaning

____ **21.** LEG or LEGIS in words like **legal** and **legislate** means:
  A wrong
  B branch or arm
  C place
  D law or bind in purpose

____ **22.** PON or POS in words like **postpone** and **positive** means:
  A ability
  B act
  C to place or put
  D speak or declare

____ **23.** MAN or MANU in words like **manipulate** or **manual** means:
  A hand
  B mind
  C head
  D back

____ **24.** LOC in words like **relocate** and **locative** means:
  A to bring
  B place
  C to seek or aim for
  D to arrange or pile up

Part III. Write the letter of the correct interpretation of each word.

___ **25.** Ben was **reassigned** to a job in Nevada. Ben:

A was told to move to Nevada

B left Nevada to go somewhere else

C decided that he wanted to stay in Nevada

D had never had a job before moving to Nevada

___ **26.** Aunt Mariah was aware that **dementia** was beginning to appear. Aunt Mariah:

A knew it was starting to be summer again

B heard the neighbor who was walking his dog

C could not use her hands as well as she once did

D had trouble remembering or thinking

___ **27.** Rollin made an **exclamatory** remark at the town meeting. Rollin:

A shouted out the remark

B whispered his remark to someone nearby

C had an opinion but did not express it

D asked a question quietly

___ **28.** The townspeople **observed** a festival in October. The townspeople:

A did not believe in having festivals in October

B always kept up their October festival

C thought that they might start up a festival after October

D tried to stop the October festival

___ **29.** Judy and Julie are **adherents** of the belief "live and let live." Judy and Julie:

A do not like this belief

B think that others should not have this belief

C strongly stick to this belief

D do not express anything about this belief

___ **30.** The **reenactment** of the battle interested Harold. Harold:

A asked others to write about the battle

B enjoyed only reading about the battle

C wanted to find ways to stop the battle

D liked watching the battle being performed again as a show

___ **31.** Nina and Matt met several **viators** during their vacation. **Viators** are

A thieves

B musicians

C travelers

D people who make jewelry

___ **32.** Some animals have **regenerative** organs. These organs:

A can be created again after they are injured

B serve two or more usesg

C are located in the neck or above

D die as soon as the animal dies

___ **33.** Jonathan could tell that Jennifer **misconstrued** what he had said. Jennifer:

A knew exactly what Jonathan meant

B agreed with what Jonathan had said

C did not understand what Jonathan had said

D did not want Jonathan to repeat what he had said

___ **34.** The waterfront homeowners were **prograding** the bay. They were:

A causing pollution and mess around the bay

B admiring the bay

C using up all the water in the bay

D making ways for their land to go farther out into the bay

___ **35.** The autumn bluegrass plants are very **flexuous**. These plants:

A live only for a short time

B have stems that turn in different directions

C grow to be very tall

D stick together in small clumps

___ **36.** Ida says that Margaret is very **petulant**. According to Ida, Margaret :

A saves her money carefully

B reads a lot and enjoys telling stories

C makes a very good friend because she is polite

D is pushy and forces her way into people's business

WordBuild Elements Level 2
Full Course Assessment

ANSWER KEY

1. **B** - transformation
2. **B** - telegraph
3. **A** - inquisitively
4. **D** - impartiality
5. **C** - devalued
6. **B** - supportable
7. **D** - unseparated
8. **A** - conjurors
9. **C** - legible
10. **C** - equilaterals
11. **A** - effusions
12. **B** - perimeters
13. **C** - to cut or divide
14. **B** - head or chief
15. **D** - to bring
16. **A** - to throw
17. **A** - to push or beat
18. **B** - to breathe
19. **D** - to roll or turn
20. **C** - to stand or stop
21. **C** - law or bind in purpose
22. **C** - to place or put
23. **A** - hand
24. **B** - place

25. **A** - was told to move to Nevada
26. **D** - had trouble remembering or thinking
27. **A** - shouted out the remark
28. **B** - always kept up their October festival
29. **C** - strongly stick to this belief
30. **D** - liked watching the battle being performed again as a show
31. **C** - travelers
32. **A** - can be created again after they are injured
33. **C** - did not understand what Jonathan had said
34. **D** - making ways for their land to go farther out into the bay
35. **B** - have stems that turn in different directions
36. **D** - is pushy and forces her way into people's business